THE RECENT PAST

THE RECENT PAST
Readings on America Since World War II

ALLAN M. WINKLER

Miami University

HarperCollins*Publishers*

Sponsoring Editor: Lauren Silverman
Project Editor: Susan Goldfarb
Cover Design: Lucy Krikorian
Production Manager: Willie Lane
Compositor: Digitype Inc.
Printer and Binder: R. R. Donnelley & Sons Company
Cover Printer: NEBC

THE RECENT PAST: Readings on America Since World War II

Copyright © 1989 by Allan M. Winkler

Library of Congress Cataloging-in-Publication Data

The recent past : readings on America since World War II / [compiled
  by] Allan M. Winkler.
      p. cm.
   Includes index.
   ISBN 0-06-047142-5
   1. United States—History—1945-   2. United States—History—1945-
—Sources. I. Winkler, Allan M., 1945-
E742.R33 1989   88-23307
973.918—dc19   CIP

      90 91 9 8 7 6 5 4 3

For David

CONTENTS

SIXTEEN   The Nuclear Question 391

PREFACE

This book provides a systematic overview of the most important social, political, and cultural patterns of the postwar years. It is a collection of essays and documents exploring the major events experienced in the United States as the nation moved from the heady days of wartime triumph through more troubled times. The selections consider everything from the Cold War and the McCarthy period to the civil rights, women's, and environmental movements; they examine presidential administrations as well as eras of social change.

The text has 16 units, each of which consists of two essays that examine different sides of an issue and a document representative of the period. The essays come from the work of the best scholars writing today; the documents, which are drawn from speeches, transcripts of conversations, government reports, and a children's book, provide a first-hand view of how the postwar years unfolded.

This book is meant to serve as a framework for American history courses dealing with the recent past. It also can be used as a supplement to a basic textbook—such as my own *Modern America: The United States from World War II to the Present*—or can serve as a core volume around which other readings are assigned. The introductory essay reflects my own sense of the postwar years; the 16 units that follow are intended to be used on a weekly basis throughout an academic term.

The Recent Past comes out of the reading, writing, and teaching I have done over the past 15 years. It derives from an effort to understand a period that spans my own lifetime. I hope that the book will provide some assistance to others in exploring the roots of questions that continue to concern us today.

This book has benefited from the assistance of a number of people. I am grateful to Elliott Gorn, Jack Kirby, and Michael O'Brien for reading my introduction and helping me think through the argument, but even more for being colleagues and friends in a way that has made a real difference to me. So too I am grateful to Stephen Day and other members of the Miami University administration for providing support and the sense that anything is possible in a well-run institution. I appreciate the help of Gerry McCauley in picking up the idea for this book and finding a suitable home. I would like to thank Barbara Mossberg for remaining a friend in spite of everything. And I owe a special debt to my children — to Jenny, for giving and sharing more than she can imagine, and to David, for going through more than anyone should have to endure. David, this one is for you.

ALLAN M. WINKLER

THE RECENT PAST

INTRODUCTION

America prospered more than any other nation after World War II. Victorious in the greatest struggle the world had known, the United States entered the postwar period confident of its mission at home and abroad. With foreign foes defeated, the nation's leaders wanted to uphold the worldwide democratic structure they had fought to preserve and to provide their constituents with the essentials of a good life. If that was a large order, most Americans believed that anything was possible, for they agreed with publisher Henry Luce that this was the "American Century."

Over the next 20 years, despite differences in their circumstances, a large majority of those living in the United States remained certain of their nation's approach. But not all of them shared in the prosperity. Class divisions persisted and racial and ethnic divisions became more visible. Most Americans, however, still accepted the assumptions of the Cold War and the anti-Communist consensus that served as the backdrop for all postwar policy. They also endorsed the expansion of governmental authority, particularly presidential power, as it sought to create an economic structure that ensured continued growth and a social framework that guaranteed equity and equality for all.

Then that design began to unravel. During the 1960s and 1970s, the United States experienced a crisis in confidence, as old assumptions were questioned and shelved. The Cold War consensus no longer seemed as compelling; presidential power threatened the delicate constitutional balance; the economic system appeared to falter; and social reform seemed to have run its course. In area after area, American leaders groped for new solutions to problems they only barely understood.

Yet if the answers were less certain and the questions themselves had changed, the areas of concern remained similar to those of the early postwar years. Critics sought reform, not revolution, and certain continuities remained. A careful assessment of attitudes and efforts in foreign and domestic affairs can help provide an understanding of the contours of policy and the configurations of mood in the years since 1945.

The Cold War was, without question, the greatest single force affecting America after World War II. Rooted in tensions that often threatened to undermine the wartime alliance among the United States, Great Britain, and the Soviet Union, the conflict between East and West became more open as the war against fascism came to an end. Each side insisted on its own priorities even more vigorously than before, and agreement became increasingly difficult to attain. Hope for cooperation faded as friction grew, and international suspicion proved to be the enduring legacy of the war.

The United States sought to generalize from its own experience and to offer the principles of liberty and free enterprise for consumption abroad. It drew on a sense of mission deeply rooted in its past. Americans subscribed to the old Puritan notion that they should be an example, "a city upon a hill." This sentiment had manifested itself in expansionary fervor in the 1840s, in imperial escapade in the 1890s, and then even more dramatically in support of Europe in the First and Second World Wars. Now Americans wanted the rest of the world to follow their democratic lead.

At the same time, they viewed the world as an interdependent whole in which each nation played a necessary part. They wanted freedom from economic restraints so that the fruits of their industry could be accessible. Without foreign markets, they feared the specter of depression once more. Continued prosperity depended on access overseas.

The Soviet Union had an altogether different notion. Worn-out by the war, the Soviets became obsessively concerned with their own security. They were determined to head off another attack, and, with the German invasion of 1941 firmly in mind, they insisted on defensible borders and friendly regimes on their western flank. They demanded stable and submissive governments in the eastern European states that would be receptive to their military and political demands. Harry Truman, president after Franklin Roosevelt died, took a tough approach toward the Russians. He insisted unsuccessfully that they subscribe to the American interpretation of the elastic Yalta accords. He accepted the framework of George Kennan, second-ranking officer at the American Embassy in Moscow, who suggested that "the whole Soviet governmental machine, including the mechanism of diplomacy, moves inexorably along the prescribed path, like a persistent toy automobile wound up and headed in a given direction, stopping only when it meets with unanswerable force." Containment was the necessary counter to the Soviet threat.

Containment became American policy in the early postwar years. The Truman Doctrine of 1947 provided economic and military aid to Greece and

Turkey to assist them in resisting Communist penetration. The Marshall Plan of 1948 went still further in offering $17 billion over a 4-year period to 16 European nations in an effort to fight against "hunger, poverty, desperation, and chaos," all of which led to radical upheaval. In 1949, NATO (the North Atlantic Treaty Organization) bound 12 member nations together with the injunction that an attack against any one would be considered an attack against all, to be met by appropriate armed force.

Following the fall of China and the Soviet detonation of an atomic bomb in 1949, Truman called for a full review of America's foreign and defense policies. Conducted by the National Security Council, NSC–68—the paper that resulted—gave shape to American policy for the next 20 years. It viewed the international arena in polar terms, with conflict endemic between East and West. "The issues that face us are momentous," the document stated, "involving the fulfillment or destruction not only of this Republic but of civilization itself." Russia had to be resisted at all cost.

That stance provided the justification for American involvement when North Korea invaded South Korea in mid-1950. Although North Korea planned and executed the initiative, American commentators insisted the Russians had masterminded the attack, and believed that national security and world peace were at stake. Thus, the United States came to interpret independence movements not as indigenous nationalistic uprisings but as examples of a massive Communist conspiracy at work.

As the United States became increasingly concerned with the perceived Communist threat, it witnessed the steady expansion of government power. The process really had begun in the midst of the Great Depression, when Franklin Roosevelt's New Deal had brought major changes to bureaucratic structure in Washington, D.C. The White House became an initiator of legislation and worked hand in hand with Congress to get things done. New agencies administered the relief programs and recovery schemes. Americans quickly became familiar with the alphabet agencies—the NRA, CCC, AAA, PWA, WPA, among others. These agencies touched the lives of all and became an accepted part of the administrative framework.

The war brought an even greater centralization of command. Increasing numbers of Americans went to work in government jobs. Between 1940 and 1945, the number of civilian employees in government posts rose from 1 million to 3.8 million. They assumed new responsibilities and provided the coordination necessary in an economy geared for war. After the war, the process continued. Truman's Fair Deal followed on the heels of Roosevelt's New Deal and served notice that the changes of the past 15 years had become permanent parts of American life. Government continued to grow during the 1950s, and became even more important in the 1960s with the proliferation of new programs that were part of Lyndon Johnson's Great Society.

Meanwhile, the presidency itself became increasingly important. Roosevelt extended his power to make executive agreements in a deal trading destroyers for bases that helped Britain in 1940. He enhanced his own reputation, and that of his office, by his attendance at wartime summits—at Casablanca, Teheran, and Yalta—as he exercised his constitutional power as commander-in-chief.

Truman, aware of what his predecessor had done, intended to pass on the power of the presidency unimpaired. He pushed personally for the Truman Doctrine, quite literally "scaring hell out of the country," as Senator Arthur Vandenberg had said he must. In the Korean crisis, Truman met with his advisers, went to the United Nations to ask for support, and only then briefed congressional leaders to tell them what he had done. He chose not to ask for a joint congressional resolution authorizing American intervention, but instead relied on his own authority as commander-in-chief. On the home front, when Truman feared a nationwide steel strike in 1952 would slow the flow of military supplies to Korea, he directed his Secretary of Commerce to seize and operate the mills. Treading on new ground, he argued that the president had the authority to do what was necessary to meet national emergencies. Although the Supreme Court decided otherwise, Truman had still moved a step beyond FDR.

Even as Dwight Eisenhower sought to restore what he thought was a proper constitutional balance, he took actions that increased presidential power. Under his leadership, the United States entered into a network of treaties around the world. Ike made extensive use of the CIA, set up in 1947, as an instrument of intervention in other lands. At home, he followed in Truman's footsteps in withholding documents sought by Congress on grounds of "executive privilege."

The process accelerated in the 1960s under John Kennedy. After Eisenhower's 8 years in office, Kennedy was determined to get the country moving again. Young, vigorous, aggressive, Kennedy asserted that the president "must be prepared to exercise the fullest powers of his office—all that are specified and some that are not." The president "must serve as a catalyst, an energizer," who performs "in the very thick of the fight." Kennedy sought to use his presidential power most fully in foreign affairs. He authorized the Bay of Pigs invasion in Cuba that promised glorious triumph but ended in disastrous defeat. In the Cuban missile crisis, Kennedy and his closest advisers made all the crucial decisions themselves, and only later informed congressional leaders. His action provided a model for future presidential direction of the war in Vietnam.

Government expanded in the economic realm as well. During the Great Depression, English economist John Maynard Keynes had predicted that recovery would come only when deliberate, sustained spending occurred. The American efforts, first for defense, then for war, proved Keynes correct. When the United States began to mobilize in 1940, the economy improved nearly overnight. As the nation became, in Roosevelt's phrase, "the great arsenal of democracy," most Americans had money in their pockets once more.

After the war, economists wanted to apply the lessons learned. Liberals in particular wanted to require the use of countercyclical tools—spending programs or tax cuts — to head off future disruptions before they became severe. A congressional bill in 1945 sought to mandate that the government promote full employment by monitoring the economy and then taking the necessary monetary and fiscal measures to maintain equilibrium. In the end, Congress gutted the proposal, and the Employment Act of 1946 that emerged created a Council of Economic Advisers to make recommendations but did little more. Yet even if the measure neglected Keynesian policies, it was a symbolic first step.

A decade and a half later, Kennedy embraced the Keynesian approach. Budget deficits had promoted prosperity during World War II. Why could they not work in peacetime too? Spending for defense and for the space program that sought to put a man on the moon pumped money into the economy, but now Kennedy began to argue for an even more focused effort to spur economic growth. At the Yale University commencement in 1962, he voiced his awareness that deficits, properly used, might help the economy improve. At the start of 1963, Kennedy called for a $13.5 billion cut in personal and corporate taxes over the next three years. The capital provided would stimulate the economy and offset whatever short-term deficits were created. Although it was an innovative suggestion, the measure was pigeon-holed in congressional committee when Kennedy was assassinated.

Lyndon Johnson took Kennedy's program and made it his own. Lobbying furiously, he got his way. Several months after he assumed the presidency, the tax-cut bill became law. For the first time, the government was about to embark on the aggressive use of fiscal policy to keep the economy buoyant. The tax cut worked just as intended. After passage, the Gross National Product (GNP) went steadily up — 7.1 percent in 1964, 8.1 percent in 1965, and 9.5 percent in 1966 — while the deficit dropped at the same time. Unemployment fell and inflation remained firmly in control.

As the United States experimented with ways of stabilizing the economic system, it became similarly concerned with guaranteeing equality for all. Black Americans built on a start made during World War II. Facing continued discrimination as they sought positions in the military services and in the industrial sector, they responded then by launching a "Double V" campaign   V for victory in the war against the dictators abroad, and V for victory in their own struggle for fair treatment at home. By the war's end, black Americans had moved up to better jobs and gained greater opportunities in the military. More important, they had begun to manifest a new militancy that brought continued results.

During Harry Truman's administration, the civil rights issue became a national concern. Court cases moved quietly through legal channels as the National Association for the Advancement of Colored People (NAACP) sought to overcome the judicial justification for segregation. The racial question became more visible in 1947, when Jackie Robinson broke the racial boundaries in baseball by signing with the Brooklyn Dodgers. On a larger stage, the United States found its racial problems intertwining with those of the Cold War. As leader of the free world, it sought to appeal for support in Africa and Asia where its discriminatory policies cast it in an unfortunate light. There was now a larger reason to confront the problem of change at home.

Harry Truman endorsed legal, though not social, equality. By executive order, he barred discrimination in the federal establishment and took the first steps to bring an end to segregation in the military forces. The United States Navy, Air Force, and Marine Corps responded most quickly. Segregation in the United States Army persisted until the Korean War, when the army needed more power and proved willing to set blacks alongside whites in combat as long as military effectiveness remained unimpaired.

More dramatic changes came in the Eisenhower years. In 1954, in the landmark *Brown* v. *Board of Education* case concerning school segregation, the United States Supreme Court ruled that the "separate but equal" doctrine propounded in 1896 was unconstitutional. In 1955, the Supreme Court declared that local school boards, acting with the guidance of lower courts, should move "with all deliberate speed" to desegregate the nation's schools. The court decision brought resistance from the South and confrontation in Little Rock, Arkansas, and elsewhere but gradually effected change.

Similar change came on the transportation front. In Montgomery, Alabama, near the end of 1955, Rosa Parks, a 43-year-old black seamstress, sat down in the front of a city bus in a section reserved by law and custom for whites. When she refused to move to the rear of the bus and was arrested, black leaders launched a massive boycott of the bus system that finally led to a Supreme Court ruling that bus segregation, like school segregation, violated the Constitution.

Blacks agitated for equal access to public facilities and to the polls as well. Hotels, restaurants, and other accommodations remained segregated in parts of the North and throughout the South. The constitutional right to vote was similarly blocked. Although the Civil Rights Acts of 1957 and 1960 began to address the voting issue, they left major loopholes.

Pressure mounted as sit-ins and freedom rides began in the South. At the 1963 March on Washington, 200,000 people heard Martin Luther King, Jr., proclaim, "I have a dream that one day this nation will rise up and live out the true meaning of its creed: 'We hold these truths to be self-evident, that all men are created equal.'"

Finally, Lyndon Johnson used his legislative genius to push through the Civil Rights Act of 1964, outlawing racial discrimination in public accommodations and prohibiting discriminatory hiring on grounds of race, sex, religion, or national origin. The next year he pushed successfully for the Voting Rights Act of 1965, which finally authorized the Attorney General to appoint federal examiners to register voters where there were pockets of discrimination and local officials were not doing the job. The measure helped change the American political balance. The year after passage, over 400,000 blacks registered to vote in the Deep South. By 1968, that number reached 1 million.

Black candidates could now be elected and black constituencies could make themselves heard.

But then, in civil rights as in other areas, the sense of constant progress disappeared. In the mid-1960s, as large parts of America seemed more prosperous and more successful than ever before, the nation found that the old assumptions no longer seemed to work. In every major area of foreign and domestic policy, challenges occurred, and as those challenges intersected with one another, they compounded a crisis in confidence that lasted for the next 10 years. The war in Vietnam undermined the assumptions that had sustained the Cold War. It led to serious criticisms of excessive executive authority, even as it spawned an inflationary cycle that eroded the economic stability just achieved. Radical criticisms forced confrontations, and those in turn led to a backlash that encouraged resistance to further reform.

The war in Vietnam was rooted in the framework of the Cold War. Although Ho Chi Minh's version of communism was rigorously nationalistic, Americans insisted on seeing it as part of a monolithic Communist crusade. Concerned about the fate of Southeast Asia as the Vietnamese struggle for independence continued, John Kennedy increased the number of civilian and military advisers. When that failed to stem the tide, Lyndon Johnson dispatched a far greater number of soldiers.

Johnson, like his predecessors, was wedded to Cold War assumptions. Soon after becoming president, he declared: "I am not going to lose Vietnam. I am not going to be the President who saw Southeast Asia go the way China went." Johnson responded to events in Vietnam on the basis of his understanding of the lessons of the past. Aggression before World War II had gone unchecked with tragic results. Johnson was convinced that to refuse to respond now would lead to World War III. Aggressors had to be stopped, he felt, for "if you let a bully come into your front yard one day, the next day he'll be up on your porch and the day after that he'll rape your wife in your own bed." But Johnson's escalation failed to bring even the stalemate achieved in the Korean War. Half a million American troops were in Vietnam at the peak of involvement in 1969, and eventually more than 50,000 died, but no resolution was apparent. The war fostered first frustration, then violent protest in American streets. "Hey, hey, LBJ. How many kids did you kill today?" opponents of the war chanted. Some 300,000 marched in New York City and 100,000 in Washington, D.C. The media dramatized both the brutal fighting and the turbulence at home, and further polarized the nation.

The war in Vietnam shattered the foreign policy consensus that had governed since World War II. Most Americans—Democrats and Republicans, old and young—had believed in positions taken during the Cold War. Some had been frustrated during the struggle in Korea, when it proved difficult to understand the demands of limited war. Some had protested the ruthless anti-Communist crusade of Senator Joseph McCarthy. But fundamentally, Americans had felt they were engaged in an important mission that demanded their support. The Vietnam War changed that view. Increasing numbers of Americans questioned the conduct of the war, particularly as they learned of atrocities at My Lai and elsewhere. Even more important, they questioned the basic policies that had led the United States into Vietnam. Was American involvement misguided? What did the United States hope to achieve? What role should the nation play in the world at large?

The war in Vietnam led Americans to question the use of presidential authority as well. Lyndon Johnson had never secured a legitimate declaration of war. During the presidential campaign of 1964, he had quietly gained the authorization he wanted in an almost underhanded way. He announced that North Vietnamese torpedo boats had, without provocation, attacked American destroyers in the international waters of the Gulf of Tonkin, 30 miles from North Vietnam. Only later did the truth emerge, that the American ships had been engaged in surveillance in combat zones close to shore, in support of South Vietnamese commando raids. Before the details of the attack were known, however, Johnson used the episode to his own advantage. He asked Congress for a resolution giving him authority to respond to aggression. Not aware that he had been carrying the resolution around for some time, Congress passed it by votes of 416–0 in the House and 88–2 in the Senate. This gave Johnson all the leverage he wanted, for, as he noted, it was "like grandma's nightshirt—it covered everything." Several years later, Americans argued that Johnson had gone too far, with charges that discouraged him from running for reelection in 1968.

Challenges continued unabated as successor Richard Nixon took office. Although Nixon sought to extricate America from the Vietnam War, at crucial moments he widened it as well, as with incursions into Cambodia and Laos that brought renewed criticism. More pointed still were the challenges to Nixon's actions in the Watergate affair. Even more than his predecessors, Nixon insisted on the trappings of presidential power. On a personal level, he used government funds to improve his own property. More important, he tried to use his office to contain his political enemies, sometimes by illegal means. As the scandal surrounding the Republican wiretapping of the Democratic National Headquarters unfolded, many Americans began to ask whether the executive establishment had become too strong, to question whether the "Imperial Presidency" had any place in the United States. After watching impeachment proceedings, then Nixon's resignation in disgrace, Americans sought, particularly at the congressional level, a more acceptable governmental equilibrium.

As Americans struggled with questions of constitutional balance, they also had to deal with issues of economic stability. The Vietnam War thoroughly disrupted the American economy. By 1966, the cost was more than $2 billion a month. The effort to finance the struggle gave rise to inflation and economic chaos. Lyndon Johnson's effort to support the Great Society and the war at the same time overheated an economy already warm from the tax cut. As the defense budget rose, the productive system of the country could not meet demand. With more dollars chasing limited goods, prices began to rise. Johnson's refusal to raise taxes let inflation get out of control and it remained a problem for the next decade and a half.

Nixon hoped to cap inflation, even at the expense of unemployment levels. Yet both seemed to rise hand in hand. When in frustration he embarked on an expansionary policy to extricate the nation from its slump and announced "I am now a Keynesian in economics," critics quipped that his assertion was a demonstration that the doctrine was dead. Nixon did move to impose wage and price controls in 1971, but then capitulated to pressures from both business and labor interests and watched instability return. With matters still out of control, the Arab nations of the Middle East and other oil-producing countries began to cut back on oil production and to raise prices. Soon the industrialized nations of the world, heavily dependent on oil, began to feel the devastating effects. Inflation rose even faster than it had before.

Meanwhile, the civil rights movement ran out of steam. The campaign had already begun to shift direction after passage of the Voting Rights Act. Blacks pressed for further gains, with less patience than before. Stokely Carmichael, head of the now aggressive Student Nonviolent Coordinating Committee (SNCC), began to talk about "black power" in mid-1966, and the new slogan drowned out the older cry for "freedom now." Riots erupted, first in Watts, in Los Angeles, then in other cities, fueling a backlash on the part of many white working-class Americans who felt that enough progress had been made. Polarized American attitudes appeared most clearly in the growing controversy over busing to achieve racial balance. Although transporting students from one area to another was not new, it became a touchier question when intertwined with integration. In 1971, the Supreme Court ruled that busing could be used to achieve desegregation, but Nixon gave legitimacy to the protest that ensued with his own stated opposition. Progress slowed, as it seemed that the real impetus for reform was gone.

A crisis of confidence had occurred. Godfrey Hodgson, a perceptive English journalist and longtime observer of America, pointed to "the crisis in the mind and spirit of the country" in the 1960s and early 1970s. The real crisis, he wrote, was that "for the first time since the Civil War and Reconstruction, a generation of Americans were compelled to ask not, as people asked in the Depression, how to solve their problems, but whether problems could be solved."

In the mid-1970s, the United States struggled to right itself. As extrication from Vietnam occurred, Congress began to reassert its own priorities, particularly in foreign affairs. Uncomfortable with the erosion of its power to executive gain, Congress passed the War Powers Act, over a presidential veto, in 1973. It provided the legislative branch the authority to oversee intervention abroad and to call a halt if it saw fit. Congress asserted that power to forbid moving back into Cambodia and Vietnam, and asserted its prerogative again to refuse to provide aid in Turkey and Angola when trouble threatened there during Gerald Ford's presidency. When Jimmy Carter entered office in 1977, he was committed to restoring global stability. Under his direction, the United States made strides in the Middle East and in the Panama Canal Zone, but proved less successful with the Soviet Union. Hopes for détente crumbled in the face of Carter's passionate commitment to human rights and the Soviet Union's invasion of Afghanistan.

During Ronald Reagan's tenure in the 1980s, the nation began a major military build-up, with rhetoric about the "evil empire" — the Soviet Union — that recalled the sloganeering of the more difficult days of the Cold War. Only near the end of his administration did Reagan's wish to secure his place in history lead to progress in arms control. In the Middle East, the nation remained unsure about how to deal with the revolutionary regime in Iran or with growing threats to regional stability. In Central America, Reagan sought to support rebel groups trying to challenge established governments over the objections of an increasingly vocal Congress. When Middle Eastern-Central American initiatives became intertwined in the Iran-Contra affair, many Americans questioned governmental policy, just as they had in the angry protests over Vietnam.

Other segments of the society questioned the size and structure of government. Reagan seized on an issue of concern in the 1980 campaign as he criticized spiraling budgets and expanding bureaucracies. Using his considerable political and theatrical skills to enhance his authority, he cut domestic spending at the very time Americans depended more on government to provide basic security and support in an increasingly complex age. And yet, in one of the ultimate ironies of the recent past, presidential power grew under Reagan even as he called for a circumscribed governmental stance.

Questions about the government's role resonated with questions about whether the United States still had the ability to control its own economy. The certainties of the immediate post – World War II years were gone. In the 1970s, as stagnation and inflation proceeded at the same time, some economists began to question the ideas of John Maynard Keynes. Old economic doctrines seemed dead, but where were the new ones to take their place? Nobel Prize winner Friedrich A. Hayek, looking at the performance of economic advisers, said that "one sometimes feels that untaught common sense would probably have done better." As *The Economist* of London noted, the decade of the 1970s was "a bad decade for economics." The 1980 midyear review by Congress's Joint Economic Committee concluded that fine-tuning by short-term monetary and fiscal adjustments no longer worked. The growing budget deficits provided evidence that things were out of control. Reagan managed to limit inflation, but after initial support for his supply-side policy of promoting business activity in the expectation that all groups would then benefit, many Americans began to ask whether they were being well served by his approach.

On the reform front, though the civil rights movement slowed, it had a major and continuing impact on other struggles. In the late 1960s, it spawned a women's movement that focused on another area of discrimination in American society. Women had found themselves economically and politically circumscribed in the early postwar years. Their role then, as presidential candidate Adlai Stevenson told them in a commencement address at Smith College in 1955, was "to influence us, man and boy" in the "humble role of housewife." That assignment, he said, "you can do in the living room with a baby in your lap or in the kitchen with a can opener in your hand." In the 1960s, women working in the civil rights movement began to question the discrimination they too faced. They bristled at sexually suggestive comments like that of black activist Stokely Carmichael, who said, "The only place for women in SNCC is prone." They were similarly concerned that the average working female in 1963 earned only 63 percent of what the average male might expect to earn. Women were able to use reform legislation that came out of the civil rights movement in their own struggle. Title VII of the 1964 Civil Rights Act prohibited discrimination on the basis of gender as well as race. It provided a tool to open doors and gave a legal grounding to the insistence on equality. Women began to organize, just as blacks had done. In 1966, they established the National Organization for Women (NOW) "to take action to bring American women into full participation in the mainstream of American society *now*." Within four years, its membership reached 15,000. Consciousness-raising groups, small and large, sprang up around the country and made women aware of the need for change.

Other groups—Hispanics and Native Americans in particular— followed that lead. Like blacks, they came to feel a sense of ethnic identity and shared commitment that slowly began to affect the material and social circumstances of their lives.

An environmental movement grew out of the agitation of the 1960s, as did a consumer movement. Critics attacked everything from automobile safety to atomic power, and called attention to dangers from asbestos and DDT. Their questioning of established attitudes and structures caused upheaval but slowly brought change.

Today, even as the sense of crisis has subsided, the United States remains beset with problems. Budget deficits mount, the stock market falters, and the nation no longer seems as authoritative in its diplomatic stance. Concerns vary according to class and economic orientation. Those well served by Reagan's economic initiatives have been willing to support other programs as well. Members of the New Right—often working class or middle-class Americans—have sought implementation of a social agenda to revive morality in personal and public life, to prohibit abortion, to restore prayer in schools. Old-time liberals, tempered in the New Deal, have objected but offered only plans that may have run their course.

Many Americans, in political as well as social arenas, have appeared increasingly concerned with a quest for solutions. One reflection of that quest was *Time* magazine's 1982 nomination of the computer as its "man of the year." As microcomputers found their way into millions of American homes, *Time* seemed to imply that machines alone might best help people understand the modern world and its demands.

Whether with computers or other tools, Americans have struggled to come to terms with changing times. After the heady optimism of the postwar years when everything went their way, they have had to realize that not everyone benefited from a traditional American stance. Both at home and abroad, they have confronted chaos and crisis as new groups have raised their voices and demanded that adjustments be made. Slowly, as Americans have realized that some problems have no easy solutions, they have had to accept that Henry Luce may have been right in 1941 — this was the "American Century" — but only for some and only for a time.

one

THE COLD WAR

Who started the Cold War? How did it begin? Why did the positions of former allies harden and their rhetoric turn shrill? Historians have been debating these questions since World War II ended. At first they accepted the views of policymakers who justified the American stance as a courageous counter to the Soviet threat. Later, particularly as the war in Vietnam led to criticism of American foreign policy, revisionist historians began to argue that American policy was provocative, insensitive to legitimate Soviet needs, and at least a contributing factor to the diplomatic breakdown.

In the first selection, "Origins of the Cold War," Arthur Schlesinger, Jr., argues that tensions among members of the Grand Alliance during World War II contributed to the later Cold War. "It was the product," he writes, "not of a decision but of a dilemma." And yet, at the end of his essay, Schlesinger suggests that Soviet paranoia and the instability of leader Joseph Stalin were really the compelling causes for the inability of the major powers to reach an accommodation.

In "American Foreign Policy and the Origins of the Cold War," Barton J. Bernstein presents a revisionist case. Postwar American policymakers had a vision of the world they hoped to create. They were often unwilling or unable to recognize Soviet requirements, and so took increasingly intransigent positions. The Cold War, Bernstein suggests, resulted when leaders "allowed their fears to distort their perceptions and their ideology to blur reality."

NSC–68 was a report to the National Security Council by the Departments of State and Defense. Prepared after the detonation of the Soviet Union's first atomic bomb, the report was largely the work of Secretary of

State Dean Acheson. Although President Harry S Truman never explicitly approved the recommendations, NSC–68 nonetheless became the basis for American policy, particularly after the outbreak of the Korean War.

To pursue the Cold War further, Walter LaFeber, *America, Russia, and the Cold War, 1945–1980* (5th ed., 1987), is a good starting point. John Lewis Gaddis, *The United States and the Origins of the Cold War, 1941–1947* (1972), is a well-argued account of the tensions that caused the breakdown in relations, and his *Strategies of Containment: A Critical Appraisal of Postwar American National Security Policy* (1982) is an even more perceptive synthesis. See also Daniel Yergin, *Shattered Peace: The Origins of the Cold War and the National Security State* (1977); Stephen Ambrose, *Rise to Globalism: American Foreign Policy Since 1938* (1980); and Gabriel Kolko and Joyce Kolko, *The Limits of Power* (1972), for other perspectives. Thomas H. Etzold and John Lewis Gaddis, *Containment: Documents of American Policy and Strategy, 1945–1950* (1978), is a useful collection of the major documents of the period.

Origins of the Cold War

ARTHUR SCHLESINGER, JR.

The Cold War in its original form was a presumably mortal antagonism, arising in the wake of the Second World War, between two rigidly hostile blocs, one led by the Soviet Union, the other by the United States. For nearly two somber and dangerous decades this antagonism dominated the fears of mankind; it may even, on occasion, have come close to blowing up the planet. In recent years, however, the once implacable struggle has lost its familiar clarity of outline. With the passing of old issues and the emergence of new conflicts and contestants, there is a natural tendency, especially on the part of the generation which grew up during the Cold War, to take a fresh look at the causes of the great contention between Russia and America.

Some exercises in reappraisal have merely elaborated the orthodoxies promulgated in Washington or Moscow during the boom years of the Cold War. But others, especially in the United States (there are no signs, alas, of this in the Soviet Union), represent what American historians call "revisionism"—that is, a readiness to challenge official explanations. No one should be surprised by this phenomenon. Every war in American history has been followed in due course by skeptical reassessments of supposedly sacred assumptions. So the War of 1812, fought at the time for the freedom of the seas, was in later years ascribed to the expansionist ambitions of Congressional war hawks; so the Mexican War became a slaveholders' conspiracy. So the Civil War has been pronounced a "needless war," and Lincoln has even been accused of manœuvring the rebel attack on Fort Sumter. So too the Spanish-American War and the First and Second World Wars have, each in its turn, undergone revisionist critiques. It is not to be supposed that the Cold War would remain exempt.

In the case of the Cold War, special factors reinforce the predictable historiographical rhythm. The outburst of polycentrism in the communist empire has made people wonder whether communism was ever so monolithic as official theories of the Cold War supposed. A generation with no vivid memories of Stalinism may see the Russia of the forties in the image of the relatively mild, seedy and irresolute Russia of the sixties. And for this same generation the American course of widening the war in Viet Nam—which even non-revisionists can easily regard as folly—has unquestionably stirred doubts about the wisdom of American foreign policy in the sixties which younger historians may have begun to read back into the forties.

It is useful to remember that, on the whole, past exercises in revisionism have failed to stick. Few historians today believe that the war hawks caused the War of 1812 or the slaveholders the Mexican War, or that the Civil War was needless, or that the House of Morgan brought America into the First World War or that Franklin Roosevelt schemed to produce the attack on Pearl Harbor. But this does not mean that one should deplore the rise of Cold

From Arthur M. Schlesinger, Jr., "Origins of the Cold War," in *Foreign Affairs*, 46 (October 1967). Reprinted by permission of the author.

War revisionism. For revisionism is an essential part of the process by which history, through the posing of new problems and the investigation of new possibilities, enlarges its perspectives and enriches its insights.

More than this, in the present context, revisionism expresses a deep, legitimate and tragic apprehension. As the Cold War has begun to lose its purity of definition, as the moral absolutes of the fifties become the moralistic clichés of the sixties, some have begun to ask whether the appalling risks which humanity ran during the Cold War were, after all, necessary and inevitable; whether more restrained and rational policies might not have guided the energies of man from the perils of conflict into the potentialities of collaboration. The fact that such questions are in their nature unanswerable does not mean that it is not right and useful to raise them. Nor does it mean that our sons and daughters are not entitled to an accounting from the generation of Russians and Americans who produced the Cold War.

The orthodox American view, as originally set forth by the American government and as reaffirmed until recently by most American scholars, has been that the Cold War was the brave and essential response of free men to communist aggression. Some have gone back well before the Second World War to lay open the sources of Russian expansionism. Geopoliticians traced the Cold War to imperial Russian strategic ambitions which in the nineteenth century led to the Crimean War, to Russian penetration of the Balkans and the Middle East and to Russian pressure on Britain's "lifeline" to India. Ideologists traced it to the Communist Manifesto of 1848 ("the violent overthrow of the bourgeoisie lays the foundation for the sway of the proletariat"). Thoughtful observers (a phrase meant to exclude those who speak in Dullese about the unlimited evil of godless, atheistic, militant communism) concluded that classical Russian imperialism and Pan-Slavism, compounded after 1917 by Leninist messianism, confronted the West at the end of the Second World War with an inexorable drive for domination.

The revisionist thesis is very different. In its extreme form, it is that, after the death of Franklin Roosevelt and the end of the Second World War, the United States deliberately abandoned the wartime policy of collaboration and, exhilarated by the possession of the atomic bomb, undertook a course of aggression of its own designed to expel all Russian influence from Eastern Europe and to establish democratic-capitalist states on the very border of the Soviet Union. As the revisionists see it, this radically new American policy — or rather this resumption by Truman of the pre-Roosevelt policy of insensate anti-communism — left Moscow no alternative but to take measures in defense of its own borders. The result was the Cold War.

These two views, of course, could not be more starkly contrasting. It is therefore not unreasonable to look again at the half-dozen critical years between June 22, 1941, when Hitler attacked Russia, and July 2, 1947, when the Russians walked out of the Marshall Plan meeting in Paris. . . . Any honest reappraisal of the origins of the Cold War requires the imaginative leap — which should in any case be as instinctive for the historian as it is prudent for the statesman — into the adversary's viewpoint. We must strive to see how, given Soviet perspectives, the Russians might conceivably have misread our signals, as we must reconsider how intelligently we read theirs. . . .

Peacemaking after the Second World War was not so much a tapestry as it was a hopelessly raveled and knotted mess of yarn. Yet, for purposes of clarity, it is essential to follow certain threads. One theme indispensable to an understanding of the Cold War is the contrast between two clashing views of world order: the "universalist" view, by which all nations shared a common interest in all the affairs of the world, and the "sphere-of-influence" view, by which each great power would be assured by the other great powers of an acknowledged predominance in its own area of special interest. The universalist view assumed that national security would be guaranteed by an international organization. The sphere-of-interest view assumed that national security would be guaranteed by the balance of power. While in practice these views have by no means been incompatible (indeed, our shaky peace has been based on a combination of the two), in the abstract they involved sharp contradictions.

The tradition of American thought in these matters was universalist. . . .

The Kremlin, on the other hand, thought *only* of spheres of interest; above all, the Russians were determined to protect their frontiers, and especially their border to the west, crossed so often and so bloodily in the dark course of their history. These western frontiers lacked natural means of defense — no great oceans, rugged mountains, steaming swamps or impenetrable jungles. The history of Russia had been the history of invasion, the last of which was by now horribly killing up to twenty million of its people. The protocol of Russia therefore meant the enlargement of the area of Russian influence. . . .

The more consistent Russian purpose was revealed when Stalin offered the British a straight sphere-of-influence deal at the end of 1941. Britain, he suggested, should recognize the Russian absorption of the Baltic states, part of Finland, eastern Poland and Bessarabia; in return, Russia would support any special British need for bases or security arrangements in Western Europe. There was nothing specifically communist about these ambitions. If Stalin achieved them, he would be fulfilling an age-old dream of the tsars. The British reaction was mixed. "Soviet policy is amoral," as Anthony Eden noted at the time; "United States policy is exaggeratedly moral, at least where non-American interests are concerned." If Roosevelt was a universalist with occasional leanings toward spheres of influence and Stalin was a sphere-of-influence man with occasional gestures toward universalism, Churchill seemed evenly poised between the familiar realism of the balance of power, which he had so long recorded as an historian and manipulated as a statesman, and the hope that there must be some better way of doing things. . . .

Meanwhile Eastern Europe presented the Alliance with still another crisis that same September. Bulgaria, which was not at war with Russia, decided to surrender to the Western Allies while it still could; and the English and Americans at Cairo began to discuss armistice terms with Bulgarian envoys. Moscow, challenged by what it plainly saw as a Western intrusion into its own zone of vital interest, promptly declared war on Bulgaria, took over the surrender negotiations and, invoking the Italian precedent, denied its Western Allies any role in the Bulgarian Control Commission. In a long and thoughtful cable, Ambassador Harriman meditated on the problems of communication with the Soviet Union. "Words," he reflected, "have a different connotation to the Soviets than they have to us. When they speak of insisting on 'friendly governments' in their neighboring countries, they have in mind something quite different from what we would mean." The Russians, he surmised, really believed that Washington accepted "their position that although they would keep us informed they had the right to settle their problems with their western neighbors unilaterally." But the Soviet position was still in flux: "the Soviet Government is not one mind." The problem, as Harriman had earlier told Harry Hopkins, was "to strengthen the hands of those around Stalin who want to play the game along our lines." The way to do this, he now told [Secretary of State Cordell] Hull, was to

> be understanding of their sensitivity, meet them much more than half way, encourage them and support them wherever we can, and yet oppose them promptly with the greatest of firmness where we see them going wrong. . . . The only way we can eventually come to an understanding with the Soviet Union on the question of non-interference in the internal affairs of other countries is for us to take a definite interest in the solution of the problems of each individual country as they arise.

. . . Churchill, increasingly fearful of the consequences of unrestrained competition in Eastern Europe, decided in early October to carry . . . [a] sphere-of-influence proposal directly to Moscow. Roosevelt was at first content to have Churchill speak for him too and even prepared a cable to that effect. But Hopkins, a more rigorous universalist, took it upon himself to stop the cable and warn Roosevelt of its possible implications. Eventually Roosevelt sent a message to Harriman in Moscow emphasizing that he expected to "retain complete freedom of action after this conference is over." It was now that Churchill quickly proposed—and Stalin as quickly accepted—the celebrated division of southeastern Europe: ending (after further haggling between Eden and Molotov) with 90 percent Soviet predominance in Rumania, 80 percent in Bulgaria and Hungary, fifty-fifty in Jugoslavia, 90 percent British predominance in Greece. . . .

It is now pertinent to inquire why the United States rejected the idea of stabilizing the world by division into spheres of influence and insisted on an East European strategy. One should warn against rushing to the conclusion that it was all a row between hard-nosed, balance-of-power realists and starry-eyed Wilsonians. Roosevelt, Hopkins, Welles, Harriman, Bohlen, Berle, Dulles and other universalists were tough and serious men. Why then did they rebuff the sphere-of-influence solution?

The first reason is that they regarded this solution as containing within itself the seeds of a third world war. The balance-of-power idea seemed inherently unstable. It had always broken down in the past. It held out to each power the permanent temptation to try to alter the balance in its own favor, and it built this temptation into the international order. It would turn the great powers of 1945 away from the objective of concerting common policies toward competition for postwar advantage. As Hopkins told Molotov at Teheran, "The President feels it essential to world peace that Russia, Great Britain and the United States work out this control question in a manner which will not start each of the three powers arming against the others." "The greatest likelihood of eventual conflict," said the Joint Chiefs of Staff in 1944 (the only conflict which the J.C.S., in its wisdom, could then glimpse "in the foreseeable future" was between Britain and Russia), ". . . would seem to grow out of either nation initiating attempts to build up its strength, by seeking to attach to herself parts of Europe to the disadvantage and possible danger of her potential adversary." The Americans were perfectly ready to acknowledge that Russia was entitled to convincing assurance of her national security — but not this way. "I could sympathize fully with Stalin's desire to protect his western borders from future attack," as Hull put it. "But I felt that this security could best be obtained through a strong postwar peace organization."

Hull's remark suggests the second objection: that the sphere-of-influence approach would, in the words of the State Department in 1945, "militate against the establishment and effective functioning of a broader system of general security in which all countries will have their part." The United Nations, in short, was seen as the alternative to the balance of power. Nor did the universalists see any necessary incompatibility between the Russian desire for "friendly governments" on its frontier and the American desire for self-determination in Eastern Europe. Before Yalta the State Department judged the general mood of Europe as "to the left and strongly in favor of far-reaching economic and social reforms, but not, however, in favor of a left-wing totalitarian regime to achieve these reforms." Governments in Eastern Europe could be sufficiently to the left "to allay Soviet suspicions" but sufficiently representative "of the center and *petit bourgeois* elements" not to seem a prelude to communist dictatorship. The American criteria were therefore that the government "should be dedicated to the preservation of civil liberties" and "should favor social and economic reforms." A string of New Deal states — of Finlands and Czechoslovakias — seemed a reasonable compromise solution.

Third, the universalists feared that the sphere-of-interest approach would be what Hull termed "a haven for the isolationists," who would advocate America's participation in Western Hemisphere affairs on condition that it did not participate in European or Asian affairs. Hull also feared that spheres of interest would lead to "closed trade areas or discriminatory systems" and thus defeat his cherished dream of a low-tariff, freely trading world.

Fourth, the sphere-of-interest solution meant the betrayal of the principles for which the Second World War was being fought—the Atlantic Charter, the Four Freedoms, the Declaration of the United Nations. Poland summed up the problem. Britain, having gone to war to defend the independence of Poland from the Germans, could not easily conclude the war by surrendering the independence of Poland to the Russians. Thus, as Hopkins told Stalin after Roosevelt's death in 1945, Poland had "become the symbol of our ability to work out problems with the Soviet Union." Nor could American liberals in general watch with equanimity while the police state spread into countries which, if they had mostly not been real democracies, had mostly not been tyrannies either. The execution in 1943 of Ehrlich and Alter, the Polish socialist trade union leaders, excited deep concern. "I have particularly in mind," Harriman cabled in 1944, "objection to the institution of secret police who may become involved in the persecution of persons of truly democratic convictions who may not be willing to conform to Soviet methods."

Fifth, the sphere-of-influence solution would create difficult domestic problems in American politics. Roosevelt was aware of the six million or more Polish votes in the 1944 election; even more acutely, he was aware of the broader and deeper attack which would follow if, after going to war to stop the Nazi conquest of Europe, he permitted the war to end with the communist conquest of Eastern Europe. As Archibald MacLeish, then Assistant Secretary of State for Public Affairs, warned in January 1945, "The wave of disillusionment which has distressed us in the last several weeks will be increased if the impression is permitted to get abroad that potentially totalitarian provisional governments are to be set up without adequate safeguards as to the holding of free elections and the realization of the principles of the Atlantic Charter." Roosevelt believed that no administration could survive which did not try everything short of war to save Eastern Europe, and he was the supreme American politician of the century.

Sixth, if the Russians were allowed to overrun Eastern Europe without argument, would that satisfy them? Even Kennan, in a dispatch of May 1944, admitted that the "urge" had dreadful potentialities: "If initially successful, will it know where to stop? Will it not be inexorably carried forward, by its very nature, in a struggle to reach the whole—to attain complete mastery of the shores of the Atlantic and the Pacific?" His own answer was that there were inherent limits to the Russian capacity to expand—"that Russia will not have an easy time in maintaining the power which it has seized over other people in Eastern and Central Europe unless it receives both moral and material assistance from the West." Subsequent developments have vindicated Kennan's argument. By the late forties, Yugoslavia and Albania, the two East European states farthest from the Soviet Union and the two in which communism was imposed from within rather than from without, had declared their independence of Moscow. But, given Russia's success in maintaining centralized control over the international communist movement for a quarter of a century, who in 1944 could have had much confidence in the idea of communist revolts against Moscow? . . .

The atmosphere of mutual suspicion was beginning to rise. In January 1945 Molotov formally proposed that the United States grant Russia a $6 billion credit for postwar reconstruction. With characteristic tact he explained that he was doing this as a favor to save America from a postwar depression. The proposal seems to have been diffidently made and diffidently received. Roosevelt requested that the matter "not be pressed further" on the American side until he had a chance to talk with Stalin; but the Russians did not follow it up either at Yalta in February (save for a single glancing reference) or during the Stalin-Hopkins talks in May or at Potsdam. Finally the proposal was renewed in the very different political atmosphere of August. This time Washington inexplicably mislaid the request during the transfer of the records of the Foreign Economic Administration to the State Department. It did not turn up again until March 1946. Of course this was impossible for the Russians to believe; it is hard enough even for those acquainted with the capacity of the American government for incompetence to believe; and it only strengthened Soviet suspicions of American purposes.

The American credit was one conceivable form of Western contribution to Russian reconstruction. Another was lend-lease, and the possibility of reconstruction aid under the lend-lease protocol had already been discussed in 1944. But in May 1945 Russia, like Britain, suffered from Truman's abrupt termination of lend-lease shipments—"unfortunate and even brutal," Stalin told Hopkins, adding that, if it was "designed as pressure on the Russians in order to soften them up, then it was a fundamental mistake." A third form was German reparations. Here Stalin in demanding $10 billion in reparations for the Soviet Union made his strongest fight at Yalta. Roosevelt, while agreeing essentially with Churchill's opposition, tried to postpone the matter by accepting the Soviet figure as a "basis for discussion"—a formula which led to future misunderstanding. In short, the Russian hope for major Western assistance in postwar reconstruction foundered on three events which the Kremlin could well have interpreted respectively as deliberate sabotage (the loan request), blackmail (lend-lease cancellation) and pro-Germanism (reparations).

Actually the American attempt to settle the fourth lend-lease protocol was generous and the Russians for their own reasons declined to come to an agreement. It is not clear, though, that satisfying Moscow on any of these financial scores would have made much essential difference. It might have persuaded some doves in the Kremlin that the U.S. government was genuinely friendly; it might have persuaded some hawks that the American anxiety for Soviet friendship was such that Moscow could do as it wished without inviting challenge from the United States. It would, in short, merely have reinforced both sides of the Kremlin debate; it would hardly have reversed deeper tendencies toward the deterioration of political relationships. Economic deals were surely subordinate to the quality of mutual political confidence; and here, in the months after Yalta, the decay was steady.

The Cold War had now begun. It was the product not of a decision but of a dilemma. Each side felt compelled to adopt policies which the other could not but regard as a threat to the principles of the peace. Each then felt compelled to undertake defensive measures. Thus the Russians saw no choice but to consolidate their security in Eastern Europe. The Americans, regarding Eastern Europe as the first step toward Western Europe, responded by asserting their interest in the zone the Russians deemed vital to their security. The Russians concluded that the West was resuming its old course of capitalist encirclement; that it was purposefully laying the foundation for anti-Soviet régimes in the area defined by the blood of centuries as crucial to Russian survival. Each side believed with passion that future international stability depended on the success of its own conception of world order. Each side, in pursuing its own clearly indicated and deeply cherished principles, was only confirming the fear of the other that it was bent on aggression.

Very soon the process began to acquire a cumulative momentum. The impending collapse of Germany thus provoked new troubles: the Russians, for example, sincerely feared that the West was planning a separate surrender of the German armies in Italy in a way which would release troops for Hitler's eastern front, as they subsequently feared that the Nazis might succeed in surrendering Berlin to the West. This was the context in which the atomic bomb now appeared. Though the revisionist argument that Truman dropped the bomb less to defeat Japan than to intimidate Russia is not convincing, this thought unquestionably appealed to some in Washington as at least an advantageous side-effect of Hiroshima.

So the machinery of suspicion and counter-suspicion, action and counter-action, was set in motion. But, given relations among traditional national states, there was still no reason, even with all the postwar jostling, why this should not have remained a manageable situation. What made it unmanageable, what caused the rapid escalation of the Cold War and in another two years completed the division of Europe, was a set of considerations which this account has thus far excluded.

Up to this point, the discussion has considered the schism within the wartime coalition as if it were entirely the result of disagreements among national states. Assuming this framework, there was unquestionably a failure of communication between America and Russia, a misperception of signals and, as time went on, a mounting tendency to ascribe ominous motives to the other side. It seems hard, for example, to deny that American postwar policy created genuine difficulties for the Russians and even assumed a threatening aspect for them. All this the revisionists have rightly and usefully emphasized.

But the great omission of the revisionists—and also the fundamental explanation of the speed with which the Cold War escalated—lies precisely in the fact that the Soviet Union was *not* a traditional national state. This is where the "mirror image," invoked by some psychologists, falls down. For the Soviet Union was a phenomenon very different from America or Britain: it was a totalitarian state, endowed with an all-explanatory, all-consuming ideology, committed to the infallibility of government and party, still in a somewhat messianic mood, equating dissent with treason, and ruled by a dictator who, for all his quite extraordinary abilities, had his paranoid moments.

Marxism-Leninism gave the Russian leaders a view of the world according to which all societies were inexorably destined to proceed along appointed roads by appointed stages until they achieved the classless nirvana. Moreover, given the resistance of the capitalists to this development, the existence of any non-communist state was *by definition* a threat to the Soviet Union. "As long as capitalism and socialism exist," Lenin wrote, "we cannot live in peace: in the end, one or the other will triumph — a funeral dirge will be sung either over the Soviet Republic or over world capitalism."

Stalin and his associates, whatever Roosevelt or Truman did or failed to do, were bound to regard the United States as the enemy, not because of this deed or that, but because of the primordial fact that America was the leading capitalist power and thus, by Leninist syllogism, unappeasably hostile, driven by the logic of its system to oppose, encircle and destroy Soviet Russia. Nothing the United States could have done in 1944–45 would have abolished this mistrust, required and sanctified as it was by Marxist gospel — nothing short of the conversion of the United States into a Stalinist despotism; and even this would not have sufficed, as the experience of Jugoslavia and China soon showed, unless it were accompanied by total subservience to Moscow. So long as the United States remained a capitalist democracy, no American policy, given Moscow's theology, could hope to win basic Soviet confidence, and every American action was poisoned from the source. So long as the Soviet Union remained a messianic state, ideology compelled a steady expansion of communist power. . . .

Stalin alone could have made any difference. Yet Stalin, in spite of the impression of sobriety and realism he made on Westerners who saw him during the Second World War, was plainly a man of deep and morbid obsessions and compulsions. When he was still a young man, Lenin had criticized his rude and arbitrary ways. A reasonably authoritative observer (N. S. Khrushchev) later commented, "These negative characteristics of his developed steadily and during the last years acquired an absolutely insufferable character." His paranoia, probably set off by the suicide of his wife in 1932, led to the terrible purges of the mid-thirties and the wanton murder of thousands of his Bolshevik comrades. "Everywhere and in everything," Khrushchev says of this period, "he saw 'enemies,' 'double-dealers' and 'spies.'" The crisis of war evidently steadied him in some way, though Khrushchev speaks of his "nervousness and hysteria . . . even after the war began." The madness, so rigidly controlled for a time, burst out with new and shocking intensity in the postwar years. "After the war," Khrushchev testifies, the situation became even more complicated. Stalin became even more capricious, irritable and brutal; in particular, his suspicion grew. His persecution mania reached unbelievable dimensions. . . . He decided everything, without any consideration for anyone or anything.

Stalin's wilfulness showed itself . . . also in the international relations of the Soviet Union. . . . He had completely lost a sense of reality; he demonstrated his suspicion and haughtiness not only in relation to individuals in the USSR, but in relation to whole parties and nations.

A revisionist fallacy has been to treat Stalin as just another Realpolitik statesman, as Second World War revisionists see Hitler as just another Stresemann or Bismarck. But the record makes it clear that in the end nothing could satisfy Stalin's paranoia. His own associates failed. Why does anyone suppose that any conceivable American policy would have succeeded?

An analysis of the origins of the Cold War which leaves out these factors—the intransigence of Leninist ideology, the sinister dynamics of a totalitarian society and the madness of Stalin—is obviously incomplete. It was these factors which made it hard for the West to accept the thesis that Russia was moved only by a desire to protect its security and would be satisfied by the control of Eastern Europe; it was these factors which charged the debate between universalism and spheres of influence with apocalyptic potentiality.

Leninism and totalitarianism created a structure of thought and behavior which made postwar collaboration between Russia and America—in any normal sense of civilized intercourse between national states—inherently impossible. The Soviet dictatorship of 1945 simply could not have survived such a collaboration. Indeed, nearly a quarter-century later, the Soviet régime, though it has meanwhile moved a good distance, could still hardly survive it without risking the release inside Russia of energies profoundly opposed to communist despotism. As for Stalin, he may have represented the only force in 1945 capable of overcoming Stalinism, but the very traits which enabled him to win absolute power expressed terrifying instabilities of mind and temperament and hardly offered a solid foundation for a peaceful world.

The difference between America and Russia in 1945 was that some Americans fundamentally believed that, over a long run, a modus vivendi with Russia was possible; while the Russians, so far as one can tell, believed in no more than a short-run modus vivendi with the United States. . . .

In retrospect, if it is impossible to see the Cold War as a case of American aggression and Russian response, it is also hard to see it as a pure case of Russian aggression and American response. "In what is truly tragic," wrote Hegel, "there must be valid moral powers on both the sides which come into collision. . . . Both suffer loss and yet both are mutually justified." In this sense, the Cold War had its tragic elements. The question remains whether it was an instance of Greek tragedy—as Auden has called it, "the tragedy of necessity," where the feeling aroused in the spectator is "What a pity it had to be this way" — or of Christian tragedy, "the tragedy of possibility," where the feeling aroused is "What a pity it was this way when it might have been otherwise."

Once something has happened, the historian is tempted to assume that it had to happen; but this may often be a highly unphilosophical assumption. The Cold War could have been avoided only if the Soviet Union had not been possessed by convictions both of the infallibility of the communist word and of the inevitability of a communist world. These convictions transformed an impasse between national states into a religious war, a tragedy of possibility into one of necessity. One might wish that America had preserved the poise and proportion of the first years of the Cold War and had not in time succumbed to its own forms of self-righteousness. But the most rational of American policies could hardly have averted the Cold War. Only today, as Russia begins to recede from its messianic mission and to accept, in practice if not yet in principle, the permanence of the world of diversity, only now can the hope flicker that this long, dreary, costly contest may at last be taking on forms less dramatic, less obsessive and less dangerous to the future of mankind.

American Foreign Policy and the Origins of the Cold War

BARTON J. BERNSTEIN

There is no nation which has attitudes so pure that they cannot be bettered by self-examination.

JOHN FOSTER DULLES (1946)

We are forced to act in the world as it is, and not in the world as we wish it were, or as we would like it to become.

HENRY L. STIMSON (1947)

Despite some dissents, most American scholars have reached a general consensus on the origins of the Cold War. As confirmed internationalists who believe that Russia constituted a threat to America and its European allies after World War II, they have endorsed their nation's acceptance of its obligations as a world power in the forties and its desire to establish a world order of peace and prosperity. Convinced that only American efforts prevented the Soviet Union from expanding past Eastern Europe, they have generally praised the containment policies of the Truman Doctrine, the Mar-

From Barton J. Bernstein, "American Foreign Policy and the Origins of the Cold War," in *Politics and Policies of the Truman Administration,* edited by Barton J. Bernstein. Copyright © 1970 by Quadrangle Books, Inc. Reprinted by permission of the publisher, Franklin Watts, Inc.

shall Plan, and NATO as evidence of America's acceptance of world responsibility. While chiding or condemning those on the right who opposed international involvement (or had even urged preventive war), they have also been deeply critical of those on the left who have believed that the Cold War could have been avoided, or that the United States shared substantial responsibility for the Cold War.

Whether they are devotees of the new realism or open admirers of moralism and legalism in foreign policy, most scholars have agreed that the United States moved slowly and reluctantly in response to Soviet provocation, away from President Franklin D. Roosevelt's conciliatory policy. The Truman administration, perhaps even belatedly, they suggest, abandoned its efforts to maintain the Grand Alliance and acknowledged that Russia menaced world peace. American leaders, according to this familiar interpretation, slowly cast off the shackles of innocence and moved to courageous and necessary policies.

Despite the widespread acceptance of this interpretation, there has long been substantial evidence (and more recently a body of scholarship) which suggests that American policy was neither so innocent nor so nonideological; that American leaders sought to promote their conceptions of national interest and their values even at the conscious risk of provoking Russia's fears about her security. In 1945 these leaders apparently believed that American power would be adequate for the task of reshaping much of the world according to America's needs and standards.

By overextending policy and power and refusing to accept Soviet interests, American policy-makers contributed to the Cold War. There was little understanding of any need to restrain American political efforts and desires. Though it cannot be proved that the United States could have achieved a *modus vivendi* with the Soviet Union in these years, there is evidence that Russian policies were reasonably cautious and conservative, and that there was at least a basis for accommodation. But this possibility slowly slipped away as President Harry S. Truman reversed Roosevelt's tactics of accommodation. As American demands for democratic governments in Eastern Europe became more vigorous, as the new administration delayed in providing economic assistance to Russia and in seeking international control of atomic energy, policy-makers met with increasing Soviet suspicion and antagonism. Concluding that Soviet-American cooperation was impossible, they came to believe that the Soviet state could be halted only by force or the threat of force.

The emerging revisionist interpretation, then, does not view American actions simply as the necessary response to Soviet challenges, but instead tries to understand American ideology and interests, mutual suspicions and misunderstandings, and to investigate the failures to seek and achieve accommodation.

During the war Allied relations were often marred by suspicions and doubts rooted in the hostility of earlier years. It was only a profound "accident" —

the German attack upon the Soviet Union in 1941 — that thrust that leading anti-Bolshevik, Winston Churchill, and Marshal Josef Stalin into a common camp. This wartime alliance, its members realized, was not based upon trust but upon necessity; there was no deep sense of shared values or obvious similarity of interests, only opposition to a common enemy. "A coalition," as Herbert Feis has remarked, "is heir to the suppressed desires and maimed feelings of each of its members." Wartime needs and postwar aims often strained the uneasy alliance. In the early years when Russia was bearing the major burden of the Nazi onslaught, her allies postponed for two years a promised second front which would have diverted German armies. In December 1941, when Stalin requested recognition of 1941 Russian borders as they had been before the German attack (including the recently annexed Baltic states), the British were willing to agree, but Roosevelt rebuffed the proposals and aroused Soviet fears that her security needs would not be recognized and that her allies might later resume their anti-Bolshevik policies. So distrustful were the Allies that both camps feared the making of a separate peace with Germany, and Stalin's suspicions erupted into bitter accusations in March 1945, when he discovered (and Roosevelt denied) that British and American agents were participating in secret negotiations with the Germans. In anger Stalin decided not to send Vyacheslav Molotov, the Foreign Minister, to San Francisco for the April meeting on the founding of the United Nations Organization.

So suspicious were the Americans and British that they would not inform the Soviet Union that they were working on an atomic bomb. Some American leaders even hoped to use it in postwar negotiations with the Russians. In wartime, American opposition to communism had not disappeared, and many of Roosevelt's advisers were fearful of Soviet intentions in Eastern Europe. In turn, Soviet leaders, recalling the prewar hostility of the Western democracies, feared a renewed attempt to establish a *cordon sanitaire* and resolved to establish a security zone in Eastern Europe.

Though Roosevelt's own strategy often seems ambiguous, his general tactics are clear: they were devised to avoid conflict. He operated often as a mediator between the British and Russians, and delayed many decisions that might have disrupted the wartime alliance. He may have been resting his hopes with the United Nations or on the exercise of America's postwar strength, or he may simply have been placing his faith in the future. Whatever future tactics he might have been planning, he concluded that America's welfare rested upon international peace, expanded trade, and open markets:

> . . . it is our hope, not only in the interest of our own prosperity, but in the interest of the prosperity of the world, that trade and commerce and access to materials and markets may be freer after this war than ever before in the history of the world. . . . Only through a dynamic and soundly expanding world economy can the living standards of individual nations be advanced to levels which will permit a full realization of our hopes for the future.

His efforts on behalf of the postwar world generally reflected this understanding.

During the war Roosevelt wavered uneasily between emphasizing the postwar role of the great powers and minimizing their role and seeking to extend the principles of the Atlantic Charter. Though he often spoke of the need for an open postwar world, and he was reluctant to accept spheres of influence (beyond the Western hemisphere, where American influence was pre-eminent), his policies gradually acknowledged the pre-eminence of the great powers and yielded slowly to their demands. By late 1943 Roosevelt confided to Archbishop Francis Spellman (according to Spellman's notes) that "the world will be divided into spheres of influence: China gets the Far East; the U.S. the Pacific; Britain and Russia, Europe and Africa." The United States, he thought, would have little postwar influence on the continent, and Russia would probably "predominate in Europe," making Austria, Hungary, and Croatia "a sort of Russian protectorate." He acknowledged "that the European countries will have to undergo tremendous changes in order to adapt to Russia; but he hopes that in ten or twenty years the European influence would bring the Russians to become less barbarous."

In 1944 Roosevelt recognized the establishment of zones of influence in Europe. The Italian armistice of the year before had set the pattern for other wartime agreements on the control of affairs of liberated and defeated European nations. When Stalin requested the creation of a three-power Allied commission to deal with the problems of "countries falling away from Germany," Roosevelt and Churchill first rebuffed the Russian leader and then agreed to a joint commission for Italy which would be limited to information gathering. By excluding Russia from sharing in decision-making in Italy, the United States and Great Britain, later concluded William McNeill, "prepared the way for their own exclusion from any but a marginal share in the affairs of Eastern Europe."

When Roosevelt refused to participate in an Anglo-American invasion of southeastern Europe (which seemed to be the only way of restricting Russian influence in that area), Churchill sought other ways of dealing with Russian power and of protecting British interests in Greece. In May 1944 he proposed to Stalin that they recognize Greece as a British "zone of influence" and Rumania as a Russian zone; but Stalin insisted upon seeking Roosevelt's approval and refused the offer upon learning that the United States would not warmly endorse the terms. When the Soviets liberated Rumania in September they secured temporarily the advantages that Churchill had offered. They simply followed the British-American example in Italy, retained all effective power, and announced they were "acting in the interests of all the United Nations." From the Soviet Union, W. Averell Harriman, the American ambassador, cabled, "The Russians believe, I think, that we lived up to a tacit understanding that Rumania was an area of predominant Soviet interest in which we should not interfere. . . . The terms of the armistice give the Soviet command unlimited control of Rumania's economic life" and effective control over political organization.

With Russian armies sweeping through the Balkans and soon in a position to impose similar terms on Hungary and Bulgaria, Churchill renewed his efforts. "Winston," wrote an associate, "never talks of Hitler these days; he is always harping on the dangers of Communism. He dreams of the Red Army spreading like a cancer from one country to another. It has become an obsession, and he seems to think of little else." In October Churchill journeyed to Moscow to reach an agreement with Stalin. "Let us settle our affairs in the Balkans," Churchill told him. "Your armies are in Rumania and Bulgaria. We have interests, missions and agents there. Don't let us get at cross-purposes in small ways." Great Britain received "90 per cent influence" in Greece, and Russia "90 per cent influence" in Rumania, "80 per cent" in Bulgaria and Hungary, and "50 per cent" in Yugoslavia. . . .

While accepting the inevitable and acknowledging Russian influence in these areas, Roosevelt had not been tractable on the major issue confronting the three powers: the treatment of postwar Germany. All three leaders realized that the decisions on Germany would shape the future relations of Europe. A dismembered or permanently weakened Germany would leave Russia without challenge on the continent and would ease her fears of future invasion. As Anthony Eden, the British Foreign Minister, explained, "Russia was determined on one thing above all others, that Germany would not again disturb the peace of Europe. . . . Stalin was determined to smash Germany so that it would never again be able to make war." A strong Germany, on the other hand, could be a partial counterweight to Russia and help restore the European balance of power on which Britain had traditionally depended for protection. Otherwise, as Henry Morgenthau once explained in summarizing Churchill's fears, there would be nothing between "the white snows of Russia and the white cliffs of Dover. . . .

. . . Yielding to the pleas of the War and State Departments, Roosevelt decided upon a plan for a stronger postwar Germany, and Churchill, under pressure from advisers, also backed away from his earlier endorsement of the Morgenthau Plan and again acted upon his fears of an unopposed Russia on the continent. At Yalta, he resisted any agreement on the dismemberment of Germany. Stalin, faced with Anglo-American solidarity on this issue, acceded. . . .

Roosevelt's successor was less sympathetic to Russian aspirations and more responsive to those of Roosevelt's advisers, like Admiral William Leahy, Chief of Staff to the Commander in Chief; Harriman; James Forrestal, Secretary of the Navy; and James F. Byrnes, Truman's choice for Secretary of State, who had urged that he resist Soviet efforts in Eastern Europe. As an earlier self-proclaimed foe of Russian communism, Truman mistrusted Russia. ("If we see that Germany is winning the war," advised Senator Truman after the German attack upon Russia in 1941, "we ought to help Russia, and if Russia is winning we ought to help Germany and in that way kill as many as possible.") Upon entering the White House, he did not seek to follow Roosevelt's tactics of adjustment and accommodation. Only eleven days in the presidency and virtually on the eve of the United Nations conference, Truman moved to a showdown with Russia on the issue of Poland.

Poland became the testing ground for American foreign policy, as Truman later said, "a symbol of the future development of our international relations." At Yalta the three powers had agreed that the Soviet-sponsored Lublin Committee (the temporary Polish government) should be "reorganized on a broader democratic basis with the inclusion of democratic leaders from Poland itself and from Poland abroad." The general terms were broad: there was no specific formula for the distribution of power in the reorganized government, and the procedures required consultation and presumably unanimity from the representatives of the three powers. The agreement, remarked Admiral Leahy, was "so elastic that the Russians can stretch it all the way from Yalta to Washington without ever technically breaking it." ("I know, Bill—I know it. But it's the best I can do for Poland at this time," Roosevelt replied.)

For almost two months after Yalta the great powers haggled over Poland. The Lublin Committee objected to the Polish candidates proposed by the United States and Great Britain for consultation because these Poles had criticized the Yalta accord and refused to accept the Soviet annexation of Polish territory. . . . In early April Stalin had offered a compromise—that about 80 per cent of the cabinet posts in the new government should be held by members of the Lublin Committee, and that he would urge the committee to accept the leading Western candidates if they would endorse the Yalta agreement. . . . By proposing a specific distribution of power, Stalin cut to the core of the issue that had disrupted negotiations for nearly three months, and sought to guarantee the victory he probably expected in Poland. Roosevelt died before replying, and it is not clear whether he would have accepted this 4 to 1 representation; but he had acknowledged that he was prepared to place "somewhat more emphasis on the Lublin Poles."

Now Truman was asked to acknowledge Soviet concern about countries on her borders and to assure her influence in many of these countries by granting her friendly (and probably nondemocratic) governments, and even by letting her squelch anticommunist democrats in countries like Poland. To the President and his advisers the issue was (as Truman later expressed Harriman's argument) "the extension of Soviet control over neighboring states by independent action; we were faced with a barbarian invasion of Europe." The fear was not that the Soviets were about to threaten all of Europe but that they had designs on Eastern Europe, and that these designs conflicted with traditional American values of self-determination, democracy, and open markets. . . .

Having heard his advisers' arguments, Truman resolved to force the Polish question: to impose his interpretation of the Yalta agreement even if it destroyed the United Nations. He later explained that this was the test of Russian cooperation. If Stalin would not abide by his agreements, the U.N. was doomed, and, anyway, there would not be enough enthusiasm among the

American electorate to let the United States join the world body. "Our agreements with the Soviet Union so far . . . [have] been a one-way street." That could not continue, Truman told his advisers. "If the Russians did not wish to join us, they could go to hell." ("FDR's appeasement of Russia is over," joyously wrote Senator Arthur Vandenberg, the Republican leader on foreign policy.) Continuing in this spirit at a private conference with Molotov, the new President warned that economic aid would depend upon Russian behavior in fulfilling the Yalta agreement. Brushing aside the diplomat's contention that the Anglo-American interpretation of the Yalta agreement was wrong, the President accused the Russians of breaking agreements and scolded the Russian Foreign Minister. When Molotov replied, "I have never been talked to like that in my life," Truman warned him, "Carry out your agreement and you won't get talked to like that." . . .

The Soviets were further embittered when the United States abruptly curtailed lend-lease six days after V-E Day. Though Truman later explained this termination as simply a "mistake," as policy-making by subordinates, his recollection was incomplete and wrong. Leo Crowley, the director of lend-lease, and Joseph Grew, the Under Secretary of State, the two subordinates most closely involved, had repeatedly warned the President of the likely impact of such action on relations with Russia, and the evidence suggests that the government, as Harriman had counseled, was seeking to use economic power to achieve diplomatic means. Termination of lend-lease, Truman later wrote, "should have been done on a gradual basis which would not have made it appear as if somebody had been deliberately snubbed." Yet, despite this later judgment, Truman had four days after signing the order in which to modify it before it was to be implemented and announced, and the lend-lease administrator (in the words of Grew) had made "sure that the President understands the situation." The administrator knew "that we would be having difficulty with the Russians and did not want them to be running all over town for help." After discussing the decision with Truman, Grew, presumably acting with the President's approval, had even contrived to guarantee that curtailment would be a dramatic shock. When the Soviet chargé d'affaires had telephoned Grew the day before the secret order was to become effective, the Under Secretary had falsely denied that lend-lease to Russia was being halted. Harriman, according to Grew's report to the Secretary of State, "said that we would be getting 'a good tough slashback' from the Russians but that we would have to face it." . . .

There is considerable evidence that American actions clearly changed after Roosevelt's death. Slowly abandoning the tactics of accommodation, they became even more vigorous after Hiroshima. The insistence upon rolling back Soviet influence in Eastern Europe, the reluctance to grant a loan for Russian reconstruction, the inability to reach an agreement on Germany, the maintenance of the nuclear monopoly—all of these could have contributed to the sense of Russian insecurity. The point, then, is that in 1945 and 1946 there may still have been possibilities for negotiations and settlements, for accommodations and adjustments, if the United States had been willing to recognize Soviet fears, to accept Soviet power in her areas of influence, and to ease anxieties.

In October 1945 President Truman delivered what Washington officials called his "getting tough with the Russians" speech. Proclaiming that American policy was "based firmly on fundamental principles of righteousness and justice," he promised that the United States "shall not give our approval to any compromise with evil." In a veiled assault on Soviet actions in Eastern Europe, he declared, "We shall refuse to recognize any government imposed on any nation by the force of any foreign power." Tacitly opposing the bilateral trading practices of Russia, he asserted as a principle of American foreign policy the doctrine of the "open door" — all nations "should have access on equal terms to the trade and the raw materials of the world." At the same time, however, Truman disregarded the fact of American power in Latin America and emphasized that the Monroe Doctrine (in expanded form) remained a cherished part of American policy there: " . . . the sovereign states of the Western Hemisphere, without interference from outside the Western Hemisphere, must work together as good neighbors in the solution of their common economic problems." . . .

As early as February 1946 [George] Kennan had formulated the strategy — later called "containment" — which became acknowledged official policy in 1947. . . . In explaining Soviet behavior Kennan expressed the emerging beliefs of American leaders about Soviet irrationality and the impossibility of achieving agreements. Kennan disregarded the history of Western hostility to the Soviet Union and concluded that Soviet policy was *unreasonably* based upon a fear of Western antagonism. Russian leaders, he warned, had a "neurotic view of world affairs. And they have learned to seek security only in patient but deadly struggle for total destruction of rival power, *never in compacts and compromises with it.*"

Soviet power, however, "is neither schematic nor adventuristic," he said. "It does not take unnecessary risks. For this reason it can easily withdraw — and usually does — when strong resistance is encountered at any point. Thus, if the adversary has sufficient force and makes clear his readiness to use it, he rarely has to do so." (In an extended development of the same theme in 1947, Kennan warned that the Soviets move "inexorably along the prescribed path, like a persistent toy automobile wound up and headed in a given direction, stopping only when it meets unanswerable force." It was necessary to "confront the Russians with unalterable counterforce at any point where they show signs of encroaching," to stop the Russians with "superior force.")

Read eagerly by policy-makers, Kennan's message seemed to represent only a slight shift in emphasis from [Secretary of State James F.] Byrnes's policies. In 1945 and early 1946 the Secretary sought through diplomacy (and apparently "implied threats") to roll back Soviet influence in Eastern Europe.

Kennan apparently accepted the situation in Eastern Europe, seemed to recommend military resistance to future expansion, and, by implication, supported a stronger military force and foreign bases. In late 1946, as Byrnes moved reluctantly toward accepting the governments of Eastern Europe, he seemed temporarily to accede to Soviet power there. But he never surrendered his hope of pushing the Soviets back, and he was prepared to resist Soviet expansion. The containment doctrine, by urging continued pressure and predicting that Soviet power would either mellow or disintegrate, promised the success that Byrnes sought; but the doctrine, according to Kennan's conception, did not emphasize the heavy reliance upon armaments and alliances that developed. (Though Kennan never explicitly discussed in his famous cable the issue of economic aid to the Soviet Union, it was clear from his analysis and from his other recommendations that disintegration could be speeded by denying economic assistance.) To the goals that Byrnes and most American officials shared, Kennan added a tactic — patience. . . .

The fear of communism, often mixed with a misunderstanding of Munich and the sense that compromise may be appeasement, has led policy-makers generally to be intransigent in their response to communism. They have allowed their fears to distort their perceptions and their ideology to blur reality. This is part of the legacy of the Truman administration in the development of the Cold War.

In these years American liberal democracy became visibly defensive. Though espousing humanitarian ideals and proclaiming the value of self-determination, Americans have often failed to exhibit a tolerance or understanding of the methods of other people in pursuing social change and establishing governments in their own (non-American) way. Revolutions have been misunderstood, seldom accepted, never befriended. Fearing violence, respecting private property, and believing in peaceful reform, Americans have become captives of an ideology which interprets revolution as dysfunctional and dangerous to American interests. Opposing these radical movements in the name of freedom, America has turned often to oligarchies and dictators instead. By falsely dividing the world into the free and the unfree, and by making alliances in the name of freedom (not security) with the enemies of freedom, America has often judged world events by the standards of the crusade against communism, and thus it has been unable to understand the behavior and problems of the underdeveloped nations. It is this defective world view, so visible in the early Cold War, that has led some to lament that the American self-conception has lost its utopian vision.

NSC–68: A Report to the National Security Council

THE EXECUTIVE SECRETARY ON UNITED STATES OBJECTIVES AND PROGRAMS FOR NATIONAL SECURITY

April 14, 1950

I. BACKGROUNDS OF THE PRESENT WORLD CRISIS

Within the past thirty-five years the world has experienced two global wars of tremendous violence. It has witnessed two revolutions — the Russian and the Chinese — of extreme scope and intensity. It has also seen the collapse of five empires — the Ottoman, the Austro-Hungarian, German, Italian and Japanese — and the drastic decline of two major imperial systems, the British and the French. During the span of one generation, the international distribution of power has been fundamentally altered. For several centuries it had proved impossible for any one nation to gain such preponderant strength that a coalition of other nations could not in time face it with greater strength. The international scene was marked by recurring periods of violence and war, but a system of sovereign and independent states was maintained, over which no state was able to achieve hegemony.

Two complex sets of factors have now basically altered this historical distribution of power. First, the defeat of Germany and Japan and the decline of the British and French Empires have interacted with the development of the United States and the Soviet Union in such a way that power has increasingly gravitated to these two centers. Second, the Soviet Union, unlike previous aspirants to hegemony, is animated by a new fanatic faith, antithetical to our own, and seeks to impose its absolute authority over the rest of the world. Conflict has, therefore, become endemic and is waged, on the part of the Soviet Union, by violent or non-violent methods in accordance with the dictates of expediency. With the development of increasingly terrifying weapons of mass destruction, every individual faces the ever-present possibility of annihilation should the conflict enter the phase of total war.

On the one hand, the people of the world yearn for relief from the anxiety arising from the risk of atomic war. On the other hand, any substantial further extension of the area under the domination of the Kremlin would raise the possibility that no coalition adequate to confront the Kremlin with greater strength could be assembled. It is in this context that this Republic and its citizens in the ascendancy of their strength stand in their deepest peril.

The issues that face us are momentous, involving the fulfillment or destruction not only of this Republic but of civilization itself. They are issues which will not await our deliberations. With conscience and resolution this Government and the people it represents must now take new and fateful decisions.

From *Foreign Relations of the United States: 1950*, I, pp. 237–292.

II. FUNDAMENTAL PURPOSE OF THE UNITED STATES

The fundamental purpose of the United States is laid down in the Preamble to the Constitution: ". . . to form a more perfect Union, establish Justice, insure domestic Tranquility, provide for the common defence, promote the general Welfare, and secure the Blessings of Liberty to ourselves and our Posterity." In essence, the fundamental purpose is to assure the integrity and vitality of our free society, which is founded upon the dignity and worth of the individual.

Three realities emerge as a consequence of this purpose: Our determination to maintain the essential elements of individual freedom, as set forth in the Constitution and Bill of Rights; our determination to create conditions under which our free and democratic system can live and prosper; and our determination to fight if necessary to defend our way of life, for which as in the Declaration of Independence, "with a firm reliance on the protection of Divine Providence, we mutually pledge to each other our lives, our Fortunes and our sacred Honor."

III. FUNDAMENTAL DESIGN OF THE KREMLIN

The fundamental design of those who control the Soviet Union and the international communist movement is to retain and solidify their absolute power, first in the Soviet Union and second in the areas now under their control. In the minds of the Soviet leaders, however, achievement of this design requires the dynamic extension of their authority and the ultimate elimination of any effective opposition to their authority.

The design, therefore, calls for the complete subversion or forcible destruction of the machinery of government and structure of society in the countries of the non-Soviet world and their replacement by an apparatus and structure subservient to and controlled from the Kremlin. To that end Soviet efforts are now directed toward the domination of the Eurasian land mass. The United States, as the principal center of power in the non-Soviet world and the bulwark of opposition to Soviet expansion, is the principal enemy whose integrity and vitality must be subverted or destroyed by one means or another if the Kremlin is to achieve its fundamental design.

IV. THE UNDERLYING CONFLICT IN THE REALM OF IDEAS AND VALUES BETWEEN THE U.S. PURPOSE AND THE KREMLIN DESIGN

A. Nature of Conflict

The Kremlin regards the United States as the only major threat to the achievement of its fundamental design. There is a basic conflict between the idea of freedom under a government of laws, and the idea of slavery under the grim oligarchy of the Kremlin, which has come to a crisis with the polarization of power described in Section I, and the exclusive possession of atomic weapons by the two protagonists. The idea of freedom, moreover, is peculiarly and intolerably subversive of the idea of slavery. But the converse is not true. The implacable purpose of the slave state to eliminate the challenge of freedom has placed the two great powers at opposite poles. It is this fact which gives the present polarization of power the quality of crisis. . . .

Thus unwillingly our free society finds itself mortally challenged by the Soviet system. No other value system is so wholly irreconcilable with ours, so implacable in its purpose to destroy ours, so capable of turning to its own uses the most dangerous and divisive trends in our own society, no other so skillfully and powerfully evokes the elements of irrationality in human nature everywhere, and no other has the support of a great and growing center of military power. . . .

VI. U.S. INTENTIONS AND CAPABILITIES—ACTUAL AND POTENTIAL

A. Political and Psychological

Our overall policy at the present time may be described as one designed to foster a world environment in which the American system can survive and flourish. It therefore rejects the concept of isolation and affirms the necessity of our positive participation in the world community.

This broad intention embraces two subsidiary policies. One is a policy which we would probably pursue even if there were no Soviet threat. It is a policy of attempting to develop a healthy international community. The other is the policy of "containing" the Soviet system. . . .

IX. POSSIBLE COURSES OF ACTION

Introduction. Four possible courses of action by the United States in the present situation can be distinguished. They are:

  a. Continuation of current policies, with current and currently projected programs for carrying out these policies;
  b. Isolation;
  c. War; and
  d. A more rapid building up of the political, economic, and military strength of the free world than provided under *a*, with the purpose of reaching, if possible, a tolerable state of order among nations without war and of preparing to defend ourselves in the event that the free world is attacked. . . .

A more rapid build-up of political, economic, and military strength and thereby of confidence in the free world than is now contemplated is the only course which is consistent with progress toward achieving our fundamental purpose. The frustration of the Kremlin design requires the free world to develop a successfully functioning political and economic system and a vigorous political offensive against the Soviet Union. These, in turn, require an adequate military shield under which they can develop. It is necessary to have the military power to deter, if possible, Soviet expansion, and to defeat, if necessary, aggressive Soviet or Soviet-directed actions of a limited or total character. The potential strength of the free world is great; its ability to develop these military capabilities and its will to resist Soviet expansion will be determined by the wisdom and will with which it undertakes to meet its political and economic problems. . . .

In summary, we must, by means of a rapid and sustained build-up of the political, economic, and military strength of the free world, and by means of an affirmative program intended to wrest the initiative from the Soviet Union, confront it with convincing evidence of the determination and ability of the free world to frustrate the Kremlin design of a world dominated by its will. Such evidence is the only means short of war which eventually may force the Kremlin to abandon its present course of action and to negotiate acceptable agreements on issues of major importance.

The whole success of the proposed program hangs ultimately on recognition by this Government, the American people, and all free peoples, that the cold war is in fact a real war in which the survival of the free world is at stake. Essential prerequisites to success are consultations with Congressional leaders designed to make the program the object of non-partisan legislative support, and a presentation to the public of a full explanation of the facts and implications of the present international situation. The prosecution of the program will require of us all the ingenuity, sacrifice, and unity demanded by the vital importance of the issue and the tenacity to persevere until our national objectives have been attained. . . .

two

THE McCARTHY YEARS

In the 1950s, the United States embarked on a vigorous, and vicious, anti-Communist crusade at home. As contention with the Soviet Union increased, Americans seized on charges of internal subversion to help explain the difficulties of the Cold War. Troubled by disclosures of espionage during World War II and worried about stalemate in the Korean War, they sought scapegoats to take the blame. Joseph R. McCarthy, a Republican senator from Wisconsin, was the focal point of the anti-Communist campaign. He took center stage with a speech before the Ohio County Women's Republican Club in Wheeling, West Virginia, on February 9, 1950 and held it for the next four years. With little or no evidence, McCarthy smeared those suspected of harboring radical or even liberal sympathies, and destroyed careers with his unfounded and unproved accusations.

What was the source of McCarthy's appeal? Commentators have asked that question ever since he assumed prominence. For a time, historians and other social scientists suggested that status resentments accounted for McCarthy's following, that working-class Americans, following the populist tradition of the late nineteenth century, viewed McCarthy as a hero and gave him the support he needed to proceed. Michael Paul Rogin effectively demolishes this argument in *The Intellectuals and McCarthy: The Radical Specter*, which is excerpted here in "McCarthyism as Mass Politics." In this selection, the second essay in this section, Rogin acknowledges McCarthy's popular following among poorer Americans, but argues that the resentments of Republican elites, out of power for the past 20 years, created and sustained the base for the anti-Communist crusade.

Robert Griffith, in "American Politics and the Origins of 'McCarthyism,'" sketches the background of antiradicalism in the American past. He shows how the Cold War contributed to deep-rooted fears, describes congressional actions taken before 1950, and suggests that an anti-Communist movement was under way well before McCarthy launched his public campaign.

Joseph McCarthy's targets and techniques can best be seen through his own words. A selection from McCarthy's Wheeling, West Virginia, speech shows his perception of the Communist threat and his willingness to use sharp rhetoric to put his opponents on the defensive.

To examine the McCarthy period further, Richard H. Rovere, *Senator Joe McCarthy* (1960), remains a good introduction to the man and his methods. Thomas C. Reeves, *The Life and Times of Joe McCarthy* (1982), is a broad-based treatment of the senator, while David M. Oshinsky, *A Conspiracy So Immense: The World of Joe McCarthy* (1983), is an even more vivid account of the anti-Communist movement. Another useful book is Robert Griffith, *The Politics of Fear: Joseph R. McCarthy and the Senate* (1970), which goes even further than his essay reprinted here in noting the way McCarthy used his political base in the Senate to sustain his public campaign.

American Politics and the Origins of "McCarthyism"

ROBERT GRIFFITH

For nearly two decades American scholars and journalists have described "McCarthyism" in terms of a popular uprising, a mass movement of the "radical right" that threatened the very fabric of American society. Inchoate, irrational, it swept across the political landscape like an elemental force of nature carrying all before it. Its sources, these scholars maintained, lay not so much in the emergent cold war, but in the "social strains" and status tensions produced by a century of modernization. McCarthyism, like populism, was seen as an attack by paranoid provincials upon the educated and the wealthy. Politicians, in this view, were but the passive instruments of the popular will, reflecting the hysteria that welled up from the grass roots. McCarthy himself, of course, was something of an exception. Indeed, he was credited with a demonic talent for probing "the dark places of the American mind." He was "the most gifted" demagogue in American history, succeeding where others had failed in arousing the American masses and inciting them to action "outside of and against the established channels of constitutional government." . . .

But was McCarthyism really a popular movement? Probably not. To be sure, anti-Communism was an element in the American political culture, and popular attitudes toward Communism, conditioned as they were by several decades of misinformation and strident propaganda, were mostly negative. It is also true that public opinion polls showed a rather high level of support for McCarthy (around 35 percent for most of 1953–54), combined with frequently intolerant attitudes toward nonconformists and dissenters. But popular intolerance and anti-Communism, however important, have tended to be constants. Even in the supposedly radical thirties, for example, most Americans seemed to favor denying freedom of speech, press, and assembly to native Communists. What needs to be explained, therefore, is not the mere existence of such attitudes, but how, during the late 1940's and early 1950's, they were mobilized and became politically operational.

Second, . . . intense negative feelings about McCarthy were usually more common than strongly favorable ones. McCarthy aroused more opposition than support. Third, . . . the most common characteristic of McCarthy supporters was not class, religion, or ethnicity, but political affiliation. Support for McCarthy was strongest among Republicans. Socioeconomic factors were not unimportant — when party affiliation was held constant, those with lower status, less education, and of the Catholic faith tended to support McCarthy disproportionately. But these last factors seem clearly less signifi-

From Robert Griffith, "American Politics and the Origins of 'McCarthyism,'" in *The Specter: Original Essays on the Cold War: and the Origins of McCarthyism*, edited by Robert Griffith and Athan Theoharis. Copyright © 1974 by Franklin Watts, Inc. Reprinted by permission of the publisher.

cant than party. There was, moreover, no continuity between populism and McCarthyism. . . . Indeed, . . . nearly the reverse was true — agrarian radicalism, where cohesive, contributed not to the Republican right, but to the constituency of Democratic liberalism.

Fourth, while the polls did show substantial support for McCarthy and extremely negative feelings about Communism, as well as a low level of support for the civil liberties of Communists and other political dissidents, the intensity of these feelings was apparently not very strong. When people were asked, for example, whether they favored allowing Communists to teach in their schools, the response (both in the thirties and in the fifties) was largely and unsurprisingly negative. But in 1953, at the height of the McCarthy era, when people were asked a simple, nondirective question ("What kinds of things do you worry about most?"), less than 1 percent listed the threat of Communism as a major concern and only 8 percent mentioned the tangentially related area of world problems. Even when the interviewer sought to lead the respondent ("Are there other problems you worry about or are concerned about, especially political or world problems?"), the level of concern was not great. The number expressing anxiety about Communism increased only from 1 percent to 6 percent. The number concerned over international affairs rose more substantially, from 8 percent to 30 percent. Significantly, more than half of those so questioned added nothing to their initial response. Thus, . . . Americans were not very deeply concerned over domestic Communism. . . .

Finally, what is all too often overlooked is the congruence between popular attitudes toward Communism and the attitudes of influential public figures. Many prominent Republicans, for example, were constantly accusing the Roosevelt and Truman Administrations of selling out to Communism at home and abroad. Nor were such charges limited to conservatives. Some liberal Republicans, such as Senator Ralph Flanders of Vermont who would later lead the movement to censure McCarthy, believed that "our late departed saint Franklin Delano Roosevelt was soft as taffy on the subject of Communism and Uncle Joe." Even Democrats such as Massachusetts Congressman John F. Kennedy attacked the Truman Administration's foreign policies, charging that "what our young men saved [in World War II], our diplomats and our President have frittered away." The Truman Administration itself used the Red issue against Henry Wallace and the Progressives and occasionally even against the Republicans. McCarthy, the President charged at one point, was the Kremlin's "greatest asset." In denouncing Communism, then, Joe McCarthy, despite his occasional attacks on "the bright young men who are born with silver spoons in their mouths," was adopting a political issue already sanctioned by much of the nation's political leadership.

The commonly accepted portrait of McCarthyism as a mass movement and McCarthy as a charismatic leader is, thus, badly overdrawn. People were less concerned about the threat of Communism and less favorably inclined toward McCarthy than is generally thought. Support for McCarthy, moreover, was closely identified with partisan Republicanism. Finally, popular

attitudes about Communism generally mirrored the views of many prominent political leads, and McCarthy's use of the issue was unexceptional. . . .

But if McCarthyism is not to be understood primarily in terms of popular
passion, then how do we explain the contentious and tumultuous politics of
the mid-twentieth century? A partial answer to this problem involves a political definition of McCarthyism and . . . the actions and inactions of political
elites. McCarthyism may not have been only a political phenomenon; it may
indeed have reflected the "social strains" of modern American society. . . .
But it was primarily a product of the political system and its leaders. The
latter did not simply respond to popular protest, but rather helped to generate
the very sense of concern and urgency that came to dominate the decade.

This is not to argue that the politics of McCarthyism was born solely of
the postwar period. There was a long history of anti-radicalism in America, a
history produced both by conservative resistance to social change and by
nativist fears of strangers in the land. It was not a history created by protean
mass movements, however, but by the complicated interplay of political
manipulation and popular myth and stereotype. The Red Scare of 1919–20 is
instructive in this regard both as analogy and as legacy.

The Red Scare was made possible by hostile popular attitudes toward
Communists and other radicals — what has been called the "anti-Communist
persuasion." The intolerant atmosphere of World War I politics, the triumph
of the Bolsheviks in Russia, the organization of the American Communist
Party, and widespread labor unrest all served as proximate causes. The Red
Scare itself was created, however, by the vigorous activities of conservative
businessmen, organized veterans, patriotic societies, and by ambitious politicians in Congress and especially in the federal government. Business organizations such as the National Association of Manufacturers, the National
Metal Trades Association, the National Founders Association all worked hard
to stir up public opinion against labor unions as part of their crusade for the
"American plan," as they called the open shop. Conservative patriotic groups,
such as the National Security League, the American Defense Society, the
American Protective League, and the National Civic Federation, sought to
promote 100 percent Americanism, as did the newly organized American
Legion. Even the American Federation of Labor (AFL) joined the crusade,
partially to stifle leftist activities within the labor movement and partially to
deflect conservative attacks [away] from the AFL. Sensational reporting by
conservative newspapers, a category that included most of the American
press, further aroused popular anxieties. Finally, the impulses created by these
and other groups were mobilized by such politicians as Attorney General A.
Mitchell Palmer and translated into political action — the Palmer raids, de-
portation of alien radicals, and a flood of sedition bills including one designed
to attack what Palmer called "the real menace of evil-thinking." Following
the federal lead, more than thirty states hurriedly passed criminal syndical-
ism, criminal anarchy, and red flag laws.

The Red Scare finally subsided, of course. Most Americans were probably not deeply troubled by the imminence of a red revolution and were aroused only fitfully by politicians and the press. The Red Scare left as its legacy, however, both a substantial body of law and precedent and a reinforced set of popular myths and stereotypes susceptible to future manipulation by interest groups and politicians.

During the depression thirties the rise of domestic radicalism and the reform programs of the New Deal prompted nervous conservatives to again raise the specter of Communism. Anti-Communism, of course, was a traditional tactic of conservative opponents of social reform — used in response to the general railroad strike of the 1870's, the Populists in the 1890's, and the IWW in the early 1900's. During the thirties it simply became sound conservative doctrine to attack the New Deal as the forerunner of an American bolshevism. "If Roosevelt is not a Communist today," charged Robert A. Taft of Ohio, "he is bound to become one." Roosevelt, echoed the Republican National Committee in 1936, was "the Kerensky of the American Revolutionary Movement."

In 1930 and again in 1934, Congress launched investigations into "un-American activities," and in 1938 Congressman Martin Dies, with the support of Democratic House leaders Sam Rayburn and William B. Bankhead and the endorsement of Vice President John Nance Garner, proposed the creation of a Special Committee on Un-American Activities. Approved by a vote of 191 to 41, the committee, under Dies's flamboyant leadership, set out on a celebrated search for Communists in the Roosevelt Administration. In the process it pioneered almost all of the techniques that would later be associated with Senator McCarthy. The committee's activities were generously reported by the press, and popular reaction appeared to be generally favorable. Liberal opposition to the committee, never very potent, virtually disintegrated; and by the end of the decade one-time critic John M. Coffee (Democrat-Washington) was campaigning on the slogan "The Dies Committee endorses John Coffee's reelection."

At the same time, growing concern over domestic radicalism, combined with increasing international tensions, led to a mass of anti-radical and anti-alien bills, three of which were finally enacted into law. The first of these was the McCormack Act of 1938, which required all agents of foreign governments to register with the Department of Justice and which later served as partial precedent for the Communist registration section of the McCarran Internal Security Act of 1950. The following year Congress passed the Hatch Act, which was primarily intended to restrict the political activities of federal employees, but which also excluded from federal employment members of any organization that advocated the forcible overthrow of the government. Finally, the Smith Act of 1940, designed mainly to compel the registration of aliens, also made it illegal to advocate the overthrow of the government by force or violence.

Most of these measures were sponsored and supported by anti–New Deal conservatives. The Roosevelt Administration itself, however, was an indifferent champion of civil liberties. Thus Secretary of Labor Frances Perkins confined her testimony on the Smith bill to relatively minor points, while the Justice Department, under whose jurisdiction the sedition provisions fell, did not testify at all. The Navy Department, which was responsible for placing in the bill a section aimed at pacifists that made it illegal to interfere with or influence adversely the loyalty, morale, or discipline of the armed forces, warmly supported the measure. Roosevelt himself defended the bill's sedition provisions, replying to a critic that "they can hardly be considered to constitute an improper encroachment on civil liberties in the light of the present world conditions."

The activities of the federal government inspired imitation at the state and local level. These activities peaked, as did their national models, during the "little Red Scare" of the mid-thirties and again toward the end of the decade. Spurred on by the American Legion and other zealously anti-Communist groups, a half dozen states initiated investigations of "un-American activities," and several passed bills requiring loyalty oaths for teachers. A few states sought to exclude Communists from the ballot, while others attempted, following the example of the Hatch Act, to bar from public office anyone thought to advocate the violent overthrow of the government.

Although the success of such activities often depended on the acquiescence or even passive support of liberals, the anti-Communist impulse of the thirties remained primarily anti-reformist, the product of conservative Republican and Democratic attacks on the New Deal. Its appeal was, therefore, always limited by the widespread popularity of the Roosevelt program. All this changed, however, with the advent of the cold war and the subsequent shift from domestic to international concerns. . . .

The cold war transformed the climate of American politics, overlaying traditional political issues with a new and emotionally charged set of concerns. The growing power of the Soviet Union and its challenge to American supremacy served to focus previously diffuse fears and anxieties over Communism. So did the arrest of men and women accused of spying for the U.S.S.R. But the anti-Communist protest of the late 1940's was more than a simple response to external events. It also sprang from the goals that American leaders set for postwar foreign policy, the manner in which they perceived the Soviet challenge to that policy, and the methods they chose to meet that challenge.

For a variety of reasons — idealism, self-interest, the hubris of the very powerful — American leaders defined United States policy in sweeping terms: the creation of a global system of stability, peace, and prosperity. The Soviet challenge to this new order was seen as a threat to world peace and to American security, a threat to which the United States was compelled to respond. The character of this response, in turn, helped to create a climate in which anti-Communist politics gained a vastly heightened potency and appeal. In part, this was because the Truman Administration itself couched its policies in a rhetoric of crusading anti-Communism, which stressed American innocence, Soviet depravity, and the necessity for confrontation.

Such views, of course, were scarcely unique to the Truman Administration. Rather they were shared by a broad segment of America's political leadership—liberal and conservative, Democratic and Republican. Both Truman and his conservative critics were influenced to a great extent by the legacy of prewar anti-Communism. Both shared illusions concerning the limits of American power and the nature of Soviet foreign policy. Truman's critics, however, generally proposed more drastic policies and justified them with greater militance than did the Administration. Even Robert Taft, a frequently incisive critic of containment, denounced the Administration for being "soft on Communism," advocated greater assistance for Chiang Kai-shek, and supported General Douglas MacArthur in the controversy over the Korean War. The Truman Administration, committed to an interventionist policy abroad, stressed anti-Communism as a means of winning support from such nationalistic but fiscally cautious conservatives. As a result, most conservatives joined the Administration in a bipartisan anti-Communist consensus, while the rest, including Taft, were left isolated and impotent. A second, and unintended consequence of this tactic, however, was the generation of a new and conservative political climate, resistant to social change at home and to negotiation and compromise abroad.

The new political climate inspired conservative businessmen, organized veterans, patriotic societies, and other zealous anti-Communists and made their efforts appear more plausible and relevant. The Chamber of Commerce, for example, through its Committee on Socialism and Communism, prepared and distributed a series of pamphlets designed to expose Communists in government and labor, to discredit New Deal social legislation, and to help businessmen reassert themselves at the community level. The American Legion was even more active. Led by its Americanism Division and active at both the state and federal levels, the Legion campaigned vigorously to arouse the nation to the perils of Communism. The Legion played an important role in creating and sustaining the Special House Committee on Un-American Activities and in the establishment of "little Dies Committees" in the states. The Legion lobbied hard for new anti-Communist legislation, supporting the Mundt-Nixon Communist registration bill as well as a wide variety of restrictive measures at the state level. Finally, the Legion became deeply involved in the colorful crusade against Communism in Hollywood and in the subsequent spread of blacklisting in the film, radio, and television industries.

The Legion and the Chamber of Commerce were only two among a welter of anti-Communist organizations, which included patriotic societies such as the Daughters of the American Revolution, Catholic groups such as the Knights of Columbus and the Catholic War Veterans, ethnic groups such as the Polish-American Congress, and a host of smaller right-wing organizations. The activities of these groups included lobbying, propaganda, and on occasion picketing and other forms of public protest. The concerns of such groups were amplified by the press. The conservative McCormick, Hearst, and Gannett chains were especially active in this undertaking, though overwrought anti-Communism was not limited to them alone. As early as

1945, for example, *Life* magazine complained that "The 'fellow traveler' is everywhere, in Hollywood, on college faculties, in government bureaus, in publishing companies, in radio offices, even on the editorial staffs of eminently capitalistic journals." From here it was but a short step to the demand that such "fellow travelers" be purged from American life.

This was not, of course, "mass" politics but "interest group" politics, a typical expression of the American political culture and not an aberrational one. The group base of American politics was not aligned . . . against a mass politics of anti-Communism. Instead, interest groups themselves lay at the heart of the anti-Communist politics of the era.

The aggressive actions of right-wing interest groups were not, moreover, met by countervailing pressures from the left. Instead, the same broad forces that lent strength and legitimacy to the postwar right served to undermine and destroy the postwar left. In 1945 the American left was a relatively large and potentially powerful movement, which included a wide assortment of liberals, socialists, and Communists. Though scarred by the memory of past betrayals and sharply divided among themselves, these leftists nevertheless shared a consensus on two fundamental points: the necessity for radical social change at home and for a conciliatory and pacific foreign policy abroad. The rise of the cold war and the resurgence of conservatism, however, led to bitter divisions within the left over American policy toward the Soviet Union and over the role of Communism in American life. The precarious unity of the popular front was shattered, both by the Communists who repudiated the wartime leadership of Earl Browder and by cold-war liberals who supported the foreign policies of the Truman Administration and sought to purge Communists from labor unions, political parties, and other voluntary associations. The overwhelming rejection of Henry Wallace in the 1948 campaign and the emergence of Americans for Democratic Action (ADA) marked the beginning of a new political era in which the left was in virtual eclipse and in which the distinction between liberals and conservatives became one of method and technique, not fundamental principle. Divided, demoralized, and after 1948 led by men who shared many of the anti-Communist assumptions of the right, the American left was unable to withstand the mounting demands of McCarthyite conservatives. . . .

The political climate of postwar America was thus shaped by the cold war, by the agitation of conservative interest groups, and by the disintegration of liberalism. It remained, however, for politicians to mobilize the support necessary for a politics of anti-Communism. Foremost among such politicians were those Republican and Democratic conservatives who had championed the anti-Communist issues since the thirties and who had maintained all along that Democratic liberalism was leading the country down the road to Communism. After 1945, however, this anti-reformist impulse was joined with the new foreign policy and internal security issues bred by the cold war. Congressional conservatives now charged that the Roosevelt and Truman Administrations were "soft" on Communism abroad and tolerant of subversion and disloyalty at home; and beginning in 1945 they launched a series of investigations into Communist activities designed in part to embarrass the government.

The frequency of such investigations was one measure of the rise of the Communist issue in American politics. There were four investigations during the 79th Congress (1945–47); twenty-two during the Republican 80th Congress (1947–49); twenty-four during the 81st Congress (1949–51); thirty-four during the 82nd Congress (1951–53); and fifty-one, an all-time high, during the Republican 83rd Congress (1953–55). Throughout the forties most of these investigations were conducted by the House Committee on Un-American Activities, led, following the retirement of Martin Dies, by J. Parnell Thomas (Republican-New Jersey) and by John S. Wood (Democrat-Georgia). More important, the focus and character of these investigations changed. Before December 1948 most of HUAC's investigations seemed to be linked to domestic concerns—the committee's primary targets were left-wing New Deal personnel, New Deal agencies such as the Federal Theatre Project and the Office of Price Administration, trade unions whose leadership included Communists, and Hollywood. But after 1948, the year in which Whittaker Chambers accused Alger Hiss first of having been a Communist and then, later, of having spied for the Soviet Union, the committee began increasingly to emphasize the internal security issues of espionage, subversion, and "Communists in government."

The Communist issue was injected into the 1946 elections and was apparently a factor in the Republican triumph, especially among urban Catholics. In 1947–48 the Truman Administration responded to these pressures by justifying its foreign policies with a crusading anti-Communist rhetoric, by instituting a federal loyalty-security program, by prosecuting Communist party leaders under the Smith Act, and in general by stressing its own firm anti-Communist credentials. Indeed, by 1948 the Administration had succeeded, if only temporarily, in using the Communist issue to its own advantage against both the Progressives and the Republicans. Crusades, however, are more easily begun than halted, and by early 1950 those conservative politicians whom Truman had sought to outflank once again held the initiative, now denouncing the Administration for the "loss" of China and demanding a sweeping purge within the government.

The rise of anti-Communism as an issue in national politics was accompanied by the growth of a derivative anti-Communist politics at the state and local levels. In part this was because many of the organizations that had agitated for restrictive measures at the federal level were also active in the states and in the communities. Some of these groups, the Chamber of Commerce and the American Legion, for example, labored not only to arouse others to the menace of Communism, but also to popularize techniques and methods for combating it. The Chamber sponsored anti-Communist seminars for local businessmen, while the American Legion held conferences for state legislators anxious to learn what the federal government and other states were doing to safeguard the Republic. Catholic Church groups and the conservative Hearst press also helped agitate the issue, as did the coterie of staff and witnesses that surrounded the House Committee on Un-American Activities.

More important, state legislatures responded almost slavishly to the force of federal law and precedent and to the anxieties aroused by national leaders. Anti-radical legislation was not, of course, new to most states. Yet what was remarkable about the great outpouring of the late forties was that so many legislatures acted at the same time and in the same way. In 1949, for example, the Maryland legislature passed a Subversive Activities Act, popularly known as the Ober Law. There was little original in the new law, however, for it had been drawn from the Smith Act of 1940, from Truman's Loyalty Program of 1947, and from portions of the Mundt-Nixon bill then pending before Congress. The Ober Law was in turn copied in part or entirely by the states of Mississippi, New Hampshire, Washington, and Pennsylvania. In the case of Pennsylvania, the legislature in 1951 established as the criteria for dismissing state employees not the Ober Law's standard—"reasonable grounds . . . to believe that any person is a subversive person"—but instead "reasonable doubt as to the loyalty of the person involved." The Maryland law had followed the criteria set forth in Truman's March 1947 loyalty order (Ex. Order 9835); the Pennsylvania legislature incorporated a generally unheralded but highly significant change in that criteria, in effect reversing the burden of proof, which Truman had ordered in April 1951 (Ex. Order 10241).

During the late forties, nearly thirty states enacted laws seeking to bar from public employment those who advocated the violent overthrow of the government, or who belonged to organizations which so advocated. In only one instance did such a state statute predate the Truman loyalty order; all of them, of course, came after the 1939 Hatch Act, which had provided such restrictions for federal employment. The Attorney General's list, institutionalized by Truman's 1947 loyalty order, was quickly adopted as a test of loyalty by states (including Arizona, New York, Michigan, Texas, Oklahoma), by municipalities (among them Detroit and New York City), and even by private employers (including the Columbia Broadcasting System). Following the passage in September 1950 of the McCarran Internal Security Act, more than a half dozen states rushed to enact so-called Communist Control Laws. Even cities passed municipal ordinances directed against Communists.

Thus state and local anti-Communist legislation, though widespread, is best understood as a reflection, not a cause, of national priorities. Unlike populism, the impact of which was felt first at the local and state level and only later at the national level, the politics of anti-Communism originated at the national level and then spread to the states.

By 1950, then, political leaders had succeeded, through the manipulation of popular myths and stereotypes, in creating a mood conducive to demagogues such as Joseph R. McCarthy. The Wisconsin senator's crude attacks on American policy and policymakers resonated through the political system not because of their uniqueness, but because of their typicality. To call this political impulse "McCarthyism," however, is to exaggerate the senator's importance and to misunderstand the politics that he came to symbolize. McCarthy was the product of anti-Communist politics, not its progenitor. Had he never made that speech in Wheeling, West Virginia, had his name never become a household word, what people came to call "McCarthyism" would nevertheless have characterized American politics at the mid-century.

McCarthyism as Mass Politics

MICHAEL PAUL ROGIN

In the decade that has elapsed since Joseph McCarthy of Wisconsin dominated American politics, the atmosphere of the McCarthy years has tended to fade from the public consciousness. But to forget the impact of McCarthyism is a mistake. . . . McCarthy's impact on public policy hardly exhausted his influence. Directly or indirectly he shattered countless lives and seemed to inflict a mood of fear and suspicion on American life as a whole. Rarely has one man in this country cast so long or so dark a shadow.

McCarthy's power, if overwhelming, was comparatively short-lived. But his impact on the intellectual community has lasted far longer. There are those who charge that the McCarthy atmosphere continues to stifle intellectual dissent. But McCarthyism has not so much suppressed opinions as changed them; it has significantly altered the tone of intellectual discussion about politics in general and American politics in particular.

A loosely coherent social theory, substantially concerned with comprehending McCarthyism, emerged in the 1950's. My interest is in that social theory, as it explains McCarthy, as it reinterprets the reform tradition, as it refracts American history through the myopia of a traumatized intelligentsia.

When McCarthy first became prominent, most liberals interpreted the danger he posed in fairly straightforward terms. To them McCarthy was simply the most successful of a number of conservative Republicans capitalizing on the Communist threat to attack the New Deal at home and the Fair Deal abroad. "McCarthyism" was a synonym for smear attacks on liberals, its roots were in traditional right-wing politics, and its principal targets were innocent individuals and liberal political goals. Liberals hardly minimized McCarthy's political importance, although they had little difficulty explaining either his roots or the danger he posed.

But to many writers such traditional analysis failed to account for McCarthy's strength. In their eyes, McCarthy was getting support not from the established groups with which traditional conservatism had been associated but rather from the dispossessed and discontented. One had to wonder about any inevitable association between popular discontent and support for progressive movements of economic reform. Moreover, McCarthy continually appealed to the mass of people for direct support over the heads of their elected leaders. And the established eastern elite, unsympathetic to the Wisconsin senator, was one of his important targets. All this suggested that popular democracy constituted a real threat to the making of responsible political decisions. McCarthy appeared not in the guise of a conservative smearing innocent liberals but in the guise of a democrat assaulting the political fabric. . . .

In this new view, McCarthyism was a movement of the radical Right that grew out of movements of the radical Left. For traditional liberals, the New Deal and contemporary liberalism had grown out of the protest politics of the pre-Roosevelt years. The newer view produced a very different history. Left-wing protest movements, democratic in their appeal to the popular masses, radical in the discontent they mobilized, had borne fruit in McCarthyism. To some, McCarthy was directly descended from an agrarian radical tradition. To others he had conservative roots as well, but his power derived from his ability to form an alliance between traditional conservatism and agrarian radicalism. . . .

The present study challenges the notion that McCarthy had agrarian radical roots. Examination of the empirical evidence finds no correlation between support for agrarian radicals and support for McCarthy; consideration of the reform tradition uncovers no unique reform appeals on which McCarthy capitalized. Investigation of the McCarthy movement discloses no agrarian radical flavor but rather a traditional conservative heritage. Analysis of the new social theory questions its relevance to American history. . . .

From 1950 through 1954, Joseph McCarthy disrupted the normal routine of American politics. But McCarthyism can best be understood as a product of that normal routine. McCarthy capitalized on popular concern over foreign policy, communism, and the Korean War, but the animus of McCarthyism had little to do with any less political or more developed *popular* anxieties. Instead it reflected the specific traumas of conservative Republican activists—internal Communist subversion, the New Deal, centralized government, left-wing intellectuals, and the corrupting influences of a cosmopolitan society. The resentments of these Republicans and the Senator's own talents were the driving forces behind the McCarthy movement.

Equally important, McCarthy gained the protection of politicians and other authorities uninvolved in or opposed to the politics motivating his ardent supporters. Leaders of the GOP saw in McCarthy a way back to national power after twenty years in the political wilderness. Aside from desiring political power, moderate Republicans feared that an attack on McCarthy would split their party. Eisenhower sought for long months to compromise with the Senator, as one would with any other politician. Senators, jealous of their prerogative, were loath to interfere with a fellow senator. Newspapers, looking for good copy, publicized McCarthy's activities. When the political institutions that had fostered McCarthy turned against him, and when with the end of the Korean War his political issue became less salient, McCarthy was reduced to insignificance.

Politics alone does not explain McCarthyism; but the relevant sociopsychology is that which underpins normal American politics, not that of radicals and outsiders. Psychological insights are not relevant alone to the peculiar politics of the American Right. Equally important, the ease with which McCarthy harnessed himself to the everyday workings of mainstream politics illuminates the weaknesses of America's respectable politicians.

Attention to sociology and psychology must be concentrated within the political stratum, not among the populace as a whole. It is tempting to explain the hysteria with which McCarthy infected the country by the hysterical preoccupations of masses of people. But the masses did not levy an attack on their political leaders; the attack was made by a section of the political elite against another and was nurtured by the very elites under attack. The populace contributed to McCarthy's power primarily because it was worried about communism, Korea, and the cold war. . . .

In January 1954, a majority of the American population approved of Senator McCarthy. For the next eleven months, one third of the total population consistently supported him; eliminate those with no opinion, and the figure rises to 40 percent. . . . This man, terribly dangerous in the eyes of sophisticated observers of American politics, had obtained the backing of millions of American people. . . .

. . . [P]erhaps the single most important characteristic of supporters of McCarthy in the national opinion polls was their party affiliation; Democrats opposed McCarthy, and Republicans supported him. In April 1954, Democrats outnumbered Republicans more than two to one among those having an unfavorable opinion of McCarthy; 16 percent more Republicans than Democrats had a favorable opinion of the Senator. Totaling support for McCarthy in a series of Gallup Polls in the early 1950's reveals that 36 percent of the Democrats favored McCarthy while 44 percent opposed him. The comparable Republican figures were 61 percent for and 25 percent against. Democrats were 8 percentage points more against McCarthy than for him, Republicans 36 points more for him than against him. The total percentage point spread by party was 44 points. In these polls, . . . no other single division of the population (by religion, class, education, and so forth) even approached the party split. . . .

The data, in sum, do not suggest intense, active, mass involvement in a McCarthyite movement. Efforts to relate status frustrations and psychological malformations to McCarthyism have not proved very successful. Party and political issue cleavages structured McCarthy's support. . . . But the ignorant, the deprived, and the lower classes did support McCarthy disproportionately. Were they expressing their animus against respectable groups and institutions?

To answer this question, we must ask two others: Why did McCarthyism attract a large popular following of this character, and what impact did support for the Senator have on political behavior?

Most people supported McCarthy because he was identified in the public mind with the fight against communism. In June 1952, a national sample was asked whether, taking all things into consideration, they thought committees of Congress investigating communism, like Senator McCarthy's, were doing more good than harm. In a period when less than 20 percent of the population had a favorable personal opinion of the Senator, 60 percent were for the committees and only 19 percent against them. The more McCarthy's name was identified with anticommunism, the more support he got from the population. . . . McCarthy's appeal was the functionally specific appeal of a single-issue promoter, not the diffuse appeal which mobilizes the "mass man." McCarthy's stress on communism may have suggested "the weakness of a single issue" for building a right-wing mass movement, but by the same token it explained the strength of McCarthyism.

Popular concern over communism could have symbolized a basic uneasiness about the health of American institutions. So it did for McCarthy and his most vociferous supporters, who saw a government overrun with dupes and traitors. For them, the Communist issue was the issue of Communists in government; internal subversion was the danger. For the American people, however, communism was essentially a foreign policy issue. In the 1952 election, less than 3 percent expressed concern over Communists in government — fewer than referred to the Point Four program. Foreign policy, on the other hand, was an extremely salient issue, and those concerned over foreign policy were more likely to vote Republican. The external Communist threat and the fear of war benefited the GOP at the polls in the 1950's: the internal Communist danger, salient to committed Republicans alone, did not. Moreover, mass concern about foreign policy did not appear over the loss of China, which the right-wing invested with such peculiar moral significance. It was only when American soldiers went to Korea that foreign policy became salient at the mass level. And the desire there — as expressed in the election of Eisenhower — was for peace not for war.

Why then, if McCarthy's appeal had specifically to do with foreign policy and the Korean War, did he receive greater support among the poorer and less-educated groups? Had the working class been actively concerned about McCarthy, we might expect this support to overcome the relative lack of political knowledge among those of low socioeconomic status. But asked to name the man who had done the best job of fighting communism, the less-educated and poorer strata volunteered McCarthy's name no more than did the better-educated and rich. Highly conscious pro-McCarthy sentiments were as prevalent among the upper as the lower classes. (Those of higher socioeconomic status, with more political information and sophistication, were more likely to name McCarthy as someone who had done a particularly bad job.) Disproportionate working-class support for McCarthy thus only manifested itself when his name was actually mentioned in the polls; it was not powerful enough to emerge when workers had to volunteer his name on their own.

The evidence does not suggest that the Communist issue preoccupied the lower classes, or that they were using that issue to vent general grievances about their position in society. More likely, they simply had less information about McCarthy's methods, a less sophisticated understanding of their nature and less concern in the abstract about possible victims of the Senator's techniques. Therefore, when the pollsters specifically mentioned McCarthy's name, it tapped among the middle-class revulsion over McCarthy's crudities and opposition to his infringements of individual rights. Among the working class, it tapped an anticommunism relatively less restrained by these concerns. . . .

What are we to conclude, then, about McCarthy's "mass" appeal? McCarthy's popular following apparently came from two distinct sources. There was first the traditional right wing of the midwestern Republican Party. Here was a group to whom McCarthy was a hero. He seemed to embody all their hopes and frustrations. These were the militants in the McCarthy movement. They worked hardest for him and were preoccupied with his general targets. To them, communism was not the whole story; their enemies were also the symbols of welfare capitalism and cosmopolitanism. These militants were mobilized by McCarthy's "mass" appeal. Yet this appeal had its greatest impact upon activists and elites, not upon the rank-and-file voters. And while McCarthy mobilized the Republican right wing, he did not change its traditional alliances. This was not a "new" American Right, but rather an old one with new enthusiasm and new power.

McCarthy's second source of popular support were those citizens mobilized because of communism and the Korean war. Concern over these issues throughout the society increased Republican strength, although this increase in popular support accrued not so much to McCarthy as to Eisenhower. McCarthy's strength here was not so much due to "mass," "populist," or "status" concerns as it was to the issues of communism, Korea, and the cold war. At the electoral level, there was little evidence that those allegedly more vulnerable to "mass" appeals were mobilized by McCarthy to change their traditional voting patterns.

McCarthy had real support at the grass roots, but his was hardly a "movement in which popular passions wreaked their aggression against the structure of the polity." In a period in which the populace gave overwhelming support to Eisenhower, it can hardly be accused of failing to show deference to responsible political leadership. In so arguing, I by no means wish to minimize the danger of McCarthyism. . . . In fact, McCarthy did immense damage to the lives and careers of countless individuals. He exercised an inordinate influence over policy making. But popular enthusiasm for his assault on political institutions simply cannot explain the power he wielded.

Insofar as McCarthy challenged political decisions, political individuals, and the political fabric, he was sustained not by a revolt of the masses so much as by the actions and inactions of various elites. . . .

Conservative Republican activists provided McCarthy with the core of his enthusiastic support. In addition, groups ranging from Catholic Democratic workers to conservative southern senators contributed to McCarthy's power—the workers by verbal approval in the polls, the senators by their actions and silences in Washington. Having examined the contribution of the masses to McCarthyism, we turn now to the elites. . . .

. . . The existence of a powerful Republican right wing, the new appeal of the issues of communism and foreign policy, and McCarthy's own tactical brilliance raised McCarthyism to a place of national prominence. But there was more to McCarthy's success than this. The response of a variety of political elites—by no means simply allies of the Wisconsin senator—enabled him to harness himself to the everyday workings of American politics. Those already part of this machinery often did not approve of McCarthy. Some, like moderate Republicans in their battle with the Democrats, congressmen in their battle with the executive, newspapers in their search for news, thought they could use him. Others, like southern Democrats, saw no need to treat McCarthy differently than they treated other senators. Still others, moderate Republicans in their desire for party unity, liberal Democrats in their desire for reelection, were afraid of him. Political and psychological reasons made a variety of political elites anxious to avoid a confrontation with McCarthy. Until it became clear to them that McCarthyism was more than politics as usual, they failed effectively to challenge it.

We have already pointed to the importance of the political structure in influencing McCarthy's mass support. Regardless of attitudes toward civil liberties and even toward McCarthy in the abstract, traditional political allegiances kept the workers in the Democratic Party in the 1950's and business and professional men in the GOP. McCarthy's "mass" appeal did not register directly in politics because many who supported him cared more about the Democratic Party, the New Deal, their trade unions, or their wives and families than they cared about McCarthy. They therefore did not break their traditional political habits.

Just as the political structure limited the sustenance McCarthy could derive from the grass roots, so it influenced the behavior of political elites. We look now at conservative Republicans and GOP moderates, at the Senate and the southern Democrats, at the press and at the liberals.

Most of those who mobilized behind McCarthy at the national level were conservative politicians and publicists, businessmen, and retired military leaders discontented with the New Deal, with bureaucracy, and with military policy. . . .

. . . The evolution of politics in the Middle West and the nation had had two political consequences for conservatives. They were in heretofore unprecedented positions of political power at the state level and political weakness at the national level. Their desperation is suggested by [Senator Robert A.] Taft's famous advice to McCarthy, "If one case doesn't work, then bring up another." This political elite sustained McCarthy. It helped dramatize his issues and fight his fights. Conservative Republican activists provided money and enthusiasm for the Senator's cause. . . .

Document
Speech, Wheeling, West Virginia

JOSEPH R. McCARTHY

Ladies and gentlemen, tonight as we celebrate the one hundred and forty-first birthday of one of the greatest men in American history, I would like to be able to talk about what a glorious day today is in the history of the world. As we celebrate the birth of this man who with his whole heart and soul hated war, I would like to be able to speak of peace in our time, of war being outlawed, and of world-wide disarmament. These would be truly appropriate things to be able to mention as we celebrate the birthday of Abraham Lincoln. . . .

Five years after a world war has been won, men's hearts should anticipate a long peace, and men's minds should be free from the heavy weight that comes with war. But this is not such a period—for this is not a period of peace. This is a time of the "cold war." This is a time when all the world is split into two vast, increasingly hostile armed camps—a time of a great armaments race.

Today we can almost physically hear the mutterings and rumblings of an invigorated god of war. You can see it, feel it, and hear it all the way from the hills of Indochina, from the shores of Formosa, right over into the very heart of Europe itself. . . .

While Lincoln was a relatively young man in his late thirties, Karl Marx boasted that the Communist specter was haunting Europe. Since that time, hundreds of millions of people and vast areas of the world have fallen under Communist domination. Today, less than 100 years after Lincoln's death, [Soviet leader Joseph] Stalin brags that this Communist specter is not only haunting the world, but is about to completely subjugate it.

Today we are engaged in a final, all-out battle between communistic atheism and Christianity. The modern champions of communism have selected this as the time. And, ladies and gentlemen, the chips are down—they are truly down. . . .

Ladies and gentlemen, can there be anyone here tonight who is so blind as to say that the war is not on? Can there be anyone who fails to realize that the Communist world has said, "The time is now"—that this is the time for

From *Congressional Record*, 81 Congress, 2nd session, pp. 1954–1957.

the show-down between the democratic Christian world and the Communist atheistic world?

Unless we face this fact, we shall pay the price that must be paid by those who wait too long.

Six years ago, at the time of the first conference to map out the peace — Dumbarton Oaks — there was within the Soviet orbit 180,000,000 people. Lined up on the antitotalitarian side there were in the world at that time roughly 1,625,000,000 people. Today, only 6 years later, there are 800,000,000 people under the absolute domination of Soviet Russia — an increase of over 400 percent. On our side, the figure has shrunk to around 500,000,000. In other words, in less than 6 years the odds have changed from 9 to 1 in our favor to 8 to 5 against us. This indicates the swiftness of the tempo of Communist victories and American defeats in the cold war. As one of our outstanding historical figures once said, "When a great democracy is destroyed, it will not be because of enemies from without, but rather because of enemies from within."

The truth of this statement is becoming terrifyingly clear as we see this country each day losing on every front.

At war's end we were physically the strongest nation on earth and, at least potentially, the most powerful intellectually and morally. Ours could have been the honor of being a beacon in the desert of destruction, a shining living proof that civilization was not yet ready to destroy itself. Unfortunately, we have failed miserably and tragically to arise to the opportunity.

The reason why we find ourselves in a position of impotency is not because our only powerful potential enemy has sent men to invade our shores, but rather because of the traitorous actions of those who have been treated so well by this Nation. It has not been the less fortunate or members of minority groups who have been selling this Nation out, but rather those who have had all the benefits that the wealthiest nation on earth has had to offer — the finest homes, the finest college education, and the finest jobs in Government we can give.

This is glaringly true in the State Department. There the bright young men who are born with silver spoons in their mouths are the ones who have been worst. . . .

I have in my hand 57 cases of individuals who would appear to be either card carrying members or certainly loyal to the Communist Party, but who nevertheless are still helping to shape our foreign policy.

One thing to remember in discussing the Communists in our Government is that we are not dealing with spies who get 30 pieces of silver to steal the blueprints of a new weapon. We are dealing with a far more sinister type of activity because it permits the enemy to guide and shape our policy. . . .

This brings us down to the case of one Alger Hiss who is important not as an individual any more, but rather because he is so representative of a group in the State Department. . . .

As you know, very recently the Secretary of State [Dean Acheson] proclaimed his loyalty to a man [Alger Hiss] guilty of what has always been considered as the most abominable of all crimes — of being a traitor to the people who gave him a position of great trust. The Secretary of State in attempting to justify his continued devotion to the man who sold out the Christian world to the atheistic world, referred to Christ's Sermon on the Mount as a justification and reason therefor, and the reaction of the American people to this would have made the heart of Abraham Lincoln happy.

When this pompous diplomat in striped pants, with a phony British accent, proclaimed to the American people that Christ on the Mount endorsed communism, high treason, and betrayal of a sacred trust, the blasphemy was so great that it awakened the dormant indignation of the American people.

He has lighted the spark which is resulting in a moral uprising and will end only when the whole sorry mess of twisted, warped thinkers are swept from the national scene so that we may have a new birth of national honesty and decency in Government.

three

THE FAIR DEAL

The Fair Deal was Harry Truman's domestic program. Based on the liberal initiatives of the New Deal, it sought to extend the American version of the welfare state Franklin Roosevelt had begun. Continuities notwithstanding, the Fair Deal unfolded in a different political environment and branched out in directions of its own. FDR had faced the problems of depression; Truman confronted the difficulties of inflation instead. Roosevelt had listened to blacks' demands for equality but for the most part had responded to white Southerners whose votes he needed on other issues. Truman, in contrast, took active steps to affirm legal equality. Roosevelt had created a coalition that endorsed his goals; for most of his presidency, Truman faced political opposition that challenged him at every turn. Even so, the Fair Deal enjoyed a number of successes as it extended the framework created under FDR. But historians have disagreed in their assessments of just how far Truman's program went and could have gone.

In "America in War and Peace: The Test of Liberalism," one of the essays in this section, Barton J. Bernstein is critical of the limited aims and achievements of the Truman administration. Liberal scholars, he suggests, have hailed the political and social reforms that accompanied postwar prosperity, but have been unwilling to accept flaws in the liberal vision itself. He is critical, too, of Truman's frequent unwillingness to use his authority for causes he claimed to support.

In the other selection, "The Fair Deal and Liberal Politics," Alonzo L. Hamby is more sympathetic to Truman. Examining the Democratic party's effort to seize the middle of the political spectrum, he considers the "nearly insuperable obstacles" faced by policymakers dealing with agricultural and economic issues. Hamby examines the impact of the Korean War on the effort at reform. And, he concludes, the Fair Deal made significant progress in building on a New Deal foundation and adapting the liberal vision to different times.

The document in this section is an excerpt from Harry Truman's 1949 State of the Union Message. Delivered after his extraordinary upset victory in the 1948 presidential race, it reaffirms his vision, reiterates his legislative agenda, and underscores the right of all citizens to a "fair deal" from their government.

For a full assessment of the Truman years, see Robert J. Donovan, *Conflict and Crisis: The Presidency of Harry S Truman, 1945–1948* (1977), and *Tumultuous Years: The Presidency of Harry S Truman, 1949–1953* (1982). Cabell Phillips, *The Truman Presidency: The History of a Triumphant Succession* (1966), is a somewhat dated but still useful narrative. Robert H. Ferrell, *Harry S. Truman and the Modern American Presidency* (1983), is the best short biography. Barton J. Bernstein and Allen J. Matusow, *The Truman Administration: A Documentary History* (1966), remains an outstanding collection of documents. Alonzo L. Hamby, *Harry S. Truman and the Fair Deal* (1974), contains a good selection of essays and documents about various sides of the Truman presidency.

The Fair Deal and Liberal Politics

ALONZO L. HAMBY

"Every segment of our population and every individual has a right to expect from our government a fair deal," declared Harry S. Truman in early 1949. In 1945 and 1946 the Truman administration had almost crumbled under the stresses of postwar reconversion; in 1947 and 1948 it had fought a frustrating, if politically rewarding, battle with the Republican Eightieth Congress. Buoyed by his remarkable victory of 1948 and given Democratic majorities in both houses of Congress, Truman hoped to achieve an impressive record of domestic reform. The president systematized his past proposals, added some new ones, and gave his program a name that would both connect his administration with the legacy of the New Deal and give it a distinct identity. The Fair Deal, while based solidly upon the New Deal tradition, differed from its predecessor in significant aspects of mood and detail. It reflected not only Truman's own aspirations but also a style of liberalism that had begun to move beyond the New Deal during World War II and had come to maturity during the early years of the Cold War—"the vital center." . . .

Arthur M. Schlesinger, Jr. gave the new liberalism a name with the publication of *The Vital Center.* An exercise in political philosophy and an exhortation to American progressives, the volume won an impressive reception. "It seemed to me one of those books which may suddenly and clearly announce the spirit of an age to itself," wrote Jonathan Daniels. Deeply influenced personally and intellectually by Reinhold Niebuhr, Schlesinger castigated the popular-front liberals as sentimental believers in progress and human perfectionism who, yearning for utopias, had been seduced by the surface idealism of communism and the Soviet experiment. Awake only to the evils of fascism, they had sympathized with at least some aspects of the Soviet experience and had accepted the Communists as allies in a common struggle, not understanding that such a tactic could lead only to self-destruction. The "restoration of radical nerve" had come with the rise of a non-Communist left in Europe and the United States, largely through the efforts of younger liberals whose impressions of the Soviet Union stemmed from the Stalinist purges of the 1930s rather than the idealism of the Russian Revolution. The new liberalism—or "radicalism" as Schlesinger preferred to call it—unconditionally rejected all varieties of totalitarianism. Applied to foreign affairs it stood for a dual policy of vigilantly containing communism and encouraging the democratic left abroad. Believing "in the integrity of the individual, in the limited state, in due process of law, in empiricism and gradualism," it was acutely aware of the weaknesses of human nature and of the dangers of excessive concentration of power. Devoted to the furtherance of individual liberty, it stood for a mixed economy, featuring partial government planning and ownership, antitrust action to discipline private big busi-

From Alonzo L. Hamby, "The Vital Center, the Fair Deal, and the Quest for a Liberal Political Economy," *The American Historical Review,* 77 (June 1972). Copyright © 1972 by Alonzo L. Hamby. Reprinted by permission of the author.

ness, and welfare programs to provide a minimum of security and subsistence to all. . . .

The legislative goals Truman announced for his administration, while not devised to meet the needs of an abstract theory, were well in tune with the vital-center approach: anti-inflation measures, a more progressive tax structure, repeal of the Taft-Hartley Act, a higher minimum wage, a farm program based on the concepts of abundant production and parity income, resource development and public power programs, expansion of social security, national medical insurance, federal aid to education, extensive housing legislation, and civil rights bills. The president's most controversial request was for authority to increase plant facilities in such basic industries as steel, preferably through federal financing of private enterprise but through outright government construction if necessary. Roundly condemned by right-wing opponents as "socialistic" and soon dropped by the administration, the proposal was actually intended to meet the demands of a prosperous, growing capitalist economy and emerged from the Fair Deal's search for the proper degree of government intervention to preserve the established American economic structure. "Between the reactionaries of the extreme left with their talk about revolution and class warfare, and the reactionaries of the extreme right with their hysterical cries of bankruptcy and despair, lies the way of progress," Truman declared in November 1949.

The Fair Deal was a conscious effort to continue the purpose of the New Deal but not necessarily its methods. Not forced to meet the emergencies of economic depression, given a solid point of departure by their predecessors, and led by a president more prone than FDR to demand programmatic coherence, the Fair Dealers made a systematic effort to discover techniques that would be at once more equitable and more practical in alleviating the problems of unequal wealth and opportunity. Thinking in terms of abundance rather than scarcity, they attempted to adapt the New Deal tradition to postwar prosperity. Seeking to go beyond the New Deal while preserving its objectives, the Truman administration advocated a more sweeping and better-ordered reform agenda. Yet in the quest for political means, Truman and the vital-center liberals could only fall back upon one of the oldest dreams of American reform — the Jacksonian-Populist vision of a union of producing classes, an invincible farmer-labor coalition. While superficially plausible, the Fair Deal's political strategy proved too weak to handle the burden thrust upon it.

The Fair Deal seemed to oscillate between militancy and moderation. New Dealers had frequently gloried in accusations of "liberalism" or "radicalism"; Fair Dealers tended to shrink from such labels. The New Dealers had often lusted for political combat; the Fair Dealers were generally more low keyed. Election campaigns demanded an aggressiveness that would arouse the Democratic presidential party, but the continued strength of the conservative coalition in Congress dictated accommodation in the postelection efforts to secure passage of legislative proposals. Such tactics reflected Truman's personal political experience and instincts, but they also developed naturally out of the climate of postwar America. The crisis of economic depression had produced one style of political rhetoric; the problems of prosperity and inflation brought forth another.

The Fair Deal mirrored Truman's policy preferences and approach to politics; it was no more the president's personal creation, however, than the New Deal had been Roosevelt's. Just as FDR's advisers had formulated much of the New Deal, a group of liberals developed much of the content and tactics of the Fair Deal. For the most part these were the men who had formed a liberal caucus within the administration in early 1947 shortly after the Republican triumph in the congressional elections of 1946, had worked to sway the president toward the left in his policy recommendations and campaign tactics, and had played a significant, if not an all-embracing, role in Truman's victory in 1948. Truman's special counsel, Clark M. Clifford, was perhaps the most prominent member of the group, but Clifford, although a shrewd political analyst, a persuasive advocate, and an extremely valuable administrative chief of staff, was neither the caucus's organizer nor a creative liberal thinker. Others gave the Fair Deal its substance as a program descending from the New Deal yet distinct from it.

The founder of the liberal caucus, Oscar R. Ewing, exemplified better than any other prominent member of the Truman administration the linkage between the New Deal and the Fair Deal. Even as a young man in turn-of-the-century Indiana he had possessed a consuming interest in Democratic politics and social welfare problems. At the age of sixteen he was secretary to the state Democratic committee, and for a time he planned to become a social worker. Instead, after graduating from the Harvard Law School, he settled in New York and pursued a highly successful practice as a partner of first the elder, then the younger, Charles Evans Hughes. By the 1940s he had also become one of the most prominent Democrats in the state and was frequently mentioned as a possible candidate for high office. During Robert E. Hannegan's tenure as chairman of the Democratic National Committee (1944–1947), Ewing was vice-chairman and, after Hannegan's health collapsed, acting chairman. Appointed administor of the Federal Security Agency in 1947, he began a drive to revitalize the agency and secure cabinet status for it. It was he who took the initiative in mobilizing the liberals within the Truman administration for the crucial struggles of 1947 and 1948.

Ewing's advocacy of comprehensive social welfare legislation—a popular magazine described him as "Mr. Welfare State himself"—was the end result of a tradition that had begun with the social workers of the Progressive era, had found partial realization during the New Deal, and was now struggling for complete fulfillment. Ewing also represented a type of Democrat who had developed during the New Deal—the staunch, partisan regular who was nevertheless committed to social welfare liberalism and identified his party with it. The strongest fighter within the administration for expanded welfare programs, he did not shrink from debate with the opposition. . . .

While Ewing represented continuity, Leon H. Keyserling and Charles F. Brannan gave the Fair Deal much of its distinctive approach. Both men served their political apprenticeships during the New Deal, but both formulated important criticisms of it and sought new techniques to achieve the objectives of liberal reform.

Keyserling, educated at Columbia University—where he was influenced by Rexford G. Tugwell—and the Harvard Law School, had gone to Washington in the early days of the Roosevelt administration to work for Jerome Frank in the Agricultural Adjustment Administration. He attracted the attention of Senator Robert F. Wagner, who made him an administrative assistant; during the next several years he was a central figure in the drafting of some of the most important legislation of the 1930s, including the National Labor Relations Act. Subsequently he was general counsel of the U.S. Housing Authority, later the National Housing Agency. In 1944 he took second prize in a widely publicized contest on the achievement of postwar prosperity with an essay urging an expansion of the economy to provide jobs for all. In 1945 he was active in the struggle for full-employment legislation. With Senator Wagner's backing he was a natural choice for the new Council of Economic Advisers, established by the Employment Act of 1946.

During 1947 and 1948 Keyserling was a valuable member of the administration liberal caucus. At the same time he was gaining a public reputation as the most imaginative and articulate economist in the government. When the bland and moderate Edwin Nourse resigned as chairman of the Council of Economic Advisers in October 1949, Keyserling was automatically the liberals' candidate for the post, and the ADA spearheaded an intensive lobbying campaign in his behalf. After a long delay, in the spring of 1950 the president gave Keyserling the appointment. . . .

Keyserling's critique of New Deal economics had several themes. First of all, the New Deal had failed to grasp the virtual impossibility of the task it had undertaken: the lifting of the nation out of the depression. Those who argued that the New Deal would have been successful with a more massive spending effort were probably wrong. Government alone simply could not solve great economic crises, and if the New Deal could not be blamed for its failure, the New Dealers could be blamed for not learning the lessons of that failure. . . .

American capitalism, as Keyserling envisioned it, had virtually unlimited opportunities for growth; an ever-expanding economy could produce undreamed-of abundance and material gain for all classes. The liberals should concentrate not on reslicing the economic pie but rather on enlarging it. Business could expect higher profits, labor better wages, farmers larger incomes, and, above all, those at the bottom of the economic scale could experience a truly decent life. The federal government should publicize these possibilities; it should provide education and guidance to the private forces whose responsible cooperation would be imperative. Keyserling recommended the initiation of a "National Prosperity Budget" in which the government would lay down targets for employment and production, indicate priority needs, and sketch out price and wage recommendations. It would be purely advisory, depending upon the cooperation of the private sectors for implementation.

The government would not be passive. It would continue to police the economy against monopolistic abuses, dictate minimum wages, use Keynesian fiscal and monetary techniques, and even impose selective controls if conditions demanded. It would provide important programs and services — such as low-cost housing, social insurance, education, and resource development — that fell outside the realm of private enterprise. Washington, however, could not keep the economy growing by itself. Expansion demanded voluntary cooperation: "The widening of this area of voluntary cooperation, through common study of common problems, is the only way that our highly industrialized and integrated economy can steer between the danger of periodic collapse and the danger of excessive governmental centralization of power." . . .

During the first half of 1949 Keyserling transformed his vision of abundance to solid figures. Assuming an annual growth rate of 3 percent and constant dollar values, the gross national product could rise from $262 billion in 1948 to $350 billion in 1958, national income from $226 billion to $300 billion. In 1948 almost two-thirds of all American families had lived on incomes of less than $4,000 a year; by 1958, $4,000 could be the minimum for all families. It would require only about half of the GNP increase to attain this goal, leaving a substantial sum for government programs and the enhancement of private incomes at other levels. Poverty thus could be eliminated without a redistribution of wealth. Progressive reform did not necessarily mean social conflict; rather it required intelligent cooperation.

Truman adopted Keyserling's figures and rhetoric. Speaking to a Kansas City audience in the fall of 1949, he acclaimed the nation's history of economic growth and increasingly higher standards of living and declared his determination to continue the process. He talked of the $300 billion national income and the $4,000 family minimum. "That is not a pipe dream," he asserted. "It can be done." . . .

Charles F. Brannan, who was as much a product of the New Deal as Keyserling, had begun his career in Colorado politics as a disciple of the old progressive, Edward Costigan, and an associate of Oscar L. Chapman, a dedicated liberal whom Truman appointed secretary of the interior in 1949. During the Roosevelt era Brannan had worked as an attorney for the Resettlement Administration and had been a regional director of the Farm Security Administration. Long close to the neo-Populist National Farmers Union, he was a personal friend of its president, James G. Patton. Moving to Washington as assistant secretary of agriculture in 1944, Brannan quickly established himself as a loyal and capable lieutenant. In 1948 he took command of the department with the blessings of the outgoing secretary, the moderate Clinton Anderson, and the enthusiastic endorsement of the Farmers Union, which had bitterly fought Anderson. No man, not even the elder or the younger

Henry Wallace, had entered the office of secretary of agriculture with clearer credentials as an aggressive liberal. Like Keyserling, Brannan used the concept of abundance as an intellectual foundation. The politicoeconomic strategy that he formulated constituted the Fair Deal's clearest break with the New Deal.

In the fall of 1948 Brannan's astute advice on political strategy and his vigorous campaigning won the attention of Truman and brought him into the White House inner circle. Almost alone Brannan grasped that Midwestern farmers were apprehensive about the future of price supports and that the Republican Eightieth Congress, by failing to enlarge government storage facilities, had practically guaranteed that grain prices would decline during the presidential campaign. Truman and his liberal advisers quickly adopted Brannan's counsel of attacking the GOP as the party of opposition to price supports, and the secretary himself carried the message into farm areas with a tirelessness that shamed other cabinet members. Truman's unexpected success in the rural Midwest made Brannan one of the major figures of the administration. It also suggested new political strategies to liberals both inside and outside the government.

Many progressives believed that the farm results represented a new trend in liberal politics. To the influential columnist Samuel Grafton, 1948 had been "a year of deep and quiet decision" for farmers; the election indicated that they had overcome their conservative biases in favor of their practical need for government support and would turn increasingly to the Democratic party. If such were the case, then the task of the liberals was to encourage and consolidate this trend. The ultimate result would be a new Democratic party with a more solidly liberal base than ever before, a liberalism that would fuse the outlook and voting power of labor with an apparently reborn Midwestern agrarian insurgency. The liberal cause would be greatly strengthened and the conservative forces proportionately weakened. Within the Republican party the number of Midwestern reactionaries would decline; within the Democratic party the Southern conservatives would have less leverage.

The first imperative was to establish lines of communication between the farmers and the liberal-labor forces. . . .

The administration took the next step in April with the introduction in Congress of a new farm program, which had been drawn up under Brannan's direction. The Brannan Plan was difficult and complex in detail, but essentially it was an effort to maintain farm income at the record high level of the war and immediate postwar periods while letting market prices fall to a natural supply-demand level. Brannan thus proposed to continue the New Deal policy of subsidizing the farmers, but he broke dramatically with the New Deal technique of restricting production and marketing in order to achieve artificially high prices.

Many agrarian progressives, including Henry A. Wallace himself, had long been troubled by the price-support mechanisms and had sought methods of unleashing the productive capacity of the farms. Brannan seemed to show the way. He proposed the maintenance of farm income through direct payments to farmers rather than through crop restriction. In order to encourage and protect the family farm, moreover, he recommended supporting a maximum of about $26,100 worth of production per farm. To the consumer he promised milk at fifteen cents a quart, to the dairy farmer a sustained high income. To the Democratic party he offered an apparently ingenious device that would unite the interests of farmers and workers.

Liberals generally were enthusiastic over both the principles and the politics of the Brannan proposals. "The new plan lets growers grow and eaters eat, and that is good," commented Samuel Grafton. "If Brannan is right, the political miracle of 1948 will become a habit as farmers, labor and consumers find common political goals," wrote agricultural columnist Angus MacDonald. James Patton called the Brannan Plan "a milestone in the history of American agriculture," and the *Nation* asserted that the average consumer should devote all his spare time to support of the program.

The plan immediately ran into the opposition of the conservatives who dominated Congress. Republicans feared that the political coalition Brannan was trying to build would entrench the Democrats in power. Large producers, most effectively represented by the powerful Farm Bureau Federation, regarded the plan as discriminatory, and many Democrats with ties to the Farm Bureau refused to support it, among them Senate majority leader Scott Lucas and Clinton Anderson, now the freshman senator from New Mexico. By June it was obvious to most political analysts that the Brannan Plan had no chance of passage in 1949. The administration and most liberals nevertheless remained optimistic. The issue seemed good, the alignment of interests logical and compelling: enough political education and campaigning could revive the scheme and revolutionize American politics. . . . Brannan campaigned extensively for his program. "Farm income equals jobs for millions of American workers," he told a labor gathering in a typical effort. "Together, let workers and farmers unite in achieving a full employment, full production economy." The administration sponsored regional farmer-labor conferences around the country. The one attracting the most attention was held in June at Des Moines, Iowa, and featured prominent labor leaders, important Democratic congressmen, and Vice-President Alben Barkley. Other such grass-roots meetings were organized as far east as upstate New York, and the Democratic National Committee prepared a pamphlet on the Brannan Plan for mass distribution. On Labor Day the president devoted two major appearances, one in Pittsburgh and the other in Des Moines, to the Brannan Plan and to farmer-labor unity. "Those who are trying to set these two great groups against each other just have axes of their own to grind," he warned his Pittsburgh audience. "Price supports must . . . give consumers the benefit of our abundant farm production," he told his Des Moines listeners.

Many liberals and Democratic politicians remained convinced that they had an overwhelming political strategy. "In 1950 and '52, the Brannan Plan will be the great issue in the doubtful states," wrote journalist A. G. Mezerik. "After that, Congress will enact a new farm bill — one which is based on low prices for consumers and a high standard of living for family farmers." In early 1950 the Brannan Plan seemed to be gaining popular support. Liberals inside and outside the administration continued to hope for vindication at the polls in November. They could not, of course, foresee the Korean War and the ways in which it would change the shape of American politics.

Even without the Korean War, however, even without the disruptive impact of McCarthyism, it is doubtful that the Brannan Plan would have worked the miracles expected of it. The liberals inside and outside the administration who had created or worked for it assumed that urban and rural groups could be united simply on grounds of mutual self-interest. They failed to understand that these groups were not deeply concerned with *mutual* self-interest; both sides had practiced with some success methods that had taken care of their own self-interest. The rhetoric about urban-rural interdependence was extremely superficial, talked but not deeply felt. Most farm and labor leaders, even those progressive in their outlook, hardly had a basis for communication. The ADA conference of February 1949 included some of the best-informed figures from the unions and the farms. Yet one of the labor leaders had to ask for an explanation "in simple language" of the concept of parity. One of the farm leaders then admitted that he had no idea what the dues check-off was or how it worked. The farm leaders also frankly commented that their constituents were strongly against such things as a minimum wage applied to farm workers, the extension of social security to cover farm labor and farmers in general, and especially the reestablishment of any sort of price controls. The situation at Des Moines seems to have been much the same. Even some of the Farmers Union officials at the conference were annoyed by the presence of the labor people. "Some farmers wondered if they weren't being sucked in to help the forces of labor fight the Taft-Hartley Act," reported journalist Lauren Soth. Such ideas, of course, were not entirely fanciful. Most of the observers at Des Moines sensed the artificiality of the whole affair, but they continued to hope that further contacts would consummate the union of city and country. . . .

For a time in carly 1950 declining farm prices seemed to generate a surge of support for the Brannan Plan. At the beginning of June, Albert Loveland, the undersecretary of agriculture, won the Iowa Democratic senatorial primary on a pro-Brannan platform and thereby encouraged the administration to believe that the Midwest was moving in its direction. Just a few weeks later, however, the Korean War began, creating situations and pressures that doomed most of the Fair Deal. . . .

During 1949 and early 1950 the Truman administration managed a record of substantial legislative accomplishment, but it consisted almost entirely of additions to such New Deal programs as the minimum wage, social security, and public power. The Housing Act of 1949, with its provisions for large-scale public housing, appeared to be a breakthrough, but weak administration, local opposition, and inadequate financing subsequently vitiated hopes that it would help the poor. Acting on his executive authority, Truman took an important step by forcing the army to agree to a policy of desegregation. The heart of the Fair Deal, however — repeal of the Taft-Hartley Act, civil rights legislation, aid to education, national medical insurance, and the Brannan Plan — failed in Congress. Given the power of the well-entrenched conservative coalition and a widespread mood of public apathy about big new reforms, Truman could only enlarge upon the record of his predecessor.

Democratic strategists hoped for a mandate in the congressional elections of 1950. In the spring Truman made a successful whistle-stop tour of the West and Midwest, rousing party enthusiasm and apparently demonstrating a solid personal popularity. Loveland's victory provided further encouragement, and in California the aggressive Fair Dealer Helen Gahagan Douglas won the Democratic nomination for the Senate by a thumping margin. Two incumbent Fair Deal supporters — Frank Graham of North Carolina and Claude Pepper of Florida — lost their senatorial primaries, but, as Southerners who had run afoul of the race issue, they did not seem to be indicators of national trends. Nevertheless, the hope of cutting into the strength of the conservative opposition ran counter to the historical pattern of midterm elections. The beginning of the Korean War at the end of June destroyed any chances of success.

The most immediate impact of Korea was to refuel an anti-Communist extremism that might otherwise have sputtered out. . . .

The war hurt the administration in other ways. It touched off a brief but serious inflation, which caused widespread consumer irritation. By stimulating demand for agricultural products it brought most farm prices up to parity levels and thereby undercut whatever attractiveness the Brannan Plan had developed in rural areas. Finally it removed the Democratic party's most effective spokesman — the president — from active participation in the campaign. Forced to play the role of war leader, Truman allowed himself only one major partisan speech, delivered in St. Louis on the eve of the balloting. . . .

Yet even the Korean War was not entirely inimical to reform. Its exigencies forced the army to transform its policy of integration into practice. Korea also provided a test for one of the basic underpinnings of the Fair Deal — Leon Keyserling's philosophy of economic expansion. Truman did not in the end fully embrace Keyserling's policies, but in the main he followed the guidance of his chief economic adviser. . . .

From the outbreak of the fighting, most liberals favored either immediate strong economic controls akin to those that had held down inflation in World War II or at least the establishment of standby machinery that could impose them rapidly. Truman disliked such measures on the basis of both principle and politics. He and his diplomatic advisers also wanted to signal the Soviet Union that the United States regarded the North Korean attack as a limited challenge meriting a limited response. Keyserling's expansionary economics provided an attractive alternative to the liberal clamor for controls. . . .

The president . . . steered a course between the orthodox liberal obsession with inflation and Keyserling's easy disregard of its perils; perhaps as a result the economy failed to expand at the rate Keyserling had hoped. On balance, however, Truman's approach to the political economy of the Korean War was closer to Keyserling's, and the conflict produced a dramatic economic growth. Before the war the peak gross national product had been $285 billion in 1948; by the end of 1952 the GNP (measured in constant dollar values) had reached a rate of $350 billion. The production index of durable manufactured goods had averaged 237 in 1950; by the last quarter of 1952 it had reached 313. The expansion, even if less than Keyserling had wanted, was breathtaking. Moreover, aside from the probably unavoidable inflation that accompanied the early months of the war, this remarkable growth had occurred in a climate of economic stability. Using a somewhat more orthodox approach than Keyserling preferred, the administration had achieved one of the central goals of the Fair Deal.

In its effort to carry on with the reforming impulse of the New Deal the Truman administration faced nearly insuperable obstacles. A loosely knit but nonetheless effective conservative coalition had controlled Congress since 1939, successfully defying Franklin Roosevelt long before it had to deal with Truman. Postwar prosperity muted economic liberalism and encouraged a mood of apathy toward new reform breakthroughs, although Truman's victory in 1948 indicated that most of the elements of the old Roosevelt coalition were determined to preserve the gains of the New Deal. The Cold War probably made it more difficult to focus public attention upon reform and dealt severe blows to civil liberties. It did, however, give impetus to the movement for Negro equality.

The Fair Deal attempted to adapt liberalism to the new conditions. Under the intellectual leadership of Leon Keyserling it formulated policies that sought to transcend the conflicts of the New Deal era by encouraging an economic growth that could provide abundance for all Americans. With Charles Brannan pointing the way, the Truman administration tried to translate abundance into a political coalition that could provide the votes for its social welfare policies. The political strategy, ambitious but unrealistic, collapsed under the weight of the Korean War. Keyserling's economics, on the other hand, received a lift from Korea; in a period of adversity the Fair Deal was able to achieve at least one of its objectives.

America in War and Peace: The Test of Liberalism

BARTON J. BERNSTEIN

The domestic events of the war and postwar years have failed to attract as much scholarly effort as have the few years of the New Deal. The reforms of the thirties and the struggle against depression have captured the enthusiasm of many liberal historians and have constituted the major themes shaping their interpretations. Compared with the excitement of the New Deal years, the events at home during the next decade seem less interesting, certainly less dramatic.

The issues of these years also seem less clear, perhaps because the period lacks the restrictive unity imposed upon the New Deal. Despite the fragmentary scholarship, however, the major issues are definable: economic policies, civil rights, civil liberties, and social welfare policies. The continued dominance by big business, the consolidation of other groups within the economy, the challenge of racial inequality — these are the themes of the wartime Roosevelt administration. Toward the end of Roosevelt's years, they are joined by another concern, the quest for social reform, and in Truman's years by such themes as economic readjustment, the renewed struggle against inflation, and the fear of disloyalty and communism. These problems are largely the legacy of the New Deal: the extension of its limited achievements, the response to its shortcomings, the criticism of its liberalism. . . .

When the nation joined the Allies, Roosevelt had explained that "Dr. Win-the-War" was taking over from "Dr. New Deal," and there were few liberal legislative achievements during the war years. Those benefits that disadvantaged groups did receive were usually a direct result of the labor shortage and the flourishing economy, not of liberal politics. By 1944, however, Roosevelt was prepared to revive the reform spirit, and he revealed his liberal vision for the postwar years. Announcing an "Economic Bill of Rights," he outlined "a new basis for security and prosperity": the right to a job, adequate food, clothing, and recreation, a decent home, a good education, adequate medical care, and protection against sickness and unemployment.

Noble as was his vision of the future society, Roosevelt was still unprepared to move far beyond rhetoric, and the Congress was unsympathetic to his program. While approving the GI Bill of Rights, including educational benefits and extended unemployment pay, Congress resisted most liberal programs during the war. Asserting its independence of the executive, the war Congress also thwarted Roosevelt in other ways — by rejecting a large tax bill designed to spread the cost of war and to reduce inflationary pressures. and by liquidating the National Resources Planning Board, which had originated the "second bill of rights" and also studied postwar economic planning.

By its opposition to planning and social reform, Congress increased the anxieties of labor and liberals about the postwar years and left the new Truman administration poorly prepared for the difficult transition to a peace-time economy when the war suddenly ended. Fearing the depression that most economists forecast, the administration did, however, propose a tax cut of $5 billion. While removing many low-income recipients from the tax rolls, the law was also of great benefit to large corporations. Charging inequity, organized labor found little support in Congress or the executive, for the government was relying upon business activity, rather than on consumer purchasing power, to soften the economic decline. Significantly, despite the anticipated $30 billion deficit (plus the $5 billion tax), no congressman expressed any fear of an unbalanced budget. Clearly fiscal orthodoxy did not occupy a very high place in the scale of values of congressional conservatives, and they accepted in practice the necessity of an unbalanced budget.

Before the tax bill passed, the wartime harmony of the major interest groups had crumbled: each struggled to consolidate its gains and advance its welfare before the anticipated economic collapse. Chafing under the no-strike pledge and restrictions on wage raises, organized labor compelled the admin-istration to relax its policy and free unions to bargain collectively. Farmers, fearful of depression, demanded the withdrawal of subsidies which artificially depressed prices. Big business, despite anticipated shortages, secured the re-moval of most controls on the allocation of resources.

As the economic forecasts shifted in late autumn, the administration discovered belatedly that inflation, not depression, was the immediate eco-nomic danger. The President acted sporadically to restrain inflationary pres-sures, but his efforts were too occasional, often misguided, and too weak to resist the demands of interest groups and the actions of his own subordinates.

Beset by factionalism and staffed often by men of limited ability, Tru-man's early government floundered. By adopting the practice of cabinet responsibility and delegating excessive authority to department chiefs, Tru-man created a structure that left him uninformed: problems frequently devel-oped unnoticed until they had swelled to crises, and the choice then was often between undesirable alternatives. Operating in a new politics, in the politics of inflation, he confronted problems requiring greater tactical skill than those Roosevelt had confronted. Seeking to maintain economic controls, and com-pelled to deny the rising expectations of major interest groups, his administra-tion found it difficult to avoid antagonizing the rival groups. In the politics of depression, the Roosevelt administration could frequently maintain political support by bestowing specific advantages on groups, but in the politics of inflation the major interest groups came to seek freedom from restrictive federal controls.

So difficult were the problems facing Truman that even a more experi-enced and skilled president would have encountered great difficulty. Inherit-ing the hostile Congress that had resisted occasional wartime attempts at social reform, Truman lacked the skill or leverage to guide a legislature seeking to assert its independence of the executive. Unable to halt fragmentation of the Democratic coalition, and incapable of ending dissension in his government, he also found that conservative subordinates undercut his occasional liberalism. Though he had gone on record early in endorsing a reform program ("a declaration of independence" from congressional conservatives, he called it), he had been unsuccessful in securing most of the legislation — a higher minimum wage, public housing, expanded unemployment benefits, and FEPC. Even the employment act was little more, as one congressman said, than a license to look for a job. The President, through ineptitude or lack of commitment, often chose not to struggle for his program. Unable to dramatize the issues or to command enthusiasm, he was an ineffectual leader.

So unsuccessful was his government that voters began jibing, "To err is Truman." Despairing of a resurgence of liberalism under Truman, New Dealers left the government in droves. By the fall of 1946, none of Roosevelt's associates was left in a prominent position. So disgruntled were many liberals about Truman and his advisers, about his unwillingness to fight for price controls, housing, benefits for labor, and civil rights, that some turned briefly to serious consideration of a new party.

Achieving few reforms during his White House years, Truman, with the notable exception of civil rights, never moved significantly beyond Roosevelt. The Fair Deal was largely an extension of earlier Democratic liberalism, but Truman's new vigor and fierce partisanship ultimately made him more attractive to liberals who despairingly watched the GOP-dominated Eightieth Congress and feared a repeal of the New Deal.

Their fears were unwarranted, as was their enthusiasm for the Fair Deal program. In practice it proved very limited — the housing program only provided for 810,000 units in six years of which only 60,000 were constructed; social security benefits were extended to ten million and increased by about 75 percent, and the minimum wage was increased to 75 cents, but coverage was reduced by nearly a million. But even had all of the Fair Deal been enacted, liberal reform would have left many millions beyond the benefits of government. The very poor, the marginal men, those neglected but acknowledged by the New Deal, went ultimately unnoticed by the Fair Deal.

While liberals frequently chafed under Truman's leadership and questioned his commitment, they failed generally to recognize how shallow were his reforms. As the nation escaped a postwar depression, American liberals gained new faith in the American economy. Expressing their enthusiasm, they came to extoll big business for its contributions. Believing firmly in the success of progressive taxation, they exaggerated its effects, and congratulated themselves on the redistribution of income and the virtual abolition of poverty. Praising the economic system, they accepted big agriculture and big labor as evidence of healthy pluralism that protected freedom and guaranteed an equitable distribution of resources.

Despite the haggling over details and the liberals' occasional dismay at

Truman's style, he expressed many of their values. Like Roosevelt, Truman never challenged big business, never endangered large-scale capitalism. Indeed, his efforts as well as theirs were directed largely to maintaining and adjusting the powers of the major economic groups.

Fearing that organized labor was threatened with destruction, Truman, along with the liberals, had been sincerely frightened by the postwar rancor toward labor. What they failed to understand was that most Americans had accepted unions as part of the political economy. Certainly most major industrialists had accepted organized labor, though smaller businessmen were often hostile. Despite the overwrought rhetoric of debates, Congress did not actually menace labor. It was not seeking to destroy labor, only to restrict its power.

Many Americans did believe that the Wagner Act had unduly favored labor and was creating unions indifferent to the public welfare and hostile to corporate power. Capitalizing on this exaggerated fear of excessive union power, and the resentment from the postwar strikes, businessmen secured the Taft-Hartley Act. Designed to weaken organized labor, it tried but failed to protect the membership from leaders; it did not effectively challenge the power of established unions. However, labor chiefs, recalling the bitter industrial warfare of the thirties, were still uneasy in their new positions. Condemning the legislation as a "slave-labor" act, they responded with fear, assailed the Congress, and declared that Taft-Hartley was the major political issue.

Within a few years, when unions discovered that they were safe, Taft-Hartley faded as an issue. But in 1948 it served Truman well by establishing the GOP's hostility to labor and casting it back into the Democratic ranks. Both the President and union chiefs conveniently neglected his own kindling of antilabor passions (as when he had tried to draft strikers). Exploiting Taft-Hartley as part of his strategy of patching the tattered Democratic coalition, Truman tied repeal of the "slave-labor" law to price controls, farm benefits, anticommunism, and civil rights in the campaign which won his election in his own right. . . .

In courting the Negro the Truman administration in 1948 made greater promises to black citizens than had any previous federal government in American history. Yet, like many Americans, Truman as a senator had regarded the Negro's plight as peripheral to his interests, and with many of his generation he believed that equality was compatible with segregation. As President, however, he found himself slowly prodded by conscience and pushed by politics. He moved cautiously at first and endorsed only measures affirming legal equality and protecting Negroes from violence.

Reluctant to fragment the crumbling Democratic coalition, Truman, in his first year, had seemed to avoid taking positions on civil rights which might upset the delicate balance between Northern and Southern Democrats. While he endorsed legislation for a statutory FEPC that the Congress would not grant, his efforts on behalf of the temporary FEPC (created by Roosevelt's executive order) were weaker. Having already weakened the power of the temorary agency, he also acquiesced in the legislative decision to kill it. Despite the fears of Negro leaders that the death of FEPC would leave Negroes virtually unprotected from discrimination in the postwar job market, Truman would not even issue an order requiring nondiscrimination in the federal service and by government contractors.

Though Truman was unwilling to use the prestige or power of his great office significantly on behalf of Negroes, he did assist their cause. While sidestepping political conflict, he occasionally supported FEPC and abolition of the poll tax. When Negroes were attacked, he did condemn the racial violence. Though generally reluctant to move beyond rhetoric during his early years, Truman, shortly before the 1946 election, found conscience and politics demanding more. So distressed was he by racial violence that when Walter White of the NAACP and a group of white liberals urged him to assist the Negro, he promised to create a committee to study civil rights.

The promise of a committee could have been a device to resist pressures, to delay the matter until after the election. And Truman could have appointed a group of politically safe men of limited reputation — men he could control. But instead, after the election, perhaps in an effort to mobilize the liberals for 1948, he appointed a committee of prominent men sympathetic to civil rights. They were men he could not control and did not seek to control.

The committee's report, undoubtedly far bolder than Truman's expectations, confirmed charges that America treated its Negroes as second-class citizens. It called for FEPC, an antilynching law, an anti-poll tax measure, abolition of segregation in interstate transportation, and the end of discrimination and segregation in federal agencies and the military. By atacking Jim Crow, the committee had moved to a redefinition of equality and interpreted segregation as incompatible with equality.

Forced by the report to take a position, he no longer could easily remain an ally of Southern Democrats and maintain the wary allegiance of Negro leaders and urban liberals. Compelled earlier to yield to demands for advancement of the Negro, pressures which he did not wish fully to resist, Truman had encouraged these forces and they were moving beyond his control. On his decision, his political future might precariously rest. Threatened by Henry Wallace's candidacy on a third-party ticket, Truman had to take a bold position on civil rights or risk losing the important votes of urban Negroes. Though he might antagonize Southern voters, he foresaw no risk of losing Southern Democrats, no possibility of a bolt by dissidents, and the mild Southern response to the Civil Rights Report seemed to confirm this judgment.

On February 2, 1948, Truman asked the Congress to enact most of the recommendations of his Civil Rights Committee (except most of those attacking segregation). Rather than using his executive powers, as the committee had urged, to end segregation in federal employment or to abolish segregation and discrimination in the military, he *promised* only to issue orders ending discrimination (but not specifying segregation) in the military and in federal agencies. Retreating to moderation, the administration did not submit any of the legislation, nor did Truman issue the promised executive orders. "The strategy," an assistant later explained, "was to start with a bold measure and then temporize to pick up the right-wing forces. Simply stated, backtrack after the bang."

Truman sought to ease Southern doubts by inserting in the 1948 platform the party's moderate 1944 plank on civil rights. Most Negro leaders, fearing the taint of Wallace and unwilling to return to the GOP, appeared stuck with Truman and they praised him. Though they desired a stronger plank, they would not abandon him at the convention, for his advocacy of rights for Negroes was unmatched by any twentieth-century president. To turn their backs on him in this time of need, most Negroes feared, would be injuring their own cause. But others were prepared to struggle for a stronger plank. Urban bosses, persuaded that Truman would lose, hoped to save their local tickets, and prominent white liberals sought power and principle. Triumphing at the convention, they secured a stronger plank, but it did not promise social equality. By promising equality when it was still regarded as compatible with segregation, they were offering far less than the "walk forthrightly into the bright sunshine of human rights," which Hubert Humphrey, then mayor of Minneapolis, had pledged in leading the liberal effort.

When some of the Southerners bolted and formed the States Rights party, Truman was freed of any need for tender courtship of the South. He had to capture the Northern vote. Quickly he issued the long-delayed executive orders, which established a federal antidiscrimination board, declared a policy of equal opportunity in the armed forces, and established a committee to end military discrimination and segregation. (In doing so, Truman courted Negro voters and halted the efforts of A. Philip Randolph to lead a Negro revolt against the draft unless the military was integrated.) Playing politics carefully during the campaign, Truman generally stayed away from civil rights and concentrated on inflation, public housing, and Taft-Hartley.

In the new Democratic Congress Truman could not secure the civil rights program, and a coalition of Southern Democrats and Northern Republicans blocked his efforts. Though liberals were unhappy with his leadership, they did not question his proposed legislation. All agreed on the emphasis on social change through legislation and judicial decisions. The liberal way was the legal way, and it seldom acknowledged the depth of American racism or even considered the possibility of bold new tactics. Only occasionally—in the threatened March on Washington in 1941, in some ride-ins in 1947, and in the campaign of civil disobedience against the draft in 1948—had there been bolder means. In each case Negroes had devised and carried out these tactics. But generally they relied upon more traditional means: they expected white America to yield to political pressure and subscribe to the dictates of American democracy. By relying upon legal change, however, and by emphasizing measures to restore a *modicum* of human dignity, Negroes and whites did not confront the deeper problems of race relations which they failed to understand.

Struggling for moderate institutional changes, liberals were disappointed by Truman's frequent unwillingness to use his executive powers in behalf of the cause he claimed to espouse. Only after considerable pressure did he create an FEPC-type agency during the Korean War. His loyalty-and-security program, in its operations, discriminated against Negroes, and federal investigators, despite protests to Truman, apparently continued to inquire into attitudes of interracial sympathy as evidence relevant to a determination of disloyalty. He was also slow to require the Federal Housing Administration to stop issuing mortgages on property with restrictive covenants, and it continued, by its policies, to protect residential segregation.

Yet his government was not without significant achievements in civil rights. His special committee had quietly acted to integrate the armed forces, and even the recalcitrant Army had abolished racial quotas when the President secretly promised their restoration if the racial imbalance became severe. And the Department of Justice, despite Truman's apparent indifference, had been an active warrior in the battle against Jim Crow. Entering cases as an *amicus curiae,* Justice had submitted briefs arguing the unconstitutionality of enforcing restrictive covenants and of requiring separate-but-equal facilities in interstate transportation and in higher education. During the summer of 1952, the Solicitor-General's Office even won the administration's approval for a brief directly challenging segregated primary education.

The accomplishments of the Truman years were moderate, and the shortcomings left the nation with a great burden of unresolved problems. Viewed from the perspective of today, Truman's own views seem unduly mild and his government excessively cautious; viewed even by his own time he was a reluctant liberal, troubled by terror and eager to establish limited equality. He was ahead of public opinion in his legislative requests, but not usually in his actions. By his occasional advocacy, he educated the nation and held high the promise of equality. By kindling hope, he also may have prevented rebellion and restrained or delayed impulses to work outside of the system. But he also unleashed expectations he could not foresee, and forces which future governments would not be able to restrain.

Never as committed to civil rights as he was opposed to communism at home and abroad, Truman ultimately became a victim of his own loyalty-and-security policies. Mildly criticized in 1945 and 1946 for being "soft on communism," the administration belatedly responded after the disastrous election of 1946. Truman appointed a committee to investigate loyalty and security, promptly accepted its standard of judgment ("reasonable grounds of belief in disloyalty"), and created a system of loyalty boards.

Outraging many liberals, his loyalty program provoked vigorous criticisms — for its secret investigations, for the failure to guarantee the accused the right to know the identity of and cross-examine the accuser, for its loose standards of proof, for its attempt to anticipate disloyal behavior by inquiring into attitudes. In seeking to protect the nation, the government seemed to be searching for all who *might* be disloyal — "potential subversives," Truman called them.

Dangerously confusing the problems of loyalty and security, the administration, in what might seem a burst of democratic enthusiasm, decided to apply the same standards to diplomats and gardeners. Disloyalty at any level of government would endanger the nation. "The presence within the government of any disloyal or subversive persons constitutes a threat to democratic processes," asserted Truman in launching the program. Anxious to remove communism in government as a possible issue, Truman had exaggerated the dangers to the nation. And by assuming that disloyalty could be determined and subversives discovered, Truman seemed also to be promising *absolute* internal security.

Shocked by earlier lax security procedures and unwilling to rely exclusively upon counterintelligence to uncover spies, the administration had responded without proper concern for civil liberties. So extreme was the program that it should have removed loyalty and security as a political issue. But by failing to distinguish between radical political activity and disloyalty, the administration endangered dissent and liberal politics: it made present or past membership in organizations on the Attorney-General's list evidence of possible disloyalty. Thus, in justifying investigations of political activity, it also legitimized occasional right-wing attacks on the liberal past and encouraged emphasis on the radicalism of a few New Dealers as evidence of earlier subversion.

In their own activities, many liberals were busy combatting domestic communism. Taking up the cudgels, the liberal Americans for Democratic Action (ADA) came often to define its purpose by its anticommunism. As an enemy of those liberals who would not renounce association with Communists, and, hence, as vigorous foes of the Progressive party, the ADA was prepared to do battle. Following Truman's strategy, ADA members assailed Wallace and his supporters as Communists, dupes of the Communists, and fellow travelers. To publicize its case the ADA even relied upon the tactic of guilt by association and paid for advertisements listing the Progressive party's major donors and the organizations on the Attorney-General's list with which they were or had been affiliated. (Truman himself also red-baited. "I do not want and will not accept the political support of Henry Wallace and his Communists. . . . These are days of high prices for everything, but any price for Wallace and his Communists is too much for me to pay.") In the labor movement liberals like the Reuther brothers led anticommunist crusades, and the CIO ultimately expelled its Communist-led unions. ("Granting the desirability of eliminating Communist influence from the trade union movement," later wrote Irving Howe and Louis Coser, "one might still have argued that mass expulsions were not only a poor way of achieving this end but constituted a threat to democratic values and procedures.")

Expressing the administration's position, Attorney-General J. Howard McGrath proclaimed a "struggle against pagan communist philosophies that seek to enslave the world." "There are today many Communists in America," he warned. "They are everywhere—in factories, offices, butcher stores, on street corners, in private business. And each carries in himself the death of our society." ("I don't think anybody ought to be employed as instructors [sic] for the young people of this country who believes in the destruction of our form of government," declared Truman.)

Calling for a crusade against evil, viewing communism as a virulent poison, the administration continued to emphasize the need for *absolute* protection, for *absolute* security. By creating such high standards and considering their fulfillment easy, by making success evidence of will and resolution, the administration risked assaults if its loyalty-and-security program was proved imperfect. To discredit the administration, all that was needed was the discovery of some red "spies," and after 1948 the evidence seemed abundant — Alger Hiss, William Remington, Judith Coplon, Julius and Ethel Rosenberg.

In foreign policy, too, Truman, though emphasizing the danger of communism, had promised success. Containment could stop the spread of communism: military expansion could be restrained and revolutions prevented. Since revolutions, by liberal definition, were imposed on innocent people by a small minority, a vigilant American government could block them. By his rhetoric, he encouraged American innocence and left many citizens little choice but to believe in their own government's failure when America could not thwart revolution — when the Chinese Communists triumphed. If only resolute will was necessary, as the administration suggested, then what could citizens believe about America's failure? Was it simply bungling? Or treason and betrayal?

By his rhetoric and action, Truman had contributed to the loss of public confidence and set the scene in which Joseph McCarthy could flourish. Rather than resisting the early movement of anticommunism, he had acted energetically to become a leader, and ultimately contributed to its transformation into a crusade which threatened his administration. But the President could never understand his own responsibility, and his failure handicapped him. Because he had a record of vigorous anticommunism, Truman was ill-prepared to respond to McCarthy's charges. At first the President could not foresee any danger and tried to dispense with McCarthy as "the greatest asset the Kremlin has." And later, as the Senator terrorized the government, Truman was so puzzled and pained that he retreated from the conflict and sought to starve McCarthy without publicity. Rather than responding directly to charges, the President tried instead to tighten his program. But he could not understand that such efforts (for example, revising the loyalty standard to "reasonable doubt as to the loyalty of the individual") could not protect the administration from charges of being soft on communism. He only encouraged these charges by seeming to yield to criticism, admitting that the earlier program was unnecessarily lax.

The President was a victim of his own policies and tactics. But bristling anticommunism was not simply Truman's way, but often the liberal way. And the use of guilt by association, the discrediting of dissent, the intemperate rhetoric — these, too, were not simply the tactics of the Truman administration. The rancor and wrath of these years were not new to American politics, nor to liberals. Indeed, the style of passionate charges and impugning opponents' motives may be endemic to American democratic politics. Submerging the issues in passion, using labels as substitutes for thought, questioning motives, these tactics characterized much of the foreign policy debate of the prewar and postwar years as well — a debate in which the liberals frequently triumphed. Developing a more extreme form of this rancorous style, relying upon even wilder charges and more flagrant use of guilt by association, McCarthy and his cohorts flailed the liberals and the Democratic administration.

In looking at the war and postwar years, liberal scholars have emphasized the achievements of democratic reform, the extension of prosperity, the movements to greater economic and social equality. Confident that big business had become socially responsible and that economic security was widespread, they have celebrated the triumph of democratic liberalism. In charting the course of national progress, they frequently neglected or minimized major problems, or they interpreted them as temporary aberrations, or blamed them on conservative forces.

Yet the developments of the sixties — the rediscovery of poverty and racism — suggest that the emphasis has been misplaced in interpreting these earlier years. In the forties and fifties white racism did not greatly yield to the dictates of American democracy, and the failure was not only the South's. The achievements of democratic liberalism were more limited than its advocates believed, and its reforms left many Americans still without adequate assistance. Though many liberal programs were blocked or diluted by conservative opposition, the liberal vision itself was dim. Liberalism in practice was defective, and its defects contributed to the temporary success of McCarthyism. Curiously, though liberalism was scrutinized by some sympathizers who attacked its faith in progress and by others who sought to trace McCarthyism to the reform impulses of earlier generations, most liberals failed to understand their own responsibility for the assault upon civil liberties or to respond to the needs of an "other America" which they but dimly perceived.

Document

Annual Message to the Congress on the State of the Union, January 5, 1949

HARRY S TRUMAN

Mr. President, Mr. Speaker, Members of the Congress:

I am happy to report to this 81st Congress that the state of the Union is good. Our Nation is better able than ever before to meet the needs of the American people, and to give them their fair chance in the pursuit of happiness. This great Republic is foremost among the nations of the world in the search for peace.

During the last 16 years, our people have been creating a society which offers new opportunities for every man to enjoy his share of the good things of life.

In this society, we are conservative about the values and principles which we cherish; but we are forward-looking in protecting those values and principles and in extending their benefits. We have rejected the discredited theory that the fortunes of the Nation should be in the hands of a privileged few. We have abandoned the "trickle-down" concept of national prosperity. Instead, we believe that our economic system should rest on a democratic foundation and that wealth should be created for the benefit of all.

The recent election shows that the people of the United States are in favor of this kind of society and want to go on improving it.

The American people have decided that poverty is just as wasteful and just as unnecessary as preventable disease. We have pledged our common resources to help one another in the hazards and struggles of individual life. We believe that no unfair prejudice or artificial distinction should bar any citizen of the United States of America from an education, or from good health, or from a job that he is capable of performing.

The attainment of this kind of society demands the best efforts of every citizen in every walk of life, and it imposes increasing responsibilities on the Government.

The Government must work with industry, labor, and the farmers in keeping our economy running at full speed. The Government must see that every American has a chance to obtain his fair share of our increasing abundance. These responsibilities go hand in hand. . . .

[G]reat as our progress has been, we still have a long way to go.

As we look around the country, many of our shortcomings stand out in bold relief.

We are suffering from excessively high prices.

Our production is still not large enough to satisfy our demands.

Our minimum wages are far too low.

From *Public Papers of the Presidents of the United States: Harry S Truman, 1949,* pp. 1–7.

Small business is losing ground to growing monopoly.

Our farmers still face an uncertain future. And too many of them lack the benefits of our modern civilization.

Some of our natural resources are still being wasted.

We are acutely short of electric power, although the means for developing such power are abundant.

Five million families are still living in slums and firetraps. Three million families share their homes with others.

Our health is far behind the progress of medical science. Proper medical care is so expensive that it is out of the reach of the great majority of our citizens.

Our schools, in many localities, are utterly inadequate.

Our democratic ideals are often thwarted by prejudice and intolerance.

Each of these shortcomings is also an opportunity—an opportunity for the Congress and the President to work for the good of the people.

Our first great opportunity is to protect our economy against the evils of "boom and bust." . . .

At the present time, our prosperity is threatened by inflationary pressures at a number of critical points in our economy. And the Government must be in a position to take effective action at these danger spots. . . .

One of the most important factors in maintaining prosperity is the Government's fiscal policy. At this time, it is essential not only that the Federal budget be balanced, but also that there be a substantial surplus to reduce inflationary pressures, and to permit a sizable reduction in the national debt, which now stands at $252 billion. I recommend, therefore, that the Congress enact new tax legislation to bring in an additional $4 billion of Government revenue. . . .

If we want to keep our economy running in high gear, we must be sure that every group has the incentive to make its full contribution to the national welfare. At present, the working men and women of the Nation are unfairly discriminated against by a statute that abridges their rights, curtails their constructive efforts, and hampers our system of free collective bargaining. That statute is the Labor-Management Relations Act of 1947, sometimes called the Taft-Hartley Act.

That act should be repealed! . . .

The health of our economy and its maintenance at high levels further require that the minimum wage fixed by law should be raised to at least 75 cents an hour. . . .

Our national farm program should be improved—not only in the interest of the farmers, but for the lasting prosperity of the whole Nation. Our goals should be abundant farm production and parity income for agriculture. Standards of living on the farm should be just as good as anywhere else in the country.

Farm price supports are an essential part of our program to achieve these ends. Price supports should be used to prevent farm price declines which are out of line with general price levels, to facilitate adjustments in production to consumer demands, and to promote good land use. Our price support legislation must be adapted to these objectives. . . .

Our growing population and the expansion of our economy depend upon the wise management of our land, water, forest, and mineral wealth. In our present dynamic economy, the task of conservation is not to lockup our resources but to develop and improve them. Failure, today, to make the investments which are necessary to support our progress in the future would be false economy.

We must push forward the development of our rivers for power, irrigation, navigation, and flood control. We should apply the lessons of our Tennessee Valley experience to our other great river basins. . . .

The Government has still other opportunities — to help raise the standard of living of our citizens. These opportunities lie in the fields of social security, health, education, housing, and civil rights.

The present coverage of the social security laws is altogether inadequate; the benefit payments are too low. One-third of our workers are not covered. Those who receive old-age and survivors insurance benefits receive an average payment of only $25 a month. Many others who cannot work because they are physically disabled are left to the mercy of charity. We should expand our social security program, both as to the size of the benefits and the extent of coverage, against the economic hazards due to unemployment, old age, sickness, and disability.

We must spare no effort to raise the general level of health in this country. In a nation as rich as ours, it is a shocking fact that tens of millions lack adequate medical care. We are short of doctors, hospitals, nurses. We must remedy these shortages. Moreover, we need — and we must have without further delay — a system of prepaid medical insurance which will enable every American to afford good medical care.

It is equally shocking that millions of our children are not receiving a good education. Millions of them are in overcrowded, obsolete buildings. We are short of teachers, because teachers' salaries are too low to attract new teachers, or to hold the ones we have. All these school problems will become much more acute as a result of the tremendous increase in the enrollment in our elementary schools in the next few years. I cannot repeat too strongly my desire for prompt Federal financial aid to the States to help them operate and maintain their school systems.

The governmental agency which now administers the programs of health, education, and social security should be given full departmental status.

The housing shortage continues to be acute. As an immediate step, the Congress should enact the provisions for low-rent public housing, slum clearance, farm housing, and housing research which I have repeatedly recommended. . . .

The driving force behind our progress is our faith in our democratic institutions. That faith is embodied in the promise of equal rights and equal

opportunities which the founders of our Republic proclaimed to their countrymen and to the whole world.

The fulfillment of this promise is among the highest purposes of government. The civil rights proposals I made to the 80th Congress, I now repeat to
the 81st Congress. They should be enacted in order that the Federal Government may assume the leadership and discharge the obligations clearly placed
upon it by the Constitution.

I stand squarely behind those proposals. . . .

We stand at the opening of an era which can mean either great achievement or terrible catastrophe for ourselves and for all mankind.

The strength of our Nation must continue to be used in the interest of all
our people rather than a privileged few. It must continue to be used unsel-
fishly in the struggle for world peace and the betterment of mankind the world
over.

This is the task before us.

It is not an easy one. It has many complications, and there will be strong
opposition from selfish interests.

I hope for cooperation from farmers, from labor, and from business.
Every segment of our population and every individual has a right to expect
from our Government a fair deal.

In 1945, when I came down before the Congress for the first time on
April 16, I quoted to you King Solomon's prayer that he wanted wisdom and
the ability to govern his people as they should be governed. I explained to you
at that time that the task before me was one of the greatest in the history of the
world, and that it was necessary to have the complete cooperation of the
Congress and the people of the United States.

Well now, we are taking a new start with the same situation. It is
absolutely essential that your President have the complete cooperation of the
Congress to carry out the great work that must be done to keep the peace in
this world, and to keep this country prosperous.

The people of this great country have a right to expect that the Congress
and the President will work in closest cooperation with one objective — the
welfare of the people of this Nation as a whole.

In the months ahead I know that I shall be able to cooperate with this
Congress.

Now, I am confident that the Divine Power which has guided us to this
time of fateful responsibility and glorious opportunity will not desert us now.

With that help from Almighty God which we have humbly acknowledged at every turning point in our national life, we shall be able to perform
the great tasks which He now sets before us.

four

THE 1950s

Affluence was the dominant motif of the 1950s. Most Americans were more prosperous than ever before. The economy was booming, and economic indicators promised continued material comfort. There were occasional downturns, to be sure, but the dismal days of the Great Crash and Great Depression now seemed safely past. Once the disruptions of World War II had been weathered, Americans wanted to enjoy the visible trappings of the good life. While not all shared the benefits of what economist John Kenneth Galbraith called "the affluent society," the culture paid the outsiders little heed. Self-confident in this age of consensus, most Americans sought to provide for their own stability and security and assumed that others would do the same. Yet even in comfortable times, occasional problems surfaced. The society became increasingly homogeneous, and some critics pointed to the anxiety and alienation that conformity brought.

In "Affluence and Anxiety," reprinted from his book *Holding the Line: The Eisenhower Era, 1952–1961,* Charles C. Alexander recognizes anxieties but focuses on the material benefits of prosperity. His statistical profile of the economy reveals its fundamental strength, even as his assessment of the standardization it brought reflects the consequences of untrammeled growth.

Sociologist C. Wright Mills is far more critical. In the selection reprinted here from *White Collar: The American Middle Classes,* published in 1951, Mills provides a scathing indictment of the patterns middle-class Americans accepted without question. Conformity, he suggests, breeds malaise, for "when white-collar people get jobs, they sell not only their time and energy but their personalities as well."

The document in this section is a children's story. *Tootle,* by Gertrude Crampton, is the tale of a locomotive who needs to be taught to stay on the tracks and always do what he is told. Published in 1945, the story was popular throughout the 1950s and served, according to sociologist David Riesman, as a "cautionary tale" instructing American children in the patterns of conformity that became so pronounced.

For further background on the 1950s, William E. Leuchtenburg, *A Troubled Feast: American Society Since 1945* (1983), describes the consumer culture that developed after World War II. Paul A. Carter, *Another Part of the Fifties* (1983), captures the mood of the period. John Kenneth Galbraith, *The Affluent Society* (1958), is a contemporary assessment of American prosperity. Sloan Wilson, *The Man in the Gray Flannel Suit* (1955), is a novel, made into a film, that underscores the materialistic values of the 1950s. David Riesman, in *The Lonely Crowd: A Study of Changing American Character* (1950), presents a perceptive sociological analysis of the implications of conformity.

Affluence and Anxiety

CHARLES C. ALEXANDER

For the American people as a whole, the two salient, overriding features of life in the decade of the 1950s were "affluence and anxiety," as the historian Carl Degler has phrased it. Never had Americans—never had any people—been so generally and spectacularly prosperous. On all sides were the evidences of widely distributed wealth and enormous national power. In the midst of their unparalleled abundance, however, Americans also had to get used to the constant threat of nuclear annihilation. They had to learn to live with perilous and frequent international crisis, with radioactive fallout from nuclear weapons tests in the atmosphere, and with a steady barrage of scientific doomsday prophecies. However much they might dim their consciousness before their television sets, travel to places their parents had only dreamed of seeing, increase their consumption of alcohol and other drugs, or otherwise engage in the collective pursuit of pleasure, the American people could never really escape the reality that their country could be largely destroyed within a matter of an hour or so. Yet if the specter of total destruction could not be completely banished, Americans could still find some solace in the mounting array of goods and gadgets available during this time of wealth unprecedented in the nation's history.

The United States had experienced periods of widespread prosperity before, notably during the 1920s and under the full-production economy of the Second World War. Not until the 1950s, however, did the nation truly arrive at what John Kenneth Galbraith has called "the affluent society." By the fifties the American economy seemed to have overcome man's historic struggle to secure the basic necessities of life—food, clothing, shelter. Despite the persistence of substantial poverty, the pertinent question no longer seemed to be whether America could feed, clothe, and house its citizens, but how it could sustain the steady advances in living standards under way since 1945. By 1956 American business corporations were paying out some $12 billion a year in dividends. Economists pegged the net worth of all Americans at $875 billion, and people were saving at the rate of 7½ percent of their incomes. Average personal income, figured after taxes and at 1956 prices, had grown to $5,050, up $530 since 1947. By 1960, although unemployment remained at about 6 percent of the work force, a record 66½ million Americans held jobs. Gross national product (GNP) had climbed from $322 billion in 1947 to more than half a trillion. Inflation, after slowing down considerably with the end of the Korean war, continued to nibble at the purchasing power of the dollar; nonetheless, real income had increased 29 percent since 1947. Because corporations had come to finance their expansion primarily out of profits rather than from stock sales, the stock market was no longer the key business barometer it had once been. Still significant, however, was the fact that late in 1954 stock averages finally regained their 1929 peak of 381.

Whereas before World War II the commonly used measures of economic health had been the volume of employment and industrial productivity, by the mid-1950s, many economists had come to place primary emphasis on the rate of overall economic growth, measured in terms of increases in GNP. To be sure, the Eisenhower administration, little influenced by Keynesian economic theory and generally inclined toward fiscal conservatism, was less concerned with growth rates than would be the succeeding Democratic administrations in the 1960s. Under Eisenhower little effort was made to manipulate federal fiscal policy as a way to stimulate economic growth; from 1953 to 1960 GNP grew at a modest annual rate of 2.9 percent, considerably below the increments of the 1920s or the period 1879–1919. Yet if the rate of overall economic expansion was generally sluggish in the post-Korean period, there could be little doubt that the United States was still experiencing the greatest peacetime prosperity in its history.

One of the key factors behind the economic surge of the 1950s was public spending. The decade saw no notable rise in federal transfer payments (expenditures for Social Security benefits, unemployment compensation, veterans' benefits, and the like) in relation to the rest of the national budget. Under a Republican administration the momentum toward the welfare state generated in the thirties and forties by the New Deal and Fair Deal, while by no means reversed, did slacken somewhat. Even so, state and local expenditures, particularly for public services, rose steadily—from 7 percent of GNP in 1950 to 9.4 percent by 1960. More importantly, because of continuing huge outlays for military purposes, overall federal expenditures remained at a high level despite the end of the Korean war and the Eisenhower administration's dogged pursuit of balanced budgets. Defense Department allocations accounted for more than half the total national budget each year of Eisenhower's Presidency.

Another key to the boom was the rapid expansion of private credit, which made it possible for Americans to buy a great deal more of almost everything with relatively less in the way of savings. For example, while family homeownership rose from 40 percent to 60 percent and disposable income increased 3½ times between 1939 and 1955, mortgage and installment indebtedness grew fivefold. Early in 1953 only about 6 percent of all Veterans Administration loans were secured without down payments, as opposed to nearly 40 percent two years later. By 1955 some 60 percent of all automobile purchases, usually cited as the single most important element in the consumer economy, took place under credit terms, which were often as generous as $100 down and three years to pay. Such terms, along with the drastic depreciation characteristic of the automobile market, commonly made it more advantageous for buyers to let their cars be repossessed than to pay them off. By the mid-fifties installment indebtedness in the United States had reached $27 billion, ten times what it had been in the 1920s. Although total personal indebtedness was still only 12 percent of total personal income, indebtedness was growing considerably faster than income.

Unprecedented private indebtedness, freely entered into and often casually borne, was one of the most important economic realities of the fifties — as was the appearance of a sizable new industry whose concern it was to investigate, report, and maintain files on the credit rating of individuals. Frequently secured at the expense of personal privacy, a good or at least passable standing with the credit agencies might be worth more than an individual's capital assets. Credit-buying made it possible for the great majority of Americans to share at least to some degree in the material abundance of the fifties. By 1956, 81 percent of American families had managed to acquire television sets, 96 percent had refrigerators, nearly 67 percent had vacuum cleaners, and almost 89 percent had washing machines. Only in the United States did such luxuries seem essential. At the end of the decade nearly 74 million automobiles were in operation in the United States, while millions more rested in junk heaps along the streets and highways of the country.

In short, the American economy had completed a fifty-year process of transformation — first recognized in the 1920s and then obscured by the Great Depression and the Second World War — from a production economy in which the primary task was to meet basic human needs, to a consumer economy which presupposed that basic needs were already being met and that the primary task was constantly to expand consumption in order to push profits to higher and higher levels. In the new consumer economy, advertising played an indispensable role in convincing consumers that they had numerous — in fact theoretically unlimited — "unconscious needs" which must somehow be satisfied. Another feature of the consumer economy was the ephemerality of goods, whether because of planned obsolescence or because mass production for mass consumption inevitably meant less durable products.

Still another feature was the relative decline in the number of people working to produce goods, and the employment of greater and greater numbers of Americans to sell, distribute, and maintain what factories and plants turned out. By the 1950s, for the first time, the "service industries" employed more than half of all wage-earners. This changeover resulted not only from the emergence of the consumer economy but also from the increasing automation of industrial processes. Labor leaders and some economists worried that automated production methods would displace great numbers of workers; other economists, as well as business leaders, believed automation would mean safer and better work, more leisure time, and an actual increase in jobs.

Accompanying the boom was a literature of praise for the American capitalist system which was strikingly similar to the self-congratulatory outpourings of the twenties. The major difference was that those who eulogized the new economy of abundance generally accepted the emergence since the thirties of the "umpire state" to promote, police, and mediate between economic interests. Among those leading the applause was David E. Lilienthal, once damned by right-wingers as a mortal enemy of private enterprise when he was a Director of the Tennessee Valley Authority and subsequently, as the first Chairman of the Atomic Energy Commission, accused of being soft on

Communism. Now Lilienthal wrote lyrically that big business had entered a "new era" of maturity, responsibility, and public service, an era in which the stereotypes of the depression years had become irrelevant. In the thirties the economist Adolph A. Berle had been a sharply critical observer of the concentration of corporate power in the hands of a managerial elite; now he described the modern corporation as "a social institution" whose "aggregate economic achievement is unsurpassed." "Taking all elements (including human freedom) into account," proclaimed Berle, the corporation's "system of distributing benefits, though anything but perfect, has nevertheless left every other system in recorded history far behind." Having once written a perceptively critical history of the confident and complacent twenties, Frederick Lewis Allen had become convinced by 1953 that the United States had built "an orderly and successful substitute" for socialism and Communism. Americans were blessed with "a system which not only helps the underdog, and brings about a dynamic redistribution of income in his favor, but also maintains the freedom of business enterprise and other private institutions, in all their fruitful diversity, to compete, invent, experiment and create. . . ."

Why did the system work so well? According to John Kenneth Galbraith, it worked because of American capitalism's built-in "countervailing power"—the economic and political interaction of such massive elements as corporate producers, sellers, and buyers; labor unions; organized agriculture; and government itself to balance and block the abuse of power. And what about poverty? Galbraith and many other experts freely acknowledged that it still existed. The usual judgment, however, was that offered by Galbraith in 1958 in *The Affluent Society:* Not a "massive affliction," poverty in America was "more nearly an afterthought." Galbraith also insisted that even vestigial poverty in the midst of plenty was a "disgrace." His prescription for eliminating poverty was a moderate, "qualitative" extension of the social welfare directions taken under the New Deal and Fair Deal but slowed under the Eisenhower administration. Others contended that the "problem" could be "solved" by new federal policies designed to accelerate economic growth, which would in turn sweep up the poor in the overall process of expansion.

Yet for all the glowing statistics attesting to the undeniable material well-being of most Americans and all the self-congratulatory paeans in behalf of the new capitalism, the American economic system revealed a number of fundamental shortcomings and weaknesses in the 1950s. For one thing, the American people went on something of an ecological binge, blissfully and wastefully expanding across the national landscape with little concern for the injury they were doing to their physical environment or for the accelerating depletion of their energy resources. It would remain for a succeeding generation to assess and work to remedy the ecological damage Americans had systematically wrought throughout their history, but especially under the heedless boosterism of the fifties.

Even in the midst of this obsessive growthmanship, the economic system still was not able to maintain unbroken prosperity. The business cycle remained a fact of American economic life. To be sure, certain structural changes in the economy—notably the rise of big government spending and massive government intervention—served to cushion the impact of economic downturns. At the same time, the economic history of the Eisenhower years suggests how sensitive the economy had become to fluctuations in the federal budget. A rather sharp recession followed the drop in military expenditures accompanying the end of the Korean war in 1953, although the economy had generally recovered by the middle of the next year. A more severe recession came in 1957–1958, this one following substantial budget cuts during the "budget battle" of 1957. Unemployment, which had hovered around 4 percent of the civilian labor force since the 1954 recovery, climbed to 7½ percent by mid-1958, the peak for the fifties. Recovery was again well under way by the end of 1958, but two years later unemployment still stood at 6 percent. Thus each recovery period after the Korean war left a higher proportion of the work force without jobs than had been true before the downturn.

Those who had jobs were more likely than ever to be working for someone other than a business employer. Whereas in 1929 only 15 percent of the labor force had worked outside private enterprise, by the early 1960s about one-third of all jobholders were employed by government, in education, or by nonprofit organizations. In the midst of effusive claims that American capitalism had eliminated the threat of massive unemployment, private enterprise in the years 1950–1960 was able to account for only one-tenth of all the new jobs generated in the economy.

Accompanying the relative decline in private-sector employment was a drop in the amount of wealth produced by American business corporations alongside other elements in the economy. The growth in national income attributable to corporations reached a peak at 55.8 percent in 1955 and then began a slow decline to the 1948 level of 53.8 percent. Nevertheless, the trend toward the concentration of corporate power, which had been under way since the last decades of the nineteenth century, continued apace during the fifties. Between 1947 and 1958 the 200 biggest industrial firms increased their proportion of total manufacturing output from 30 percent to 38 percent, while the 50 biggest upped their share from 17 percent to 23 percent. By 1961 the 100 biggest corporations had come to control 31 percent of all industrial wealth in the United States.

On the surface, it is true, concentration seemed to be shrinking in about as many industries as it was increasing. This paradox is explained by the spectacular appearance in the post–World War II period of the business conglomerate, marking a new phase and offering a new instrument in the historic movement to centralize economic power in America. Unlike earlier forms of business combination, which had sought to consolidate producers within a single industry, the conglomerate featured industrial and mercantile diversification. Ostensibly the conglomerate seemed not to threaten the existing competitive situation because it did not aim to monopolize a particular industry or segment of trade. Actually it made fewer and fewer parent firms more powerful than ever by extending their operations into areas of the economy having no apparent relation to each other. Thus one conglomerate of businesses might be involved in manufacturing numerous different products, in operating resort hotels, in mining and lumbering operations, and in various other ventures.

On the whole, the Department of Justice was not disposed to interfere with conglomerate mergers. As a consequence, between 1950 and 1961 the 500 largest corporations in America merged with and absorbed a total of 3,404 smaller companies operating in a bewildering variety of areas of manufacturing and merchandising. Meanwhile the 50 biggest corporations acquired 471 firms, all without objection from the Justice Department. Two main arguments were used to justify or at least mitigate the increasing centralization of corporate power. The first was the longstanding one that concentration was inevitable and in the long run productive of order, efficiency, and better service to the consumer. The second argument was initially advanced in rudimentary form in the twenties and then refurbished and elaborated in the post–World War II years: The modern corporation, according to its defenders, had taken on a new sense of "public conscience" and a new obligation to serve the public interest even, so the rhetoric of both corporate managers and lay advocates seemed to suggest, at the expense of turning a profit.

Yet turning a profit remained the raison d'être of American business, and during the Eisenhower years there were repeated instances showing the conflict between the incessant pressure for private profit and power and the vaunted public conscience of corporate management. The most dramatic was the scandal in the electrical manufacturing industry which was uncovered in the last year of the Eisenhower administration. Officials of the General Electric Corporation, a firm hailed by Adolph Berle and others as almost a paragon of corporate responsibility, conspired with executives of twenty-nine smaller companies making electrical machinery to set prices on a wide range of products, from turbine generators to kilowatt-hour meters. In 1960 the Department of Justice prosecuted the price-fixing companies for violating the antitrust laws and overcharging customers by several billion dollars. Of twenty indictments secured, GE officials were named in nineteen. Ultimately seven executives, including a GE vice president and two general managers, served short prison terms. Eight other GE officials received suspended sentences; five more were fined individually. The federal courts imposed nearly $2 million in fines on the 30 offending companies, of which GE paid $437,500. . . .

Such episodes should have helped discredit the carefully nurtured image of the benevolent corporation dedicated to serving the public interest. Similarly, even a rudimentary knowledge of the realities of taxation should have been enough to puncture the myth that the United States had an equitable, graduated income tax system. For example, in 1959, of nineteen Americans with incomes of more than $5 million, five paid no federal taxes at all, and not one of the nineteen paid taxes at the nominal legal rate. By the 1950s the federal tax system had become so complex, so full of loopholes, and so geared to encourage property ownership and capital investment that the more money a person made the smaller the percentage of his income he was likely to pay in federal taxes. . . .

The economic history of the fifties also should have shown the hollowness of the claim that poverty in America was either insignificant or was in the process of evaporating. Far from being swept up in the expansionary surge, poverty remained one of the stubbornest features of American life. Living conditions, income levels, and employment opportunities were generally bad among four groups: the rapidly growing number of black people living near the center of cities; white, commonly "old-stock" Americans in the Appalachian coal regions from western Pennsylvania to northern Georgia; mill workers in the declining industrial towns of New England; and rural people, both white and black, in the southern states. Of course it is true that economists used different measures of poverty, and that even the poorest Americans were in better shape than much of the world's population. But it was cold comfort for a black ghetto resident to be told that his standard of living was higher than that of the average European, when from every side he was bombarded by reminders that as Americans he and his family were supposed to have all sorts of things he simply could not afford, and that he should be working regularly, when some 30 percent of black city dwellers were unemployed. By any measure it was clear that many millions of citizens lived far below the general level of material affluence. . . .

On one matter, however, there was general agreement in the 1950s: The average American industrial workingman was better off than he had ever been. Pay was higher and hours were shorter than during any previous period. Workers had been protected by law in their right to organize and enter into collective bargaining with employers since the 1930s. One of the major legacies of the New Deal–World War II years, "big labor," seemingly possessed great economic leverage, even though the 1947 Taft-Hartley Act had restricted certain kinds of union activity, had outlawed compulsory union membership before employment (the closed shop), and had sanctioned state "right-to-work" laws prohibiting compulsory union membership after employment (the union shop).

Big labor became even bigger in February 1955, when the American Federation of Labor (AFL) and the Congress of Industrial Organizations (CIO), archrivals since the rise of the CIO in the mid-thirties, merged their combined memberships of 15 million. The merger did not entirely end jurisdictional disputes between AFL craft unions and CIO industrial unions, but organized labor could now function better than ever to gain regular wage increases, greater job security, and even profit-sharing agreements. . . .

[T]he American people as a whole . . . were certainly dedicated to the frenzied pursuit of material accumulation and upward social mobility. Social mobility in America had always been closely linked to geographical mobility.

But whereas that had once meant the steady push of the population westward and the accelerating migration of rural people to towns and cities, by the middle decades of the twentieth century social mobility usually meant escape from, not to, an urban existence. By 1960 about 70 percent of all Americans lived in urban areas. Even more notable, though, was the fact that approximately half the population lived not in the inner cities but in peripheral suburban regions.

The flight from the inner city became epidemic in the fifties, as rising personal incomes and easy home financing enabled tens of millions of families, mostly middle-class and almost entirely white, to move into treeless, monotonous housing developments recently scraped out of the rural landscape. Left behind were most working-class whites, anxiously awaiting the time when they too could afford a house in the suburbs, and the vast number of urban blacks, forced by economic necessity and social discrimination to crowd into old and usually deteriorating tenements and neighborhoods near the city's central business district. A number of the older cities — New York, Chicago, Boston, Philadelphia, Detroit — actually lost population during the fifties. . . .

America, . . . [critics argued] had once been a land of exciting diversity and new beginnings — a magnet for the adventurer, the dissenter, the free individual. But now Americans had come to worship the cult of comformity, to settle comfortably for a homogenized existence, to carry on an obsessive quest for personal security. . . . Instead of following his own internalized life goals, the archetypal American of the mid-twentieth century continually adapted and readapted his personality and behavior to the changing collective aspirations, life styles, and idea patterns of peer groups and society as a whole. . . .

One new feature of the social criticism of the fifties was its focus on the expanding suburbs. A host of social scientists, popular writers, and novelists turned their attentions to the manners, mores, and anxieties of the inhabitants of "suburbia." Suburbia was supposed to be the breeding ground of other-directedness, the locus of the Organization Man, the place where the troubled careerist in Sloan Wilson's best-selling novel, *The Man in the Gray Flannel Suit,* slept and spent his weekends. Of course not all suburban areas were architecturally monotonous, choked with children, settled by rootless, driven adults. Suburbs could and did vary considerably in age, appearance, and the life styles of their inhabitants. Still, there remained much truth in the stereotype of suburbia and its people. Suburbia was where nearly everyone either already lived or seemed to want to live. A house in the suburbs had become the chief symbol of success for many millions of Americans. That success — translated as a comfortable income, job security, perhaps a chance for advancement — increasingly was achievable only within a bureaucratic framework. Americans were in fact becoming organization men, and organization women as well. . . .

Those who worried about conformity, standardization, and other-directedness commonly blamed the mass media — the popular press, advertising, television, radio, motion pictures—even more than public education for what was wrong with American life. By pandering to the lowest common denominator of public taste in an incessant drive for profit, the media had supposedly perverted and debased the fine arts and molded an unthinking and unfeeling mass mind. . . .

Broadly speaking, the focus on mass culture was only part of the spreading concern over the putatively coercive, enervating effects of modern mass society. There was, though, a more specific reason why after 1950 more words were spent in discussion of mass culture than every before—the arrival of television as a central fact of American existence. The availability of cheap electricity and the affluence of the period enabled the great majority of Americans to acquire television sets much sooner than they had radio in the twenties and thirties. . . . By 1956, . . . more than 500 stations were in operation, serving some 40 million homes. Nearly all local television stations were affiliated with the three networks—CBS, NBC, and ABC—which had previously dominated radio and had quickly come to control television. By mid-decade advertisers were paying out a billion dollars yearly to the TV networks and their affiliates, twice as much as was going to radio.

Americans exulted in, argued about, and were generally more fascinated by the images on the small glowing screens in their homes than they would ever be again. Except for the drab offerings of the publicly owned stations usually connected with colleges and universities, television programming depended on profit considerations. Among other things, that meant that both networks and local stations followed the pattern of pre-1950 radio programming, presenting a potpourri of soap operas, children's features, newscasts, quiz shows, variety (basically music and comedy) programs, dramatic series, and sports events. Most of what appeared on the picture tube either repeated the stale formulas of radio or plumbed new depths of inanity and tastelessness. . . .

White Collar: The American Middle Classes

C. WRIGHT MILLS

The white-collar people slipped quietly into modern society. Whatever history they have had is a history without events; whatever common interests they have do not lead to unity; whatever future they have will not be of their own making. If they aspire at all it is to a middle course, at a time when no middle course is available, and hence to an illusory course in an imaginary society. Internally, they are split, fragmented; externally, they are dependent on larger forces. Even if they gained the will to act, their actions, being unorganized, would be less a movement than a tangle of unconnected contests. As a group, they do not threaten anyone; as individuals, they do not practice an independent way of life. So before an adequate idea of them could be formed, they have been taken for granted as familiar actors of the urban mass.

Yet it is to this white-collar world that one must look for much that is characteristic of twentieth-century existence. By their rise to numerical importance, the white-collar people have upset the nineteenth-century expectation that society would be divided between entrepreneurs and wage workers. By their mass way of life, they have transformed the tang and feel of the American experience. They carry, in a most revealing way, many of those psychological themes that characterize our epoch, and, in one way or another, every general theory of the main drift has had to take account of them. For above all else they are a new cast of actors, performing the major routines of twentieth-century society:

At the top of the white-collar world, the old captain of industry hands over his tasks to the manager of the corporation. Alongside the politician, with his string tie and ready tongue, the salaried bureaucrat, with brief case and slide rule, rises into political view. These top managers now command hierarchies of anonymous middle managers, floorwalkers, salaried foremen, county agents, federal inspectors, and police investigators trained in the law.

In the established professions, the doctor, lawyer, engineer, once was free and named on his own shingle; in the new white-collar world, the salaried specialists of the clinic, the junior partners in the law factory, the captive engineers of the corporation have begun to challenge free professional leadership. The old professions of medicine and law are still at the top of the professional world, but now all around them are men and women of new skills. There are a dozen kinds of social engineers and mechanical technicians, a multitude of girl Fridays, laboratory assistants, registered and unregistered nurses, draftsmen, statisticians, social workers.

In the salesrooms, which sometimes seem to coincide with the new society as a whole, are the stationary salesgirls in the department store, the mobile salesmen of insurance, the absentee salesmen — ad-men helping others sell from a distance. At the top are the prima donnas, the vice presidents who say that they are 'merely salesmen, although perhaps a little more creative than others,' and at the bottom, the five-and-dime clerks, selling commodities at a fixed price, hoping soon to leave the job for marriage.

In the enormous file of the office, in all the calculating rooms, accountants and purchasing agents replace the man who did his own figuring. And in the lower reaches of the white-collar world, office operatives grind along, loading and emptying the filing system; there are private secretaries and typists, entry clerks, billing clerks, corresponding clerks — a thousand kinds of clerks; the operators of light machinery, comptometers, dictaphones, addressographs; and the receptionists to let you in or keep you out.

Images of white-collar types are now part of the literature of every major industrial nation: Hans Fallada presented the Pinnebergs to pre-Hitler Germany. Johannes Pinneberg, a bookkeeper trapped by inflation, depression, and wife with child, ends up in the economic gutter, with no answer to the question, 'Little Man, What Now?' — except support by a genuinely proletarian wife. J. B. Priestley created a gallery of tortured and insecure creatures from the white-collar world of London in *Angel Pavement.* Here are people who have been stood up by life: what they most desire is forbidden them by reason of what they are. George Orwell's Mr. Bowling, a salesman in *Coming Up for Air,* speaks for them all, perhaps, when he says: 'There's a lot of rot talked about the sufferings of the working class. I'm not so sorry for the proles myself. . . . The prole suffers physically, but he's a free man when he isn't working. But in every one of those little stucco boxes there's some poor bastard who's never free except when he's fast asleep and dreaming that he's got the boss down the bottom of a well and is bunging lumps of coal at him. Of course the basic trouble with people like us is that we all imagine we've got something to lose.'

Kitty Foyle is perhaps the closest American counterpart of these European novels. But how different its heroine is! In America, unlike Europe, the fate of white-collar types is not yet clear. A modernized Horatio Alger heroine, Kitty Foyle (like Alice Adams before her) has aspirations up the Main Line. The book ends, in a depression year, with Kitty earning $3000 a year, about to buy stock in her firm, and hesitating over marrying a doctor who happens to be a Jew. While Herr Pinneberg in Germany was finding out, too late, that his proletarian wife was at once his life fate and his political chance, Kitty Foyle was busy pursuing an American career in the cosmetics business. But twenty-five years later, during the American postwar boom Willy Loman appears, the hero of *The Death of a Salesman,* the white-collar man who by the very virtue of his moderate success in business turns out to be a total failure in life. Frederic Wertham has written of Willy Loman's dream: 'He succeeds with it; he fails with it; he dies with it. But why did he have this dream? Isn't it true that he had to have a false dream in our society?'

The nineteenth-century farmer and businessman were generally thought to be stalwart individuals—their own men, men who could quickly grow to be almost as big as anyone else. The twentieth-century white-collar man has never been independent as the farmer used to be, nor as hopeful of the main chance as the businessman. He is always somebody's man, the corporation's, the government's, the army's; and he is seen as the man who does not rise. The decline of the free entrepreneur and the rise of the dependent employee on the American scene has paralleled the decline of the independent individual and the rise of the little man in the American mind.

In a world crowded with big ugly forces, the white-collar man is readily assumed to possess all the supposed virtues of the small creature. He may be at the bottom of the social world, but he is, at the same time, gratifyingly middle class. It is easy as well as safe to sympathize with his troubles; he can do little or nothing about them. Other social actors threaten to become big and aggressive, to act out of selfish interests and deal in politics. The big businessman continues his big-business-as-usual through the normal rhythm of slump and war and boom; the big labor man, lifting his shaggy eyebrows, holds up the nation until his demands are met; the big farmer cultivates the Senate to see that big farmers get theirs. But not the white-collar man. He is more often pitiful than tragic, as he is seen collectively, fighting impersonal inflation, living out in slow misery his yearning for the quick American climb. He is pushed by forces beyond his control, pulled into movements he does not understand; he gets into situations in which his is the most helpless position. The white-collar man is the hero as victim, the small creature who is acted upon but who does not act, who works along unnoticed in somebody's office or store, never talking loud, never talking back, never taking a stand.

When the focus shifts from the generalized Little Man to specific white-collar types whom the public encounters, the images become diverse and often unsympathetic. Sympathy itself often carries a sharp patronizing edge; the word 'clerk,' for example, is likely to be preceded by 'merely.' Who talks willingly to the insurance agent, opens the door to the bill collector? 'Every-body knows how rude and nasty salesgirls can be.' Schoolteachers are stan-dard subjects for businessmen's jokes. The housewife's opinion of private secretaries is not often friendly — indeed, much of white-collar fiction capital-izes on her hostility to 'the office wife.'

These are images of specific white-collar types seen from above. But from below, for two generations sons and daughters of the poor have looked forward eagerly to becoming even 'mere' clerks. Parents have sacrificed to have even one child finish high school, business school, or college so that he could be the assistant to the executive, do the filing, type the letter, teach school, work in the government office, do something requiring technical skills: hold a white-collar job. In serious literature white-collar images are often subjects for lamentation; in popular writing they are often targets of aspiration.

Images of American types have not been built carefully by piecing together live experience. Here, as elsewhere, they have been made up out of tradition and schoolbook and the early, easy drift of the unalerted mind. And they have been reinforced and even created, especially in white-collar times, by the editorial machinery of popular amusement and mass communications.

Manipulations by professional image-makers are effective because their audiences do not or cannot know personally all the people they want to talk about or be like, and because they have an unconscious need to believe in certain types. In their need and inexperience, such audiences snatch and hold to the glimpses of types that are frozen into the language with which they see the world. Even when they meet the people behind the types face to face, previous images, linked deeply with feeling, blind them to what stands before them. Experience is trapped by false images, even as reality itself sometimes seems to imitate the soap opera and the publicity release.

Perhaps the most cherished national images are sentimental versions of historical types that no longer exist, if indeed they ever did. Underpinning many standard images of The American is the myth, in the words of the eminent historian, A. M. Schlesinger, Sr., of the 'long tutelage to the soil' which, as 'the chief formative influence,' results in 'courage, creative energy and resourcefulness. . . .' According to this idea, which clearly bears a nineteenth-century trademark, The American possesses magical independence, homely ingenuity, great capacity for work, all of which virtues he attained while struggling to subdue the vast continent.

One hundred years ago, when three-fourths of the people were farmers, there may have been some justification for engraving such an image and calling it The American. But since then, farmers have declined to scarcely more than one-tenth of the occupied populace, and new classes of salaried employees and wage-workers have risen. Deep-going historic changes resulting in wide diversities have long challenged the nationalistic historian who would cling to The American as a single type of ingenious farmer-artisan. In so far as universals can be found in life and character in America, they are due less to any common tutelage of the soil than to the leveling influences of urban civilization, and above all, to the standardization of the big technology and of the media of mass communication.

America is neither the nation of horse-traders and master builders of economic theory, nor the nation of go-getting, claim-jumping, cattle-rustling pioneers of frontier mythology. Nor have the traits rightly or wrongly associated with such historic types carried over into the contemporary population to any noticeable degree. Only a fraction of this population consists of free private enterprisers in any economic sense; there are now four times as many wage-workers and salary workers as independent entrepreneurs. 'The stuggle for life,' William Dean Howells wrote in the 'nineties, 'has changed from a free fight to an encounter of disciplined forces, and the free fighters that are left get ground to pieces. . . .'

If it is assumed that white-collar employees represent some sort of continuity with the old middle class of entrepreneurs, then it may be said that for the last hundred years the middle classes have been facing the slow expropriation of their holdings, and that for the last twenty years they have faced the spectre of unemployment. Both assertions rest on facts, but the facts have not been experienced by the middle class as a *double* crisis. The property question is not an issue to the new middle class of the present generation. That was fought out, and lost, before World War I, by the old middle class. The centralization of small properties is a development that has affected each generation back to our great-grandfathers, reaching its climax in the Progressive Era. It has been a secular trend of too slow a tempo to be felt as a continuing crisis by middle-class men and women, who often seem to have become more commodity-minded than property-minded. Yet history is not always enacted consciously; if expropriation is not felt as crisis, still it is a basic fact in the ways of life and the aspirations of the new middle class; and the facts of unemployment *are* felt as fears, hanging over the white-collar world.

By examining white-collar life, it is possible to learn something about what is becoming more typically 'American' than the frontier character probably ever was. What must be grasped is the picture of society as a great salesroom, an enormous file, an incorporated brain, a new universe of management and manipulation. By understanding these diverse white-collar worlds, one can also understand better the shape and meaning of modern society as a whole, as well as the simple hopes and complex anxieties that grip all the people who are sweating it out in the middle of the twentieth century.

The troubles that confront the white-collar people are the troubles of all men and women living in the twentieth century. If these troubles seem particularly bitter to the new middle strata, perhaps that is because for a brief time these people felt themselves immune to troubles.

Before the First World War there were fewer little men, and in their brief monopoly of high-school education they were in fact protected from many of the sharper edges of the workings of capitalist progress. They were free to entertain deep illusions about their individual abilities and about the collective trustworthiness of the system. As their number has grown, however, they have become increasingly subject to wage-worker conditions. Especially since the Great Depression have white-collar people come up against all the old problems of capitalist society. They have been racked by slump and war and even by boom. They have learned about impersonal unemployment in depressions and about impersonal death by technological violence in war. And in good times, as prices rose faster than salaries, the money they thought they were making was silently taken away from them.

The material hardship of nineteenth-century industrial workers finds its parallel on the psychological level among twentieth-century white-collar employees. The new Little Man seems to have no firm roots, no sure loyalties to sustain his life and give it a center. He is not aware of having any history, his past being as brief as it is unheroic; he has lived through no golden age he can recall in time of trouble. Perhaps because he does not know where he is going, he is in a frantic hurry; perhaps because he does not know what frightens him, he is paralyzed with fear. This is especially a feature of his political life, where the paralysis results in the most profound apathy of modern times.

The uneasiness, the malaise of our time, is due to this root fact: in our politics and economy, in family life and religion — in practically every sphere of our existence — the certainties of the eighteenth and nineteenth centuries have disintegrated or been destroyed and, at the same time, no new sanctions or justifications for the new routines we live, and must live, have taken hold. So there is no acceptance and there is no rejection, no sweeping hope and no sweeping rebellion. There is no plan of life. Among white-collar people, the malaise is deep-rooted; for the absence of any order of belief has left them morally defenseless as individuals and politically impotent as a group. Newly created in a harsh time of creation, white-collar man has no culture to lean upon except the contents of a mass society that has shaped him and seeks to manipulate him to its alien ends. For security's sake, he must strain to attach himself somewhere, but no communities or organizations seem to be thoroughly his. This isolated position makes him excellent material for synthetic molding at the hands of popular culture — print, film, radio, and television. As a metropolitan dweller, he is especially open to the focused onslaught of all the manufactured loyalties and distractions that are contrived and urgently pressed upon those who live in worlds they never made.

In the case of the white-collar man, the alienation of the wage-worker from the products of his work is carried one step nearer to its Kafka-like completion. The salaried employee does not make anything, although he may handle much that he greatly desires but cannot have. No product of craftsmanship can be his to contemplate with pleasure as it is being created and after it is made. Being alienated from any product of his labor, and going year after year through the same paper routine, he turns his leisure all the more frenziedly to the *ersatz* diversion that is sold him, and partakes of the synthetic excitement that neither eases nor releases. He is bored at work and restless at play, and this terrible alternation wears him out.

In his work he often clashes with customer and superior, and must almost always be the standardized loser: he must smile and be personable, standing behind the counter, or waiting in the outer office. In many strata of white-collar employment, such traits as courtesy, helpfulness, and kindness, once intimate, are now part of the impersonal means of livelihood. Self-alienation is thus an accompaniment of his alienated labor.

When white-collar people get jobs, they sell not only their time and energy but their personalities as well. They sell by the week or month their smiles and their kindly gestures, and they must practice the prompt repression of resentment and aggression. For these intimate traits are of commercial relevance and required for the more efficient and profitable distribution of goods and services. Here are the new little Machiavellians, practicing their personable crafts for hire and for the profit of others, according to rules laid down by those above them.

In the eighteenth and nineteenth centuries, rationality was identified with freedom. The ideas of Freud about the individual, and of Marx about society, were strengthened by the assumption of the coincidence of freedom and rationality. Now rationality seems to have taken on a new form, to have its seat not in individual men, but in social institutions which by their bureaucratic planning and mathematical foresight usurp both freedom and rationality from the little individual men caught in them. The calculating hierarchies of department store and industrial corporation, of rationalized office and governmental bureau, lay out the gray ways of work and stereotype the permitted initiatives. And in all this bureaucratic usurpation of freedom and of rationality, the white-collar people are the interchangeable parts of the big chains of authority that bind the society together.

White-collar people, always visible but rarely seen, are politically voice-less. Stray politicians wandering in the political arena without party may put 'white collar' people alongside businessmen, farmers, and wage-workers in their broadside appeals, but no platform of either major party has yet referred to them directly. Who fears the clerk? Neither *Alice Adams* nor *Kitty Foyle* could be a *Grapes of Wrath* for the 'share-croppers in the dust bowl of business.'

But while practical politicians, still living in the ideological air of the nineteenth century, have paid little attention to the new middle class, theore-ticians of the left have vigorously claimed the salaried employee as a potential proletarian, and theoreticians of the right and center have hailed him as a sign of the continuing bulk and vigor of the middle class. Stray heretics from both camps have even thought, from time to time, that the higher-ups of the white-collar world might form a center of initiative for new political begin-nings. In Germany, the 'black-coated worker' was one of the harps that Hitler played on his way to power. In England, the party of labor is thought to have won electoral socialism by capturing the votes of the suburban salaried workers.

To the question, what political direction will the white-collar people take, there are as many answers as there are theorists. Yet to the observer of American materials, the political problem posed by these people is not so much what the direction may be as whether they will take any political direction at all.

Between the little man's consciousness and the issues of our epoch there seems to be a veil of indifference. His will seems numbed, his spirit meager. Other men of other strata are also politically indifferent, but electoral victories are imputed to them; they do have tireless pressure groups and excited captains who work in and around the hubs of power, to whom, it may be imagined, they have delegated their enthusiasm for public affairs. But white-collar people are scattered along the rims of all the wheels of power: no one is enthusiastic about them and, like political eunuchs, they themselves are without potency and without enthusiasm for the urgent political clash.

Estranged from community and society in a context of distrust and manipulation; alienated from work and, on the personality market, from self; expropriated of individual rationality, and politically apathetic—these are the new little people, the unwilling vanguard of modern society. These are some of the circumstances for the acceptance of which their hopeful training has quite unprepared them.

What men are interested in is not always what is to their interest; the troubles they are aware of are not always the ones that beset them. It would indeed be a fetish of 'democracy' to assume that men immediately know their interests and are clearly aware of the conditions within themselves and their society that frustrate them and make their efforts misfire. For interests involve not only values felt, but also something of the means by which these values might be attained. Merely by looking into himself, an individual can neither clarify his values nor set up ways for their attainment. Increased awareness is not enough, for it is not only that men can be unconscious of their situations; they are often falsely conscious of them. To become more truly conscious, white-collar people would have to become aware of themselves as members of new strata practicing new modes of work and life in modern America. To know what it is possible to know about their troubles, they would have to connect, within the going framework, what they are interested in with what is to their interest.

If only because of its growing numbers, the new middle class represents a considerable social and political potential, yet there is more systematic information available on the farmer, the wage-worker, the Negro, even on the criminal, than on the men and women of the variegated white-collar worlds. Even the United States census is now so arranged as to make very difficult a definitive count of these people. Meanwhile, theorizing about the middle class on the basis of old facts has run to seed, and no fresh plots of fact have been planted. Yet the human and political importance of the white-collar people continues to loom larger and larger. . . .

Document
Tootle

GERTRUDE CRAMPTON

Far, far to the west of everywhere is the village of Lower Trainswitch. All the baby locomotives go there to learn to be big locomotives. The young locomotives steam up and down the tracks, trying to call out the long, sad *ToooOooot* of the big locomotives. But the best they can do is a gay little *Tootle*.

Lower Trainswitch has a fine school for engines. There are lessons in Whistle Blowing, Stopping for a Red Flag Waving, Puffing Loudly When Starting, Coming Around Curves Safely, Screeching When Stopping, and Clicking and Clacking Over the Rails.

Of all the things that are taught in the Lower Trainswitch School for Locomotives, the most important is, of course, Staying on the Rails No Matter What.

The head of the school is an old engineer named Bill. Bill always tells the new locomotives that he will not be angry if they sometimes spill the soup pulling the diner, or if they turn the milk to butter now and then. But they will never, never be good trains unless they get 100 A+ in Staying on the Rails No Matter What. All the baby engines work very hard to get 100 A+ in Staying On the Rails. After a few weeks not one of the engines in the Lower Train-

switch School for Trains would even think of getting off the rails, no matter—well, no matter what.

One day a new locomotive named Tootle came to school.

"Here is the finest baby I've seen since old 600," thought Bill. He patted
the gleaming young locomotive and said, "How would you like to grow up to
be the Flyer between New York and Chicago?"

"If a Flyer goes very fast, I should like to be one," Tootle answered. "I
love to go fast. Watch me."

He raced all around the roundhouse.

"Good! Good!" said Bill. "You must study Whistle Blowing, Puffing
Loudly When Starting, Stopping for a Red Flag Waving, and Pulling the
Diner without Spilling the Soup.

"But most of all you must study Staying on the Rails No Matter What.
Remember, you can't be a Flyer unless you get 100 A+ in Staying on the
Rails."

Tootle promised that he would remember and that he would work very
hard.

He did, too.

He even worked hard at Stopping for a Red Flag Waving. Tootle did not
like those lessons at all. There is nothing a locomotive hates more than
stopping.

But Bill said that no locomotive ever, ever kept going when he saw a red
flag waving.

One day, while Tootle was practicing for his lesson in Staying on the
Rails No Matter What, a dreadful thing happened.

He looked across the meadow he was running through and saw a fine,
strong black horse.

"Race you to the river," shouted the black horse, and kicked up his
heels.

Away went the horse. His black tail streamed out behind him, and his
mane tossed in the wind. Oh, how he could run!

"Here I go," said Tootle to himself.

"If I am going to be a Flyer, I can't let a horse beat me," he puffed.
"Everyone at school will laugh at me."

His wheels turned so fast that they were silver streaks. The cars lurched
and bumped together. And just as Tootle was sure he could win, the tracks
made a great curve.

"Oh, Whistle!" cried Tootle. "That horse will beat me now. He'll run
straight while I take the Great Curve."

Then the Dreadful Thing happened. After all that Bill had said about
Staying on the Rails No Matter What, Tootle jumped off the tracks and raced
alongside the black horse!

The race ended in a tie. Both Tootle and the black horse were happy.
They stood on the bank of the river and talked.

"It's nice here in the meadow," Tootle said.

When Tootle got back to school, he said nothing about leaving the rails. But he thought about it that night in the roundhouse.

"Tomorrow I will work hard," decided Tootle. "I will not even think of leaving the rails, no matter what."

And he did work hard. He practiced tootling so much that the Mayor Himself ran up the hill, his green coattails flapping, and said that everyone in the village had a headache and would he please stop TOOTLING.

So Tootle was sent to practice Staying on the Rails No Matter What.

As he came to the Great Curve, Tootle looked across the meadow. It was full of buttercups.

"It's like a big yellow carpet. How I should like to play in them and hold one under my searchlight to see if I like butter!" thought Tootle. "But no, I am going to be a Flyer and I must practice Staying on the Rails No Matter What!"

Tootle clicked and clacked around the Great Curve. His wheels began to say over and over again, "Do you like butter? Do you?"

"I don't know," said Tootle crossly. "But I'm going to find out."

He stopped much faster than any good Flyer ever does, unless he is stopping for a Red Flag Waving. He hopped off the tracks and bumped along the meadow to the yellow buttercups.

"What fun!" said Tootle.

And he danced around and around and held one of the buttercups under his searchlight.

"I do like butter!" cried Tootle. "I do!"

At last the sun began to go down, and it was time to hurry to the roundhouse.

That evening while the Chief Oiler was playing checkers with old Bill, he said, "It's queer. It's very queer, but I found grass between Tootle's front wheels today."

"Hmm," said Bill. "There must be grass growing on the tracks."

"Not on our tracks," said the Day Watchman, who spent his days watching the tracks and his nights watching Bill and the Chief Oiler play checkers.

Bill's face was stern. "Tootle knows he must get 100 A+ in Staying on the Rails No Matter What, if he is going to be a Flyer."

Next day Tootle played all day in the meadow. He watched a green frog and he made a daisy chain. He found a rain barrel, and he said softly, "Toot!" "TOOT!" shouted the barrel. "Why, I sound like a flyer already!" cried Tootle.

That night the First Assistant Oiler said he had found a daisy in Tootle's bell. The day after that, the Second Assistant Oiler said that he had found hollyhock flowers floating in Tootle's eight bowls of soup.

And then the Mayor Himself said that he had seen Tootle chasing butterflies in the Meadow. The Mayor Himself said that Tootle had looked very silly, too.

Early one morning Bill had a long, long talk with the Mayor Himself.

When the Mayor Himself left the Lower Trainswitch School for Loco-motives, he laughed all the way to the village.

"Bill's plan will surely put Tootle back on the track," he chuckled.

Bill ran from one store to the next, buying ten yards of this and twenty yards of that and all you have of the other. The Chief Oiler and the First, Second, and Third Assistant Oilers were hammering and sawing instead of oiling and polishing. And Tootle? Well, Tootle was in the meadow watching the butterflies flying and wishing he could dip and soar as they did.

Not a store in Lower Trainswitch was open the next day and not a person was at home. By the time the sun came up, every villager was hiding in the meadow along the tracks. And each of them had a red flag. It had taken all the red goods in Lower Trainswitch, and hard work by the Oilers, but there was a red flag for everyone.

Soon Tootle came tootling happily down the tracks. When he came to the meadow, he hopped off the tracks and rolled along the grass. Just as he was thinking what a beautiful day it was, a red flag poked up from the grass and waved hard. Tootle stopped, for every locomotive knows he must Stop for a Red Flag Waving.

"I'll go another way," said Tootle.

He turned to the left, and up came another waving red flag, this time from the middle of the buttercups.

When he went to the right, there was another red flag waving.

There were red flags waving from the buttercups, in the daisies, under the trees, near the bluebirds' nest, and even one behind the rain barrel. And, of course, Tootle had to stop for each one, for a locomotive must always Stop for a Red Flag Waving.

"Red flags," muttered Tootle. "This meadow is full of red flags. How can I have any fun?

"Whenever I start, I have to stop. Why did I think this meadow was such a fine place? Why don't I ever see a green flag?"

Just as the tears were ready to slide out of his boiler, Tootle happened to look back over his coal car. On the tracks stood Bill, and in his hand was a big green flag. "Oh!" said Tootle.

He puffed up to Bill and stopped.

"This is the place for me," said Tootle. "There is nothing but red flags for locomotives that get off their tracks."

"Hurray!" shouted the people of Lower Trainswitch, and jumped up from their hiding places. "Hurray for Tootle the Flyer!"

Now Tootle is a famous Two-Miles-a-Minute Flyer. The young loco-motives listen to his advice.

"Work hard," he tells them. "Always remember to Stop for a Red Flag Waving. But most of all, Stay on the Rails No Matter What."

five

DWIGHT D. EISENHOWER

Dwight D. Eisenhower was what the American people wanted in the 1950s. A World War II hero who had kept the Grand Alliance intact, he conveyed a sense of confidence that all was well. His easy manner and broad smile reflected American prosperity and strength. Conservative, like many of his contemporaries, he had a more limited view of the role of government than Truman or FDR. Ike also appeared to take a passive approach to the presidency. The office, he believed, had grown too strong, and he was intent on restoring what he considered a delicate constitutional balance. Critics joked about the Eisenhower doll—once wound up, it did nothing at all. Yet historians have come to recognize both Eisenhower's own understated political perspicacity and his importance in ratifying New Deal social reforms.

In "Dwight D. Eisenhower and Republican Conservatism," Alonzo L. Hamby recognizes Eisenhower's accomplishment in preserving Republican values while at the same time working to harmonize those with the liberal consensus created by FDR. Eisenhower, he suggests, was intent on holding the line rather than branching out in new directions, and in so doing provided a sense of continuity with the past in a time of change.

Fred I. Greenstein, in "Eisenhower as Leader," argues persuasively that Eisenhower was a much more astute political leader than his critics understood. Despite his seemingly casual approach to his office, he was well-prepared, persuaded of his priorities, and able to convince those around him to follow his lead. His "hidden-hand presidency" took him where he wanted to go.

The document reprinted in this section, "On Leadership," is a statement by Eisenhower himself, as quoted in the memoir of his aide Emmet John Hughes. In it, Eisenhower reflects on leadership and what it entails, and provides evidence for Greenstein's argument.

To examine Eisenhower further, see Stephen E. Ambrose, *Eisenhower: The President* (1984), the most complete assessment of the White House years. Charles C. Alexander, *Holding the Line: The Eisenhower Era, 1952–1961* (1975), is a good brief account of the period. Gary W. Reichard, *The Reaffirmation of Republicanism: Eisenhower and the 83rd Congress* (1975), is a similarly useful study of political and policy questions. Herbert S. Parmet, *Eisenhower and the American Crusades* (1972), provides a detailed picture of domestic policy. Robert Griffith, "Dwight D. Eisenhower and the Corporate Commonwealth," in *The American Historial Review,* 87 (February 1982), is a perceptive assessment of Eisenhower's ideological orientation. Peter Lyon, *Eisenhower: Portrait of the Hero* (1974), offers still another view of Eisenhower, and Eisenhower's own memoirs — *Mandate for Change, 1953–1956* (1963) and *Waging Peace* (1965) — are helpful as well.

Dwight D. Eisenhower
and Republican Conservatism

ALONZO L. HAMBY

Dwight D. Eisenhower was the last of the twentieth-century American presidents to be nurtured in the Victorian climate of opinion that had produced [Franklin D.] Roosevelt and [Harry S] Truman. He was also the only twentieth-century president, other than Theodore Roosevelt, to have experienced public celebration as a military hero, and he possessed a more tangible democratic touch than any of his predecessors save Truman. These attributes coalesced to make his administration an oasis of placidity between eras of extraordinary turbulence in American politics. Eisenhower's espousal of the values of a cherished past provided Americans with a sense of continuity in a troubled, changing time. His status as a hero blended with his image as a democrat to secure him a combination of reverence and trust that made him all but invulnerable to political sniping.

Eisenhower's career as a politician, even more than his career as a soldier, was one of almost storybook individual success, as measured by landslide election victories and remarkable popularity ratings. His larger goals, however, were much more elusive. He sought the presidency because he felt a duty to save his party and his country from forces of irrational extremism. Ultimately, he gave the nation a badly needed breathing spell and time of adjustment to the realities of the post–New Deal, post-atomic, postcolonial world, and he made a modest beginning in his more ambitious objective of establishing a moderate-to-conservative political tradition and a cadre of political leaders who could carry on after him. If less than creative, his leadership may have served a useful purpose in times that did not demand creativity. . . .

Eisenhower . . . and the people around him wanted to preserve the essence of traditional Republicanism and at the same time make it palatable to mid-twentieth-century America. They wanted to impart a fresh tone to old values, produce policies that would somehow reconcile the needs of the present with the outlook of the past, and eventually develop the new personalities that would carry their effort into the future. They hoped to use his administration as the springboard for a viable new conservative tradition that would assimilate much of the accomplishment of the New Deal–Fair Deal tradition while drawing a line against its extension.

Eisenhower's management of the presidency reflected this larger aspiration. Conditioned by Roosevelt and Truman — and before that by the earlier Roosevelt and Woodrow Wilson — both contemporary observers and scholars since have been most impressed by the weak, passive, negative character of the Eisenhower leadership. Generally liberal-Democratic in their orientation, they have assumed that activism in the pursuit of social change is a commendable norm and that words such as *weak, passive,* and *negative* may be used almost as synonyms. Whatever the merits of this outlook, it is useful more as a point of departure for criticism than in aiding understanding.

Eisenhower's handicaps as president are obvious. His political experience was severely limited, and he had little working knowledge of the civilian Washington bureaucracy. What he eventually gained in experience may have been more than countered by the deterioration of his health through a heart attack, a stroke, and a major abdominal operation; there can be little question that he had lost substantial vigor and capacity for work by the end of his second term. Moreover, his well-established distaste for detail no doubt served him less well in the White House than it had in the military. He handled the presidency in the role of a supreme commander, reserving only the larger issues for his personal attention and engaging in compromise and conciliation as the major tools of leadership. If one accepts him and his objectives on his own terms, however, it really is not meaningful to characterize him . . . as a "passive-negative" president. He moved with vigor against excessive social activism when the occasion demanded and worked hard to remake the Republican party. Ultimately more successful than ["Mr. Republican," Ohio Senator Robert A.] Taft, he nevertheless fell short of establishing Republicanism as a credible alternative to New Deal – Fair Deal Democracy.

However much he rejected vigorous Roosevelt-Truman – style leadership in some areas, Eisenhower never doubted that the presidency was a post that called for vigorous moral leadership. By preachment and deed, he sought to bring America back to the values of his youth — pietistic religion and self-help. Although he never before had displayed signs of having absorbed the devout faith of his parents, he assuredly had absorbed their broader outlook. He presented his political campaign as a "crusade." He took formal membership in the Presbyterian church. He began his inaugural address with a prayer and opened cabinet meetings in the same way. The custom spread quickly throughout the conformist atmosphere of the executive branch. (Soon a joke was making the rounds to the effect that a high-level official had exclaimed in the midst of an important meeting: "Dammit! We forgot the prayer!")

The religion that Eisenhower projected was the religion of a conservative, the classical — if misnamed — "Protestant ethic" with its connection between piety and worldly success, its affirmation of individualism and self-help as keys to salvation as well as riches. It provided both a sense of continuity with the past and a moral alternative to liberal welfarism. It also had a heavy dose of nationalistic patriotism, stemming from the assumption that the United States was a nation favored by God and that the atheistic Soviet Union represented a force that God's Nation had to crusade against. From the mouths of vulgar, right-wing demagogues, such assumptions had appeared ludicrous. Expressed in a benign, fatherly way by a beloved hero, they took on respectability.

The Eisenhower years witnessed a superficial religious revival of impressive proportions. Its most representative leaders were moderately conservative ministers, such as Rev. Norman Vincent Peale or Bishop Fulton J. Sheen, who doubled as personal advice writers and connected religion to getting ahead in the world. The result—when compared to the high philosophy of the theologians or the intense quest for salvation that had once characterized American Protestantism—was little more than a bland affirmation of faith, a homogenized, bloodless American religion that perfectly suited the yearnings of Eisenhower and of much of the American middle class in the fifties. In the end, it was less a search for redemption than a form of national self-congratulation.

This reassuring vision was only a small part of the new political appeal that Eisenhower attempted to develop. He must have understood that his presidency was a national tribute to him as an individual, not to the appeal of his party. The Republicans had won control of Congress only by a hairsbreadth in 1952, lost it in 1954, and never regained it. The old values of individualism and self-help had been grievously discredited by Herbert Hoover and could never be resuscitated in their starkest form. Eisenhower seems instinctively to have realized that a public willing to pay homage to the old values was unwilling to accept them in undiluted form.

He never was foolish enough to advocate a return to the 1920s and was apt to be curt with those who did. A sharp, private reprimand to his right-wingish brother, Edgar, vividly illustrates his grasp of reality:

> Should any political party attempt to abolish social security and eliminate labor laws and farm programs, you would not hear of that party again in our political history. There is a tiny splinter group, of course, that believes that you can do those things. Among them are H. L. Hunt, . . . a few other Texas oil millionaires, and an occasional politician and businessman from other areas. Their number is negligible and they are stupid.

He was even careful about applying the term *conservative* to himself, more often using such words as *moderate* or *middle-of-the-road,* and at times adopting the phrase *dynamic conservatism.* Not a theoretician, he could do little more than grope for ways to express a new mood.

The most conspicuous administration intellectual was Arthur Larson, a presidential speechwriter and subcabinet official with an academic background. In his widely read book *A Republican Looks at His Party* (1956), Larson set forth the principles of a "New Republicanism." He described it as a mean between the political principles of 1896 (McKinley Republicanism) and those of 1936 (Rooseveltian Democracy), based upon the ideological and tactical premise that "in politics—as in chess—the man who holds the center holds a position of almost unbeatable strength." The New Republicanism aimed at the preservation of the federal-state balance in American federalism, encouraged business enterprise as a legitimate, progressive force in American life, extended the same tolerance to labor (whether organized or unorganized), and accepted broad government responsibility for the general welfare. It professed a belief in God and a divine order of things. It cited the special American historical and political experience of national development without revolution or intense class conflict. Larson's thinking appealed strongly to Eisenhower, but the task of translating it into political experience and a usable political tradition was more formidable than either could have realized at the euphoric midpoint of Ike's reign.

In his personal values and preferences on most specific domestic issues, Eisenhower was actually a bit more conservative than Taft (with whom he developed a cordial relationship before Taft's sudden death in 1953). Yet the political tradition that Roosevelt and Truman had built emerged from his administration largely unscathed, cut back a bit here and there perhaps, but also advanced in other areas. This occurred even though the administration openly aligned itself with the only group in American life that had opposed Roosevelt and Truman with near unanimity—the business community. The counterrevolution never came and was never even attempted.

One can find no single answer for the smooth emergence of the New Republicanism and the widespread GOP acceptance of the works of the party's political enemies. Several considerations appear important. The New and Fair Deals were too woven into the fabric of society to be torn out; moreover, it was obviously unwise to contemplate such a step. The dispensing of benefits throughout society, whether or not it was just and enlightened, had surely been politically popular; any effort to take them away would be doubly unpopular. It was in any case conservatism at its simplest and most elemental to accept social and political arrangements much as they existed and to assume that change in any direction had to be a slow process. The New Republicanism reflected Eisenhower's well-developed style of leadership with its emphasis upon realism, accommodation, and compromise. It also reflected the changed character of American business, at least at the level of elite leadership.

The corporate tone of the Eisenhower administration was never in doubt. The president surrounded himself with successful financiers, corporate lawyers, and high-level business executives; those of his advisers who did not fit those categories usually possessed the values of the people who did. There were, to be sure, some characters in this group. Secretary of Defense Charles Wilson, the former president of General Motors, compared advocates of social welfare spending to kennel dogs that bayed for food rather than hunting dogs that worked for it; he announced to the world that the interests of GM were those of the United States. Secretary of the Treasury George M. Humphrey, a vehement fiscal conservative, in a moment of dismay at a substantial Eisenhower budget deficit predicted in public that continued large-scale spending would lead to a "hair-curling" depression.

But whatever the occasional tendency of a Wilson or a Humphrey to sound like political primitives, the Eisenhower business executives actually tended to represent the values and aspirations of the mid-twentieth-century corporate executive suite. They were torn between the inner-directed, individualistic ethos of the entrepreneurial past and the other-directed, adaptive values of the managerial present, capable of feeling nostalgia for Herbert Hoover while making the compromises necessary to run an organization in the real world. The new corporate outlook and experience mirrored Eisenhower's to a remarkable degree, gave coherence to his politics, and more than anything else accounted for his choice of the Republican party and the importance of the "millionaires" in his administration.

Much like executives who had learned to live with labor unions and government regulations even while grumbling about them, the president and those around him resignedly adapted themselves to the social-political structure of a new America. They reflected the values of both the managerial subclass and much of the broader middle class by working hard to govern efficiently, control costs, and thereby contain inflation. Within these limits, they displayed little resistance to government activism, social welfarism, or the continuing prosperity of those who had reaped benefits from the New Deal.

No group had received more from Roosevelt and Truman than organized labor; union spokesmen were thus persistently critical of the Eisenhower administration, just as they were of individual managements from whom they nonetheless received recognition and with whom they engaged in negotiations. Yet Eisenhower never posed the slightest threat to the position that the trade unions had achieved; like the American corporate elite, he had no foolish hope of turning back the clock. It is inevitably recalled that his first secretary of labor, Martin Durkin, resigned in protest against the administration's failure to recommend major changes in the Taft-Hartley Act. It is often forgotten that Durkin's successor, James P. Mitchell, a former personnel executive with vast business and government experience, enjoyed the respect of the labor establishment and much of the liberal community. The administration's only significant move in labor legislation, the Landrum-Griffin Act, was a mild, barely effective regulatory measure aimed primarily at mobster infiltration of unions. In general, Eisenhower and his team dealt with labor much as the management of a large, mature organization might deal with a well-established bargaining agent.

Farmers, the beneficiaries of increasingly expensive and decreasingly effective price support programs, fared less well for several reasons. They were a declining segment of the population, lacked organizational solidarity, and had failed to establish a home in either party. They never had achieved an ideological consensus about their own identity, thinking of themselves at times as the neglected, downtrodden yeoman backbone of America, and at times as entrepreneurs engaged in a business enterprise. Democratic liberalism, predominantly urban in its orientation and offended by the general failure of the farm community to support trade union objectives, became ever cooler to agricultural subsidies as the fifties progressed. The corporate managerial outlook of the Eisenhower administration rather naturally responded negatively to petty entrepreneurs who demanded government aid rather than practice self-help.

Eisenhower and his secretary of agriculture, Ezra Taft Benson, were able to secure legislation establishing ever lower price support levels. Although the program remained horrendously expensive, its cost grew at a much lower rate than would have been the case with the continuance of high supports. One result was the liquidation of many marginal farmers and the augmentation of urban social problems by a rural migration to the cities. Benson expressed the hope that the federal government could extricate itself entirely from agriculture, but neither he nor Eisenhower actually proposed withdrawal as anything more than a long-term objective. Instead they moved cautiously back from what they considered an overextended position.

Social welfarism as such did not give the Eisenhower administration grave difficulties so long as it met the tests of efficiency and reasonable costs. It was Eisenhower who obtained the creation of the Department of Health, Education and Welfare, an objective Truman had failed to achieve. He went along with a higher minimum wage (not a cost to the government), extensive increases in Social Security (a self-funded program), a limited program of medical care for the indigent elderly (a vital social duty with carefully controlled costs), and the National Defense Education Act (a response to Sputnik wrapped in the protective cloak of national security). Such positions, of course, pleased neither liberal Democrats nor hard-core conservative Republicans, a fact that doubtless confirmed the administration's faith in the rightness of its course.

Governmental activism held few terrors for Eisenhower so long as it met the same tests. His administration, for example, acceded to the St. Lawrence Seaway project (self-funded) and the interstate highway system (underwritten by a trust fund financed by new taxes). Both were monumental public works projects that spendthrift New Dealers would have envied, but established in such a way that neither would put a drain on the budget. When pressed to state some sort of philosophical principle, the president and most of his associates would declare themselves states' righters and deplore the size of the federal bureaucracy. From time to time, as in the return of the Tidelands oil claims to the states, they acted upon this intuition; in other cases, when the need for federal action appeared established and the expense could be managed, they ignored it.

Eisenhower's moderation had a powerful appeal to a nation ready for a period of peace and tranquility after years of domestic change and bitterness. But it also was a style of leadership incapable almost by definition of dealing with extreme situations that required something more than bland, moderate treatment. Perhaps the two major failures of the domestic side of Ike's administration were his treatments of McCarthyism and the black revolution.

In [Joseph R.] McCarthy, Eisenhower faced a nihilist and verbal terrorist for whom immersion in the administration atmosphere of compromise and moderation would have been akin to political suffocation. Having achieved fame and a sizable following with charges of Communism in government, McCarthy had no intention of disappearing from public attention just because his own party had won the White House. Like all terrorists, he had to be handled forcefully; this Eisenhower was unwilling to do, in part because the president himself had sanctioned the continued use of the Communist issue against the Democrats by high officials of his own administration, in part because a strong denunciation of McCarthy would have conflicted with his own concept of party and national leadership. He did not want to alienate McCarthy's disciples on the Republican Right, and he wanted to avoid an unseemly public fight with one of the most accomplished of bare-knuckle brawlers. Unopposed by the one public leader who could have discredited him, McCarthy ran amok for almost two years, harassing and embarrassing his own party while the Democrats looked on in mingled delight and dismay. Finally, the Senate disciplined him with covert encouragement from the White House, and he slipped into a well-deserved obscurity.

However grievous, the damage that McCarthy had been permitted to cause was not irreparable; but it is hard to make the same statement about Eisenhower's indifference to the black revolution. In order to understand his attitude toward the American Negro, one must recall the narrowness of his professional experience. He had spent almost his entire life as a career soldier, breathing an atmosphere in which blacks were universally considered inferior, segregated, and kept in their very low place. He rarely, if ever, dealt with blacks on his own level; and unlike the professional politician who must build coalitions, he never had to negotiate with black leaders and discuss their aspirations. Intellectually and socially, he was about as unprepared for the explosion of the civil rights movement as a president could have been.

As the Supreme Court pondered its decision in the school desegregation case in 1954, the president invited the new chief justice, Earl Warren, to dinner at the White House. He expressed his personal hope that the Court's decision would not result in any fundamental change. At no time after the Court had ruled against "separate but equal" educational facilities did Eisenhower speak out in support of the decision. He saw the presidency as a place of moral leadership, but he clearly did not conceive of segregation as a moral issue. Moreover, any strong advocacy of civil rights might have damaged growing Republican strength in the South. His support of black objectives was quite limited and resulted mostly from the urgings of his Department of Justice; its most tangible fruits were two civil rights bills universally recognized as ineffective as soon as they were passed. It is often remembered that Eisenhower sent federal troops to Little Rock to enforce a desegregation order, but it is also frequently forgotten that he took no action in other cases, such as the expulsion of black student Autherine Lucy from the University of Alabama, a situation in which defiance was more subtle and hence more capable of being ignored.

Eisenhower was of course hardly the first political leader to temporize on the position of blacks in American life — and scarcely the last. His inaction was consistent with the entire tenor of his presidency, and it is perhaps foolish to assume that any political leaders will grasp the banner of a social revolution unless they are forced to make a choice. One may nevertheless regret that finding himself at a turning point in American history, Eisenhower could do no more than retreat from positions staked out by his predecessor.

Eisenhower's greatest failure by his own lights was his inability to make the New Republicanism into a movement of the American majority. As a hero, he enjoyed immunity from political defeat, but his status as a hero also blinded the public to both his partisan affiliation and to the ideological perspective he sought to advance. Moreover, his presidency demonstrated anew the old, sound political axiom that popularity is very hard to transfer. Even during the headiest days of the Eisenhower ascendancy, the New Republicanism as a doctrine had to stand on its own merits. However interesting it might have been as a social-intellectual phenomenon, politically it was a flop, incapable of producing the numbers of legislators, governors, and congressmen it needed to establish itself as an enduring force. Neither Eisenhower nor his partisans could persuade the public that the New Republicanism really differed from the Old.

The central problem was the uninspiring performance of the economy in the 1950s—slow economic growth, periodic recession, creeping inflation. The nation never approached a disaster akin to that of the 1930s; most Americans, in fact, perceptibly bettered their lot. Still, the lackluster performance of the economy generated a substantial upward trend in unemployment and created considerable apprehension in a nation not that far from the trauma of the Depression. The persistence of inflation, albeit at a modest rate that would have been welcomed as a salvation two decades later, added both to public irritation and to the problems of the administration. From the perspective of Eisenhower and his aides, inflation was the worst danger; they fought it relentlessly with conservative fiscal and monetary policies that contributed to the prolonged economic slowdown of the fifties and cast doubt upon their argument that the Republicans could bring the country prosperity as well as peace.

This doubt received considerable reinforcement from the failure of the New Republicanism to produce fresh new moderate faces on a national basis. The Old Hero, like Roosevelt or Truman, could do little to speed up the slow pace of change at the state and local levels of party organization; consequently, whatever the desires of the White House, the GOP faces before the electorate usually appeared a bit more reminiscent of Herbert Hoover than Arthur Larson. Here and there, the administration achieved a breakthrough. In the Illinois of the late fifties, Charles Percy, a successful young corporate executive, emerged as the up-and-coming figure in the Republican party of the appropriately named Everett McKinley Dirksen; the White House saw to it that Percy achieved maximum visibility by making him chairman of the platform committee at the 1960 Republican convention. An achiever in business, moderate in ideology, articulate, and handsome, Percy was the New Republicanism personified.

Unfortunately, few like him had emerged by the end of Eisenhower's second term, and fewer still (Percy included) had won election to major offices. . . . Gradually, of course, the old generation would give way to the inexorable certainties of death or defeat, thereby clearing the path for younger moderates. In the meantime, it could fairly be said that Eisenhower had most clearly succeeded in bringing to a position of fame and strength only a dynamic young Republican whose moderation was questionable and about whom he seems to have entertained periodic doubts — Richard M. Nixon. . . .

Any evaluation of Eisenhower's presidency must be equivocal. While he was not a professional politician, neither was he a "captive hero," taken in tow by the professionals. Even after his health became a problem, he remained a man in control, working with a definite sense of purpose toward broad objectives. If his leadership seemed at times less than forceful, it was because his style had always been accommodationist rather than combative. Seeking in the main to hold the line, he did not go in quest of new vistas for social policy or government activity. He was a moderate conservative who accepted American society as it existed while encouraging the nurture of traditional values. This led him to give scant attention to important new currents, such as the black revolution, but it also gave the nation and the Republican party time to digest most of the New and Fair Deals and make them part of the national consensus. Neither Eisenhower nor any imaginable substitute could manage the activist side of his goal, the remaking of the Republican party in his own image. Hindered like Roosevelt by the fragmented nature of the American party system, he could do little more than begin a time-consuming process.

Oddly, his diplomacy was less effective. His leadership style, which had in many respects met the needs of the nation domestically, was not so well attuned to a rapidly changing world. American foreign policy in the fifties required a process of adjustment, not an institutionalization and rigidification of the concepts and impulses of the early Cold War. To hold the line in diplomacy was increasingly to ignore the nature of a new international environment. To adjust to a world in flux is of course never easy, and it would be folly to assume that any president could have handled the task without error or reverses. It is not too much, however, to expect one to recognize what is happening.

Eisenhower was assuredly successful in the one area of politics where it matters most, at the ballot box. The recipient of landslide victories in 1952 and 1956, he almost certainly could have been elected by another overwhelming margin had he been able to run in 1960. Whatever shortcomings critics may find in his administration, he possessed the trust and love of the American people in a way that transcended party politics. It was in many respects more impressive than the esteem FDR had enjoyed, for that was based heavily upon the wholesale dispensation of benefits to the needy. Eisenhower offered Americans not tangible help but rather a sense of reassurance emanating from the qualities he embodied. Most visible among them were the qualities of the hero — strength, authority, command, identification with the aspirations and triumphs of the nation itself. Less visible but probably more fundamental were the qualities of the managerial conservative as this type had evolved halfway through this century — organization, adaptation, cooperation—coexisting uneasily with a nostalgia for a simpler, more individualistic past. They were qualities that in the aggregate made Eisenhower a father figure to a nation that wanted a breathing spell from the relentless pace of twentieth-century change.

Eisenhower as Leader

FRED I. GREENSTEIN

From January 1953 to January 1961, . . . the United States [had] a uniquely popular president, Dwight D. Eisenhower. He was the sole chief executive to serve the two terms permitted by the Constitution since ratification of the Twenty-second Amendment. He averaged 64 percent approval in Dr. Gallup's monthly soundings of how Americans rate the president's performance, exceeding all of the post–World War II presidents except [John F.] Kennedy, who did not live to face the cost of such policies as his administration's increasing military involvement in Vietnam.

Eisenhower's unique record in winning and holding public support provides one reason why students of American politics have begun to dissect the way this man, who in his time was widely thought of as politically inept and indifferent, carried out the tasks of presidential leadership. . . .

The unique characteristic of Eisenhower's approach to presidential leadership was his self-conscious use of political strategies that enabled him to carry out both presidential roles without allowing one to undermine the other. These strategies derived from leadership style that explicitly departed from the emphasis of most presidents since Franklin D. Roosevelt on establishing what Richard Neustadt calls professional reputation—the impression of being a skilled, tough politician. On the assumption that a president who is predominantly viewed in terms of his political prowess will lose public support by not appearing to be a proper chief of state, Eisenhower went to great lengths to conceal the political side of his leadership.

He did this so well and played the part of nonpolitical chief of state so convincingly that until recently most writers on the presidency viewed him through the lens of his 1950s liberal critics as an aging hero who reigned more than he ruled and lacked the energy, motivation, and political know-how to have a significant impact on events. During Eisenhower's time in office most president watchers would have agreed with the *New Yorker*'s Richard Rovere, who saw his personality as blandly "standard American," his mind as "unschematic" and "distrustful of fine distinctions," and his performance as that of a man who "most of the time" was bored by "the whole operating side of government." Nor was Rovere alone in his low estimate of Eisenhower. In 1962, Arthur Schlesinger, Sr., asked seventy-five academic authorities on the presidency to list thirty-one chief executives from Washington to Eisenhower in order of "greatness." Eisenhower ranked twenty-first, tied with Chester Arthur. To these scholars, if Eisenhower served as an exemplar of anything it was of how *not* to conduct the presidency.

Some of the revival of interest in Eisenhower derives from no more than nostalgia for what in retrospect seems to have been an untroubled era presided over by a kindly, simple man. Eisenhower nostalgia, by stressing his political innocence, reinforces the impression that there is nothing to be learned from how he did his job.

A more important source of new interest is appreciation of his actions and goals. At the time he left office, Republican boasts of an administration that ended the Korean War and presided over seven-and-a-half years in which not a soldier was lost in combat sounded like standard campaign rhetoric. After Vietnam, however, this could readily be viewed as an accomplishment. Eisenhower's caution in expanding domestic welfare programs seemed uncreative to the authorities Arthur Schlesinger polled in 1962, the great bulk of whom were liberals. In our present postliberal era of disillusionment with the fruits of the Great Society's programs, however, his go-slow social policy has begun to appear more attractive. Similarly, Eisenhower's horror of inflation no longer sounds quaint in light of soaring inflation in the 1970s and 1980s. And his struggle to hold down military expenditures, which in the 1950s was castigated by many liberal Democrats as contributing to bomber and missile gaps, now is open to favorable reassessment as a policy that might have averted the arms race which escalated in the Kennedy and Johnson years.

Not all policy reevaluations have endorsed Eisenhower's goals and actions. In the 1950s, his administration's covert intervention brought about the overthrow of the Mossadegh government in Iran (1953) and the Arbenz government in Guatemala (1954). The political climate of the 1970s and 1980s has not produced retrospective idealization of secretly engineered overthrows by the United States of regimes that the president views as potentially hostile to American interests.

Both the positive and the negative reevaluations of Eisenhower's policies contribute to still another source of renewed interest in him — his approach to leadership. That he not only had policies worthy of reassessment but pursued his political goals in unique ways undermines the 1950s view of his incumbency as no more than an interregnum of leaderless drift. It is not then a contradiction in terms (as contemporary critics would have said) to speak of "Eisenhower leadership." Instead, it is a challenge — the one to which this [essay] is addressed — to unravel, characterize, and illustrate his leadership style.

Even during Eisenhower's presidency some political observers sensed that there were aspects of Eisenhower's leadership, and of the man himself, that did not meet the eye. Rovere, for example, while sharing the liberal view that Eisenhower was not seriously committed to leading, acknowledged that his presence in office had helped to neutralize the poisonous internal security controversy epitomized in Senator Joseph McCarthy's allegations that domestic subversion was rampant. Moreover, in spite of powerful pressures, Eisenhower had refused to become involved in military conflict in Asia. "One hesitates to attribute political adroitness to a man who has revealed so much political ineptitude as Eisenhower," Rovere concluded, "but it happens to be a fact that he has achieved, through luck or good management, a number of things that are commonly thought to be the product of skill."

The *New York Times*'s Arthur Krock, in a 1957 article on the difference between "impressions of the President" and Eisenhower "the man," came close to identifying Eisenhower's approach of publicly displaying the warm, benign qualities of an uncontroversial head of state, while shielding his coolly detached, politically informed prime ministerial attributes. What Krock called the "outer man" exhibited all the head of state qualities, including those of personal appearance, that helped make him so appealing to the public.

> The President's stature is a happy compromise between the short and the tall. His usual complexion is ruddy under the golfing tan. His blue eyes are kindly, but penetrating. His voice has the rough grain that is accepted as the token of virility, and his accent is the kind known as "Midwestern" that is prevalent in North America.
>
> His manner is genial; his ways and reflexes are kindly; his bearing is soldierly, yet his well-tailored civilian clothes never seem out of character. His smile is attractively pensive, his frequent grin is infectious, his laughter ready and hearty. He fairly radiates "goodness," simple faith and the honest, industrious background of his heritage.

This public Eisenhower, Krock acknowledged, seemed problematic as a presidential technician. Perhaps, Krock suggested, his "staff system make[s] him too dependent on subordinates for the choice and synthesis of public matters laid before him, and for the selection of those to be admitted to his presence." That Eisenhower's personal friends were businessmen and military men seemed to reflect "at least a mild distaste for the company of professional politicians." And Krock wondered whether his "frequent changes of scene and recreation . . . imply that he is irked by his heavy and incessant duties." Krock also reminded his readers of the well known grammatical disorders of Eisenhower's press conference prose "in which numbers and genders collide, participles hang helplessly and syntax is lost forever."

In spite of such outer appearances, Krock, whose prominence in Washington journalism won him numerous off-the-record conversations with Eisenhower, was persuaded of his political ability. "[T]he President is remarkably well informed in a vast field of government operations," Krock wrote. "[H]is occasional unawareness of a major event is merely the result of special concentration at the same time on some difficult administrative problem, and . . . while perhaps he wishes he were not the President more often than some of his predecessors did, he enjoys the power and the glory and is absorbed in his task." Moreover, Krock acknowledged that he periodically sensed in the inner Eisenhower facets not reflected in his normally visible image. There seemed to be more steel and less folksy, idiomatic warmth to the private man than to the public man. Eisenhower, at a press conference, for example, "froze at an implication that helicopters were being bought by public funds for his recreational use."

> And when a reporter asked if he had been "filled in" on a large affair of government—a phrase revealing unconscious acceptance of the critical line that the President doesn't know what is going on in Washington unless someone chooses to tell him—he chillingly remarked that this was a "strange locution". . . . The instant effect . . . of the language employed was one of the many demonstrations provided by the press questioning periods that the President's mental process is penetrating and alert.

Several years after Eisenhower left office, another journalist, the *New York Post*'s Murray Kempton, provided the first re-examination of Eisenhower that explicitly delineated an Eisenhower approach to leadership based on complementing the public appearance of political innocence with private toughness. Kempton concluded that he and other 1950s observers had deliberately been misled into "the underestimation of Dwight D. Eisenhower." Reading between the lines of Eisenhower's memoirs and rethinking the episodes of his presidency, Kempton was persuaded that behind the warm outward appearance there was an Eisenhower who never lost the disposition to calculate, consider options, and accept casualties as well as victories required of a supreme commander.

Eisenhower's unsentimental political realism, Kempton felt, was revealed in his easy acknowledgement in 1960 that the Soviet Union had captured a U-2 spy plane and its pilot only because a mechanical failure had prevented the plane from disintegrating and therefore the pilot inadvertently survived. Kempton believed that Richard Nixon was on the mark in his explanation of why Eisenhower had seemed ready to abandon him as a running mate in 1952 and 1956 for political expediency. Eisenhower, Nixon notes, "was a far more complex and devious man than most people realized."

Since the 1970s, direct sources for reevaluating the man and his leadership have been uncovered. It is no longer necessary to speculate as to whether Eisenhower was the simple "Kansas farmer-boy"-turned soldier he claimed to be, rather than a politician whose operations were deliberately shielded from contemporaries other than his immediate associates. . . .

Eisenhower's vice-president, Richard Nixon, was not the only one to remark on his complexity; many others acquainted with the nonpublic man made similar observations. What most of them appear to have recognized was the obvious intricacy of the political psychology of a leader who in many respects displayed antithetical qualities in public and in private. The testimonies of three such observers — a journalist, a congressman, and a presidential advisor — point to an array of Eisenhower's personal qualities, each differing in its public and private manifestations, that shaped his leadership style.

Journalist Theodore White reports that in the course of covering Eisenhower at NATO in 1951 and observing him closely he was forced to reverse the impression he had formed on the basis of Eisenhower's public persona. "I made the mistake," White confessed, "so many observers did of considering Ike a simple man, a good straightforward soldier."

> Yet Ike's mind was not flaccid; and gradually, reporting him as he performed, I found his mind was tough, his manner deceptive; that the rosy private smile could give way, in private, to furious outbursts of temper; that the tangled rambling rhetoric of his off-the-record remarks could, when he wished, be disciplined by his own pencil into clean hard prose.

Congressman Stuyvesant Wainwright, an Eisenhower Republican, discovered a world of difference between the impression left by the *New York Times,* which "always made him out to be a mediocre, fumbling, ignorant boob," and the informed, issue-involved president with whom he had periodic conferences. Moreover, his bond as an Eisenhower loyalist was strengthened by his awareness of the president's depth of knowledge about public affairs:

> When I went in there to talk with him, I used to come away on cloud nine, I was so impressed. And not just by the man. I was impressed because he knew exactly what he was talking about. I'd read about how he had been out in the morning taking putting practice, but when we went there he knew his business. He would ask us about paragraph three of section 4B. And I used to say, "Mr. President, someone must have briefed you pretty well five minutes ago," and he would say, "No, I looked it over last night." He knew what was in the bill, and he knew what to ask. It was just the opposite from what the papers said!

. . . Since Eisenhower's press conference transcripts were the single most influential source of his reputation for vague expressions and muddled thinking, it is well to keep in mind . . . that, even when Eisenhower's sentences did not parse, his meaning was hammered home by the force and vividness of his personality. Compare the transcript of an Eisenhower press conference with a recording of it. In the recording, the muddled syntax recedes and his voice emphatically and persuasively conveys his message. The films of Eisenhower, which became regular fare for the television viewers — who by the mid-1950s included virtually the entire electorate — are even more effective. His mobile, expressive face and dignified but comfortable comportment emerge as the expression of a manifestly warm human being who speaks earnestly of his and the nation's ideals. He comes across as solid and full of common sense — a reassuring figure who lived up to his own premise that, as the visible symbol of the nation, the president should exhibit a "respectable image of American life before the world."

By no stretch of the imagination, however, could the bulk of his press conference discourse be said to reveal sharply honed reasoning. Even when he dealt with some of the complexities of an issue, he usually did so through broad simplifications and in a colloquial manner. And asserting that he was not informed about them, he often refused to discuss complexities. He conveyed the impression of a leader who took it for granted that much of the detailed content of contemporary issues was "non-presidential," frequently referring questioners to cabinet secretaries for answers to issues that he said were in their domain, not his, or had not yet been sufficiently studied by subordinates to come to his attention.

The intellectual thinness and syntactical flaws in press conference texts, Eisenhower would later write, resulted from caution. With press conferences open to quotation and broadcast, "an inadvertent misstatement in public would be a calamity." But, he continued, realizing that "it is far better to stumble or speak guardedly than to move ahead smoothly and risk imperilling the country," by consistently focusing on ideas rather than on phrasing, he "was able to avoid causing the nation a serious setback through anything I said in many hours, over eight years of intensive questioning." Then, in the understated mode he used when he chose to draw attention to one of his strengths, he went on to add, "I soon learned that ungrammatical sentences in the transcripts caused many to believe I was incapable of using good English: indeed, several people who have my private papers, many in my handwriting, have expressed outright astonishment that in my writings syntax and grammatical structure were at least adequate."

They were, as he well knew, more than adequate. The Eisenhower Library files contain many letters and memoranda he composed, some marked "private and confidential," others classified for security purposes, reflecting the clean, hard writing, and, by extension, thinking, to which White refers. They include dispassionate, closely reasoned assessments of contemporary issues and personalities that belie the amiable, informal, and often vague usages of his press conference discourse. Startlingly, for a man who seemed, to as acute an observer as Richard Rovere, to have an "unschematic" mind, many of his confidential writings display geometric precision in stating the basic conditions shaping a problem, deducing their implications, and weighing the costs and benefits of alternative possible responses. . . .

. . . Eisenhower . . . had a capacity for practical political thought. He assessed the political motivations of others, anticipating their likely responses to alternative courses of action, and had an explicit decision-making criterion — a decision must be in the long-term public interest *and* must be acceptable domestically so that congressional support can be assured. In short, the Eisenhower who was widely thought of as nonpolitical, who himself insisted that he was not a politician, and who in private used the words "politics" and "politician" pejoratively employed reasoning processes that bespoke political skill and sensitivity. . . .

Every World War II buff knows that a crucial part of Eisenhower's contribution to the Axis defeat was holding together the strongminded, diverse leaders of the Western alliance. When asked to explain how Eisenhower managed this, his associates often sought recourse in such ambiguities as "the mystery of leadership." . . .

Clearly this personal force in face-to-face leadership was palpable to those who worked with him even though they had difficulty finding precise words to express the experience of working with Eisenhower. One cabinet aide, for example, characterizes Eisenhower's presence in meetings as "electric." Harvard law and political science professor Robert Bowie, an observer whose accounts of events usually subordinate personal feelings to analytic interpretation, recounts his first meeting with Eisenhower (in 1945, during Eisenhower's brief stint as military governor of Germany) not in terms of its content, but of the emotions induced in him and others by Eisenhower's manner. "What struck me," Bowie recalls, "was the vibrant personality, the very magnetic appeal which he had, even in dealing with people that he hadn't met or known before." Although he had just defeated them, he even "created an immediate sense of friendliness with the Germans and avoided any memory or recollection of prior relationships which could have made it awkward." . . .

Eisenhower's ability to win support in group settings may have seemed artless, but it actually represented a conscious application of what he realized were proven tactics for effective leadership, although his use of such tactics no doubt became second nature to him, requiring little conscious forethought. One of the closest observers of Eisenhower's practices over an extended period of demanding leadership, his World War II Chief of Staff, Walter Bedell Smith, explained that Eisenhower consulted subordinates as much to win them over as to canvass their views:

> His personality is such that it impresses itself immediately upon senior subordinates as completely frank, completely honest, very human and very considerate. . . . He has great patience, and he disdains no advice regardless of source. One of his most successful methods in dealing with individuals is to assume that he himself is lacking in detailed knowledge and liable to make an error and is seeking advice. This is by no means a pose, because he actually values the recommendations and suggestions he receives, although his own better information and sounder judgment might cause them to be disregarded.

Subordinates so consulted, Smith observed, tended to be highly loyal and to accept Eisenhower's policies readily, presumably because they were flattered to be taken seriously and to feel that whatever line of action Eisenhower embarked upon had been informed by consultation with them.

C. D. Jackson, the Time Inc. executive who in 1953 and early 1954 worked closely with Eisenhower as a national security consultant and speech writer, also noted Eisenhower's habitual close attentiveness to others, by observing that "the only time his features seem to sag is when he is bored." But it was clear to Jackson that Eisenhower took pains to master this appearance. Even the sag in his features, Jackson commented, "is only momentary, because his almost fantastically patient courtesy comes into play almost instantly in order to give the bore the impression that he is being listened to with interest."

Appointments Secretary Robert Gray also noted that Eisenhower's skill and ease in dealing with visitors to his office was built on experience and technique. Eisenhower's meetings with visitors were "never stiff," Gray reported, though he "could manage a near complete schedule of important appointments at quarter-hour intervals, clear his mind in the seconds it took me to escort out his old visitor and bring in the new, and be locked on the fresh subject in full concentration by the time I withdrew." If the visitor became tongue-tied in Eisenhower's presence, "the President could carry the conversation single-handedly," finding common ground through small talk until "the visitor had settled back on his chair prepared to discuss the . . . business that had brought him." . . .

Eisenhower's equal success in rallying and sustaining public support also was not arrived at without effort, though it was based on a personal public attractiveness to people with which few leaders are endowed. Films of Eisenhower's public appearances reveal an animated, enthusiastic man inspiring in the public a reciprocal enthusiasm. This is evident in the wartime newsreels showing a smiling, confident, unpretentious general, easily making his way through formations of troops; in the ticker-tape parades celebrating his return to the United States in 1945; and finally in films showing the motorcades with Eisenhower, both as a candidate and president, standing in open cars, beaming, waving, and signaling the familiar V for victory as he entered the cheering communities where he was making appearances. . . .

Eisenhower the man shaped the distinctive Eisenhower leadership style. His personal makeup was permeated by contrasts. Each element in his makeup had the same duality between what the public saw in him and the private man. As a thinker, the public saw a folksy, common-sense replica of the man on the street. The confidential records show a man with extraordinary capacities for detached, orderly examination of problems and personalities. In public he seemed to be removed from the political arena. But the inner Eisenhower reasoned about political contingencies with greater rigor and readiness than many political professionals and drew on a long-standing acquaintance with the labyrinths of national and international governance. His ability to win friends and influence people—both face to face and in the mass—seemed to result simply from the magnetism of his sunny personality. But he worked at his apparent artlessness, consciously choosing strategies that made people want to support him. And on occasion the sunny personality masked anger or despondency, since he viewed it as a duty of the responsible leader to exude optimism.

As president, he conveyed a warm, reassuring presence and presided over a peaceful and reasonably prosperous decade while seeming not to work at it. In fact, he pushed and disciplined himself relentlessly. Finally, his political convictions were more intense than those of many who spend their entire careers in party or elective office. But he curbed his strongly felt conservatism to profess the extent of domestic liberalism that seemed necessary to win his party middle-of-the-road support. And he moderated the harsh side of his cold war world view by taking the lead in making peace initiatives.

This was a man with a striking propensity to establish "space" between his private and public self. While this propensity also characterizes hypocrites, Eisenhower, in no letter, conversation, or diary entry, reveals the mark of a hypocrite, if that term is taken to connote contradictory public and private behavior informed by cynicism. Responding to a war correspondent's description of Eisenhower's use of profanity, one letter writer suggested that a supreme commander's language ought to reflect his dependence on divine guidance. Eisenhower expostulated: "Why, dammit, I *am* a religious man!" His private political comments show a similar impatiently intense idealism, as he chafed at politicians and business and labor leaders whom he viewed as too shortsighted to act in the national interest.

Compartmentalizing public and private elements of his personal makeup required considerable effort, self-discipline, and a conception of his duties in which eschewing expression of impolitic impulses was taken for granted as an obligation of responsible leadership. Many of the Eisenhower dichotomies reflect a reassuringly benign-seeming public self and a private one with a well-developed capacity for tough-minded political realism. A personality capable of maintaining this division is perfectly suited for adapting to the contradictory public expectations that the president serve both as uncontroversial chief of state and potentially divisive prime minister. Such a person is also well suited to carry out the organizational procedures necessary to rationalize the official routines of public leadership while maintaining a capacity to develop flexible unofficial means for adapting organizational leadership to the complexities and idiosyncracies of the people he is leading.

Document

On Leadership

DWIGHT D. EISENHOWER

. . . Now, look, I happen to *know* a little about leadership. I've had to work with a lot of nations, for that matter, at odds with each other. And I tell you this: you do not *lead* by hitting people over the head. Any damn fool can do that, but it's usually called "assault"—not "leadership." . . . I'll tell you what leadership is. It's *persuasion*—and *conciliation*—and *education*—and *patience.* It's long, slow, tough work. That's the only kind of leadership I know — or believe in — or will practice. . . .

    . . . *They* talk and write and prate about leadership. And they'd be happy and cheering — if I knocked some congressional heads together. Well, I *won't* — not even the thickest heads in my own party — not if I can possibly avoid it. For that will not be leadership, and I'll tell you *why.* In the first place, you don't "lead" a man by yelling at him in public or forcing him to say publicly, "Yes, it's true — I've been voting like a damn fool ever since I came to Congress twenty years ago." In the second place, if I forced some of these fellows to go through that kind of public penance and conversion — how long do you think they would *stay* converted? I'll tell you — long enough to get off their knees, run a short distance, and curse me for humiliating them. And in the third place, when Senator X or Senator Z does something I think is just deplorable, more than half the time that means he's a Republican — *supposed* to be helping me, not working against me. So if I tell him off in public, what am I accomplishing? Just this much: I am yelling to the world, "Please come and look, all of you, at the knucklehead I have representing me and my party and my program on Capitol Hill." . . .

    . . . Look, I know how good I could make *myself* look. Everyone who's yapping now would be cheering . . . if only I would do my "leading" in public — where they could *see* me. . . . Well, I can't do that. I will spend the hours here, quietly, in this office, staring out these windows, sometimes a little hopelessly — with [legislators] Dirksen or Millikin or Knowland here, to tell me what industries I have to protect with higher tariffs — or how the folks back home don't like these big bills for Mutual Security — or how to put Chiang Kai-Shek back in Peiping. . . . So I'll listen. And I'll answer. And I'll try to get them to understand, to *give.* I'll try to get them to give not everything, but — a little here, a little there. And I'll hope that maybe something I say *does* get through — and stays with them. . . . I don't know any other way to lead.

six

JOHN F. KENNEDY

John F. Kennedy captured the public's imagination in the early 1960s. The youngest elected president, his vigor and vitality provided a contrast to Eisenhower's low-key approach. To an America worried about the Soviet Union's post-Sputnik advantages in space, Kennedy offered hope that the United States could reaffirm its national purpose and move toward what he called a "new frontier." As he appointed intellectuals to office, invited Nobel Prize winners to dinner, and played touch football with his family on the lawn, his administration came to appear like the legendary Camelot of King Arthur's day. Assassinated in November 1963, his premature death enhanced the Kennedy myth.

Unfortunately, Kennedy's record of accomplishment was thin. In foreign affairs, he took a confrontational approach that exacerbated Cold War tensions. His hard-line stance toward Russia in the Cuban missile crisis of 1962 was initially hailed as his finest hour, but critics later charged that his rigid posture came close to catalyzing nuclear war. On the domestic front, Kennedy proved to have little ability to provide legislative leadership and managed to achieve few of his goals. Even his personal life glowed less with rumors of his extramarital affairs.

The selections reprinted in this section reflect changing assessments of Kennedy. The first piece, "The Kennedy Promise" by journalist James Reston, sums up the prevailing view of Kennedy a year after his death. Reston acknowledges Kennedy's difficulties—his handling of foreign policy produced a "spotty record" and he proved to be a better campaigner than legislative leader—but concludes that he provided a sense of hope that could continue even after he was gone.

Twenty years later, as Kennedy came under severe attack for his provocative Cold War stance, his waffling on civil rights, and his unwillingness to push harder for social reform, historian Herbert S. Parmet provides a more balanced view of his strengths and weaknesses in "John F. Kennedy: Idealism and Cynicism." Parmet argues that Kennedy did make a difference. "Promises," he writes, "*were* being fulfilled. The nation *was* going forward." But even he must admit in the end that "glamour overshadowed quality" and could not compensate entirely for the limitations of substance.

Kennedy's own approach is revealed in his January 1961 Inaugural Address, reprinted here. Concerned almost entirely with foreign affairs, it was a clarion call for a strong Cold War stance. With ringing rhetoric, it enlisted Americans in the national cause, but may have drawn the lines too sharply, aroused too many expectations, and so led to confrontations that might have been avoided.

The literature about Kennedy records the changing views. Not long after his death, two assistants wrote accounts that portrayed Kennedy just as James Reston had seen him. Arthur M. Schlesinger, Jr., *A Thousand Days: John F. Kennedy in the White House* (1965), and Theodore C. Sorensen, *Kennedy* (1965), are two highly sympathetic treatments. In the next decade, critics began to surface. Richard Walton, *Cold War and Counterrevolution* (1972), is a sharp assessment of Kennedy's foreign policy. Henry Fairlie, *The Kennedy Promise: The Politics of Expectation* (1972), is a critical account by an English journalist of a crisis-oriented approach that aroused expectations that could not be fulfilled. Garry Wills, *The Kennedy Imprisonment* (1981), is an equally critical work that includes other members of the Kennedy clan in its analysis. For a straightforward overview of aims and limitations, see Jim F. Heath, *Decade of Disillusionment: The Kennedy–Johnson Years* (1975).

The Kennedy Promise

JAMES RESTON

Time seems to be trying to make amends to John Fitzgerald Kennedy. Robbed of his years, he is being rewarded and honored in death as he never was in life. Deprived of the place he sought in history, he has been given in compensation a place in legend. What was a monstrous personal and historic crime a year ago is now something even more elemental and enduring: It is a symbol of the tragedy and caprice of life, and is likely to be remembered by the novelists and the dramatists long after the historians have gone on to other things.

Will he seem different to the historians from the way the dramatists will see him? What are they likely to say of his conduct of foreign affairs, domestic affairs, the Presidency itself? Are we already confusing myth with reality, as he was always telling us we should not do?

Probably we are, but this is only fair and maybe even natural. For there was always something vaguely legendary about him. He was a story-book President, younger and more handsome than mortal politicians, remote even from his friends, graceful, almost elegant, with poetry on his tongue and a radiant young woman at his side.

He was a sudden and surprising person. He never did things when other men were doing them. He went to Congress and the White House earlier than most. He married much later than his contemporaries. His war record, his political record and his personal life were marked by flashes of crisis and even by a vague premonition of tragedy. He always seemed to be striding through doors into the center of some startling triumph or disaster. He never reached his meridian: we saw him only as a rising sun.

Accordingly, it is not easy to make an estimate of his 1,000 days in the White House. He didn't have a fair chance and he didn't even give himself a fair chance. He often made his decisions alone after a series of private talks with several individuals, none of whom shared the whole process of his thought.

Oddly in one who had such an acute sense of history, he was disorderly about keeping records of what led up to his decisions, and though he had a great gift for conversation, he seems to have spent little time talking to his closest associates about how he had decided things in the past.

All this complicates the task of placing him in the catalogue of the Presidents. We do not have the record. We do not have the full story of the two Cuban crises, or his meeting with Khrushchev in Vienna, or the reasoning behind his gambles in Vietnam, or the communications that led up to the atomic test-ban treaty with the Soviets. We have only our clippings, memories, and impressions, and these can be uncertain guides.

I—FOREIGN POLICY

Historians—and here we are in the realm of opinion—will probably rate President Kennedy's handling of foreign policy higher than his contemporaries did. It is a spotty record. He dreamed occasionally of an interdependent Atlantic world and this has become part of the legend, but the reality is that the alliance was in poor shape during most of his Administration. He courted Latin America like a thoughtful lover, but, again, the Alliance for Progress was more dream than reality.

Even so, he had a feeling for the way the world was going. He understood the challenge of change. He was fascinated by the political revolution produced by the liberation of the colonial peoples: sometimes too fascinated with it, and too inclined to give it a higher priority than it deserved. He studied and understood the intricate problems of the atomic revolution and the scientific revolution, probably better than any of his predecessors.

Yet this keen, analytical intelligence was not always a help. It enabled him to see the problems, but it often depressed him about finding the answers. I always thought—perhaps wrongly—that his intelligence made him pessimistic. The evidence that science was transforming the world seemed so clear and overwhelming to him that he was irritated by the failure of men and institutions to adapt and keep up.

In his very first State of the Union message, 10 days after he had been sworn in, he told the Congress and the nation: "Before my term has ended, we shall have to test anew whether a nation organized and governed such as ours can endure. The outcome is by no means certain. The answers are by no means clear."

His bungling of his first foreign-policy gamble, when he tried to help the Cuban refugees overthrow the Castro Government, made him all the more conscious, not only of the complexities of political decision, but of the possible consequences of failure.

The events at the Bay of Pigs contributed to his natural caution, and added to his problems with the Communists for most of the rest of his days in the White House. It is impossible to be sure about this, but I was in Vienna when he met Khrushchev shortly after the fiasco of the Bay of Pigs, and saw him 10 minutes after his meeting with the Soviet leader. He came into a dim room in the American Embassy shaken and angry. He had tried, as always to be calm and rational with Khrushchev, to get him to define what the Soviet Union could and would not do, and Khrushchev had bullied him and threatened him with war over Berlin.

We will have to know much more about that confrontation between Kennedy and Khrushchev, one now deprived of life and the other of power, before we can be sure, but Kennedy said just enough in that room in the embassy to convince me of the following: Khrushchev had studied the events of the Bay of Pigs; he would have understood if Kennedy had left Castro alone or destroyed him; but when Kennedy was rash enough to strike at Cuba but not bold enough to finish the job, Khrushchev decided he was dealing with an inexperienced young leader who could be intimidated and blackmailed. The Communist decision to put offensive missiles into Cuba was the final gamble of this assumption.

The missile crisis brought out what always seemed to me to be Kennedy's finest quality and produced the events on which Kennedy's place in history probably depends. There is a single fact that repeats itself in the Kennedy story like the major theme in a symphony: He was at his best in the highest moment of crisis.

He could be ambiguous and even indecisive on secondary questions. He obviously trifled with the first Cuban crisis. He also temporized with the Vietnamese crisis, partly supporting those who wanted to intervene "to win," partly going along with those who reminded him that the French had suffered 175,000 casualties against the same Communist army, but never really defining his aims or reconciling his power with his objectives.

Yet always in his political life he acted decisively when faced with total defeat. He was supremely confident, almost presumptuous, in going for the Presidency in the first place against the opposition of the most powerful elements in his party. He was bold and effective when first Hubert Humphrey, then Harry Truman and finally Lyndon Johnson challenged him publicly during the campaign for the nomination. He probably won the Presidency in the critical debates with Richard Nixon. And this same quality came out in the missile crisis in Cuba.

Then he was, as Robert Frost had urged him to be, "more Irish than Harvard" but with a dash of Harvard intelligence, too. If the first Cuban crisis was the worst example of the uses of American power and diplomacy in this generation, the second Cuban crisis was the best. And the significance of this fact can be understood only in relation to the longer perspective of war in this century.

Twice in this century, the leaders of the free world have been confronted by the menacing power of a totalitarian state. From 1912 until 1914, and again from 1935 to 1939, Germany made a series of moves that clearly threatened the peace and order of the world, and during those critical testing periods, Britain, France and the United States failed either to raise enough military power or to show enough will power to avoid the holocaust. The resulting tragedies of the two great wars transformed the history of the world.

The Soviet decision to place long-range missiles in Cuba, capable of firing atomic rockets into almost any part of the United States, was a similar and in some ways even more ominous test. This lunge into the Western Hemisphere was clearly an effort to change the world balance of power in Moscow's favor, and Kennedy faced it at the risk of war and turned it back.

It is ironic that he went to his grave with many of his fellow countrymen condemning him for failing to get rid of all the Communists and all the defensive missiles in Cuba as well as all the offensive missiles. Yet this view has not been shared by most of the political leaders and historians of the world.

I saw Prime Minister Macmillan of Britain just before he resigned and before President Kennedy was murdered. "If Kennedy never did another thing," Macmillan remarked, "he assured his place in history by that single act. He did what we failed to do in the critical years before the two German wars."

Within a year of Kennedy's death, Khrushchev was removed from power, partly as a result of his humiliating defeat in the Cuban missile crisis, but something important and maybe even historic remained: The Communist world was relieved of the illusion that the United States would not risk atomic war to defend its vital interests. This new awareness greatly reduced the danger of miscalculating American intentions and led almost at once to the first really serious steps to bring atomic weapons under control.

II—THE HOME FRONT

Mr. Kennedy was more at ease in the larger world of diplomacy and the struggle between nations than he was in the world of Congressional politics and the struggle between contending national forces. He had more freedom of action in foreign than in domestic policy. He did not seem to mind the small talk of ceremonial meetings with heads of state or foreign students at the White House, and he had a rare combination of informality and dignity that made him very effective in this role. But blarneying with pompous Congressmen bored him and he simply would not take time to do it, as his successor, President Johnson, has with such marked success.

This was odd, in a way. He was a superb politician in planning and running a Presidential campaign, but he didn't really know the deck on Capitol Hill and he did not really like to play the political game there. Even though he spent most of his political life in the House and the Senate, he was always sort of a nonresident member of those peculiar clubs, always a backbencher with a high truancy record and an excessive respect for the chairmen of the committees and the other elders of the Congress.

The very qualities of appearance, style and cast of mind that won him the admiration of the intellectual and diplomatic worlds somehow marked him as an outsider in his dealings with the Congress. He had little patience for the tiresome loquacity and endless details of legislation, and he never cared much for the boisterous bantering and backslapping of the cloakrooms.

He had a kind of gay magic as a political speaker, most of it as carefully contrived as it seemed spontaneous. He was good at the arts of Hollywood and Madison Avenue, and this delighted his fellow politicians, but he was a little too polished, ambitious and out of the ordinary to escape the envy and criticism of The Hill.

Congress likes typical Americans and Kennedy was not one. In his mature life, he probably crossed the Atlantic more often than he crossed the Allegheny range. He never seemed at home in the West. The America he understood best was bounded by Harvard Yard, the State Department, Park Avenue and Palm Beach. His political style and humor were not based on the exaggerated language and gymnastics of the American hustings but on the gentler models of the House of Commons.

Maybe these things had nothing to do with his troubles in getting a legislative program through the Congress; maybe it was just the old stubborn resistance of the Congress to change—"the government of the living by the dead"—but the fact remains that his domestic program was in deep trouble when he was killed, and some of us despaired that Capitol Hill would ever be his field of triumph.

Part of the Kennedy legend is connected with his introduction of the most radical legislation in behalf of Negro equality in this century. But again the reality is less romantic. He did not normally like to take on anything more than he had to tackle, no matter how worthy. Oddly for a man who wrote a book celebrating the heroes of lost causes ("Profiles in Courage"), he was always saying: "Why fight if you are not sure to win?" The Negro demonstrations in the summer of 1963, however, forced his hand, and he went along when some Republican leaders and his brother Robert urged that action was necessary.

Yet, on the home front, as in the foreign field, he did start one major innovation of transcending importance. At the urging of Walter Heller, the chairman of the Council of Economic Advisers, he broke with the traditional economic concepts of Capitol Hill and plunged for a large tax cut and a planned deficit. Liberal economists in Europe and in the American universities had been arguing for years that it was no longer necessary to redistribute the wealth of the rich in order to elevate the poor, but that the total production of wealth could be increased to the benefit of everybody if modern technology and fiscal measures were applied.

Kennedy was not by temper a fiscal reformer. He came to the White House as a rather timid liberal, but the longer he was in office the more he cried out against the restraining economic and fiscal traditions of the past and the more he appealed to the country to deal with the world as it is. He never saw his tax bill go through; he died before it was passed. But he was largely responsible for heading the country into the most prolonged period of peacetime prosperity since the last World War. There was a recession when he took over in 1961. Unemployment was up to almost 7 per cent of the work force. There was a balance-of-payments deficit of nearly $4 billion. The outflow of gold to other countries in 1960 totaled $1.7 billion. But by the time he died, this trend had been reversed, at least in part as a result of his initiatives.

III—THE IMPONDERABLES

Yet even if he turned the tide of the cold war toward the control of nuclear arms, and started the trend toward acceptance of the new economics of increased production and general prosperity, this is not the Kennedy story that is likely to be remembered.

These things were only dramatic symbols of his critical mind. He was a critic of his age. He did not think we could deal with the menace of nuclear weapons unless we searched constantly for means of accommodation with the Communists. He did not think we could employ our people in the midst of a revolution in labor-saving machinery unless we changed our attitude toward Federal budgets and Federal deficits.

He did not think we could deal with the pressures of communism, rising population, or galloping automation, or that we could contain the rising expectations of the non-white races and the new nations unless we moved faster to integrate the races at home and the nations of the free world abroad. In short, he did not believe we could deal effectively with a transformed world unless we transformed ourselves — our attitudes of mind and our institutions.

This was a youthful mind asking the big questions. He was not one for big plans and grand designs, though contemporary writers often professed to see such things in some of the speeches of Ted Sorensen. Incidentally, it was always difficult to tell where the soaring rhetoric of Sorensen's bolder and more liberal mind left off and the more cautious Kennedy mind picked up, but Kennedy was not a great planner.

I once asked him in a long private talk at Hyannis Port what he wanted to have achieved by the time he rode down Pennsylvania Avenue with his successor. He looked at me as if I were a dreaming child. I tried again: Did he not feel the need of some goal to help guide his day-to-day decisions and priorities? Again a ghastly pause. It was only when I turned the question to immediate, tangible problems that he seized the point and rolled off a torrent of statistics about the difficulty of organizing nations at different levels of economic development.

Yet there is a puzzle in all this. For while he wanted to transform the thought and institutions of the nation, and regarded the machinery of the Congress as almost an anachronism, he concentrated on working — not, on the whole, very successfully — with the Congress, and he never really exploited his considerable gifts as a public educator.

"Give me the right word and the right accent," said Joseph Conrad, "and I will move the world." This was Churchill's way and nobody admired it more than Kennedy. But while he made a few glorious trial flights, something held him back, some fear of appealing to the people over the heads of the Congress, some fear of too much talk (he hated verbosity), some modesty, maybe — always so apparent in his embarrassment before applauding crowds.

The essence of the tragedy, however, is perfectly clear. What was killed in Dallas was not only the President but the promise. The death of youth and the hope of youth, of the beauty and grace and the touch of magic.

The heart of the Kennedy legend is what might have been. His intelligence made people think that the coming generation might make the world more rational. It even made it hard for the intellectuals of Europe to be anti-American. His good looks and eloquence put a brighter shine on politics, and made his world relevant and attractive to young people all over the world.

All this is apparent in the faces of the people who come to his grave daily on the Arlington hill. In the world of their dreams, Presidents would be young and heroic, with beautiful wives, and the ugly world would be transformed by their examples.

John Finley, the master of Eliot House at Harvard, sent me a letter which sums up this sense of loss better than anything else:

"No doubt like innumerable people, I feel suddenly old without Mr. and Mrs. Kennedy in the White House. On reflection, ours seems a society of older people; it takes a while to reach the top in science, law, business and most other things. Yet, paradoxically, only the young have the freshness to enjoy and not be wearied by the profusion of vitality of present American life.

"Not only by ability, but by sheer verve and joy, the Kennedys imparted their youth to everyone and put a sheen on our life that made it more youthful than it is. Mr. Johnson now seems Gary Cooper as President — 'High Noon,' the poker game, the easy walk and masculine smile. But even Gary Cooper was growing older, and the companions and adversaries around the poker table reflect a less fresh, if no doubt practical and effective, mood. All will be well, I feel sure . . . but it is August, not June. . . ."

Always we come back to the same point. The tragedy of John Fitzgerald Kennedy was greater than the accomplishment, but in the end the tragedy enhances the accomplishment and revives the hope.

Thus the law of compensation operates. "The dice of God are always loaded," wrote Emerson. "For everything you have missed you have gained something else. . . . The world looks like a multiplication table, or a mathematical equation, which, turn it how you will, balances itself. . . . Every secret is told, every crime is punished, every virtue rewarded, every wrong redressed, in silence and certainty."

John F. Kennedy: Idealism and Cynicism

HERBERT S. PARMET

Together with [John F.] Kennedy's personality, the challenge to "get America moving again" had penetrated the nation's conscience, and that meant confronting enemies wherever they existed and transforming them into allies. If there was no longer such a reality as monolithic international communism, if nationalistic versions had gone beyond Kremlin control, the potential danger was even greater. The split was not something America ought to "look forward to with comfort." "It could bring us harm," Kennedy told an off-the-record briefing of journalists at the State Department, "if Khrushchev has to prove his revolutionary intensity." For too long American policy had reacted, not initiated. Like prewar England the "free world" was too lethargic. An

Excerpts from *JFK: The Presidency of John F. Kennedy* by Herbert S. Parmet. Copyright © 1983 by Herbert S. Parmet. Reprinted by permission of Doubleday, a division of Bantam, Doubleday, Dell Publishing Group, Inc.

active America, demonstrating the blessings of liberty, could sell values that fostered confidence and respect. There was enough potential for the excitement and satisfaction of natural desires without Communist authoritarianism. All this Kennedy believed, but he also knew it was easy to rhapsodize.

He had gone from plateau to plateau. He had overcome the hurdles and was not about to stop. He was a hard man to know. His exterior revealed very little of what churned inside. One European visitor, an especially perceptive student of character and minds who had the opportunity to engage him in long talks, perceived an inner struggle that was constantly working to retain self-control. Drift and boredom were perhaps the greatest, unaffordable indulgences. He knew exactly what he wanted. From his parents he had unceasingly absorbed the inevitability of success.

Still, he never got very far from the realization that disaster was waiting, that all his margins of survival — from the *Amigari* that sliced open *PT 109* to the victory over Nixon — had been exceedingly narrow. More than any other President since Abe Lincoln, thought Walt Rostow, Kennedy combined that sense of tragedy and the possibility of tragedy, "but the idealism in his stance was another counterpoint in him." He was, after all, the man who was going to bring sense to the chaos. Queries directed to the White House about Kennedy's favorite quotations received the standard response that the one he liked best of all came from Edmund Burke, the great English Whig: "The only thing necessary for the triumph of evil is for good men to do nothing." "The White House intrigued him," remembered Kennedy's journalist friend, Charles Bartlett. "He was just burning with the things he could do. He really was challenged by the opportunity to do something for the country."

After the Eisenhower fifties Americans were ready to "honeymoon" with the Kennedys. The First Family becomes the republic's Royal Family. In a world of electronic images constantly communicating life-styles and values, the White House sets the pace. Kennedy was the first telegenic President of a people who knew that "seeing is believing." So, for all the reverence for Ike and Mamie, there was a seamless transition to the semi-aristocratic chic of Jack and Jackie. When presidential Press Secretary Pierre Salinger and Mrs. Kennedy's personal secretary, Pamela Turnure, announced that the new First Lady was having the White House sponsor a program for the creative arts, the change seemed authentic. Eleanor, Bess, Mamie — they belonged to the past.

In a very few words Fred Dutton spelled out what ultimately became the most characteristic mark of the Kennedy presidency, the one element that defied all the *Congressional Quarterly* boxscores of legislation proposed and accepted. At Bobby's urging Dutton, a thirty-seven-year-old Californian, had joined Kennedy's staff after two years as executive secretary to Governor Pat Brown. "The nature of the overriding task for this Office," he wrote in a memorandum, "remains not so much just more legislation, nor more executive orders, but to evoke more of a willingness by people to give of themselves to accomplish all the hard things which need to be done."

The innovative Hundred Days of Roosevelt, a time when the entire nation had to be rescued from despair, had created new criteria for judging early success. With Eisenhower there were different ground rules. He came into office surrounded by every kind of contention *except* economic, and so becoming the great conciliator earned him a place in history. These two men, the one offering new departures to save the system and the other pacifiers, were the most successful of recent Presidents.

For Kennedy the Inaugural Address had done its job. He needed only to build on that tone.

A solemn journey, a mission of revitalization and reform, had begun. The glow lent the "honeymoon" an almost magical aura; if not the dynamic, somber rolling up of sleeves and restructuring of Roosevelt's time, there at least was another kind of appeal: the spark of confidence. America really seemed to be "moving again." Both within and outside the White House there was a new kind of bravado or even audacity. While news and analysis columns did not hesitate to delineate just how cautious the new administration really was, the *Times* nevertheless declared, after he had been in office sixty days, that the "Kennedy personality has turned the White House into a beehive of action and ideas." "Our faith in him and in what he was trying to do was absolute," Pierre Salinger later wrote, "and he could impart to our work together a sense of challenge and adventure—a feeling that he was moving, and the world with him, toward a better time."

There were areas where Kennedy could get immediate and substantive results. He had only to place his name on a document to boost the quantity and quality of food for the needy. His first executive order directed Orville Freeman to use funds already available to expand food distribution to the needy, thereby fulfilling a pledge made during the West Virginia primary. On Inauguration Day he had noted few black faces among the Coast Guard contingent that marched along Pennsylvania Avenue, so one of his first acts was to pick up the telephone and personally ask the Coast Guard commander whether that reflected an exclusionary policy. Assured that none existed, he replied, "Well, I didn't see any yesterday in the parade." Before the week was out, he sent a memo to Chester Bowles directing the undersecretary to investigate the small number of minorities in the Foreign Service and throughout the State Department. He also dispatched Arthur Goldberg to New York to settle a costly tugboat strike that had stymied much of the nation's commerce, and within fourteen hours of his arrival the secretary of labor was able to announce a settlement. But the most dramatic breakthrough came on the last day of January, and that seemed to demonstrate that the Kennedyites were as good as their word. On Capitol Hill, after a fight led by Sam Rayburn, with close monitoring by Kennedy since he and the speaker had discussed the strategy at Palm Beach, the administration won its vote to enlarge the Rules Committee. Their margin was only five votes, as slim as most Kennedy crucial battles seemed to be, but it meant that the addition of two Democrats and one Republican might weaken the grip of Chairman Howard W. Smith and expedite the flow of vital legislation. With the administration only eleven days old, whether this would have any substantial future effect was secondary to the symbolic impact.

One gain seemed certain. Doubts about Kennedy's youth and inexperience had been neutralized. Headiness had bolstered his staff and assured the nation, and the staging of his first press conference on January 25 further stimulated the popular acceptance. From the Indian Treaty Room of the Old State Department Building where Eisenhower's conferences had been held, the quasi-theatrical event was moved to the amphitheater of the New State Department Building. On hand were all the paraphernalia of modern electronics. Kennedy, in a pin-striped suit and white shirt, strode to the lectern at 6:00 P.M., dinner hour on the East Coast. He stood apart from the more than four hundred people in the auditorium, separated by a spacious hollow, beyond which his live audience sat in elevated tiers ready to record and interrogate. The scene, wrote Russell Baker, was about as warm as "an execution chamber"; but with that performance Kennedy brought presidential press conferences into the realm of effective public relations. He sold himself even more than his views.

His spontaneous and televised news conferences became an integral part of a public relations "blitz," and he held ten during those first three months. From the start he became an instant champion of the art. He stood there, confident, cameras focused on his tanned face, triumphant and in command. His opening statement told of early decisions — to delay the Geneva atomic test ban negotiations until the American position could be more adequately prepared; to substantially increase food assistance for civil war–torn Congo. Then, with no real change in demeanor, came his coup: The Soviet government had ordered the release of both survivors from an RB-47, which had been shot down over the USSR while on an "electro-magnetic survey." This removed "a serious obstacle to improvement of Soviet-American relations." Offering no additional interpretation, he merely said the matter had been under discussion with Llewellyn Thompson, the American ambassador in Moscow, and that the men were en route home. He neither thanked Khrushchev nor offered any apologies for possible intrusion into Soviet air space, which the Eisenhower administration had denied, but volunteered that, like his predecessor, he had banned additional flights. Offering no hint of new departures, he left an impression of prudent continuity.

Nor did he extend an olive branch. Less than three weeks before Kennedy came to power the Eisenhower administration increased the Havana–Washington tensions by breaking diplomatic relations. Acting in the immediate afterglow of the inauguration, Castro warned that Cubans were ready to meet the "threat of imminent aggression," a matter that had become plain to all with open eyes in the entire region from Miami to Guatemala, and challenged the new American President to "make the first move" in restoring friendly relations. That, replied Kennedy, was "a matter that should be negotiated," and then proceeded to declare that the Cubans were repugnant to American interests because they were less concerned about the welfare of their own people than in "imposing an ideology which is alien to this hemisphere." Castro was not a legitimate force but an intruder who threatened the "security" and "peace" of the Americas.

There was no softening when Kennedy faced his first joint session of Congress on January 30 and spoke on the State of the Union. The language was portentous, the style of a man with a mission — Lincoln at Gettysburg, Churchill during the Battle of Britain. "It is one of the ironies of our time," he declared, "that the techniques of a harsh and repressive system should be able to instill discipline and ardor in its servants — while the blessings of liberty have too often stood for privilege, materialism and a life of ease."

Self-consciously, then, he girded himself for the test and loaded his message with the cataclysmic tones of a man about to preside either over a new creation or Armageddon:

> I speak today in an hour of national peril and national opportunity. . . . We shall have to test anew whether a nation organized and governed such as ours can endure. . . . our national household is cluttered with unfinished and neglected tasks. . . . Each day we draw nearer the hour of maximum danger, as weapons spread and hostile forces grow stronger. . . . the tide of events has been running out and time has not been our friend. . . . We cannot escape our dangers — neither must we let them drive us into panic or narrow isolation. . . . There will be further setbacks before the tide is turned. But turn it must. The hopes of mankind rest upon us.

Walt Rostow likes to recall that they belonged to an extended family, each with his own official title but each prepared to pitch in with whatever had to be done. Assignments sometimes landed on the fellow who happened to be in the Oval Office at the particular moment of need. "The informality was amazing,"recalled Dutton. "Kennedy really didn't get himself involved in what might be called housekeeping functions; he didn't care about them." He had little patience for the niceties of administration, for the pipelines that structured bureaucracies. Especially at the start, he would use his own telephone to make those calls to surprised subordinates. He wanted action above all.

Delegations of authority were minimal. The Cabinet, the National Security Council, and the whole chain of command were all transformed from the carefully structured Eisenhower format to Kennedy's personal style. He shunned long-winded discussions, preferring to question and get right to the point. He was the best interrogator they had ever met. He learned much by listening, but more by reading, digesting every possible document. "As soon as it got around to the town that Kennedy was reading our memos," Roger Hilsman has recalled, "everybody in town began to read our memos." Aides quickly caught on that the best route to "the boss" was through the written word. Even so he was not isolated behind a wall of paper. "We were few enough so that the President had some idea of who we were and what we were doing," Carl Kaysen says when contemplating how White House staffs have grown since Kennedy's time. "There wasn't anybody there who had not some personal contact with Kennedy from time to time."

"The Kennedy Administration is an odd mixture of idealism and cynicism," wrote James Reston, "of liberals and conservatives, of professors and politicians, of Harvard grafted on to the Boston Irish." He had, Rostow recalls, "a marvelous gift for orchestrating people. The people he wove together represented almost geological layers in Kennedy's experiences — old friends from pre-war days, college friends, the PT boat friends, and these people all respected one another." His administrative technique in handling was indeed the skill of a man who had grown up in a big family, and it "appeared almost an extension of that style and experience." They had their jealousies, their territorial prerogatives, that occasionally marred the superficial appearance of perfect harmony, but, almost to a man, their loyalty to Jack Kennedy was the great unifier.

Afterward the veterans of the New Frontier read the retrospective views of "Camelot." Increasingly they found themselves on the defensive, criticizing detractors as writers of "pseudohistory" who failed to understand what the New Frontier was really like. They did not doubt that, in that early post-Eisenhower era, they had something to offer a world headed toward either nuclear annihilation or totalitarianism. America was also about to decide whether the Second Reconstruction would collapse like the first, with similar consequences, or whether, in their hands, the pattern would be broken, rational solutions achieved; and unlike the backlashes against abolitionism and "black Republicanism," this time there could be racial civility. They liked the challenges (*challenge* was one of the boss's favorite words) of maneuvering in a complex and dangerous world. Literary critic Alfred Kazin, skeptical that all the intellectuality was but power wrapped in tinsel, approached them warily. But even Kazin came away convinced that they gave "the glow of those who have not merely conceived a great work but are in a position to finish it." . . .

All told, Kennedy's legislative objectives were closely tuned to what was possible. In March, during a conversation with Dean Acheson, Kennedy cited the following comment from Lord Acton's "An Essay on Nationality": "The pursuit of a remote and ideal object, which captivates the imagination by its splendor and the reason by its simplicity, evokes an energy which would not be inspired by a rational, possible end, limited by many antagonistic claims, and confined to what is reasonable, practical and just." By that standard Kennedy succeeded magnificently. On May 1 he signed into law the Area Redevelopment Act to pump federal funds toward the rejuvenation of depressed areas. Only four days later minimum wages were raised to $1.25 an hour. Social Security benefits were also widened. A $4.88 billion ominibus housing bill was the most comprehensive measure in that field since the Taft–Ellender Act of 1949, and was aimed largely for the benefit of low- and moderate-income families. There was also more aid for localities to battle water pollution, and more money toward public works.

But, as with any presidency, the inevitable prices had to be paid. Minimum-wage legislation was almost decimated by the traditional Republican–Southern Democratic conservative coalition, and the administration's victory had to come at the price of sacrificing tens of thousands of the most miserably paid, including 150,000 laundry workers. Few were more in need of such protection, but a well-organized laundry association lobby made their desperation quite irrelevant. When at last Area Redevelopment grants started, the first were targeted not toward the most vital areas, but [instead] "to serve a shirt factory deep in the Ozark Mountains of Senator Fulbright's Arkansas. . . . a nonunion, low-wage enterprise of the very type whose competition has been so keenly felt in the depressed manufacturing centers of the North." Other major parts of the program requested in February—health care, aid to education—were either in jeopardy or without any chance of success.

Kennedy's critics would later focus on such things and lament the absence of "real" accomplishments. But mostly they were voicing their own frustrations, speaking out about a people, a Congress, and a President not out to achieve New Deal–style reforms for American society but a modification of the past decade's mild conservatism. Among those expressing other preferences, the tilt was toward the right.

But promises *were* being fulfilled. The nation *was* going forward. At the start of March, Kennedy sent a special message, creating a Peace Corps and signed an executive order establishing the agency on a temporary basis. His brother-in-law, R. Sargent Shriver, began serving as its director. The suite that opened to serve as its headquarters, at 806 Connecticut Avenue, was immediately inundated by mail and phone calls from eager young people. Then on March 13 the President addressed Latin American diplomats at the White House and called "on all of the people of the hemisphere to join in a new Alliance for Progress—*Alianza para Progreso*—a vast cooperative effort, unparalleled in magnitude and nobility of purpose, to satisfy the basic needs of the American people for homes, work and land, health and schools." "It was quite an occasion," career diplomat Thomas Mann remarked years later when recalling that scene. The Alliance held out the hope of a middle way in Latin America, the promotion of popular democracies capable of countering Castroite revolutionary sentiments seeking to overturn the hemisphere's rightist dictatorships. That and the Peace Corps were imbued with missionary nobility, tapping latent desires to assert the universality of the American dream.

All that combined with a very visible presidency boosted Kennedy's standing far above November's figures. A *Newsweek* survey reported that the "new, young, and untried President—one who had been elected by only 49.7 per cent of the electorate—now had the great part of the American people behind him." In a confidential analysis, Kennedy's own pollster wrote that the ability to "get things done" was winning the highest rating of popular approval. While critics duly pointed out that Kennedy had not set his sights very high, both the Gallup pollsters and Lou Harris, who made confidential studies for the White House, concluded that the expectations of most Americans had been "exceeded." Harris's calculations had Kennedy's favorable ratings at an incredibly high ninety-two to eight, and the Gallup organization's somewhat more modest figures still showed a substantially impressive seventy-two to six margin among those with an opinion.

On Capitol Hill, Kennedy had managed to achieve a fairly reliable working majority through a coalition of northern and western Democrats and liberal Republicans. Still, the steps were tempered, the requests moderate, the compromises forthcoming. Why, then, was he so cautious? Why did he fail to exert his personal leadership to achieve a more impressive legislative record? "It is true," Walter Heller explained in 1980, "that, for all his national popularity, for all the effective troops that he had in the White House in terms of relations with Congress, he was not confident of his ability to get things through Congress." In sharp contrast to Kennedy's responses to global events, in the realm of domestic politics, Heller explained, "I think he had a deep-seated belief that he had to condition and educate the country in his first term and he'd get his payoff in the second term." The need to postpone action until reelection became a common explanation, almost giving the impression that the man who had run for the presidency on the theme of getting the country "moving again" was guilty of the same kind of procrastination as his predecessor.

If Kennedy was cautious, hesitant, calculating the probable cost of each move, he managed to approach foreign policy with a freer hand. Certainly, it was in the nature of the presidency, and the Founding Fathers had made clear the Chief Executive's responsibility. There in the very arena where the stakes risked nuclear disaster rather than the alienation of some domestic interest group, Kennedy was less hesitant about using those powers. Foreign crises were, of course, also more urgent and far less likely to permit delay. Moreover, the international order was of much greater personal interest and, from the start of his presidency, not a day passed without reminders of its primacy. In late March, Adolf Berle wrote in his diary that Kennedy "has had more rough crises thrown at him in the first sixty days of his Administration than any President since Lincoln." Before the anti-Castro brigade even attempted to land on Cuban soil, a writer for *The Nation* praised Kennedy for his "ability to live with chaos." Springtime had come, bringing out the cherry blossoms in Washington, and the President was finding his challenges. . . .

The John F. Kennedy who became President was the survivor of what had been a "brutal filter." To become worthy of his father, he had overcome the natural inhibitions of his personality. He had endured persistent pain and escaped a premature death sentence. The public view of Jack was as a "golden boy," but the original "golden boy" for the Kennedys was Joe Jr., the "lost prince," and the second son had surmounted a multitude of barriers to become a worthy replacement.

Joseph P. Kennedy, the former ambassador, had done his work behind the scenes, but in significant ways he was as much a liability as an asset. Jack had to get there by his own wiles, and he had few illusions about the process. He is not known to have said so directly, but he would have agreed with the fiery, red-bearded spoilsman of gilded age New York, Roscoe Conkling, who reminded reformers that "parties are not built up by deportment, or by ladies' magazines, or gush!" Those who thought Kennedy cynical and crafty had a point, but in his pursuit of goals he could be as cautious and indecisive as anyone else.

Jack Kennedy never thought of the world as a moral place, which is what he had in mind when he said that "life isn't fair." All of life was a test, each new obstacle a trial. His escapades, his sexual adventures, were respites from constant crises, and were moreover as much a privilege of aristocracy as any other symbol of rank. Yet there was a great dichotomy between the playboy and the somber, quiet desperation that characterized his discipline and determination to meet challenges. He was forever meeting challenges. They were the aspirations of an aristocratic responsibility, a burden especially great for one first establishing the claim to such credentials.

If he was to become that leader, an American Churchill, perhaps, the tests would be crucial. All of his trials had been won by small margins. At the head of the government the latitude would not be much greater. He saw the world as the battleground of a civil war between the extremes of Right and Left. He asked for sacrifices, and that distinguished him from his Democratic and Republican rivals.

It was the missionary approach, the sailing-against-the-wind romanticism that conveys a masculine, messianic quality and portrays the stakes as choices between freedom and slavery, between extinction and survival. Implicit throughout, and sometimes specified, was whether this challenge—to him the highest calling—was within the ability of a democratic society forced to compete with the single-minded, efficient, centrally directed advantages inherent in totalitarianism. This basic Kennedy preoccupation foreshadowed his subsequent global policies. Always it was the exporting of democracy, at once doubting its ability to resist the forces of evil and, at the same time, remaining convinced that it represented the preferred choice among the options available to man.

Just as it has often been suggested that only Nelson Rockefeller's heritage made him a Republican, and that his true place and certainly his more likely means of fulfilling political ambitions would have been as a Democrat, so may it be said that Jack Kennedy was a Democrat by culture and geography only. Having come to power by that route, his only way to move ahead was by mobilizing the remnants of the New Deal, trying to resurrect and reorder that coalition through a style that fused moderation with idealism.

He was, as Presidents tend to be, primarily interested in global affairs. Kennedy's belief in democratic self-determination was backed up by an extensive American military commitment. His infatuation with paramilitary operations, counterinsurgency, and inability to rationalize intelligence operations made a mockery of rhetoric that appealed to reason. Subsequent revelations about secret wars did much to establish JFK as a man who had actually brought international tensions to their most dangerous moments. His constant need to demonstrate toughness had helped to manufacture potential

disasters everywhere. In Southeast Asia, in particular, he left behind a prescription for even greater disasters to come.

He "stood up" to Khrushchev but capitulated to Congress. He followed
a domestic course that precluded battling for the fulfillment of the economic
and social welfare needs of the Democratic Party's postdepression constituency. His effectiveness on Capitol Hill was limited, and he even appeared
submissive. He had vowed to "get America moving again" but failed to
deliver in key ways.

Glamour overshadowed quality. JFK appeared too handsome, too
witty, too intelligent; Jackie was too beautiful, too cultivated, and much too
elegant. So was Sorensen's lofty prose, which began to seem like the tinsel
wrapped around an artificial world that posed as a modern Camelot.

Kennedy had struggled to reach the top. Once there he paused, looked at
the barriers to further progress, and, rather than press forward with his
momentum, accommodated himself to the new realities. Where others may
have seen opportunities, he found that the much-advertised "corridors of
power" were really Byzantine labyrinths. His assessment argued for caution,
for harnessing resources to fight the real battles some other day. Explanations
for the meagerness of output held that he needed more time and more
support from Capitol Hill and the American public. If he developed more
popular strength and could be reelected decisively in 1964, unlike the narrow
victory of 1960, he could then go on to reach those "new frontiers." He was,
they reasoned, learning and growing as he went along.

Like Adlai Stevenson, however, John F. Kennedy attracted architects
more impressed than he by the efficacy of new designs. Also, as in Stevenson's
case, they were convinced that a man so civilized, so quick to grasp the
intricacies, would surely adopt their view of an America less preoccupied with
the powerful and more concerned with the displaced. Their confidence in his
growth largely spoke for their own commitment to his leadership. As with
Stevenson, Kennedy enchanted not only those who worked on his New
Frontier but a generation of young people who found themselves similarly
inspired by a man who seemed convinced that democracy and quality were
not incompatible. From them Kennedy derived much of his political and
quantitative strength. In turn he told them what they wanted to hear. Kennedy "did not ride the tide of intellectualism," Arthur Schlesinger, Jr., wrote
to a critical Alfred Kazin in 1962, "he drew it with him." He knew how easily
women could be seduced, and he understood that men were not very different. He dazzled a generation of intellectuals accustomed to having a "nitwit"
in the White House, and when they recovered from his charm and reviewed
the era, they resented the deception.

They had been used. His thousand days led to the nightmare years that
followed. The rage that destroyed neighborhoods and the endless search for
the "light at the end of the tunnel" only resulted in an "age of disillusionment." And Jack Kennedy, to whom the torch had been passed, became the
orphan of failure. At best he was an "interim" President who had promised
but not performed. He was rejected along with his era.

Memories, however, are notoriously short. The point has been made many times before, but it is worth repeating: If Kennedy was a "cold warrior," who was not in his day? Who, that is, among those who could have plausibly risen to the presidency? He believed that strength was the most effective producer of reason, and that has yet to be disproved. He saw the world as a dangerous place, and reacted accordingly. If he had not, his inevitable replacement would have been someone who would have promised to really get tough. When the course gave signs that it could be altered, Kennedy responded accordingly and tried to lead toward a more rational accommodation. He convinced much of the world that his purpose was peace. His American University speech and the test ban treaty were bold moves for those cold-war years, and they began a round of arms limitations agreements and more dialogue that at least psychologically (an element that cannot be minimized) seemed to move the world away from having to think the unthinkable. At his death he was involved in sounding out a new, saner relationship with Cuba. The face that he put on the national purpose through such programs as the Peace Corps and the Alliance for Progress, whatever their limitations, was at least consistent with the idealism much of the world preferred to associate with America.

That was strengthened by his identification with the civil rights movement. There, too, he was cautious; but, finally caught up in a revolution against the great cancer in American life, his Justice Department worked to enforce the laws already passed. The President withheld the full power of the Executive Office for too long. There were, as usual, too many reasons for delay. He had to be pressed too hard, but when the time came, he provided the leadership that the struggle for equality had always needed from the White House.

When President Johnson faced the nation in his first address after the assassination and said, "Let us continue," the meaning was clear. Almost despite himself, defying his own calculations, at his death Jack Kennedy had already become identified with the universal aspirations that are elusive to so many. Had he been given more than a thousand days, there is no telling how far he might have gone in that direction. Much depended on what he thought the American people would accept.

He was, finally, a moderate conservative and a rational idealist. Above all Jack Kennedy, trained to be a politician, was a politician. His self-discipline, combined with hereditary assets, had taken him far. His life, his rise to power, and the White House years reflect his struggle to govern in a democratic society. During his brief period in the White House he established a new style and tone for the presidency, one that evoked national pride and hope. That made his limitations all the more painful.

Document
Inaugural Address, January 20, 1961

JOHN F. KENNEDY

We observe today not a victory of party but a celebration of freedom—symbolizing an end as well as a beginning—signifying renewal as well as change. For I have sworn before you and Almighty God the same solemn oath our forebears prescribed nearly a century and three quarters ago.

The world is very different now. For man holds in his mortal hands the power to abolish all forms of human poverty and all forms of human life. And yet the same revolutionary beliefs for which our forebears fought are still at issue around the globe—the belief that the rights of man come not from the generosity of the state but from the hand of God.

We dare not forget today that we are the heirs of that first revolution. Let the word go forth from this time and place, to friend and foe alike, that the torch has been passed to a new generation of Americans—born in this century, tempered by war, disciplined by a hard and bitter peace, proud of our ancient heritage—and unwilling to witness or permit the slow undoing of those human rights to which this nation has always been committed, and to which we are committed today at home and around the world.

Let every nation know, whether it wishes us well or ill, that we shall pay any price, bear any burden, meet any hardship, support any friend, oppose any foe to assure the survival and the success of liberty.

This much we pledge—and more.

To those old allies whose cultural and spiritual origins we share, we pledge the loyalty of faithful friends. United, there is little we cannot do in a host of cooperative ventures. Divided, there is little we can do—for we dare not meet a powerful challenge at odds and split asunder.

To those new states whom we welcome to the ranks of the free, we pledge our word that one form of colonial control shall not have passed away merely to be replaced by a far more iron tyranny. We shall not always expect to find them supporting our view. But we shall always hope to find them strongly supporting their own freedom—and to remember that, in the past, those who foolishly sought power by riding the back of the tiger ended up inside.

To those peoples in the huts and villages of half the globe struggling to break the bonds of mass misery, we pledge our best efforts to help them help themselves, for whatever period is required—not because the communists may be doing it, not because we seek their votes, but because it is right. If a free society cannot help the many who are poor, it cannot save the few who are rich.

To our sister republics south of our border, we offer a special pledge—to convert our good words into good deeds—in a new alliance for progress—

From *Public Papers of the Presidents of the United States: John F. Kennedy, 1961*, pp. 1–3.

to assist free men and free governments in casting off the chains of poverty. But this peaceful revolution of hope cannot become the prey of hostile powers. Let all our neighbors know that we shall join with them to oppose aggression or subversion anywhere in the Americas. And let every other power know that this Hemisphere intends to remain the master of its own house.

To that world assembly of sovereign states, the United Nations, our last best hope in an age where the instruments of war have far outpaced the instruments of peace, we renew our pledge of support—to prevent it from becoming merely a forum for invective—to strengthen its shield of the new and the weak—and to enlarge the area in which its writ may run.

Finally, to those nations who would make themselves our adversary, we offer not a pledge but a request: that both sides begin anew the quest for peace, before the dark powers of destruction unleashed by science engulf all humanity in planned or accidental self-destruction.

We dare not tempt them with weakness. For only when our arms are sufficient beyond doubt can we be certain beyond doubt that they will never be employed.

But neither can two great and powerful groups of nations take comfort from our present course—both sides overburdened by the cost of modern weapons, both rightly alarmed by the steady spread of the deadly atom, yet both racing to alter that uncertain balance of terror that stays the hand of mankind's final war.

So let us begin anew—remembering on both sides that civility is not a sign of weakness, and sincerity is always subject to proof. Let us never negotiate out of fear. But let us never fear to negotiate.

Let both sides explore what problems unite us instead of belaboring those problems which divide us.

Let both sides, for the first time, formulate serious and precise proposals for the inspection and control of arms—and bring the absolute power to destroy other nations under the absolute control of all nations.

Let both sides seek to invoke the wonders of science instead of its terrors. Together let us explore the stars, conquer the deserts, eradicate disease, tap the ocean depths and encourage the arts and commerce.

Let both sides unite to heed in all corners of the earth the command of Isaiah—to "undo the heavy burdens . . . (and) let the oppressed go free."

And if a beach-head of cooperation may push back the jungle of suspicion, let both sides join in creating a new endeavor, not a new balance of power, but a new world of law where the strong are just and the weak secure and the peace preserved.

All this will not be finished in the first one hundred days. Nor will it be finished in the first one thousand days, nor in the life of this Administration, nor even perhaps in our lifetime on this planet. But let us begin.

In your hands, my fellow citizens, more than mine, will rest the final success or failure of our course. Since this country was founded, each generation of Americans has been summoned to give testimony to its national loyalty. The graves of young Americans who answered the call to service surround the globe.

Now the trumpet summons us again — not as a call to bear arms, though arms we need — not as a call to battle, though embattled we are — but a call to bear the burden of a long twilight struggle, year in and year out, "rejoicing in hope, patient in tribulation"—a struggle against the common enemies of man: tyranny, poverty, disease and war itself.

Can we forge against these enemies a grand and global alliance, North and South, East and West, that can assure a more fruitful life for all mankind? Will you join in that historic effort?

In the long history of the world, only a few generations have been granted the role of defending freedom in its hour of maximum danger. I do not shrink from this responsibility — I welcome it. I do not believe that any of us would exchange places with any other people or any other generation. The energy, the faith, the devotion which we bring to this endeavor will light our country and all who serve it — and the glow from that fire can truly light the world.

And so, my fellow Americans: ask not what your country can do for you — ask what you can do for your country.

My fellow citizens of the world: ask not what America will do for you, but what together we can do for the freedom of man.

Finally, whether you are citizens of America or citizens of the world, ask of us here the same high standards of strength and sacrifice which we ask of you. With a good conscience our only sure reward, with history the final judge of our deeds, let us go forth to lead the land we love, asking His blessing and His help, but knowing that here on earth God's work must truly be our own.

seven

LYNDON B. JOHNSON AND THE GREAT SOCIETY

Lyndon Johnson was the most effective political leader in post–World War II America. First a congressman, then a senator, and finally vice president under John Kennedy, he assumed the presidency after JFK's assassination in 1963. Almost immediately, Johnson moved to push Kennedy's programs to passage, and, with his reelection in 1964, he proclaimed his own vision of the "Great Society" the United States could become.

Johnson was extraordinarily successful. His legislative record was the most impressive since the New Deal of FDR. There was something for everyone — laws passed mandated a tax cut, protected civil rights, provided aid to education, established a medicare system, and reformed immigration policy. Johnson had reason to be proud, but even before his commitment to protect South Vietnam intruded on his domestic program, the Great Society came under attack. Conservatives felt that it went too far; radicals argued compellingly that it failed to go far enough.

In "From the Great Society to Black Power," Frederick F. Siegel describes Johnson and his unique approach to the presidency. He shows how LBJ moved quickly to assert his legitimacy after the assassination and then marshaled support for his own program once reelected in his own right. Underscoring the triumphs, Siegel also notes the seeds of discontent.

Tom Hayden was one of Johnson's critics in the 1960s. Committed to the social and political transformation of the United States. Hayden charged that little meaningful progress was being made. In "Welfare Liberalism and Social Change," which appeared first in *Dissent* (1966), Hayden argues that the Great Society welfare state "is more machinery than substance." Piece-meal improvements, he suggests, undermine the prospects for real reform.

Johnson's own commitment to social reform appears in a speech he delivered in May 1964 at the University of Michigan. In it, he spells out for the first time his full vision of the Great Society and defines the framework for the legislative initiatives of the next few years.

To follow the Great Society further, Doris Kearns, *Lyndon Johnson and the American Dream* (1976), is a good starting point. Journalists Rowland Evans, Jr., and Robert Novak provide a useful assessment of the early years of Johnson's presidency in *Lyndon B. Johnson: The Exercise of Power* (1966). Sar A. Levitan and Robert Taggart's *The Promise of Greatness* (1976), a detailed account of Great Society programs, argues that goals were realistic and progress was made. Eric Goldman, *The Tragedy of Lyndon Johnson* (1969), is the personal view of a historian who worked in the White House. *The Vantage Point: Perspectives of the Presidency* (1971) is Johnson's own account of the presidential years, but it lacks the vividness of his personal approach.

From the Great Society to Black Power

FREDERICK F. SIEGEL

On November 22, 1963, in the same plane that carried the slain chief executive's body back to Washington, Lyndon Baines Johnson was sworn in as the thirty-sixth President of the United States. Lyndon Johnson was a Rabelaisian, larger-than-life figure. A tall man from Texas, a state with a reputation for producing outsized characters, Johnson had the face of a riverboat gambler and the political skills of a master politician. He was only ten years older than Kennedy, but he came from a different generation and a different world. A product of Depression era poverty, Johnson's political views had been shaped in part by his political hero, Franklin Delano Roosevelt. Styling himself after FDR, Johnson liked to be called LBJ. If Kennedy had been born with a silver spoon in his mouth, Johnson grew up with the taste of dirt in his. He came from the desperately poor hill country of West Texas. "When I was young," Johnson told reporters, "poverty was so common that we didn't know it had a name."

A self-made man, Johnson fought his way to the top of the Texas political heap. A man of wildly conflicting impulses, he was driven on the one hand by greed and an unquenchable thirst for success and on the other by a genuine concern for the plight of those who had shared his childhood poverty. Johnson's Texas was a one-party state. The Democratic Party in Texas was a circus tent organization that included everyone from right to left, from business big and little to labor, blacks, and Mexican-Americans. The key to success in that situation was to create a consensus everyone could live with. Johnson became a master of using his extraordinary persuasive skills to engineer agreement between diverse interests. Elected to Congress in 1937, he made his mark bringing together within the Democratic Party rapacious nouveau riche Texas oil millionaires and conscious-stricken Northern liberals whose political divisions paralleled those of his own vast personality. He was elected to the Senate in 1948 by the narrowest of margins, leading his detractors to joke about "Landslide Lyndon." But once there, he rose, with the support of his fellow Texan and mentor, Speaker of the House Sam Rayburn, to become Majority Leader of the Senate in 1955 after serving only one term.

Johnson became one of the most powerful and effective Majority Leaders the Hill has ever known. He was an overpowering figure with the psychic energy of a natural phenomenon. When a congressman was asked why he had changed his mind on a key vote, he answered: "Well, it's this way. Lyndon got me by the lapels and put his face on top of mine and talked and talked and talked. I figured it was either getting drowned or joining." Extremely intelligent without being an intellectual, he was a reader of men, not books. Johnson, as an English reporter described it, "comes into a room slowly and warily, as if he means to smell out the allegiances of everyone in it." He combined a rare ability to look inside his fellow politicians with a near-photographic memory for details, so that, as one aide put it, "not a sparrow falls on Capitol Hill" without LBJ knowing.

The Kennedy loyalists and intellectuals were among the few who seemed totally immune to his political sway. They viewed the roughhewn Johnson as a boor and a usurper, much as FDR's retinue looked down on the man from Missouri, Harry S. Truman. For the Kennedyites, brother Bobby was the true heir to the throne, so that the Johnson presidency was simply an unfortunate interregnum. Kennedy's intellectual camp followers were exhilarated by a President who brought taste to the White House and recognition for them. Enthralled by the magic of Camelot, "they received his words and images," said literary critic Alfred Kazin, "as children 'read' the pictures in a storybook." Johnson, on the other hand, reminded intellectuals of what the rest of the country was like. He reminded us of who we were—and some, said Richard Whalen, conceived their dislike of him in that moment.

For his part, Johnson brushed aside the snubs and moved quickly to calm the nation by proclaiming his intent to carry on Kennedy's noble mission. As powerful as he was, Johnson was somewhat in awe of his Ivy League advisers, something that worried Rayburn. After an obviously impressed Johnson recited the extraordinary academic credentials of his Cabinet, the Speaker snorted, "I just wish one of them had been elected anything, even deputy sheriff."

To prove he was worthy of the office and not just another parochial Southerner, Johnson moved quickly to push Kennedy's civil rights legislation, long blocked by his fellow Dixie politicians. As Johnson explained it: "If I didn't get out in front of this issue" the liberals "would get me . . . I had to produce a civil rights bill that was even stronger than the one they'd have gotten if Kennedy had lived." And produce he did. Defying all the writers, politicians, and analysts who spoke of the "deadlock of democracy," Johnson used his unparalleled skills to break the Southern filibuster. He pushed through Congress the most sweeping civil rights legislation since the end of the First Reconstruction. The 1964 Civil Rights Act, described by Supreme Court Justice Arthur Goldberg as "the vindication of human dignity," became the cornerstone of civil rights law. It provided legal and financial support for cities desegregating their schools, banned discrimination by businesses and unions, created an Equal Opportunities Commission to enforce that ban, and outlawed discrimination in places of public accommodation.

With the Civil Rights Act passed and his own legitimacy established, Johnson turned to putting his own stamp on the presidency. Declaring, "We are not helpless before the iron law of [traditional] economics," Johnson called for a "War on Poverty" as Kennedy had called for a war on Communism.

The "War," wrote *Time* magazine, reflected the "uniquely American belief" that "evangelism, money and organization can lick just about anything." Americans generally believed that "a rising tide lifts all boats," but a spate of books on poverty, particularly Michael Harrington's powerful *The Other America*, showed that a substantial number of Americans, black and white, silently suffered from such serious deprivation that they would be unaided by the general prosperity. The very poor, argued anthropologist Oscar Lewis, were trapped in a culture of poverty, a culture which, in the words of Harrington, meant that "the poor are not like us. . . . They are a different kind of people."

Social science promised a way to reach the culturally distant world of severe poverty. On assuming the presidency Johnson inherited an economic growth rate that had more than doubled from 2.1 percent to 4.5 percent since 1960 and which, with mild inflation, was pouring extraordinary amounts of money into federal coffers. This "social surplus," the excess of revenues over expenditures, provided nearly four billion dollars a year for new public spending. The flow of money was so great that Governor Earl Long of Louisiana whimsically suggested massive spending for two highway systems, one reserved for drunks. Johnson's economic advisers assured him that the unprecedented surpluses would continue indefinitely. Pointing to the great success of the 1964 tax cut, which seemed to demonstrate their ability to put their theories into practice, the "new" economists claimed that, through Keynesian "demand management," they had discovered the secret of constant noninflationary growth. In short, the continuing surplus created by "demand management" meant that poverty could be abolished without undue sacrifice from the rest of the population. There would be a "maximum of reform with a minimum of social disruption."

While the economists were guiding the fiscal ship of state, their fellow experts, the sociologists, devised programs to provide the poor with nutritional aid, health and schooling benefits, job training, and even dignity and respect. The programs were institutionalized as part of Johnson's Economic Opportunity Act of 1964. The act appropriated nearly a billion dollars for projects such as the Head Start program to assist disadvantaged preschoolers, the Job Corps for high school dropouts, a domestic Peace Corps — Volunteers in Service to America (VISTA) — a Neighborhood Youth Corps, and a Community Action Program designed for the "maximum feasible participation" by the poor it was meant to aid.

Flushed by his legislative successes, LBJ headed into the 1964 presidential campaign by asking for even broader social measures as part of what he called "The Great Society." Like Kennedy's New Frontier, the Great Society was a presidential answer to the quest for national and thus in many cases individual purpose in an increasingly secular age. It was to be the fulfillment of the American creed of equal opportunity — a grand mobilization of expertise, this time to fight poverty and disease, as depression, fascism, and Communism had been fought previously. In LBJ's own inspiring words: "This nation . . . has man's first chance to create a Great Society: a society of success without squalor, beauty without barrenness, of genius without the wretchedness of poverty. We can open the doors of learning. We can open the doors of opportunity and closed community — not just to the privileged few, but, thank God, we can open doors to everyone." Rhetoric (glorious though it was) aside, Johnson's proposals for a Great Society hinged on passing a twenty-five-year backlog of liberal Democratic legislation on health, education, racial discrimination, and conservation that had been sitting on the rear burner ever since the New Deal flame was snuffed out by the Republican/ Dixiecrat coalition in 1937.

The Great Society program, which vested vast new powers in the federal government, promised to rearrange the relationship between Washington and the rest of the nation. For American liberals the growth of federal power meant the chance to complete the racial reforms begun by Reconstruction and the economic reforms begun by the New Deal without a fundamental restructuring of American society. But for many others, those who "understood the American creed, not as a common set of national values, but as a justification for their particular set of local values," the Great Society proved to be deeply unsettling. Their fears, however, were never fully aired, nor was Johnson given the chance to build a national consensus for the Great Society, because Barry Goldwater, his opponent in 1964, gave LBJ the enormous advantage of running as a social reformer while still seeming to be the less radical of the two.

Johnson's Republican opposition came from a group of youth activists deeply opposed to American policies in Vietnam and bitterly hostile to what they called the "Establishment," symbolized by Nelson Rockefeller. Their movement was directed by Stephen Shadeg, who had been heavily influenced by the thought and tactics of Chairman Mao. Their candidate, described by conservative William Buckley as one of "the few genuine radicals in American life," was Barry Morris Goldwater, junior senator from Arizona.

The Goldwater movement was built on the strength of the old Taftite right, the "veterans of the thirty years' war with the New Deal." Like Taft, Goldwater would say, "Yes, I fear Washington, more than I fear Moscow." But most of all Goldwater feared what he saw as Moscow's influence in Washington, so that as a first-term senator he was one of the diehards who opposed the censure of McCarthy after almost the entire Senate had turned against the demagogue from Wisconsin. The old right had been repeatedly defeated, in its struggle to control the Republican Party, by what it called the Eastern establishment, otherwise known as the "two-bit New Dealers" or "me-too Republicans." But in 1964 the Goldwater movement defeated the Rockefeller Republicans by mobilizing two new political elements: nouveau riche anti-union oilmen and aerospace men of the Southwest, and ideologically charged conservative youth.

Like their left-wing counterparts, these young conservatives disdained the soft society of welfarism with all its compromises and government paternalism. They complained of a "sickness in our society and the lack of a common purpose" that might "restore inner meaning to every man's life in a time too often rushed, too often obsessed with petty needs and material greeds." Contemptuous of businessmen who placed profit before free market ethics, they dreamed of a world made whole by the heroic deeds of rugged individuals untrammeled by the heavy hand of the state. Their allies, the Texas oilmen and aerospace entrepreneurs, however, were beneficiaries of vast government subsidies such as the oil-depletion allowance. But both were united in their hostility to the Rockefeller wing of the Republican Party. And both subscribed to the notion that only a laissez-faire economy could create the disciplined individuals with the character and fortitude necessary to sustain democracy. Politics for the activists was not so much a matter of pursuing material interests as a national screen on which to project their deepest cultural fears. They were part of a mood, a mood of deluxe puritanism, as much as an ideology, and in the words of Richard Whalen, "Barry Goldwater was the favorite son of their state of mind."

But even with his activists and oilmen, Goldwater, like Taft before him, might have lost the nomination if it hadn't been for the first nationwide stirrings of a white backlash against the civil rights movement. Interest in Goldwater was flagging when Alabama's Governor George Wallace, a flaming segregationist, made a surprising showing in liberal Wisconsin's Democratic primary. The Wallace showing revived interest in Goldwater, who was seen as the Republican most opposed to federal intervention on behalf of Afro-Americans. When Goldwater was nominated, Wallace's candidacy collapsed, suggesting a considerable overlap in the two men's donors and constituencies. Tall, trim, and handsome, the altogether affable Goldwater was not personally a bigot. A member of the NAACP, Goldwater was the kind of terribly sincere fellow everyone likes to have for a neighbor or fraternity brother. He came to popular attention by spearheading congressional criticism of Walter Reuther and by his outspoken calls for a holy crusade against Communism in general and Castro in particular. But as Goldwater told reporter Joseph Alsop: "You know, I haven't really got a first-class brain." And it showed. His combination of bland and outrageous statements alienated all but the right wing of the Republican Party from his candidacy. He could in the same speech assert that "where fraternities are not allowed, Communism flourishes" and then, warming to his message, suggest that nuclear weapons be used against Cuba, China, and North Vietnam if they refused to accede to American demands. Goldwater was unafraid of voicing unpopular views. He called for the abolition of the TVA, an end to the graduated income tax, and the elimination of Social Security, while campaigning forthrightly for the elimination of the union shop. "My aim," he said, "is not to pass laws but to repeal them." Here, in the words of Phyllis Schlafly, was "a choice and not an echo."

There was really no need for Johnson to criticize Goldwater's campaign for being too radical. Goldwater did it for him, proclaiming on national TV that "extremism in the defense of liberty is no vice." When the Goldwaterites adopted the slogan "In your hearts you know he's right," Democrats responded with "In your guts you know he's nuts." Johnson replied to Goldwater's "no substitute for victory" rhetoric on Vietnam with a proclamation of restraint. "We are not," LBJ told the American people, "about to send

American boys nine or ten thousand miles from home to do what Asian boys ought to be doing for themselves." It is a virtual replay of the Truman-Mac-Arthur struggle, with the same outcome.

With the successful focusing of the campaign on Goldwater's artless "shoot from the lip" pronouncements—"The child has no right to an education; in most cases he will get along very well without it"—Johnson's own measures at home and abroad went undebated. It was a curious consequence of the 1964 campaign that the fundamental issues raised by both Johnson's social innovations and Goldwater's ideological thrust went almost unnoticed, producing a curiously empty campaign which ironically denied Johnson the opportunity to build support for the Great Society. The consensus that emerged instead was that Barry Goldwater was unfit for office. The reaction to Goldwater was so broadly negative that the party which once denounced "economic royalists" now found Wall Street and big business flocking to its banner. Johnson attracted the nation's corporate elite in creating what Oscar Gass has called a Grossblock, a coalition of upper-middle-class professionals and lower-middle-class blue-collar workers, big business and labor, Catholics and Protestants, blacks and whites outside the Deep South, in a national replication of the Texas Democratic Party's "one big tent."

LBJ swept to victory with 61 percent of the vote, only 5 points short of doubling Goldwater's total. The Democrats gained 2 seats in the Senate and 37 in the House, creating enormous Democratic majorities.

LBJ's victory was so overwhelming that commentators openly speculated about the impending death of both conservatism and the Republican Party. We are left, said one observer, with a "one and a half party system." But an analysis of local voting patterns revealed something very different. On a host of social issues, ranging from prayer in the public schools to calls for cutting federal expenditures and reducing welfare spending, the electorate was far closer to Goldwater than to Johnson. Goldwater the candidate was repudiated, but on a local level conservatism was intact and even thriving. In California, for instance, areas which went strongly for LBJ also voted to repeal the state's anti-discriminatory fair housing laws by a better than two-to-one margin. Similarly, in Maryland, areas which had supported George Wallace when he made his strong showing in the Democratic primary there went overwhelmingly for LBJ in the general election. These Maryland voters were in favor of the civil rights bill even as they feared black militancy.

Goldwater's defeat was of such proportion that ironically it served to break the hold conservative Democrats held over their own party. So many Northern liberals triumphed in congressional races against Republicans "dragged down by Barry" that for the first time the Democrats had clear majorities in both houses without having to rely on their Dixiecrat allies. On the other hand, Goldwater, by piggybacking his right-to-work rhetoric on George Wallace's states' rights racism, had carried the Deep South, breaking the Democrats' century-long hold over that region. And while the Goldwater campaign rhetoric was most noted for its fire-eating foreign policy, it was

Goldwater's appeal to the white backlash against black militancy that had garnered most of his votes North and South.

Lyndon Johnson was keenly aware that the American political system's balance of powers had been designed for stalemate. As a young congressman, he had seen FDR, at the height of his power, humbled when he tried to pack the Supreme Court. Johnson realized that unless he moved quickly to take advantage of his landslide victory, the naturally parochial tendencies of the Congress would block his Great Society initiatives. Johnson moved rapidly to circumvent the established interests in Congress. Instead of asking congress-men for legislative proposals, he organized task forces composed of adminis-tration aides and social reform academics to draw up legislation which would then be presented to the sachems as a fait accompli. Or as LBJ put it to his aides, "I want to see a whole bunch of coonskins on the wall."

The programs Johnson deemed most important were Medicare to pro-tect the elderly from catastrophic losses and aid to elementary education to upgrade the schooling for both black and white poor. Legislation for Medicare and aid to elementary education had been proposed by Democrats ever since the mid-1940s but had always met fierce opposition from the American Medical Association and proponents of states' rights. Johnson knew that if he won on these two issues, "the momentum," as historian Jim Heath has put it, "would carry over, making it relatively easy to enact the rest of his legislative program." As before, the powerful AMA put up a tenacious fight against any form of federally guaranteed health insurance for the elderly, portraying it as a step on the road to socialized medicine. But Johnson, aided by the wily Wilbur Mills, of the House Ways and Means Committee, not only got Medi-care passed; in a little-noticed maneuver, Medicaid, health care for the indi-gent, was tacked on. LBJ flew to Independence, Missouri, to sign the bill in front of a smiling Harry S. Truman. On January 12, 1965, only five days after the Medicare legislation was approved, LBJ sent the politically explosive aid to elementary education bill to the Congress. Part and parcel of the War on Poverty, the bill was opposed by Protestant fundamentalists who wanted to deny federal money to the Catholic schools and by segregationists who saw Washington's money as the beginning of federal control over local schools. Here Johnson, aided by Senator Wayne Morse, achieved what the senator called a "back-door victory," by overtly ignoring racial and religious ques-tions in order to target money regionally on the basis of population below the poverty level in a given area.

With Medicare and aid to education passed, Johnson moved quickly to complete what critics called his "revolution from above." If the word "revolu-tion" was overblown, the critics were right to see that LBJ made unprece-dented use of the federal budget. "No previous budget had ever been so contrived to do something for every major economic interest in the nation." But LBJ offered something for almost all his supporters: tax cuts for big business; billions of dollars for Appalachian social and economic development; the first major additions to our national parks and the first comprehensive air and water pollution standards for environmentalists; truth in packaging legislation for consumers; federal aid for mass transit for city dwellers; a subsidy boost for farmers; a National Arts and Humanities Foundation for academics; and, in LBJ's own words, "the goddamnedest toughest voting rights act" and Model Cities, low-cost housing, job-training programs, and slum clearance for blacks. At the end of this spate of legislation, the Democratic leadership on the Hill spoke jubilantly of the "fabulous 89th" Congress as "the Congress of fulfillment," "the Congress of accomplished hopes," "the Congress of realized dreams."

In the words of liberal policy analyst Sar Levitan, a great deal of LBJ's agenda involved "unabashedly class legislation . . . designating a special group in the population as eligible to receive the benefits of American law." Class legislation was nothing new in American politics—federal insurance for overseas corporate investments and the mortgage tax deduction for homeowners are examples. What was different about the Great Society was that it extended such special benefits to those who were least well off. Johnson's left-wing critics complained that in order to aid the poor, his legislation provided a windfall for a multitude of contractors and middlemen who ultimately were the greatest beneficiaries. There is a good deal of truth to this charge. The doctors who fought Medicaid so bitterly were to number among its prime beneficiaries. Building contractors often became wealthy through Model Cities renewal efforts. This said, however, it is unlikely that any of the legislation directed at alleviating poverty could have passed a Congress composed of men representing American business and middle-class interests unless they too were cut in on federal largess.

Johnson, the adventurous conservative, was denounced as a "Red" by fiscal conservatives and simply a pork-barrel New Dealer by leftists, but both charges were wide of the mark. The New Deal was designed to aid widows, orphans, and the indigent; in short, it represented help for those worst off without addressing the underlying issues of social fairness. The Great Society, without being socialist, tried to partially redefine the structure of opportunity in America. Its aim was not simply to provide handouts to the poor; rather, it attempted to make the competitive race of life a bit fairer. The Great Society had a dramatic effect in relieving poverty. From 1964 to 1968 more than 14 million Americans moved out of poverty as the proportion of the impoverished was halved from 22 to 11 percent of the nation. Just as FDR's New Deal had incorporated working-class immigrants and organized them into the mainstream of American life, LBJ's Great Society tried to do the same for blacks and the poverty-stricken.

By 1945 black demands for civil rights had become undeniable. The reasoned and dignified struggle for full citizenship, pursued with great courage and nobility, evoked widespread admiration. The black leadership and particularly Dr. King came to be revered by liberals eager to atone for past failings and awed by King's combination of shrewdness and moral grandeur. With formal freedoms attained, the focus shifted to the equivalent of the nineteenth century's "forty acres and a mule" — that is, to economic citizenship, and in particular to the problems of the Northern ghettos, where, in the words of Martin Luther King, there was the threat of "social catastrophe."

In June 1965 Lyndon Johnson was an uncrowned monarch at the height of his power. Respected, if not idolized, by liberals who found him too vulgar, he enjoyed an extraordinary sway over Congress, and the country enjoyed an unprecedented prosperity. The initial agenda for the Great Society had been nearly completed, and amid projections of greater budget surpluses to come there were promises of even more sweeping social programs. It seemed that the small war raging in Asia could be brought to a successful conclusion. On June 4, 1965, Johnson, responding to fears about the social disintegration of the black city slums, gave a memorable address at Howard University, an address that records the highwater mark of the possibilities for an American social democracy. Referring to the Voting Rights Act, which was generally taken to be the keystone of civil rights legislation, Johnson declared that it was not an end but a beginning: "Freedom is not enough. You do not wipe away the scars of centuries by saying, 'Now you are free to go where you want, do as you desire' . . . You do not take a person who for years has been hobbled by chains and liberate him, bring him up to the starting line of a race and say, 'You are free to compete with all the others,' and still believe that you have been completely fair." "The country," he said, "had to move beyond opportunity to achievement. . . . This is the next and more profound stage of the battle for civil rights. We do not seek just freedom, but opportunity. Not just equality as a right and theory, but equality as fact and as result."

On August 6, LBJ signed legislation for a comprehensive voting rights bill whose sweep and enforcement powers were barely dreamed of a decade earlier. On August 9, large-scale rioting broke out in Watts, the black section of Los Angeles. Remarkably enough and unrealized at the time, Johnson's kingdom had begun to crumble. . . .

The 1966 mid-term congressional elections revealed just how much the nation's anti-poverty effort owed to the Goldwater debacle which allowed LBJ to ram major reforms through the Congress. The grass-roots opposition to statism and extensive social welfare programs was undiminished even when the Great Society rode high in the Washington saddle. When the moral logic of civil rights and the political pressures produced by the riots led the government to impose itself on the organization of life at the local level through fair housing and school integration measures, hometown conservatism moved back into the national arena and the groundwork was laid for a right-wing revival.

The Republicans, implying that Johnson's poverty programs were largely responsible for the riots, turned the election into a referendum on the Great Society and "crime in the streets." House Republican leader Gerald R. Ford captured the tone of the campaign when he asked, "How long are we going to abdicate law and order — the backbone of civilization — in favor of a social theory that the man who heaves a brick through your window is simply the misunderstood and underprivileged product of a broken home?" It was a theme that played brilliantly on the resentments of white urban ethnics who were angered by the way the riots, which often took place on the edge of their neighborhoods, produced more financial rewards than arrests. But it was the "theories" that Ford referred to, the tendency of guilt-ridden reformers to rationalize all black demands, which infuriated urban ethnics most and threatened to divide the Democratic Party between low-income "bread and butter" white Democrats trapped in the burning cities and the New Politics heirs of the Stevensonian tradition of high-minded reform.

The elections were a disaster for the Democrats. Forty-five members of the House who had supported the poverty programs lost their seats, "an emphatic message to the survivors." The GOP gained 47 seats in the House and 3 in the Senate, while the balance in the statehouses shifted from a 33 – 17 Democratic advantage to an even split. Most unnerving for liberals was that longtime civil rights advocate Senator Paul Douglas of Illinois was defeated by a "determined" white rebellion against "open occupancy housing." The election brought forth a panoply of new conservative spokesmen, including Ronald Reagan, who became governor of California in a landslide. Reagan had directed his campaign against welfare chiselers and big government.

The political meaning of the election was obscured, however, because it was soon overshadowed by the increasingly unpopular war in Vietnam and the spectacular efflorescence of the "youth culture."

Welfare Liberalism and Social Change

TOM HAYDEN

Americans find it unthinkable that their country can be corrupt at the center, guilty as a society of inhuman behavior. This is true even among American reformers, most of whom hold that discrimination, poverty, and foreign intervention are simply flaws in a generally humanitarian record. While the massacre of the Vietnamese grinds on, while Negro uprisings spread to every city, while the public looks back on August 6 as Luci's wedding and Hiroshima is forgotten, the progressive American — he may be a liberal businessman, university president, technical assistance expert, or trade unionist — is perhaps uneasy but remains basically complacent, secure in the justness of our objectives at home and abroad.

From Tom Hayden "Welfare Liberalism and Social Change," in *The Great Society Reader: The Failure of American Liberalism*, edited by Marvin E. Gettleman and David Mermelstein. Copyright © 1966 by Tom Hayden. Reprinted by permission of Random House, Inc.

Since early in the century, the task of American leaders has been to make "peace," "self-determination" and the promise of a better life the language that explains American purposes. Probably none of them has ever willfully deprived a man of food or killed another in cold blood; they order political and economic suppression and murder — by gas, napalm, or nuclear weapons — only as a means of realizing peace and preserving democracy.

Until the day their language changes to that of naked power, it is easy to assume they are not fiends but honorable men. This is the assumption that makes reformers hope for their country. But it is sheer indulgence not to confront the consequences of our leaders' actions. We need to stop giving weight to protestations of good intentions, and to examine instead the worth of American words in the light of American deeds.

The general contradiction most worth examining is between the philosophy and the practice of the liberal – welfare state that has been constructed at home and is now being forcibly exported to other parts of the world. It is the belief in our commitment to welfare that, more than anything else, allows our honorable men to sleep at night while other men are murdered, jailed or hungry.

The legitimacy gained by the industrial unions, the welfare legislation passed in the thirties and forties, and now the civil rights and antipoverty reforms of the sixties — these are seen as part of a long sweep toward a society of economic and social justice. But there is, in fact, little evidence to justify the view that the social reforms of the past thirty years actually improved the quality of American life in a lasting way, and there is much evidence which suggests that many of the reforms gained were illusory or token, serving chiefly to sharpen the capacity of the system for manipulation and oppression.

Look closely at the social legislation upon which the notion of domestic improvement is based. The Wagner Act was supposed to effect unionization of workers; but today the unionized labor force is shrinking with the automation of the mass-production industries, and millions of other workers, never organized, are without protection. The Social Security laws were supposed to support people in distress, but today many are still not covered, and those who are solely dependent on Social Security payments cannot make ends meet. Unemployment compensation policies were supposed to aid men in need of jobs, but today many are still without coverage, while benefits represent a smaller and smaller share of the cost of living. The Employment Act of 1946 was supposed to guarantee federal action to provide a job for every American who needed one, but in 1966 the official (understated) unemployment rate is close to 5 per cent, and may be over 30 per cent for young men in the ghettos. The 1949 Public Housing Act, sponsored by conservative Robert Taft, was to create 800,000 low-cost units by 1953, but today less than half that number have been constructed, and many of them are beyond reach of the poor. The difficult struggle to enact even a token policy of public medical care, the hollow support for public education, the stagnation and starvation of broader programs for health, recreation and simple city services — all this suggests that the welfare state is more machinery than substance.

The trend is *toward*, not away from, increased racial segregation and division, greater unemployment for Negroes than whites, worse educational facilities in the slums, less job security for whites, fewer doctors for nearly everyone: in essence, the richest society in all history places increasing pressures on its "have nots" despite all talk of the "welfare state" and "Great Society." The real subsidies go to the housebuilders, farmers, businessmen, scholars, while comparatively, there are only scraps for the poor. The welfare recipient who cannot purchase decent furniture will not take much comfort in knowing she is one of the "richest" poor people in the world. America's expanding affluence is still built on a system of deep inequalities. . . .

Seen in this context, the 1965 antipoverty program should evoke little optimism. The amount of money allotted is a pittance, and most of it is going to local politicians, school boards, welfare agencies, housing authorities, professional personnel and even the police; its main thrust is to shore up sagging organizational machinery, not to offer the poor a more equitable share of income and influence. Meaningful involvement of the poor is frustrated by the poverty planners' allegiance to existing local power centers. In reality, the poor only flavor the program. A few are co-opted into it, but only as atomized individuals. They do not have independent organizational strength, as do the machines and social agencies.

Some of the more sophisticated poverty planners believe that the involvement of the poor is essential to effective programs; thus the heavy emphasis on, and debate about, the need for "maximum feasible participation" of the poor. This policy concept rests upon the conviction that the modern poor cannot be socialized upward and into the mainstream of American life in the tradition of the earlier immigrants. . . .

Many of the poverty planners concede that progress will involve some element of conflict and that the poor cannot be painlessly assimilated into the greater society. The feeling is that change can be accomplished through a "dialogue" between the poor and the powerful, in which the poor assert their needs as clearly as necessary. But while dialogue is promoted, final decisions remain in traditional hands. Sargent Shriver encourages "representative neighborhood advisory organizations" to give "advice on programs," which can then be "channeled" to the community action agency. This is all Shriver sees as necessary to give neighborhood people "an effective voice in the conduct and administration of neighborhood-based programs."

The poverty program, in short, assumes the poor are groups of damaged individuals who need charity, relief, technical aid, or retraining. What the program cannot accept is the possibility that the poor are "natives" pitted against "colonial" structures at home that exclude and exploit them. . . .

Welfare liberalism has brought new insecurities to the American exploited. The poor are without the effective ability to control any economic resources in the welfare state. Antipoverty funds are controlled "from above" by city or federal officials. There is no unionization of tenants or welfare clients to provide financing and protection. Unable to gather independent capital from the public sector, the poor are considered unqualified for credit by banks and lending institutions. This lack of meaningful economic power divides the contemporary poor from earlier immigrant generations, who entered an expanding economy and formed unions and co-ops to advance their interests. Lacking any security or power, the "left out" whites and the poor Negroes are more likely to vote for their "masters"—those who control the public housing, welfare, and unemployment checks—or not vote at all, rather than risk an independent political initiative.

The "colonial power" maintains control of the ghetto from the outside, through the police, social agencies, and a cultivated group of colonized natives ("Uncle Toms"). The idea is conveyed, by every means, that only the governors are qualified to govern, that the only chance for self-gain, even survival, lies in trying to be like the governors, that protest is a sign of maladjustment and furthermore can never succeed. This colonialism is as real as the more traditional colonialism of Britain and France, despite our official national ideology of equality. . . .

One way of understanding the welfare state is through its processes of institutionalized reform. Perhaps because of its Madisonian political traditions or its prosperity, America allows substantial dissent, as shown, for example, in the history of the labor or civil rights movements. Yet there are profound continuities that the tradition of dissent has not interrupted significantly: private corporation privilege, imperialist intervention abroad, racial and class prejudice. Reform seems to follow a typical pattern, challenging the society for a time but always adjusting to these status quo facts.

In the postwar period, reformers have tended to be of two types. The first are the professionals, men located in government agencies, teaching, journalism, law, social work. The second are the activists, located in reform, civil rights, and labor politics. Their types often blend, for instance, as former civil rights activists take desk jobs in the War on Poverty, or as professors begin to join demonstrations. Both the professional and the activist assume that the leadership of American society can be "enlightened" and improved through a combination of political pressure and skilled maneuver.

The term "professionalized reform" was coined by Daniel Moynihan to describe one part of this postwar pattern of change. In his view, the poverty program was created by a handful of concerned professionals rather than by an existing or threatening social movement. These poverty planners typify a "new class" precisely because they plan, they study the general needs of the system rather than defending a narrow interest. Less and less do they require "the masses" to bring issues to their attention; research makes possible a kind of "early warning system" for the country's elite.

Certainly this view reflects a real development. The poverty legislation was conceived by a small circle of men, just as New Deal reforms were conceived by a "brain trust." Michael Harrington's book helped to inspire it, just as earlier muckrakers focused attention on social needs. The personal compassion of JFK and LBJ made the programs possible, just as the plight of "one-third of a nation" troubled FDR. Such opportunities for "professionalized reform" are becoming more numerous than in earlier periods because of the expanding class of professional and service personnel taking part in the administration of society.

But it is not clear that these groups add more than sophistication and a white collar image to the status quo. They in fact develop their own "vested interests," as do even the social workers. Not being "of" the ghetto or the working class, they depend on information about the poor filtered through organizations of people similar to themselves. Their proposals for reform are developed not by the people who must live with the reforms (the poor themselves), but by planners with one eye on the census data and another on the political barometer. The consequence of the "new professionalism" tends to be, at best, patchwork (a young woman receives a skill through the Neighborhood Youth Corps, but her new earning power leads to a separation from her husband who is earning less) and, at worst, new public funds to shore up existing bureaucracies of the "welfare industry." . . .

The perilous position of the [liberal] movement, due to attacks from centralized business and political forces, adds a further incentive for a top-down system of command. The need for alliances with other groups, created in large part through the trust which sets of leaders develop for each other, also intensifies the trend toward vertical organization. Finally, the leaders see a need to screen out anyone with "Communist-oriented" views, since such individuals are presumably too skilled to be allowed to operate freely within the movement. Slowly an elite is formed, calling itself the liberal-labor community. It treats the rank-and-file as a mass to be molded; sometimes thrust forward into action, sometimes held back. A self-fulfilling pattern emerges: because the nature of the organization is elitist, many people react to it with disinterest or suspicion, giving the leadership the evidence it needs to call the masses apathetic. . . .

Some on the left tend to see each piece of social legislation as a victory which strengthens the "progressive" forces. They see a step-by-step transformation of society as the result of pushing for one "politically acceptable" reform after another. But it appears that the American elite has discovered a long-term way to stabilize or cushion the contradictions of our society. It does this through numerous forms of state intervention, the use of our abundant capacity for material gratification, and the ability to condition nearly all the information which people receive. And if this is the case, then more changes of the New Deal variety will not be "progressive" at all. Except for boosting the relative income of a few, this entire reformist trend has weakened the poor under the pretense of helping them and strengthened elite rule under the slogan of curbing private enterprise. In fostering a "responsible" Negro and labor leadership and bringing it into the pseudo pluralist system of bargaining and rewards, a way has been found to contain and paralyze the disadvantaged and voiceless people.

Defenders of the welfare state—professional or activist—say that its critics overlook (1) the political and material gains that have been made for the poor under its auspices, and (2) the relative freedom to continue organizing protest that it guarantees. The point, however, is not to deny the gains. No economic improvement or civil liberty, however small, should be underestimated. But it is something else to point to those gains in defense of an entire system. In the first place, the gains are minute in relation to what the American productive system could make available to its people. Second, the very security of those gains is not guaranteed without continuous militant pressure. Third, the struggle for those gains left most white workers with more security but at the price of remaining racist in outlook, while still working under alienating conditions. Fourth, the process of reform seemed to undermine the spirit of insurgency itself by institutionalizing and limiting it. . . .

We see, then, that welfare liberalism is more than a system of co-optation, more than an air-conditioned nightmare. It is also a system that punishes, with whatever violence is necessary, those who balk at its embrace. In this sense its liberalism is a facade over a more coercive conservative core.

The need is not to expand the welfare state, not to incorporate the "backward" parts into it, but to replace it altogether with a political economy that serves, rather than denies, the needs of the poor and millions of other people in this country and abroad. But replacing the political economy is not a negotiable issue arrived at through institutional reform. It is a revolutionary issue, resolved by building new institutions to replace the old. What then can be done? . . .

. . . [H]umane opposition to the American welfare empire must be constructed not in speculative theory, but in action. Ideas, after all, are welcome commodities, easily absorbed in the new system. Only through combined action will ordinary men create the beginning of a different society. The experience and practice of solidarity is a deeper form of opposition to the welfare empire than any radical critique. Only a community contributing its own movements and institutions can fill the vacuum of local political life that the authoritarian society creates. Only men who know themselves to be capable decision-makers can consider fighting for a thoroughly democratic society. Only men able to improvise and invent vocations of their own will be prepared to demand, and live in, a decentralized, automated society of the future. Only men with experience in a universe of mixed races and cultures will be able to shed national chauvinism and ethnocentrism. Furthermore, masses of men will only be persuaded of change when some of them create a compelling, if very imperfect, example of what the future might be.

The real alternative to bureaucratic welfarism is to be found budding in the experience of men who form communities—whether a freedom school, a community union, a teach-in, or a wildcat strike—to struggle as equals for their own self-determination. Such communities come and go, existing at their best during intense periods of solidarity. But even where they fail to achieve institutional reality, these communities become a permanent part of this generation's consciousness of the possible. The new society still takes shape in the womb of the old.

Document

Remarks at the University of Michigan, May 22, 1964

LYNDON B. JOHNSON

. . . I have come today from the turmoil of your Capital to the tranquility of your campus to speak about the future of your country.

The purpose of protecting the life of our Nation and preserving the liberty of our citizens is to pursue the happiness of our people. Our success in that pursuit is the test of our success as a Nation.

For a century we labored to settle and to subdue a continent. For half a century we called upon unbounded invention and untiring industry to create an order of plenty for all of our people.

The challenge of the next half century is whether we have the wisdom to use that wealth to enrich and elevate our national life, and to advance the quality of our American civilization.

Your imagination, your initiative, and your indignation will determine whether we build a society where progress is the servant of our needs, or a society where old values and new visions are buried under unbridled growth. For in your time we have the opportunity to move not only toward the rich society and the powerful society, but upward to the Great Society.

The Great Society rests on abundance and liberty for all. It demands an end to poverty and racial injustice, to which we are totally committed in our time. But that is just the beginning.

The Great Society is a place where every child can find knowledge to enrich his mind and to enlarge his talents. It is a place where leisure is a welcome chance to build and reflect, not a feared cause of boredom and restlessness. It is a place where the city of man serves not only the needs of the body and the demands of commerce but the desire for beauty and the hunger for community.

It is a place where man can renew contact with nature. It is a place which honors creation for its own sake and for what it adds to the understanding of the race. It is a place where men are more concerned with the quality of their goals than the quantity of their goods.

But most of all, the Great Society is not a safe harbor, a resting place, a

From *Public Papers of the Presidents: Lyndon B. Johnson, 1963–1964*, pp. 704–707.

final objective, a finished work. It is a challenge constantly renewed, beckoning us toward a destiny where the meaning of our lives matches the marvelous products of our labor.

So I want to talk to you today about three places where we begin to build the Great Society—in our cities, in our countryside, and in our classrooms.

Many of you will live to see the day, perhaps 50 years from now, when there will be 400 million Americans—four-fifths of them in urban areas. In the remainder of this century urban population will double, city land will double, and we will have to build homes, highways, and facilities equal to all those built since this country was first settled. So in the next 40 years we must rebuild the entire urban United States. . . .

The catalog of ills is long: there is the decay of the centers and the despoiling of the suburbs. There is not enough housing for our people or transportation for our traffic. Open land is vanishing and old landmarks are violated. . . .

Our society will never be great until our cities are great. Today the frontier of imagination and innovation is inside those cities and not beyond their borders. . . .

A second place where we begin to build the Great Society is in our countryside. We have always prided ourselves on being not only America the strong and America the free, but America the beautiful. Today that beauty is in danger. The water we drink, the food we eat, the very air that we breathe, are threatened with pollution. Our parks are overcrowded, our seashores overburdened. Green fields and dense forests are disappearing.

A few years ago we were greatly concerned about the "Ugly American." Today we must act to prevent an ugly America. . . .

A third place to build the Great Society is in the classrooms of America. There your children's lives will be shaped. Our society will not be great until every young mind is set free to scan the farthest reaches of thought and imagination. We are still far from that goal. . . .

These are three of the central issues of the Great Society. While our Government has many programs directed at those issues, I do not pretend that we have the full answer to those problems.

But I do promise this: We are going to assemble the best thought and the broadest knowledge from all over the world to find those answers for America. I intend to establish working groups to prepare a series of White House conferences and meetings—on the cities, on natural beauty, on the quality of education, and on other emerging challenges. And from these meetings and from this inspiration and from these studies we will begin to set our course toward the Great Society. . . .

For better or for worse, your generation has been appointed by history to deal with those problems and to lead America toward a new age. You have the chance never before afforded to any people in any age. You can help build a society where the demands of morality, and the needs of the spirit, can be realized in the life of the Nation.

So, will you join in the battle to give every citizen the full equality which

God enjoins and the law requires, whatever his belief, or race, or the color of his skin?

Will you join in the battle to give every citizen an escape from the crushing weight of poverty?

Will you join in the battle to make it possible for all nations to live in enduring peace—as neighbors and not as mortal enemies?

Will you join in the battle to build the Great Society, to prove that our material progress is only the foundation on which we will build a richer life of mind and spirit?

There are those timid souls who say this battle cannot be won; that we are condemned to a soulless wealth. I do not agree. We have the power to shape the civilization that we want. But we need your will, your labor, your hearts, if we are to build that kind of society.

Those who came to this land sought to build more than just a new country. They sought a new world. So I have come here today to your campus to say that you can make their vision our reality. So let us from this moment begin our work so that in the future men will look back and say: It was then, after a long and weary way, that man turned the exploits of his genius to the full enrichment of his life. . . .

eight

THE WAR IN VIETNAM

The war in Vietnam was a disaster for the United States. Southeast Asia had long been turbulent, as Vietnam fought for independence against French colonial authorities. On defeating the French, however, Vietnam found itself partitioned, and a bitter civil war continued as North Vietnam, led by Ho Chi Minh, sought to reunify the country. American policymakers, working within a Cold War consensus, provided more and more aid to South Vietnam, as they responded to the World War II lesson that aggression had to be stopped at all costs. Escalation continued gradually until the mid-1960s, when Lyndon Johnson authorized an American army in Vietnam that included half a million troops. But that army never had orders to fight an all-out war, and so, despite the destruction wrought, the struggle continued with no end in sight. Meanwhile, an ever-growing protest movement in the United States challenged American assumptions and actions in the war.

How did America become involved in the Vietnam War? And why did the war become such an albatross to the United States? Scholars have continued the debate that began in the 1960s with new materials and with a sense of perspective that was not possible until the American presence in Vietnam came to an end.

Leslie H. Gelb, a Defense Department official responsible for compiling the Pentagon Papers—the government's own study of the war—suggests in "Vietnam: The System Worked" that American aims led directly to involvement in Vietnam. American leaders, Gelb argues, perceived a real need to stop Communist expansion in Southeast Asia, and so chose consciously to

171

take the steps to stave off defeat. While unwilling to launch a full-scale war, they were determined to persevere.

Writing a decade later, historian George C. Herring, in "The War in Vietnam," examines both contemporary assessments and subsequent analyses of American conduct in the war. He describes the debate between hawks and doves that occurred in the 1960s, and notes the strategic and diplomatic difficulties that culminated in American defeat.

As scholars have examined the Vietnam War, they have been able to rely on a growing collection of memoirs and personal accounts by those who fought in the war. Ron Kovic, a young Marine from Long Island, describes in "Born on the Fourth of July" how he went to Southeast Asia to do whatever John Kennedy asked and returned home paralyzed from the waist down. Writing both in first- and third-person narratives, Kovic provides a vivid first-hand account of the events that led to his wound.

George C. Herring, *America's Longest War: The United States and Vietnam, 1950–1975* (1979), is the best place to begin a full examination of the Vietnam War. Frances FitzGerald, in *Fire in the Lake* (1972), underscores cultural differences between Vietnamese and Americans and shows how they conflicted. David Halberstam, *The Best and the Brightest* (1972), is a lengthy account of American assumptions that includes sharply drawn portraits of officials responsible for the war. Guenter Lewy, *America in Vietnam* (1978), argues that the Johnson administration was justified in intervening, and then claims that its conduct of the war led to ultimate defeat. Stanley Karnow, *Vietnam: A History* (1983), is an account written to accompany the superb public television series about the war. Al Santoli, *Everything We Had: An Oral History of the Vietnam War by Thirty-three American Soldiers Who Fought It* (1981), offers first-person voices reflecting on the struggle. For documents, see *The Pentagon Papers*, available in different versions after publication in the *New York Times* in 1971. The collection provides a detailed account of America's growing involvement as far back as 1945, with particular emphasis on decisions for escalation in the mid-1960s.

Vietnam: The System Worked

LESLIE H. GELB

The story of United States policy toward Vietnam is either far better or far worse than generally supposed. Our Presidents and most of those who influenced their decisions did not stumble step by step into Vietnam, unaware of the quagmire. U.S. involvement did not stem from a failure to foresee consequences.

Vietnam was indeed a quagmire, but most of our leaders knew it. Of course there were optimists and periods where many were genuinely optimistic. But those periods were infrequent and short-lived and were invariably followed by periods of deep pessimism. Very few, to be sure, envisioned what the Vietnam situation would be like by 1968. Most realized, however, that "the light at the end of the tunnel" was very far away—if not finally unreachable. Nevertheless, our Presidents persevered. Given international compulsion to "keep our word" and "save face," domestic prohibitions against "losing," and their personal stakes, our leaders did "what was necessary," did it about the way they wanted, were prepared to pay the costs, and plowed on with a mixture of hope and doom. They "saw" no acceptable alternative.

Three propositions suggest why the United States became involved in Vietnam, why the process was gradual, and what the real expectations of our leaders were:

First, U.S. involvement in Vietnam is not mainly or mostly a story of step by step, inadvertent descent into unforeseen quicksand. It is primarily a story of why U.S. leaders considered that it was vital not to lose Vietnam by force to Communism. Our leaders believed Vietnam to be vital not for itself, but for what they thought its "loss" would mean internationally and domestically. Previous involvement made further involvement more unavoidable, and, to this extent, commitments were inherited. But judgments of Vietnam's "vitalness"—beginning with the Korean War—were sufficient in themselves to set the course for escalation.

Second, our Presidents were never actually seeking a military victory in Vietnam. They were doing only what they thought was minimally necessary at each stage to keep Indochina, and later South Vietnam, out of Communist hands. This forced our Presidents to be brakemen, to do less than those who were urging military victory and to reject proposals for disengagement. It also meant that our Presidents wanted a negotiated settlement without fully realizing (though realizing more than their critics) that a civil war cannot be ended by political compromise.

Third, our Presidents and most of their lieutenants were not deluded by optimistic reports of progress and did not proceed on the basis of wishful thinking about winning a military victory in South Vietnam. They recognized that the steps they were taking were not adequate to win the war and that

From Leslie H. Gelb, "Vietnam: The System Worked," *Foreign Policy* 3 (Summer 1971). Copyright © 1971 by the Carnegie Endowment for International Peace. Reprinted by permission of *Foreign Policy*.

unless Hanoi relented, they would have to do more and more. Their strategy was to persevere in the hope that their will to continue—if not the practical effects of their actions—would cause the Communists to relent.

Each of these propositions is explored below.

ENDS: "WE CAN'T AFFORD TO LOSE"

Those who led the United States into Vietnam did so with their eyes open, knowing why, and believing they had the will to succeed. The deepening involvement was not inadvertent, but mainly deductive. It flowed with sureness from the perceived stakes and attendant high objectives. U.S. policy displayed remarkable continuity. There were not dozens of likely "turning points." Each postwar President inherited previous commitments. Each extended these commitments. Each administration from 1947 to 1969 believed that it was necessary to prevent the loss of Vietnam and, after 1954, South Vietnam by force to the Communists. The reasons for this varied from person to person, from bureaucracy to bureaucracy, over time and in emphasis. For the most part, however, they had little to do with Vietnam itself. A few men argued that Vietnam had intrinsic strategic military and economic importance, but this view never prevailed. The reasons rested on broader international, domestic, and bureaucratic considerations.

Our leaders gave the *international* repercussions of "losing" as their dominant explicit reason for Vietnam's importance. During the Truman Administration, Indochina's importance was measured in terms of French-American relations and Washington's desire to rebuild France into the centerpiece of future European security. After the cold war heated up and after the fall of China, a French defeat in Indochina was also seen as a defeat for the policy of containment. In the Eisenhower years, Indochina became a "testing ground" between the Free World and Communism and the basis for the famous "domino theory" by which the fall of Indochina would lead to the deterioration of American security around the globe. President Kennedy publicly reaffirmed the falling domino concept. His primary concern, however, was for his "reputation for action" after the Bay of Pigs fiasco, the Vienna meeting with Khrushchev, and the Laos crisis, and in meeting the challenge of "wars of national liberation" by counterinsurgency warfare. Under President Johnson, the code word rationales became Munich, credibility, commitments and the U.S. word, a watershed test of wills with Communism, raising the costs of aggression, and the principle that armed aggression shall not be allowed to succeed. There is every reason to assume that our leaders actually believed what they said, given both the cold war context in which they were all reared and the lack of contradictory evidence.

With very few exceptions, then, our leaders since World War II saw Vietnam as a vital factor in alliance politics, U.S.-Soviet-Chinese relations, and deterrence. This was as true in 1950 and 1954 as it was in 1961 and 1965. The record of United States military and economic assistance to fight Communism in Indochina tells this story quite clearly. From 1945 to 1951, U.S.

aid to France totaled over $3.5 billion. Without this, the French position in Indochina would have been untenable. By 1951, the U.S. was paying about 40 percent of the costs of the Indochina war and our share was going up. In 1954, it is estimated, U.S. economic and technical assistance amounted to $703 million and military aid totaled almost $2 billion. This added up to almost 80 percent of the total French costs. From 1955 to 1961, U.S. military aid averaged about $200 million per year. This made South Vietnam the second largest recipient of such aid, topped only by Korea. By 1963, South Vietnam ranked first among recipients of military assistance. In economic assistance, it followed only India and Pakistan.

The *domestic* repercussions of "losing" Vietnam probably were equally important in Presidential minds. Letting Vietnam "go Communist" was undoubtedly seen as:

- opening the floodgates to domestic criticism and attack for being "soft on Communism" or just plain soft;
- dissipating Presidential influence by having to answer these charges;
- alienating conservative leadership in the Congress and thereby endangering the President's legislative program;
- jeopardizing election prospects for the President and his party;
- undercutting domestic support for a "responsible" U.S. world role; and
- enlarging the prospects for a right-wing reaction—the nightmare of a McCarthyite garrison state.

U.S. domestic politics required our leaders to maintain both a peaceful world and one in which Communist expansion was stopped. In order to have the public support necessary to use force against Communism, our leaders had to employ strong generalized, ideological rhetoric. The price of this rhetoric was consistency. How could our leaders shed American blood in Korea and keep large numbers of American troops in Europe at great expense unless they were also willing to stop Communism in Vietnam?

Bureaucratic judgments and stakes were also involved in defining U.S. interests in Vietnam. Most bureaucrats probably prompted or shared the belief of their leaders about the serious repercussions of losing Vietnam. Once direct bureaucratic presence was established after the French departure, this belief was reinforced and extended. The military had to prove that American arms and advice could succeed where the French could not. The Foreign Service had to prove that it could bring about political stability in Saigon and "build a nation." The CIA had to prove that pacification would work. AID had to prove that millions of dollars in assistance and advice could bring political returns.

The U.S. commitment was rationalized as early as 1950. It was set in 1955 when we replaced the French. Its logic was further fulfilled by President Kennedy. After 1965, when the U.S. took over the war, it was immeasurably hardened.

There was little conditional character to the U.S. commitment—except for avoiding "the big war." Every President talked about the ultimate responsibility resting with the Vietnamese (and the French before them). This "condition" seems to have been meant much more as a warning to our friends than a real limitation. In every crunch, it was swept aside. The only real limit applied to Russia and China. Our leaders were not prepared to run the risks of nuclear war or even the risks of a direct conventional military confrontation with the Soviet Union and China. These were separate decisions. The line between them and everything else done in Vietnam always held firm. With this exception, the commitment was always defined in terms of the objective to deny the Communists control over all Vietnam. This was further defined to preclude coalition governments with the Communists.

The importance of the objective was evaluated in terms of cost, and the perceived costs of disengagement outweighed the cost of further engagement. Some allies might urge disengagement, but then condemn the U.S. for doing so. The domestic groups which were expected to criticize growing involvement always were believed to be outnumbered by those who would have started down the road if they knew this would mean over half a million men in Vietnam, over 40,000 U.S. deaths, and the expenditure of well over $100 billion is historically irrelevant. Only Presidents Kennedy and Johnson had to confront the possibility of these large costs. The point is that each administration was prepared to pay the costs it could foresee for itself. No one seemed to have a better solution. Each could at least pass the baton on to the next.

Presidents could not treat Vietnam as if it were "vital" without creating high stakes internationally, domestically, and within their own bureaucracies. But the rhetoric conveyed different messages:

To the Communists, it was a signal that their actions would be met by counteractions.

To the American people, it set the belief that the President would ensure that the threatened nation did not fall into Communist hands—although without the anticipation of sacrificing American lives.

To the Congress, it marked the President's responsibility to ensure that Vietnam did not go Communist and maximized incentives for legislators to support him or at least remain silent.

To the U.S. professional military, it was a promise that U.S. forces would be used, if necessary and to the degree necessary, to defend Vietnam.

To the professional U.S. diplomat, it meant letting our allies know that the U.S. cared about their fate.

To the President, it laid the groundwork for the present action and showed that he was prepared to take the next step to keep Vietnam non-Communist.

Words were making Vietnam into a showcase—an Asian Berlin. In the process, Vietnam grew into a test case of U.S. credibility—to opponents, to allies, but perhaps most importantly, to ourselves. Public opinion polls seemed to confirm the political dangers. Already established bureaucratic judgments about the importance of Vietnam matured into cherished convictions and organizational interests. The war dragged on.

Each successive President, initially caught by his own belief, was further ensnarled by his own rhetoric, and the basis for the belief went unchallenged. Debates revolved around how to do things better, and whether they could be done, not whether they were worth doing. Prior to 1961, an occasional senator or Southeast Asian specialist would raise a lonely and weak voice in doubt. Some press criticism began thereafter. And later still, wandering American minstrels returned from the field to tell their tales of woe in private. General Ridgway as Chief of Staff of the Army in 1954 questioned the value of Vietnam as against its potential costs and dangers, and succeeded in blunting a proposed U.S. military initiative, although not for the reasons he advanced. Under Secretary of State George Ball raised the issue of international priorities in the summer of 1965 and lost. Clark Clifford as Secretary of Defense openly challenged the winnability of the war, as well as Vietnam's strategic significance, and argued for domestic priorities. But no systematic or serious examination of Vietnam's importance to the United States was ever undertaken within the government. Endless assertions passed for analysis. Presidents neither encouraged nor permitted serious questioning, for to do so would be to foster the idea that their resolve was something less than complete. The objective of a non-Communist Vietnam, and after 1954 a non-Communist South Vietnam, drove U.S. involvement ever more deeply each step of the way.

MEANS: "TAKE THE MINIMAL NECESSARY STEPS"

None of our Presidents was seeking total victory over the Vietnamese Communists. War critics who wanted victory always knew this. Those who wanted the U.S. to get out never believed it. Each President was essentially doing what he thought was minimally necessary to prevent a Communist victory during his tenure in office. Each, of course, sought to strengthen the anti-Communist Vietnamese forces, but with the aim of a negotiated settlement. Part of the tragedy of Vietnam was that the compromises our Presidents were prepared to offer could never lead to an end of the war. These preferred compromises only served to reinforce the conviction of both Communist and anti-Communist Vietnamese that they had to fight to the finish in their civil war. And so, more minimal steps were always necessary.

Our Presidents were pressured on all sides. The pressures for victory came mainly from the inside and were reflected on the outside. From inside the administrations, three forces almost invariably pushed hard. *First*, the military establishment generally initiated requests for broadening and intensifying U.S. military action. Our professional military placed great weight on the strategic significance of Vietnam; they were given a job to do; their prestige was involved; and of crucial importance (in the 1960's) — the lives of many American servicemen were being lost. The Joint Chiefs of Staff, the MAAG (Military Assistance Advisory Group) Chiefs and later the Commander of U.S. forces in Vietnam were the focal points for these pressures. *Second*, our Ambassadors in Saigon, supported by the State Department, at times pressed for and often supported big steps forward. Their reasons were similar to those of the military. *Thirdly*, an ever-present group of "fixers" was making urgent demands to strengthen and broaden the Saigon government in order to achieve political victory. Every executive agency had its fixers. They were usually able men whose entire preoccupation was to make things better in Vietnam. From outside the administration, there were hawks who insisted on winning and hawks who wanted to "win or get out." Capitol Hill hawks, the conservative press, and, for many years, Catholic organizations were in the forefront.

The pressures for disengagement and for de-escalation derived mostly from the outside with occasional and often unknown allies from within. Small for most of the Vietnam years, these forces grew steadily in strength from 1965 onward. Isolated congressmen and senators led the fight. First they did so on anticolonialist grounds. Later their objections developed moral aspects (interfering in a civil war) and extended to non-winnability, domestic priorities, and the senselessness of the war. Peace organizations and student groups in particular came to dominate headlines and air time. Journalists played a critical role — especially through television reports. From within each administration, opposition could be found: (1) among isolated military men who did not want the U.S. in an Asian land war; (2) among some State Department intelligence and area specialists who knew Vietnam and believed the U.S. objective was unattainable at any reasonable price; and (3) within the civilian agencies of the Defense Department and isolated individuals at State and CIA, particularly after 1966, whose efforts were trained on finding a politically feasible way out.

Our Presidents reacted to the pressures as brakemen, pulling the switch against both the advocates of "decisive escalation" and the advocates of disengagement. The politics of the Presidency largely dictated this role, but the personalities of the Presidents were also important. None were as ideological as many persons around them. All were basically centrist politicians.

Their immediate aim was always to prevent a Communist takeover. The actions they approved were usually only what was minimally necessary to that aim. Each President determined the "minimal necessity" by trial and error and his own judgment. They might have done more and done it more rapidly if they were convinced that: (1) the threat of a Communist takeover were more immediate, (2) U.S. domestic politics would have been more permissive, (3) the government of South Vietnam had the requisite political stability and military potential for effective use and (4) the job really would have gotten done. After 1965, however, the minimal necessity became the maximum they could get given the same domestic and international constraints.

The tactic of the minimally necessary decision makes optimum sense for the politics of the Presidency. Even our strongest Presidents have tended to shy away from decisive action. It has been too uncertain, too risky. They derive their strength from movement (the image of a lot of activity) and building and neutralizing opponents. Too seldom has there been forceful moral leadership; it may even be undemocratic. The small step that maintains the momentum gives the President the chance to gather more political support. It gives the appearance of minimizing possible mistakes. It allows time to gauge reactions. It serves as a pressure-relieving valve against those who want to do more. It can be doled out. Above all, it gives the President something to do next time.

The tactic makes consummate sense when it is believed that nothing will fully work or that the costs of a "winning" move would be too high. This was the case with Vietnam. This decision-making tactic explains why the U.S. involvement in Vietnam was gradual and step by step.

While the immediate aim was to prevent a Communist victory and improve the position of the anti-Communists, the longer term goal was a political settlement. As late as February 1947, Secretary of State Marshall expressed the hope that "a pacific basis of adjustment of the difficulties" between France and the Vietminh could be found. After that, Truman's policy hardened, but there is no evidence to suggest that until 1950 he was urging the French not to settle with the Vietnamese Communists. Eisenhower, it should be remembered, was the President who tacitly agreed (by not intervening in 1954) to the creation of a Communist state in North Vietnam. President Kennedy had all he could do to prevent complete political collapse in South Vietnam. He had, therefore, little basis on which to compromise. President Johnson inherited this political instability, and to add to his woes, he faced in 1965 what seemed to be the prospect of a Communist military victory. Yet, by his standing offer for free and internationally supervised elections, he apparently was prepared to accept Communist participation in the political life of the South.

By traditional diplomatic standards of negotiations between sovereign states, these were not fatuous compromises. One compromise was, in effect, to guarantee that the Communists could remain in secure control of North Vietnam. The U.S. would not seek to overthrow this regime. The other compromise was to allow the Communists in South Vietnam to seek power along the lines of Communist Parties in France and Italy, i.e. to give them a "permanent minority position."

But the real struggle in Vietnam was not between sovereign states. It was among Vietnamese. It was a civil war and a war for national independence.

Herein lies the paradox and the tragedy of Vietnam. Most of our leaders and their critics did see that Vietnam was a quagmire, but did not see that the real stakes—who shall govern Vietnam—were not negotiable. Free elections, local sharing of power, international supervision, cease-fires—none of these could serve as a basis for settlement. What were legitimate compromises from Washington's point of view were matters of life and death to the Vietnamese. For American leaders, the stakes were "keeping their word" and saving their political necks. For the Vietnamese, the stakes were their lives and their lifelong political aspirations. Free elections meant bodily exposure to the Communist guerrillas and likely defeat to the anti-Communists. The risk was too great. There was no trust, no confidence.

The Vietnam war could no more be settled by traditional diplomatic compromises than any other civil war. President Lincoln could not settle with the South. The Spanish Republicans and General Franco's Loyalists could not have conceivably mended their fences by elections. None of the post-World War II insurgencies—Greece, Malaya, and the Philippines—ended with a negotiated peace. In each of these cases, the civil differences were put to rest—if at all—only by the logic of war.

It is commonly acknowledged that Vietnam would have fallen to the Communists in 1945–46, in 1954, and in 1965 had it not been for the intervention of first the French and then the Americans. The Vietnamese Communists, who were also by history the Vietnamese nationalists, would not accept only part of a prize for which they had paid so heavily. The anti-Communist Vietnamese, protected by the French and the Americans, would not put themselves at the Communists' mercy.

It may be that our Presidents understood this better than their critics. The critics, especially on the political left, fought for "better compromises," not realizing that even the best could not be good enough, and fought for broad nationalist governments, not realizing there was no middle force in Vietnam. Our Presidents, it seems, recognized that there was no middle ground and that "better compromises" would frighten our Saigon allies without bringing about a compromise peace. And they believed that a neutralization formula would compromise South Vietnam away to the Communists. So the longer-term aim of peace repeatedly gave way to the immediate needs of the war and the next necessary step.

EXPECTATIONS: "WE MUST PERSEVERE"

Each new step was taken not because of wishful thinking or optimism about its leading to a victory in South Vietnam. Few of our leaders thought that they could win the war in a conventional sense or that the Communists would be decimated to a point that they would simply fade away. Even as new and further steps were taken, coupled with expressions of optimism, many of our leaders realized that more—and still more—would have to be done. Few of these men felt confident about how it would all end or when. After 1965, however, they allowed the impression of "winnability" to grow in order to justify their already heavy investment and domestic support for the war.

The strategy always was to persevere. Perseverance, it seemed, was the only way to avoid or postpone having to pay the domestic political costs of failure. Finally, perseverance, it was hoped, would convince the Communists that our will to continue was firm. Perhaps, then, with domestic support for perseverance, with bombing North Vietnam, and with inflicting heavy casualties in the South, the Communists would relent. Perhaps, then, a compromise could be negotiated to save the Communists' face without giving them South Vietnam.

Optimism was a part of the "gamesmanship" of Vietnam. It had a purpose. Personal-organizational optimism was the product of a number of motivations and calculations:

- Career services tacitly and sometimes explicitly pressured their professionals to impart good news.
- Good news was seen as a job well done; bad news as personal failure.
- The reporting system was set up so that assessments were made by the implementors.
- Optimism bred optimism so that it was difficult to be pessimistic this time if you were optimistic the last time.
- People told their superiors what they thought they wanted to hear.
- The American ethic is to get the job done.

Policy optimism also sprang from several rational needs:

- To maintain domestic support for the war.
- To keep up the morale of our Vietnamese allies and build some confidence and trust between us and them.
- To stimulate military and bureaucratic morale to work hard.

There were, however, genuine optimists and grounds for genuine optimism. Some periods looked promising: the year preceding the French downfall at Dienbienphu; the years of the second Eisenhower Presidency when most attention was riveted on Laos and before the insurgency was stepped up in South Vietnam; 1962 and early 1963 before the strategic hamlet pacification program collapsed; and the last six months of 1967 before the 1968 Tet offensive.

Many additional periods by comparison with previous years yielded a sense of real improvement. By most conventional standards—the size and firepower of friendly Vietnamese forces, the number of hamlets pacified, the number of "free elections" being held, the number of Communists killed, and so forth—reasonable men could and did think in cautiously optimistic terms.

But comparison with years past is an illusory measure when it is not coupled with judgments about how far there still is to go and how likely it is that the goal can ever be reached. It was all too easy to confuse short-term breathing spells with long-term trends and to confuse "things getting better" with "winning." Many of those who had genuine hope suffered from either a lack of knowledge about Vietnam or a lack of sensitivity toward politics or both.

The basis for pessimism and the warning signals were always present. Public portrayals of success glowed more brightly than the full range of classified reporting. Readily available informal and personal accounts were less optimistic still. The political instability of our Vietnamese allies—from Bao Dai through Diem to President Thieu has always been apparent. The weaknesses of the armed forces of our Vietnamese allies were common knowledge. Few years went by when the fighting did not gain in intensity. Our leaders did not have to know much about Vietnam to see all this.

Most of our leaders saw the Vietnam quagmire for what it was. Optimism was, by and large, put in perspective. This means that many knew that each step would be followed by another. Most seemed to have understood that more assistance would be required either to improve the relative position of our Vietnamese allies or simply to prevent a deterioration of their position. Almost each year and often several times a year, key decisions had to be made to prevent deterioration or collapse. These decisions were made with hard bargaining, but rapidly enough for us now to perceive a preconceived consensus to go on. Sometimes several new steps were decided at once, but announced and implemented piecemeal. The whole pattern conveyed the feeling of more to come.

With a tragic sense of "no exit," our leaders stayed their course. They seemed to hope more than expect that something would "give." The hope was to convince the Vietnamese Communists through perseverance that the U.S. would stay in South Vietnam until they abandoned their struggle. The hope, in a sense, was the product of disbelief. How could a tiny, backward Asian country *not* have a breaking point when opposed by the might of the United States? How could they not relent and negotiate with the U.S.?

And yet, few could answer two questions with any confidence: Why should the Communists abandon tomorrow the goals they had been paying so dear a price to obtain yesterday? What was there really to negotiate? No one seemed to be able to develop a persuasive scenario on how the war could end by peaceful means.

Our Presidents, given their politics and thinking, had nothing to do but persevere. But the Communists' strategy was also to persevere, to make the U.S. go home. It was and is a civil war for national independence. It was and is a Greek tragedy. . . .

WHERE DO WE GO FROM HERE?

If Vietnam were a story of how the system failed, that is, if our leaders did not do what they wanted to do or if they did not realize what they were doing or what was happening, it would be easy to package a large and assorted box of policy-making panaceas. For example: Fix the method of reporting from the field. Fix the way progress is measured in a guerrilla war. Make sure the President sees all the real alternatives. But these are all third-order issues, because the U.S. political-bureaucratic system did not fail; it worked.

Our leaders felt they had to prevent the loss of Vietnam to Communism, and they have succeeded so far in doing just that. Most of those who made Vietnam policy still believe that they did the right thing and lament only the domestic repercussions of their actions. It is because the price of attaining this goal has been so dear in lives, trust, dollars, and priorities, and the benefits so intangible, remote, and often implausible, that these leaders and we ourselves are forced to seek new answers and new policies. . . .

The War in Vietnam

GEORGE C. HERRING

For Lyndon Johnson, the Vietnam War represented a personal as well as a national tragedy. Johnson had not created the commitment in Vietnam, and he would have preferred to shun what he once called "that bitch of a war" and concentrate on "the woman I really loved," his cherished Great Society. But the war he took on so reluctantly and struggled unsuccessfully to conclude eventually destroyed the Great Society, tore the nation apart, and inflicted great pain on Johnson himself. "The only difference between the Kennedy assassination and mine," he lamented in 1968, is that "I am alive and it has been more torturous." Johnson could console himself only with the hope that history would vindicate him for taking up the thankless burden of defending South Vietnam and for persevering in the face of a stalemated war and relentless pressures at home. . . .

The Johnson administration maintained that it had escalated the war in response to North Vietnamese aggression. Hanoi had instigated the insurgency in South Vietnam and had supported it with steadily increasing quantities of personnel and supplies. The United States had patiently endured North Vietnamese interference for years, responding only by sending aid and advisers to South Vietnam. But in 1964 and 1965, Hanoi had sharply stepped up its aggression, even dispatching regular units to the South. The United States had no choice but to carry the war to North Vietnam and to send its own combat forces to hold the line in South Vietnam.

The administration justified each major step it took as a response to a specific enemy provocation. The first bombing raids against North Vietnam in August 1964 were in retaliation for "unprovoked attacks" by North Vietnamese gunboats on U.S. destroyers engaged in "routine patrols" in the Gulf of Tonkin. The President also used this Gulf of Tonkin incident to secure a congressional resolution authorizing him to "take all necessary measures" to "prevent further aggression." Rolling Thunder, the systematic bombing campaign initiated in February 1965, came in response to Vietcong raids on the United States air base at Pleiku. The commitment of major increments of American ground forces in July 1965 was necessary to counter North Vietnamese infiltration of regulars, specifically the 325th Infantry Division, a crack unit whose presence posed a mortal threat to South Vietnam.

Johnson and his advisers insisted that by intervening in Vietnam they were defending vital interests of the United States. The administration stressed that a noncommunist South Vietnam was necessary to contain an expansionist Communist China. It resurrected the "domino theory," first publicized by Eisenhower in 1954, warning that the fall of South Vietnam

Reprinted from "The War in Vietnam" by George C. Herring, in *Exploring the Johnson Years*, Robert A. Divine, editor. Copyright © 1981 by the University of Texas Press. Reprinted by permission of the author and the publisher.

would cause the loss of all of Southeast Asia with disastrous economic, political, and strategic consequences for the United States. Johnson and Secretary of State Dean Rusk repeatedly emphasized that failure to stand firm in the face of aggression, as in the 1930s, would encourage further aggression, upsetting the international order the United States had established after World War II and perhaps provoking a third world war.

A group of so-called doves questioned the official explanation of the war from the outset. Included among them were prominent journalists, former government officials, and scholars—representatives of the most important segments of the nation's foreign policy elite. The doves ranged over the political spectrum. Liberals protested that the massive, indiscriminate use of military power in Vietnam was undermining America's moral position in the world. Conservatives deplored Johnson's neo-Wilsonian crusade and warned that by attempting to impose its will on the world the United States was "inviting a disaster beyond anything yet known to mankind." The radical New Left proclaimed that Vietnam was but the most blatant manifestation of a reactionary America's commitment to destroy revolution in the third world. From 1965 to 1973, the doves subjected Johnson and his successor, Richard Nixon, to a steady barrage of sometimes vicious criticism.

Doves differed among themselves in assessing American interests in Vietnam. Radicals agreed with the President's conclusion but reached it from a very different set of premises. Stressing the economic sources of American foreign policy, they argued that the survival of the capitalist system depended upon maintenance of the exploitative trade arrangements by which the United States had gained hegemony over the world economy. Conceding that U.S. economic interests in Vietnam were small, they nevertheless contended that the revolution there was symbolic of a larger, world-wide challenge to American dominance. The United States had gone to war in Vietnam, Gabriel Kolko concluded, to "stop every form of revolutionary movement which refuses to accept the predominant role of the United States. . . . On the outcome of this epic contest rests the future of peace and social progress in the world for the remainder of the twentieth century."

Liberals and conservatives, on the other hand, vigorously challenged the administration's contention that Vietnam was vital to the United States. In the light of the Sino-Soviet split, they argued, the Cold War had ended or at least entered a new phase, rendering outmoded the assumptions of the policy of containment. Some doves questioned whether China in fact had expansionist aims; others insisted that Chinese influence was inevitable in Southeast Asia. Most dismissed the domino theory as a sham and contended that, in any event, local nationalism rather than U.S. military power was the most effective barrier to any domino effect in a pluralistic world. In this context, they concluded, Vietnam was of no more than marginal importance to the United States.

All doves flatly rejected Johnson's explanation of the origins of the war. They conceded Ho Chi Minh's communist background but argued that he was primarily a nationalist whose fundamental goal was to complete the anticolonial revolution he had launched against the French in 1945. Radicals agreed that the insurgency in South Vietnam was an extension of Ho's revolution but accepted its legitimacy. Liberals stressed that it had erupted spontaneously in the South in response to the corrupt and oppressive American-sponsored regime of Ngo Dinh Diem. Preoccupied with its own problems and fearful of provoking war with the United States, North Vietnam had ignored the southern insurgents' pleas for aid until American escalation of the conflict had forced it to respond. Even then, doves concluded, Hanoi's support was not crucial to the success of the Vietcong.

The doves dismissed as blatant falsehoods the administration's accusations of North Vietnamese aggression. . . .

Holding the United States primarily responsible for the escalation, doves charged that the bombing and the dispatch of ground troops were desperate attempts of the Johnson administration to stave off the collapse of South Vietnam from within. The succession of puppets following the overthrow of Diem in November 1963 had been unable to rally the fragmented population of South Vietnam, and vocal elements were demanding peace and reconciliation with the Vietcong. The Tonkin Gulf reprisals were designed to shore up the embattled government of Nguyen Khanh and to distract attention from the breakdown in the South. Some argued that Johnson also took advantage of the contrived crisis to secure passage of a resolution making possible an escalation to which he was already committed. Once the presidential election of 1964 was safely past, he initiated the bombing of North Vietnam and dispatched combat forces to head off the impending collapse of the South Vietnamese government. . . .

The doves thus accused Johnson of lying to get the nation to accept war. He misrepresented the situation in Vietnam and the reasons for escalation. While continually insisting that he was merely following the policies of his predecessors, he was in fact ordering drastic changes. He deliberately obscured the significance of these changes by portraying them as reprisals. He refused to take his case directly to Congress and the public, presumably because he perceived the weakness of his position. Johnson and his advisers "manipulated the public, the Congress, and the press from the start," [author] David Halberstam concluded.

Most doves agreed that intervention in Vietnam had been disastrous, but they differed among themselves about why it had occurred. Some argued that the administration had perceived war was not the answer to the "realities" in Vietnam but had acted to escalate conflict anyway. Conservatives stressed the "arrogance of power," the unwillingness of the policymakers to accept frustration and failure. . . .

Most liberals were more charitable, stressing misperception as the basic cause of intervention. Despite the enormous changes that had taken place in the world, they argued, Johnson and his advisers continued to be guided by the Cold War certitudes of the 1950s: a rigid, militant, anticommunism and an unwavering faith that aggression, whatever its form, must be met forcibly. Any tendency to deviate from these views was countered by the lingering effects of McCarthyism. The "right wing of the Republican party tattooed on the skins of politicians and bureaucrats alike some vivid impressions of what could happen to a liberal administration that chanced to be in office the day a red flag rose over Saigon," [defense analyst] Daniel Ellsberg observed.

Liberal doves differed in assigning blame for the misperception. Some early writers advanced the "quagmire thesis" that overoptimistic advisers had misled unsuspecting Presidents step by step into the war in Vietnam. Others argued that Johnson's lack of experience in foreign affairs, the shallowness and rigidity of his intellect, and a temperament that could not stand the thought of anything resembling defeat were decisive factors in the escalation of the war. Many of these same writers theorized, to Johnson's rage, that the more perceptive John F. Kennedy, who had become disenchanted with Vietnam at the time of his death, would have found a better solution.

Liberals also focused on bureaucratic factors in explaining the commitment in Vietnam. The nation's leading Asian specialists had been purged from the government in the McCarthy era, they argued, and Vietnam policy-making suffered from a chronic lack of expertise. Time-worn assumptions went unquestioned year after year because of the natural bureaucratic tendency toward conformity. Those who doubted or questioned either left government service; were "domesticated," that is, permitted to speak out but ignored when decisions were made; or dissented only in measured tones for fear of losing their effectiveness. Most writers agreed that conformity was common to all bureaucracies, but some argued that Lyndon Johnson was particularly intolerant of dissent and imposed a tightly closed system in which debate was always about means rather than ends or basic assumptions. "Through a variety of procedures, both institutional and personal, doubt, dissent and expertise were effectively neutralized in the making of policy," [administration official] James Thomson concluded. . . .

Johnson's handling of the war has also provoked controversy, the debate closely following the positions staked out on the question of intervention. Those who defend American involvement as necessary or at least unavoidable criticize Johnson and his advisers for employing means that assured failure. Those who regard intervention as misguided question the morality of the means used and express doubts whether there was any acceptable way to preserve an independent, noncommunist South Vietnam. . . .

As with the decision to intervene, postwar controversy on the war itself closely parallels the contemporary debate. Determined to prevail in Vietnam without involving the United States in all-out war, Johnson deliberately chose a middle course of "enough, but not too much" military pressure, provoking fire from both sides. Hawks urged the pursuit of victory and relentlessly pressed him to use the level of force required to end the war quickly and decisively. Doves bitterly protested the militarization of United States policy, denouncing the bombing of North Vietnam and of search-and-destroy operations in the South as at best ineffective, at worst immoral. . . .

Most postwar commentators agree that American strategy was inherently unworkable. The search-and-destroy strategy was based on a gross miscalculation of North Vietnam's determination to resist and its capacity to replace its losses; as long as the United States would not attack the sanctuaries, it could not succeed. The strategy was counterproductive, moreover, causing enormous economic and social dislocation in South Vietnam, the country the United States was trying to save, and resulting in high draft rates and heavy U.S. casualties which caused growing unrest at home. . . . [T]he gradual escalation of the bombing produced minimal gains at a high price. North Vietnam was given time to disperse its population and resources, protect its infiltration routes, and develop an air defense system that took a large toll in American aircraft. Hanoi effectively exploited the bombing for propaganda advantage in world and even American opinion. . . .

The full story of the diplomacy of the war will not be known for many years. Little reliable evidence is available from the North Vietnamese side, and interpretations of Hanoi's position remain highly speculative. The voluminous White House and State Department files dealing with negotiations are still classified. The most important available source is that section of *The Pentagon Papers* dealing with diplomatic contacts, only recently released in "sanitized" form. The historical analyses are not nearly as comprehensive or as penetrating as the other parts of the papers, and many documents have been deleted in whole or in part because of "national security" restrictions. Nevertheless, these documents, along with several of the oral histories in the Johnson Library and recent scholarly works, shed considerable light on American handling of the major peace initiatives.

A brief survey cannot do justice to the impossibly complex diplomatic maneuvering, but several generalizations may be ventured. Johnson was unquestionably sincere in his desire for peace, and, in any event, domestic and international pressures required that he respond to initiatives from third parties and even the faintest signals from Hanoi. The administration dutifully pursued countless overtures and made determined efforts to open direct contacts with North Vietnam in Paris, Moscow, and Rangoon. The United States gradually backed away from its demand for the immediate withdrawal of all North Vietnamese troops, eventually agreeing to stop the bombing with the "understanding" that such action would lead to "prompt and productive" discussions and that Hanoi would not take military advantage of the American concession. In several vaguely worded proposals, the administration also modified at least slightly its opposition to Vietcong participation in a political settlement.

Washington did handle several major peace initiatives badly. To cite but one example, the United States undercut British Prime Minister Harold Wilson's efforts to enlist the cooperation of Soviet Premier Alexei Kosygin in arranging talks with Hanoi by failing to communicate accurately to London a recent change in its conditions for a bombing halt. An enraged Wilson was left out on a limb when the new, harsher terms became apparent, and the initiative quickly collapsed. Johnson was essentially correct, however, when he later pointed out that the North Vietnamese had already privately rejected the earlier, more favorable American offer. The major result was to exacerbate Anglo-American relations and give critics an occasion to charge the United States with bad faith.

In the final analysis, the administration's skepticism and its rigid bargaining position seem to have been more responsible for the failure of diplomacy than its ineptitude. Johnson's attitude toward the various peace initiatives was at best ambivalent. He dismissed many third-party overtures as "Nobel Prize fever." Although desirous of peace and determined to show his willingness to negotiate, he suspected that Hanoi was using the prospect of talks to increase domestic and international pressures on the United States. He was reluctant to appear too conciliatory lest he play into Hanoi's hands or convey an impression of weakness. Most important, he was determined to secure a noncommunist South Vietnam, and he remained confident, at least until 1967, that he could achieve this goal by increasing military pressure. Thus, although he made concessions, they represented, as George Ball later conceded, "little more than rejuggling of words so as to make our own objectives seem more palatable without materially changing our basic position."

It seems entirely likely, however, that the doves exaggerated the possibility of serious negotiations during this period. Johnson's assessment of the third-party initiatives may not have been off the mark. A former Hungarian diplomat has testified that at least one of them was based on a gross misrepresentation of Hanoi's position and was designed to enhance the prestige of its author, the Hungarian foreign minister. He has also speculated that the Soviet Union on several occasions may have misled the United States about the prospect of negotiations in order to do Hanoi a favor by getting the bombing stopped. The firmness with which North Vietnam clung to its goals in the face of subsequent U.S. concessions and military punishment suggests that it was unlikely to enter serious negotiations unless convinced that it could get what it wanted by political means. Like Washington, Hanoi could not afford to ignore pleas for peace, and it probably appeared conciliatory on occasion to get the bombing stopped and to put the United States at a propaganda disadvantage. The North Vietnamese modified their bargaining position a bit over the years, but never to the extent that their basic goals would be jeopardized. They too seem to have remained certain that they could achieve their goals by military means and regarded major concessions as unnecessary and potentially dangerous. The diplomatic stalemate merely reflected the stalemate on the battlefield.

Among the many issues raised by the Vietnam War, few have caused greater controversy than the Tet Offensive of 1968. Westmoreland and others have compared North Vietnam's strategy to that of Hitler in the Ardennes campaign. In a desperate, last-ditch effort to snatch victory from the jaws of defeat, a battered enemy hurled its best units against the cities of South Vietnam. The move failed disastrously. Although caught by surprise, the United States and South Vietnam quickly recovered, inflicting crippling losses on the attackers. Had the United States exploited its advantage, the war could have been ended. Westmoreland blames the media for the U.S. failure to do so. Ignoring massive evidence to the contrary, panicky and spiteful journalists portrayed Tet as an enemy victory, creating widespread disillusionment at home and forcing Johnson to seek a negotiated settlement. "It was like two boxers in a ring," Westmoreland concludes, "one having the other on the ropes, close to a knockout, when the apparent winner's second inexplicably throws in the towel."

Doves have taken a very different view of the events of February 1968. Despite the huge losses suffered by the Vietcong, they question whether Tet significantly altered the balance of forces in South Vietnam. The offensive was designed primarily for its impact on public opinion in the United States, they contend, and in this it succeeded. Some doves hail Johnson's decisions to end the gradual escalation of the war as long overdue and give Clark Clifford the credit. Others question the extent to which Johnson really changed his policy, arguing that he merely shifted tactics to preserve a position that was becoming untenable, permitting an unnecessary and destructive war to go on for four more years. . . .

Historical writing on Johnson's management of the Vietnam War is obviously still in an embryonic stage. Little material is open in the Johnson files for the period after 1965. State Department and Defense Department records remain closed. Scholars must therefore rely on *The Pentagon Papers*, memoirs of participants, such material as can be gleaned from interviews, and older accounts by journalists. Despite the extensive secondary literature, many important topics remain virtually uninvestigated. Most of the work done thus far has been by participants, journalists, and international relations specialists, many of whom have had a particular axe to grind, lesson to proclaim, or doctrine to promote.

In fairness to Johnson, it must be stressed that the situation he inherited in Vietnam lent itself to no easy solution—perhaps to no solution at all. Those who argue that a more decisive use of military power, a deeper commitment to negotiations, or greater stress on pacification would have brought the desired results conveniently overlook what appear from this perspective the harsh realities of the conflict. Those realities included (1) a determined, indeed fanatical foe, willing to sacrifice everything for its cause and driven by the centuries-old impulses of Vietnamese nationalism; (2) the threat of Soviet and Chinese intervention, heightened during the Johnson era by the fierce rivalry between the two communist giants; (3) a weak ally, lacking most of the basic ingredients for nationhood, eager for the United States to assume the burden of its defense but resentful of American domination; and (4) a domestic consensus which wanted success in Vietnam without paying a high price. The President was poorly served by his advisers, none of whom displayed exceptional imagination in perceiving, much less coping with, these admittedly intractable problems. Moreover, as Johnson himself repeatedly pointed out, his critics offered no viable solutions.

This much being said, it is still clear that the vindication Johnson hoped for has not come. Historical judgments to a large degree rest on perceptions of success or failure or commitment to a cause regarded as worthy. The events of April 1975 leave little room for debate on the outcome of the war. Although Hanoi's subsequent actions have led some writers to reaffirm the essential morality of the commitment in Vietnam, this view has not gained wide acceptance. Johnson was wise to avoid a larger war, a policy for which he should be given full credit, especially in view of the pressures he withstood and the disastrous actions of his successor. Yet he miscalculated drastically in assuming that his goals could be attained by limited means. He imposed restrictions on the military, but he provided little direction to American military strategy. Even after it was evident that the chosen instruments were not working, he refused to resolve the contradictions or clear up the ambiguities, continuing instead to pursue an improvised consensus approach that could not work. Johnson once observed of Vietnam that if "I have to turn back I want to make sure I am not in too deep to do so." Yet this is precisely the position he found himself in by 1967. Indeed, the longer the war went on and the more unlikely a favorable solution became, the more resistant he became to turning back. What he saw as courage and perseverance now seem more like rigidity and stubbornness. Lyndon Johnson no longer appears an evil or sinister figure, the warmonger of the rhetoric of protest, but rather a tragic figure, trapped in a dilemma not entirely of his own making and stubbornly persisting despite the enormous pain he was inflicting on the nation and himself.

Document
Born on the Fourth of July

RON KOVIC

I am the living death
the memorial day on wheels
I am your yankee doodle dandy
your john wayne come home
your fourth of july firecracker
exploding in the grave

All his life he'd wanted to be a winner. It was always so important to win, to be the very best. He thought back to high school and the wrestling team and out on Lee Place and Hamilton Avenue when he and the rest of the boys had played stickball or football. He thought back to that and remembered how hard he'd tried to win even in those simple games.

But now it all seemed different. All the hopes about being the best marine, winning all those medals. They all seemed crushed now, they were gone forever. Like the man he had just killed with one shot, all these things had disappeared and he knew, he was very certain, they would never come back again. It had been so simple when he was back on the block with Richie or running down to the deli to pick up a pack of Topps baseball cards, even working in the food store that summer before he went to the war now seemed like a real nice thing. It seemed like so much nicer a thing than what was happening around him now, all the faces, the torn green fatigues, and just below his foot was the guy's head with a gaping hole through his throat. . . .

It was his friend the major who gave him his second chance. He called him into the command bunker one day and told him he wanted him to become the leader of his new scout team. The major who understood him told him he liked the way he operated and said he knew the sergeant could do a good job.

Here was his chance, he thought, to make everything good again. This young, strong marine was getting a second crack at becoming a hero. He knew, he understood, the thing the major was doing for him, and he left the tent feeling stronger and better than he'd felt for a long time. Here was his chance, he thought over and over again.

He walked down the twisting ammo-box sidewalk and saluted one of the officers as smartly as ever, much too smartly for anyone who had been over there as long as him. The thoughts of the night he'd killed the corporal were already becoming faded as he began to think more and more about the scout team, how he would train them and the things they would do to make up for all the things that had come before.

He wrote in his diary that night how proud he was to have been made the leader of the scouts, to be serving America in this its most critical hour, just like President Kennedy had talked about. He might get killed, he wrote, but so had a lot of Americans who had fought for democracy. It was very important to be there putting his life on the line, to be going out on patrol and lying in the rain for Sparky the barber and God and the rest. He was proud. He was real proud of what he was doing. This, he thought, is what serving your country is supposed to be about. . . .

I remember we all sort of stopped and watched for a moment. Then all of a sudden the cracks were blasting all around our heads and everybody was running all over the place. We started firing back with full automatics. I emptied a whole clip into the pagoda and the village. I was yelling to the men. I kept telling them to hold their ground and keep firing, though no one knew what we were firing at. I looked to my left flank and all the men were gone. They had run away, all run away to the trees near the river, and I yelled and cursed at them to come back but nobody came. I kept emptying everything I had into the village, blasting holes through the pagoda and ripping bullets into the tree line. There was someone to my right lying on the ground still firing.

I had started walking toward the village when the first bullet hit me.

There was a sound like firecrackers going off all around my feet. Then a real loud crack and my leg went numb below the knee. I looked down at my foot and there was blood at the back of it. The bullet had come through the front and blew out nearly the whole of my heel.

I had been shot. The war had finally caught up with my body. I felt good inside. Finally the war was with me and I had been shot by the enemy. I was getting out of the war and I was going to be a hero. I kept firing my rifle into the tree line and boldly, with my new wound, moved closer to the village, daring them to hit me again. For a moment I felt like running back to the rear with my new million-dollar wound but I decided to keep fighting out in the open. A great surge of strength went through me as I yelled for the other men to come out from the trees and join me. I was limping now and the foot was beginning to hurt so much, I finally lay down in almost a kneeling position, still firing into the village, still unable to see anyone. I seemed to be the only one left firing a rifle. Someone came up from behind me, took off my boot and began to bandage my foot. The whole thing was incredibly stupid, we were sitting ducks, but he bandaged my foot and then he took off back into the tree line.

For a few seconds it was silent. I lay down prone and waited for the next bullet to hit me. It was only a matter of time, I thought. I wasn't retreating, I wasn't going back, I was lying right there and blasting everything I had into the pagoda. The rifle was full of sand and it was jamming. I had to pull the bolt back now each time trying to get a round into the chamber. It was impossible and I started to get up and a loud crack went off next to my right ear as a thirty-caliber slug tore through my right shoulder, blasted through my lung, and smashed my spinal cord to pieces.

I felt that everything from my chest down was completely gone. I waited to die. I threw my hand back and felt my legs still there. I couldn't feel them but they were still there. I was still alive. And for some reason I started believing, I started believing I might not die, I might make it out of there and live and feel and go back home again. I could hardly breathe and was taking short little sucks with the one lung I had left. The blood was rolling off my flak jacket from the hole in my shoulder and I couldn't feel the pain in my foot anymore, I couldn't even feel my body. I was frightened to death. I didn't think about praying, all I could feel was cheated.

All I could feel was the worthlessness of dying right here in this place at this moment for nothing.

nine

THE 1960s

The United States underwent enormous upheaval in the 1960s. Despite the promise of the Great Society, criticism of means and assumptions became more intense, and the war in Vietnam galvanized the growing protest. Cultural norms shifted too, as young Americans in particular began to express their individuality in new ways.

The changes of the 1960s occurred simultaneously. A new counterculture developed, with different styles of behavior and dress. Rock music became popular; drug use became widespread; and sexual codes became more liberal than before. Soon the example of the "hippies" infiltrated the culture at large. Political activity, meanwhile, became increasingly aggressive as it took aim at the Vietnam War. Students, on campuses around the country, were in the forefront of the campaign. Not all protesters shared countercultural assumptions, nor were all students politically active, but shifts unfolded side by side and reinforced each other in turbulent times.

Historian William L. O'Neill, in "The Counter-Culture," one section of his book on America in the 1960s, traces the roots of cultural change back to the "beats" of the decade before and shows the different manifestations of the movement.

Godfrey Hodgson, an English journalist, describes the volatile political atmosphere of the period in "The Great Schism," a selection from his book *America in Our Time*. He traces the roots of the New Left back to prior protests, and then outlines the origins and activities of SDS—Students for a Democratic Society.

Tom Hayden, one of the early SDS activists, was the primary author of

193

the group's political manifesto, the "Port Huron Statement," which is excerpted here. Twenty thousand copies of the 64-page document were mimeographed and circulated in 1962. A second printing of about the same number of copies occurred in 1964, and a third printing followed in 1966. The "Port Huron Statement" sums up the assumptions of young radicals of the time and sketches their vision of a new society in which Americans would be less alienated and more involved. It speaks of participatory democracy as the basis for a legitimate political system.

For other views of the decade, Milton Viorst, *Fire in the Streets: America in the 1960's* (1979), is a good starting point. Theodore Roszak, *The Making of a Counter Culture* (1968), reveals the roots of cultural change, while Charles Reich, *The Greening of America* (1970), is a good example of a highly popular work of the period. Tom Wolfe, *The Electric Kool-Aid Acid Test* (1968), describes Ken Kesey and the drug culture of the 1960s. For a sense of the political transitions taking place, see Allen J. Matusow, *The Unraveling of America: A History of Liberalism in the 1960s* (1984). Kirkpatrick Sale, *SDS* (1973), and James Miller, *"Democracy Is in the Streets": From Port Huron to the Siege of Chicago* (1987), both describe radical political activity. Todd Gitlin, *The Sixties: Years of Hope, Days of Rage* (1987), is another account of the period by an influential activist.

The Counter-Culture

WILLIAM L. O'NEILL

Counter-culture as a term appeared rather late in the decade. It largely replaced the term "youth culture," which finally proved too limited. When the sixties began, youth culture meant the way adolescents lived. Its central institutions were the high school and the mass media. Its principal activities were consuming goods and enacting courtship rituals. Critics and students of the youth culture were chiefly interested in the status and value systems associated with it. As time went on, college enrollments increased to the point where colleges were nearly as influential as high schools in shaping the young. The molders of youthful opinion got more ambitious. Where once entertainers were content to amuse for profit, many began seeing themselves as moral philosophers. Music especially became a medium of propaganda, identifying the young as a distinct force in society with unique values and aspirations. This helped produce a kind of ideological struggle between the young and their elders called the "generation gap." It was the first time in American history that social conflict was understood to be a function of age. Yet the young were not all rebellious. Most in fact retained confidence in the "system" and its norms. Many older people joined the rebellion, whose progenitors were as often over thirty (where the generation gap was supposed to begin) as under it. The attack on accepted views and styles broadened so confusingly that "youth culture" no longer described it adequately. Counterculture was a sufficiently vague and elastic substitute. It meant all things to all men and embraced everything new from clothing to politics. Some viewed the counter-culture as mankind's best, maybe only, hope; others saw it as a portent of civilization's imminent ruin. Few recalled the modest roots from which it sprang.

Even in the 1950's and very early sixties, when people still worried about conformity and the silent generation, there were different drummers to whose beat millions would one day march. The bohemians of that era (called "beatniks" or "beats") were only a handful, but they practiced free love, took drugs, repudiated the straight world, and generally showed which way the wind was blowing. They were highly publicized, so when the bohemian impulse strengthened, dropouts knew what was expected of them. While the beats showed their contempt for social norms mostly in physical ways, others did so intellectually. Norman Mailer, in "The White Negro," held up the sensual, lawless hipster as a model of behavior under oppressive capitalism. He believed, according to "The Time of Her Time," that sexual orgasm was the pinnacle of human experience, perhaps also an approach to ultimate truth. Norman O. Brown's *Life Against Death*, a psychoanalytic interpretation of history, was an underground classic which argued that cognition

From *Coming Apart: An Informal History of America in the 1960's* by William L. O'Neill. Copyright © 1971 by William L. O'Neill. Reprinted by permission of Times Books/Random House, Inc.

subverted intuition. Brown called for a return to "polymorphous perversity," man's natural estate. The popularity of Zen Buddhism demonstrated that others wished to slip the bonds of Western rationalism; so, from a different angle, did the vogue for black humor.

The most prophetic black humorist was Joseph Heller, whose novel *Catch-22* came out in 1960. Though set in World War II the book was even more appropriate to the Indochinese war. Later Heller said, "That was the war I had in mind; a war fought without military provocation, a war in which the real enemy is no longer the other side, but someone allegedly on your side. The ridiculous war I felt lurking in the future when I wrote the book." *Catch-22* was actually written during the Cold War, and sold well in the early sixties because it attacked the perceptions on which that war, like the Indochinese war that it fathered, grew. At the time reviewers didn't know what to make of *Catch-22*. World War II had been, as everyone knew, an absolutely straightforward case of good versus evil. Yet to Heller there was little moral difference between combatants. In fact all his characters are insane, or carry normal attributes to insane lengths. They belong to a bomber squadron in the Mediterranean. Terrified of combat, most hope for ground duty and are free to request it, but: "There was only one catch and that was Catch-22, which specified that a concern for one's own safety in the face of dangers that were real and immediate was the process of a rational mind. Orr was crazy and could be grounded. All he had to do was ask; and as soon as he did, he would no longer be crazy and would have to fly more missions. Orr would be crazy to fly more missions and sane if he didn't, but if he was sane he had to fly them. If he flew them he was crazy and didn't have to; but if he didn't want to he was sane and had to."

The squadron's success depends more on having a perfect bomb pattern than hitting the target. Milo Minderbinder is the key man in the Theater, though only a lieutenant, because he embodies the profit motive. He puts the entire war on a paying basis and hires the squadron out impartially to both sides. At the end Yossarian, the novel's hero, resolves his dilemma by setting out for neutral Sweden in a rubber raft. This was what hundreds of real deserters and draft evaders would be doing soon. It was also a perfect symbol for the masses of dropouts who sought utopian alternatives to the straight world. One day there would be hundreds of thousands of Yossarians, paddling away from the crazed society in frail crafts of their own devising. *Catch-22* was not just black comedy, nor even chiefly an anti-war novel, but a metaphor that helped shape the moral vision of an era.

Although children and adolescents watched a great deal of television in the sixties, it seemed at first to have little effect. Surveys were always showing that youngsters spent fifty-four hours a week or whatever in front of the tube, yet what they saw was so bland or predictable as to make little difference. The exceptions were news programs, documentaries, and dramatic specials. Few watched them. What did influence the young was popular music, folk music first and then rock. Large-scale enthusiasm for folk music began in 1958 when the Kingston Trio recorded a song, "Tom Dooley," that sold two million records. This opened the way for less slickly commercial performers. Some, like Pete Seeger, who had been singing since the depression, were veteran performers. Others, like Joan Baez, were newcomers. It was conventional for folk songs to tell a story. Hence the idiom had always lent itself to propaganda. Seeger possessed an enormous repertoire of message songs that had gotten him blacklisted by the mass media years before. Joan Baez cared more for the message than the music, and after a few years devoted herself mainly to peace work. The folk-music vogue was an early stage in the politicalization of youth, a forerunner of the counter-culture. This was hardly apparent at the time. Folk music was not seen as morally reprehensible in the manner of rock and roll. It was a familiar genre. Folk was gentle music for the most part, and even when sung in protest did not offend many. Malvina Reynolds' "What Have They Done to the Rain?" complained of radioactive fallout which all detested. Pete Seeger's anti-war song "Where Have All the Flowers Gone?" was a favorite with both pacifists and the troops in Vietnam.

Bob Dylan was different. Where most folk singers were either cleancut or homey looking, Dylan had wild long hair. He resembled a poor white dropout of questionable morals. His songs were hard-driving, powerful, intense. It was hard to be neutral about them. "The Times They Are a-Changing" was perhaps the first song to exploit the generation gap. Dylan's life was as controversial as his ideology. Later he dropped politics and got interested in rock music. At the Newport Jazz Festival in 1965 he was booed when he introduced a fusion of his own called "folk-rock." He went his own way after that, disowned by the politically minded but admired by a great cult following attracted as much, perhaps, by his independent life as by his music. He advanced the counter-culture in both ways and made money too. This also was an inspiration to those who came after him.

Another early expression, which coexisted with folk music, though quite unlike it, was the twist. Dance crazes were nothing new, but the twist was remarkable because it came to dominate social dancing. It used to be that dance fads were here today and gone tomorrow, while the two-step went on forever. Inexpert, that is to say most, social dancers had been loyal to it for generations. It played a key role in the traditional youth culture. Who could imagine a high school athletic event that did not end with couples clinging to one another on the dimly lit gym floor, while an amateur dance band plodded gamely on? When in 1961 the twist became popular, moralists were alarmed. It called for vigorous, exhibitionistic movements. Prurient men were reminded of the stripper's bumps and grinds. They felt the twist incited lust. Ministers denounced it. Yet in the twist (and its numerous descendants), bodies were not rubbed together as in the two-step, which had embarrassed millions of schoolboys. Millions more had suffered when through awkwardness they bumped or trod on others. The twist, by comparison, was easy and safe. No partner was bothered by the other's maladroitness. It aroused few passions. That was the practical reason for its success. But there was an ideological impulse behind it also. Amidst the noise and tumult each person danced alone, "doing his own thing," as would soon be said. But though alone, the dancer was surrounded by others doing their own thing in much the same manner. The twist celebrated both individuality and communality. This was to become a hallmark of the counter-culture, the right of everyone to be different in much the same way. The twist also foretold the dominance of rock, to which it was so well suited.

No group contributed more to the counter-culture than the Beatles, though, like folk music and the twist, their future significance was not at first apparent. Beatlemania began on October 13, 1963, when the quartet played at the London Palladium. The police, caught unawares, were hardly able to control the maddened throngs. On February 9, 1964, they appeared on U.S. television. The show received fifty thousand ticket requests for a theater that seated eight hundred. They were mobbed at the airport, besieged in their hotel, and adored everywhere. Even their soiled bed linen found a market. Their next recording, "Can't Buy Me Love," sold three million copies in advance of release, a new world's record. Their first movie, *A Hard Day's Night* (1964), was both a critical and a popular success. Some reviewers compared them with the Marx brothers. They became millionaires overnight. The Queen decorated them for helping ease the balance-of-payments deficit. By 1966 they were so rich that they could afford to give up live performances.

For a time the Beatles seemed just another pop phenomenon, Elvis Presley multiplied by four. Few thought their music very distinguished. The reasons for its wide acceptance were hard to fathom. Most felt their showmanship was the key factor. They wore their hair longer than was fashionable, moved about a lot on stage, and avoided the class and racial identifications associated with earlier rock stars. Elvis had cultivated a proletarian image. Other rock stars had been black, or exploited the Negro rhythm-and-blues tradition. The Beatles were mostly working class in origin but sang with an American accent (like other English rock stars) and dressed in an elegant style, then popular in Britain, called "mod." The result was a deracinated, classless image of broad appeal.

The Beatles did not fade away as they were supposed to. Beatlemania continued for three years. Then the group went through several transformations that narrowed its audience to a smaller but intensely loyal cult following in the Dylan manner. The group became more self-consciously artistic. Their first long-playing record took one day to make and cost £400. "Sergeant Pepper's Lonely Hearts Club Band" took four months and cost £25,000. They were among the first to take advantage of new recording techniques that enabled multiple sound tracks to be played simultaneously. The Beatles learned new instruments and idioms too. The result was a complex music that attracted serious inquiry. Critics debated their contributions to musicology and argued over whether they were pathfinders or merely gifted entrepreneurs. In either case, they had come a long way aesthetically from their humble beginnings. Their music had a great effect on the young; so did their styles of life. They led the march of fashion away from mod and into the hairy, mustached, bearded, beaded, fringed, and embroidered costumes of the late sixties. For a time they followed the Maharishi, an Indian guru of some note. They married and divorced in progressively more striking ways. Some were arrested for smoking marijuana. In this too they were faithful to their clientele.

John Lennon went the farthest. He married Yoko Ono, best known as an author of happenings, and with her launched a bizarre campaign for world peace and goodness. Lennon returned his decoration to the Queen in protest against the human condition. Lennon and Ono hoped to visit America but were denied entry, which, to the bureaucratic mind, seemed a stroke for public order and morality. They staged a bed-in for peace all the same. They also formed a musical group of their own, the Plastic Ono Band, and circulated nude photographs and erotic drawings of themselves. This seemed an odd way to stop the war in Indochina, even to other Beatles. The group later broke up. By then they had made their mark, and, while strange, it was not a bad mark. Whatever lasting value their music may have, they set a good example to the young in most ways. Lennon's pacifism was nonviolent, even if wildly unorthodox. At a time when so many pacifists were imitating what they protested against, that was most desirable. They also worked hard at their respective arts and crafts, though others were dropping out and holding up laziness as a socially desirable trait. The Beatles showed that work was not merely an Establishment trick to keep the masses in subjection and the young out of trouble.

Beatlemania coincided with a more ominous development in the emerging counter-culture — the rise of the drug prophet Timothy Leary. He and Richard Alpert were scientific researchers at Harvard University who studied the effects of hallucinogenic drugs, notably a compound called LSD. As early as 1960 it was known that the two were propagandists as well as scientists. In 1961 the University Health Service made them promise not to use undergraduates in their experiments. Their violation of this pledge was the technical ground for firing them. A better one was that they had founded a drug cult. Earlier studies of LSD had failed, they said, because the researchers had not themselves taken the drug. In order to end this "authoritarian" practice, they "turned on" themselves. Their work was conducted in quarters designed to look like a bohemian residence instead of a laboratory. This was defended as a reconstruction of the natural environment in which social "acid-dropping" took place. They and many of their subjects became habitual users, not only of LSD but of marijuana and other drugs. They constructed an ideology of sorts around this practice. After they were fired the *Harvard Review* published an article of theirs praising the drug life: "Remember, man, a natural state is ecstatic wonder, ecstatic intuition, ecstatic accurate movement. Don't settle for less."

With some friends Leary and Alpert created the International Foundation for Internal Freedom (IF-IF) which published the *Psychedelic Review.* To advertise it a flyer was circulated that began, "Mescaline! Experimental Mysticism! Mushrooms! Ecstasy! LSD-25! Expansion of Consciousness! Phantastica! Transcendence! Hashish! Visionary Botany! Ololiuqui! Physiology of

Religion! Internal Freedom! Morning Glory! Politics of the Nervous System!"
Later the drug culture would generate a vast literature, but this was its
essential message. The truth that made Western man free was only obtainable
through hallucinogenic drugs. Truth was in the man, not the drug, yet the
drug was necessary to uncover it. The natural state of man thus revealed was
visionary, mystical, ecstatic. The heightened awareness stimulated by "con-
sciousness-expanding" drugs brought undreamed-of sensual pleasures, according to Leary. Even better, drugs promoted peace, wisdom, and unity with
the universe.

Alpert soon dropped from view. Leary went on to found his own sect,
partly because once LSD was banned religious usage was the only ground left
on which it could be defended, mostly because the drug cult *was* a religion.
He wore long white robes and long blond hair. And he traveled about the
country giving his liberating message (tune in, turn on, drop out) and having
bizarre adventures. His personal following was never large, but drug use
became commonplace among the young anyway. At advanced universities
social smoking of marijuana was as acceptable as social drinking. More so, in
a way, for it was better suited to the new ethic. One did not clutch one's
solitary glass but shared one's "joint" with others. "Grass" made one gentle
and pacific, not surly and hostile. As a forbidden pleasure it was all the more
attractive to the thrill-seeking and the rebellious. And it helped further distinguish between the old world of grasping, combative, alcoholic adults and the
turned-on, cooperative culture of the young. Leary was a bad prophet. Drug-
based mystical religion was not the wave of the future. What the drug cult led
to was a lot of dope-smoking and some hard drug-taking. When research
suggested that LSD caused genetic damage, its use declined. But the effects of
grass were hard to determine, so its consumption increased.

Sometimes "pot" smokers went on to other drugs—a deadly compound called "speed," and even heroin. These ruined many lives (though it
was never clear that the lives were not already ruined to begin with). The
popularity of drugs among the young induced panic in the old. States passed
harsher and harsher laws that accomplished little. Campaigns against the drug
traffic were launched periodically with similar results. When the flow of grass
was interrupted, people turned to other drugs. Drug use seemed to go up
either way. The generation gap widened. Young people thought marijuana
less dangerous than alcohol, perhaps rightly. To proscribe the one and permit
the other made no sense to them, except as still another example of adult
hypocrisy and the hatred of youth. Leary had not meant all this to happen,
but he was to blame for some of it all the same. No one did more to build the
ideology that made pot-smoking a morally constructive act. But though a
malign influence, no one deserved such legal persecution as he experienced
before escaping to Algeria from a prison farm.

In Aldous Huxley's prophetic novel *Brave New World*, drug use was
promoted by the state as a means of social control. During the sixties it
remained a deviant practice and a source of great tension between the generations. Yet drugs did encourage conformity among the young. To "turn on
and drop out" did not weaken the state. Quite the contrary, it drained off

potentially subversive energies. The need for drugs gave society a lever should it ever decide to manipulate rather than repress users. Pharmacology and nervous strain had already combined to make many adult Americans dependent on drugs like alcohol and tranquilizers. Now the young were doing the same thing, if for different reasons. In a free country this meant only that individual problems increased. But should democracy fail, drug abuse among both the young and old was an instrument for control such as no dictator ever enjoyed. The young drug-takers thought to show contempt for a grasping, unfeeling society. In doing so they opened the door to a worse one. They scorned their elders for drinking and pill-taking, yet to outsiders their habits seemed little different, though ethically more pretentious. In both cases users were vulnerable and ineffective to the extent of their addiction. Of such ironies was the counter-culture built.

Another sign of things to come was the rise and fall of Ken Kesey and his Merry Pranksters. Kesey graduated from college in Oregon in 1958 and came to Stanford University. There he studied creative writing and absorbed the local bohemian atmosphere, which was still pretty traditional. People drank wine, lamented the sad state of American culture, and looked to Europe for relief in the classic manner. Kesey found work in a mental hospital, which was the subject of his first published novel, *One Flew over the Cuckoo's Nest.* It enjoyed a great success in 1962. He also figured in medical experiments conducted at the hospital. One of the drugs tested on him was LSD. Soon he was moving in psychedelic drug circles. In 1963, with the profits from his book, he bought a log house and some land near La Honda, about fifteen miles from Palo Alto.

Among the restless types who joined him was Neal Cassidy, a legendary figure who had been the model for Dean Moriarty in Jack Kerouac's famous beat-generation novel *On the Road.* The Merry Pranksters, as they became known, developed a unique life style. Sex played a part in it (a lean-to called the Screw Shack was added to the cabin for this purpose), but music and drugs more so. Everyone was also involved in The Movie—a continuing film record of their experiences. In the spring of 1964 the Pranksters bought a school bus, fitted it out with camping facilities, loaded the refrigerator with orange juice and acid, painted it in psychedelic colors, wired it for sound, and set off for the World's Fair in New York. One freaked out along the way (suffered a drug-induced breakdown) and was lost, but the rest made it to New York and then to Timothy Leary's borrowed estate in Millbrook. Leary refused to see them, but the contrast in drug subcultures was strikingly demonstrated all the same. Leary's League for Spiritual Discovery was cool and devotional. He was, literally, the high priest of a religious movement. The Pranksters were hot and crazy on principle. They visited the meditation rooms in Leary's basement and promptly termed it the Crypt Trip. They also made fun of the Tibetan Book of the Dead, one of the Learyites' most revered texts. Though a fiasco in one sense, the trip to New York helped define the Pranksters' secular identity in the semimystical drug world.

They went back to La Honda and wired it ever more extravagantly for light and sound. The Movie got more elaborate. The group expanded. Then, on April 23, 1965, they entered history with the most psychedelic drug bust ever. The county sheriff, federal agent Wong, eight police dogs, and wave upon wave of cops and squad cars stormed La Honda and arrested thirteen unarmed drug freaks. Eventually charges were dropped against all but Kesey, who was tagged for possession of marijuana. Overnight his status as a folk hero was established. In August he went so far as to invite the Hell's Angels to La Honda, and to everyone's amazement the visit came off nicely. There was only one gang-bang, and that voluntary. The Angels left without smashing everything up, even though high on beer and acid. It was practically an unnatural event. Soon after, Kesey was invited to the annual California Unitarian Church conference, where he seduced the young and appalled the old. An appearance at Berkeley's Vietnam Day in October was less successful. He had a theory about ending the war by having everyone turn his back on it. The Vietnam Day Committee thought stronger measures were in order.

What really put Kesey at the center of the new culture, however, were the "acid tests." These were big public gatherings with light shows, rock music, mad dancing, and, of course, acid-dropping. "Can you pass the acid test?" was their motto. These were the first important multimedia happenings, combining light shows, tapes, live rock bands, movie and slide projectors, strobe lights, and other technical gimmicks. Their climax was reached at the San Francisco Tripps Festival in January 1966. It was meant to release all the new forms of expression in the cultural underground. Bill Graham, who had managed the San Francisco Mime Troupe, was its organizer. Kesey and the Pranksters gave the acid test. The Tripps Festival was a great success. Several rock groups (The Grateful Dead and Big Brother and the Holding Company) proclaimed the emergence of a new musical genre—acid rock. Graham began staging such affairs regularly in the Fillmore Auditorium in San Francisco. Out of this came the "San Francisco Sound," which made the city a provincial capital in the music industry. Hippie culture, with its drugs, rock groups, psychedelic folk art, and other apparatus, was well and truly launched.

None of this did Kesey himself much good. Just before the Tripps Festival he was arrested for possession again. To escape a stiff jail term he fled to Mexico. Thereafter the new culture had to do without him. Mexico was a bad trip and he returned a chastened man. He talked about "going beyond acid" and gave a poorly received Acid Test Graduation. Many thought he was just copping out to avoid prison. Thanks to good lawyers and hung juries he finally got only six months at a work camp near his old place in La Honda. On being released he went back to Oregon with his family and started another novel. (His third. The second, *Sometimes a Great Notion,* was published while he was still a Prankster. It is a lovely book, though not so successful as his first.)

Kesey was not well known outside of California at the time except as a novelist. He owed his nonliterary folk-freak reputation to Tom Wolfe's book *The Electric Kool-Aid Acid Test,* which came out afterward. Hence Kesey was not so much influential as archetypal. His progression from student to artist to acidhead and crazy commune leader to jail and repentance was a course many would later take, in part anyway. He foreshadowed the hippies and yippies. He also showed how hazardous the psychedelic drug life was. Kesey lost his freedom for a while, and only time would tell what remained of his talent. Yet the somber end of his trip did not have much effect. The local media gave his revels much publicity, their dénouement relatively little. Wolfe, his Boswell, added to the Kesey legend by writing it up in the breathless, adulatory, highly colored prose of the "new journalism." It made insanity seem romantic and the tawdry glamorous. Nothing contemporary was alien to it if sufficiently bizarre. Wolfe's book was a best-seller. Kesey's activities sold a lot of newspapers. Everyone made money from his adventures but Kesey himself. This moral was not lost on the folk heroes who came after him. A striking feature of the mature counter-culture was the facility with which its leading figures made deviance pay off, usually by writing nonbooks. Even so, their profits were small compared with what the rock kings made.

. . .

To see how far the youth culture had progressed in a few years, one had only to compare the careers of Joan Baez and Janis Joplin. Miss Baez remained as delicately beautiful and as clear-voiced as ever. In 1964 she and Bob Dylan had been the "fantasy lovers of the folk revival." But by 1968 her vogue was long since gone. She still sang in much the same manner as before. She was even more dedicated to peace and nonviolence. Miss Baez was a tax resister on moral grounds, and she married a draft resister who went to prison rather than accept induction. Yet neither her music nor her beliefs nor her style of life was "relevant" to young people any longer. The place she once occupied was taken by Janis Joplin, a wholly different kind of woman. Miss Joplin was a hard-drinking, tough-talking, ugly but dynamic power for a San Francisco rock band called Big Brother and the Holding Company. A wild, passionate, totally involved performer, she was not much different as a person. Miss Joplin was what the groupies would have become if talented. She did exactly what she pleased, took lovers freely, owned a psychedelic sports car and a closet full of costumes, and, when her reputation eclipsed that of Big Brother and the Holding Company, struck out on her own. "If I miss," she told a reporter, "I'll never have a second chance on nothing. But I gotta risk it. I never hold back, man. I'm always on the outer limits of probability." What was her philosophy of life? "Getting stoned, staying happy, and having a good time. I'm doing just what I want with my life, enjoying it." She burned her candle at both ends and it did not last the night.

Miss Joplin was far more candid than many rock stars. One of their most tiresome habits was insisting on having it both ways. They wanted to be rich and famous while also radical and culturally momentous. What made the Beatles so attractive was that having become rich beyond the dreams of avarice, they abandoned it. And (Lennon excepted) they did not moralize much, however seriously they took themselves. The Rolling Stones, on the other hand, called for revolution in 1968 and the following year made millions with a whirlwind tour of the U.S. As time went on, the commercial aspects increasingly dominated rock. Few went so far as the coalition of groups in St. Louis who refused demands that they offer free, or at least reduced-price, tickets to the needy because doing so would be contrary to the American principle of free enterprise. But time was on their side. The evolution of the San Francisco Sound showed how quickly culture could give way to commerce. At their inception the hippie rock groups were products of the Haight-Ashbury subculture and dedicated to its precepts. But those who prospered soon succumbed to the cash nexus. Bill Graham got rich from his rock palaces, the Fillmore West in San Francisco and Fillmore East in New York. The Carousel Ballroom in San Francisco, funded by the indigenous Grateful Dead and the Jefferson Airplane, went broke. Before long San Francisco was only a regional music center, the New Rock's Nashville, as one critic put it. It was not so much an independent musical capital as a branch office of the music industry. As rock became less a movement and more a business, its impact, though not its popularity, declined. It seemed unlikely that rock would soon become a television staple. But some day its fans would be middle-aged, so even that possibility could not be permanently excluded.

. . .

The greatest event in counter-cultural history was the Woodstock Festival in Bethel, New York. It was organized on the pattern of other large rock festivals. Big-name groups were invited for several days of continuous entertaining in the open. A large crowd was expected, but nothing like the 300,000 or 400,000 youngsters who actually showed up on August 15, 1969. Everything fell apart in consequence. Tickets could not be collected nor services provided. There wasn't enough food or water. The roads were blocked with abandoned autos, and no one could get in or out for hours at a time. Surprisingly, there were no riots or disasters. The promoters chartered a fleet of helicopters to evacuate casualties (mostly from bad drug trips) and bring in essential supplies. Despite the rain and congestion, a good time was had by all (except the boy killed when a tractor accidentally drove over his sleeping bag). No one had ever seen so large and ruly a gathering before. People stripped down, smoked pot, and turned on with nary a discouraging word, so legend has it. Afterward the young generally agreed that it was a beautiful experience proving their superior morality. People were nicer to each other than ever before. Even the police were impressed by the public's order (a result of their wisely deciding not to enforce the drug laws). . . .

The rock festival at Altamont [California] that winter was . . . [a] disaster. It was a free concert that climaxed the Rolling Stones' whirlwind tour of the U.S. They called it their gift to the fans. Actually it was a clever promotion. The Stones had been impressed with the moneymaking potential of Woodstock. While Woodstock cost the promoters a fortune, they stood to recoup their losses with a film of the event. This inspired the Stones to do a Woodstock themselves. At the last minute they obtained the use of Dick

Carter's Altamont Raceway. It had been doing poorly and the owner thought the publicity would help business. Little was done to prepare the site. The police didn't have enough notice to bring in reserves, so the Stones hired a band of Hell's Angels as security guards (for $500 worth of beer). The Stones did their thing and the Angels did theirs.

The result was best captured by a *Rolling Stone* magazine photograph showing Mick Jagger looking properly aghast while Angels beat a young Negro to death on stage. A musician who tried to stop them was knocked unconscious, and he was lucky at that. Before the day was over many more were beaten, though no others fatally. Sometimes the beatings were for aesthetic reasons. One very fat man took off his clothes in the approved rock festival manner. This offended the Angels who set on him with pool cues. No one knows how many were clubbed that day. The death count came to four. Apart from Meredith Hunter, who was stabbed and kicked to death, they mostly died by accident. A car drove off the road into a clump of people and killed two. A man, apparently high on drugs, slid into an irrigation canal and drowned. The drug freak-outs were more numerous than at Woodstock. The medical care was less adequate. Not that the physicians on hand didn't try; they just lacked the support provided at Woodstock, whose promoters had spared no expense to avert disaster. Oddly enough the press, normally so eager to exploit the counter-culture, missed the point of Altamont. Early accounts followed the customary rock festival line, acclaiming it as yet another triumph of youth. In the East it received little attention of any kind. . . .

While it was difficult in 1969 to tell where the counter-culture would go, it was easy to see where it came from. Artists and bohemians had been demanding more freedom from social and artistic conventions for a long time. The romantic faith in nature, intuition, and spontaneity was equally old. What was striking about the sixties was that the revolt against discipline, even self-discipline, and authority spread so widely. Resistance to these tendencies largely collapsed in the arts. Soon the universities gave ground also. The rise of hedonism and the decline of work were obviously functions of increased prosperity, and also of effective merchandising. The consumer economy depended on advertising, which in turn leaned heavily on the pleasure principle. This had been true for fifty years at least, but not until television did it really work well. The generation that made the counter-culture was the first to be propagandized from infancy on behalf of the pleasure principle.

But though all of them were exposed to hucksterism, not all were convinced. Working-class youngsters especially soon learned that life was different from television. Limited incomes and uncertain futures put them in touch with reality earlier on. Middle-class children did not learn the facts of life until much later. Cushioned by higher family incomes, indulged in the same way as their peers on the screen, they were shocked to discover that the world was not what they had been taught it was. The pleasure orientation survived this discovery; the ideological packaging it came in often did not. All this had happened before, but in earlier years there was no large, institutional-ized subculture for the alienated to turn to. In the sixties hippiedom provided one such, the universities another. The media publicized these alternatives and made famous the ideological leaders who promoted them. So the deviant young knew where to go for the answers they wanted, and how to behave when they got them. The media thus completed the cycle begun when they first turned youngsters to pleasure. That was done to encourage consumption. The message was still effective when young consumers rejected the products TV offered and discovered others more congenial to them.

Though much in the counter-culture was attractive and valuable, it was dangerous in three ways. First, self-indulgence led frequently to self-destruc-tion. Second, the counter-culture increased social hostility. The generation gap was one example, but the class gap another. Working-class youngsters resented the counter-culture. They accepted adult values for the most part. They had to work whether they liked it or not. Beating up the long-haired and voting for George Wallace were only two ways they expressed these feelings. The counter-culture was geographical too. It flourished in cities and on campuses. Elsewhere, in Middle America especially, it was hated and feared. The result was a national division between the counter-culture and those adults who admired or tolerated it—upper-middle-class professionals and intellectuals in the Northeast particularly—and the silent majority of workers and Middle Americans who didn't. The tensions between these groups made solving social and political problems all the more difficult, and were, indeed, part of the problem.

Finally, the counter-culture was hell on standards. A handful of bohe-mians were no great threat to art and intellect. The problem was that a generation of students, the artists and intellectuals of the future, was infected with romanticism. Truth and beauty were in the eye of the beholder. They were discovered or created by the pure of heart. Formal education and training were not, therefore, merely redundant but dangerous for obstructing channels through which the spirit flowed. It was one thing for hippies to say this, romanticism being the natural religion of bohemia. It was quite another to hear it from graduate students. Those who did anguished over the future of scholarship, like the critics who worried that pop art meant the end of art. These fears were doubtlessly overdrawn, but the pace of cultural change was so fast in the sixties that they were hardly absurd.

Logic seemed everywhere to be giving way to intuition, and self-disci-pline to impulse. Romanticism had never worked well in the past. It seemed to be doing as badly in the present. The hippies went from flower power to death-tripping in a few years. The New Left took only a little longer to move from participatory democracy to demolition. The counter-cultural ethic re-mained as beguiling as ever in theory. In practice, like most utopian dreams, human nature tended to defeat it. At the decade's end, young believers looked forward to the Age of Aquarius. Sensible men knew there would be no Aquarian age. What they didn't know was the sort of legacy the counter-cul-ture would leave behind. Some feared that the straight world would go on as before, others that it wouldn't.

The Great Schism

GODFREY HODGSON

On May 11, 1965, Dean Rusk called the Soviet ambassador to the United States, Anatoly Dobrynin, down to the State Department. He told him that the United States was willing to stop bombing North Vietnam, which it had then been doing for just over two months, if Hanoi would order the Viet Cong to halt its activity in the South. It was the beginning of what was to be a weary, seven-year dialogue of the deaf, doomed to frustration. Each side saw the other as a blackmailer, cynically asking to be paid to stop doing what it should not have started in the first place. But there was another, ironic resonance to the conversation. Rusk strove to convince the Russian that the United States was in deadly earnest. "Hanoi appears to have the impression they may succeed," he said, "but the U.S. will not get tired." One illusion in particular Rusk did all he could to dispel. The Russians would be making a bad mistake if they supposed that the U.S. Government would be affected in the slightest by what Rusk dismissed as the "very small domestic pressure" against the war.

It was a startling misreading of the situation. The truth was that Lyndon Johnson and his advisers underestimated the political cost of the war even more disastrously than they underestimated its economic cost. Precisely in the two months before Rusk's conversation with Dobrynin, domestic opposition to American involvement in Vietnam made a quantum jump. It broke out of the tiny shell of the traditional peace movement and began to reach its first wider constituency, on college campuses. For the first time since the beginning of the Cold War, the foreign policy of the liberal consensus met serious opposition from the Left. Within less than three years, the opinion polls were to show more than half the population opposed to the war. Vietnam would make it impossible for Lyndon Johnson to fulfill his plans for building a Great Society, impossible for him to be re-elected, impossible, even, for him to travel freely around the country.

The war became the organizing principle around which all the doubts and disillusionments of the years of crisis since 1963, and all the deeper discontents hidden under the glossy surface of the confident years, coalesced into one great rebellion. Those "very small domestic pressures" grew and grew until the United States did get tired of the war. And then they grew and grew again until they had polarized the country into two opposed camps, two mutually hostile cultures, even: those who accepted and those who rejected the assumptions of 1960. That evening, as Rusk tried to impress upon Dobrynin the unity of American purpose, the age of consensus was on the very eve of giving way to the Great Schism.

On Lincoln's Birthday in 1947, between four and five hundred American

men publicly destroyed their draft cards in protest against the imminent
passage of the new Selective Service Act. Sixty-three of them did so at a
meeting in New York City where the speakers included A. J. Muste, Dwight
Macdonald, David Dellinger and Bayard Rustin. Muste, veteran preacher
and pacifist, had founded the American Workers Party in the 1930s and had
helped to found CORE in the 1940s. Macdonald had by 1947 successively
renounced the Communists, the Trotskyites and Marxism itself but was still
to perform his greatest service to the American Left when his *New Yorker*
article drew President Kennedy's attention to the problem of poverty and put
it on the agenda of American politics. Dellinger had been to jail as a conscien-
tious objector in World War II, and in 1947 Rustin still had a thirty-day
sentence on a Georgia chain gang hanging over him for his part in the
Journey of Reconciliation, precursor of the Freedom Rides, earlier the same
year.

That 1947 meeting is a reminder that the New Left of the 1960s had its
roots in an older tradition. Even its most spectacular techniques were not
always new. The peace movement in the United States was older than the
Vietnam War, older than the draft, older than the Cold War. Indeed there had
been a radical peace movement in America for a hundred years. At times
there have been conservative peace movements as well: Copperhead in the
Civil War, German- or Irish-American in the First World War, isolationist
between the wars.

The roots of the radical peace movement have always been entangled
with those of the civil rights movement. The ideals, and many of the idealists,
have been common to both. They have been ideals of personal conscience
and liberation, perhaps, more than aspirations to acquire political power in
order to change society. But they have had a political base of sorts in two,
uneasily allied, minority traditions: the Marxist Left, and the tradition of
radical religious conscience—especially, though not exclusively, Jewish,
Quaker and Unitarian.

This is the native American Left. It can claim, and for me persuasively,
to represent much of what is truest and best in the American political tradition. But in so far as it has represented itself as a peace movement and nothing
more, it has been disingenuous. It has always been a critique of the moral
justification of the American *status quo,* and of the morality of those who
wielded power in America.

The influence of this radical peace movement has ebbed and flowed
according to the degree to which the times favored its ability to recruit
support from other, less conscience-directed groups. In 1947, with fear of
Stalinism building up to a climax, the peace movement was near its lowest
ebb. Its influence hardly stretched beyond the tiny circulation of A. J. Muste's
paper *Liberation.*

By the late 1960s, it seemed to have reached a zenith. More than half the
population opposed the war. But that was deceptive. It did not mean that half
the population had joined the peace movement. The draft, the war, and the
crisis had indeed led millions to re-examine the moral basis of American

power. But millions of those who opposed the war had no sympathy for any such re-examination. They simply wanted the war to end.

In the late 1950s, as the fear of McCarthyism and of the Soviet Union began to recede, the peace movement slowly began to expand beyond these twin bases on the Left and in the church groups. A more affluent strain had been added by the World Federalists. One of the founders, Cord Meyer, went on to become a senior official at the CIA. Another was Norman Cousins, editor of *Saturday Review.* With Norman Thomas of the Socialist Party and Clarence Pickett of the American Society of Friends — the Left and the churches again — Cousins was behind the founding of the National Committee for a Sane Nuclear Policy (SANE), which put its first advertisement in the New York *Times* on November 15, 1957.

"Sociologically," SANE's director, Sanford Gottlieb, told me, "SANE recruited from the business and professional middle class. These were issue-oriented, educated, middle-class people. They were concerned about nuclear weapons, nuclear testing, fall-out and related issues."

The best-known of these converts, and yet quite typical of them, was Dr. Benjamin Spock, pediatrician to a generation. "I was a hawk in 1960," Dr. Spock said in an interview. "I thought there was a missile gap. There was nothing pacifist about me then. I thought we had to be strong to stand up to the Soviet Union."

In 1962 he joined SANE — at the *third* invitation. It was a small thing that changed his mind. President Kennedy had announced that he would meet with his experts to decide whether the United States needed to go on testing nuclear weapons or not. The experts met, and the President announced that they all agreed that the United States was ahead in nuclear weapons technology . . . but that he was going to go on testing anyway, so as not to fall behind.

"I thought that was odd," said Dr. Spock. "You were damned if you didn't, and damned if you did. It was quite clear that if all the experts said we were behind, we would go on testing. But we were also going to go on testing when the experts said we were ahead. So when would we stop? I thought of all the children who would die of leukemia and cancer, and of the ultimate possibility of nuclear war, and I joined SANE."

He was asked to collaborate with Bill Bernbach, of the Doyle Dane Bernbach agency, in writing the copy for an advertisement in the New York *Times.* "I was thrown into intellectual and emotional turmoil," he told me. "It was having to write that ad which made me examine all aspects of American foreign policy."

"Dr. Spock is worried," the text began. And he was. The next year, he became one of the two cochairmen of SANE. The other was the Harvard history professor H. Stuart Hughes, who ran for the Senate against Edward Kennedy on the peace issue in November 1962. The Hughes campaign was the first attempt to inject the peace issue into mainstream electoral politics.

In the advertisement, Dr. Spock wore a suit with a waistcoat, and he was looking down at a little girl with a frown of concern. The furrowed brow was the style of SANE and the other middle-class peace groups in the early sixties. But even before the Kennedy assassination, another wing of the peace movement was growing up, whose style was the clenched fist of anger. The Student Peace Union was founded in Chicago in 1959. By 1962 it had seventy chapters and more than thirty-five hundred members. Affiliated to it were radical groups at the two most influential universities in the country, TOCSIN at Harvard and SLATE at Berkeley.

A breath was stirring the elms on campus. The young people who joined the SPU were concerned with more than just the issue of "peace" as such. They joined peace groups partly because there were no other radical groups for them to join. (The Communists' Labor Youth League, for example, was dissolved in 1957; the Trotskyite Young People's Socialist League, the once famous YPSL, had almost ceased to exist.) The concern of the SPU was with building a new society, not just with protecting the existing one from fall-out and nuclear war.

Yet the Student Peace Union was short-lived. It disbanded in 1964. Many of its members moved on to the group—organization is not, perhaps, the right word—that eventually took up the running as the spearhead of the radical peace movement: Students for a Democratic Society.

SDS was born in wedlock as the child of those poor but honest parents the Old Left and the American labor movement. But it wasn't long before, like many another child of the sixties, it ran away from home. It didn't like the compromises it felt the old folks had to make to earn their living. And it needed to find its own identity.

To grasp how the New Left and the peace movement developed, you need to understand their parentage. The New York socialist Left at the beginning of the 1960s was a tiny world. It was riven by family quarrels and love-hate relationships that no outsider can quite hope to fathom. And yet, through its influence over parts of the labor movement and over certain intellectuals, it exercised infinitely more power than its numbers warranted, or than most Americans imagined.

One of the obsolescent institutions of the Old Left was the League for Industrial Democracy. It had known more glorious days, as a platform for Jack London, for Upton Sinclair, and later for Norman Thomas. But now it existed on the charity of the New York needle-trades unions. A group of socialists, including Michael Harrington, now proposed to revitalize it as a center for discussions among labor people, blacks and intellectuals. They were what was called in the family the Schachtmanites: followers of the veteran Marxist theoretician Max Schachtman.

In 1960, as part of their plans for revamping the LID, they equipped it with a student wing. In 1961 this was taken over by a group of students led by Al Haber, a radical from the University of Michigan.

Over the winter, a good deal of energy went into discussing drafts of a paper written by the editor of the student newspaper at Michigan, Tom

Hayden. In June 1962 fifty-nine members from a dozen campuses met with Harrington (who had then just finished writing *The Other America*) as a sort of camp counselor, at a UAW conference center at Port Huron, north of Detroit. There they issued a sixty-four-page statement, largely written by Hayden, which has often been called the manifesto of the New Left.

The most often-quoted passage (partly perhaps because it is the first!) stresses the perplexity of a new generation before the twin issues of race and peace:

> We are people of this generation, bred in at least modest comfort, housed now in universities, looking uncomfortably to the world we inherit.
>
> When we were kids the United States was the wealthiest and strongest country in the world . . . many of us began maturing in complacency.
>
> As we grew, however, our comfort was penetrated by events too troubling to dismiss. First, the permeating and victimizing fact of human degradation, symbolized by the Southern struggle against racial bigotry, compelled most of us from silence to activism. Second, the enclosing fact of the Cold War, symbolized by the presence of the Bomb, brought awareness that we ourselves, and our friends, and millions of abstract "others" we knew more directly because of our common peril, might die at any time.

There was little in what the statement had to say about these two grand issues that could have troubled their mentors in the labor movement. It was when it touched on the immediate experience of students, that is, on the university, that the statement's analysis departed most sharply from orthodoxy.

In the past few years, it noted, thousands of students had begun to demonstrate against racial injustice and the threat of war. The real significance of these demonstrations lay in the fact that students were at last "breaking the crust of apathy and overcoming the inner alienation that remain the defining characteristics of American college life." It is an interesting formulation: it comes close to implying that the causes of student concern over peace or civil rights lay in the unhappiness of their own lives. And what were the causes of apathy and alienation? Again, the statement answers that they are to be found, at least partly, in the university: in "cumbersome academic bureaucracy" and in "social and physical scientists" who work "for the corporate economy" or "accelerate the arms race." Five years before the accusation became commonplace that universities were guilty of complicity in Vietnam, and more than two years before the first student revolt at Berkeley, SDS was already depicting the university and its (predominantly liberal) professors as substantially to blame for student alienation. From the start, the New Left had a tendency to be more outraged by what it conceived as the hypocrisies of the liberals than by the grosser sins of the Right.

In the next section of the Port Huron statement, the key passage in the entire document, the liberal intellectuals are even more explicitly treated as mere apologists for a structure of oppression:

> Some regard this national doldrum [*sic:* i.e. apathy] as a sign of healthy approval of the established order—but is it approval by consent or manipulated acquiescence? Others declare that the people are withdrawn because compelling issues are fast disappearing—perhaps there are fewer breadlines in America, but is Jim Crow gone, is there enough work, is world war a diminishing threat, and what of revolutionary new peoples? Still others think the national quietude is a necessary consequence of the need for elites to resolve the complex and specialized issues of modern industrial society—but why then should *business* elites decide foreign policy, and who controls the elites anyway, and are they solving mankind's problems?
>
> The apathy here is, first, *subjective*—the felt powerlessness of ordinary people. . . . But subjective apathy is encouraged by the *objective* American situation, the actual structural separation of people from power.

Long before the escalation of the Vietnam War, then; before the disillusionment of the civil rights movement in 1964; even before the assassination; *some* young people, when they looked at the institution they knew best, which was the university, were ready to question the liberal ideology and its ever-prompt apologetics for the *status quo.* Something in the air that generation had breathed—television quiz shows, perhaps, or the revolution of rising expectations, or sheer boredom with the pious repetitions of consensus—had predisposed it to skepticism.

Yet it was so far only a predisposition. Tom Hayden's long and candid account of the evolution of his own political states of mind, in an interview in *Rolling Stone* in 1972, has something of the pathos of an archaeological dig. Right at the bottom of the trench, under all the strata of his later radical career, beneath the Chicago trial, and the peace movement, and community organizing, there nestled the unmistakable fragments of the lost innocence of a Kennedy liberal. Lower still lie the carbonized traces of a rebel who was once without a cause.

> I was a college editor, very influenced by the Beat Generation. My thing was to hitchhike all over the country. . . .
>
> And so that summer [it was 1960] I went to North Beach [where the Beats had lived on love and poetry and cheap red wine, in San Francisco] and my justification for it as an editor was that I was going to cover the Democratic convention [in Los Angeles]. I was always very divided between being what now you would call a radical and what then didn't have a name . . . it was mainly like trying to mimic the life of James Dean or something like that. . . . And then the other half of me was in the Establishment—ambitious young reporter who wanted to be a famous correspondent.
>
> I got to Berkeley and immediately went to the first person who was giving out leaflets, because I'd never seen anything like this before . . . and being political, they took me home and gave me a room to stay in for a few weeks and tried to educate me politically. . . .

Brought up in a working-class family in the suburbs of once-militant

Detroit, and after three years at one of the best universities in the country, Hayden had never come in contact with the Left. To question the ethics of nuclear war, to organize unorganized workers, these were new thoughts.

> You know what they were doing? They were organizing farm workers. . . .
>
> He drove me out to Livermore one day and showed me the nuclear reactor, where all the hydrogen bombs were made. And then another day [he] drove me out into the fields and the valleys, and he told me about the Chicanos. . . .
>
> On the other hand, I was in part tied to the Kennedy image also, the appeal of the New Frontier and the Peace Corps was pretty great.

There would be causes . . . to spare for rebels in the sixties. No doubt, if he had gone into the Peace Corps, it would have made him a rebel just the same. That was what it did for Paul Cowan, a representative figure of upper-middle-class dissent if ever there was one. Son of the producer who thought up quiz shows, alumnus of Choate and Harvard, he wrote an angry, strangely self-pitying book about the Peace Corps called *The Making of an Un-American.* But whether you grew up at Choate or in working-class Detroit, it was hard not to be "in part tied to the Kennedy image." They all started out as believers. Or at least they all once wanted to believe.

It is usual to speak of a generation radicalized by external events: by Dallas, and Mississippi, and Vietnam. And the relentless succession of external traumas did have its effect. Hayden mentions all those three among the stations of his personal journey. But even more, perhaps, they were driven into radical rebellion by their personal experience of those whom they expected to be their allies: by what they saw as the liberals' equivocations and manipulations. Hayden was no exception.

In the summer of 1961 he and his Michigan friend Paul Potter, a future president of SDS, visited McComb, Mississippi, with Bob Moses. While they were watching a nonviolent demonstration, they were pulled from their car by whites whom they believed had been set on them by the sheriff. Then they were told to leave town, or go to jail, by a high state official. They flew to Washington, expecting to be met with indignation and help from the Justice Department. Politely they were told by John Doar that there was nothing the federal government could do and that they should stay away from Mississippi. "From that time on," Hayden comments, "it was clear."

An even more embittering lesson was to come. That same autumn, Hayden and several others of those who later became the national leadership of SDS ran for national office in the National Student Association. They had no means of knowing that it was controlled by the CIA. But they did come up against what they described, with more truth than they realized at the time, as "the foreign policy elite" of the NSA: mysteriously well-heeled and well-briefed "students" in their thirties who always seemed to have plenty of money for flying around Europe.

> It all became a little more chilling [Hayden added] when one day we were in the

office of the president of the NSA just before the congress and found on his desk a chart written in his hand. His name was Richard Rettig. He was a CIA agent from the University of Wisconsin, and he had a chart of the congress. Me, Haber, and other people, SDS people, were listed as being the Left on this chart, and there was a Right and a Center, in terms of power blocs. And at the top there was a group called the control group.

Eleven years later, Hayden laughed as he remembered the shock and disillusionment of that discovery.

"Control group," he repeated. "Capital C, capital G!"

This, as the young radicals saw it, more than any other factor meant that there had to be a New Left. For a long time they hoped that they would be able to work with labor and the Left liberals, that they shared common ideals about peace and civil rights. But what was unmistakable was that in practice those whom they expected to be their allies were afraid of them. The Old Left "retained a liberal or radical rhetoric, but their real job was to be the Left gatekeeper of American radicalism."

And so the next SDS manifesto, *America and the New Era,* published in 1963, was more radical than the Port Huron statement. And the main difference was precisely on the issue of the liberal establishment:

. . . the capture of liberal rhetoric and the liberal power base by the corporate liberalism of the New Frontiersmen means that the reformers and the democratically oriented liberals are trapped by the limitations of the Democratic Party, but afraid of irrelevancy outside it.

The young radicals refused to limit themselves to writing pamphlets. They believed in action. "The whole soul of the New Left idea of politics," Carl Oglesby, another of the pioneers, wrote later, was the "concentration on process rather than on institutional end-points." And so they decided to try to contact the working class directly, in the most literal sense: by knocking on doors.

This was the logic behind the next phase of SDS's activity: "community organizing." It might be true, as Todd Gitlin, president of SDS from 1963 to 1964, wrote, that "the under-class has its most abrasive contacts with the ruling elites less at the point of production than outside it." The unions, in any case, controlled contacts at "the point of production," and they were not about to let young student radicals interfere with their power there. And so the community organizer knocked on doors, and talked about "bad housing, meager and degrading welfare, irrelevant schools, inadequate community facilities." As it happened, SDS was helped to do this with a grant from the UAW. But the constituency the young radicals were trying to reach was not the same as that of the big unions. The "communities" where they worked— defined, in fact, by their sad lack of community—were not inhabited by members of the UAW, the Teamsters or the building-trades unions, but by the unorganized and, all too often, by the unemployed. Rennie Davis and Todd Gitlin worked with poor white Appalachian migrants in the Uptown neighborhood of Chicago, Tom Hayden and Carl Wittman mainly with blacks in Newark. They discovered a world that had simply not been described by the liberal social scientists: a world where alienation meant not apolitical complacency but anger, deprivation, and poverty every bit as desperate as they had witnessed in the South.

The idea that a mass movement for social change through participatory democracy could be built by organizing the unorganized around local issues has proved to be a delusion. But it was a heady and a transforming experience for those who threw themselves into it. It was a time of apostolic hope and purity of motive. And for a while it distracted the attention of young radicals from what was happening in Vietnam.

In the late summer of 1964, shocked by the bombing of North Vietnam after the Tonkin Gulf incident, SDS did call a protest demonstration, to be held in Washington the following spring. When it took place, on April 17, 1965, the war had been escalated, and at least fifteen thousand young people joined the SDS march. It was one of the first signs that opposition to the war was spreading beyond the ranks of committed radicals. Yet, even then, SDS remained reluctant to give the war priority over the attempt to build a grass-roots radical movement in the United States. At the SDS national convention at Kewadin, Michigan, as late as June 1965, the foreign policy workshop, chaired by Todd Gitlin, recommended *against* concentrating on Vietnam. So, far from whipping up the movement against the Vietnam War, SDS took a leading part in it only with reluctance and after it was clear that there would be a mass movement against the war among young people anyway.

The dream of a multi-issue coalition lay behind the reasons why older radicals, too, were slow to take up the issue of Vietnam. But where the New Left had plunged into community organizing because they were pessimistic about the chances that labor would ever give a radical lead, the older Left was deterred from speaking out against the war for the opposite reason.

"In 1964 and 1965," Michael Harrington has written, "it seemed to us socialists that political realignment in America was about to come true. . . . The landslide of 1964 had elected the most liberal Congress within a generation. With an activist president of New Deal inclinations, that provided the setting for the most hopeful period of reform since Franklin Roosevelt." The anguished debate within the New York Left paralleled the dilemma with which liberals in general wrestled as the war gathered momentum and seemed to threaten the prospects of the Great Society.

Harrington has described one particular meeting at which Max Schachtman "launched into a Marxist attack on pacifism and the moralistic approach to politics. In Max's view, a condemnation of the Vietnam war primarily on the grounds that it was immoral was an exercise in phase-mongering." Schachtman and his friends argued, on spurious Marxist grounds, that because the peace movement was largely middle class, which it was, *ergo* it must be acting in a manner contrary to the interests of the working class.

There was a profoundly pessimistic assumption that the mass of the working class would inevitably support the war: an assumption that was, in spite of some dramatic and highly publicized symbolic events, only partially borne out, and which might have been even less justified if the Left, in 1965 or even earlier, had thrown its considerable influence with organized labor into the scales against the war.

That did not happen. The Left was to be divided on this issue as bitterly as the country as a whole. Certainly, even within his own immediate circle, Max Schachtman's arguments did not go unchallenged. Michael Harrington, in the end, broke with Schachtman on this issue and finally resigned his cochairmanship of the Socialist Party rather than "pretend any solidarity with people who, in the name of Marxism, were helping Richard Nixon." Bayard Rustin, on the other hand, found himself in the tragic posture, for a lifelong pacifist, of justifying the war in the name of a radical coalition that never materialized. Puzzling and even perverse as these almost theological arguments may seem to outsiders, they do explain why the Old Left did not take the lead, as it might have been expected to do, in the movement against the war.

If people on the Left were reluctant to attack the war because of their high hopes for Lyndon Johnson's domestic programs, the same was even more true of the liberals. The negative form of the proposition carried most weight: if we don't back Johnson, we might get Goldwater.

Even the hard-core peace movement felt the force of this. "We were outspoken enough about Johnson and the war in 1964," David McReynolds of the War Resisters' League acknowledged in an interview, "but we did discourage demonstrations. We thought it important to elect Johnson."

"We were so eager to have Johnson over Goldwater," Dr. Spock told me, "that there was what the psychologists call a halo effect. If you think someone is on your side, you ignore his defects. I campaigned actively on radio and TV for President Johnson."

SANE had organized two demonstrations on Vietnam in front of the White House when President Kennedy was still in it, but in those days the issue was Diem's autocratic behavior as much as it was American involvement. In Washington, under the influence of the Franco-American writer Bernard Fall, *The New Republic* had taken up the issue even earlier, with a special issue, in April 1962, headlined "No Win in Vietnam." In 1964 there had been a SANE petition, organized by Hans Morgenthau among others, calling for the neutralization of both Vietnams. Nevertheless few liberals were deeply concerned before the escalation decisions of early 1965.

"There wasn't very much evidence that we had cause to be worried until February of 1965," Sanford Gottlieb of SANE told me. "On the morning of February 7, Bernard Fall called me at 7 o'clock in the morning and said, 'They did it.'"

"Sandy Gottlieb called up early that Sunday morning," Dr. Spock remembers, "and said the U.S. was bombing North Vietnam. He read over the text of a denunciatory telegram he wanted Hughes and me to send to Johnson. . . . In the end I agreed, and he sent it in our name. A commentator said the White House says the move is approved by all Americans except Dr. Spock and Professor Hughes."

That was a considerable error on the White House's part. But the reaction to the decision to escalate the war did not explode all at once. "The successive nations in this country reacted to the war one after another," Sanford Gottlieb put it, "and the big sophisticated universities were first."

As it happened, the first of them was the University of Michigan. It was at Michigan that the technique was invented that linked the peace movement to the mass of students who were uneasy about the morality of the war and threatened by the draft. The technique was the teach-in, and it happened by accident.

Dr. William Gamson, a sociologist, was one of the four leaders of the teach-in movement at Ann Arbor. "The idea came from something that happened in the civil rights movement," he said. "I was a Democrat but not actively involved in politics, but I had been vice-chairman of CORE in Boston. There was a school boycott in the Boston area. As well as asking children to stay away from school, a Freedom School was set up to teach black history and civil rights: this was more positive than just asking kids to stay away from school."

"After the bombing in February 1965," Gamson went on, "a group of about fifteen faculty members met at one of our homes on March 11 to discuss what action we should take." The group included the philosopher Arnold Kaufman, who had actually been the chairman of the local Citizens for Johnson/Humphrey group three months before.

"Some wanted to put a protest ad in the paper. Some called for a hunger strike. Most of us wanted something more drastic than an ad. We hit on the idea of a one-day cancellation of classes and the holding of an all-day Vietnam symposium on the model of the Freedom School I just mentioned."

On March 17 the *Michigan Daily* reported that thirty-five faculty members were willing to walk out on March 24 to protest the Administration's policy in Vietnam. Selma was also mentioned. Two days later, the headline was "Faculty Group Cuts Off Walkout, Plans Teach-in." It was a new word. What had happened in the intervening two days was that there had been an angry reaction from the state legislature. The university administration, scenting trouble, persuaded Kaufman, Gamson and their friends to modify their plans.

On March 24 the following ad appeared in the *Michigan Daily*, signed by 216 members of the faculty.

AN APPEAL TO OUR STUDENTS

We the faculty are deeply worried about the war in Vietnam.

We think its moral, political and military consequences are very grave, and that we must examine them and find new alternatives before irreparable actions occur.

We are devoting this night, March 24–25, to seminars, lectures, informal discussions and a protest rally to focus attention on the war, its consequences, and ways to stop it.

It was an appeal from the faculty to the students, moderate in tone and signed by many who could not by any stretch of the imagination be called radicals. There was even a note at the bottom of the ad that today has a period flavor: "Women may obtain overnight permission from their house directors" to attend the teach-in. It went off peacefully. Two speakers from the State Department were given a hearing. It was, in fact, a pretty mild affair.

And yet the idea spread as if a spark had been thrown onto dry straw. "It spread because the mood at Michigan prevailed in other places," says Gamson simply. Michigan faculty called friends at fifty other universities. The very next day, there was a letter in the *Daily* from ten Stanford professors saying they planned to hold a teach-in there. Within a couple of weeks teach-ins had taken place at dozens of colleges. The movement culminated in a national, televised teach-in from Washington in June.

A few days after the first teach-in at Michigan, there was one at the University of Wisconsin. A graduate student, James Gilbert, later described what he had found so impressive about it. Not all the lectures were about Vietnam, he said; in fact, the most important was probably a speech on the meaning of commitment by the French existentialist and *résistante* Germaine Brée. He added:

This, I think, hints at the central meaning of the teach-ins; that the Vietnam war has implications for every aspect of life; that it actually means something for the university itself. . . . Vietnam was for some, then, a symbol for the deeper ills of American society.

Document
Port Huron Statement

TOM HAYDEN ET AL.

INTRODUCTION: AGENDA FOR A GENERATION

We are people of this generation, bred in at least modest comfort, housed now in universities, looking uncomfortably to the world we inherit.

When we were kids the United States was the wealthiest and strongest country in the world; the only one with the atom bomb, the least scarred by modern war, an initiator of the United Nations that we thought would distribute Western influence throughout the world. Freedom and equality for

From Students for a Democratic Society, *Port Huron Statement.* 1962. A copy of the third printing is available in the Labadie Collection, Hatcher Graduate Library, University of Michigan.

each individual, government of, by, and for the people—these American values we found good, principles by which we could live as men. Many of us began maturing in complacency.

As we grew, however, our comfort was penetrated by events too troubling to dismiss. First, the permeating and victimizing fact of human degradation, symbolized by the Southern struggle against racial bigotry, compelled most of us from silence to activism. Second, the enclosing fact of the Cold War, symbolized by the presence of the Bomb, brought awareness that we ourselves, and our friends, and millions of abstract "others" we knew more directly because of our common peril, might die at any time. We might deliberately ignore, or avoid, or fail to feel all other human problems, but not these two, for these were too immediate and crushing in their impact, too challenging in the demand that we as individuals take the responsibility for encounter and resolution.

While these and other problems either directly oppressed us or rankled our consciences and became our own subjective concerns, we began to see complicated and disturbing paradoxes in our surrounding America. The declaration "all men are created equal . . ." rang hollow before the facts of Negro life in the South and the big cities of the North. The proclaimed peaceful intentions of the United States contradicted its economic and military investments in the Cold War status quo.

We witnessed, and continue to witness, other paradoxes. With nuclear energy whole cities can easily be powered, yet the dominant nation-states seem more likely to unleash destruction greater than that incurred in all wars of human history. Although our own technology is destroying old and creating new forms of social organization, men still tolerate meaningless work and idleness. While two-thirds of mankind suffers undernourishment, our own upper classes revel amidst superfluous abundance. Although world population is expected to double in forty years, the nations still tolerate anarchy as a major principle of international conduct and uncontrolled exploitation governs the sapping of the earth's physical resources. Although mankind desperately needs revolutionary leadership, America rests in national stalemate, its goal ambiguous and tradition-bound instead of informed and clear, its democratic system apathetic and manipulated rather than "of, by, and for the people."

Not only did tarnish appear on our image of American virtue, not only did disillusion occur when the hypocrisy of American ideals was discovered, but we began to sense that what we had originally seen as the American Golden Age was actually the decline of an era. The worldwide outbreak of revolution against colonialism and imperialism, the entrenchment of totalitarian states, the menace of war, overpopulation, international disorder, supertechnology—these trends were testing the tenacity of our own commitment to democracy and freedom and our abilities to visualize their application to a world in upheaval.

Our work is guided by the sense that we may be the last generation in the experiment with living. But we are a minority—the vast majority of our people regard the temporary equilibriums of our society and world as eternally-functional parts. In this is perhaps the outstanding paradox: we ourselves are imbued with urgency, yet the message of our society is that there is no viable alternative to the present. Beneath the reassuring tones of the politicians, beneath the common opinion that America will "muddle through," beneath the stagnation of those who have closed their minds to the future, is the pervading feeling that there simply are no alternatives, that our times have witnessed the exhaustion not only of Utopias, but of any new departures as well. Feeling the press of complexity upon the emptiness of life, people are fearful of the thought that at any moment things might be thrust out of control. They fear change itself, since change might smash whatever invisible framework seems to hold back chaos for them now. For most Americans, all crusades are suspect, threatening. The fact that each individual sees apathy in his fellows perpetuates the common reluctance to organize for change. The dominant institutions are complex enough to blunt the minds of their potential critics, and entrenched enough to swiftly dissipate or entirely repel the energies of protest and reform, thus limiting human expectancies. Then, too, we are a materially improved society, and by our own improvements we seem to have weakened the case for further change.

Some would have us believe that Americans feel contentment amidst prosperity—but might it not better be called a glaze above deeply-felt anxieties about their role in the new world? And if these anxieties produce a developed indifference to human affairs, do they not as well produce a yearning to believe there *is* an alternative to the present, that something *can* be done to change circumstances in the school, the workplaces, the bureaucracies, the government? It is to this latter yearning, at once the spark and engine of change, that we direct our present appeal. The search for truly democratic alternatives to the present, and a commitment to social experimentation with them, is a worthy and fulfilling human enterprise, one which moves us and, we hope, others today. On such a basis do we offer this document of our convictions and analysis: as an effort in understanding and changing the conditions of humanity in the late twentieth century, an effort rooted in the ancient, still unfulfilled conception of man attaining determining influence over his circumstances of life.

VALUES

Making values explicit—an initial task in establishing alternatives—is an activity that has been devalued and corrupted. The conventional moral terms of the age, the politician moralities—"free world," "people's democracies"—reflect realities poorly, if at all, and seem to function more as ruling myths than as descriptive principles. But neither has our experience in the universities brought us moral enlightenment. Our professors and administrators sacrifice controversy to public relations; their curriculums change more slowly than the living events of the world; their skills and silence are purchased by investors in the arms race; passion is called unscholastic. The questions we might want raised — what is really important? can we live in a different and better way? if we wanted to change society, how would we do it? — are not thought to be questions of a "fruitful, empirical nature," and thus are brushed aside. . . .

Men have unrealized potential for self-cultivation, self-direction, self-understanding, and creativity. It is this potential that we regard as crucial and to which we appeal, not to the human potentiality for violence, unreason, and submission to authority. The goal of man and society should be human independence: a concern not with image of popularity but with finding a meaning in life that is personally authentic; a quality of mind not compulsively driven by a sense of powerlessness, nor one which unthinkingly adopts status values, nor one which represses all threats to its habits, but one which has full, spontaneous access to present and past experiences, one which easily unites the fragmented parts of personal history, one which openly faces problems which are troubling and unresolved; one with an intuitive awareness of possibilities, an active sense of curiosity, an ability and willingness to learn.

This kind of independence does not mean egotistic individualism — the object is not to have one's way so much as it is to have a way that is one's own. Nor do we deify man — we merely have faith in his potential.

Human relationships should involve fraternity and honesty. Human interdependence is contemporary fact; human brotherhood must be willed, however, as a condition of future survival and as the most appropriate form of social relations. Personal links between man and man are needed, especially to go beyond the partial and fragmentary bonds of function that bind men only as worker to worker, employer to employee, teacher to student, American to Russian.

Loneliness, estrangement, isolation describe the vast distance between man and man today. These dominant tendencies cannot be overcome by better personnel management, nor by improved gadgets, but only when a love of man overcomes the idolatrous worship of things by man. As the individualism we affirm is not egoism, the selflessness we affirm is not self-elimination. On the contrary we believe in generosity of a kind that imprints one's unique individual qualities in the relation to other men, and to all human activity. Further, to dislike isolation is not to favor the abolition of privacy; the latter differs from isolation in that [it] occurs or is abolished according to individual will.

We would replace power rooted in possession, privilege, or circumstance by power and uniqueness rooted in love, reflectiveness, reason, and creativity. As a *social system* we seek the establishment of a democracy of individual participation, governed by two central aims: that the individual share in those social decisions determining the quality and direction of his life; that society be organized to encourage independence in men and provide the media for their common participation. . . .

ten

NIXON AND WATERGATE

Richard Nixon was one of the most tenacious politicians of the postwar period. First a representative, then a senator from California, he became vice president under Eisenhower in 1953. Defeated by John Kennedy in his bid for the presidency in 1960, Nixon looked as though he had reached the end of the line after losing another election in California in 1962. But he remained politically involved, and as the Democratic party fragmented over the Vietnam War in 1968, he portrayed himself as a unifying force and won the office he had sought for so long.

Nixon's tenure in office included a number of notable accomplishments. He boldly opened the way to the People's Republic of China by making a personal visit there and moving a step closer toward formal diplomatic ties, which had been severed after the revolution of 1949. He extricated the United States from Vietnam, though at the cost of added polarization at home. And he promoted détente—and a more peaceful mood—in American dealings with the Soviet Union.

But all the while there was a darker side to the Nixon administration. The White House operated in a state of siege. Never a warm or easygoing individual, Nixon appeared even more defensive as he consolidated his power and insulated himself from his liberal critics. Finally, he overreached himself as his reelection campaign became embroiled in the Watergate affair. An attempt by employees of the Committee to Reelect the President to tap the telephones of the Democratic National Committee in the Watergate office and apartment complex backfired when the conspirators were caught in the act. Over the course of the next two years, the administration's cover-up unraveled. As impeachment threatened, evidence that Nixon himself had authorized the effort to head off an investigation culminated in his resignation in disgrace.

The first selection reprinted here—"Nixon in the White House," an excerpt from Rowland Evans, Jr., and Robert D. Novak's book of the same name—describes the closed atmosphere in the White House. The two well-known journalists give a sense of the smugness that characterized the inner circle, as they delineate the problems that later brought the president down.

In "Watergate," journalist and social critic Jonathon Schell reflects on the political crisis that disrupted the American constitutional system in the 1960s and 1970s. He sees the roots in the war in Vietnam, with a growing effort to act secretly that finally went too far. Within that context, Schell tells the story of the break-in and cover-up that caught up with Nixon at last.

The document in this section is an excerpt from a taped conversation held on June 23, 1972 between President Nixon and H. R. Haldeman, his chief of staff. In the passage reprinted here, Nixon authorizes using the CIA to head off the FBI's investigation of the Watergate break-in. In so doing, he becomes guilty of obstruction of justice. This tape, when finally released, proved to be the "smoking gun" that persuaded Nixon that he could not escape an impeachment conviction and led him to resign.

For further examination of Nixon, Garry Wills, *Nixon Agonistes: The Crisis of the Self-Made Man* (1969), is a scathing assessment of the early years. Stephen Ambrose, *Nixon: The Education of a Politician, 1913–1962* (1987), is a good survey of the prepresidential period. Bruce Mazlish, *In Search of Nixon: A Psychohistorical Inquiry* (1972), and Fawn M. Brodie, *Richard Nixon: The Shaping of His Character* (1981), are psychological studies. Nixon's own autobiographies—*Six Crises* (1962) and *RN: The Memoirs of Richard Nixon* (1978)—are useful for a sense of how Nixon saw himself. The most complete account of Watergate and the background that made it possible is J. Anthony Lukas, *Nightmare: The Underside of the Nixon Years* (1976).

Nixon in the White House

ROWLAND EVANS, JR., AND ROBERT D. NOVAK

In the second week of January 1971 the Republican National Committee was assembling in Washington for its midwinter meeting. It was nearly two years since the inauguration of Richard Milhous Nixon, the first authentic Republican politician to become President of the United States since Calvin Coolidge was elected in 1924, the heyday of the Grand Old Party. Whatever Nixon's identification problems with the rest of the country, he should have had none whatever here with the members of the National Committee, so many of whom he knew so well.

One Western committeeman, in particular, was a tried-and-true Nixon man, a party man who was called a member of the Old Guard in an earlier day and who now backed Richard Nixon as he once backed Robert Alphonso Taft. But on the evening of January 13, 1971, as members of the National Committee gathered for cocktails at the Washington Hilton Hotel, this Westerner was preoccupied with thoughts about a most-un-Republican letter to the editor published in that morning's *Washington Post* and signed by the distinguished historian and biographer Irving Brant. It was typical of the hard, sometimes brutal criticism that the academic community had leveled at Richard Nixon for a generation.

"Richard Nixon," wrote Brant, "in spite of his tremendously hard work and overwhelming ambition to be well thought of, is at bottom a synthetic figure." By contrast, he continued, each of the first five American Presidents had faults, but "each man was a genuine person — himself — presenting a definite personality and clear-cut character. Who and what is Richard Nixon?"

The Western Republican politician, an unquestionably loyal Nixon man, remarked that he thought the author of that letter was a little unfair, a little rough, but still, that fellow had something. "I wonder myself," he said slowly. "Who and what *is* Richard Nixon?"

That Irving Brant should have asked the question was neither surprising nor significant. That a conservative member of the Republican National Committee should agree was both surprising and significant. Nor was he alone, and therein lay the central irony of Richard Nixon, who had swept to office, after so many years of frustration, as Mr. Republican, successor to Taft, comrade-in-arms to party workers.

Never having made his reputation as a politician emotionally wedded to controversial or powerful causes — as, by contrast, Barry Goldwater made his reputation as ideologue of the right — Nixon came to the Presidency curiously unfathomed as a human being even by the party stalwarts who composed his base of support. For Nixon the politician, far more than Lyndon Johnson or John F. Kennedy or Dwight Eisenhower, concealed Nixon the man, and the man was, even to some of his close friends, an unbelievably complex, shy, remote and tense figure whose iron control seldom permitted anyone to glimpse the tumult inside. He was also a man cursed to live without the appearance of charm. He waged an endless battle to overcome that lack, but the effort usually fell short. At the root of this incapacity was his loneliness, and the loneliness was partly an inheritance of birth in a poor and undistinguished family, partly his environment as a poor boy, partly the harsh way politics had dealt with him. Having never attached himself to powerful causes, he lacked the political intimacies and camaraderies that so often joined politicians in common undertakings. His closest friends were not great leaders in the academic, business or political worlds or childhood pals, but a newly rich real estate speculator in Florida and the millionaire inventor of the aerosol valve.

But this was no Warren Harding, bewitched by vulgar wealth. His idols were not captains of industry but heroes of state — Winston Churchill, above all. Late one evening the last week of November 1970, at a low point in his Presidency, he had finished writing the finishing touches for a speech (working as ever on a yellow legal pad), and turned to an aide to talk about the kind of President he admired and would like to emulate. He eliminated the recent past: they were too close at hand to judge. But looking back, he mentioned these as Presidents who *did* something: Andrew Jackson, nemesis of the banks; Abraham Lincoln, who saved the Union; Grover Cleveland, who restored the power of the Presidency after all those stalwart Republicans; Theodore Roosevelt, who fought the trusts; Woodrow Wilson, the great reformer and internationalist; Franklin D. Roosevelt, who engineered a peaceful revolution. Four Democrats and two Republicans — one of whom bolted his party — scarcely a pantheon for Mr. Republican.

Richard Nixon's personal reputation was that of a hard man, bordering on meanness. It was bolstered as stories leaked out of the inner sanctum of the White House about his intemperate attitude toward his greatest nemeses: liberal Republicans who did not support their President, and the press. Oddly, he could have been a good newspaperman himself, with a taste for journalistic voyeurism in observing and, from a detached viewpoint, analyzing sports events and politics alike. But his wife, Pat, and his two daughters, Tricia and Julie, had never sought to hide the anguish induced by a story critical of him, and that had its effect on the President himself, adding to his own annoyance.

That ill temper, in bygone days, had displayed itself frequently and publicly, as during his 1956 campaign for reelection as Vice President when a mass resignation of his staff threatened. On the last day of campaigning for President in 1960, on the eve of defeat, a fatigued, worried Richard Nixon lashed out in a television studio at his staff in front of press and television technicians. But now, as President, not once had he lost his temper — never castigating an underling, except perhaps in the inmost intimacy of his personal staff and his family. He was, moreover, almost compulsively unable to fire or dress down an aide, whether Cabinet member or middle-level policymaker. Although a college debater, he now detested confrontation with an opponent and would do anything to avoid it. To blow off steam at an aide or to confront an enemy was the soul and substance of the political life of a Harry Truman or a Lyndon Johnson or a Huey Long or even of a John F. Kennedy. But not President Richard Nixon.

His lack of wit and humor was a cliché both in and outside the White House, but he was capable of practical jokes of a rather high order, one of which he pulled off following his European trip in early 1969, when he ordered the White House police force to wear elegant ceremonial uniforms like the household guard in a European court. The first appearance of the costumes, which were straight from Central European comic opera, unleashed a public torrent of abuse, and the President quickly retreated. A few days later his two most intimate White House aides, H. R. (Bob) Haldeman and John Ehrlichman, both of whom had thought the new uniform a great idea, each received an embossed hat box tied in gold ribbon and decked out like a Christmas tree. Inside was one of the new gold-ribboned stovepipe hats with the patent-leather visor. There was no note, and the President never mentioned his little gifts to Bob and John. Considering Nixon's genuine love for ceremony and ritual, that bit of humorous self-deprecation was remarkable.

There were, too, many midnight telephone calls, friendly and intimate, to close aides, friends and occasionally a journalist. They would come sometimes as late as two in the morning, and could go on for many minutes and on a variety of subjects. In one such call to Donald Rumsfeld, a Presidential Counsellor, Nixon mentioned his great friend Whittaker Chambers, whose help had been indispensable to Nixon in breaking the Alger Hiss case, and Rumsfeld sought to learn more about him. The President discoursed brilliantly on Chambers, the tortured intellectual who had joined and then deserted the Communist Party. It was one of many midnight chats that revealed a side of Nixon the public knew nothing about.

Often the precise idiom or choice of words to make a point or to make an apt response seemed just beyond the President's grasp—a fault that badly hurt his public reputation. That was true when, during his campaign in St. Petersburg, Fla., in October 1970, a motorcycle policeman was thrown from his vehicle in the Presidential caravan and severely injured. Leaving his limousine, Nixon rushed to the injured policeman and expressed his sympathies. The policeman replied that *he* was the one to be sorry that the motorcade had been delayed. Then, embarrassing silence—the President speechless for seconds. Finally he blurted out: "Do you like the work?"

Despite this inability to relate to individuals in specific, ordinary life situations, he prided himself on his skill as a master of mass communications. He worked his press conferences with neither notes nor podium; his steel-trap mind could comprehend difficult concepts and memorize great quantities of facts. Yet, no President ever prepared so diligently for a press conference as Richard Nixon, and he treated each as if it were his first exposure to the naked eye of the camera, with nerves taut as airtime neared. He would sit in a cool, dark room collecting his thoughts and calming himself, but when he entered the East Room of the White House for the press conference, he would often be bathed in sweat. He had fewer press conferences than any President since Herbert Hoover.

That added to his isolation, which was more pronounced than any President's since Hoover—isolation from the press, from most of his aides, from his Cabinet. Reclusive by nature, the Presidency heightened that characteristic and added difficulties to his Presidency.

Yet, all in all and now well into the third year of his Presidency, Richard Nixon had changed remarkably little in office. He was still, in essence, the same man who had, after so long and hard a chase for power, awaited its assumption at the Pierre Hotel in New York in November 1968. . . .

The mood in the White House—from Presidential aides on down to stenographers—was surprise bordering on shock the morning of Friday, January 28, 1972, when Barbara Walters of the National Broadcasting Company's *Today* program turned up at 1600 Pennsylvania Avenue with an NBC film crew in tow. Even Herb Klein, the director of communications for the Nixon administration, who was supposed to know about such matters, was taken by surprise. Nor could anybody have guessed Miss Walters' highly improbable mission: to interview Harry Robert Haldeman himself, the cloistered keeper of the Presidential keys and preeminent master of the White House inner sanctum. For the first time, Bob Haldeman was to be exposed to the outer world.

There was no particular crisis in the administration of Richard Nixon, now entering its fourth year, requiring Haldeman to strip aside the veils of anonymity and publicly proclaim the virtues of his chief. Far from it. An aura of optimism, of almost smug satisfaction, had drenched the White House ever since Nixon's two great surprises of the summer of 1971: the announcement on July 15 of his China trip and the announcement on August 15 of his New Economic Policy. The former, in a single stroke, had disarmed Nixon's foreign policy critics on the left and given the nation a forceful demonstration of daring and imaginative management of foreign policy; the latter, temporarily at least, had seemed to arrest both inflation at home and deterioration of the dollar abroad while robbing Democrats of ammunition for their economic attack against the President that had been building in velocity and effect. Nixon's long decline in popularity had ended, and the curve was now upward. Nine months before the election, his chances for a second term seemed to be improving. And apart from popularity polls and long-range election forecasting, the glowing self-confidence of the President and the men around him was both obvious and justified. Nixon's dramatic action on China and the economy the previous summer had been fine political tonic, arresting the decline of his administration into frustration and ineffectiveness. To much of Washington, Richard Nixon was exercising Presidential power in the grand manner.

The mood of euphoria was particularly thick at the White House the morning Miss Walters taped her Haldeman interview. Just three nights earlier, on January 25, Nixon had once again gone to the country on nationwide television with another stunning surprise, though less so than the twin shockers of China and the New Economic Policy. The impact was similar: Nixon had preempted the staggering Democrats on a key issue.

On that evening, the President revealed that the ubiquitous Henry A. Kissinger had conducted private, informal peace negotiations with North Vietnamese envoys on the outskirts of Paris on twelve occasions between August 4, 1969, and August 16, 1971. On May 31, 1971, Nixon revealed, Kissinger had offered a total American withdrawal from Vietnam in return for the release of all American prisoners and a cease-fire. In reply, he said, Hanoi's diplomats "insisted that we overthrow the Government of South Vietnam." He then revealed that after more fruitless negotiations between Kissinger and the Communists, the United States had prepared a new proposal: an offer of free elections one month *after* the resignation of General Nguyen Van Thieu as President of South Vietnam and after the withdrawal of American forces. Instead of an answer, Hanoi declined even to meet Kissinger again in Paris, reported the President. . . .

But inside the White House, this sense of political well-being was diminished by the President's irritation, obvious to close aides, over the criticism of the Senate doves. And no aide was closer than the faithful Haldeman, who reflected his President's moods as accurately as a thermometer reflects the temperature. Without careful thought, Haldeman's reflection mechanism went to work, inevitably magnifying out of all reasonable proportions the criticism from Capitol Hill that was so irritating Nixon. That the criticism was in the forefront of his mind became swiftly apparent when Miss Walters and the NBC crew entered his neat-as-a-pin Williamsburg-style office in the White House where so few journalists, politicians and even administration officials had ever been admitted. . . .

The result was memorable. With the cheery blaze in Haldeman's office fireplace providing a cozy background, Haldeman was asked by Miss Walters what kind of criticism upset President Nixon. Haldeman replied: criticism "that can get in the way of what he's doing," and immediately offered a case in point—the President's new peace plan. Before that plan had been revealed on January 25, he explained, the President's critics were *"unconsciously* echoing the line that the enemy wanted echoed" [emphasis added by Evans and Novak]. But now that the President had fully revealed the nature of Kissinger's secret negotiations, Haldeman went on, "the only conclusion you can draw is that the critics now are *consciously* aiding and abetting the enemy of the United States. . . . " With Haldeman skating perilously close to the thin ice of the definition for treason, the startled Miss Walters reminded him that these critics included United States senators. But Haldeman skated on. "In this particular posture," he said evenly, "I think they are *consciously* aiding and abetting the enemy."

The tape was not shown on the *Today* program until some ten days later, on February 7, and the instantaneous result was one of those angry furors that so delight Washington. "Back us, says Mr. Haldeman of the White

House staff," wrote James Reston in the *New York Times* the next morning, "or you are giving aid and comfort to the enemy. Dissent, even honest dissent, is unpatriotic!" Reston then went on to articulate a common theme heard around Washington that morning—that Haldeman sounded mighty like the "Old Nixon." Haldeman, wrote Reston,

> is still back in the Beverly Hilton Hotel in Los Angeles with Nixon on the morning of November 7, 1962, after he ran Mr. Nixon's campaign to defeat against Pat Brown, blaming everything on the wicked press. . . . He is a loyal Nixon man and sees opposition to his chief as opposition to the nation.
>
> . . .

The Haldeman incident, like so many transient furors in Washington, was soon forgotten. It is recounted at length because under analysis it reveals a great deal about the administration of Richard Nixon as it entered its fourth year:

1. The mood of being under siege by the liberal establishment that Nixon carried into the White House with him in 1969 still held him and his closest associates in thrall three years later. This mood, pervasive in their private conversation, popped into public consciousness in Haldeman's "aiding and abetting the enemy" accusation, and in the President's approval of it.

2. Nixon had not broken himself of the irresistible temptation to lash out at his enemies in the most venomous manner, a practice now mimicked by Haldeman. With the political momentum moving in his direction, no assault against essentially ineffective criticism of his peace plan was needed on any pragmatic grounds. Rather, it satisfied an inner compulsion.

3. Loyalty remained the paramount virtue in the upper reaches of the Nixon White House—loyalty upward to the President, loyalty downward from the President. Uncompromising loyalty to Nixon, even to the point of eschewing constructive criticism of him in the privacy of staff meetings, was highly valued among lesser staffers as a worthy characteristic of John Ehrlichman, Chuck Colson and, most particularly, Bob Haldeman. Similarly, loyalty flowed downward to them from the President. For Nixon to have criticized Haldeman for his indiscreet words, either in private or public, would have been a breach of that code.

4. Haldeman, at the apex of the most powerful, highly structured and tightly controlled White House staff system in history, wielded immense power without any accountability. As the *Today* interview showed, no colleague dared challenge him and the President chose not to monitor his activities too closely. Add to this the continuing refusal of Haldeman to give access to influential figures from the outside world—particularly the world of the press and the politicians—and the sacrosanct custom of Executive privilege, which bars Congress from calling him to testify on anything, and Haldeman's awesome power assumes its true dimension.

These four points, moreover, lead to a broader conclusion: sycophantic defenders to the contrary, not all that much had changed in the first three years of the Nixon Presidency. Its strengths and weaknesses, its foibles and its inherent characteristics, were essentially the same as they had been in the beginning. . . .

As for the President himself, he obviously felt and looked more comfortable in the job, relying somewhat less on staff advice and playing an obviously more activist role in an area he had woefully neglected for so long — the area of domestic and particularly economic policy. The New Economic Policy of August 15, 1971, had been the watershed. Besides offering a dose of much-needed confidence to an unconfident nation, and at least temporary relief from the agonizing price and wage spiral, it also brought a bright measure of confidence to the President himself, and thus visibly affected the nature of the Nixon Presidency. Such an audacious exercise of Presidential power obviously reinforced Nixon's self-esteem, on the wane going into the summer of 1971. However many more days he would spend as President, it was inconceivable that Nixon would again neglect the uses of power to permit a major problem to deteriorate as the economic situation had deteriorated for two and a half years.

But having said that, the myth that an utter metamorphosis had transformed the Nixon Presidency on August 15 was preposterous and the implication of the Haldeman Incident proved it. A mature politician does not undergo complete transformation so late in life, and the Nixon of 1972 was basically unchanged from the Nixon of 1969.

His emphasis and interests remained heavily on the foreign policy side. His love of ritual and novelty, and his zest for outrageous overstatement, remained undiminished. His hostility toward ancient enemies and hypersensitivity to criticism prevailed. His suspicion of the press was undimmed and his passion for privacy continued to make him the most inaccessible President since Herbert Hoover. The passage into the Oval Office was jealously guarded by Haldeman with the President's thorough approval and deep gratitude. In the spring of 1972 his last televised news conference had been the one in June 1971.

There persisted also an unreality about the inviolability of the Presidency — a fancy propagated in particular by Haldeman and certainly not discouraged by Nixon. When Nixon was interviewed over national television by Dan Rather of CBS on January 2, 1972, he and his senior staff were outraged that Rather should turn "A Conversion with the President" into a penetrating interview with tough (but certainly in no way unfair) cross-examination. The President's senior staff was even more incensed over Alan Drury, the best-selling Washington novelist and a thoroughgoing conservative. Drury had been granted unusual privileges, including private interviews with Nixon and Haldeman and a seat at several White House staff meetings, to help him prepare an illustrated book on the Nixon administration (*Courage and Hesitation,* Doubleday, 1971). Friendly it was, but not friendly enough for Nixon's men. They regarded the occasional critical and unfriendly material as a betrayal of trust, though no objective reader could possibly agree.

What obscured such pettiness was the fact that all indicators of popularity and approval for the President and his administration were moving upward in 1972, whereas they had been in more or less continuous decline for the preceding three years. But in no small part, this stemmed from forces beyond Nixon's control: the deepening crisis of the ideologically splintered Democratic Party, and Nixon's remarkable freedom from misfortune or serious crisis throughout late 1971 and into early 1972.

The question remained: When adversity struck, as indeed it must, would President Nixon be markedly better equipped to deal with it than he had been in his first years as President? . . .

As the cherry blossoms bloomed in Washington in the spring of 1972, the state of Richard Nixon's political health seemed stronger than at any time since his election.

A Republican Presidential-primary challenge from the right by Representative John Ashbrook of Ohio, reflecting the anger of the Buckleyite conservatives that Nixon had drifted too far leftward (particularly in foreign policy), was picking up no popular support. When Nixon broadly hinted over national television on January 2, 1972, that Spiro T. Agnew probably would be his running mate again in 1972, millions of conservatives were pacified.

In the national opinion polls, Nixon for the first time since 1969 was running far ahead of any possible Democrat, although some of his political aides well understood that much of his advantage derived from the disarray of the Democratic Party and its disorderly struggle to find a nominee.

Nevertheless, after nearly three and a half years in office, the underlying frustrations of Richard Nixon's Presidency persisted:

Instead of quietly going away, the Vietnam war continued to threaten all that Nixon had attempted and accomplished both at home and abroad.

The delicate diplomacy to establish a true era of negotiations with the Soviet Union and Communist China remained a treacherous tortuous affair with only moderate progress recorded.

The economy continued to resist administration remedies, the twin evils of inflation and unemployment persisting and the workingman increasingly discontented.

Though considerably tamer than it had been in 1969, the Democratic Congress was maddeningly balky in dealing with the President's proposals.

And finally, despite all his efforts, Richard Nixon remained an essentially unloved President—more respected and admired, surely, than three years earlier, but still unloved. Bearing that burden, he persisted in the traits that had always dogged his career of adversity: suspicion, hostility toward enemies, aloofness, and that curious inability to reach a state of empathy with his countrymen.

Perhaps if he were reelected, the second term might be different. Then, for the first time in his political life, there would not be yet another election to prepare for and other worlds to conquer.

Watergate

JONATHAN SCHELL

In the course of the last decade, the United States passed through a protracted internal political crisis that diverted the nation's energy and attention from virtually all other business, embittered every aspect of public life, and finally brought the American Constitutional system to the edge of a breakdown. The crisis had its origins in the intervention of the United States in a civil war in Indo-China—a move that, to the astonishment of the whole nation, grew in the space of a few years from a minor distraction in American foreign policy into an engulfing national obsession—and it reached its conclusion with the resignation of a President of the United States. No crisis in American political history came more unexpectedly than this one. And no crisis was more baffling to those who were caught up in it. At any given moment from the mid-nineteen-sixties until the early nineteen-seventies, most of the nation seemed to believe that the worst was over, with the result that the nation was repeatedly pitched from one phase of the crisis into the next without warning. In fact, so bewildered were Americans by what was happening to them and by what they themselves were doing that many came to believe that both in Indo-China and at home the United States had been overtaken by a wholly accidental and therefore wholly absurd fate. And when the crisis was unmistakably over, many voices were heard recommending that the nation try to forget about it immediately, as though people were ready to accept the notion that the events of recent years defied understanding in retrospect—just as they had defied anticipation and had defied understanding as they unfolded—and so were truly without any discoverable meaning whatever. Yet each phase of the crisis—the war abroad, the strife at home, and the systemic convulsion at the end—grew out of the preceding one, and all were episodes in a single story: a story that encompassed some ten years of American history. Today, looking back over events that no one foresaw, that no one fully grasped when they occurred, and that many would now like to forget, Americans are left still wondering where the trouble came from, what it did to the nation, and what, if anything, it was all for. . . .

In mid-1972, as President Nixon's reelection campaign was getting under way, the crisis of Constitutional government in the United States was deepen-

From *The Time of Illusion* by Jonathan Schell. Copyright © 1975 by Jonathan Schell. Reprinted by permission of Alfred A. Knopf.

ing rapidly. The crisis had apparently had its beginnings in the war in Vietnam. Certainly the lines connecting the crisis to the war were numerous and direct. The war had been the principal issue in the struggle between the President and his political opposition—a struggle that had provoked the Presidential Offensive, which was aimed at destroying independent centers of authority in the nation. In more specific ways, too, the evolution of the Administration's usurpations of authority had been bound up with the war. Almost as soon as the President took office, he had ordered the secret bombing campaign against Cambodia, and when details of the campaign leaked out, he had placed the warrantless wiretaps on the phones of newsmen and White House aides. And when the Director of the Federal Bureau of Investigation seemed to be on the verge of getting hold of summaries of those tapped conversations, the President, in his efforts to prevent this, had entered into his venomous hidden struggle with the Director. The White House attempt to "nail" Daniel Ellsberg was another improper action to grow out of the war. And it had been operatives first hired to carry out this project who had gone on to carry out some of the most serious crimes in the plan to spy on and disrupt the Democrats. The evolution of the warrantless-wiretap incident and of the Pentagon Papers incident illustrated one of the ways in which the crisis of the Constitutional system was deepening. Large quantities of secret information were building up in the White House, first in connection with the war policy and then in connection with the President's plans to insure his reëlection. Every day, as the White House operatives went on committing their crimes, the reservoir of secrets grew. And the very presence of so many secrets compelled still more improper maneuverings, and thus the creation of still more secrets, for to prevent any hint of all that information from reaching the public was an arduous business. There had to be ever-spreading programs of surveillance and increasing efforts to control government agencies. Only agencies that unquestioningly obeyed White House orders could be relied upon to protect the White House secrets, and since in normal times it was the specific obligation of some of the agencies to uncover wrongdoing, wherever it might occur, and bring the wrongdoers to justice, some agencies had to be disabled completely. In effect, investigative agencies such as the F.B.I. and the Central Intelligence Agency had to be enlisted in the obstruction of justice.

At some point back at the beginning of the Vietnam war, long before Richard Nixon became President, American history had split into two streams. One flowed aboveground, the other underground. At first, the underground stream was only a trickle of events. But during the nineteensixties—the period mainly described in the Pentagon Papers—the trickle grew to a torrent, and a significant part of the record of foreign affairs disappeared from public view. In the Nixon years, the torrent flowing underground began to include events in the domestic sphere, and soon a large part of the domestic record, too, had plunged out of sight. By 1972, an elaborate preëlection strategy—the Administration strategy of dividing the Democrats—was unfolding in deep secrecy. And this strategy of dividing the Democrats governed not only a program of secret sabotage and espionage but the formation of Administration policy on the most important issues facing the nation. Indeed, hidden strategies for consolidating Presidential authority had been governing expanding areas of Administration policy since 1969, when it first occurred to the President to frame policy not to solve what one aide called "real problems" but to satisfy the needs of public relations. As more and more events occurred out of sight, the aboveground, public record of the period became impoverished and misleading. It became a carefully smoothed surface beneath which many of the most significant events of the period were being concealed. In fact, the split between the Administration's real actions and policies and its pretended actions and policies was largely responsible for the new form of government that had arisen in the Nixon White House, in which images consistently took precedence over substance, and affairs of state were ruled by scenarios. The methods of secrecy and the techniques of public relations were necessary to one another, for the people, lacking access to the truth, had to be told something, and it was the public-relations experts who decided what that something would be.

When the President made his trip to Russia, some students of government who had been worried about the crisis of the American Constitutional system allowed themselves to hope that the relaxation of tensions in the international sphere would spread to the domestic sphere. Since the tensions at home had grown out of events in the international sphere in the first place, it seemed reasonable to assume that an improvement in the mood abroad would give some relief in the United States, too. These hopes were soon disappointed. In fact, the President's drive to expand his authority at home was accelerated; although the nation didn't know it, this was the period in which White House operatives advanced from crimes whose purpose was the discovery of national-security leaks to crimes against the domestic political opposition. The Presidential Offensive had not been called off; it had merely been routed underground. The President spoke incessantly of peace, and had arranged for his public-relations men to portray him as a man of peace, but there was to be no peace — not in Indo-China, and not with a constantly growing list of people he saw as his domestic "enemies." Détente, far from relaxing tensions at home, was seen in the White House as one more justification for its campaign to crush the opposition and seize absolute power.

On Sunday, June 18, 1972, readers of the front page of the [New York] *Times* learned, among other things, that heavy American air strikes were continuing over North Vietnam, that the chairman of President Nixon's Council of Economic Advisers, Herbert Stein, had attacked the economic proposals of Senator McGovern, who in less than a month was to become the Presidential nominee of the Democratic Party, and that the musical *Fiddler on the Roof* had just had its three-thousand-two-hundred-and-twenty-fifth performance on Broadway. Readers of page 30 learned, in a story not listed in the "News Summary and Index," that five men had been arrested in the headquarters of the Democratic National Committee, in the Watergate office building, with burglary tools, cameras, and equipment for electronic surveillance in their possession. In rooms that the men had rented, under aliases, in the adjacent Watergate Hotel, thirty-two hundred-dollar bills were found, along with a notebook containing the notation "E. Hunt" (for E. Howard Hunt, as it turned out) and, next to that, the notation "W. H." (for the White House). The men were members of the Gemstone team.

Most of the high command of the Nixon Administration and the Nixon reëlection committee were out of town when the arrests were made. The President and H. R. Haldeman were on the President's estate in Key Biscayne, Florida. John Dean was in Manila, giving a lecture on drug abuse. John Mitchell, who was then director of the Committee for the Re-Election of the President, and Jeb Magruder, who had become the committee's assistant director, were in California. In the hours and days immediately following the arrests, there was a flurry of activity at the headquarters of the committee, in a Washington office building; in California; and at the White House. Magruder called his assistant in Washington and had him remove certain papers—what later came to be publicly known as Gemstone materials—from his files. Gordon Liddy, by then the chief counsel of the Finance Committee to Re-Elect the President, went into the headquarters himself, removed from his files other materials having to do with the break-in, including other hundred-dollar bills, and shredded them. At the White House, Gordon Strachan, an aide to Haldeman, shredded a number of papers having to do with the setting up of the reëlection committee's undercover operation, of which the break-in at the headquarters of the Democratic National Committee was an important part. Liddy, having destroyed all the evidence in his possession, offered up another piece of potential evidence for destruction: himself. He informed Dean that if the White House wished to have him assassinated he would stand at a given street corner at an appointed time to make things easy. E. Howard Hunt went to his office in the Executive Office Building, took from a safe ten thousand dollars in cash he had there for emergencies, and used it to hire an attorney for the burglars. In the days following, Hunt's name was expunged from the White House telephone directory. On order from John Ehrlichman, his safe was opened and his papers were removed. At one point, Dean—also said to have been acting under instructions from Ehrlichman—give an order for Hunt to leave the country, but then the order was rescinded. Hunt's payment to an attorney for the burglars was the first of many. Herbert Kalmbach was instructed by Dean and, later by Ehrlichman, Haldeman, and Mitchell to keep on making payments, and he, in turn, delegated the task to Anthony Ulasewicz. Theirs was a hastily improvised operation. Kalmbach and Ulasewicz spoke to each other from phone booths. (Phone booths apparently had a strong attraction for Ulasewicz. He attached a change-maker to his belt to be sure to have enough coins for his calls, and he chose to make several of his "drops" of the payoff money in them.) He and Kalmbach used aliases and code language in their conversations. Kalmbach became Mr. Novak and Ulasewicz became Mr. Rivers—names that seem to have been chosen for no specific reason. Hunt, who had had some forty mystery stories published, was referred to as "the writer," and Haldeman, who wore

a crewcut, as "the brush." The payoff money became "the laundry," because when Ulasewicz arrived at Kalmbach's hotel room to pick up the first
installment he put it in a laundry bag. The burglars were "the players," and
the payoff scheme was "the script." Apparently, the reason the White House
conspirators spoke to one another from phone booths was that they thought
the Democrats might be wiretapping them, just as they had wiretapped the
Democrats. In late June, the President himself said to Haldeman, of the
Democrats, "When they start bugging us, which they have, our little boys will
not know how to handle it. I hope they will, though." Considerations like
these led Kalmbach, Ulasewicz, and others working for the White House to
spend many unnecessary hours in phone booths that summer.

All these actions were of the sort that any powerful group of conspirators
might take upon the arrest of some of their number. Soon, however, the
White House was taking actions that were possible only because the conspirators occupied high positions in the government, including the highest position
of all—the Presidency. For almost four years, the President had been "reor-
ganizing" the executive branch of the government with a view to getting the
Cabinet departments and the agencies under his personal control, and now he
undertook to use several of these agencies to cover up crimes committed by
his subordinates. In the early stages of the coverup, his efforts were directed
toward removing a single evidentiary link: the fact that the Watergate burglars
had been paid with funds from his campaign committee. There was a vast
amount of other information that needed to be concealed—information
concerning not just the Watergate break-in but the whole four-year record of
the improper and illegal activities of the White House undercover operators,
which stretched from mid-1969, when the warrantless wiretaps were placed,
to the months in 1972 when the secret program for dividing the Democrats
was being carried out—but if this one fact could somehow be suppressed,
then the chain of evidence would be broken, and the rest of it might go
undetected. On June 23rd, the President met with Haldeman and ordered
him to have the C.I.A. request that the F.B.I. halt its investigation into the
origin of the Watergate burglars' funds, on the pretext that C.I.A. secrets
might come to light if the investigation went forward. The problem, Haldeman told the President, was that "the F.B.I. is not under control, because
Gray doesn't exactly know how to control it." Patrick Gray was Acting
Director of the F.B.I. "The way to handle this now," he went on, "is for us to
have Walters call Pat Gray and just say, 'Stay to hell out of this.'" The
reference was to Vernon Walters, Deputy Director of the C.I.A. A moment
later, Haldeman asked the President, concerning the F.B.I., "And you seem to
think the thing to do is get them to stop?" "Right, fine," the President
answered. But he wanted Haldeman to issue the instructions. "I'm not going
to get that involved," he said. About two hours later, Haldeman and Ehrlichman met with C.I.A. Director Richard Helms and Deputy Director Walters,
and issued the order.

The maneuver gave the White House only a temporary advantage. Six
days later, on June 29th, Gray did cancel interviews with two people who

could shed light on the origin of the burglars' funds. (On the twenty-eighth, Ehrlichman and Dean had handed him all the materials taken from Hunt's safe, and Dean had told him that they were never to "see the light of day." Gray had taken them home, and later he burned them.) But soon a small rebellion broke out among officials of the F.B.I. and the C.I.A. Meetings were held, and at one point Gray and Walters told each other they would rather resign than submit to the White House pressure and compromise their agencies. Several weeks after the request was made, the F.B.I. held the interviews after all. The rebellion in the ranks of the federal bureaucracy was not the first to break out against the Nixon White House. As early as 1969, some members of the Justice Department had fought Administration attempts to thwart the civil-rights laws. In 1970, members of the State Department and members of the Office of Education, in the Department of Health, Education, and Welfare, had protested the invasion of Cambodia. In 1970, too, J. Edgar Hoover had refused to go along with the Huston plan. The executive bureaucracy was one source of the President's great power, but it was also acting as a check on his power. In some ways, it served this function more effectively than the checks provided by the Constitution, for, unlike the other institutions of government, it at least had some idea of what was going on. But ultimately it was no replacement for the Constitutional checks. A President who hired and fired enough people could in time bring the bureaucracy to heel. And although a Gray, a Walters, or a Helms might offer some resistance to becoming deeply involved in White House crimes, they would do nothing to expose the crimes. Moreover, the bureaucracy had no public voice, and was therefore powerless to sway public opinion. Politicians of all persuasions could — and did — heap abuse on "faceless," "briefcase-toting" bureaucrats and their "red tape," and the bureaucracy had no way to reply to this abuse. It had only its silent rebellions, waged with the passive weapons of obfuscation, concealment, and general foot-dragging. Decisive opposition, if there was to be any, had to come from without.

With respect to the prosecutorial arm of the Justice Department, the White House had aims that were less ambitious than its aims with respect to the F.B.I. and the C.I.A., but it was more successful in achieving them. Here, on the whole, the White House men wished merely to keep abreast of developments in the grand-jury room of the U.S. District Court, where officials of the Committee for the Re-Election of the President were testifying on Watergate, and this they accomplished through the obliging cooperation of Henry Petersen, the chief of the Criminal Division, who reported regularly to John Dean and later to the President himself. Dean subsequently described the coöperation to the President by saying, "Petersen is a soldier. He played — he kept me informed. He told me when we had problems, where we had problems, and the like. Uh, he believes in, in, in you. He believes in this Administration. This Administration has made him." What happened in the Grand Jury room was further controlled by the coördinating of perjured testimony from White House aides and men working for the campaign committee. As for the prosecutors, a sort of dim-wittedness — a failure to draw obvious conclusions, a failure to follow up leads, a seeming willingness to construe the Watergate case narrowly — appeared to be enough to keep them from running afoul of the White House.

While all these moves were being made, the public was treated to a steady stream of categorical denials that the White House or the President's campaign committee had had anything to do with the break-in or with efforts to cover up the origins of the crime. The day after the break-in, Mitchell, in California, described James McCord, one of the burglars, as "the proprietor of a private security agency who was employed by our Committee months ago to assist with the installation of our security system." Actually, McCord was the committee's chief of security at the moment when he was arrested. Mitchell added, " We want to emphasize that this man and the other people involved were not operating either in our behalf or with our consent. . . . There is no place in our campaign or in the electoral process for this type of activity, and we will not permit nor condone it." On June 19th, two days after the break-in, Press Secretary Ziegler contemptuously dismissed press reports of White House involvement. "I'm not going to comment from the White House on a third-rate burglary attempt," he said. On June 20th, when Lawrence O'Brien, the chairman of the Democratic Party, revealed that the Party had brought a one-million-dollar civil-damages suit against the Committee for the Re-Election of the President and the five burglary suspects, charging invasion of privacy and violation of the civil rights of the Democrats, Mitchell stated that the action represented "another example of sheer demagoguery on the part of Mr. O'Brien." Mitchell said, "I reiterate that this committee did not authorize and does not condone the alleged actions of the five men apprehended there."

Among the nation's major newspapers, only one, the Washington *Post,* consistently gave the Watergate story prominent headlines on the front page. Most papers, when they dealt with the story at all, tended to treat it as something of a joke. All in all, the tone of the coverage was not unlike the coverage of the Clifford Irving affair the previous winter, and the volume of the coverage was, if anything, less. "Caper" was the word that most of the press settled upon to describe the incident. A week after the break-in, for instance, the *Times* headlined its Watergate story WATERGATE CAPER. When another week had passed, and Howard Hunt's connection with the break-in had been made known, *Time* stated that the story was "fast stretching into the most provocative caper of 1972, an extraordinary bit of bungling of great potential advantage to the Democrats and damage to the Republicans in this election year." In early August, the *Times* was still running headlines like THE PLOT THICKENS IN WATERGATE WHODUNIT over accounts of the repercussions of the burglary. "Above all, the purpose of the break-in seemed obscure," the *Times* said. "But these details are never explained until the last chapter." The President held a news conference six weeks after the break-in, and by then the story was of such small interest to newsmen that not one question was asked concerning it. . . .

During the summer and early fall, a good deal of information about the origins of the break-in was made public. It became known (through interviews given to the press by Alfred Baldwin, a former F.B.I. agent and the member of the Watergate break-in team who had been in charge of the monitoring equipment) that transcripts of phone conversations tapped by the Watergate bugging team had been delivered to someone at the Committee for the Re-Election of the President. It became known (through White House and campaign-committee responses to the inquiries of reporters) that G. Gordon Liddy and E. Howard Hunt had once worked for the White House. And it became known (through the investigative reporting of the Washington *Post*) that twenty-five thousand dollars that had been given as a contribution to the Nixon campaign had been deposited in a Florida bank to the account of Bernard Barker, who was one of the Watergate burglars. These facts seemed to point to certain inescapable conclusions, but somehow the public's interest was not awakened. A poll taken in October showed that only half of the public had even heard of the break-in. Stories pertaining to the aboveground history of the country dominated the news. . . .

As Congress set about trying to recover its powers in the wake of total reorganization and the bombing of North Vietnam, the trial of the seven Watergate defendants got under way in U.S. District Court. In the months since the election, the issue of Watergate had faded, and the papers had devoted their front pages to other news. Shortly after the trial began, however, the front-page news was that all the defendants but two had pleaded guilty. In the courtroom, Judge John Sirica, who presided, found himself dissatisfied with the questioning of witnesses by the government prosecutors. The prosecutors now had a suggestion as to the burglars' motive. They suggested that it might be blackmail. They did not say of whom or over what. At the trial, the key prosecution witness, the former F.B.I. agent Alfred Baldwin, related that on one occasion he had taken the logs of the Watergate wiretaps to the headquarters of the Committee for the Re-Election of the President. But this suggested nothing to the Justice Department, one of whose spokesmen had maintained when the indictment was handed up in September that there was "no evidence" showing that anyone except the defendants was involved. Sirica demurred. "I want to know where the money comes from," he said to the defendant Bernard Barker. "There were hundred-dollar bills floating around like coupons." When Barker replied that he had simply received the money in the mail in a blank envelope and had no idea who might have sent it, Sirica commented, "I'm sorry, but I don't believe you." When the defense lawyers protested Sirica's questioning, he said, "I don't think we should sit up here like nincompoops. The function of a trial is to search for the truth."

All the Watergate defendants but one were following the White House scenario to the letter. The exception was James McCord. He was seething with scenarios of his own. He hoped to have the charges against him dismissed, and, besides, he had been angered by what he understood as a suggestion from one of his lawyers that the blame for the Watergate break-in be assigned to the C.I.A., his old outfit, to which he retained an intense loyalty. There was some irony in the fact that McCord's anger had been aroused by an Administration plan to involve the C.I.A. in its crimes. McCord believed that Nixon's removal of C.I.A. director Richard Helms, in December of 1972 — at the very time that McCord himself was being urged to lay the blame for Watergate at the door of the C.I.A. — was designed to pave the way for an attempt by the Administration itself to blame the break-in on the agency and for a takeover of the agency by the White House. He had worked for the White House, but he did not see the reorganizational wars from the White House point of view. He saw them from the bureaucrats' point of view; in his opinion, President Nixon was attempting to take over the C.I.A. in a manner reminiscent of attempts by Hitler to take control of German intelligence agencies before the Second World War. The White House, that is, belatedly discovered that it had a disgruntled "holdover" on its hands. And this particular holdover really was prepared to perform sabotage; he was prepared, indeed, to sabotage not just the President's policies but the President himself, and, what was more, he had the means to do it. McCord was putting together a scenario that could destroy the Nixon Administration. In a letter delivered in December, to his White House contact, the undercover operative John Caulfield, McCord pronounced a dread warning: If the White House continued to try to have the C.I.A. take responsibility for the Watergate burglary, "every tree in the forest will fall," and "it will be a scorched desert." Piling on yet another metaphor of catastrophe, he wrote, "Pass the message that if they want it to blow, they are on exactly the right course. I am sorry that you will get hurt in the fallout." McCord was the first person in the Watergate conspiracy to put in writing exactly what the magnitude of the Watergate scandal was. Many observers had been amazed at the extreme hard line that the President had taken since his landslide reëlection — the firings in the bureaucracies, the incomprehensible continuation of the attacks on Senator McGovern, the renewed attacks on the press, the attacks on Congress's power of the purse, the bombing of Hanoi. They could not know that at the exact moment when President Nixon was wreaking devastation on North Vietnam, James McCord was threatening to wreak devastation on him. . . .

On February 7th, the Senate, by a vote of seventy-seven to none, established a Select Committee on Presidential Campaign Activities, to look into abuses in the Presidential campaign of 1972, including the Watergate break-in; and the Democratic leadership appointed Senator Sam Ervin, of North Carolina, the author of the resolution to establish the Select Committee, to be its chairman. Three days later, the Administration secretly convened a Watergate committee of its own, in California — at the La Costa Resort Hotel and Spa, not far from the President's estate in San Clemente, with John Dean, H. R. Haldeman, John Ehrlichman, and Richard Moore, a White House aide, in attendance. The meeting lasted for two days. Its work was to devise ways of hampering, discrediting, and ultimately blocking the Ervin committee's investigation. . . .

In the latter part of March, the pace of events in . . . the coverup quickened. Under the pressure of the pending sentences, two of the conspirators were breaking ranks: James McCord and Howard Hunt. McCord, who had been threatening the White House with exposure since December, now wrote a letter to Judge Sirica telling what he knew of the coverup. Hunt, for his part, was angry because he and the other defendants and their lawyers had not been paid as much money as they wanted in return for their silence. In November, 1972, he called Charles Colson to remind him that the continuation of the coverup was a "two-way street," and shortly after the middle of March he told Paul O'Brien, an attorney for the reëlection committee, that if more funds weren't forthcoming immediately he might reveal some of the "seamy things" he had done for John Ehrlichman—an apparent reference to the break-in at the office of Daniel Ellsberg's psychiatrist. Shortly thereafter, O'Brien informed Dean of Hunt's demand. These events on one edge of the coverup had an immediate influence on the chemistry of the whole enterprise. On March 21st, John Dean, convinced now that the coverup could not be maintained, met with the President and related the story of it as he knew it from beginning to end. The President's response was to recommend that the blackmail money be paid to Hunt. "I think you should handle that one pretty fast," he said. And later he said, "But at the moment don't you agree that you'd better get the Hunt thing? I mean, that's worth it, at the moment." And he said, "That's why your, for your immediate thing you've got no choice with Hunt but the hundred and twenty or whatever it is. Right?" The President was willing to consider plans for limited disclosure, and the meeting ended with a suggestion from Haldeman, who had joined the two other men: "We've got to figure out where to turn it off at the lowest cost we can, but at whatever cost it takes."

Dean's session with the President put the President in a peculiarly difficult position. The conspirators in a coverup are caught in a web of powerful opposing forces. On the one hand, they need to keep themselves as closely informed as possible about the crimes that are being covered up and about the coverup itself, in order to be able to plan their moves. On the other hand, they need to keep themselves as ignorant as possible of these same matters, since the knowledge of crimes, if it is not reported to the responsible authorities, is itself a crime—misprision. When the conspirators are men in government with a special obligation to investigate and prosecute crimes, the tension between the need to know and the need not to know is particularly acute. In such a case, the multiplicity of roles assumed by each conspirator gives rise to a complexity of motivation so great as to befuddle even the conspirator himself. The conspirator who is a public official not only must know the facts, in order to get on with the coverup, while seeming not to know the facts, in order to escape indictment for misprision, but also must, in his public role as investigator, seem actively to seek the facts while secretly making sure he does not find them. When the sleuth and the criminal are united in one person, as they were in the person of the President during the Watergate coverup, one is presented with the spectacle of a man following his own footsteps in circles while taking care never to discover where they lead.

President Nixon was well aware of the importance of remaining ignorant of some matters, and in late February, he said to Dean, "The main thing, of course, is also the, the isolation of the President from this." (There had been much discussion in recent years about the isolation of American Presidents from reality, but no one had suggested that a President might deliberately cultivate such isolation.) Now Dean, by laying out the story of the coverup in detail, was forcing the President to take some action, because if the President did not now act, Dean would be a witness to the crime of the President's inaction.

The defection of Hunt and McCord had upset the delicate balance of roles demanded by the coverup. Information that had to be kept secret began to flow in a wide loop through the coverup's various departments. Not only Hunt and McCord but Dean and Magruder began to tell their stories to the prosecutors. The prosecutors, in turn, relayed the information to Attorney General Kleindienst and Assistant Attorney General Petersen, who then relayed it to Haldeman and Ehrlichman, who in this period were desperately attempting to avoid prosecution, and were therefore eager to know what was happening in the Grand Jury room. Any defections placed the remaining conspirators in an awkward position. In order to get clear of the collapsing coverup, they had to become public inquisitors of their former subordinates and collaborators. Such a transformation, however, was not likely to sit well with the defectors, who were far from eager to shoulder the blame for the crimes of others, and who, furthermore, were in possession of damaging information with which to retaliate.

Notwithstanding these new tensions, the President sought to continue the coverup. In the weeks following his meeting with Dean on March 21st, his consistent strategy was what might be called the hors-d'oeuvre strategy. The President described the strategy to Haldeman and Ehrlichman after a conversation with Dean on April 14th by saying, "Give 'em an hors d'oeuvre and maybe they won't come back for the main course." His hope was that by making certain public revelations and by offering a certain number of victims to the prosecutors he could satisfy the public's appetite, so that it would seek no more revelations and no more victims. (This technique, which Ehrlichman, on another occasion, called a "modified limited hang-out," was also what Haldeman had had in mind when he suggested that they should "turn it off at the lowest cost" they could.) Hors d'oeuvres of many kinds came under consideration. Some were in the form of scapegoats to be turned over to the prosecutors, and others were in the form of incomplete or false reports to be issued to the public. . . .

In the White House, the fabric of reality had disintegrated altogether. What had got the President into trouble from the start had been his remarkable capacity for fantasy. He had begun by imagining a host of domestic foes. In retaliating against them, he had broken the law. Then he had compounded his lawbreaking by concealing it. And, finally, in the same way that he had broken the law although breaking it was against his best interests, he was bringing himself to justice even as he thought he was evading justice. For, as though in anticipation of the deterioration of his memory, he had installed another memory in the Oval Office, which was more nearly perfect than his own, or anyone else's merely human equipment: he had installed the taping system. The Watergate coverup had cast him in the double role of conspirator and investigator. Though the conspirator in him worked hard to escape the law, it was the investigator in him that gained the upper hand in the end. While he was attempting to evade the truth, his machines were preserving it forever.

At the moment when the President announced "major developments" in the Watergate case, the national process that was the investigation overwhelmed the national process that was the coverup. The events that followed were all the more astounding to the nation because, at just the moment when the coverup began to explode, the President, in the view of many observers, had been on the point of strangling the "obsolete" Constitutional system and replacing it with a Presidential dictatorship. One moment, he was triumphant and his power was apparently irresistible; the next moment, he was at bay. For in the instant the President made his announcement, the coverup cracked — not just the Watergate coverup but the broader coverup, which concealed the underground history of the last five years — and the nation suffered an inundation of news. The newspaper headlines now came faster and thicker than ever before in American history. The stories ran backward in time, and each day's newspaper told of some event a little further in the past as reporters traced the underground history to the early days of the Administration, and even into the terms of former Administrations. With the history of half a decade pouring out all at once, the papers were stuffed with more news than even the most diligent reader could absorb. Moreover, along with the facts, non-facts proliferated as the desperate men in the White House put out one false or distorted statement after another, so that each true fragment of the story was all but lost in a maze of deceptions, and each event, true or false, came up dozens of times, in dozens of versions, until the reader's mind was swamped. And, as if what was in the newspapers were not already too much, television soon started up, and, in coverage that was itself a full-time job to watch, presented first the proceedings of the Ervin committee and then the proceedings of the House Judiciary Committee, when it began to weigh the impeachment of the President. And, finally, in a burst of disclosure without anything close to a precedent in history, the tapes were revealed — and not just once but twice. The first set of transcripts was released by the White House and was doctored, and only the second set, which was released by the Judiciary Committee, gave an accurate account of the President's conversations.

As the flood of information flowed into the public realm, overturning the accepted history of recent years, the present scene was also transformed. The Vice-President was swept from office when his bribe-taking became known, but so rapid was the pace of events that his departure was hardly noticed. Each of the institutions of the democracy that had been menaced by the President — and all had been menaced — was galvanized into action in its turn: the press, the television networks, the Senate, the House of Representatives, and, finally, in a dispute over release of the tapes, the Supreme Court. The public, too, was at least awakened, when the President fired the Special Prosecutor whom he had appointed to look into the White House crimes. In an outpouring of public sentiment that, like so much else that happened at the time, had no precedent in the nation's history, millions of letters and telegrams poured in to Congress protesting the President's action. The time of letters sent by the President to himself was over, and the time of real letters from real people had come. No one of the democracy's institutions was powerful enough by itself to remove the President; the efforts of all were required — and only when those efforts were combined was he forced from office. . . .

Document

White House Transcript

Meeting: The President and Haldeman, Oval Office, June 23, 1972 (10:04–11:39 A.M.)

H: Now, on the investigation, you know the Democratic break-in thing, we're back in the problem area because the F.B.I. is not under control, because [acting director of the F.B.I. L. Patrick] Gray [III] doesn't exactly know how to control it and they have — their investigation is now leading into some productive areas — because they've been able to trace the money — not through the money itself — but through the bank sources — the banker. And, and it goes in some directions we don't want it to go. Ah, also there have been some things — like an informant came in off the street to the F.B.I. in Miami who was a photographer or has a friend who is a photographer who developed some films through this Guy Barker and the films had pictures of Democratic National Committee letterhead documents and things. So it's things like that that are filtering in. Mitchell came up with yesterday, and John Dean analyzed very carefully last night and concludes, concurs now with Mitchell's recommendation that the only way to solve this, and we're set up beautifully to do it, ah, in that and that — the only network that paid any attention to it last night was NBC — they did a massive story story on the Cuban thing.

P: That's right.

H: That the way to handle this now is for us to have [deputy director of

From the *New York Times,* August 6, 1974.

the CIA Vernon] Walters call Pat Gray and just say, "stay to hell out of this—this is ah, business here we don't want you to go any further on it." That's not an unusual development, and ah, that would take care of it.

P: What about Pat Gray—you mean Pat Gray doesn't want to?

H: Pat does want to. He doesn't know how to, and he doesn't have, he doesn't have any basis for doing it. Given this, he will then have the basis. He'll call Mark Felt in, and the two of them—and Mark Felt wants to cooperate because he's ambitious—

P: Yeah.

WHAT WOULD BE SAID

H: He'll call him in and say, "we've got the signal from across the river to put the hold on this." And that will fit rather well because the FBI agents who are working the case, at this point, feel that's what it is.

P: This is CIA? They've traced the money? Who'd they trace it to?

H: Well they've traced it to a name, but they haven't gotten to the guy yet.

P: Would it be somebody here?

H: Ken Dahlberg.

P: Who the hell is Ken Dahlberg?

H: He gave $25,000 in Minnesota and, ah, the check went directly to this guy Barker.

P: It isn't from the committee though, from Stans?

H: Yeah. It is. It's directly traceable and there's some more through some Texas people that went to the Mexican Bank which can also be traced to the Mexican Bank—They'll get their names today.

H: —and (pause)

P: Well, I mean, there's no way—I'm just thinking if they don't cooperate, what do they say? That they were approached by the Cubans. That's what Dahlberg has to say, the Texans too, that they—

H: Well, if they will. But then we're relying on more and more people all the time. That's the problem and they'll stop if we could take this other route.

P: All right.

H: And you seem to think the thing to do is get them to stop?

P: Right, fine.

H: They say the only way to do that is from White House instructions. And it's got to be to Helms and to—ah, what's his name—? Walters.

P: Walters.

WHAT PROPOSAL WOULD BE

H: And the proposal would be that Ehrlichman and I call them in, and say, ah—

P: All right, fine. How do you call him in—I mean you just—well, we protected Helms from one hell of a lot of things.

H: That's what Ehrlichman says.

P: Of course, this Hunt, that will uncover a lot of things. You open that scab there's a hell of a lot of things and we just feel that it would be very detrimental to have this thing go any further. This involves these Cubans, Hunt and a lot of hanky-panky that we have nothing to do with ourselves. Well what the hell, did Mitchell know about this?

H: I think so, I don't think he knew the details, but I think he knew.

P: He didn't know how it was going to be handled though—with Dahlberg and the Texans and so forth? Well who was the asshole that did? Is it Liddy? Is that the fellow? He must be a little nuts.

H: He is.

P: I mean he just isn't well screwed on is he? Is that the problem?

H: No, but he was under pressure, apparently, to get more information, and as he got more pressure, he pushed the people harder to move harder—

P: Pressure from Mitchell?

H: Apparently.

P: Oh, Mitchell. Mitchell was at the point (unintelligible).

H: Yea.

P: All right, fine. I understand it all. We won't second-guess Mitchell and the rest. Thank God it wasn't Colson.

COLSON INTERVIEWED

H: The F.B.I. interviewed Colson yesterday. They determined that would be a good thing to do. To have him take an interrogation, which he did, and that—the F.B.I. guys working the case concluded that there were one or two possibilities—one, that this is a White House—they don't think that there is anything at the election committee—they think it was either a White House operation and they had some obscure reasons for it—nonpolitical, or it was a Cuban and the C.I.A. and after their interrogation of Colson yesterday, they concluded it was not the White House, but are now convinced it is a C.I.A. thing, so the C.I.A. turnoff would—

P: Well, not sure of their analysis, I'm not going to get that involved. I'm (unintelligible).

H: No, sir, we don't want you to.

P: You call them in.

H: Good deal.

P: Play it tough. That's the way they play it and that's the way we are going to play it.

H: O.K.

P: When I saw that news summary, I questioned whether it's a bunch of crap, I thought, er, well it's good to have them off us awhile, because when they start bugging us, which they have, our little boys will not know how to handle it. I hope they will though.

H: You never know.

P: Good.

eleven

THE BLACK STRUGGLE FOR EQUALITY

The black quest for equality has dominated the post–World War II period. Long treated as second-class citizens, blacks began to chip away at the "Jim Crow" system of racial segregation during the war itself, and became even more aggressive in the years that followed. They sought an end to the separation of blacks and whites in public schools and facilities and the protection of the constitutionally guaranteed right to vote. Peaceful at first, the civil rights movement became more militant as modest gains were made but real equality still seemed far away.

In "Race Relations and Social Change," Harvard Sitkoff provides a good overview of what he calls "the preconditions for racial change" in the United States. Arguing that structural changes in the socioeconomic patterns of American life had a pronounced effect on race relations, he describes how industrialization, migration, and prosperity affected black political consciousness. "Desire and will are not enough," Sitkoff states, for a major social movement to succeed. Civil rights progress grew out of the economic transformations that occurred during and after World War II.

Taking a different tack, Clayborne Carson suggests that collective action was the most important factor in the struggle for equality as he focuses on SNCC—the Student Nonviolent Coordinating Committee—in the 1960s. In "SNCC and the Black Struggle," he notes the origins of the organization in the ferment of the sit-ins in Greensboro, North Carolina, and describes its subsequent rise and fall as the civil rights movement itself built up momentum and then declined.

The most important figure in the movement—until his assassination in 1968 — was the Reverend Martin Luther King, Jr. A young black Baptist minister, King gained public attention in the Montgomery bus boycott in the 1950s. Following the nonviolent approach of Indian pacifist Mohandas Gandhi, he preached the possibility of black – white integration in American society. Although he was jailed time and again for his protests, King persisted, and the movement grew accordingly. His most dramatic moment came at the August 1963 March on Washington, where several hundred thousand people heard him describe eloquently his dream for American society. That speech, "I have a Dream," is reprinted here.

On the civil rights movement, Harvard Sitkoff, *The Struggle for Black Equality, 1954 – 1980* (1981), is a good place to begin. August Meier and Elliott Rudwick describe the Congress of Racial Equality in *CORE: A Study in the Civil Rights Movement, 1942 – 1968* (1975). On King himself, see David Lewis, *King: A Critical Biography* (1970), and David J. Garrow, *Bearing the Cross: Martin Luther King, Jr., and the Southern Christian Leadership Conference, 1955 – 1968* (1986). Anne Moody, *Coming of Age in Mississippi* (1968), is the moving autobiography of a black woman who grew up in the South. William H. Chafe, *Civilities and Civil Rights: Greensboro, North Carolina, and the Black Struggle for Freedom* (1980), provides a good treatment of the sit-ins and their consequences. Malcolm X, *The Autobiography of Malcolm X* (1964), is the angry account of a black leader who opposed the nonviolent approach.

Race Relations and Social Change

HARVARD SITKOFF

Of the interrelated causes of progress in race relations since the start of the Great Depression, none was more important than the changes in the American economy. No facet of the race problem was untouched by the elephantine growth of the Gross National Product, which rose from $206 billion in 1940 to $500 billion in 1960, and then in the 1960s increased by an additional 60 percent. By 1970, the economy topped the trillion dollar mark. This spectacular rate of economic growth produced some 25 million new jobs in the quarter of a century after World War II and raised real wage earnings by at least 50 percent. It made possible the increasing income of blacks, their entry into industries and labor unions previously closed to them, gains for blacks in occupational status, and a shortage of workers that necessitated a slackening of restrictive promotion policies and the introduction of scores of government and private industry special job training programs for Afro-Americans. It also meant that the economic progress of blacks did not have to come at the expense of whites, thus undermining the most powerful source of white resistance to the advancement of blacks. The widespread economic deprivation of whites during the Depression and before had given the near-poor majority of whites an economic stake in the repression of blacks. However, as the accelerating growth of the GNP, number of available jobs, and national income (five times in 1970 what it had been in 1945) changed the living conditions of most whites, and lessened their memories of hard times, many came to understand that black progress need not come out of their pockets.

The effect of economic changes on race relations was particularly marked in the South. The rapid industrialization of the South since 1940 ended the dominance of the cotton culture. With its demise went the need for a vast underclass of unskilled, subjugated laborers. Power shifted from rural areas to the cities, and from tradition-oriented landed families to the new officers and professional workers in absentee-owned corporations. The latter had neither the historical allegiances nor the nonrational attachment to racial mores to risk economic growth for the sake of tradition. The old system of race relations had no place in the new economic order. Time and again in the 1950s and 1960s, the industrial and business elite took the lead in accommodating the South to the changes sought by the civil rights movement. As the mayor of Atlanta, the capital of the New South, explained in 1962, "We're too busy to hate. We are free to use our talents and energies to grow and to attract industry. . . . Hate never built anything. There's nothing to be gained from hate but stagnation. Let's forget about fighting and go to work." The following year his successor journeyed to Washington to plead for passage of the proposed civil rights act. Throughout the South, in fact, one increasingly encountered the view that profits and economic expansion required a mini-

From Harvard Sitkoff, "Race Relations: Progress and Prospects," in *Paths to the Present: Interpretive Essays on American History Since 1930,* edited by James T. Patterson. Copyright © 1975 by Burgess Publishing Company. Reprinted by permission of the author.

mum of racial turmoil. Because racial disturbances hurt business, regional values had to yield, and the new Southern power structure acceded to black demands. It could safely do so because the economy had also caused major shifts in population. Industrialization accelerated urbanization and the migration into the South of millions of white collar employees and their families. These newcomers and urbanites had little stake in the perpetuation of the rural caste system. It enhanced neither their self-image as modern, progressive patriots nor their economic interests.

The existence of an "affluent society" boosted the fortunes of the civil rights movement itself in countless ways. Most obviously, it enabled millions of dollars in contributions from wealthy liberals and philanthropic organizations to pour into the coffers of the NAACP, Urban League, Southern Christian Leadership Conference headed by Dr. Martin Luther King, Jr., and countless other Negro rights groups. Without those funds it is difficult to comprehend how the movement could have accomplished those tasks so essential to its success: legislative lobbying and court litigation; nationwide speaking tours and the daily mailings of press releases all over the country; the organization of mass marches, demonstrations, and rallies; constant, rapid communication and travelling over long distances; and the convocation of innumerable public conferences and private strategy sessions.

Prosperity also increased the leisure time of many Americans and enabled them to react immediately to the changing times. The sons and daughters of the newly affluent increasingly went to college. By 1970, five times as many students were in college as in 1940. What they learned helped lead to pronounced changes in white attitudes towards racial discrimination and segregation. Many took what they had been taught out into the streets, working for the movement, participating in the Mississippi Freedom Summer of 1964, the Freedom Rides of 1961, and the rash of sit-ins in 1960. Other whites learned from the TV sets in their homes. By the time Lyndon Johnson signed the Voting Rights Act of 1965, some 95 percent of all American families owned at least one television. The race problem entered their living rooms. Tens of millions nightly watched the drama of the Negro Revolution. The growing majority of Americans favoring racial equality and justice had those sentiments reinforced by TV shots of snarling police dogs attacking black demonstrators, rowdy white hoods molesting young blacks patiently waiting to be served at a lunch counter, and hate-filled white faces in a frenzy because of the effrontery of little black children entering a previously all-white school.

Negroes viewed the same scenes on their TV sets, and the rage these scenes engendered helped transform isolated battles into a national campaign. Concurrently, the conspicuous display of white affluence on TV vividly awakened blacks to a new sense of their relative deprivation. That, too, aroused black anger. And *now* something *could* be done about it. The growing Negro middle and working classes put their money and bodies on the line: the newly educated and affluent became the backbone of the civil rights movement. In addition, because the consumer economy depended on consumer purchasing, black demands had to be taken seriously. By 1970, black buying power topped $25 billion, a large enough sum to make the threat of boycotts an effective weapon for social change. Negro economic advances also made blacks less patient in demanding alterations in their social status. They desired all the decencies and dignity they believed their full pay check promised. Lastly, nationwide prosperity contributed to more blacks entering college, which stimulated higher expectations and a heightened confidence that American society need not be static. In sum, the changes in the economy since 1940 underlay the Negro revolution of rising expectations: as blacks improved their status, and found whites less resistant to that progress, they became increasingly impatient with all remaining humiliations of second-class citizenship.

Most importantly, changes in the economy radically affected black migration. Cotton mechanization pushed blacks off the farms, and the lure of jobs pulled them to the cities. In 1930, three-quarters of the Negroes in the United States lived in or near the rural black belt. By 1973, over half the blacks lived outside the South, and, nationally, nearly 80 percent resided in urban areas. Indeed, in the two decades prior to 1970, the black population in metropolitan areas rose by more than seven million—a number greater than the total immigration by any single nationality group in American history. Such a mass migration, in conjunction with prosperity, fundamentally altered the whole configuration of the race problem. First, the issue of race became national in scope. No longer did it affect only one region, and no longer could it be left in the hands of Southern whites. Second, it modified the objective conditions of life for Negroes and changed their perceptions of what was right and how to get it. For the first time in American history the great mass of blacks were freed from the confines of a rigid caste structure. Now subject to new formative experiences, Negroes developed new norms and beliefs. In the relative anonymity and freedom of the North and the city, aggression could be turned against one's oppressor rather than against one's self, more educational and employment opportunities could be secured, and political power could be mobilized. Similarly, as expectations of racial equality increased with the size of black migration from the rural South, so the religious faith that had for so long sustained Afro-Americans working on plantations declined. The promise of a better world in the next one could not suffice. The urban black would not wait for his rewards until the afterlife.

Because Negroes could vote in the North, they stopped believing they would have to wait. Enfranchisement promised all in this life that religion did in the next. The heavenly city, to put it mildly, was not achieved; but vital legislative and legal accomplishments did flow from the growing Negro vote. Without the presence of black political power in the North, the demonstrations in the South would not have led to the civil rights laws and presidential actions necessary to realize the objectives of those protesting against Jim Crow in Montgomery, Greensboro, Birmingham, Jackson, and Selma. Although the claim of Negro publicists that the concentration of Northern black votes in the industrial cities made the Afro-American electorate a "balance of power" in national politics was never wholly accepted by either major party, the desire of every president from Franklin Roosevelt to Lyndon Johnson to win and hold the black vote made it an important factor in determining public policy. And as the Democratic party became less dependent upon Southern electoral votes, and less able to garner them, it had to champion civil rights more in order to win the populous states of the North and Midwest where blacks were increasingly becoming an indispensable component of the liberal coalition.

The prominence of the United States as a world power further pushed politicians into making race relations a matter of national concern. During World War II millions of Americans became aware for the first time of the danger of racism to national security. Japan focused on the United States' racist treatment of nonwhite citizens as the core of its propaganda appeals to win the loyalty of the colored peoples of China, India, and Latin America. Each lynching, race riot, and instance of Jim Crow in the American war effort was paraded around the world by the Axis as proof of the hypocrisy of Roosevelt's Four Freedoms. The costs of racism went even higher during the Cold War. The Soviet Union continuously undercut American appeals to the nations of Africa and Asia by publicizing American ill-treatment of Negroes. As the competition between the United States and international Communism intensified, foreign policy makers came to recognize racism as the American's own worst enemy. "The existence of discrimination against minority groups in this country," Undersecretary of State Dean Acheson stated in 1946, "has an adverse effect on our relations with other countries. We are reminded over and over by some foreign newspapers and spokesmen, that our treatment of various minorities leaves much to be desired. . . . Frequently we find it next to impossible to formulate a satisfactory answer to our critics in other countries." The following year, a presidential commission stressed the international problems caused by America's failure to grant equality to blacks, and, early in 1948, President Harry Truman justified his asking Congress for civil rights legislation squarely on the world-wide implications of American race relations. Rarely in the next twenty years did a plea for civil rights before the Supreme Court, on the floor of Congress, and emanating from the White House fail to emphasize that point. In short, fear forced the nation to hasten the redefining of the Negro's status. The more involved in world affairs the United States became, the more imperative grew the task of setting its racial affairs in order.

The rapid growth of nationalistic independence movements among the world's colored peoples had special significance for Afro-Americans. In 1960 alone, sixteen African nations emerged from under white colonial rule. Each proclamation of independence in part shamed blacks in the United States to intensify their struggle for equality and justice, and in part caused a surge of racial pride in Negroes, an affirmation of blackness. "At the rate things are going here," Negro author James Baldwin jeered during the sit-in struggles, "all of Africa will be free before we can get a lousy cup of coffee." And a year later, Eldridge Cleaver wrote from San Quentin prison: "When a black President Kwame Nkrumah of Ghana, arrayed majestically in colorful tribal robes, can stride in towering dignity and pride onto the highest rostrum of the United Nations General Assembly, and deliver a rousing, epoch-making speech — without first pausing to either 'straighten' his hair or 'bleach' his skin, the unspoken message to his brethren is unmistakable: Black is Coming Back! . . . And then when Africa asks the American Negro with what type of hair was he born, he will answer loud and clear, with dignity and pride: 'As crinkly as yours.'" Both the shame and the price contributed mightily to the Negro Revolt. The experience of African independence proved the feasibility of change and the vulnerability of white supremacy, while at the same time aiding Afro-Americans to see themselves as members of a world majority rather than as just a hopelessly outnumbered American minority.

The decline in intellectual respectability of ideas used to justify segregation and discrimination similarly provided Afro-Americans with new weapons and shields. The excesses of Nazism and the decline of Western imperialism combined with internal developments in the academic disciplines of anthropology, biology, history, psychology, and sociology to discredit notions of inherent racial differences or predispositions. First in the 1930s, then with accelerating rapidity during World War II and every year thereafter, books and essays attacking racial injustice and inequality rolled off the presses. As early as 1944, Gunnar Myrdal in his monumental *An American Dilemma* termed the pronounced change in scholarship about race "the most important of all social trends in the field of interracial relations." This conclusion overstated the power of the word, but undoubtedly the mountain of the new data, theory, and exposition at least helped to erode the pseudo-scientific rationalizations once popularly accepted as the basis for white supremacy. Every public opinion poll and attitudinal survey taken since the start of World War II emphatically underlined America's growing recognition of the harm done to blacks by racism. Indeed, racial equalitarianism had become part of the United States' official creed by the 1960s and a major theme in the teachings of the nation's media and educational systems.

In such an atmosphere, young blacks could mature without "the mark of oppression." Negroes could safely abandon the "nigger" role. To the extent that textbooks, sermons, declarations by governmental officials, advertising, and movies and TV affirmed the need to transform relationships between the races and to support Negro demands for full citizenship, blacks could confidently and openly rebel against the inequities they viewed as the source of their oppression. They could publicly express the rage their parents had been forced to internalize; they could battle for what they deemed their birthright rather than wage war against themselves. Thus, in conjunction with the migration to cities, these new cultural processes helped to produce the "New Negro" hailed by essayists ever since the Montgomery bus boycott in 1956 inaugurated a more aggressive state in the Afro-American's quest for equality.

In sum, changes in the American economy after 1940 set in motion a host of developments which made possible a transformation in race relations. The increasing income and number of jobs available to blacks and whites, and Negro migration and social mobility, coalesced with converging trends in politics, foreign affairs, and the mass media to endow those intent on improving race relations with both the resources and consciousness necessary to challenge the *status quo.* Objective conditions that had little to do with race in a primary sense thus created a context in which organizations and leaders could press successfully for racial changes. This is neither to suggest that individuals do not matter in history nor that the civil rights movement did not make an indispensable contribution to progress in race relations. It is however, to emphasize the preconditions for such an endeavor to prevail. Desire and will are not enough. Significant and long-lasting alterations in society flow neither from the barrel of a gun nor from individual conversions. Mass marches, demonstrations, and rhetoric alone cannot modify entrenched behavior and values. Fundamental social change is accomplished only when individuals seize the moment to mobilize the latent power inherent in an institutional structure suddenly in flux.

Beginning in the 1930s, blacks, no longer facing a monolithic white power structure solidly arrayed against them, demanded with numbers and a unity that had never existed before the total elimination of racial inequality in American life. For three decades, the tactics and goals of the movement steadily grew more militant as the organization, protests, and power of Negroes jumped exponentially. Each small triumph held out the promise of a greater one, heightening expectations and causing blacks to become ever more anxious about the pace of progress.

The first stage centered on securing the enforcement of the Fourteenth and Fifteenth Amendments. Supported mainly by white liberals and upper-middle-class blacks, the civil rights movement in the 1930s and 1940s relied on publicity, agitation, litigation in the courts, and lobbying in the halls of political power to gain the full inclusion of blacks in American life. Advances came in the legal and economic status of blacks, and in the minor social, political, and cultural concessions afforded Afro-Americans in the North, but the all-oppressive system of Jim Crow in the South remained virtually intact. Then a mounting awareness of the possibility and necessity of further change crystallized in a largely Negro-led middle-class movement intent on toppling the whole edifice of segregation and discrimination. A crescendo of direct action protests infused the civil rights movement with a pervasive moral fervor and forced the federal government to yield time and again to each new demand. By the mid-1960s, the civil rights movement had significantly succeeded in accomplishing its stated goals: outlawing enforced segregation and discrimination in public facilities and accommodations, improving educational and employment opportunities, ending disfranchisement, and creating a milieu in which every citizen regardless of race would be judged on his own merit. But that too no longer sufficed. Before most Americans became fully aware of the changes that had occurred, the movement shifted from stressing equality of opportunity to demanding preferential and compensatory programs needed to ensure the advancement of those left behind in a technological society, from appealing for a color-blind society to insisting on one in which blacks could be proud of their own color and would cherish their own separate institutions, and from desiring a fully integrated United States to demanding a pluralistic structure in which blacks could develop their own power to deal from a position of strength with their white counterparts.

First in the court system, then in executive actions, and finally in Congress, this unceasing and mounting pressure from the civil rights movement prodded the government consistently in the direction of *real* racial equality. In the 1930s, the Negro movement failed to secure its two major legislative goals — anti-poll tax and anti-lynching laws — but it did manage to get Franklin D. Roosevelt and other members of his official family to speak on behalf of racial justice, to increase the numbers of blacks in government, to establish a Civil Rights Section in the Justice Department, and to ensure blacks a share of the relief and recovery assistance. In part due to specific New Deal programs, the percentage of Negroes attending and graduating from college rose, black life expectancy increased from 48 to 53 years, the gap between white and black median income began to close, and the more than one million blacks taught to read and write in federally sponsored classes decreased Negro illiteracy from over 16 percent to less than 10 percent. "Conditions were far from ideal," Paul Robeson observed after spending more than a decade in Europe escaping American racism, "they were not so much changed in fact as they appeared to be, in the hopefulness of liberals and Negro leaders. But change was in the air, and this was the best sign of all." Even Ralph Bunche, perhaps Roosevelt's severest black critic in the 1930s, admitted that FDR's administration was without precedence in the manner "it granted broad recognition to the existence of the Negro as a national problem and undertook to give specific consideration to this fact in many ways." In large part, the hopes aroused by the New Deal led to the establishment of such new organizations concerned with race relations as the National Negro Congress, the Southern Conference on Human Welfare, and the Southern Negro Youth Conference, and helped the NAACP to more than double its membership to some fifty thousand in 1940.

The gains during the New Deal, however, functioned primarily as a prelude to the take-off of the civil rights movement during World War II. The ideological character of the war and the government's need for the loyalty and manpower of all Americans stimulated blacks to expect a better deal from the government; this led to a militancy never before seen in black communities. Membership in the NAACP multiplied nearly ten times; the Congress of Racial Equality, organized in 1942, experimented with various forms of nonviolent direct action confrontations to challenge segregation; and A. Philip Randolph attempted to build his March-on-Washington Committee into an all-black mass protest movement. In 1941, his threat of a march on Washington, combined with the growth in the Negro vote and the exigencies of a foreign threat to American security, forced Roosevelt to issue Executive Order 8802 (the first such order dealing with race since Reconstruction), establishing the first President's Committee on Fair Employment Practices

(FEPC). Designed to eliminate discriminatory employment practices in companies and unions with government contracts or engaged in any war-related work, the FEPC, with help from the desperate need for labor caused by the draft and booming war production, aided some two million blacks in gaining employment in defense plants and almost 200,000 more in entering the federal civil service. Black membership in labor unions doubled to 1,250,000 by the end of the war.

Still other barriers crumbled during the war. The Army integrated its officer training program and during the Battle of the Bulge called for Negro volunteers to fight in integrated combat units. The Marines and Navy opened their ranks to blacks for a variety of duties and integrated their basic and advanced training facilities. And, with increasing firmness, liberal politicians pressed for civil rights legislation and emphasized that the practices of white supremacy brought into disrepute America's stated war aims. Minimal gains to be sure, but the expectations they aroused set the stage for the greater advances in the postwar period. By 1945, Afro-Americans had benefited enough from the expansion in jobs and income, service in the armed forces and the massive migration to Northern cities to know better what they now wanted; and they had developed enough political influence, white alliances, and organizational skills to know how to go about getting their civil rights.

Equally vital, the Supreme Court began its major reversal in the 1930s. After having frustrated congressional Reconstruction policies and written into the Constitution its own Jim Crow beliefs, especially in the *Civil Rights Cases* (1883) and *Plessy v. Ferguson* (1896), the Supreme Court started to dismantle the separate-but-equal doctrine in 1938. That year, the high court ruled that Missouri could not exclude a Negro from its state university law school when it offered blacks only scholarships to an out-of-state institution as an alternative. Other Supreme Court decisions prior to World War II whittled away at discrimination in interstate travel, in employment, in judicial and police practices, and in the exclusion of blacks from jury service. During the war, the Court outlawed the white primary, holding that the nominating process of a political party constituted "state action." After various attempts by Southern state governments to circumvent this ruling, the justices in 1953 made clear their determination to void all subterfuges designed to keep blacks disfranchised. In other decisions handed down during the Truman presidency, the Supreme Court moved vigorously against all forms of segregation in interstate commerce, decided that states and the federal government cannot enforce restrictive racial covenants on housing, and so emphasized the importance of "intangible factors" in quality education that the demise of legally segregated schooling for students at all levels became a near certainty.

Meanwhile, the Truman administration emerged as a partisan of the cause of civil rights. Responding to the growth of the Negro vote, the need to blunt the Soviet Union's exploitation of the race issue, and the firmly organized campaign for the advancement of blacks, Harry Truman acted where Roosevelt had feared to. In late 1946, the President appointed a Committee on Civil Rights to recommend specific measures to safeguard the civil rights of minorities. This was the first such committee in American history, and its 1947 report, *To Secure These Rights,* eloquently pointed out all the inequities of life in Jim Crow America and spelled out the moral, economic, and international reasons for government action. It called for the end of segregation and discrimination in public education, employment, housing, the armed forces, public accommodations, and interstate transportation. Other commissions appointed by Truman stressed the need for racial equality in the armed services and the field of education. Early in 1948, Truman sent the first presidential message on civil rights to Congress. Congress failed to pass any of the measures he proposed, but Truman later issued executive orders ending segregation in the military and barring discrimination in federal employment and in work done under government contract. In addition, his Justice Department prepared *amicus curiae* briefs to gain favorable court decisions in civil rights cases, and Truman's rhetoric in behalf of racial justice helped legitimize goals of the civil rights movement. However small the meaningful accomplishments remained, the identification of the Supreme Court and the Presidency with the cause of racial equality further aroused the expectations of Negroes that they would soon share in the American Dream.

No single event did more to quicken Negro hopes than the *coup de grace* to segregated education delivered by a unanimous Supreme Court on May 17, 1954. The *Brown* ruling that separate educational facilities "are inherently unequal" struck at the very heart of white supremacy in the South. A year later, the Court called for compliance "with all deliberate speed," mandating the lower federal courts to require from local school boards "a prompt and reasonable start toward full compliance." But except in the District of Columbia and the border states, the South responded with every conceivable subterfuge to prevent enforcement of the ruling. Angered by this defiance, the Court complained in 1963 that they had "never contemplated that the concept of 'deliberate speed' would countenance indefinite delay in elimination of racial barriers in schools," and the next year the justices with all deliberate sarcasm noted that there had been "entirely too much deliberation and not enough speed." Repeatedly in the 1960s, the Court ruled against all attempts to delay full compliance as "no longer tolerable."

The end of legally mandated segregation in education started a chain reaction which led the Supreme Court ever further down the road toward the total elimination of all racial distinctions in the law. In the most sweeping terms—"As against the reserved powers of the states, Congress may use any rational means to effectuate the constitutional prohibition of racial discrimination in voting"—the Court unanimously upheld the Voting Rights Act of 1965, and struck down all attempts to limit Negro enfranchisement or block Afro-Americans from fully participating in every phase of the political process. It also unanimously declared constitutional Title II of the 1964 Civil Rights Act, barring all racial discrimination in public accommodations, and voided the convictions of Negroes engaged in direct action protests against segregation in the South. For all practical purposes, the legal quest for equality had succeeded: the emphasis on legalism had accomplished its goals. Constitutionally, blacks had become first-class citizens.

But in the decade after the *Brown* decision, the promise of change far outran the reality of it. While individual Negroes of talent desegregated most professions, the recessions of the Fifties caused black unemployment to soar and the gap between Negro and white family income to widen. And despite the rulings of the Supreme Court and the noble gestures and speeches of politicians, massive resistance to desegregation throughout the South proved the rule. This was the context for the second stage of the civil rights movement. When the nation's attempt to forestall integration and racial equality collided with both the Negro's leaping expectations and his dissatisfaction with the speed of change, blacks took to the streets in a wave of nonviolent direct action protests against every aspect of racism still humiliating them.

In each successive year in the momentous decade between the Court's desegregation ruling and congressional approval of the Voting Rights Act, the struggle against white supremacy intensified, blacks annually grew more militant, and the goals of the "Negro Revolt" kept broadening and deepening. First came the Montgomery Bus Boycott, which began on December 5, 1955, and lasted for a year until local authorities finally ended segregation. It popularized a new strategy for the civil rights movement and gave both blacks and whites dedicated to bettering race relations a towering new spokesman, Dr. Martin Luther King, Jr. King fused the precepts of Jesus, Gandhi, and the Declaration of Independence into an almost irresistible plea for racial justice, and his charisma stimulated blacks to act and whites to support those actions as no black leader had ever before been able to do. The next year, Autherine Lucy tried to desegregate the University of Alabama, and in 1957, King established the Southern Christian Leadership Conference, and President Dwight D. Eisenhower sent federal troops to Little Rock to enforce a court order desegregating Central High School. Boycotts against segregation and disfranchisement in Tallahassee, Birmingham, and Tuskegee in the following years, and the admission of Charlayne Hunter and Hamilton Holmes to the University of Georgia in 1960, all helped herald the emergence of the "New Negro," unafraid, militant, and determined to battle for every right due him.

The massive sit-in demonstrations against Jim Crow which started in 1960 further accelerated all the processes of racial change by radicalizing both the tactics and aims of the movement. The formation of the Student Nonviolent Coordinating Committee forced every established civil rights group to act more militantly or risk being despised as "Uncle Tom." In 1961, CORE sponsored a series of Freedom Rides to gain enforcement of the Court and Interstate Commerce Commission rulings against segregation in the waiting rooms, rest rooms, and restaurants of Southern bus terminals. The violence against the Freedom Riders, vividly captured on TV, compelled the Kennedy administration to come out forcefully for the desegregation of all interstate transportation facilities. Another barrier fell in 1962 when James Meredith entered the hitherto all-white University of Mississippi. And then came the dramatic events of 1963, when the civil rights movement reached the highpoint of its strength, unity, and moral fervor. Twice that year President John F. Kennedy federalized the Alabama National Guard to enforce school desegregation. In the spring, tens of thousands of blacks battled local police, fire hoses, and snarling dogs to overturn Birmingham's oppressive system of job discrimination and general segregation; that summer, almost a quarter of a million of blacks and whites participated in a March on Washington for Jobs and Freedom. Preaching to the great throng massed in front of the Lincoln Memorial, and to many millions more tuned in on their TV sets, King dreamed aloud of a United States where the color of one's skin had no meaning, where black and white children would walk together as brothers and sisters, where "all of God's children, black and white men, Jews and Gentiles, Protestants and Catholics, will be able to join hands and sing in the words of that old Negro spiritual, 'Free at last! Free at last! Thank God almighty, we are free at last!'" "Go back to Mississippi, go back to Alabama," King exhorted, and many more thousands did in the Mississippi Freedom Summer of 1964 and the march from Selma to Montgomery in 1965. No section of the country, no segment of the population, no vestige of Jim Crow went untouched by the Negro revolt. The desired responses came from clergymen, educators, and the mass media. Scores of states and municipalities passed fair housing and employment opportunity laws; universities, corporations, and labor unions modified their restrictive entrance requirements; and a public consensus clearly emerged that equality of status was the birthright of every American. . . .

SNCC and the Black Struggle

CLAYBORNE CARSON

The Student Nonviolent Coordinating Committee (SNCC, pronounced "snick") emerged from the seemingly sterile American political landscape of the 1950s, thrived in the midst of the mass struggles of the 1960s, and died in the arid atmosphere of repression, divisiveness, and self-absorption at the beginning of the 1970s. As racial discord and discontent broke through a facade of accommodation, and as black people attempted to end a heritage of racial subordination, SNCC's radicalism flowered, displaying the possible dimensions of personal freedom in pursuit of social change.

SNCC initially attracted southern black college students whose attitudes were confined within the narrow bounds of permissible political dissent of the Cold War era and the even narrower bounds imposed by the southern segregationist regimes. As black students became involved in the lunch counter sit-in movement that began in 1960, they acquired new perspectives for viewing American society and its prevailing cultural and political values. SNCC became a community in which a small but growing number of

Excerpted by permission of the author and publishers from *In Struggle: SNCC and the Black Awakening of the 1960's* by Clayborne Carson. Cambridge, Massachusetts: Harvard University Press. Copyright © 1981 by the President and Fellows of Harvard College.

activists—whites as well as blacks, nonstudents and students, northerners and southerners—attempted to create more satisfying alternatives to the prevailing American middle-class way of life. Because SNCC so clearly reflected the emergent values of an expanding social struggle, it became a gathering point for idealistic young people, who saw in it a unique outlet for expressing their resentment of racial injustice.

After the uncompromising militancy of the student "freedom riders" placed the administration of President John F. Kennedy on the defensive during the spring and summer of 1961, a group of activists left campuses and careers to become full-time SNCC staff members. With few resources other than their commitment, creativity, and youthful energy, these SNCC workers led a frontal attack on the southern strongholds of racism. While mobilizing black communities, they acquired a distinctive radicalism that was shaped by their changing experiences and aspirations. At first this radicalism took the form of an insistence that the federal government act forcefully and swiftly on behalf of civil rights workers and southern blacks seeking civil rights. By the mid-1960s, however, SNCC workers began to question not only the pace but also the prevailing strategies of change in American society. They observed that existing leaders did not initiate the most significant local struggles; instead, such struggles produced new indigenous leadership capable of sustaining them. By making southern blacks more confident of their capacity to overcome oppression, SNCC workers revived dormant feelings of racial consciousness and ultimately stimulated many of the movements that would transform American society. . . .

SNCC's development can be traced through three stages. In the first stage civil rights activists came together in SNCC to form a community with a social struggle. SNCC workers sought to create a rationale for activism by eclectically adopting ideas from the Gandhian independence movement and from the American traditions of pacifism and Christian idealism as formulated by the Congress of Racial Equality (CORE), Fellowship of Reconciliation (FOR), and Southern Christian Leadership Conference (SCLC). SNCC, however, was typically less willing than other civil rights groups to impose its ideas on local black leaders or to restrain southern black militancy. Viewed as the "shock troops" of the civil rights movement, SNCC activists established projects in areas such as rural Mississippi considered too dangerous by other organizations. As the thrust of SNCC's activities shifted from desegregation to political rights, its philosophical commitment to nonviolent direct action gave way to a secular, humanistic radicalism influenced by Marx, Camus, Malcolm X, and most of all by the SNCC organizers' own experiences in southern black communities. In the summer of 1964 SNCC's singular qualities came to national attention when it played a leading role in bringing hundreds of northern students to Mississippi for a decisive battle over voter registration in the main bastion of southern segregation.

The second stage of SNCC's development began after the defeat of an attempt by the Mississippi Freedom Democratic party (MFDP) to unseat the regular all-white delegation to the Democratic National Convention in August 1964. SNCC had by this time become a training ground for activists who would participate in the Free Speech Movement at Berkeley, the Vietnam War protests, and the women's struggle, but SNCC workers themselves had become more uncertain about the values guiding their work. Over the next two years, they looked inward, questioning whether the strategy they had followed could achieve the fundamental social changes they now viewed as necessary. Staff members debated whether southern black people could achieve lasting improvement in their lives while continuing to rely on appeals for white liberal support and federal intervention, and whether SNCC could continue to expand the black struggle while remaining tied to the rhetoric of interracialism and nonviolent direct action. They also questioned whether their remaining goals could best be achieved through continued confrontation with existing institutions or through the building of alternative institutions controlled by the poor and powerless.

The third phase of SNCC's development involved the members' efforts to resolve their differences by addressing the need for black power and black consciousness, by separating themselves from white people, and by building black-controlled institutions. After his election as chairman of SNCC in May 1966, Stokely Carmichael popularized the organization's new separatist orientation, but he and other workers were unable to formulate a set of ideas that could unify black people. As SNCC workers sought to increase black awareness of the range of available political and cultural alternatives, they became embroiled in bitter factional battles and failed to sustain local black movements in the South. Disagreements about the future direction of the struggles also divided black communities throughout the nation. Weakened by internal dissension, SNCC withered in the face of the same tactics of subtle co-optation and ruthless repression that stifled the entire black struggle. . . .

Late Monday afternoon, February 1, 1960, at a lunch counter in Greensboro, North Carolina, four black college students ignited one of the largest of all Afro-American protest movements. The initial spark of the movement was a simple, impulsive act of defiance, one that required no special skills or resources. Planned the previous night, the "sit-in" — as it would be called — was not the product of radical intellectual fement. Rather, it grew out of "bull sessions" involving college freshmen who were, in most respects, typical southern black students of the time, politically unsophisticated and socially conventional. The four students would be influenced by the decade of social struggle that unexpectedly followed their protest far more than they affected the course of that struggle. Nonetheless, the initial sit-in contained the seeds of radicalism that would flower in SNCC, the principal organization to emerge from the black student sit-ins of 1960.

The four students, like many other young activists of the 1960s, acted on the basis of suppressed resentments that preceded the development of an ideological rationale for protest. Without an organizational structure and without a coherent set of ideas to guide their actions, the Greensboro students were determined to break with the past. Only after their isolated protest had provided the stimulus for an intense, sometimes chaotic process of political education within the southern struggle would the four students become fully aware of the significance of what they had done. In the beginning, they only spoke of a modest desire: to drink a cup of coffee, sitting down.

The initial sit-in was a tentative challenge to Jim Crow. Joseph McNeil and Izell Blair, roommates at the predominantly black North Carolina Agricultural and Technical College, along with two other students, Franklin McCain and David Richmond, purchased a few items at Greensboro's downtown F. W. Woolworth store and then sat down at the lunch counter reserved by custom for whites. They asked to be served but were refused. When a waitress asked them to leave, they explained politely that as they had bought items in other sections of the store, they should be allowed to sit on the stools rather than stand. They received no sympathy from a black woman who worked behind the counter. "You are stupid, ignorant!" she chastised them. "You're dumb! That's why we can't get anywhere today. You know you are supposed to eat at the other end." Although refused service, the four students became more confident as they observed the lack of forceful opposition by the store employees. When informed that the four students were continuing to sit at the lunch counter, the store manager merely ordered his employees to ignore them. The students had expected to be arrested, but instead they discovered a tactic that not only expressed their long-suppressed anger but also apparently did not provoke severe retaliation from whites. "Now it came to me all of a sudden," McCain remembered thinking. "Maybe they can't do anything to us. Maybe we can keep it up."

They did. The four remained on the stools for almost an hour, until the store closed. After returning to campus, they contacted the student body president and recruited more students for another sit-in. The following morning a group of thirty students returned to the store and occupied the lunch counter. There were no confrontations, but the second sit-in, which lasted about two hours, attracted the attention of local reporters. A national news service carried an account of the protest, mentioning a group of "well-dressed Negro college students" who ended their sit-in with a prayer. On Wednesday morning a still larger group of students occupied most of the sixty-six seats at the lunch counter. In the afternoon three white students from Greensboro College joined them. Officials at North Carolina A. & T. resisted attempts by state officials to force them to restrict the activities of their students and by Thursday morning hundreds of black students had been drawn into the expanding protest. Many white youths had also gathered in the downtown section of Greensboro, cursing and threatening the black protesters and attempting to hold seats for white patrons. By the end of the week, after continued disruption of business activities and a telephoned bomb threat, the store manager decided to close the store. The mayor of Greensboro then called upon black students and business leaders to forgo temporarily "individual rights and financial interests" while city officials sought "a just and honorable resolution" of the controversy. The demonstrators, by this time organized as the Students' Executive Committee for Justice, agreed to halt the protests for two weeks to give local leaders a chance to find a solution.

Although the Greensboro sit-ins were discontinued temporarily, students at nearby black colleges followed news accounts of the protest and quickly organized sit-ins. Over the weekend in which a sit-in moratorium was being arranged in Greensboro, more than one hundred students met in Winston-Salem to plan a protest of their own. Before they could act, however, Carl Matthews, a black college graduate working in Winston-Salem, conducted the city's first sit-in on Monday, February 8. Later in the afternoon Matthews was joined by about twenty-five other blacks, many of them students in Winston-Salem Teachers College. The same day, seventeen students from North Carolina College and four from Duke University staged a sit-in at the Woolworth lunch counter in Durham. On Wednesday morning students in Raleigh decided to act after hearing a radio report assuring listeners that there would be no protests by college students in that locality. Two days later, when black students demonstrating at a suburban shopping center near Raleigh were arrested for trespassing, other students rushed to the scene to be arrested. In all, forty-one students were arrested and charged with trespassing in the first mass arrests of the sit-in movement. By the end of the week, more sit-ins had occurred in the North Carolina communities of Charlotte, Fayetteville, High Point, Elizabeth City, and Concord. On February 10, Hampton, Virginia, became the first community outside North Carolina to experience student sit-ins. Protests occurred soon afterward in the Virginia cities of Norfolk and Portsmouth. By the end of February, Nashville, Chattanooga, Richmond, Baltimore, Montgomery, and Lexington were among over thirty communities in seven states to experience sit-ins. The protests reached the remaining southern states by mid-April. By that time, according to one study, the movement had attracted about fifty thousand participants.

Although the initial Greensboro sit-in had been peaceful and polite, the student protests gradually became more assertive, even boisterous. As demonstrations attracted increasing crowds of participants and onlookers, they came to be perceived as threats to social order. Most sit-ins by black college students were characterized by strict discipline among the protesters, but several outbreaks of violence occurred when protests involved high school students. The first serious instance of violence took place on February 16 in Portsmouth, Virginia, where hundreds of black and white high school students fought each other after a sit-in. More extensive violence, involving over a thousand people, took place in Chattanooga, Tennessee, after a demonstration on February 23. Over thirty persons, mostly whites, were arrested and police used fire hoses to end the two days of rioting.

Even in places where sit-ins were not accompanied by violence, there was an underlying current of hostility and fear among both blacks and whites. White onlookers verbally assaulted black protesters and at times only the rapid arrest of protesters by police prevented violent physical assaults. The protesters themselves, though usually peaceful, were engaging in a form of "passively aggressive behavior—stepping over the line and waiting, rather than exhibiting overtly hostile or revolutionary behavior." Nonviolent tactics, particularly when accompanied by a rationale based on Christian principles, offered black students an appealing combination of rewards: a sense of moral superiority, an emotional release through militancy, and a possibility of achieving desegregation. The delicate balance between militancy and restraint produced tensions often released through humor. Popular jokes ridiculed the pretensions of white segregationalists:

> A Negro goes into a restaurant and asks for "pigs' feet." "Don't serve them," the counterman answers. "Chitterlings then." "Don't serve them." "Pig's necks?" "Don't serve them" "Pig's ears?" "Don't serve them." "White man," the Negro says, "you just ain't ready for integration."

> A waitress told a pair of sit-inners. "I'm sorry but we don't serve Negroes here." "Oh, we don't eat them either," came the reply.

The sit-ins brought to the surface interracial tensions that had long been suppressed in the South, and they stimulated a process of self-realization among blacks that would continue through the decade. The goal of lunch counter desegregation certainly did not exhaust the range of black aspirations; nor did the sit-in tactic fully express the dormant emotions of southern blacks. But, as many other groups had discovered both in the United States and elsewhere, nonviolent direct action was a starting point for the emergence of a new political consciousness among oppressed people. For southern black students in the spring of 1960, it offered an almost irresistible model for social action.

Never again during the decade would the proportion of students active in protest equal the level reached at southern black colleges during the period from February to June 1960. On many campuses support for the sit-ins was almost unanimous. Over 90 percent of the students at North Carolina A. & T. and three nearby colleges took part in demonstrations or aided the movement by boycotting or picketing segregated stores. Student protesters commented that it was "like a fever. Everyone wanted to go. We were so happy." . . .

Rather than indicating the existence of radicalism on black college campuses, the decision of black students to engage in protest was the outgrowth of guilt and frustration owing to their previous failure to take effective action against the humiliating Jim Crow system. Richmond recalled that, like many other blacks of his age group, he had "constantly heard about all the evils that were occurring and how black folks were mistreated and nobody was doing anything about it." The plan for the first sit-in was formulated after Richmond and three classmates denounced their own apathy and challenged each other to take action. "There were many words and few deeds," McCain remembered. "We did a good job of making each other feel bad."

Many other black youths were witnessing the same events that stimulated the emotions of the Greensboro students. The highly publicized racial controversies following the Supreme Court's *Brown* decision in 1954 illustrated the need for blacks to take resolute action to assert rights that were assumed to be theirs. Cleveland Sellers, a black high school student in South Carolina at the time of the first lunch counter sit-ins, was one of many students who felt a strong sense of identification with blacks such as Daisy Bates, Rosa Parks, and Martin Luther King who had challenged segregation in Little Rock and Montgomery. "When they spoke," Sellers recalled, "they said what I was thinking. When they suffered, I suffered with them. And on those rare occasions when they managed to eke out a meager victory, I rejoiced too."

During the 1950s some young blacks had even participated in civil rights demonstrations, though there was little news coverage of these isolated protests. Youth Marches for Integrated Schools, held in Washington, D.C., in 1958 and 1959, attracted thousands of participants. A few southern black students attended workshops sponsored by CORE or SCLC on the use of nonviolent tactics. There were even some instances of sit-in activity, most notably in Oklahoma City where in 1958 teenagers affiliated with the NAACP began to demand service at local restaurants.

The African independence movement, led by college-trained activists, also affected black youths. A black sociologist commented in 1960 that African students attending black colleges in the United States often reproached Afro-American students for "not being as aggressive as their counterparts in Africa." Students who later took part in the sit-in movement heard reports of the African independence struggle when attending an ecumenical religious conference held in Athens, Ohio, a few weeks before the initial Greensboro sit-in. A scholar at the conference noted that "hundreds" of southern black students "listened, discussed and evidently thought a great deal as militant African nationalists 'stole the show' with predictions of a 'new order.'" According to a journalist who visited black campuses during the spring of 1960, "even the most unintellectual black students were envious of the African independence movement and vaguely moved by it."

The quickening pace of events affecting blacks in the United States and Africa contributed to what has been called "a state of psychosocial readiness to protest" among young southern blacks. "In a way," one student said, "we have been planning it all our lives." Another student explained: "It's like waiting for a bus, man. You know where you're going all the time, but you can't get there 'til the right vehicle comes along." After the Greensboro students had seized the initiative, other students would claim that they had been planning sit-ins or similar protests even before February 1960. In fact, a few black students in Nashville had not only engaged in such planning, but also had schooled themselves in the philosophical doctrines of the Gandhian passive resistance movement in India. It was these Nashville activists, rather than the four Greensboro students, who had an enduring impact on the subsequent development of the southern movement.

The later lives of the four Greensboro students typified the careers of many students whose involvement in the racial struggle was only brief. Of the four, only Izell Blair attended the founding conference of SNCC, in which he never played a leadership role. After serving as student body president at North Carolina A. & T., Blair attended law school for a year, worked as a teacher in the Job Corps, and then joined a black self-help group in Boston, the Opportunity Industrialization Center. During the mid-1960s he became a member of the Nation of Islam, taking the name Jibreel Khazan. Franklin McCain moved to Charlotte after graduation and began a career as an engineer with the Celanese Corporation. David Richmond was briefly involved in voter registration work in Mississippi but returned to Greensboro, where he worked with local antipoverty programs and figured in efforts to prevent outbreaks of racial violence during the late 1960s. Joseph McNeil joined the Air Force after graduation and in 1966, while engaged in bombing missions over North Vietnam, publicly criticized the anti-war position taken by Stokely Carmichael as chairman of SNCC. McNeil was subsequently employed by International Business Machines and then took a management position with a Wall Street banking firm.

Quite inadvertently, the four students had set in motion historical forces which they and most of their fellow activists were unable to forecast or even comprehend. The southern struggle would result only gradually in a transformation of individual attitudes and beliefs. Most student activists were committed to the expressed values of the American political system, though many also began to identify with the black student movement and its own emerging values. Diane Nash remarked that the black student became a member of "a group of people suddenly proud to be called 'black,'" and in the student "was born a new awareness of himself as an individual." Another Nashville student activist, Marion Barry, noted that for "the first time in history black students sit down at the conference table with officials and are heard." Political scientist Michael Walzer was among the whites who noted the pride of black students for whom "new forms of political activity were a kind of self-testing and proving." Although white participation in protests was welcomed, he "never heard a Negro ask, or even hint, that whites should join their picket lines. It will be better for them, and for us, I was told, if *they* came unasked." Even outside the South, blacks were moved by news accounts of the student protest movement. Robert Moses, then a twenty-six-year-old high school teacher in New York, was impressed by the "sullen, angry, determined" looks on the faces of North Carolina student protesters in a newspaper photograph: "Before, the Negro in the South had always looked on the defensive, cringing. This time they were taking the initiative. They were kids of my age, and I knew this had something to do with my own life. It made me realize that for a long time I had been troubled by the problem of being a Negro and at the same time being an American. This was the answer."

Nash, Barry, Moses, and many other young blacks saw the sit-ins as the beginning of a new stage of black political development. The southern sit-in movement had demonstrated that black students could initiate a social struggle without the guidance of older black leaders and existing organizations. As

local white leaders gave into the student demands, an increasingly self-confident, able, and resourceful group of young black activists emerged as spokes-
persons for the local protest movements. Like the four Greensboro pioneers,
the emergent leaders discovered that their initial acts of defiance could be
sustained. Released from the guilt associated with accommodation, they
eagerly sought new roles to intensify the social struggle.

Some student leaders sensed the need for a protest organization to
consolidate their newly won influence. They wanted an organization that
would expand black militancy rather than restrain or control it. Many of
them believed that the movement also needed a set of guiding ideas, and the
sit-ins had spawned the notion that such ideas should come not from the
pre-existing ideologies but from the intellectual awakening that had begun on
the southern black campuses. Accordingly, in April 1960 these students
created SNCC to preserve the spontaneity and the militancy of the sit-
ins. . . .

SNCC was born during a period of extensive student protest activity. Yet its
creation indicated the culmination of the lunch counter sit-in movement
rather than the beginning of a new upsurge of student activism. SNCC exerted
little control over the ad hoc protest groups throughout the South whose
activities it was supposed to coordinate. Only as the spontaneous enthusiasm
of the early protests waned did the new organization begin to attract support.

SNCC's founding conference, held on April 16–18, 1960, in Raleigh,
North Carolina, was called by Ella Baker, executive director of SCLC. The
initiating role of SCLC might have signaled the reassertion of control over the
southern black struggle by Martin Luther King and the black ministers
associated with him, but Baker, who understood the psychological need of
student activists to remain independent of adult control, resisted efforts to
subvert their autonomy. Students at the conference affirmed their commitment to the nonviolent doctrines popularized by King, yet they were drawn to
these ideas not because of King's advocacy but because they provided an
appropriate rationale for student protest.

SNCC's founding was an important step in the transformation of a
limited student movement to desegregate lunch counters into a broad and
sustained movement to achieve major social reforms. Although many of the
students at the founding conference initially were reluctant to broaden the
focus of their activities, the existence of a South-wide coordinating committee
provided the opportunity for increasing numbers of young people to participate in a regional movement that would attack racism in all its dimensions. . . .

Stokely Carmichael's popularization of the black power slogan began a new
stage in the transformation of Afro-American political consciousness. Shat-
tering the fragile alliance of civil rights forces, the black power upsurge
challenged the assumptions underlying previous interracial efforts to achieve
national civil rights reforms. The black struggles of the 1960s had awakened

dormant traditions of black radicalism and racial separatism by fostering among black people a greater sense of pride, confidence, and racial identity. Through their increasingly positive response to the concept of black power, Afro-Americans in every section of the nation indicated their determination to use hard-won human rights to improve their lives in ways befitting their own cultural values.

Like the four Greensboro students who ignited the lunch counter protest movement, Carmichael was not an exceptional prophetic figure. He became a symbol of black militancy because he sensed a widespread preparedness among blacks to reject previous habits of accommodation. His attitudes, shaped by experiences in the southern struggle, coincided with the unarticulated feelings of many other blacks, especially in northern urban centers, whose hopes were raised but not fulfilled by the civil rights movement. Like his Greensboro precursors, Carmichael was an innovator who could not control nor fully understand the social forces he had set in motion, and he could only begin the difficult task of formulating a comprehensive political strategy for the post civil rights era. Nonetheless he set forth the broad outlines of subsequent black political development. Carmichael joined a line of audacious black leaders — Martin Delany, Marcus Garvey, Malcolm X — whose historical role was to arouse large segments of the black populace by reflecting their repressed anger and candidly describing previously obscured aspects of their racial oppression.

Only after Carmichael attracted national attention as an advocate of black power did he begin to construct an intellectual rationale for what initially was an inchoate statement of conclusions drawn from SNCC's work. He attempted to demonstrate that black power was a logical outgrowth of the southern struggle and a reasonable response to the conditions facing Afro-Americans. While he did clarify many misconceptions of his views, he could not eliminate confusion caused by biased press reports and SNCC workers' own uncertainty about future programs. Moreover, his writings and public statements were not only vague formulations of strategy but were also emotional responses to the frustrations of SNCC staff members and rebellious urban blacks. Disillusioned by their previous attempts to achieve change through nonviolent tactics and interracial alliances, Carmichael and other outspoken militants in SNCC were no longer restrained by concern for the sensibilities of white people. By forthrightly expressing previously suppressed anger, Carmichael and others experienced a sense of "release" similar to that felt by black activists during the early days of the lunch counter sit-in movement.

SNCC workers' satisfaction with the black power slogan was based largely on the extent to which it aroused blacks and disturbed whites. By using an ambiguous phrase that would stir racial emotions, they demonstrated their continued willingness to take risks on behalf of their ideals. While Carmichael felt the need to explain his ideas to whites, he wavered ambivalently between efforts to address his critics and repeated refusals to soften his rhetoric to allay white fears. "I have to address myself to black people, not to the press or the white bourgeoisie," he told journalist Paul Good. On several occasions he proposed that the civil rights movement abandon its role "as a buffer zone between the black community and the white community" and begin "to express the feeling of the black community in the tone of the black community."

Carmichael still attempted to persuade whites who were willing to listen to his arguments. During the summer of 1966, he published two essays: "What We Want," in the *New York Review of Books,* and "Toward Black Liberation," in the *Massachusetts Review.* In these often reprinted essays, Carmichael explained the reasons for SNCC's change in direction in terms that white liberals and radicals would understand, if not accept.

Carmichael argued for the cultural and political autonomy of black communities. He defended the black power concept as a response by black people to the need "to reclaim our history and our identity from the cultural terrorism and depredation of self-justifying white guilt." He argued that black people would "have to struggle for the right to create our own terms to define ourselves and our relationship to the society, and to have these terms recognized."

In his call for racial self-determination, Carmichael repeated many of the arguments of the Atlanta Project position paper written the previous spring. Although he still resisted the Atlanta separatists' demand for the expulsion of whites from SNCC, he now conveyed to a national audience many of their ideas regarding the psychological implications of the black struggle. While the Atlanta separatists used the issue of white participation in SNCC to increase their influence in the organization, Carmichael used the broader issue of white political hegemony to challenge the moderate leadership of competing civil rights organizations. "We want to decide who is our friend, and we will not accept someone who comes to us and says: 'If you do X, Y, and Z, then I'll help you.'" He insisted, "We cannot have the oppressors telling the oppressed how to rid themselves of the oppressor."

Carmichael did not preclude the possibility of interracial alliances. He rejected the criticism that the black power concept represented "a withdrawal into black nationalism and isolationism." Instead, he suggested that SNCC's policies could have the opposite effect: "When the Negro community is able to control local offices, and negotiate with other groups from a position of organized strength, the possibility of meaningful political alliances on specific issues will be increased." This was possible, however, only if white activists recognized their responsibility to organize white communities. "They admonish blacks to be nonviolent," he wrote. "Let them preach nonviolence in the white community."

Since 1964 Carmichael had urged white radicals to assume the task of organizing poor whites, but he warned that poor whites were "becoming more hostile—not less—partly because they see the nation's attention focused on black poverty and nobody coming to them." During a talk in Atlanta he commented sardonically that "the reality of it is that poor whites are very racist, because the country is racist, and that to go into a poor white community in Mississippi or Alabama and talk about integration is to invite suicide upon one's self." Aware of the enormous obstacles organizers would face in white communities, he nonetheless repeatedly complained about white activists who preferred to go to black communities—"where the action is"—rather than seeking to mobilize whites to achieve progressive social change.

Carmichael did little to encourage blacks to accept alliances on the basis of class. "The only reason [whites] suppress us is because we are black," he told an audience in the Watts section of Los Angeles. Though he identified himself with the interests of poor blacks, he did not attempt to mobilize blacks by stressing their common class interests. Sensing that they would not respond as readily to class appeals as to racial appeals, Carmichael moved ever closer to an ideology of black separatism. Carmichael probably recognized that his analytical statements were oversimplified, but support of discontented blacks rather than understanding from skeptical whites was his primary goal. In his speeches he gave little attention to the economic problems of blacks presenting instead ideas that would appeal to blacks of all classes. "The most important thing that black people have to do is to begin to come together, and to be able to do that we must stop being ashamed of being black," he said. "We are black and beautiful."

Carmichael provided little advice to his black listeners regarding the political direction they should take once they had come together under black leadership. Not yet prepared to adopt completely the notion that Afro-Americans were or should become a separate cultural or political entity, he concentrated on undermining support for the existing social order rather than describing a new one. In his few explicit references to the future of the black struggle, he invoked a group uplift model based on popular conceptions of the historical experiences of European ethnic groups. "Traditionally, for each new ethnic group, the route to social and political integration in America's pluralistic society has been through the organization of their own institutions with which to represent their communal needs within the larger society," he wrote. When he appeared on "Face the Nation," Carmichael mentioned the Irish and Jews as examples of groups that had gained local political control through the electoral process. He said that his conception of black power involved the organization of blacks as an independent force that could become a "strong block" within existing political parties to force politicians "to speak to [black] needs."

An element of dissimulation undoubtedly lay in Carmichael's defense of the black power concept. He was not prepared to state whether his call for black power was simply an extension of SNCC's previous militancy in pursuit of reformist goals or a fundamental redirection of that militancy toward radical or revolutionary objectives. That Carmichael presented his arguments to white liberals and radicals suggests that he retained some hope of building an interracial democracy founded on racial equality. Despite his vacillation between hope and despair, between pluralist and separatist models of social reality, Carmichael was nonetheless identified as a symbol of racial hostility and violence. During the months following the Mississippi march his effort to clarify his ideas was obscured by a controversy over the black power slogan that was more a clash of emotions than of ideas. . . .

The spontaneous urban uprisings of 1968 ended an era of black struggle, for unlike earlier rebellions involving SNCC and southern blacks, they dissipated quickly when confronted by powerful institutions. White political leaders responded to violent black challenges with deadly repression and anesthetizing palliatives. The uprisings failed to foster a strong enough sense of collective purpose to override the endemic selfish and vindictive motives that emerged in outbursts of racial spite. Black urban rebellions were too short-lived to transform personal anger and frustration into a sustained political movement. . . .

Optimism among blacks that racial unity was possible eroded quickly during the tumultuous year of 1968. Although many of the controversial ideas that once had defined SNCC's radicalism were widely accepted, events in the spring and summer of 1968 suggested that black unity was an illusive goal. . . .

The assassination of Martin Luther King in April 1968 revealed to the SNCC staff both the depth of black discontent and the vulnerability of black leaders. They often had disagreed with the nonviolent tactics King advocated, but they joined other black Americans in expressing their outrage over his murder. Although no longer part of SNCC's leadership, Stokely Carmichael probably expressed the sentiments of many other staff members when he publicly warned "white America" that it had made a mistake by killing King. He called King "the one man of our race that this country's older generations, the militants and the revolutionaries and the masses of black people would still listen to." Some observers expected Carmichael's influence to increase with King's death, but, rather than conveying a sense of confidence, Carmichael displayed a curious tone of fatalism when he predicted a violent struggle in which black people would "stand up on our feet and die like men. If that's our only act of manhood, then Goddammit we're going to die."

After delivering these remarks, Carmichael, along with millions of other black people, went into the streets to express their anger. In a unique display of nationwide racial unity, blacks in numerous cities burned and looted white property and battled the police and military forces sent to suppress them. Over forty blacks were killed and more than twenty thousand arrested throughout the nation. Carmichael was blamed for the destruction in Washington, but actually no leader was capable of exerting much control over the spontaneous activities. White fears and black fantasies to the contrary, the uprisings after King's death demonstrated the absence of political coordination or even communication among black militants. . . .

SNCC's rise and fall coincided with the evolution of the black struggles of the 1960s. Emerging from the black student sit-in movement of 1960, SNCC initially had drawn inspiration and ideas from the American tradition of religious radicalism, a tradition influenced by Mahatma Gandhi and intertwined with previous, isolated civil rights protests. As SNCC workers became deeply involved in an expanding social movement in the South, they acquired a distinctive style of rebellious activism and of community organizing that enabled them to mobilize large segments of black communities under indigenous leadership. SNCC workers epitomized the militant mood of black people, particularly those in the most racially repressive regions of the Black Belt, who were suddenly released from the psychological burdens of cultural and political conformity. As SNCC workers came together to form an activist community in the midst of an awakening black populace, they were transformed by their experiences. Their openness to new ideas, their brash willingness to challenge powerful institutions, their experimental approach to life allowed staff members to express the changing mood of the southern struggle. SNCC "freedom fighters" acquired a singular mystique based on their rebelliousness and their commitment to humanistic ideals. They became models for a generation of young activists, inside and outside the South, who challenged many of the assumptions that made possible the continued existence of injustice and oppression in American society.

By the mid-1960s, however, SNCC staff members had begun to question some of the assumptions underlying their own radicalism. As the focus of the southern black struggle changed from desegregation to political and economic concerns, SNCC's radicalism assumed a secular rather than religious tone, although the theme of moral outrage remained evident in SNCC's public criticisms of the federal government and of Cold War liberalism. . . .

SNCC workers failed to resolve the enduring dilemmas that had perplexed earlier radicals and revolutionaries, but they provided a surviving legacy. This legacy is most evident among black people in the deep South communities where SNCC became enmeshed in strong local struggles. Local black leaders who gained new conceptions of themselves as a result of SNCC's work carried on political movements after SNCC workers departed and the excitement of protest subsided. . . .

Black people who never participated in the collective struggles of the 1960s have also benefited from them. Indeed, blacks who chose not to participate in black struggles and who are primarily concerned with pursuing personal goals rather than assuming social responsibilities are the ones most likely to gain the rewards of American society. As Willie Ricks commented, "Black folks walking around in suits and ties, having jobs, that's an outgrowth of SNCC." Purposeful amnesia about recent Afro-American history has enabled many contemporary blacks to ignore the fact that they enjoy the benefits of sacrifices made by earlier generations and to see their personal success as solely the result of their own efforts. Black youngsters who have greater educational opportunities open to them, who can take black studies courses, who can find high-paying jobs are not more able than their parents and grandparents, but they are certainly more fortunate to live at a time when their abilities are more likely to be rewarded. . . .

Document

I Have a Dream

MARTIN LUTHER KING, JR.

I am happy to join with you today in what will go down in history as the greatest demonstration for freedom in the history of our nation.

Five score years ago, a great American, in whose symbolic shadow we stand today, signed the Emancipation Proclamation. This momentous decree came as a great beacon light of hope to millions of Negro slaves who had been seared in the flames of withering injustice. It came as a joyous daybreak to end the long night of their captivity.

But one hundred years later, the Negro still is not free; one hundred years later, the life of the Negro is still sadly crippled by the manacles of segregation and the chains of discrimination; one hundred years later, the Negro lives on a lonely island of poverty in the midst of a vast ocean of material prosperity; one hundred years later, the Negro is still languished in the corners of American society and finds himself in exile in his own land.

So, we've come here today to dramatize a shameful condition. In a sense we've come to our nation's capital to cash a check. When the architects of our republic wrote the magnificent words of the Constitution and the Declaration of Independence, they were signing a promissory note to which every American was to fall heir. This note was the promise that all men, yes, black men as well as white men, would be guaranteed the unalienable rights of life, liberty, and the pursuit of happiness.

It is obvious today that America has defaulted on this promissory note in so far as her citizens of color are concerned. Instead of honoring this sacred obligation, America has given the Negro people a bad check; a check which has come back marked "insufficient funds." But we refuse to believe that the bank of justice is bankrupt. We refuse to believe that there are insufficient funds in the great vaults of opportunity of this nation. And so we've come to cash this check, a check that will give us upon demand the riches of freedom and the security of justice.

We have also come to this hallowed spot to remind America of the fierce urgency of now. This is no time to engage in the luxury of cooling off or to take the tranquilizing drug of gradualism. Now is the time to make real the promises of democracy; now is the time to rise from the dark and desolate valley of segregation to the sunlit path of racial justice; now is the time to lift our nation from the quicksands of racial injustice to the solid rock of brotherhood; now is the time to make justice a reality for all of God's children. It would be fatal for the nation to overlook the urgency of the moment. This sweltering summer of the Negro's legitimate discontent will not pass until there is an invigorating autumn of freedom and equality.

Nineteen sixty-three is not an end, but a beginning. And those who hope that the Negro needed to blow off steam and will now be content, will have a rude awakening if the nation returns to business as usual. There will be neither rest nor tranquility in America until the Negro is granted his citizenship rights. The whirlwinds of revolt will continue to shake the foundations of our nation until the bright day of justice emerges.

But there is something that I must say to my people, who stand on the worn threshold which leads into the palace of justice. In the process of gaining our rightful place, we must not be guilty of wrongful deeds. Let us not seek to satisfy our thirst for freedom by drinking from the cup of bitterness and hatred. We must forever conduct our struggle on the high plain of dignity and discipline. We must not allow our creative protests to degenerate into physical violence. Again and again we must rise to the majestic heights of meeting physical force with soul force. The marvelous new militancy, which has engulfed the Negro community, must not lead us to a distrust of all white people. For many of our white brothers, as evidenced by their presence here today, have come to realize that their destiny is tied up with our destiny. And they have come to realize that their freedom is inextricably bound to our freedom. We cannot walk alone. And as we walk, we must make the pledge that we shall always march ahead. We cannot turn back.

There are those who are asking the devotees of Civil Rights, "When will you be satisfied?" We can never be satisfied as long as the Negro is the victim of the unspeakable horrors of police brutality; we can never be satisfied as long as our bodies, heavy with the fatigue of travel, cannot gain lodging in the motels of the highways and the hotels of the cities; we cannot be satisfied as long as the Negro's basic mobility is from a smaller ghetto to a larger one; we can never be satisfied as long as our children are stripped of their selfhood and robbed of their dignity by signs stating "For White Only"; we cannot be satisfied as long as the Negro in Mississippi cannot vote and a Negro in New York believes he has nothing for which to vote. No! No, we are not satisfied, and we will not be satisfied until "justice rolls down like waters and righteousness like a mighty stream."

I am not unmindful that some of you have come here out of great trials and tribulations. Some of you have come fresh from narrow jail cells. Some of you have come from areas where your quest for freedom left you battered by the storms of persecution and staggered by the winds of police brutality. You have been the veterans of creative suffering. Continue to work with the faith that unearned suffering is redemptive. Go back to Mississippi. Go back to Alabama. Go back to South Carolina. Go back to Georgia. Go back to Louisiana. Go back to the slums and ghettos of our Northern cities, knowing that somehow this situation can and will be changed. Let us not wallow in the valley of despair.

I say to you today, my friends, so even though we face the difficulties of today and tomorrow, I still have a dream. It is a dream deeply rooted in the American dream. I have a dream that one day this nation will rise up and live out the true meaning of its creed, "We hold these truths to be self-evident, that all men are created equal." I have a dream that one day on the red hills of Georgia, sons of former slaves and the sons of former slave owners will be able to sit down together at the table of brotherhood. I have a dream that one day even the state of Mississippi, a state sweltering with the heat of injustice, sweltering with the heat of oppression, will be transformed into an oasis of freedom and justice. I have a dream that my four little children will one day live in a nation where they will not be judged by the color of their skin, but by the content of their character.

I HAVE A DREAM TODAY!

I have a dream that one day down in Alabama — with its vicious racists, with its Governor having his lips dripping with the words of interposition and nullification — one day right there in Alabama, little black boys and black girls will be able to join hands with little white boys and white girls as sisters and brothers.

I HAVE A DREAM TODAY!

I have a dream that one day every valley shall be exalted, every hill and mountain shall be made low. The rough places will be plain and the crooked places will be made straight, "and the glory of the Lord shall be revealed, and all flesh shall see it together."

This is our hope. This is the faith that I go back to the South with. With this faith we will be able to hew out of the mountain of despair, a stone of hope. With this faith we will be able to transform the jangling discords of our nation into a beautiful symphony of brotherhood. With this faith we will be able to work together, to pray together, to struggle together, to go to jail together, to stand up for freedom together, knowing that we will be free one day. And this will be the day. This will be the day when all of God's children will be able to sing with new meaning, "My country 'tis of thee, sweet land of liberty, of thee I sing. Land where by father died, land of the pilgrim's pride, from every mountain side, let freedom ring." And if America is to be a great nation, this must become true.

So let freedom ring from the prodigious hilltops of New Hampshire; let freedom ring from the mighty mountains of New York; let freedom ring from the heightening Alleghenies of Pennsylvania; let freedom ring from the snow-capped Rockies of Colorado. But not only that. Let freedom ring from Stone Mountain of Georgia; let freedom ring from the curvaceous slopes of California; let freedom ring from Lookout Mountain of Tennessee; let freedom ring from every hill and mole hill of Mississippi. "From every mountainside, let freedom ring."

And when this happens, and when we allow freedom to ring, when we let it ring from every village and every hamlet, from every state and every city, we will be able to speed up that day when all of God's children, black men and white men, Jews and Gentiles, Protestants and Catholics, will be able to join hands and sing in the words of the old Negro spiritual: "Free at last. Free at last. Thank God Almighty, we are free at last."

twelve

THE WOMEN'S
MOVEMENT

The women's movement of the 1960s and 1970s changed the framework of American society. Active first in the effort to achieve racial equality, women became discouraged at the discrimination they faced in the struggle. Men, black and white, made policy decisions; women assumed the more menial chores. At the same time women felt sexually exploited by their male associates. The frustrations of women working for civil rights mirrored those of women throughout the society, and provided the spark that brought change.

Sara Evans was the first to locate the roots of the women's movement in the campaign for civil rights. Drawing on interviews, manifestos, and personal experiences, she provides persuasive evidence of the links between the two struggles. Her essay "Women's Consciousness and the Civil Rights Movement," is a capsule treatment of her book-length study of the origins of the modern women's movement.

Historian William H. Chafe follows with an overview of recent feminism that locates it in its twentieth-century context. In "Feminism in the 1970's," he examines social trends that provided a basis for change and explores the structural problems of the movement as well as the obstacles that had to be overcome.

The document in this section, "The Problem That Has No Name," is taken from one of the most important books of the 1960s — Betty Friedan's *The Feminine Mystique.* Pointing to a pervasive sense of discontent, Friedan provides a telling critique of the patterns of the 1950s that defined a woman's place as the home, where she aspired to little more than raising children and supporting her husband's career. Women read Friedan's book, passed it

279

around, and used it to help articulate their own grievances as the movement grew.

To explore further the origins of the contemporary women's movement, see Sara Evans, *Personal Politics: The Roots of Women's Liberation in the Civil Rights Movement and the New Left* (1979). William H. Chafe, *The American Woman: Her Changing Social, Political, and Economic Roles, 1920–1970* (1972), is a useful overview of shifts in the status of women throughout the twentieth century. Lois W. Banner, *Women in the 20th Century* (1974), is a brief history of women's activity. Sheila M. Rothman, *Women's Proper Place: A History of Changing Ideals and Practices, 1870 to the Present* (1978), analyzes changes in women's aims and undertakings in the past hundred years. Shulamith Firestone, *The Dialectic of Sex: The Case for Feminist Revolution* (1970), is a radical analysis of sex discrimination. Peter Gabriel Filene, *Him/Her/Self: Sex Roles in Modern America* (1975), examines shifts in men's as well as women's roles.

Women's Consciousness and
the Civil Rights Movement

SARA EVANS

Twice in the history of the United States the struggle for racial equality has been midwife to a feminist movement. In the abolition movement of the 1830s and 1840s and again in the civil-rights revolt of the 1960s, women experiencing the contradictory expectations and stresses of changing roles began to move from individual discontents to a social movement in their own behalf. Working for racial justice, they developed both political skills and a belief in human rights which could justify their own claim to equality.

Moreover, in each case, the racial and sexual tensions embedded in Southern culture projected a handful of white Southern women into the forefront of those who connected one cause with the other. In the 1830s, Sarah and Angelina Grimke, devout Quakers and daughters of a Charleston slave-owning family, spoke out sharply against the moral evils of slavery and racial prejudice. "The female slaves," they said, "are our countrywomen, *they are our sisters;* and to us as women, they have a right to look for sympathy with their sorrows, and effort and prayer for their rescue. . . . Women ought to feel a peculiar sympathy in the colored men's wrong, for like him, she has been accused of mental inferiority, and denied the privileges of a liberal education."

Through the nineteenth century and into the twentieth, religious commitment led a series of middle-class women to engage in social action, though they continued to accept many conventional attitudes about women and blacks. A new set of circumstances in the late 1950s and early '60s, however, forced a few young Southern white women into an opposition to Southern culture more comparable to that of the Grimke sisters than to their immediate predecessors. During this period, student ministries and the YWCA fostered a growing social concern and articulated, in the language of existential theology, a radical critique of American society and Southern segregation. The ethos of the Southern civil-rights struggle perfectly matched this spirit of religious insurgency which motivated a generation of white students. When the revolt of Southern blacks began in 1960, it touched a chord of moral idealism and brought a significant group of white Southern women into a movement which would both change their lives and transform a region.

Following the first wave of sit-ins in 1960, the Southern Christian Leadership Conference (SCLC), at the insistence of its assistant director, Ella Baker, called a conference at Shaw University in Raleigh, N.C., on Easter weekend. There black youth founded their own organization, the Student Nonviolent Coordinating Committee (SNCC) to provide a support network for direct action. SNCC set the style and tone of grass-roots organizing in the rural South and led the movement into the black belt. The spirit of adventure

From Sara Evans, "Women's Consciousness and the Southern Black Movement," in *Southern Exposure* IV (Winter 1977). Reprinted by permission of Sara Evans.

and commitment which animated the organization added new vitality to a deeply rooted struggle for racial equality.

In addition to this crucial role within the black movement, SNCC also created the social space within which women began to develop a new sense of their own potential. A critical vanguard of young women accumulated the tools for movement building: a language to describe oppression and justify revolt, experience in the strategy and tactics of organizing, and a beginning sense of themselves collectively as objects of discrimination.

Relative deprivation is an overused and overly clinical term to describe the joys, the pain, the anger, and the ambiguity of their experience.

Nevertheless, it was precisely the clash between the heightened sense of self-worth which the movement offered to its participants and the replication of traditional sex roles within it that gave birth to a new feminism. Treated as housewives, sex objects, nurturers, and political auxiliaries, and finally threatened with banishment from the movement, young white Southern women responded with the first articulation of the modern challenge to the sexual status quo.

THE DECISION

The first critical experience for most white women was simply the choice to become involved. In contrast to portions of the Northern student movement, Southern women did not join the civil-rights struggle thoughtlessly or simply as an extension of a boyfriend's involvement. Such a decision often required a break with home and childhood friends that might never heal. It meant painful isolation and a confrontation with the possibility of violence and death. Such risks were not taken lightly. They constituted forceful acts of self-assertion.

Participation in civil rights meant beginning to see the South through the eyes of the poorest blacks, and frequently it shattered supportive ties with family and friends. Such new perceptions awakened white participants to the stark brutality of racism and the depth of their own racial attitudes. One young woman had just arrived in Albany, Georgia, when she was arrested along with the other whites in the local SNCC voter registration project. By the time she left jail after nine days of fasting, the movement was central to her life. Her father suffered a nervous breakdown. But while she was willing to compromise on where she would work, she staunchly refused to consider leaving the movement. That, it seemed to her, "would be like living death."

For other women, such tensions were compounded by the fact that parents and friends lived in the same community. Judith Brown joined the staff of CORE and was sent to work in her home town. She wrote later of the anxieties she felt: "For that year I had to make a choice between the white community in which I had grown up and the black community, about which I knew very little."

Anguished parents used every weapon they could muster to stop their children. "We'll cut off your money," "You don't love us," they threatened.

The women who refused to acquiesce often responded with loving determination. On June 27, 1964, a young volunteer headed for Mississippi wrote:

> Dear Mom and Dad:
>
> This letter is hard to write because I would like so much to communicate how I feel and I don't know if I can. It is very hard to answer to your attitude that if I loved you I wouldn't do this. . . . I can only hope you have the sensitivity to understand that I can both love you very much and desire to go to Mississippi. . . . There comes a time when you have to do things which your parents do not agree with.

Even activist parents, who themselves had taken serious risks for causes they believed in, were troubled. Mimi Feingold learned years later that when she joined the freedom rides with the moral and financial support of her parents, her mother was ill with worry. Heather Tobis' uncle wrote that her work in Mississippi compared with the struggle against fascism in the 1930s and 1940s. "We are proud to claim you as our own," he said. But her parents asked angrily over the phone, "Do you know how much it takes to make a child?" Whether they kept their fears to themselves or openly opposed their children's participation, the messages from parents, both overt and subliminal, were mixed: "We believe in what you're doing—but don't do it." Their concern could only heighten their daughters' ambivalences.

The pain of such a choice, however, was eased by the sense of purpose with which the movement was imbued. The founding statement of SNCC rang with Biblical cadences:

> . . . the philosophical or religious ideal of nonviolence [is] the foundation of our purpose, the presupposition of our faith, and the manner of our action. Nonviolence as it grows from Judaic-Christian tradition seeks a social order of justice permeated by love. . . .
>
> Through nonviolence, courage displaces fear; love transforms hate. Acceptance dissipates prejudice; hope ends despair. Peace dominates war; faith reconciles doubt. Mutual regard cancels enmity. Justice for all overcomes injustice. The redemptive community supersedes systems of gross immorality.

The goals of the movement—described as the "redemptive community," or more often, the "beloved community"—constituted both a vision of the future obtained through nonviolent action and a conception of the nature of the movement itself. Jane Stembridge, daughter of a Southern Baptist minister who left her studies at Union Theological Seminary to become the first paid staff member of SNCC, expressed it in these words: ". . . finally it all boils down to human relationship. . . . It is the question of whether I shall go on living in isolation or whether there shall be a we. The student movement is not a cause . . . it is a collision between this one person and that one person. It is a *I am going to sit beside you.* . . . Love alone is radical."

Within SNCC the intensely personal nature of social action and the commitment to equality resulted in a kind of anarchic democracy and a general questioning of all the socially accepted rules. When SNCC moved into voter registration projects in the Deep South, this commitment led to a deep respect for the very poorest blacks. "Let the people decide" was about as close to an ideology as SNCC ever came. Though civil-rights workers were frustrated by the depth of fear and passivity beaten into generations of rural black people, the movement was also nourished by the beauty and courage of people who dared to face the loss of their livelihoods and possibly their lives.

One white, female civil-rights worker in Mississippi wrote that the Negroes in Holly Springs were incredibly brave, "the most real people" she had ever met. She continued, "I'm sure you can tell that the work so far has been far more gratifying than anything I ever anticipated. The sense of urgency and injustice is such that I no longer feel I have any choice . . . and every day I feel more and more of a gap between us and the rest of the world that is not engaged in trying to change this cruel system."

NEW REALITIES

The movement's vision translated into daily realities of hard work and responsibility which admitted few sexual limitations. Young white women's sense of purpose was reinforced by the knowledge that the work they did and the responsibilities they assumed were central to the movement. In the beginning, black and white alike agreed that whites should work primarily in the white community. They had an appropriate role in urban direct-action movements where the goal was integration, but their principal job was generating support for civil rights within the white population. The handful of white women involved in the early '60s either worked in the SNCC office—gathering news, writing pamphlets, facilitating communications—or organized campus support through such agencies as the YWCA.

In direct-action demonstrations, many women discovered untapped reservoirs of courage. Cathy Cade attended Spelman College as an exchange student in the spring of 1962. She had been there only two days when she joined Howard Zinn in a sit-in in the black section of the Georgia Legislature. Never before had she so much as joined a picket line. Years later she testified: "To this day I am amazed. I just did it." Though she understood the risks involved, she does not remember being afraid. Rather she was exhilarated, for with one stroke she undid much of the fear of blacks that she had developed as a high school student in Tennessee.

Others, like Mimi Feingold, jumped eagerly at the chance to join the freedom rides but then found the experience more harrowing than they had expected. Her group had a bomb scare in Montgomery and knew that the last freedom bus in Alabama had been blown up. They never left the bus from Atlanta to Jackson, Mississippi. The arrest in Jackson was anticlimactic. Then there was a month in jail where she could hear women screaming as they were subjected to humiliating vaginal "searches."

When SNCC moved into voter registration projects in the Deep South, the experiences of white women acquired a new dimension. The years of enduring the brutality of intransigent racism finally convinced SNCC to invite several hundred white students into Mississippi for the 1964 "freedom summer." For the first time, large numbers of white women would be allowed into "the field," to work in the rural South.

They had previously been excluded because white women in rural communities were highly visible; their presence, violating both racial and sexual taboos, often provoked repression. According to Mary King, "the start of violence in a community was often tied to the point at which white women appeared to be in the civil-rights movement." However, the presence of whites also brought the attention of the national media, and, in the face of the apparent impotence of the federal law enforcement apparatus, the media became the chief weapon of the movement against violence and brutality. Thus, with considerable ambivalence, SNCC began to include whites—both men and women—in certain voter registration projects.

The freedom summer brought hundreds of Northern white women into the Southern movement. They taught in freedom schools, ran libraries, canvassed for voter registration, and endured constant harassment from the local whites. Many reached well beyond their previously assumed limits: "I was overwhelmed at the idea of setting up a library all by myself," wrote one woman. "Then can you imagine how I felt when at Oxford, while I was learning how to drop on the ground to protect my face, my ears, and my breasts, I was asked to *coordinate* the libraries in the entire project's community centers? I wanted to cry 'HELP' in a number of ways."

And while they tested themselves and questioned their own courage, they also experienced poverty, oppression and discrimination in raw form. As one volunteer wrote:

> For the first time in my life, I am seeing what it is like to be poor, oppressed and hated. And what I see here does not apply only to Gulfport or to Mississippi or even to the South. . . . This summer is only the briefest beginning of this experience.

Some women virtually ran the projects they were in. And they learned to live with an intensity of fear that they had never known before. By October, 1964, there had been 15 murders, 4 woundings, 37 churches bombed or burned, and over 1,000 arrests in Mississippi. Every project set up elaborate security precautions—regular communication by two-way radio, rules against going out at night or walking downtown in interracial groups. One woman summed up the experience of hundreds when she explained, "I learned a lot of respect for myself for having gone through all that."

NEW ROLE MODELS

As white women tested themselves in the movement, they were constantly inspired by the examples of black women who shattered cultural images of appropriate "female" behavior. "For the first time," according to one white Southerner, "I had role models I could respect."

Within the movement many of the legendary figures were black women around whom circulated stories of exemplary courage and audacity. Rarely did women expect or receive any special protection in demonstrations or jails. Frequently, direct-action teams were equally divided between women and men, on the theory that the presence of women in sit-in demonstrations might lessen the violent reaction. In 1960, slender Diane Nash had been transformed overnight from a Fisk University beauty queen to a principal leader of the direct-action movement in Nashville, Tennessee. Within SNCC she argued strenuously for direct action—sit-ins and demonstrations—over voter registration and community organization. By 1962, when she was twenty-two years old and four months pregnant, she confronted a Mississippi judge with her refusal to cooperate with the court system by appealing her two-year sentence or posting bond:

> We in the nonviolent movement have been talking about jail without bail for about two years or more. The time has come for us to mean what we say and stop posting bond. . . . This will be a black baby born in Mississippi, and thus wherever he is born he will be born in prison. I believe that if I go to jail now it may help hasten that day when my child and all children will be free—not only on the day of their birth but for all their lives.

Several years later, Annie Pearl Avery awed six hundred demonstrators in Montgomery, Alabama, as a white policeman who had beaten several protesters approached her with his club raised. She reached up, grabbed his club and said, "Now what you going to do. . . . ?" Stunned, the policeman stood transfixed while Avery slipped back into the crowd.

Perhaps even more important than the daring of younger activists was the towering strength of older black women. There is no doubt that women were key to organizing the black community. In 1962, SNCC staff member Charles Sherrod wrote the office that in every southwest Georgia county "there is always a 'mama.' She is usually a militant woman in the community, out-spoken, understanding, and willing to catch hell, having already caught her share."

Stories of such women abound. For providing housing, food, and active support to SNCC workers, their homes were fired upon and bombed. Fannie Lou Hamer, the Sunflower County sharecropper who forfeited her livelihood to emerge as one of the most courageous and eloquent leaders of the Mississippi Freedom Democratic Party, was only the most famous. "Mama Dolly" in Lee County, Georgia, was a seventy-year-old, grey-haired lady "who can pick more cotton, slop more pigs, plow more ground, chop more wood, and do a hundred more things better than the best farmer in the area." For many white volunteers, they were also "mamas" in the sense of being mother-figures, new models of the meaning of womanhood.

THE UNDERTOW OF OPPRESSION

Yet new models bumped up against old ones: self-assertion generated anxiety; new expectations existed alongside traditional ones; ideas about freedom and equality bent under assumptions about women as mere houseworkers and sexual objects. These contradictory forces finally generated a feminist response from those who could not deny the reality of their new-found strength.

Black and white women took on important administrative roles in the Atlanta SNCC office, but they also performed virtually all typing and clerical work. Very few women assumed the public roles of national leadership. In 1964, black women held a half-serious, half-joking sit-in to protest these conditions. By 1965, the situation had changed enough that a quarrel over who would take notes at staff meetings was settled by buying a tape recorder.

In the field, there was a tendency to assume that housework around the freedom house would be performed by women. As early as 1963, Joni Rabinowitz, a white volunteer in the southwest Georgia Project, submitted a stinging series of reports on the "woman's role."

> Monday, 15 April: . . . The attitude around here toward keeping the house neat (as well as the general attitude toward the inferiority and "proper place" of women) is disgusting and also terribly depressing. I never saw a cooperative enterprize [*sic*] that was less cooperative.

There were also ambiguities in the position of women who had been in the movement for many years and were perceived by others as important leaders. While women increasingly became a central force in SNCC between 1960 and 1965, white women were always in a somewhat anomalous position. New recruits saw Casey Hayden and Mary King as very powerful. Hayden had been an activist since the late '50s. Her involvement in the YWCA and the Christian Faith and Life Community at the University of Texas led her to join the demonstrations which erupted in Austin in 1959. From that time on she worked full-time against segregation, sometimes through the Y, sometimes through the National Student Association or Students for a Democratic Society, but always most closely with SNCC. Mary King, daughter of a Southern Methodist minister, had visited SNCC on a trip sponsored by the Y at Ohio Wesleyan University in 1962 and soon returned to work full-time.

They and others who had joined the young movement when it included only a handful of whites knew the inner circles of SNCC through years of shared work and risk. They had an easy familiarity with the top leadership which bespoke considerable influence. Yet Hayden and King could virtually run a freedom registration program and at the same time remain outside the basic political decision-making process.

Mary King described herself and Hayden as being in "positions of relative powerlessness." They were powerful because they worked very hard. According to King, "If you were a hard worker and you were good, at least before 1965 . . . you could definitely have an influence on policy."

The key phrase is "at least before 1965," for by 1965 the position of white women in SNCC, especially Southern women whose goals had been shaped by the vision of the "beloved community," was in steep decline. Ultimately, a growing spirit of black nationalism, fed by the tensions of large numbers of whites, especially women, entering the movement, forced these women out of SNCC and precipitated the articulation of a new feminism.

RACIAL/SEXUAL TENSIONS

White women's presence inevitably heightened the sexual tension which runs as a constant current through racist culture. Southern women understood that in the struggle against racial discrimination they were at war with their culture. They reacted to the label "Southern lady" as though it were an obscene epithet, for they had emerged from a society that used the symbol of "Southern white womanhood" to justify an insidious pattern of racial discrimination and brutal repression. They had, of necessity, to forge a new sense of self, a new definition of femininity apart from the one they had inherited. Gradually they came to understand the struggle against racism as "a key to pulling down all the . . . fascist notions and mythologies and institutions in the South," including "notions about white women and repression."

Thus, for Southern women this tension was a key to their incipient feminism, but it also became a disruptive force within the civil-rights movement itself. The entrance of white women in large numbers into the movement could hardly have been anything but explosive. Interracial sex was the most potent social taboo in the South. And the struggle against racism brought together young, naive, sometimes insensitive, rebellious, and idealistic white women with young, angry black men, some of whom had hardly been allowed to speak to white women before. They sat-in together. If they really believed in equality, why shouldn't they sleep together?

In many such relationships there was much warmth and caring. Several marriages resulted. One young woman described how "a whole lot of things got shared around sexuality—like black men with white women—it wasn't just sex, it was also sharing ideas and fears, and emotional support. . . . My sexuality for myself was confirmed by black men for the first time ever in my life, see . . . and I needed that very badly. . . . It's a positive advantage to be a big woman in the black community."

On the other hand, there remained a dehumanizing quality in many relationships. According to one woman, it "had a lot to do with the fact that people thought they might die." They lived their lives at an incredible pace and could not be very loving toward anybody. "So people would go to a staff meeting and . . . sleep with whoever was there."

Sexual relationships did not become a serious problem, however, until interracial sex became a widespread phenomenon in local communities in the summer of 1964. The same summer that opened new horizons to hundreds of women simultaneously induced serious strains within the movement itself. Accounts of what happened vary according to the perspectives of the observer.

Some paint a picture of hordes of "loose" white women coming to the South and spreading corruption wherever they went. One male black leader recounted that "where I was project director we put white women out of the project within the first three weeks because they tried to screw themselves across the city." He agreed that black neighborhood youth tended to be sexually aggressive. "I mean you are trained to be aggressive in this country, but you are also not expected to get a positive response."

Others saw the initiative coming almost entirely from males. According to historian Staughton Lynd, director of the Freedom Schools, "Every black SNCC worker with perhaps a few exceptions counted it a notch on his gun to have slept with a white woman—as many as possible. And I think that was just very traumatic for the women who encountered that, who hadn't thought that was what going South was about." A white woman who worked in Virginia for several years explained, "It's much harder to say 'No' to the advances of a black guy because of the strong possibility of that being taken as racist."

Clearly the boundary between sexual freedom and sexual exploitation was a thin one. Many women consciously avoided all romantic involvements in intuitive recognition of that fact. Yet the presence of hundreds of young whites from middle- and upper-middle-income families in a movement primarily of poor, rural blacks exacerbated latent racial and sexual tensions beyond the breaking point. The first angry response came not from the surrounding white community (which continually assumed sexual excesses far beyond the reality) but from young black women in the movement.

A black woman pointed out that white women would "do all the shit work and do it in a feminine kind of way while black women . . . were out in the streets battling with the cops. So it did something to what our femininity was about. We became amazons, less than and more than women at the same time." Another black woman added, "If white women had a problem in SNCC, it was not just a male/woman problem . . . it was also a black woman/white woman problem. It was a race problem rather than a woman's problem." And a white woman, asked whether she experienced any hostility from black women, responded, "Oh tons and tons! I was very, very afraid of black women, very afraid." Though she admired them and was continually awed by their courage and strength, her sexual relationships with black men placed a barrier between herself and black women.

Soon after the 1964 summer project, black women in SNCC sharply confronted male leadership. They charged that they could not develop relationships with the black men because the men did not have to be responsible to them as long as they could turn to involvement with white women.

Black women's anger and demands constituted one part of an intricate maze of tensions and struggles that were in the process of transforming the civil-rights movement. SNCC had grown from a small band of sixteen to a swollen staff of 180, of whom 50% were white. The earlier dream of a beloved community was dead. The vision of freedom lay crushed under the weight of intransigent racism, disillusion with electoral politics and nonviolence, and differences of race, class, and culture within the movement itself. Within the rising spirit of black nationalism, the anger of black women toward white women was only one element.

It is in this context that Ruby Doris Smith Robinson, one of the most powerful black women in SNCC, is said to have written a paper on the position of women in SNCC. If a copy of this paper exists I have yet to find it. Those I have interviewed who attended the conference at which she delivered it, or who heard about it soon thereafter, have hazy and contradictory memories. Nevertheless this paper has been cited frequently in the literature of contemporary feminism as the earliest example of "women's consciousness" within the new left.

Ruby Doris Smith Robinson was a strong woman. As a teenager she had joined the early Atlanta demonstrations during her sophomore year at Spelman College. That year, as a participant in the Rock Hill, South Carolina, sit-in she helped initiate the "jail — no bail" policy in SNCC. A month in the Rock Hill jail bound her to the movement with a zeal born of common suffering, deepened commitment, and shared vision. Soon she was a battle-scarred veteran, respected by everyone and feared by many; she ran the SNCC office with unassailable authority.

As an early leader of the black nationalist faction, Robinson hated white women for years because white women represented a cultural ideal of beauty and "femininity" which by inference defined black women as ugly and unwomanly. But she was also aware that women had from time to time to assert their rights as women. In 1964, she participated in and perhaps led the sit-in in the SNCC office protesting the relegation of women to typing and clerical work. Robinson died of cancer in 1968, and we may never know her own assessment of her feelings and intentions in 1964. We do know, however, that tales of her memo generated feminist echoes in the minds of many. And Stokely Carmichael's reputed response that "the only position for women in SNCC is prone" stirred up even more.

For Southern white women who had devoted several years of their lives to the vision of a beloved community, the rejection of nonviolence and movement toward a more ideological, centralized, and black nationalist movement was bitterly disillusioning. Mary King recalled, "It was very sad to see something that was so creative and so dynamic and so strong disintegrating. . . . I was terribly disappointed for a long time. . . . I was most affected by the way that black women turned against me. That hurt more than the guys. But it had been there, you know. You could see it coming."

REBIRTH OF FEMINISM

In the fall of 1965, Mary King and Casey Hayden spent several days of long discussions in the mountains of Virginia. Both of them were on their way out of the movement, though they were not fully conscious of that fact. Finally they decided to write a "kind of memo" addressed to "a number of other women in the peace and freedom movements." In it they argued that women, like blacks, "seem to be caught in a common-law caste system that operates, sometimes subtly, forcing them to work around or outside hierarchical structures of power which may exclude them. Women seem to be placed in the same position of assumed subordination in personal situations too. It is a caste system which, at its worst, uses and exploits women."

Hayden and King set the precedent of contrasting the movement's egalitarian ideas with the replication of sex roles within it. They noted the ways in which women's position in society determined women's roles in the movement — like cleaning houses, doing secretarial work, and refraining from active or public leadership. At the same time, they observed, "having learned from the movement to think radically about the personal worth and abilities of people whose role in society had gone unchallenged before, a lot of women in the movement have begun trying to apply those lessons to their own relations with men. Each of us probably has her own story of the various results."

They spoke of the pain of trying to put aside "deeply learned fears, needs, and self-perceptions . . . and . . . to replace them with concepts of people and freedom learned from the movement and organizing." In this process many people in the movement had questioned basic institutions, such as marriage and child-rearing. Indeed, such issues had been discussed over and over again, but seriously only among women. The usual male response was laughter, and women were left feeling silly. Hayden and King lamented the "lack of community for discussion: Nobody is writing, or organizing, or talking publicly about women, in any way that reflects the problems that various women in the movement came across." Yet despite their feelings of invisibility, their words also demonstrated the ability to take the considerable risks involved in sharp criticisms. Through the movement they had developed too much self-confidence and self-respect to accept passively subordinate roles.

The memo was addressed principally to black women — long time friends and comrades-in-nonviolent-arms — in the hope that, "perhaps we can start to talk with each other more openly than in the past and create a community of support for each other so we can deal with ourselves and others with integrity and can therefore keep working." In some ways, it was a parting attempt to halt the metamorphosis in the civil-rights movement from non-violence to nationalism, from beloved community to black power. It expressed Hayden and King's pain and isolation as white women in the movement. The black women who received it were on a different historic trajectory. They would fight some of the same battles as women, but in a different context and in their own way.

This "kind of memo" represented a flowering of women's consciousness that articulated contradictions felt most acutely by middle-class white women. While black women had been gaining strength and power within the movement, white women's position — at the nexus of sexual and racial conflicts — had become increasingly precarious. Their feminist response, then, was precipitated by loss in the immediate situation, but it was a sense of loss against the even deeper background of new strength and self-worth which the movement had allowed them to develop. Like their foremothers in the nineteenth century, they confronted this dilemma with the tools which the movement had given them: a language to name and describe oppression; a deep belief in freedom, equality and community soon to be translated into "sisterhood"; a willingness to question and challenge any social institution which failed to meet human needs; and the ability to organize.

It is not surprising that the issues were defined and confronted first by Southern women whose consciousness developed in a context which inextricably and paradoxically linked the fate of women and black people. These spiritual daughters of Sarah and Angelina Grimke kept their expectations low in November, 1965. "Objectively," Hayden and King wrote, "the chances seem nil that we could start a movement based on anything as distant to general American thought as a sex-caste system." But change was in the air and youth was on the march.

In the North there were hundreds of women who had shared in the Southern experience for a week, a month, a year, and thousands more who participated vicariously or worked to extend the struggle for freedom and equality into Northern communities. These women were ready to hear what their Southern sisters had to say. The debate within Students for a Democratic Society (SDS) which started in response to Hayden and King's ideas led, two years later, to the founding of the women's liberation movement.

Thus, the fullest expression of conscious feminism within the civil-rights movement ricocheted off the fury of black power and landed with explosive force in the Northern, white new left. One month after Hayden and King mailed out their memo, women who had read it staged an angry walkout of a national SDS conference in Champaign-Urbana, Illinois. The only man to defend their action was a black man from SNCC.

Feminism in the 1970's

WILLIAM H. CHAFE

The resurgence of feminism in the 1960's represented the third incarnation of a dynamic women's rights movement in American history. The first . . . grew out of the abolitionist struggle of the 1830's and featured the legendary leadership of people like Elizabeth Cady Stanton and Susan B. Anthony. The second developed out of the social reform ethos of the early 1900's, and though the lineal descendant of the first movement, exhibited a style of leadership and a tactical approach significantly different from its

Abridged from *Women and Equality: Changing Patterns in American Culture,* by William H. Chafe. Copyright © 1977 by Oxford University Press, Inc. Reprinted by permission.

antecedent. Cresting with the battle over the suffrage amendment, it succumbed to factionalism and public indifference in the 1920's and 1930's. The contemporary movement, like its predecessors, has grown out of a period of generalized social ferment, both drawing upon and reflecting a widespread sensitivity toward discrimination and injustice. The contemporary drive for women's liberation, however, differs from its forerunners in at least three ways: it is grounded in and moving in the same direction as underlying social trends at work in the society; it has developed an organizational base that is diverse and decentralized; and it is pursuing a wide range of social objectives that strike at many of the root causes of sex inequality. Although some of these distinctive characteristics are a source of weakness as well as strength, no previous feminist movement has attempted so much, and none has been better situated to make progress toward the goal of equality.

Probably the chief advantage of contemporary feminism lies in the extent to which its goals and programs have meshed with, or addressed directly, prevailing trends in the society. . . .

. . . [T]he feminism of the 1960's and 1970's differed from previous women's movements precisely because it grew out of and built upon prevailing social trends. For the first time ideological protest and underlying social and economic changes appeared to be moving in a similar direction. . . . [F]emale work patterns were virtually transformed in the years after 1940. Prior to World War II, female employment was limited primarily to young, single women or poor, married women. Few middle-class wives held jobs. By 1975, in contrast, the two-income family had become the norm; 49 per cent of all wives worked; and the median income of families where wives were employed was nearly $17,000. Although the employment changes did not signify progress toward equality, they ensured that social norms about woman's "place" no longer had a base in reality.

As a result, feminist programs spoke more directly than ever before to the daily experience of millions of women. Female workers might not consider themselves feminists; indeed, they might shun any kind of association with the abstract cause of women's rights. But the same workers knew that they did not receive equal pay with men and that most of the higher paying jobs carried a "male only" tag. Similarly, the large number of women workers who had school-age and pre-school children understood the problems caused by inadequate day-care and after-school facilities. Discontented homemakers, who yearned for a more diverse life but saw all the barriers in the way, had a comparable sense of recognition. Thus there developed a common ground on which feminist activists and their potential constituency could stand, and that common ground provided the starting point from which some women moved toward greater collective consciousness of a sense of grievance.

A second social trend which coincided with the revival of feminism was the decline in the birth rate during the 60's and 70's. After World War II a "baby boom" swept the country, peaking in 1957 with a birth rate of 27.2 children per thousand people. There then ensued a prolonged downturn, which in 1967 resulted in a birth rate of 17.9, the lowest since the Great Depression. At the time demographers disagreed about the reasons for the decline, some citing the development of oral contraceptives, others economic and social instability. But all agreed there would be a new baby boom in the early 1970's when the children born twenty years earlier began to reproduce. Instead of rising, though, the birth rate continued to plummet, reaching an all-time low by the mid-70's and achieving the reproduction level required— over time—for Zero Population Growth.

Although many forces contributed to the continuing decline, the inter-action of female employment with changing attitudes toward women's roles appears to have been decisive. Throughout the 1960s, women married later, delayed the birth of their first child, and bore their last child at an earlier age. Whether as cause or effect, this trend coincided with many women finding occupations and interests away from the home. The rewards of having a job, as well as the desire for extra money to meet rising living standards, tended to emphasize the advantages of a small family. These values, in turn, were reinforced in the late 60's by the ideology of feminism and the population control movement. Two Gallup polls in 1967 and 1971 highlighted the shift in values. The earlier survey showed that 34 per cent of women in the prime childbearing years anticipated having four or more children. By 1971, in contrast, the figure had dropped to 15 per cent. Two years later 70 per cent of the nation's 18- to 24-year-old women indicated that they expected to have no more than two children. Thus feminist emphasis on personal fulfillment and freedom from immersion in traditional sex roles operated in tandem with long-range social developments which made such goals more objectively feasible.

Finally, changing attitudes and behavior in the realm of human sexual-ity meshed closely with feminist values concerning personal and bodily libera-tion. Although suffrage leaders in the early 20th century had exhibited little understanding or tolerance of the sexual revolution, supporters of women's liberation emphasized as one of their strongest themes the importance of women knowing their own bodies and having the freedom to use them as they saw fit. One manifestation of this emphasis was the publication by a woman's health collective of *Our Bodies, Our Selves,* a handbook which urged women to understand and appreciate their bodies. (The book had sold 850,000 copies from 1971 through 1976.) Still another manifestation was a generally sup-portive attitude toward "liberated" personal life-styles, including lesbianism, communal living, and sexual relationships outside of marriage

Significantly, such attitudes reinforced many of the social trends already developing in the culture, particularly among the young. In the eyes of many observers, a second sexual revolution occurred starting in the mid-60's. One study of women students at a large urban university showed a significant increase after 1965 in the number of women having intercourse while in a "dating" or "going steady" relationship; at the same time guilt feelings about sex sharply declined. Another nation-wide sample of freshmen college women in 1975 disclosed that one-third endorsed casual sex based on a short ac-quaintance, and over 40 per cent believed a couple should live together before getting married. Most indicative of changing mores, perhaps, was a survey of eight colleges in 1973 which showed not only that 76 per cent of women had engaged in intercourse by their junior year (the male figure was 75 per cent), but that women were appreciably more active sexually than men. Daniel Yankelovich's public opinion polls of college and non-college young people in the 60's and 70's appeared to confirm the major departure in sexual behavior and attitudes. Only a minority of women disapproved morally of pre-marital sex, homosexual relations between consenting adults, or having an abortion. Although women's liberation advocates warned that women could be victimized anew as sex objects under the guise of sexual freedom (just as they had been under a system of more repressive mores), the fact remained that the movement's support for abortion, homosexual rights, and free bodily expression placed it more in harmony with emerging cultural attitudes toward sexuality than in opposition.

In each of these areas, it seemed clear that the women's liberation movement was both drawing upon and reinforcing important changes taking place in the society. Shifts in employment patterns, demography, and sexual mores may have had a momentum of their own, but feminism introduced a powerful ingredient of ideology and activism that sought to transform these impersonal social trends and create new values and attitudes toward sex roles. In that sense, for the first time a dynamic relationship existed between "objective" social changes and feminist efforts to shape those changes in a particular direction. In contrast with each of the previous woman's movements, the women's liberation drive of the 1960's and 1970's operated in a context where the social preconditions for ideological change were present. No longer was feminism irrelevant to most people's daily lives. Instead, its message spoke to many of the realities of the contemporary society. As a result, the possibility of an audience being able to respond was greater than ever before.

The second major distinctive quality of the new feminism is that as a result of a broader social base, the organization and structure of the movement differ significantly from that of the past. When women's rights advocates were on the margin of society and alienated from the world of most women, the organizational basis of the movement was narrow. Supporters of feminism, for the most part, came from the same social class and economic background. To maximize impact, the organizations they formed were national in scope. The women's liberation movement of the 60's and 70's, in contrast, almost defied categorization. Although feminist groups such as NOW [National Organization for Women] and the Women's Equity Action League (WEAL) operated out of national offices in a style similar to that of other reform groups, the grass roots supporters of the movement fit less easily into an organizational niche. Some observers described women's liberation as a "guerilla movement," its headquarters located in every kitchen or bedroom where women developed a more critical and independent sense of self. Whether or not the description was fully accurate, the new feminism appeared both diverse and decentralized, its strength more likely to be found in local communities than in national hierarchies. Since the movement had emerged in response to social conditions affecting a large number of women, it tended to reflect the different backgrounds of its supporters and the special concerns which were of greatest interest to them. . . .

. . . In the late 60's feminism was generally associated with "liberal" university towns, student enclaves, the affluent suburbs, or the cosmopolitan urban centers of the East and West Coasts. Many supporters of the movement did come from the best universities and from well-off families, even if in the latter case, they had rejected some of the paraphernalia of affluence. (In a survey of its readers, *Ms.* magazine found that 84 per cent had been to college, and that 71 per cent worked, mostly in higher level jobs.) Others supposedly were disaffected suburban wives and mothers, bored by bridge parties and chauffeuring children to dance lessons. From the point of view of some critics, such women were indulging a fantasy desire to join the world of social protest, and in the absence of exposure to the real injustices of hunger, poverty, and racial violence had "invented" the superficial issue of sex discrimination.

Still, the charge of elitism appeared less applicable to the women's movement of the 60's and 70's than to prior manifestations of feminism. Most supporters of the movement identified with the political left and were highly conscious of the issues of class and race, seeking wherever possible to find ways of transcending those barriers. Rather than criticize or remain aloof from other dissident groups, women liberationists supported organizations like the United Farm Workers and aligned themselves with other groups seeking social change. (The early women's rights movement had done the same, of course, but the concern with racism faded by the late 19th century.) Many of the substantive demands of the movement, in turn, promised to help the poor as well as the rich and middle class. Most well-off women could afford to send their children to nursery school or hire service help. It was working-class women who would benefit most from universal day-care, equal pay, an end to job discrimination, and the availability of inexpensive abortions and birth control assistance.

In addition, there was some evidence to contradict the popular image of the women's movement as a white middle-class preserve. Despite major differences in priority and perspective between black and white women, a National Black Feminist Organization formed in 1973 both to assert the distinctive interests of black women in the struggle for women's rights and to provide a base for cooperative action on those issues which affected women across racial lines. By 1974 the NBFO had a membership of 2,000 women in ten chapters. Similarly, working-class women affirmed some identification with the concerns of the women's movement through the creation of the Coalition of Labor Union Women (CLUW). . . .

Perhaps more important, the new social base of feminism produced a thoroughly decentralized structure. . . .

The women's liberation movement of the 60's and 70's . . . was almost without any overarching structure. Despite the existence of groups like the National Organization for Women (NOW), the movement functioned primarily through small, informal groups on a local level. Its energy came from the bottom, not the top, and from the immediate ongoing concern of women with the quality of their own lives. Events or issues which were national in scope (such as the Equal Rights Amendment, or the march for equality on the 50th anniversary of the suffrage victory) were certainly not ignored, but the day-to-day direction of the movement grew out of local conditions which were central to the lives of the women most involved. Thus, as long as people in the immediate environment shared a common sense of grievance and a common desire for change, the movement was largely self-sustaining. It did not depend on national leadership. Indeed, many feminists believed deeply that "leaders" were unnecessary, that women could make decisions collectively, and that concepts of hierarchy and command were products of a male culture, hence to be avoided. In this context, the movement was decentralized for two reasons: it was rooted in local communities where women came together to deal with issues in their own lives; and it represented an ideology that viewed large organizations and leadership structures as part of the problem rather than the solution.

Not surprisingly, the absence of conventional leadership structures proved a source of considerable controversy. . . .

On balance, though, it seemed that decentralization and the lack of structure were central to the movement's strength as well as its distinctiveness. An ideal social movement might combine the discipline of a national organization with the energy of local grass roots efforts, yet such a combination appeared inconsistent—even contradictory— to the internal dynamics of the women's liberation movement. The vitality of the movement lay precisely in the proliferation of local organizations, each growing out of a particular concern or experience of different groups of women. Because such organizations reflected the immediate priorities of the women who created them, they commanded substantial loyalty and energy. It seemed at least possible, if not likely, that such an investment of local energy and initiative would be difficult to sustain in a hierarchical organization with established policies and strict procedures.

Finally, the pattern of decentralization ensured that the women's liberation movement would not rise or fall on the basis of one organization's activities or decisions. When all attention was riveted on a single national group as the embodiment of a cause, there was always the danger of defeat through internal divisions or the independent action of third parties. Thus some movements have been judged dead or alive on the basis of a single vote in Congress, or a series of public relations maneuvers. A social movement rooted in diverse local situations, however, and organized around a variety of issues, was less vulnerable to symbolic defeats. Thus, just as the movement's relevance to social trends helped to reinforce its ideological vitality, its decentralized structure accentuated its organizational strong point—grass roots support in the local community.

This, in turn, leads to the third distinguishing characteristic of the women's liberation movement, the variety and scope of its objectives. . . .

. . . Although ratification of the proposed Equal Rights Amendment to the Constitution, repeal of abortion laws, or women's political caucuses represented the most visible items on the feminist agenda, most activists understood that success in one venture only meant there would be a new problem to work on. In this sense, feminists seemed to have learned a great deal from the civil rights movement, where the achievement of some goals such as the Voting Rights Act simply disclosed the existence of additional layers of racism to be combated. Implicit in feminist activities was the perception that, as in the Chinese proverb, the problem of inequality was a box within a box within a box, with no single answer.

The spectrum of activities in one university community during the early 1970's illustrated the diversity of objectives pursued by different groups. One group of women came together to plan a course for public school teachers on eliminating sexism in the classroom. Another met weekly to edit and publish children's books which were free of invidious sex stereotypes. Still another group worked on a coalition of citizens concerned with day care. While a local woman's center sponsored a meeting for the purpose of starting a union of household workers, a NOW chapter worked to counter employment discrimination. Counseling on sexuality, birth control, and abortion occupied still others. Lesbian discussion groups provided a forum for homosexual women to talk about the politics of sex, and a socialist feminist group addressed the junction of class and sex issues. Consciousness-raising groups for divorced or widowed women attempted to deal with the specific problems growing out of those situations. Although such diversity produced conflict over priorities as well as opportunities for cooperation, it illustrates the pluralistic approach which the women's movement of the 60's and 70's brought to the problem of sex inequality—an approach which maximized the possibility of local women becoming involved in an issue important to their own immediate lives.

In the end, therefore, each of the distinctive qualities of feminism in the 60's and 70's was inextricably connected to the next. Because feminist ideas directly addressed contemporary social realities, more people perceived the movement as relevant to their own circumstances. This, in turn, helped to produce involvement in local activities which seemed pertinent to the larger issue. The extent to which the movement grew out of and related back to the immediate experience of large numbers of women made unnecessary the centralized and hierarchical structures of the past, and the absence of such structures encouraged the development of multiple activities each dealing with a particular aspect of sex inequality. . . .

As in the history of all social movements, however, contemporary feminism faced serious obstacles. Some reflected internal tensions that emerged from the very diversity and decentralization which distinguished the movement from its predecessors. Others derived from outside sources and mirrored the opposition, tacit as well as organized, which the ideas of women's liberation engendered. Together, they highlighted both the dimensions of the challenge confronting the movement and the scope of its quest for change.

Perhaps the most profound obstacle was the extent to which the movement threatened the sense of identity millions of people had derived from the culture and from the primary transmitter of social values, the family. The words "masculine" and "feminine" were as emotionally powerful in the meanings they conveyed as any other terms, including "white" and "black." People were raised to identify as almost sacred the attributes attached to each phrase, and to view any deviation as a mark of shame. For a boy to be called a "fairy," for example, represented a crushing insult, to be avoided at all costs. . . .

. . . [I]t seemed clear that feminism was attacking the entire spectrum of traditional male and female roles. Women's liberation advocates argued that the culture had denied females their right to be human, first, by insisting that they be "feminine" and, then, by defining "feminine" in such a way that women were deprived of the freedom to shape their own lives and choose their own careers. The same culture, it was charged, had denied males the right to be fully human by ruling out of bounds the idea of fatherhood as a full-time vocation and defining as inappropriate for men the expression of vulnerability, gentleness, or dependence. To correct these errors, feminists proposed to dismantle or radically alter some of the fundamental institutions of the culture. Instead of the traditional marriage ceremony, feminists suggested a marital contract, specifying the responsibilities of each partner and the prerequisites that had to be maintained for the relationship to be continued. Women's liberation advocates argued that women and men should be equally free to pursue careers, care for children, initiate sex, and select social companions. Public day-care services, they contended, should be available to assume part of the responsibility previously borne solely by parents. And individuals should be free — as individuals — to determine their own life style, sexual preference, occupation, and personal values.

Not surprisingly, both the indictment and the proposed solutions deeply offended people who had been raised to believe that existing norms of behavior were not only functional but morally inviolable. . . . To women who had spent a lifetime devoting themselves to the culturally sanctioned roles of homemaker and helpmate, the feminist charge that women had been enslaved frequently appeared as a direct attack on their own personal experience. Such women did not believe that they had wasted their lives or had been duped by malevolent husbands. Many enjoyed the nurturant and supportive roles of wife and mother, believed that the family should operate with a sexual division of labor, and profoundly resented the suggestion that the life of a homemaker somehow symbolized failure. From their point of view, the women's liberation movement was often guilty of arrogance and contempt toward the majority of women, and some expressed that view by voting against local Equal Rights amendments in New Jersey and New York or by supporting the traditional values celebrated in the "Total Woman" movement.

In a somewhat similar way, many men believed that the movement was conducting an insidious campaign to undermine their strength, deny their authority, and destroy their self-image. As they looked at feminist demands

for equal sharing of household responsibilities, affirmative action in employment, and complete freedom over personal lives, it seemed that women
activists were trying to take away their role as breadwinners and sabotage their
position of leadership in the home. Instead of helping women, many men
believed, feminists were intent on wrecking the family, turning wife against
husband, and transforming men into dishwashers and baby-sitters. Nothing
threatened men more than the belief that in movement groups women told
each other intimate details of their respective experiences with men and
hatched plans to subvert traditional marital relationships. From such a vantage point, women's liberation symbolized anarchic and amoral forces at
work in the society, seeking to untie all the knots and loosen the bonds that
gave life its security and stability.

Although such fears were exaggerated, concern about the challenge to
traditional "masculine" and "feminine" roles ran deep in the society. The
issues raised by feminism went to the root of people's personal as well as
social identity. At best such questions had the potential of making people
vulnerable and insecure. At worst, they produced bitter hostility. Moreover,
there existed a generalized anxiety that the triumph of women's liberation
might mean the destruction of human relationships as they had been known,
with impersonal competition replacing the warmth associated with woman's
traditional role, and a unisex sameness overcoming the rich distinctiveness of
previous male-female relationships. Part nostalgia and part legitimate concern about depersonalization, the anxiety provided important kindling for
those forces seeking to build a political backfire against women's liberation on
such issues as opposition to abortion and the Equal Rights Amendment. Thus
the greatest obstacle feminism faced was the commitment of millions of
people to the institutions, values, and personal self-images which were associated with traditional sex roles. As conservatives mobilized the political
potential implicit in that commitment, feminists found some of their objectives increasingly endangered.

The second major obstacle faced by the movement was that of internal
dissension. Though the absence of a centralized structure and focus on a
single issue proved to be assets in most respects, the resulting diversity of aims
and priorities constituted a seedbed of ideological conflict. Intense factional
disputes erupted over both goals and methods. Some feminists believed that
only the total abolition of the nuclear family could bring freedom to women.
Others accepted the family institution but sought to change its structure to
make it more equitable. While some traced discrimination against women to
an inherent and irrevocable male malevolence, others saw men as parallel
victims of a warped socialization process. Similar divisions developed over
the issue of style or political tactics. Should movement supporters denounce
the status quo in uncompromising terms and demand immediate radical
change? Or should they moderate their rhetoric, seek a common ground with
their audience, and attempt to move one step at a time? Clearly, such questions had no easy answers, but they produced a continuing tension which on

occasion resulted in internal disputes even more ferocious and embittered than conflicts with outside opponents. . . .

Still, what remained impressive was the degree of change that appeared to be taking place notwithstanding the obstacles. Although most American women might disavow any overt association with the movement *per se* ("I'm no women's libber," "They're too radical for my taste"), the same women supported many of the substantive programs of the movement. Day-care centers, availability of abortion services, equal career opportunities, and greater sharing of household tasks all received substantial approval in public opinion surveys of women. As late as 1962 a Gallup poll showed that a majority of female respondents did not believe American women were discriminated against. Eight years later women divided down the middle on the question of whether they supported the movement to secure greater equality. By 1974 those responding to the same question endorsed the efforts toward more equality by two to one.

The greatest impact of the movement appeared among the young and on college campuses. The Yankelovich survey of the early 70's showed a doubling in two years of the number of students viewing women as an oppressed group, with a large majority endorsing concepts of equality in sexual relations, the importance of women's relation to other women, and the notion that men and women were born with the same talents. Two-thirds of college women agreed that "the idea that a woman's place is in the home is nonsense," and only one-third felt that having children was an important personal value. Other polls showed similar results, including a rapid change over time. A 1970 survey of college freshmen indicated that half of the men and more than one-third of the women endorsed the idea that "the activities of married women are best confined to the home and family." Five years later only one-third of the men and less than one-fifth of the women took the same position.

Not surprisingly, changing attitudes toward traditional roles in the home were accompanied by shifting expectations about careers. In the 1970 survey of freshmen, males outnumbered females 8 to 1 in expressing an interest in the traditionally "masculine" fields of business, engineering, medicine, and law. By 1975, in contrast, the ratio was down to 3 to 1. In the same period, moreover, the number of women expecting to enter the "feminine" fields of elementary and secondary school teaching plummeted from 31 per cent to 10 per cent. Indicative of the general trend was one survey of eight colleges in 1973 which showed that 82 per cent of the women considered a career very important or important to their self-fulfillment, while only 67 per cent put marriage in the same category. Although such survey data described theoretical expectations rather than actual behavior, the evidence suggested that many women were following through on their announced intentions. The proportion of women in the entering classes of law school skyrocketed by 300 per cent from 1969 to 1974, and many law schools anticipated that women would make up half of each class by 1980. Women doctorates also increased significantly, with the share of Ph.D.'s earned by women growing from 11 per cent in 1970 to 21 per cent in 1975. Although working-class and older women did not share completely all the new ideas, they too seemed to be undergoing change. Non-college young women were less convinced of the value of sister-hood or the reality of discrimination than college women, but the Yankelo-vich survey showed them endorsing feminist ideas on greater equality in family decision-making, women's right to sexual pleasure, and skepticism toward the traditional homemaker ideal. Older women, in turn, displayed their involvement in change by enrolling in growing numbers in continuing education programs and seeking graduate training for new careers.

The exact nature of the change that had taken place was not easy to define. At its roots, it was a shift of consciousness, a new awareness or sensibility among women about women, and about their relation to men. . . .

There was no way to quantify such consciousness, or to know with certainty what it meant. Yet it seemed to be a palpable reality — taking root, growing, spreading. . . .

Much of the change that had taken place, of course, could be traced to non-ideological forces. Long-term trends in the economy, demographic pat-terns, and cultural values all contributed substantially. In addition, only a relatively small proportion of the total female population participated, either directly or indirectly, in the women's movement. . . .

Yet the women's movement of the 60's and 70's seems, on balance, to have been decisive to the heightened consciousness of the younger generation. Behavioral change, prompted by impersonal social forces, can go only so far. At some point ideological forces must intervene to spur a transformation of the values which help to shape and define behavioral options. In the late 60's and 70's the woman's movement provided such a spur, criticizing the as-sumptions, values, and images that had prevailed in the past and offering an alternative vision of what might prevail in the future. Although most men and women did not align themselves vigorously on the side of feminism, political discussions, media coverage, decisions on public school curriculum, employ-ment practices, and the dynamics of family living all reflected the impact of the movement's existence. It had raised questions, presented demands, and introduced ideas which compelled discussion. And even when the discussion was hostile, people were considering issues central to self and society in a way that had not happened before.

Document
The Problem That Has No Name

BETTY FRIEDAN

The problem lay buried, unspoken, for many years in the minds of American women. It was a strange stirring, a sense of dissatisfaction, a yearning that women suffered in the middle of the twentieth century in the United States. Each suburban wife struggled with it alone. As she made the beds, shopped for groceries, matched slipcover material, ate peanut butter sandwiches with her children, chauffeured Cub Scouts and Brownies, lay beside her husband at night—she was afraid to ask even of herself the silent question—"Is this all?"

For over fifteen years there was no word of this yearning in the millions of words written about women, for women, in all the columns, books and articles by experts telling women their role was to seek fulfillment as wives and mothers. Over and over women heard in voices of tradition and of Freudian sophistication that they could desire no greater destiny than to glory in their own femininity. Experts told them how to catch a man and keep him, how to breastfeed children and handle their toilet training, how to cope with sibling rivalry and adolescent rebellion; how to buy a dishwasher, bake bread, cook gourmet snails, and build a swimming pool with their own hands; how to dress, look, and act more feminine and make marriage more exciting; how to keep their husbands from dying young and their sons from growing into delinquents. They were taught to pity the neurotic, unfeminine, unhappy women who wanted to be poets or physicists or presidents. They learned that truly feminine women do not want careers, higher education, political rights—the independence and the opportunities that the old-fashioned feminists fought for. Some women, in their forties and fifties, still remembered painfully giving up those dreams, but most of the younger women no longer even thought about them. A thousand expert voices applauded their femininity, their adjustment, their new maturity. All they had to do was devote their lives from earliest girlhood to finding a husband and bearing children. . . .

The suburban housewife—she was the dream image of the young American women and the envy, it was said, of women all over the world. The American housewife—freed by science and labor-saving appliances from the drudgery, the dangers of childbirth and the illnesses of her grandmother. She was healthy, beautiful, educated, concerned only about her husband, her children, her home. She had found true feminine fulfillment. As a housewife and mother, she was respected as a full and equal partner to man in his world. She was free to choose automobiles, clothes, appliances, supermarkets; she had everything that women ever dreamed of.

In the fifteen years after World War II, this mystique of feminine fulfillment became the cherished and self-perpetuating core of contemporary American culture. Millions of women lived their lives in the image of those pretty pictures of the American suburban housewife, kissing their husbands goodbye in front of the picture window, depositing their stationwagonsful of children at school, and smiling as they ran the new electric waxer over the spotless kitchen floor. They baked their own bread, sewed their own and their children's clothes, kept their new washing machines and dryers running all day. They changed the sheets on the beds twice a week instead of once, took the rug-hooking class in adult education, and pitied their poor frustrated mothers, who had dreamed of having a career. Their only dream was to be perfect wives and mothers; their highest ambition to have five children and a beautiful house, their only fight to get and keep their husbands. They had no thought for the unfeminine problems of the world outside the home; they wanted the men to make the major decisions. They gloried in their role as women, and wrote proudly on the census blank: "Occupation: housewife." . . .

If a woman had a problem in the 1950's and 1960's, she knew that something must be wrong with her marriage, or with herself. Other women were satisfied with their lives, she thought. What kind of a woman was she if she did not feel this mysterious fulfillment waxing the kitchen floor? She was so ashamed to admit her dissatisfaction that she never knew how many other women shared it. If she tried to tell her husband, he didn't understand what she was talking about. She did not really understand it herself. For over fifteen years women in America found it harder to talk about this problem than about sex. Even the psychoanalysts had no name for it. When a woman went to a psychiatrist for help, as many women did, she would say, "I'm so ashamed," or "I must be hopelessly neurotic." "I don't know what's wrong with women today," a suburban psychiatrist said uneasily. "I only know something is wrong because most of my patients happen to be women. And their problem isn't sexual." Most women with this problem did not go to see a psychoanalyst, however. "There's nothing wrong really," they kept telling themselves. "There isn't any problem."

But on an April morning in 1959, I heard a mother of four, having coffee with four other mothers in a suburban development fifteen miles from New York, say in a tone of quiet desperation, "the problem." And the others knew, without words, that she was not talking about a problem with her husband, or her children, or her home. Suddenly they realized they all shared the same problem, the problem that has no name. They began, hesitantly, to talk about it. Later, after they had picked up their children at nursery school and taken them home to nap, two of the women cried, in sheer relief, just to know they were not alone.

Gradually I came to realize that the problem that has no name was shared by countless women in America. As a magazine writer I often interviewed women about problems with their children, or their marriages, or their houses, or their communities. But after a while I began to recognize the telltale signs of this other problem. I saw the same signs in suburban ranch houses and split-levels on Long Island and in New Jersey and Westchester

County; in colonial houses in a small Massachusetts town; on patios in Memphis; in suburban and city apartments; in living rooms in the Midwest. Sometimes I sensed the problem, not as a reporter, but as a suburban housewife, for during this time I was also bringing up my own three children in Rockland County, New York. I heard echoes of the problem in college dormitories and semi-private maternity wards, at PTA meetings and luncheons of the League of Women Voters, at suburban cocktail parties, in station wagons waiting for trains, and in snatches of conversation overheard at Schrafft's. The groping words I heard from other women, on quiet afternoons when children were at school or on quiet evenings when husbands worked late, I think I understood first as a woman long before I understood their larger social and psychological implications.

Just what was this problem that has no name? What were the words women used when they tried to express it? Sometimes a woman would say "I feel empty somehow . . . incomplete." Or she would say, "I feel as if I don't exist." Sometimes she blotted out the feeling with a tranquilizer. Sometimes she thought the problem was with her husband, or her children, or that what she really needed was to redecorate her house, or move to a better neighborhood, or have an affair, or another baby. Sometimes, she went to a doctor with symptoms she could hardly describe: "A tired feeling . . . I get so angry with the children it scares me . . . I feel like crying without any reason." (A Cleveland doctor called it "the housewife's syndrome.") A number of women told me about great bleeding blisters that break out on their hands and arms. "I call it the housewife's blight," said a family doctor in Pennsylvania. "I see it so often lately in these young women with four, five and six children who bury themselves in their dishpans. But it isn't caused by detergent and it isn't cured by cortisone."

. . .

In 1960, the problem that has no name burst like a boil through the image of the happy American housewife. In the television commercials the pretty housewives still beamed over their foaming dishpans and *Time*'s cover story on "The Suburban Wife, an American Phenomenon" protested: "Having too good a time . . . to believe that they should be unhappy." But the actual unhappiness of the American housewife was suddenly being reported—from the *New York Times* and *Newsweek* to *Good Housekeeping* and CBS Television ("The Trapped Housewife"), although almost everybody who talked about it found some superficial reason to dismiss it. . . .

It is no longer possible to ignore that voice, to dismiss the desperation of so many American women. This is not what being a woman means, no matter what the experts say. For human suffering there is a reason; perhaps the reason has not been found because the right questions have not been asked, or pressed far enough. I do not accept the answer that there is no problem because American women have luxuries that women in other times and lands never dreamed of; part of the strange newness of the problem is that it cannot be understood in terms of the age-old material problems of man: poverty, sickness, hunger, cold. The women who suffer this problem have a hunger that food cannot fill. It persists in women whose husbands are struggling interns and law clerks, or prosperous doctors and lawyers; in wives of workers and executives who make $5,000 a year or $50,000. It is not caused by lack of material advantages; it may not even be felt by women preoccupied with desperate problems of hunger, poverty or illness. And women who think it will be solved by more money, a bigger house, a second car, moving to a better suburb, often discover it gets worse. . . .

If I am right, the problem that has no name stirring in the minds of so many American women today is not a matter of loss of femininity or too much education, or the demands of domesticity. It is far more important than anyone recognizes. It is the key to these other new and old problems which have been torturing women and their husbands and children, and puzzling their doctors and educators for years. It may well be the key to our future as a nation and a culture. We can no longer ignore that voice within women that says: "I want something more than my husband and my children and my home."

thirteen

THE ENVIRONMENTAL CAMPAIGN

In the 1960s, Americans began to worry about the fate of their environment. Twice before in the twentieth century, first in the Progressive period and later during the New Deal, conservation advocates had launched crusades to protect the nation's resources. Each time the movement had made gains, then run its course. Now, with the natural preserve threatened once more, activists mounted another campaign to save the environment. Using techniques borrowed from the civil rights and women's movements, they sought to arrest the deterioration and destruction of America's landscape.

Historian Samuel P. Hays argues in "From Conservation to Environment" that environmental activism was rooted in changes that took place in American society after World War II. Americans came to value natural environments more as their standard of living rose. Increasingly concerned with health and fitness, they sought new opportunities for outdoor physical activity. With more and more leisure time, they saw the nation's forests and parks as sources of recreation and enjoyment. When such areas were threatened, they took political action to assure their preservation. Analyzing both background trends and more immediate provocations, Hays shows how the environmental campaign unfolded over an extended period of time.

The second selection focuses on the impact of naturalist Rachel Carson's brilliant *Silent Spring*. In "Chemical Fallout and the Environmental Movement," environmental educator Ralph H. Lutts begins by noting the book's tremendous impact following its 1962 publication in alerting the public to the dangers of pesticide poisoning and environmental pollution, and suggests that its reception had roots in the fears of fallout that troubled

Americans in the first decades of the atomic age. Concern about one threat translated into concern about another as the hazards of the chemical DDT became known.

The document reprinted here is the opening section of architect Peter Blake's muckraking book *God's Own Junkyard: The Planned Deterioration of America's Landscape.* Published in 1964, the largely pictorial account indicts the careless attitudes toward the environment that have led to the "uglification" of a once-beautiful land. Blake argues that public policy and the pursuit of private profit, coupled with general citizen indifference, have led to the unconscionable desecration of the American landscape.

For further examination of the environmental movement, a good starting point is Samuel P. Hays's extensive *Beauty, Health, and Permanence: Environmental Politics in the United States, 1955–1985* (1987). Roderick Nash's *Wilderness and the American Mind* (1967) and *The American Environment: Readings in the History of Conservation* (1976) provide useful background. Rachel Carson's *Silent Spring* (1962) is indispensable, and can be read in conjunction with Frank Graham, Jr.'s *Since Silent Spring* (1970), which examines reaction to Carson's book. Ralph Nader, the noted consumer advocate, turned his attention to the environment, and his own "The Profits in Pollution," published in *The Progressive* (Volume 34, April 1970), is useful, as is John C. Esposito, *Vanishing Air: The Ralph Nader Study Group Report on Air Pollution* (1970). Martin V. Melosi, *Garbage in the Cities: Refuse, Reform, and the Environment, 1880–1980* (1981), is an important survey of the efforts to dispose of waste.

From Conservation to Environment

SAMUEL P. HAYS

The historical significance of the rise of environmental affairs in the United States in recent decades lies in the changes which have taken place in American society since World War II. Important antecedents of those changes, to be sure, can be identified in earlier years as "background" conditions on the order of historical forerunners. But the intensity and force, and most of the substantive direction of the new environmental social and political phenomenon can be understood only through the massive changes which occurred after the end of the War—and not just in the United States but throughout advanced industrial societies. . . .

THE CONSERVATION AND ENVIRONMENTAL IMPULSES

Prior to World War II, before the term "environment" was hardly used, the dominant theme in conservation emphasized physical resources, their more efficient use and development. The range of emphasis evolved from water and forests in the late 19th and early 20th centuries, to grass and soils and game in the 1930's. In all these fields of endeavor there was a common concern for the loss of physical productivity represented by waste. The threat to the future which that "misuse" implied could be corrected through "sound" or efficient management. Hence in each field there arose a management system which emphasized a balancing of immediate in favor of more long-run production, the coordination of factors of production under central management schemes for the greatest efficiency. . . .

Enough has already been written about the evolution of multiple-purpose river development and sustained-yield forestry to establish their role in this context of efficient management for commodity production. But perhaps a few more words could be added for those resources which came to public attention after World War I. Amid the concern about soil erosion, from both rain and wind, the major stress lay in warnings about the loss of agricultural productivity. What had taken years to build up over geologic time now was threatened with destruction by short-term practices. . . .

Perhaps the most significant vantage point . . . was the degree to which resource managers thought of themselves as engaged in a common venture. It was not difficult to bring into the overall concept of "natural resources" the management of forests and waters, of soils and grazing lands, and of game. State departments of "natural resources" emerged, such as in Michigan, Wisconsin and Minnesota, and some university departments of forestry became departments of natural resources—all this as the new emphases on soils and game were added to the older ones on forests and waters. By the time of World War II a complex of professionals had come into being,

From Samuel P. Hays, "From Conservation to Environment: Environmental Politics in the United States Since World War II," in *Environmental Review* 6 (Fall 1982). Copyright © 1982 by the American Society for Environmental History. Reprinted by permission of the author.

with a strong focus on management as their common task, on the organization of applied knowledge about physical resources so as to sustain output for given investments of input under centralized management direction. This entailed a common conception of "conservation" and a common focus on "renewable resources," often within the rubric of advocating "wise use" under the direction of professional experts.

During these years another and altogether different strand of activity also drew upon the term "conservation" to clash with the thrust of efficient commodity management. Today we frequently label it with the term "preservation" as we seek to distinguish between the themes of efficient development symbolized by [Chief Forester] Gifford Pinchot and natural environment management symbolized by [naturalist] John Muir. Those concerned with national parks and the later wilderness activities often used the term "conservation" to describe what they were about. In the Sierra Club the "conservation committees" took up the organization's political action in contrast with its outings. And those who formed the National Parks Association and later the Wilderness Society could readily think of themselves as conservationists, struggling to define the term quite differently than did those in the realm of efficient management. Even after the advent of the term "environment" these groups continued to identify themselves as "conservationists" such as in the League of Conservation Voters, especially when they wished to draw together the themes of natural environment lands and environmental protection. The National Parks Association sought to have the best of both the old and the new when it renamed its publication, *The National Parks and Conservation Magazine: The Environmental Journal.* . . .

After the War a massive turnabout of historical forces took place. The complex of specialized fields of efficient management of physical resources increasingly came under attack amid a new "environmental" thrust. It contained varied components. One was the further elaboration of the outdoor recreation and natural environment movements of pre-War, as reflected in the Wilderness Act of 1964, the Wild and Scenic Rivers Act of 1968, and the National Trails Act of the same year, and further legislation and administrative action on through the 1970's. But there were other strands even less rooted in the past. The most extensive was the concern for environmental pollution, or "environmental protection" as it came to be called in technical and managerial circles. While smoldering in varied and diverse ways in this or that setting from many years before, this concern burst forth to national prominence in the mid-1960's and especially in air and water pollution. And there was the decentralist thrust, the search for technologies of smaller and more human scale which complement rather than dwarf the more immediate human setting. One can find decentralist ideologies and even affirmations of smaller-scale technologies in earlier years. . . . But the intensity and direction of the drive of the 1970's was of a vastly different order. The search for a "sense of place," for a context that is more manageable intellectually and emotionally amid the escalating pace of size and scale had not made its mark in earlier years as it did in the 1970's to shape broad patterns of human thought and action.

One of the most striking differences between these post-War environmental activities, in contrast with the earlier conservation affairs, was their social roots. Earlier one can find little in the way of broad popular support for the substantive objectives of conservation, little "movement" organization, and scanty evidence of broadly shared conservation values. The drive came from the top down, from technical and managerial leaders. In the 1930's one can detect a more extensive social base for soil conservation, and especially for new game management programs. But, in sharp contrast, the Environmental Era displayed demands from the grass-roots, demands that are well charted by the innumerable citizen organizations and studies of public attitudes. One of the major themes of these later years, in fact, was the tension that evolved between the environmental public and the environmental managers, as impulses arising from the public clashed with impulses arising from management. This was not a new stage of public activity per se, but of new values as well. The widespread expression of social values in environmental action marks off the environmental era from the conservation years.

It is useful to think about this as the interaction between two sets of historical forces, one older that was associated with large-scale management and technology, and the other newer that reflected new types of public values and demands. The term "environment" in contrast with the earlier term "conservation" reflects more precisely the innovations in values. The technologies with which those values clashed in the post-War years, however, were closely aligned in spirit and historical roots with earlier conservation tendencies, with new stages in the evolution from the earlier spirit of scientific management of which conservation had been an integral part. A significant element of the historical analysis, therefore, is to identify the points of tension in the Environmental Era between the new stages of conservation as efficient management, as it became more highly elaborated, and the newly evolving environmental concerns which displayed an altogether different thrust. Conflicts between older "conservation" and newer "environment" help to identify the nature of the change.

One set of episodes in this tension concerned the rejection of multiple-purpose river structures in favor of free flowing rivers; here was a direct case of irreconcilable objectives, one stemming from the conservation era, and another inherent in the new environmental era. There were cases galore. But perhaps the most dramatic one, which pinpoints the watershed between the old and the new, involved Hell's Canyon on the Snake River in Idaho. For many years that dispute had taken the old and honorable shape of public versus private power. Should there be one high dam, constructed with federal funds by the Bureau of Reclamation, or three lower dams to be built by the Idaho Power Company? These were the issues of the 1930's, the Truman years and the Eisenhower administrations. But when the Supreme Court reviewed a ruling of the Federal Power Commission on the issue in 1968, it pointed out in a decision written by Justice Douglas that another option had not been considered—no dam at all. Perhaps the river was more valuable as an undeveloped, free flowing stream. The decision was unexpected both to the immediate parties to the dispute, and also to "conservationists" in Idaho and the Pacific Northwest. In fact, those conservationists had to be persuaded to become environmentalists. But turn about they did. The decision seemed to focus a perspective which had long lain dormant, implicit in the circumstances but not yet articulated, and reflected a rather profound transformation in values which had already taken place.

There were other realms of difference between the old and the new. There was, for example, the changing public conception of the role and meaning of forests. The U.S. Forest Service, and the entire community of professional foresters, continued to elaborate the details of scientific management for wood production; it took the form of increasing input for higher yields, and came to emphasize especially even-aged management. But an increasing number of Americans thought of forests as environments for home, work and play, as an environmental rather than as a commodity resource, and hence to be protected from incompatible crop-oriented strategies. Many of them bought woodlands for their environmental rather than their wood production potential. But the forestry profession did not seem to be able to accept the new values. The Forest Service was never able to "get on top" of the wilderness movement to incorporate it in "leading edge" fashion into its own strategies. As the movement evolved from stage to stage the Service seemed to be trapped by its own internal value commitments and hence relegated to playing a rear-guard role to protect wood production. Many a study conducted by the Forest Service experiment stations and other forest professionals made clear that the great majority of small woodland owners thought of their holdings as environments for wildlife and their own recreational and residential activities; yet the service forester program conducted by the Forest Service continued to emphasize wood production rather than environmental amenities as the goal of woodland management. The diverging trends became sharper with the steadily accumulating environmental interest in amenity goals in harvesting strategies and the expanding ecological emphases on more varied plant and animal life within the forest.

There were also divergent tendencies arising from the soil conservation arena. In the early 1950's, the opposition of farmers to the high-dam strategies of the U.S. Army Corps of Engineers led to a new program under the jurisdiction of the Soil Conservation Service, known as PL 566, which emphasized the construction of smaller headwater dams to "hold the water where it falls." This put the SCS in the business of rural land and water development, and it quickly took up the challenge of planning a host of such "multiple-use" projects which combined small flood control reservoirs with flat-water recreation and channelization with wetland drainage. By the time this program came into operation, however, in the 1960's, a considerable interest had arisen in the natural habitats of headwater streams, for example for trout fishing, and wetlands for both fish and wildlife. A head-on collision on this score turned an agency which had long been thought of as riding the lead wave of conservation affairs into one which appeared to environmentalists to be no better than the Corps—development minded and at serious odds with newer natural environment objectives.

There was one notable exception to these almost irreconcilable tensions between the old and the new in which a far smoother transition occurred — the realm of wildlife. In this case the old emphasis on game was faced with a new one on nature observation or what came to be called a "non-game" or "appreciative" use of wildlife. Between these two impulses there were many potential arenas for deep controversy. But there was also common ground in their joint interest in wildlife habitat. The same forest which served as a place for hunting also served as a place for nature observation. In fact, as these different users began to be identified and counted it was found that even on lands acquired exclusively for game management the great majority of users were non-game observers. As a result of this shared interest in wildlife habitat it was relatively easy for many "game managers" to shift in their self-conceptions to become "wildlife managers." Many a state agency changed its name from "game" to "wildlife" and an earlier document, "American Game Policy, 1930," which guided the profession for many years, became "The North American Wildlife Policy, 1973.". . .

THE ROOTS OF NEW ENVIRONMENTAL VALUES

The most immediate image of the "environmental movement" consists of its "protests," its objections to the extent and manner of development and the shape of technology. From the media evidence one has a sense of environmentalists blocking "needed" energy projects, dams, highways and industrial plants, and of complaints of the environmental harm generated by pollution. Environmental action seems to be negative, a protest affair. This impression is also heavily shaped by the "environmental impact" mode of analysis which identifies the "adverse effects" of development and presumably seeks to avoid or mitigate them. The question is one of how development can proceed with the "least" adverse effect to the "environment." From this context of thinking about environmental affairs one is tempted to formulate an environmental history based upon the way in which technology and development have created "problems" for society to be followed by ways in which action has been taken to cope with those problems.

This is superficial analysis. For environmental impulses are rooted in deep seated changes in recent America which should be understood primarily in terms of new positive directions. We are at a stage in history when new values and new ways of looking at ourselves have emerged to give rise to new preferences. These are characteristic of advanced industrial societies throughout the world, not just in the United States. They reflect two major and widespread social changes. One is associated with the search for standards of living beyond necessities and conveniences to include amenities made possible by considerable increases in personal and social "real income." The other arises from advancing levels of education which have generated values associated with personal creativity and self-development, involvement with natural environments, physical and mental fitness and wellness and political autonomy and efficacy. Environmental values and objectives are an integral part of these changes.

Extensive study of attitudes and values by public opinion analysts and sociologists chart these larger changes in social values in considerable detail. Some have brought them together in comprehensive accounts. They can be best observed in the market analyses which have been sponsored by the American business community since the 1920's which gave rise to the initial interest in attitude surveys. Such analyses have identified value changes in almost every sub-group in the American population, from different ages to ethnic and religious variations, to regional differences and rural-urban distinctions. . . .

From these more general surveys, from studies specifically of environmental values, from analyses of recreational and leisure preferences undertaken by leisure research specialists, from surveys of the values expressed by those who purchase natural environment lands, and from the content of environmental action in innumerable grass-roots citizen cases one can identify the "environmental impulse" not as reactive but formative. It reflects a desire for a better "quality of life" which is another phase of the continual search by the American people throughout their history for a higher standard of living. Environmental values are widespread in American society, extending throughout income and occupational levels, areas of the nation and racial groups, somewhat stronger in the middle sectors and a bit weaker in the very high and very low groupings. There are identifiable "leading sectors" of change with which they are associated as well as "lagging sectors." They tend to be stronger with younger people and increasing levels of education and move into the larger society from those centers of innovation. They are also more associated with particular geographical regions such as New England, the Upper Lakes States, the Upper Rocky Mountain region and the Far West, while the South, the Plains States and the lower Rockies constitute "lagging" regions. Hence one can argue that environmental values have expanded steadily in American society, associated with demographic sectors which are growing rather than with those which are more stable or declining.

Within this general context one can identify several distinctive sets of environmental tendencies. One was the way in which an increasing portion of the American people came to value natural environments as an integral part of their rising standard of living. They sought out many types of such places to experience, to explore, enjoy and protect: high mountains and forests, wetlands, ocean shores, swamplands, wild and scenic rivers, deserts, pine barrens, remnants of the original prairies, places of relatively clean air and water, more limited "natural areas." Interest in such places was not a throwback to the primitive, but an integral part of the modern standard of living as people sought to add new "amenity" and "aesthetic" goals and desires to their earlier preoccupation with necessities and conveniences. These new consumer wants were closely associated with many others of a similar kind such as in the creative arts, recreation and leisure in general, crafts, indoor and household decoration, hi-fi sets, the care of yards and gardens as living space and amenity components of necessities and conveniences. Americans experienced natural environments both emotionally and intellectually, sought them out for direct personal experience in recreation, studied them as objects of scientific and intellectual interest and desired to have them within their community, their region and their nation as symbols of a society with a high degree of civic consciousness and pride.

A new view of health constituted an equally significant innovation in environmental values, health less as freedom from illness and more as physical and mental fitness, of feeling well, of optimal capability for exercising one's physical and mental powers. The control of infectious diseases by antibiotics brought to the fore new types of health problems associated with slow, cumulative changes in physical condition, symbolized most strikingly by cancer, but by the 1980's ranging into many other conditions such as genetic and reproduction problems, degenerative changes such as heart disease and deteriorating immune systems. All this put more emphasis on the non-bacterial environmental causes of illness but, more importantly, brought into health matters an emphasis on the positive conditions of wellness and fitness. There was an increasing tendency to adopt personal habits that promoted rather than threatened health, to engage in physical exercise, to quit smoking, to eat more nutritiously and to reduce environmental threats in the air and water that might also weaken one's wellness. Some results of this concern were the rapid increase in the business of health food stores, reaching $1.5 billion in 1979, the success of the Rodale enterprises and their varied publications such as *Prevention* and *Organic Gardening,* and the increasing emphasis on preventive medicine.

These new aesthetic and health values constituted much of the roots of environmental concern. They came into play in personal life and led to new types of consumption in the private market, but they also led to demands for public action both to enhance opportunities, such as to make natural environments more available and to ward off threats to values. The threats constituted some of the most celebrated environmental battles: power and petrochemical plant siting, hardrock mining and strip mining, chemicals in the workplace and in underground drinking water supplies, energy transmission lines and pipelines. Many a local community found itself faced with a threat imposed from the outside and sought to protect itself through "environmental action." But the incidence and intensity of reaction against these threats arose at a particular time in history because of the underlying changes in values and aspirations. People had new preferences and new personal and family values which they did not have before. Prior to World War II, the countryside, that area between the nation's cities and its wildlands, had been an area of rapid decline, a land much of which "nobody wanted," but in the years after the War it became increasingly occupied and hence defended. Here was a major battleground for the contending environmental and developmental antagonists. Because of these new values developmental activities which earlier might have been accepted were now considered to be on balance more harmful than beneficial.

Still another concern began to play a more significant role in environmental affairs in the 1970's — an assertion of the desirability of more personal family and community autonomy in the face of the larger institutional world of corporate industry and government, an affirmation of smaller in the face of larger contexts of organization and power. This constituted a "self-help" movement. It was reflected in numerous publications about the possibilities of self-reliance in production of food and clothing, design and construction of homes, recreation and leisure, recycling of wastes and materials, and use of energy through such decentralized forms as wind and solar. These tendencies were far more widespread than institutional and thought leaders of the nation recognized since their world of perception and management was far removed from community and grass-roots ideas and action. The debate between "soft" and "hard" energy paths seemed to focus much of the controversy over the possibilities of decentralization. But it should also be stressed that the American economy, while tending toward more centralized control and management, also generated products which made individual choices toward decentralized living more possible and hence stimulated this phase of environmental affairs. While radical change had produced large-scale systems of management it had also reinvigorated the more traditional Yankee tinkerer who now found a significant niche in the new environmental scheme of things.

Several significant historical tendencies are integral parts of these changes. One involves consumption and the role of environmental values as part of evolving consumer values. At one time, perhaps as late as 1900, the primary focus in consumption was on necessities. By the 1920's a new stage had emerged which emphasized conveniences in which the emerging consumer durables, such as the automobile and household appliances were the most visible elements. This change meant that a larger portion of personal income, and hence of social income and production facilities were now being devoted to a new type of demand and supply. By the late 1940's a new stage in the history of consumption had come into view. Many began to find that both their necessities and conveniences had been met and an increasing share of their income could be devoted to amenities. The shorter work week and increasing availability of vacations provided opportunities for more leisure and recreation. Hence personal and family time and income could be spent on amenities. Economists were inclined to describe this as "discretionary income." The implications of this observation about the larger context of environmental values is that it is a part of the history of consumption rather than of production. That in itself involves a departure from traditional emphases in historical analysis.

Another way of looking at these historical changes is to observe the shift in focus in daily living from a preoccupation with work in earlier years to a greater role for home, family and leisure in the post-War period. Public opinion surveys indicate a persistent shift in which of these activities respondents felt were more important, a steady decline in a dominant emphasis on work and a steady rise in those activities associated with home, family and leisure. One of the most significant aspects of this shift was a divorce in the physical location of work and home. For most people in the rapidly developing manufacturing cities of the 19th century the location of home was dictated by the location of work. But the widespread use of the automobile, beginning in the 1920's, enabled an increasing number of people, factory workers as well as white collar workers, to live in one place and to work in another. The environmental context of home, therefore, came to be an increasingly separate and distinctive focus for their choices. Much of the environmental movement arose from this physical separation of the environments of home and work.

One can identify in all this an historical shift in the wider realm of politics as well. Prior to World War II the most persistent larger context of national political debate involved the balance among sectors of production. From the late 19th century on the evolution of organized extra-party political activity, in the form of "interest groups," was overwhelmingly devoted to occupational affairs, and the persistent policy issues involved the balance of the shares of production which were to be received by business, agriculture and labor, and sub-sectors within them. Against this array of political forces consumer objectives were woefully weak. But the evolution of new types of consumption in recreation, leisure and amenities generated a quite different setting. By providing new focal points of organized activity in common leisure and recreational interest groups, and by emphasizing community organization to protect community environmental values against threats from external developmental pressures, consumer impulses went through a degree of mobilization and activity which they had not previously enjoyed. In many an instance they were able to confront developmentalists with considerable success. Hence environmental action reflects the emergence in American politics of a new effectiveness for consumer action not known in the years before the War.

One of the distinctive aspects of the history of consumption is the degree to which what once were luxuries, enjoyed by only a few, over the years became enjoyed by many — articles of mass consumption. In the censuses of the last half of the 19th century several occupations were identified as the "luxury trades," producing items such as watches and books which later became widely consumed. Many such items went through a similar process, arising initially as enjoyed only by a relative few and then later becoming far more widely diffused. These included such consumer items as the wringer washing machine and the gas stove, the carpet sweeper, indoor plumbing and the automobile. And so it was with environmental amenities. What only a few could enjoy in the 19th century came to be mass activities in the mid-20th, as many purchased homes with a higher level of amenities around them and could participate in outdoor recreation beyond the city. Amid the tendency for the more affluent to seek out and acquire as private property the more valued natural amenity sites, the public lands came to be places where the opportunity for such activities remained far more accessible to a wide segment of the social order.

A major element of the older, pre–World War II "conservation movement," efficiency in the use of resources, also became revived in the 1970's around the concern for energy supply. It led to a restatement of rather traditional options, as to whether or not natural resources were limited, and hence one had to emphasize efficiency and frugality, or whether or not they were unlimited and could be developed with unabated vigor. Environmentalists stressed the former. It was especially clear that the "natural environments" of air, water and land were finite, and that increasing demand for these amid a fixed supply led to considerable inflation in price for those that were bought and sold in the private market. Pressures of growing demand on limited supply of material resources appeared to most people initially in the form of inflation; this trend of affairs in energy was the major cause of inflation in the entire economy. The great energy debates of the 1970's gave special focus to a wide range of issues pertaining to the "limits of growth." Environmentalists stressed the possibilities of "conservation supplies" through greater energy productivity and while energy producing companies objected to this as a major policy alternative, industrial consumers of energy joined with household consumers in taking up efficiency as the major alternative. In the short run the "least cost" option in energy supply in the private market enabled the nation greatly to reduce its energy use and carried out the environmental option.

In accounting for the historical timing of the environmental movement one should emphasize changes in the "threats" as well as in the values. Much of the shape and timing of environmental debate arose from changes in the magnitude and form of these threats from modern technology. That technology was applied in increasing scale and scope, from enormous drag-lines in strip mining, to 1000-megawatt electric generating plants and "energy parks," to superports and large-scale petrochemical plants, to 765-kilovolt energy transmission lines. And there was the vast increase in the use and release into the environment of chemicals, relatively contained and generating a chemical "sea around us" which many people considered to be a long-run hazard that was out of control. The view of these technological changes as threats seemed to come primarily from their size and scale, the enormity of their range of impact, in contrast with the more human scale of daily affairs. New technologies appeared to constitute radical influences, disruptive of settled community and personal life, of a scope that was often beyond comprehension, and promoted and carried through by influences "out there" from the wider corporate and governmental world. All this brought to environmental issues the problem of "control," of how one could shape more limited personal and community circumstance in the face of large-scale and radical change impinging from afar upon daily life.

STAGES IN THE EVOLUTION OF ENVIRONMENTAL ACTION

Emerging environmental values did not make themselves felt all in the same way or at the same time. Within the context of our concern here for patterns of historical change, therefore, it might be well to secure some sense of stages of development within the post–World War II years. The most prevalent notion is to identify Earth Day in 1970 as the dividing line. There are other candidate events, such as the publication of Rachel Carson's *Silent Spring* in 1962, and the Santa Barbara oil blowout in 1969. But in any event definition of change in these matters seems to be inadequate. Earth Day was as much a result as a cause. It came after a decade or more of underlying evolution in attitudes and action without which it would not have been possible. Many environmental organizations, established earlier, experienced considerable growth in membership during the 1960's, reflecting an expanding concern. The regulatory mechanisms and issues in such fields as air and water pollution were shaped then; for example the Clean Air Act of 1967 established the character of the air quality program more than did that of 1970. General public awareness and interest were expressed extensively in a variety of public forums and in the mass media. Evolving public values could be observed in the growth of the outdoor recreation movement which reached back into the 1950's and the search for amenities in quieter and more natural settings, in the increasing number of people who engaged in hiking and camping or purchased recreational lands and homes on the seashore, by lakes and in woodlands. This is not to say that the entire scope of environmental concerns emerged fully in the 1960's. It did not. But one can observe a gradual evolution rather than a sudden outburst at the turn of the decade, a cumulative social and political change that came to be expressed vigorously even long before Earth Day.

We might identify three distinct stages of evolution. Each stage brought a new set of issues to the fore without eliminating the previous ones, in a set of historical layers. Old issues persisted to be joined by new ones, creating over the years an increasingly complex and varied world of environmental controversy and debate. The initial complex of issues which arrived on the scene of national politics emphasized natural environment values in such matters as outdoor recreation, wildlands and open space. These shaped debate between 1957 and 1965 and constituted the initial thrust of environmental action. After World War II the American people, with increased income and leisure time, sought out the nation's forests and parks, its wildlife refuges, its state and federal public lands, for recreation and enjoyment. Recognition of this growing interest and the demands upon public policy which it generated, led Congress in 1958 to establish the National Outdoor Recreation Review Commission which completed its report in 1962. Its recommendations heavily influenced public policy during the Johnson administration, leading directly to the Land and Water Conservation Fund of 1964 which established, for the first time, a continuous source of revenue for acquisition of state and federal outdoor recreation lands. It accelerated the drive for the National Wilderness Act of 1964 and the Wild and Scenic Rivers and National Trails Acts of 1968.

These laws reflected in only a limited way a much more widespread interest in natural environment affairs which affected local, state and federal policy. During the 1950's many in urban areas had developed a concern for urban overdevelopment and the need for open space in their communities. This usually did not receive national recognition because it took place on a more local level. But demands for national assistance for acquisition of urban open space led to legislation in 1960 which provided federal funds. The concern for open space extended to regional as well as community projects, involving a host of natural environment areas ranging from pine barrens to wetlands to swamps to creeks and streams to remnants of the original prairies. Throughout the 1960's there were attempts to add to the national park system which gave rise to new parks such as Canyonlands in Utah, new national lakeshores and seashores and new national recreation areas.

These matters set the dominant tone of the initial phase of environmental concern until the mid-1960's. They did not decline in importance, but continued to shape administrative and legislative action as specific proposals for wilderness, scenic rivers or other natural areas emerged to be hotly debated. Such general measures as the Eastern Wilderness Act of 1974, the Federal Land Planning and Management Act of 1976 and the Alaska National Interest Lands Act of 1980 testified to the perennial public concern for natural environment areas. So also did the persistent evolution of indigenous western wilderness groups in almost every state and the formation of a western umbrella organization, the Wilderness Alliance, headquartered in Denver, in 1978. One might argue that these were the most enduring and fundamental environmental issues throughout the two decades. While other citizen concerns might ebb and flow, interest in natural environment areas persisted steadily. That interest was the dominant reason for membership growth in the largest environmental organizations. The Nature Conservancy, a private group which emphasized acquisition of natural environment lands, grew in activity in the latter years of the 1970's and reached 100,000 members in 1981; this only further emphasized the persistent and enduring public concern for natural environment areas as an integral and important element of American life.

Amid this initial stage of environmental politics there evolved a new and different concern for the adverse impact of industrial development with a special focus on air and water pollution. This had long evolved slowly on a local and piecemeal basis, but emerged with national force only in the mid-1960's. In the early part of the decade air and water pollution began to take on significance as national issues and by 1965 they had become highly visible. The first national public opinion poll on such questions was taken in that year, and the President's annual message in 1965 reflected, for the first time, a full fledged concern for pollution problems. Throughout the rest of the decade and on into the 1970's these issues evolved continually. Federal legislation to stimulate remedial action was shaped over the course of these seven years, from 1965 to 1972, a distinct period which constituted the second phase in the evolution of environmental politics, taking its place alongside the previously developing concern for natural environment areas.

The legislative results were manifold. Air pollution was the subject of new laws in 1967 and 1970; water pollution in 1965, 1970 and 1972. The evolving concern about pesticides led to revision of the existing law in the Pesticides Act of 1972. The growing public interest in natural environment values in the coastal zone, and threats to them by dredging and filling, industrial siting and offshore oil development first made its mark on Congress in 1965 and over the next few years shaped the course of legislation which finally emerged in the Coastal Zone Management Act of 1972. Earth Day in the spring of 1970 lay in the middle of this phase of historical development, both a result of the previous half-decade of activity and concern and a new influence to accelerate action. The outline of these various phases of environmental activity, however, can be observed only by evidence and actions far beyond the events of Earth Day. Such more broad-based evidence identifies the years 1965 to 1972 as a well-defined phase of historical development in terms of issues, emphasizing the reaction against the adverse effects of industrial growth as distinct from the earlier emergence of natural environment issues.

Yet this new phase was shaped heavily by the previous period in that it gave primary emphasis to the harmful impact of pollution on ecological systems rather than on human health — a concern which was to come later. In the years between 1965 and 1972 the interest in "ecology" came to the fore to indicate the intense public interest in potential harm to the natural environment and in protection against disruptive threats. The impacts of highway construction, electric power plants and industrial siting on wildlife, on aquatic ecosystems and on natural environments in general played a major role in the evolution of this concern. One of the key elements of evolving public policy was the enhanced role of the U.S. Fish and Wildlife Service in modifying decisions by developmental agencies to reduce their harmful actions. The effects of pesticides were thought of then in terms of their impact on wildlife and ecological food chains, rather than on human health. The major concern for the adverse effect of nuclear energy generation in the late 1960's involved its potential disruption of aquatic ecosystems from thermal pollution rather than the effect of radiation on people. The rapidly growing ecological concern was an extension of the natural environment interests of the years 1957 to 1965 into the problem of the adverse impacts of industrial growth.

Beginning in the early 1970's still a third phase of environmental politics arose which brought three other sets of issues into public debate: toxic chemicals, energy and the possibilities of social, economic and political decentralization. These did not obliterate earlier issues, but as some natural environment matters and concern over the adverse effects of industrialization shifted from legislative to administrative politics, and thus became less visible to the general public, these new issues emerged often to dominate the scene. They were influenced heavily by the seemingly endless series of toxic chemical episodes, from PBB's in Michigan to kepone in Virginia to PCB's on the Hudson River, to the discovery of abandoned chemical dumps at Love Canal [in New York State] and near Louisville, Kentucky. These events, however, were only the more sensational aspects of a more deep-seated new twist in public concern for human health. Interest in personal health and especially in preventive health action took a major leap forward in the 1970's. It seemed to focus especially on such matters as cancer and environmental pollutants responsible for a variety of health problems, on food and diet on the one hand and exercise on the other. From these interests arose a central concern for toxic threats in the workplace, in the air and water, and in food and personal habits that came to shape some of the overriding issues of the 1970's on the environmental front. It shifted the earlier emphasis on the ecological effects of toxic pollutants to one more on human health effects. Thus, while proceedings against DDT in the late 1960's had emphasized adverse ecological impacts, similar proceedings in the 1970's focused primarily on human health.

The energy crisis of the winter of 1973-74 brought a new issue to the fore. Not that energy matters had gone unnoticed earlier, but their salience had been far more limited. After that winter they became more central. They shaped environmental politics in at least two ways. First, energy problems brought material shortages more forcefully into the realm of substantive environmental concerns and emphasized more strongly the problem of limits which these shortages imposed upon material growth. The physical shortages of energy sources such as oil in the United States, the impact of shortages on rising prices, the continued emphasis on the need for energy conservation all helped to etch into the experience and thinking of Americans the "limits" to which human appetite for consumption could go. Second, the intense demand for development of new energy sources increased significantly the political influence of developmental advocates in governmental, corporate and technical institutions which had long chafed under both natural environment and pollution control programs. This greatly overweighted the balance of political forces so that environmental leaders had far greater difficulty in being heard. In the face of energy issues environmental leaders formulated their own energy proposals which they sought to inject into the debates, but not yet with overriding success amid an overwhelming emphasis on traditional approaches to increasing energy supply.

Lifestyle issues also injected a new dimension into environmental affairs during the course of the 1970's. They became especially visible in the energy debates, as the contrast emerged between highly centralized technologies on the one hand, and decentralized systems on the other. Behind these debates lay the evolution of new ideas about organizing one's daily life, one's home, community and leisure activities and even work—all of which had grown out of the changing lifestyles of younger Americans. It placed considerable emphasis on more personal, family and community autonomy in the face of the forces of larger social, economic and political organization. The impact and role of this change was not always clear, but it emerged forcefully in the energy debate as decentralized solar systems and conservation seemed to be appropriate to decisions made personally and locally—on a more human scale—contrasting markedly with high-technology systems which leaders of technical, corporate and governmental institutions seemed to prefer. Issues pertaining to the centralization of political control played an increasing role in environmental politics as the 1970's came to a close.

To define stages in the evolution of environmental affairs in this manner helps to interweave those affairs with broader patterns of social change. One should be wary, perhaps, of the temptation to argue that by 1980 a "full-scale" set of environmental issues had emerged, bit by bit, to form a coherent whole. For there were many different strands which at times went off in different directions. Those whose environmental experience was confined to the urban context did not always share the perspective and interest in issues of those who were preoccupied with the wildlands. Yet it was rather striking the degree to which working relationships had developed amid the varied strands. What was especially noticeable was the degree to which the challenge posed by the Reagan administration tended to mobilize latent values and strengthen cooperative tendencies. From the beginning of that administration, the new governmental leaders made clear their conviction that the "environmental movement" had spent itself, was no longer viable, and could readily be dismissed and ignored. During the campaign the Reagan entourage had refused often to meet with citizen environmental groups, and in late November it made clear that it would not even accept the views of its own "transition team" which was made up of former Republican administration environmentalists who were thought to be far too extreme. Hence environmentalists of all these varied hues faced a hostile government that was not prone to be evasive or deceptive about that hostility. Its anti-environmental views were expressed with enormous vigor and clarity.

We can well look upon that challenge as an historical experiment which tested the extent and permanence of the changes in social values which lay at the root of environmental interest. By its opposition the Reagan administration could be thought of as challenging citizen environmental activity to prove itself. And the response, in turn, indicated a degree of depth and persistence which makes clear that environmental affairs stem from the extensive and deep-seated changes we have been describing. Most striking perhaps have been the public opinion polls during 1981 pertaining to revision of the Clean Air Act. On two occasions, in April and in September the Harris poll found that some 80% of the American people favor at least maintaining that Act or making it stricter, levels of positive environmental opinion on air quality higher than for polls in the 1960's or 1970's. One can also cite the rapid increases in membership which have occurred in many environmental organizations, most notably the Sierra Club, as well as financial contributions to them. And the initial forays into electoral politics which environmentalists have recently undertaken seem to have tapped activist predispositions mobilized by the fear of the new administration. . . .

THE ENVIRONMENTAL ECONOMY AND
ENVIRONMENTAL IDEOLOGY

. . . We might . . . profitably identify the environmental impulse more precisely in terms of its ideological component. What is the place of environmental ideas amid the political ideologies inherited from the recent past? These customarily divide political forces between the "liberal" and the "conservative." The corporate business community and critics of growth in government are thought of as "conservatives," while more subordinate sectors of society who look to government to aid them are thought of as "liberal." While these ideological patterns have roots deeper in history than the 1930's, they were given a new twist during the New Deal when controversies over public spending for social programs such as welfare and social security were added to those of earlier vintage which involved disputes among business, labor and agriculture over the distribution of the fruits of production.

Environmental issues and environmental ideas are difficult to classify in this way. If one raised the question as to whether or not environmentalists favored public or private enterprise in principle, one would have to observe that while they called for greater governmental initiatives in behalf of their objectives such as in public land management or environmental controls on private production, they were as skeptical of public as they were of private enterprise. The Tennessee Valley Authority, the major example of public ownership of the means of industrial production in recent times, was roundly condemned when its actions with respect to air pollution, dam building and coal and uranium mining were environmentally detrimental and was applauded when it took up innovative energy measures during the Carter administration. . . .

Environmental values and ideas tended not to fit into traditional political ideologies, but to cut across them. They tended to define corporate leaders as radicals, as responsible for massive, rapid and deep-seated transformations in modern society that threatened to destroy prized natural environments, that uprooted stable ways of life, and generated pervasive and persistent chemical threats. Corporate leaders were ever demanding that people change their lives markedly in order to accommodate developmental objectives, and to accept the risks of their proposals for rapid and far-reaching changes. In response to these demands, environmentalists sought to slow up the pace of innovation, to restrain it. Hence they were conservative. It would not be accurate to describe them as one industry leader did as "stone-age neanderthals," for environmentalists shared, with approval, the material benefits of modern production. But they were willing to argue that the pace of change in America in the 1960's and 1970's was far too rapid and should be slowed down so as not to destroy values important to a society of modern patterns of life.

They were also often fiscal conservatives when the use of public funds was an important instrument of material development and engaged in many a political struggle to cut back public spending. The 1960's and 1970's were decades of rapid economic "growth" in which jobs and product increased dramatically and public programs with public funding played a major role in it: construction of dams and highways, rebuilding on flood plains after floods, channelization of streams and rivers, development of barrier islands, a host of "rural development" programs which had become extended from the "depressed" area of the Appalachians to the entire nation. All these tended to encourage more rapid economic development. The most widely known cases of environmental action on this score pertained to funds for construction of public works in rivers and harbors under the auspices of the U.S. Army Corps of Engineers. It was no wonder that in fashioning coalitions to scale back such expenditures environmentalists joined with the National Taxpayers Union and other "fiscal conservatives" in Congress who tended to give ideological support to reduced public spending.

At the same time, in social values environmentalists could be thought of as innovative rather than conservative. Their views about natural environments and human health were associated with newer rather than older ideas about human wants and needs; they had a larger association with other innovations in values such as the more autonomous role of women, more cosmopolitan rather than traditional ways of life, and "freer" ways of thinking that were associated with social modernization. Such value changes had taken place at a number of times in the nation's past and these historians understand by sorting out newer values from older, distinguishing those people who espoused the newer with enthusiasm from those who drew back in defense and fear against cultural change. In the mid-19th century, for example, the Republican party had been associated with innovations in cultural values and the Democratic party with a defense of older ones. But in the mid-20th century, the party roles were reversed, as the Democrats seemed to harbor cultural innovation and the Republicans spoke out in defense of older values. These patterns of cultural change tended to define what was "conservative" and what was "liberal" in terms different from the issues of economic controversy. And so it was with environmental values in which environmentalists both expressed the defense of daily life from technological radicalism and espoused innovations in cultural values.

Within the context of these more "modern" and more innovative values, however, there was in environmental affairs a deeply conservative streak in a different sense that went far beyond the role of corporations and their defense to the larger ideology of conservatism—a search for wider human meaning. Environmentalists tended to work out their values amid a "sense of place" that provided roots to life's meaning much in the same way as "local" community values long had displayed. It was their involvement with the natural environments of given places that had engaged emotions and minds. It was the threat to that "place" of home, work and play from large-scale developments, from air and water pollution, and from toxic chemical contamination which aroused them to action. Environmentalists sought roots in the less developed and more natural world, and rapid change threatened those roots with impairment and destruction. Insofar as one could describe conservatism as more generally a search for roots, for stability and order amid the larger world of rapid change, then environmentalists shared that impulse.

SUMMARY

This article has constituted an attempt to place the environmental affairs of the past three decades in the perspective of historical evolution. . . . I have argued that these cannot be understood adequately unless they are associated with the newer society, the newer economy and the newer politics of the decades after World War II. Moreover, they can be understood only as an evolving phenomenon within those post-War decades, amid the patterns of change in the advanced consumer society as it steadily took shape. American society today is far different than it was in the 1930's. It can best be understood not as an implication of the New Deal years, but as a product of vast social and economic transformations which took place after World War II which brought many new values and impulses to the American political scene. And so it is with environmental affairs. While displaying some roots in earlier times they were shaped primarily by the rapidly changing society which came into being after the War which, in so many ways, constitutes a watershed in American history.

Chemical Fallout and the Environmental Movement

RALPH H. LUTTS

The landmark book *Silent Spring* played a vitally important role in stimulating the contemporary environmental movement. Never before or since has a book been so successful in alerting the public to a major environmental pollutant, rooting the alert in a deeply ecological perception of the issues, and promoting major public, private and governmental initiatives to correct the problem. It was exceptional in its ability to combine a grim warning about pesticide poisoning with a text that celebrated the living world. *Silent Spring* has been compared in its social impact to *Uncle Tom's Cabin;* John Kenneth Galbraith described it as one of the most important books of Western literature and Robert Downs listed it as one of the "books that changed America."

Rachel Carson's case against the indiscriminate use of pesticides prevailed in the face of powerful, well-financed opposition by the agricultural and chemical industries. Despite this opposition she prompted national action to regulate pesticides by mobilizing a concerned public. The book established a broad constituency for addressing the problem — broader, perhaps, than that enjoyed by any previous environmental issue. Never before had so diverse a body of people, from bird watchers, to wildlife managers and public health professionals, to suburban homeowners, been joined together to deal with a common national and international environment threat. Her success in the face of what might have been overwhelming opposition suggests there

From Ralph H. Lutts, "Chemical Fallout: Rachel Carson's *Silent Spring*, Radioactive Fallout, and the Environmental Movement," in *Environmental Review* 9 (Fall 1985). Copyright © 1985 by the American Society for Environmental History. Reprinted by permission of the author.

was something significantly different between the response to *Silent Spring* in 1962 and the pesticide control efforts of the first half of the century.

The issue of pesticide pollution was not new. Since the introduction of Paris green around 1867 highly toxic compounds of lead and arsenic were widely used in agriculture despite the significant health hazards they pre-sented. As one example, 75 million lbs. of lead arsenate were applied within the U.S. in 1944; 8 million lbs. were even used in the 1961–62 crop year when DDT was preeminent. In the early decades of their use these toxic chemicals could sometimes be found as visible coatings on farm produce in retail markets. Over the years stories of acute poisonings and warnings of the dangers of chronic toxicity appeared in the press. Everyone was warned to scrub or peel fruits and vegetables before they were eaten. Many public health officials attempted to institute strong regulations and strict residue tolerances, but the general public, medical profession and agriculture industry showed only limited concern. This relative indifference to the hazards of pesticides in the first half of the century stands in stark contrast to the vocal outcry following the publication of *Silent Spring.*

Why is it that the book's publication in 1962 had such a major impact upon the public? The answer to this question might reveal a good deal about the origins of contemporary environmental concerns, but no one has exam-ined it systematically. A number of answers have been suggested, focussing most often upon Carson's extraordinary skill and reputation as a writer, the general circumstances surrounding the risk of pesticide use and misuse, the publisher's marketing strategy, and the chemical industry's response. Many authors also noted the growing public awareness of a variety of environmental problems, including water and air pollution. One of the major events to bring the hazards of pesticides to public attention was the "Cranberry Scandal" of 1959 when people were warned against eating this traditional fruit during the Thanksgiving season because of pesticide contamination. The thalidomide syndrome also came to the public's attention shortly before the publication of *Silent Spring* and the pictures of the distorted infant limbs caused by a supposedly beneficial drug certainly made people pay greater attention to Carson's message.

There was another issue, however, that played an equal or greater role in preparing the public to accept Carson's warning—an issue that has been largely overlooked. She was sounding an alarm about a kind of pollution that was invisible to the senses; could be transported great distances, perhaps globally; could accumulate over time in body tissues; could produce chronic as well as acute poisoning; and could result in cancer, birth defects and genetic mutations that may not become evident until years or decades after exposure. Government officials, she also argued, were not taking the steps necessary to control this pollution and protect the public. Chemical pesticides were not the only form of pollution fitting this description. Another form, far better known to the public at the time, was radioactive fallout.

People in the United States and throughout the world were prepared, or pre-educated, to understand the basic concepts underlying Rachel Carson's

Silent Spring by the decade-long debate over radioactive fallout preceding it. They had already learned that poisons, in this case radioactive ones, could create a lasting global danger. To understand the deep impact of this debate upon the public we must review the history of the fallout controversy.

THE BEGINNING

During the heady days of the late 1940s, when the United States was the only nation possessing the atomic bomb, Americans did not worry much about this symbol of international status and power. The major cultural contribution of the 1946 U.S. A-bomb tests at the Bikini Atoll in the Pacific was the name of a new French bathing suit. The Soviet Union's detonation of its own atomic bomb in 1949 destroyed this complacency and the post-war nuclear arms race began. In 1951 the USSR exploded another two devices and the United States sixteen. By the end of 1953 both nations had conducted a total of 26 more tests. In November 1952 the U.S. government exploded the world's first thermonuclear device, followed by the Soviet's detonation of their own device in August 1953. In March 1954 the U.S. tested its first portable superbomb.

By the early 1950s the public was extraordinarily interested in atomic weapons. This early interest reflected a nationalistic pride, fear of the Soviets, and fascination with the bombs and the mysteries of radioactivity, rather than a major concern about public health. The majority of United States A-Bomb tests were conducted in Nevada and the resulting clouds of radioactive materials, which passed over populated areas of nation, led to growing public anxiety despite reassuring statements by the AEC [Atomic Energy Commission]. In March 1953, for example, a *New York Times* writer reported that the AEC had determined there was no danger to American cities from the tests. The explanation may not have instilled great confidence, however. "Radioactivity in the atmosphere," he wrote, "decreases rapidly and the 'fall-out,' or settling of airborne radioactive particles, is hastened by rain or snow. The latter factor has caused upstate New York areas such as Rochester and Buffalo to be called 'radiation sewers.'"

In May 1953 Utah stockmen blamed the Nevada tests for the unexpected deaths of more than 1,000 ewes and lambs. The AEC investigated the complaints and assured the stockmen that although they did not know what was responsible for the deaths, it was certainly not atomic tests. A rancher and the wife of another rancher filed suit, claiming they had been injured by the same tests. The woman charged that "radioactive dust from the blasts had caused her hair to fall out, her skin and fingernails to peel off, and gave her recurrent nausea." The man complained of losing all his body hair.

Although these events received national publicity, it was not until the "Bravo" test of the U.S. superbomb in the Pacific that the scope of the danger of fallout became widely known. Weather forecasts for this March 1, 1954 explosion were wrong and the fallout was blown in an unexpected direction. Rep. Chet Holifeld (D., Calif.), a member of the Joint Atomic Energy Committee, later characterized the test as "out of control," a charge that the chairman of the AEC denied. This denial was little consolation to the 28 Americans and 236 natives of the Marshall Islands who were exposed to radioactive fallout. Fortunately they were quickly decontaminated and relocated to a safe area. The fishermen on a Japanese tuna boat wandering near the Bikini test area were not so lucky.

The 23 seamen on the *Lucky Dragon* had no knowledge that a test was about to take place, but the distant, brilliant light in the sky reminded them of stories of Hiroshima and Nagasaki. Nevertheless, they did not recognize the subsequent four hour snow of strange whitish dust upon their vessel as a special threat. When they soon became ill and began to lose their hair, however, they became alarmed and turned homeward. It was two weeks before they reached Japan and more days passed before the nature of their illness was discovered. During this period they worked, ate and slept in the midst of the fallout dust. After months of illness most of the men recovered, but Aikichi Kuboyama, the radioman, died on September 23rd.

The tragedy was compounded by its impact upon the fishing industry. Many of the fish brought back to the *Lucky Dragon* were found to be contaminated, but not until after they had been sold. Radioactive fish were also discovered on other tuna boats, creating near panic in a nation dependent upon the sea for protein. One boat in eight returned with contaminated fish as ocean currents spread radiation from the Bikini test through the Pacific. The national consumption of fish and fish prices plummeted, and the industry suffered terribly. All of these events were followed closely by the world press.

The bomb that dropped fallout upon the *Lucky Dragon* was very dirty, much more so than one would expect in theory from a hydrogen bomb. It was the first of a new kind of device that used inexpensive Uranium-238 in massive quantities. Its deadly fission products and other debris were injected into the upper atmosphere by the blast to circle the globe. Independent scientists identified the nature of the bomb soon after the test and also discovered the presence of Strontium-90, a particularly dangerous and long lasting radioactive isotope. This was not officially announced, however, until a June 1955 speech delivered by AEC Commissioner Willard Libby. He added the reassuring suggestion that after a nuclear war fallout could be removed from cities with "ingenious devices such as street sweepers, in which the driver sits on a bag of sand or a thick metal slab to protect him from radiation."

The public was now less willing blindly to accept statements like this. The information and apprehensions originally shared by a few scientists were finding their way into the popular press and everyday conversation. Americans became increasingly alarmed when they discovered that their own food was contaminated.

STRONTIUM-90

Oh where, oh where has the fallout gone, oh where can the poison be, why right in the milk and the other things that the milkman brings to me.

Senator George Aiken (R., Vermont) was displeased with this and other songs sung by "certain pacifist groups." In 1962 he asked a congressional hearing witness whether he did not think "it was a great calamity that the critics of the use of milk and other dairy products did not advise the Maker before He set up the original milk program?" The Senator's pique was prompted by the universal presence of Strontium-90 in milk products, the resulting public anxiety regarding their wholesomeness, and the tremendous emotional leverage that the fear of radioactive milk gave the opponents of nuclear weapons.

A radioactive isotope, Strontium-90 (Sr-90) has a half-life of 28 years, making it a long lasting component of fallout. Soon after World War II the Atomic Energy Commission recognized that Sr-90, which is chemically similar to calcium, can accumulate in bones and possibly lead to cancer. In August 1953 its presence in animal bones, milk and soil was first confirmed by the Lamont Geological Observatory. Lamont established a worldwide network for sampling human bone and within a few years found Sr-90 present in "all human beings, regardless of age or geographic locations." Sr-90 found its way into humans via the ecological food chain as fallout in the soil, was picked up by plants, further concentrated in herbivorous animals, and eventually consumed by humans.

The news that Sr-90 was a dangerous component of fallout received wide publicity in 1954 when Japanese scientists discovered that it was a part of the dust sampled from the *Lucky Dragon.* The new superbombs created Sr-90 in far greater quantities than did the old A-bombs. Public concern increased as the 1950s progressed, the bomb tests continued and radiation levels rose, and the issue received a great deal of press attention. In 1956, for example, *Newsweek* announced, "The testing of hydrogen bombs may have *already* propelled enough strontium 90 . . . into the stratosphere to doom countless of the world's children to inescapable and incurable cancer." The magazine characterized Sr-90 as "the invisible bone-hitting particles" that "can never be removed." The federal government established an elaborate system to monitor food and water for Sr-90 and other radioisotopes. In addition, there were a number of private research projects that added to knowledge of this pollutant. Some were also designed to increase public awareness of the hazard.

The Consumer's Union, for example, conducted a major national study of Sr-90 concentrations in milk — a highly emotional topic, because of the importance of milk in the diet of growing children. Sr-90 was found in a variety of foods in addition to milk, so the organizations also conducted an annual study of Sr-90 levels in the total diet, based upon typical menus of citizens living in a number of cities throughout the United States. The results of these tests were published in a series of articles in *Consumer Reports,* which had a readership in the millions.

Another study, the Baby Tooth Survey, was a particularly imaginative combination of research and public education. In 1958 Herman Kalckar proposed an international study of the concentration of radioisotopes in baby teeth. The special advantages of baby teeth were that their age could be precisely established; they could, unlike bones, be collected as they were shed without injury to the donors; and they were readily available, insuring a large and continuous supply. Although a coordinated international program was never established a number of smaller projects were eventually conducted around the world, beginning in St. Louis, Missouri.

In 1958 the newly created Greater St. Louis Citizens' Committee for Nuclear Information decided to undertake a survey of Sr-90 in the teeth of children. The survey started in earnest at the beginning of 1959. Since they would require the assistance of the citizenry and in order to prevent unreasonable public fears as a result of the study itself, the committee initiated a public education campaign and successfully gained the support of schools, medical institutions, libraries, Scout groups, and other community organizations. Initially they received teeth at the rate of 1,000 each month, but the collection rate rapidly increased. By 1961 one million tooth survey forms had been distributed and teeth were being received at the rate of 750 each week; a total of over 67,500 by the end of the year. Nearly 10% of these were coming from outside the St. Louis region. They received nearly 160,000 teeth by the end of 1964. Each child was given an "I Gave My Tooth To Science" button.

The study became a model for similar projects around the world. Over the years the scope of the committee broadened. The organization had a strong biological and ecological perspective and its interests expanded from fallout to wider environmental problems. The name of its newsletter was changed to *Scientist and Citizen,* which eventually metamorphosed into *Environment.* What began as a mimeographed newsletter about fallout had turned into one of the nation's major sources of environmental information and one of the committee's founders and best known members, Barry Commoner, had achieved national prominence in the environmental movement.

These and other studies, and the wide publicity they received, brought the issue of radioactive fallout very close to home. No longer was fallout a problem limited to a few Japanese fishermen or western ranchers. People around the nation knew that invisible radioactive material was in the air they breathed and lodged within their very own bones and those of their children. In learning about this hazard they also learned about the ecological food chain, the biological concentration of these materials, and the cancer and other radiation-induced effects that might strike them in future years.

ON THE BEACH

Public anxiety about the effects of nuclear tests and atomic radiation was expressed in a series of science fiction motion pictures that were long on fiction and short on science. These 1950s masterpieces of the cinematic art included *The Beast From 20,000 Fathoms* (1953; resurrected dinosaur), *Them!* (1954; giant ants), *Tarantula* (1955; giant spider), and *The Incredible Shrinking Man* (1957; tiny man). Rather than representing true science fiction, these films were a modern version of gothic horror. A literary or cinematic journey from the world of normal, everyday experience to one of fantasy and terror requires some device to encourage belief. Radioactive fallout provided such a device, an excuse for conjuring up demons in the form of mutants, monsters and nature run amuck. The fall of radiation had become the modern equivalent of the fall of darkness and the stroke of midnight.

Beginning with the 1951 film *Five,* there also arose a new film genre examining the theme of survival after World War III. Other films of this sort included *The World, The Flesh, and the Devil* (1959), *On the Beach* (1959) and *Panic in Year Zero* (1960). Each considered the plight of the survivors of nuclear war: facing one's certain death as radiation spread across the earth; being the last human beings on earth and bearing the responsibility for the future of the species; and surviving in the face of overwhelming disaster and the collapse of social order. Although most of these films were not of the highest quality they presented to millions of people a terrifying image of the future and expressed the anxieties of their society.

On the Beach was an exception to the rule. It was a high budget, prestige film designed to attract international attention to the issues of nuclear war and fallout. The novel, written by the well known author Nevil Shute, was published in 1957 and became a best seller with over 2,000,000 copies in print by 1960. It portrayed the despair and resignation of the citizens of Australia following a 1962 nuclear war in the northern hemisphere. They had to wait over a year until the radioactive air mass of the northern hemisphere mixed sufficiently with the southern air mass to bring their certain death; more than enough time to consider what lay ahead and for each to find his or her own way of coming to terms with the inevitable.

Many reviewers found it difficult to accept the calmness with which Shute's characters faced their doom. The Australians went about the business of their lives, adjusted to the shortage of supplies, and considered whether or not they would take the government-issued suicide pills that promised a quick death as an alternative to slow radiation poisoning. The trout season was opened early, because few would be alive when the traditional date arrived. "But there was no orgy of immorality, no riots and looting of the haves by the have nots, no mass religious revival," wrote one reviewer with some disappointment. Another, however, wrote, "If this thriller is ever televised, there may be a wilder stampede than Orson Wells wrought two decades ago with his Martians."

The film version of *On the Beach,* produced and directed by Stanley Kramer, was released by United Artists two years after the book's publication. With over $4,000,000 invested, a large figure at that time, Kramer had the difficult task of making a box office success out of a movie about a terribly depressing subject. He hired big name stars: Gregory Peck as the American submarine commander, Dwight Tower; Ava Gardner as the less than glamorous alcoholic, Moira Davidson; and dancer Fred Astaire as the physicist, Julian Osborn. Casting Gardner and Astaire against type helped attract attention. The promotion of the film emphasized its relevance to major issues of the time — nuclear fallout and the survival of humanity in a nuclear age. This was, as *Variety* noted, "part of United Artists' campaign to make the film what's termed 'a status symbol,' meaning something to be seen despite its grim nature." On December 17, 1959 the film premiered in 18 cities around the world, with versions in eight languages. Gregory Peck and one thousand others attended the premier in Moscow. With this kind of promotion it is not surprising that *On the Beach* was a major success. Two months after its release it was still on top.

Perhaps the most moving of the film's scenes were those of the dead cities of the U.S. west coast. Tower and his crew were sent to investigate strange radio signals coming from the area, hoping they were a sign that some human life remained. Raising the periscope to examine the coast, they found cities devoid of life. The images of San Francisco, its streets empty and without movement, were haunting. The final disappointment came when they discovered that the radio signals, which they had traveled halfway around the world to investigate, were created as a window shade randomly flapping in the breeze jiggled a Coke bottle against a telegraph key.

The film's final scenes of Melbourne's vacant, lifeless streets recalled Dwight Tower's thoughts in the novel as he drove through the city. "'Very soon,' he mused, 'perhaps in a month's time, there would be no one here, no living creatures but the cats and dogs that had been granted a short reprieve. Soon they too would be gone; summers and winters would pass by and these houses and these streets would know them. . . . The human race was to be wiped out and the world made clean again for wiser occupants without undue delay.'"

In addition to widespread and strong praise for the film there were notes of criticism. Some reviewers leveled the same charge as had been directed at the book, arguing that the characters accepted their fate too calmly. Others complained that the film did not show the violence of the war or the physical agony of its victims. A *Time* reviewer wrote that the film "turns out to be a sentimental sort of a radiation romance, in which the customers are considerately spared any scenes of realistic horror. . . ." Lodging a different criticism, New York's Governor Nelson Rockefeller feared the film might diminish the nation's "will to resist . . . some of my kids saw the picture and came away with the feeling of 'what's the use?'"

After a decade of preparation the American public was ready to believe what *On the Beach* had to say. People understood that fallout can circle the globe and this invisible poison, which they were unable to detect with their own senses, could threaten their lives and future. At a congressional hearing in mid-1961, [atomic theorist] Herman Kahn spoke of the scientists in the 1950s, who did not believe nuclear war was survivable. "In other words," he said, "the belief in the 'end of history' was an expert's belief, rather than a layman's belief. In fact, if the layman had been told fully and frankly what the experts believed, he would have been horrified. . . . The picture and book, 'On the Beach,' reflected these views." The "end of history," however, was no longer a concept known only to experts.

SEEKING SHELTER

Americans did not accept the "end of history" passively. The mid- and late 1950s witnessed growing public and congressional interest in fallout shelters.

Governor Rockefeller was a vocal advocate and in the spring of 1960 he announced plans to build one in the basement of his New York Fifth Avenue apartment building. He made a special effort to influence the new president, John F. Kennedy. Given the well known hazards of fallout and nuclear war it was difficult for the president not to take steps to protect the population from this potentially disastrous threat. In a special message to Congress on May 25, 1961 he announced a major step-up in the nation's civil defense program.

In June Kennedy met with USSR Premier Khrushchev, who told him of the Soviet's intention to end the West's access to Berlin. In response Kennedy made a radio and television report to the nation announcing an increase of $207 million above the $104 million already appropriated for civil defense — a total of five times the previous year's funding. This was only one part of a major mobilization of U.S. defense in preparation for the likelihood that the Soviet Union would sign a separate peace treaty with East Germany, thus isolating West Berlin. This was a grim message, in which he raised the specter of nuclear war with the USSR. The president's speech prompted an outpouring of national concern. In July the Office of Civil and Defense Mobilization received 16,994 inquiries from the public, with a major increase following the speech — 5,382 letters on August 1st alone.

In the night of August 13th East Germany began constructing the Berlin wall. The Soviet Union resumed testing nuclear weapons on August 31st. Since the end of 1958 the two nations had tacitly agreed to suspend nuclear testing and between that time and August 1961 neither the USA nor the USSR had conducted tests. By the end of 1961, though, the Soviets had detonated over 30 devices. The United States re-established its own testing program and by the end of 1962 had detonated nearly 90 devices, compared to about 40 of the Soviets' in the same year. The world of 1962 witnessed the largest annual number of nuclear explosions in history. The background radiation level, which had dropped since 1958, again began to climb as nuclear debris was injected into the atmosphere.

The hostilities between the two nations reached a peak in October, 1962, when Kennedy decided to confront the USSR over its attempt to base nuclear missiles in Cuba. Five years after the publication of *On the Beach,* in the year of the novel's fictional holocast, the world held its breath as the two superpowers poised on the edge of a terrifyingly real nuclear war.

Through the autumn of 1961 the administration had continued to promote the creation of public and private fallout shelters. *Life* magazine published a major article on fallout shelters in September, complete with an introductory letter from the president. "Nuclear weapons and the possibility of nuclear war," he wrote, "are facts of life we cannot ignore today. . . . The ability to survive coupled with the will to do so therefore are essential to our country." The article claimed "97 out of 100 people can be saved" and provided diagrams of home shelters (including one soon to be available from Sears, Roebuck & Co. for $700) and tips on shelter living. In December the Defense Department published a brochure promoting home shelters and other forms of fallout protection. 25,000,000 copies were distributed free from post offices and civil defense offices throughout the nation.

The country was swept up into a "shelter mania" as citizens with the means constructed fallout shelters in their basements and backyards. Entrepreneurs marketed kits of food and survival equipment for the well-outfitted shelter and clothing stores catered to the special needs of doomsday. One Manhattan dress shop recommended "gay slacks and dress with a cape that could double as an extra blanket."

The shelter mania showed its dark side as citizens armed their home shelters to fight off neighbors who, in the event of a war, might want to share their limited space and provisions. A Nevada civil defense official announced that it might become necessary to rely on vigilantes to defend his state from World War III California refugees. "There is evidence that the Administration policies, which seem to emphasize an every-man-for-himself approach," wrote *Newsweek,* "have succeeded in bringing out the worst side of human nature. Some citizens are behaving as if they were cavemen already."

Criticism of the program grew. In November Kennedy's advisor Arthur Schlesinger warned the president, "Everywhere the shelter program seems to be emerging as the chief issue of domestic concern — and as one surrounded by an alarming amount of bewilderment, confusion and, in some cases (both pro and con) of near-hysteria." *Newsweek* and *Consumer Reports* pointed out that the administration's program did not provide protection from blast, heat or firestorm, and did not provide for dispersing targets. In December the American Medical Association urged the nation to "stop worrying about radioactive fall-out and concentrate on getting ready for Christmas." It went on to say, "There really isn't very much that us average folks can do about it anyway." . . .

As the mania abated and cooler heads prevailed, Congress pared the President's civil defense budget request for fiscal year 1962–63 from $695 million down to $80 million. Steps were taken to reduce the hazards of nuclear weapons with the signing in June 1963 of a treaty to install a "hot line" between Moscow and Washington, and in August 1963 of the Limited Test Ban Treaty to halt above ground testing. The U.S. government would continue to support fallout shelters, but never again would the public display the kind of obsession that had characterized this period.

Kennedy's civil defense program left a lasting impression upon the nation. The "end of history," nuclear war, and radioactive fallout were no longer simply items of uncomfortable conversation. They were threats against which individual citizens had physically prepared. Worse still, the actions that their government urged were not designed for prevention. Instead, they were based upon accepting and accommodating to this overshadowing doom. In the following years the ubiquitous fallout shelter sign and its radiation symbol became part of the landscape as it graced school, public buildings, subway tunnels, and many privately owned structures. It became a reminder of a terrifying, inescapable threat.

CHEMICAL FALLOUT

Silent Spring was published on September 27, 1962 — one month before the Cuban missile crisis and one year before the signing of the Limited Test Ban Treaty; almost three years after the release of the film version of *On the Beach,* and two years before the release of Stanley Kubrick's *Dr. Strangelove: or How I Learned to Stop Worrying and Love the Bomb.* The nation was steeped in years of debate about nuclear weapons and fallout which served as a point of reference to help people understand the hazards of pesticides and as a fearful symbol to motivate action.

The environmental and health hazards of radioactive materials were on Rachel Carson's mind as she wrote the book. In the summer of 1960, while deeply involved in writing *Silent Spring,* she also worked on a revised edition of *The Sea Around Us.* In a new preface she wrote about the impacts of fallout and the ocean disposal of nuclear wastes upon the marine environment. She described how marine organisms can concentrate radioisotopes and wrote that, "By such a process tuna over an area of a million square miles surrounding the Bikini bomb test developed a degree of radioactivity enormously higher than that of the sea water." In creating these materials, she warned, we must face the question of whether we "can dispose of these lethal substances without rendering the earth uninhabitable."

It is no accident, then, that the first pollutant mentioned by name in *Silent Spring* was not a pesticide, but Strontium-90. Well known to the American public, Sr-90 was a tool to help her explain the properties of pesticides. Early in *Silent Spring* she wrote: "Strontium 90, released through nuclear explosions into the air, comes to earth in rain or drifts down as fallout, lodges in soil, enters into the grass or corn or wheat grown there, and in time takes up its abode in the bones of a human being, there to remain until his death. **Similarly,** chemicals sprayed on croplands or forests or gardens lie long in soil, entering in a chain of poisoning and death."

Although this was the book's first reference to a specific pollutant, it was not its first allusion to fallout. The opening chapter, "A Fable for Tomorrow," painted a picture of a lovely rural Midwestern town struck by a mysterious blight. People, animals, fish, and birds sickened and many died. Roadside vegetation withered. What had happened to this town now lifeless and without even the song of birds? In the nooks and crannies of the town's buildings one could find a white powder that "had fallen like snow upon the roofs and the lawns, the fields and streams" a few weeks before. "No witchcraft," she wrote, "no enemy action had silenced the rebirth of new life in this stricken world. The people had done it themselves." This fall of pesticides upon the town conjures up the specter of radioactive fallout — a specter created intentionally by the author. In an early draft Carson wrote that the powder reminded the townspeople of the dust that fell upon the *Lucky Dragon.* She also wrote that visitors to the town wondered if perhaps the wind had carried fallout from a bomb test and dropped it on the town. Not only does this chapter present a frightening description of potential pesticide hazards, it evokes the image of a town dying from nuclear fallout. On an even more subtle level it recalls the images of lifeless American cities shown so graphically less than three years before in *On the Beach.*

Elsewhere in her book Carson made an even more direct comparison between fallout and pesticides. Writing of a Swedish farmer who had died of pesticide poisoning and recalling the unfortunate radioman of the *Lucky Dragon,* she wrote, "Like Kuboyama, the farmer had been a healthy man, gleaning his living from the land as Kuboyama had taken his from the sea. For each man a poison drifting out of the sky carried a death sentence. For one, it was radiation-poisoned ash; for the other, chemical dust." A few pages later she wrote that, "Certain chemicals, again reminding us of radiation products like Strontium 90, have a peculiar affinity for the bone marrow." She also referred to the leukemia victims of the Hiroshima A-bomb to illustrate a similar hazard from pesticides. Other references to radiation are sprinkled throughout the book.

Lois and Louis Darling, *Silent Spring*'s illustrators, also had radiation in mind as they explored ideas for drawings. Their marginal notes on a draft manuscript include a mushroom cloud sketch in one place and a note to illustrate the Swedish farmer/*Lucky Dragon* comparison in another. I have found no evidence that Rachel Carson directly suggested either of these possibilities to the Darlings. Although neither of these ideas found their way into the final book, they demonstrate the images the book brought to mind.

I am not suggesting that using fallout as an analogy for pesticides was a central part of the design of this very sophisticated book. Indeed, the topic was not a major part of the conversations between Rachel Carson and her editor, nor have I found reference to it in her notes and correspondence about *Silent Spring.* As a thoughtful person who was aware of the issues of her time, however, it was impossible for Carson not to have been influenced by the decade of public discussion and debate. She and her book were products and representatives of their time, as well as shapers of it.

Fallout, one might say, was "in the air" and it is a tribute to Carson's perceptive skill as an author that she was able to recognize and take advantage of the deep-seated cluster of social concerns surrounding it in the public's mind. Not only did she tap into this anxiety and direct it toward pesticides; she also used the public's existing understanding about the hazards of fallout to teach about the similar hazards of chemical poisons. Just as Strontium-90 could travel great distances, enter the food chain and accumulate in human tissue, so too could pesticides. Just as radioactive materials may produce chronic rather than acute poisoning, so too with pesticides. And just as exposure to radiation may produce cancer, birth defects and mutations, so might pesticides. The public already knew the basic concepts—all it needed was a little reminding.

A common motive of the contemporary environmental movement is a profound and pervasive element of fear. It is a fear that, for good or ill, colors and sometimes distorts virtually every popular analysis of major environmental problems. This is not simply a fear that we will deplete a particular natural resource, lose pristine wilderness, or be poisoned. It is the belief that we may well be facing the "end of history," that we as a species might be doomed. This anxiety burst to the surface with the destruction of Hiroshima and Nagasaki. It is rooted in the omnipresent threat of nuclear destruction.

The generation that promoted Earthday 1970 grew up in the shadow of nuclear destruction. This threat became a tacit part of the way in which people understood their world. It is no surprise then, that the belief in the imminent end of the earth became integrated with more traditional conservation concerns. This younger generation did not create the anxiety, nor did its elder, Rachel Carson. She did, though, write one of the first and most eloquent of books bridging the gap between the environmental movement and this new fearful vision of Armageddon.

Document
God's Own Junkyard

PETER BLAKE

PREFACE

This book is not written in anger. It is written in fury—though not, I trust, in blind fury. It is a deliberate attack upon all those who have already befouled a large portion of this country for private gain, and are engaged in befouling the rest.

Some of these latter-day vandals are well organized and well financed— such as the billboard industry whose profitable creations along our highways have been implicated in a staggering number of automobile accidents. . . . Some of our latter-day vandals are "little people"—tradesmen and shop-keepers trying to make a modest living—people without ties to the landscape or townscape in which they live, people whose eyes have lost the art of seeing. And still others among our latter-day vandals are all the rest of us—all of us who no longer care, or no longer care enough.

A very cynical acquaintance of mine said to me recently: "The national purpose of the United States, from the very beginning, has been to let everyone make as much money as he possibly can. If they found oil under St. Patrick's Cathedral, they would put a derrick smack in the center of the nave, and nobody would give the matter a second thought."

This is perhaps a rather naïve book. It is based on the assumption that our national purpose, or purposes, are somewhat more idealistic. It is based on the further assumption that it is not too late for us to learn to see again, and to learn to care again about the physical aspects of our environment. And it is

*based, finally, on the assumption that ours could be a reasonably civilized
society—if enough of us could be stirred into action.*

*This is, therefore, a muckraking book, not because muckraking is a
particularly enjoyable activity, but because there seems to be so much muck
around that needs to be raked so that this country may be made fit again to
live in. . . .*

GOD'S OWN JUNKYARD

No people has inherited a more naturally beautiful land than we: within an
area representing a mere 6 per cent of the land surface of the globe we can
point to mountain ranges as spectacular as those of the Dolomites and to
jungles as colorful as those of the Amazon valley; to lake-studded forests as
lovely as those of Finland and to rolling hills as gentle as those around
Salzburg; to cliffs that rival those of the French Riviera and to sandy beaches
that are unexcelled even by the shores of Jutland; in short, to about as varied
and thrilling a geography as has ever been presented to man.

The only trouble is that we are about to turn this beautiful inheritance
into the biggest slum on the face of the earth. "The mess that is man-made
America," as a British magazine has called it, is a disgrace of such vast
proportions that only a concerted national effort can now hope to return
physical America to the community of civilized nations.

Our towns and cities boast many isolated handsome buildings—but
very, very few handsome streets, squares, civic centers, or neighborhoods.
(Even such rare exceptions as Rockefeller Center in New York, now twenty-
five years old, have become disfigured as they have expanded beyond their
original limits.) Our suburbs are interminable wastelands dotted with millions
of monotonous little houses on monotonous little lots and crisscrossed by
highways lined with billboards, jazzed-up diners, used-car lots, drive-in
movies, beflagged gas stations, and garish motels. Even the relatively un-
spoiled countryside beyond these suburban fringes has begun to sprout more
telephone poles than trees, more trailer camps than national parks. And the
shores of oceans, lakes, and rivers are rapidly becoming encrusted with the
junkiness of industries that pollute the water on which they depend.

This seems a strange state of affairs in a nation co-founded, and presided over
for eight years, by a great architect, Thomas Jefferson. It seems a strange state
of affairs in a nation that has, since Jefferson, produced some of the Western
world's most creative architects—H. H. Richardson, Louis Sullivan, Frank
Lloyd Wright, to name only a few—and some of its most dedicated conservationists, including another President, Theodore Roosevelt.

These men, and many others like them—writers, poets, painters,
pamphleteers—believed that America represented not merely a political
challenge, but also an esthetic one: a challenge to preserve (and, quite possibly, to improve upon) what someone called "God's Own Country."

Alas, except for National and State Parks not much of the natural beauty of this country remains preserved. And unhappily those fine National Forests and State Parks tend to do to the landscape what National and State Museums do to painting and sculpture: that is, embalm it. (They tend to "elevate" us on Sundays and holidays, rather than enrich our lives all year round.) However praiseworthy such conservation efforts may be in helping to protect parts of the American countryside, they do little to protect those areas in which most of us live or spend our free time—the areas nearest to cities and suburbs.

As for the preservation of man-made improvements, this is almost nonexistent: except for a few isolated structures of well-established historic value (or, at any rate, interest), and a few isolated blocks in some of our older cities, none of our impressive architectural heritage is protected. In Manhattan, the magnificent, nineteenth-century iron-and-glass façades south of Bleeker Street are defaced, demolished, or neglected; in Chicago, the Mecca of modern architects the world over, important structures by Louis Sullivan have been destroyed to make way for more profitable enterprises; in Buffalo, New York, Frank Lloyd Wright's world-famous Larkin Building, designed in 1904 and honored in every single history book on modern architecture, was sold by the city fathers in 1949 to a wrecking firm for a few thousand dollars; the new owners replaced it with a parking lot.

And so it goes—in St. Louis, San Francisco, Baltimore, Philadelphia, Boston, Pittsburgh—everywhere. When a building—whether handsome or of indifferent quality—has ceased to be a "money-maker," down it comes to make way for a bowling alley or a supermarket.

The total indifference on the part of our city fathers toward this country's man-made heritage was never more clearly shown than when New York's stately Pennsylvania Station, built by McKim, Mead and White, was condemned to bite the dust: the Mayor, a former Chairman of the City Planning Commission (and, hence, a man not entirely untutored in matters of architecture), did not even bother to ask his advisory committee on historical preservation to render an opinion on the significance of the old Station—until it was too late. And then he ignored the opinion of his distinguished committee; for, after all, the committee had no power at all!

"History," of course, "is bunk." History can also be politically inconvenient: the syndicate which desired to replace Penn Station with a mammoth amusement center was not without significant political connections.

Yet it would be unfair to place on the politicians all blame for permitting the destruction of our cultural heritage, or to imply that such acts are invariably motivated by sinister backroom shenanigans. Except for a very small (and generally ineffective) minority, few citizens of our great urban centers really care. On April 11, 1955, that popular mouthpiece of New York the *Daily News* (circulation: phenomenal), published a rousing editorial which suggested that another wonderful relic of America's neoclassic period, the New York Public Library built by Carrère & Hastings in 1911, be topped off with a super-skyscraper so the revenue from millions of square feet of rentable office space thus created would put the city into the black. Not content, however, with advocating one act of vandalism-per-page-per-day, the *News* printed in its adjoining letters column an even more spectacular proposal from an irate reader who anonymously signed him- (or her-) self "Overtaxed." "These city fathers make me sick," wrote Mr., Mrs. or Miss Overtaxed, "raising fares, taxes, and so forth in order to get money. They should chop down the Central Park trees, sell the wood, and then pave the place over. Set up a race track in the northern part, a Coney Island at the south end, and a mambo palace in the center. The remaining space could be rented for parking."

On that memorable morning in 1955, the editorial page of the *News* seemed more entertaining than it had for some time. In retrospect, the joke appears to have been on those of us who thought that New York was a reasonably civilized place. It is true that there is no office skyscraper astride the Public Library (as we go to press); but there is one — the biggest in the world, by God! — astride Warren & Wetmore's beautiful 1913 Grand Central Station, just a couple of blocks to the east. And it is true that Central Park has not been paved over completely just yet, but the bulldozers are at its gates, making ugly noises; and a few forays into Olmsted's preserve have been successfully attempted.

If history is indeed bunk, as our city fathers announce by their actions everywhere and every day, is it really so surprising that most of our fellow citizens show very little pride in their hometowns? Is it really so surprising that they don't care a hoot about what their diner, their parking lot, their cut-rate store, their cocktail lounge, their poolroom, and their movie marquee do to the streetscape? Is it really so surprising that the average citizen, deprived of lasting symbols of a community, begins to create his own graven images — things of which he can be (perhaps justly) proud?

After all, isn't this a free country? "In the name of culture, in the name of esthetics, whatever that is," said the late Robert S. Kerr of Oklahoma on the floor of the Senate of the United States in March, 1958 (only he pronounced it "ass-thetics"), "it will be a grave day in this country when we reach so high an *'ass-thetic'* pinnacle that men are willing and able . . . to deprive citizens of their vested rights. . . . What kind of culture [is this?] . . . It is the kind of culture one can find in Russia. It is the kind of culture Hitler went down the drain trying to implement in Germany. . . ." The late, distinguished Senator from Oklahoma can rest in peace; no one has yet succeeded in putting over "ass-thetics" in the cities of the United States. The Republic is safe; it is, instead, our cities that are going down the drain.

fourteen

THE REAGAN YEARS

Ronald Reagan swept into office determined to turn the government and the nation around. He scored an overwhelming victory over the hapless Jimmy Carter in the election of 1980, as he called for reduced federal spending, elimination of the budget deficit, and a stronger national defense. A conservative with strong ideological views, Reagan sought to reestablish his own vision of the American dream.

Although Reagan was almost 70 years old when he assumed the presidency, he appealed to Americans eager for change. His background in radio, film, and television served him well in his effort to forge a new consensus. He was reassuring in his public appearances and conveyed the impression that the government was in good hands.

At the start, it seemed as though Reagan could do no wrong. With Republican majorities in both houses of Congress, he was able to push through major tax cuts and larger defense expenditures as he moved to fulfill campaign promises. When scandals surfaced and critics pointed to the "sleaze factor" in the administration, Reagan managed to escape the taint. He survived an assassination attempt and appeared personally and professionally indestructible.

In Reagan's second term, after another overwhelming victory in 1984, his administration began to unravel. The budget deficit weakened the stock market, which tumbled in 1987. That same year, revelations of a secret National Security Council effort aimed at freeing hostages by selling arms to Iran and then using the profits to fund the Contras — rebels fighting against the left-wing government in Nicaragua — shook the country. Congress had

343

been neither consulted nor informed. As the inner struggles of the administration became visible in nationally televised hearings, the Iran-Contra scandal took the shine off Reagan's image.

In "An Early Appraisal of the Reagan Presidency," political scientist Fred I. Greenstein assesses the early Reagan years and then provides a useful summary of the background that led to the presidency. Although Greenstein's essay appeared before the Iran-Contra affair surfaced, he notes the tendency to delegate too much authority that got Reagan into trouble later on.

Garry Wills, a well-known journalist, columnist, and historian, argues in "Reagan in Office" that the president's roots and interests lay at home. Whereas past presidents, Kennedy and Nixon in particular, had been consumed by foreign affairs, Reagan had a different agenda, and Wills shows how he moved to implement it. Wills underscores the president's bond with the American people and reveals how Reagan played on that tie in his policy initiatives.

The document in this section offers still another view of Reagan. It comes from the "Report of the President's Special Review Board," headed by former Senator John Tower, investigating the Iran-Contra affair. The report reveals a president out of touch with his administration, unsure of what was being done, and too willing to allow aides to take unwarranted actions at his expense.

In addition to the works excerpted here, there are a number of other good assessments of the Reagan years. Lou Cannon, *Reagan* (1982), is a thorough account of background and early presidency by the highly regarded White House correspondent from the *Washington Post*. Lawrence I. Barrett, *Gambling with History: Reagan in the White House* (1983), is an equally good survey of the early period by the *Time* correspondent. Rowland Evans, Jr., and Robert D. Novak, both veteran journalists, focus on the transition in *The Reagan Revolution: An Inside Look at the Transformation of the U.S. Government* (1981). Ronnie Dugger, *On Reagan: The Man & His Presidency* (1983), is a detailed survey of Reagan's policies by a respected investigative reporter and author. For a fuller view of Reagan's first electoral victory, see Gerald Pomper and colleagues, *The Election of 1980: Reports and Interpretations* (1981). For a first-hand account of the New Right and its influence, written by a major fundraiser, see Richard Viguerie, *The New Right: We're Ready to Lead* (1981).

An Early Appraisal of the Reagan Presidency

FRED I. GREENSTEIN

THE DISTINCTIVENESS OF THE REAGAN PRESIDENCY

The Reagan presidency needs to be tracked while under way because it is in some ways unique and in others extraordinary, even in the limited universe of nine modern presidencies. As a rare specimen it provides special perspective on what is and is not possible in public policy and presidential leadership. The Reagan presidency stands out by virtue of the chief executive's ideological closure, his propensity to act on his principles, his success in doing so, and the consequences of his success in transforming ideology into policy.

1. Extent and extremity of Reagan's ideological closure. . . . [N]o other president has come to office after a remotely comparable prior career of making public an ideologically consistent (if very general) commitment to a political philosophy. Not only has Reagan been more devoted to and more uncompromising in his political principles than have previous presidents, but he has also departed from convention in the kinds of stands he takes. His abstract positions on issues are not centrist, even though at strategic times he has taken pains to avoid divisiveness by practicing the art of the possible and by dealing with his adversaries in a conciliatory manner. Anticipating the sketch of Reagan-the-man and of the political context of his accession to the presidency that concludes this [selection], we may simply note that his long-articulated, noncentrist views took shape during the mid-1950s and early 1960s phase of his post-Hollywood career. During this period, which coincided with the culmination of his transformation from youthful New Deal enthusiast to middle-aged conservative, he crystallized his new views while working as a circuit-riding speaker to the many units of the vast General Electric company (GE) and to innumerable civic groups.

As a conservative orator, Reagan honed to perfection a talk couched in uncomplicated *Reader's Digest* prose that came to be known as "The Speech." A primer of conservative doctrine, it set forth a consistent, strongly stated series of admonitions: eliminate government restraint on the free market, devolve power from federal to lower jurisdictions, decrease taxes, and maintain a tough stance toward the Soviet Union. Delivered in the 1964 campaign, "The Speech" earned the erstwhile sports announcer, film actor, union leader, and public speaker a dominant position among conservatives who remained true to [Republican presidential nominee Barry] Goldwater's cause but sought a candidate with broad appeal.

Ideologues have regularly had their supporters in American politics, but to most observers of American politics, the 1964 defeat of an outspoken conservative vindicated the proposition that realistic American politicians would not choose true believers (much less noncentrist ones) as presidential nominees, a perception that was further reinforced by the overwhelming defeat of an outspoken liberal candidate, George McGovern, in 1972. But both Goldwater and McGovern lost support for reasons connected with such factors as their personalities, campaign styles, and strategies, as well as because citizens viewed them as too extreme. Reagan's attractive personality and style as political performer commended him as a candidate who might present an ideologically clear, strongly conservative choice rather than a centrist echo, but nevertheless be electable.

2. Reagan's proclivity once in office to transform faith into works. If on taking office Reagan had revealed himself to be only a campaign ideologue and had shifted to the middle-of-the-road policy proposals of Ford or Nixon, his distinctiveness as a position-taker while out of office would be of modest significance. Candidates with strong positions sometimes abandon them in office.

Reagan, however, sought to be true not only to the more orthodox conservative principles he had been propounding for years but also to a later appendage to his ideology — the beguiling supply-side doctrine that tax reductions would provide a painless remedy for the nation's economic woes. Especially in 1981, Reagan acted decisively to put his principles into practice in . . . spending and tax-cutting legislation . . . and to implement his campaign demands for drastic deregulation of the private sector. . . . And he has been broadly consistent with his principles in his foreign as well as domestic policy practices, although . . . with tactical exceptions and . . . by building incrementally on a commitment [Jimmy] Carter had already made to increase military expenditures.

3. Reagan's initial success in putting his programs into practice. Though not unique among modern presidencies, the Reagan administration's early success in achieving its policy goals, notably in the case of economic and domestic programs and defense appropriations, was impressively distinctive. Modern presidents consistently propose policies, but usually Congress blocks or substantially alters their efforts. [Harry] Truman's 1948 campaign was run on a platform calling for major domestic policy changes. None of consequence was enacted. Those portions of [John] Kennedy's campaign promises to move the nation "forward" which called for congressional action were largely unachieved by the time of his death. Indeed, of the nine modern presidents only [Franklin] Roosevelt and [Lyndon] Johnson had striking legislative success — until 1981.

When Reagan took office, it had become truistic among students of the presidency that while two of the previous four presidents (Johnson and [Richard] Nixon) may have striven, to their ultimate regret, for "imperial" hegemony in the political system, the post-Watergate presidency was a distinctly nonimperial, "imperiled" institution. By 1980 presidency-curbing statutes and extralegal changes in institutions and practices appeared to have significantly sapped the president's ability to exercise influence.

Reagan and company reversed the notion that presidents were becoming increasingly powerless. By the summer of 1981, in a striking display of political skill that took advantage of such circumstances as a Republican-controlled Senate and a Democratic party in disarray, Reagan forces had administratively induced changes introduced by presidential appointees. And, while Reagan's results have been less dramatic since then, he has resisted welfare program restorations and sharp cuts in his defense spending requests. He and his aides have also been ingenious in maintaining his "success" record by advance negotiations that lead to legislative outcomes Reagan is prepared to accept and claim as accomplishments, even if they are not as striking as his 1981 achievements.

Of Reagan's first-year victories, the most significant were two enactments he signed on the same day in August — a major reduction in domestic expenditures and the Economic Recovery Tax Act of 1981. The massive tax cut — designed to reduce federal revenues by $737 billion over a five-year period — is of special interest to policy analysts because, to a degree extraordinary in American politics, it constitutes a massive policy change based on ideological premises.

To say that the tax cut has been consequential, however, is not to say it has been successful or even that there was prior evidence that it would succeed. . . . [T]he rationale behind the tax cut was based on empirically untested political theory. The very groups the cut was designed to galvanize — investors and businesses — were from the start skeptical about the supply-side assumptions that underpinned such a drastic reduction in federal revenues. The assumptions of supply-side economics, which George Bush had most conspicuously criticized during the 1980 nomination campaign, were that funds made available to prosperous Americans by tax cuts would then be invested and that these investments would set off a chain reaction of increased productivity, higher employment, less need for public assistance subsidies, and a higher individual and corporate income base on which to collect taxes. The result would be a balanced federal budget. The failure of this scenario to take place is the single most conspicuous cause of the fourth way in which the Reagan presidency stands out.

4. The tension between principles and practice in Reagan's leadership. The Reagan presidency provides political analysts with a historically unique opportunity to examine the practicality of ideologically informed policy-making in the American context. American politicians have been both belabored and praised for their opportunism — for their disposition to advocate equivocal positions of the sort A. Lawrence Lowell epitomized in his sardonic 1897 reference to "a tariff for revenue only, so adjusted as to protect American industries."

Heretofore, American politics has yielded little evidence of the consequences of ideologically informed policy-making. None of the modern presidents, nor for that matter their precursors, entered office with Reagan's degree of commitment to political abstractions. The Great Society was an extension of the New Deal. The New Deal was . . . an ideological hodgepodge.

By putting abstractly conceived policies into practice, the Reagan presidency constitutes a case study for the continuing controversy between planners and incrementalists about the desirability of basing policy on comprehensive political theories. In this debate the word "planner" includes not only visionaries of the Left who want to construct new institutions on the basis of their principles, but also policy advocates like President Reagan who propose radically conservative departures. . . .

THE BACKGROUND OF THE REAGAN PRESIDENCY

. . .

Reagan: Political Man—Late Entry Political Career

In contrasting the long governmental careers of European parliamentary leaders with the American candidate selection process in which a political novice can achieve high office, [British political scientist] Anthony King has characterized Ronald Reagan as just such a political *arriviste:* "a retired film actor and professional after-dinner speaker" who "fought his first election in 1966 when he was already 55 years old."

Yes, but. . . . If King's observations were all one knew about Reagan, it would be difficult to imagine that, once in office, he could have achieved a reputation among other political leaders as an impressively effective political operator. King's characterization, written before Reagan took office, appears in a discussion of why the presidential nominating system Americans developed in the 1970s permits the emergence of presidents who, once in Washington, perform with predictable ineptness. The then-incumbent Jimmy Carter, King noted, had previously been a "small-town businessman and former naval officer," whose governmental experience had consisted of two terms as state senator and one as governor of a state much less analogous to the nation than is California in size, complexity, and politics. It was not surprising that as national chief executive Carter had been spectacularly unsuccessful in enunciating and winning support for a political program.

Reagan has been far from apolitical, as [journalist] Lou Cannon, the best-informed observer of his career, has made clear. In government, as a union leader, and even as an undergraduate campus leader, Reagan has been politically active, politically involved, and consistently drawn to partake of the generic enterprise of politics, in the sense of "who gets what, when, and how." He has been an enthusiastic political partisan for the entire period of the modern presidency, casting his first ballot in 1932 for Franklin Roosevelt, his idol of the Depression years and the model for his political style of reaching out rhetorically to the American people through the electronic media.

From the 1930s through the early postwar period, he held the view common among liberal Democrats that "Red-baiting" attacks on communism were covert attempts to smear liberals and trade unions. By 1948, however, he had shifted to the then equally common stance of cold war anti-Communist liberalism and made election speeches in support of Truman. His political views had evolved from non-Communist to anti-Communist liberalism.

Reagan's political activism was spurred by his trade union activism. Shortly after arriving in Hollywood in the 1930s, he became an official of the Screen Actors' Guild and began to participate in its political position-taking and jurisdictional politics, as well as in its negotiations with the film studios. Reagan plunged into union activities with the cheerful affinity for politicking he had earlier displayed as campus politician. As a man whose profession called for persuasive public performances, who took politics seriously, and who (at some cost to his movie career) was deep in union activity, it was quite natural for him to become a political campaigner. In 1950, the last year he campaigned for Democrats, Reagan spoke for the entire California Democratic slate, in effect rejecting Richard Nixon's "pink lady" campaign efforts to brand his senatorial opponent, Helen Gahagan Douglas, as "soft on communism." His transition to conservatism was not yet consummated, but his principal avocational interests were following public affairs and engaging in grass-roots and union politicking.

The relative importance to Reagan of film acting and politicking even in his Hollywood years is suggested by the tone and distribution of chapters in his 1965 autobiographical memoir, *Where's the Rest of Me?* The first nine chapters are a breezy, fast-paced account of his youth in Illinois, college antics, radio sportscasting, and life as an actor.

The final nine chapters shift pace. Several are almost pedantically devoted to the pull and haul of interests and personalities in the Screen Actors' Guild and the labor movement generally. All of the final chapters intertwine career narrative with references to union politics and national political issues. Appended to the book is the text of "The Speech," documenting the transformation Reagan made during the Eisenhower years to conservatism and to devoting his time to public exposition of conservative doctrine.

Reagan's GE experience as a business spokesman crystallized his conservatism. During this period he also became outstandingly successful as a political communicator, learning to convey his views equally persuasively in face-to-face conversation and in smooth, but not slick, speeches to large audiences. Rather than being a mere "after-dinner speaker," moreover, Reagan took on a virtually 'round-the-clock regimen of public appearances that were an outstanding preparation for political campaigning. He sometimes appeared before as many as a dozen forums in a day, repeating his basic message, but modifying it extemporaneously.

His GE years led in 1960 to his official transfer of loyalties to the Republican party. After the GE connection ended, he became generally available as a speaker to conservative audiences. This extended to his impressive 1964 campaign performance, which in turn persuaded a group of conservative California businessmen to back his successful 1966 campaign for governor.

Reagan's Prepresidential Career as Politician

In short, although Reagan first ran for elective office at age fifty-five, his affinity for politics was long-standing. Moreover, he had already built and sharpened skills that were highly appropriate for winning office and for use in political persuasion once in office. His skills, it must be stressed, were not well-attuned to the detailed side of policy-making and analysis. As a rhetorician who preferred anecdote to analysis he could be sold on policies or even political strategies without exploring their implications. Moreover, his stock-in-trade was general issues, not specific policy proposals. A generic politician may be gifted but may nevertheless invent square wheels out of inexperience with the problems of public policy.

Reagan spent eight years as governor of a state which, if it were a country, would have the seventh-largest gross national product in the world. Close accounts by Lou Cannon and others of the Reagan governorship illustrate that although Reagan's political enzymes and experience on the mashed-potato lecture circuit helped him politically, they did not make him into an instant gubernatorial success. His first term, in particular, was replete with episodes revealing a facet of his political style — the extensive use of delegation — that has been at once a strength and a source of one of the most persistent criticisms of his leadership, whether in the State House or the White House.

Because as governor-elect Reagan knew little about details of government and initially chose poor advisers, he assumed office with a flawed understanding of such fundamentals as the status of the state's finances, the requirements of preparing a budget, and even of what positions he should take on legislative proposals that directly impinged on his core ideological values. Moreover, at first he worked poorly with the legislature. The reader should turn to Lou Cannon's *Reagan* and to the many sources he cites for an account of the evolution of Reagan's state leadership. Suffice it to say that at age fifty-five he was capable of learning to operate as an effective political professional. In doing so, he developed a style of operation that closely presaged his White House procedures.

This style included regular use of advanced polling technology geared to media presentations that were timed to serve his purposes, a readiness to communicate with adversaries and to keep ideological cleavage from extending to the personal level, but an overall tendency to act on his ideological principles when possible. He also acquired governmental savvy and, perhaps more important, learned how to identify loyal aides who could handle the aspects of leadership that either did not interest him or were not his strength. A number of the devoted, technically able veterans of his California staff — Edwin Meese III, Michael Deaver, and William Clark, for example — were to follow him to Washington.

During the early seventies, when the impediments to presidential leadership were again the standard theme in writings about the presidency and proposals to reform it, one common assertion was that modern presidential recruitment too rarely produced chief executives with previous comparable executive experience. The argument was that former legislators and vice-presidents (and presumably also one-term governors such as Jimmy Carter of states such as Georgia having archaic institutions and practices) were not as well suited for presidential leadership as the former New York governor (and assistant secretary of the Navy), Franklin Roosevelt, had been.

The ex-actor, ex-banquet speaker elected in 1980 had been governor for eight years. The duration and scope of his prepresidential experience as a state-level chief executive exceeded that of any other president. Still, he lacked exposure to federal-level issues and foreign policy. Moreover, neither he nor his aides had Washington experience. In this connection, it will be remembered that Richard Nixon's difficulties were in part a result of too much reliance on a "California mafia."

Nomination, Election, and Transition to Office

By the 1970s the American way of nominating presidents had evolved into an inordinately demanding and erratic enterprise. That decade saw a proliferation of state presidential primary elections and party caucuses running from the winter through the spring of the election year and making candidate selection a frenetic sequence of choices shaped by publicity, advertising, and campaigning in many highly diverse jurisdictions. What was always a decentralized nominating system became virtually atomized.

The system, as often is said, is best suited for the sort of would-be nominee who fits Reagan's status in 1976 — that of an unemployed millionaire. After completing his second term as governor in 1974, Reagan returned to public speaking, supplementing his current rendition of "The Speech" with accounts of how he had successfully employed conservative leadership practices in his two terms as California governor. Meanwhile, Richard Nixon's unelected successor was struggling to "put Watergate behind," working with deliberate speed to create his own administration. Ford was also seeking to rally from the plunge in public support that followed his pardon of Nixon and, saddled with a poorly performing economy, was preparing for the marathon nominating process that would consume the first half of 1976.

Ford's experience in 1976 was worlds apart from that of Harry Truman, the previous modern president to seek nomination despite low Gallup ratings. Indeed, Truman had far less backing among his party colleagues than Ford had with his. In 1948, Truman was quite easily nominated at the Democratic party convention. By 1976, however, conventions were little more than sites for satisfying the outcome of the previous half-year's gauntlet of state primaries and caucuses.

It was not difficult for Reagan the lecturer to begin seeking to become Reagan the presidential candidate, traversing the country to challenge his party's incumbent. Running against the conservative president, Reagan had to be a superconservative in 1976. He castigated the détente elements in the Ford-Kissinger foreign policy and opposed the Panama Canal sovereignty treaty on nationalistic grounds ("We bought it, we paid for it, it's ours, and we're going to keep it"). In addition, he raised the social issues dear to the fundamentalist right-wing movements that were gaining strength in the 1970s.

After a lackluster start, in which he was defeated by Ford in the initial New England primaries, Reagan carried North Carolina and a sufficient number of other conservative states, plus his own California, to remain in the race until the convention. Much like Reagan's first term as governor, his 1976 nominating campaign gave him on-the-job training. Moreover, it made him the most visible Republican after Ford and the discredited Nixon.

By 1978 Reagan was campaigning for the 1980 nomination. In the foundering Jimmy Carter he had a readier target than he had had in Ford. Prenomination surveys showed that Reagan was well ahead of the field in Republican party supporters' preferences for the 1980 Republican nomination, a field that included Ford. There was, however, a harbinger of the difficulties he would face during his presidency as the myth that the outcome of the 1980 election had been a mandate for his specific economic policies began to dissolve. Polls of the general electorate, however, found slightly more support for Ford than for Reagan against Carter. In short, Reagan was a party favorite, but his strong conservatism diminished his ability to appeal to the entire public.

In 1980, Reagan sought to temper his image as another Goldwater. Moreover, since he was running as the principal conservative in a field of less well known Republican moderates, he had the luxury of being able to moderate his conservative rhetoric, conducting . . . a trifocal campaign — one designed first to win the nomination, then to unify the party, and finally to put the party in a favorable position to win the general election.

After an initial gaffe in Iowa, where he refused to participate in a debate with the other candidates and seemed about to lose his lead to George Bush, Reagan's race was nearly flawless. In the early sequence of primaries he won decisively in New Hampshire; ran better than expected in Massachusetts; was an upset winner in Vermont; overwhelmingly carried the four southern states of South Carolina, Georgia, Florida, and Alabama; and, after decisively beating Anderson in the Illinois congressman's home state on March 18, was widely conceded to be the certain nominee, despite the twenty-five remaining primaries. By the time of the convention he was to win twenty-nine primaries, losing only six — all of them to Bush. Bush was his leading moderate contender, apart from Ford, who had run in no primaries but had made it known that he was available for a draft if the convention became deadlocked.

. . . Reagan's conciliatory rhetoric on accepting the Republican nomination in 1980 ("this convention has shown a party united, with positive programs for solving the nation's problems") [contrasts] with Goldwater's divisive acceptance speech of 1964 ("those who do not care for our cause, we don't expect to enter our ranks. . . ."). In contrast to other ideologues, Left as well as Right, Reagan, when pressed, has consistently put results over ideological purity. While he has used divisive rhetoric, he has shown a remarkable ability — aided by his winning personal style and a seeming lack of the burning anger that normally accompanies intense commitment to issues — to put conflicts behind him. A case in point: His abortive effort at the 1980 convention to arrange a Ford vice-presidency, followed by his offer of that position to Bush, suggested that he harbored no resentment of the latter's talk of "voodoo economics." As he had in Sacramento, Reagan acted on the old saw that in politics there come times when it is necessary to rise above principle and do what is right.

The 1980 Campaign and Election

No president has ever had lower Gallup Poll ratings than did Jimmy Carter. He was widely viewed as a good man who had no sense of direction and who consequently was responsible for what, by Election Day 1980, was the least satisfactorily performing national economy since the Great Depression. If the Iranian hostage crisis had not produced a temporary surge of patriotic support for Carter and given him an excuse not to debate Edward Kennedy, he might readily have been the first twentieth-century incumbent to be denied renomination.

With a unified Republican party behind him and [John] Anderson's third-party candidacy threatening Carter's support, Reagan might well have expected a landslide victory. Carter's weak appeal and the foundering economy put him in a league with Herbert Hoover as a highly vulnerable incumbent. Reagan had softened, if not obliterated, the divisively conservative themes in his appeal; he had gone to great lengths to reach ethnic and blue-collar members of the Democratic constituency; and all indicators suggested that as a television debater he had been more persuasive than Carter.

Nevertheless, the election was widely viewed as a toss-up. Carter's unpopularity was clear, as was the powerful sense that the economy demanded new guidance. Yet, even watered down, Reagan's rhetoric and the baggage of his past commitments aroused fears that he might precipitate World War III or eliminate basic welfare benefits such as social security. Some voters were also skeptical of electing a septuagenarian president, and others presumably took into account Reagan's penchant for factual gaffes. In no other election on which survey data are available have more Americans indicated that they were unenthusiastic about both major party candidates.

In the event, a Reagan victory that encompassed more than 90 percent of the electoral vote and carried with it the first Republican control of the Senate since 1954 and a thirty-three-seat Republican surge in the House *looked* like a landslide. Reagan's aides inevitably treated the outcome as a mandate for his specific policy proposals, and, with far less justification, much of the press and many members of Congress accepted this reading of the election results. In fact, conservatism was at best a minor determinant of Reagan's election. The 1980 outcome was more a rejection of Carter than a demonstration of popular enthusiasm for Reagan or his policies. . . .

Reagan's 51 percent of the three-way vote in 1980 represented a mere 2 percent increase over Ford's 1976 Republican tally. It is true that when

Anderson, who clearly denied Carter victory in states such as Massachusetts and thus contributed to the landslide impression of the electoral college outcome, is excluded, Reagan did receive 55 percent of the two-party vote, but he won against a president whose stewardship of the economy had been discredited. The increases in Republican congressional strength that proved an absolute necessity in carrying through the 1981 legislative strategies were far from evidence of a conservative surge. Surveys generally showed little change between 1980 and earlier years in public approval of existing government spending levels and other issues that were part of the Reagan platform and taken by him to be elements of his mandate. The increase of 8 percent in House seats resulted from an increase of only 3 percent (from 50.6 percent to 53.5 percent) in votes for Republican House candidates, scarcely a Republican surge. Although the Republicans gained twelve seats in the Senate, they did so well in large part because more Democrats than Republicans were up for reelection: in twenty-four of the thirty-four Senate elections, Democratic incumbents were running. Overall, fewer votes were cast for Republican than Democratic senators.

From Election to Inauguration: Strategic Consolidation

Reagan not only seized the nomination, unified the party, and won the election, but he also, in the common parlance, landed on his feet. In offering the vice-presidency first to Ford and then to Bush, he demonstrated his ecumenical commitment to include Republican moderates in his administration. Then, with remarkable speed, he and his chief aides began putting together the strategy for carrying out what [journalists Rowland] Evans[, Jr.,] and [Robert] Novak have only slightly hyperbolically called *The Reagan Revolution.* Between the election and Inauguration Day, Reagan's forces prepared a package of domestic and economic policy proposals, and a strategy for rapidly enacting them, with a degree of technical skill that was to make the president's first year in office seem like a deliberate inversion of the standard catalogue of explanations of stalemated presidential leadership. That is, he was effective in legislative liaison, shaping the political agenda, and many of the other aspects of presidential politics that his immediate predecessors had not handled with favorable results. In effect, he set the stage for what two former Carter administration officials have concluded was needed for the presidency in the 1980s and what they realized their former boss had lacked—"a strategic approach to domestic affairs."

Reagan promptly assembled a staff that was both congenial to him and Washington-wise. At its core, taking a central part in shaping the substance of and enactment strategy for the 1981 budget and tax cuts was the famous triumvirate of Meese, Deaver, and Baker. Edwin Meese and Michael Deaver, both Californians, know intimately the Reagan operating style. Meese is the man Reagan's conservative backers believe to be most ideologically "pure." Within the White House, he is the specialist in staff organization and in reducing issues to options for presidential choice. Deaver is nominally the scheduling aide, but more fundamentally serves as the personal friend and confidant of the president and the first lady. Reagan, however, did not content himself with employing Californians at the nerve center of his presidency. He appointed a skilled, effective Washington operator, George Bush's former chief of staff, James Baker III, to head the strategic effort of moving Reagan's principles through the Washington policymaking labyrinth.

In a similar matching of a long-time, California-based Reagan loyalist with an experienced Washington aide, the president appointed Lynn Nofziger, a veteran of all of his electoral campaigns, to the White House office specializing in grass-roots politicking. Nofziger's job was to influence legislators via their constituents, coordinating his efforts with direct appeals to the Hill by experienced Ford White House lobbyist Max Friedersdorf. The Nofziger-Friedersdorf combination was ideally suited for simultaneous persuasion of legislators in Washington and through their districts.

Reagan's appointment of Congressman David Stockman to head the Office of Management and Budget was critical for both the detailed domestic and economic policies and the operations of the new administration. A virtual Talmudic scholar of the federal budget, Stockman was relentless in identifying targets for cutting expenditures. His knowledge of budget minutiae and his ability to synthesize diverse economic projections of the consequences of cuts in spending and taxes was equaled by his appreciation for the possibilities of using congressional rules innovatively in the enactment of policy. Only a shrewd strategist of the current Congress could have conceived the plan to achieve expenditure cuts by employing the reconciliation provisions of the congressional budgeting procedures instituted in the wake of Watergate, thus permitting a single vote on an omnibus bill that had the effect of reducing or eliminating programs that inevitably would have survived had members of Congress been forced to vote on them singly.

In the transition period, Reagan assiduously built cordial relations with congressional leaders. The cooperation of Howard Baker, the first Republican Senate majority leader since William Knowland in 1954, was vital to the strategy of initiating legislation in the Republican-controlled Senate and then winning its passage by forming a coalition of Republicans and southern Democrats in the House. But Reagan was broadly conciliatory to both parties and all factions in Congress, perhaps signaling his awareness that he would eventually have to play conventional, bipartisan, coalition politics to get legislative results.

We now know that Reagan's aides served him less well on substance than on procedure. It may be that the president entertained fewer doubts than did his advisers about the feasibility, and even the technical adequacy, of the analyses used to justify the first year's economic and social programs. In foreign policy, Reagan's appointments were fated to produce . . . extraordinarily fractious first-year intramural conflicts. . . . Nevertheless, except for the foreign policy shambles, the administration took office displaying skill and team work that exceeded anything Washington had experienced in the previous decade. Moreover, just as there was seeming consensus among the president's policy advisers, there was a widespread sense of acceptance by other public figures of Reagan's claims that his election had been the result of strong public support for the specific details of his program.

Far more than most political observers would have imagined just after Reagan's election, or even at the time of his inauguration, the president and his associates entered office prepared to cut through the thicket that normally prevents the president from exercising substantial influence on Capitol Hill. The organizational and conceptual preparation of the Reagan forces for conducting foreign policy was not at all promising, however. And even in the case of the domestic and economic programs, which were based more on doctrinal reasoning than on experience, there was danger of the kind of boomeranging policy against which the incrementalists warn. By the same token, daring policy departures might just prove to be the necessary medicine for a profoundly ailing economy. In short, the Reagan administration took office with the potential, for better or worse, of making a unique contribution to American politics and policy. . . .

Reagan in Office

GARRY WILLS

Ronald Reagan, the actor who took up politics in his mid-fifties, confounded expectation in California, where he retained the voters' esteem through two terms as governor. This distinguished him from both his predecessor and his successor, each of whom had been seasoned in California politics — Brown senior by training, Brown junior by birth and domestic influence. But Reagan's success in California was a minor feat by comparison with his sustained popularity as President. He entered the White House when the completion of a second term had come to seem a disappearing art. [Richard] Nixon had fallen from the office, after [Lyndon] Johnson fled it. [Gerald] Ford could not be renominated, nor [Jimmy] Carter reelected. The presidency was being called an impossible assignment, just when Reagan came along and treated it as a part-time job — with the public's hearty approval.

This performance rested on the paradox of Reagan's accessible yet legendary status, similar to [Dwight] Eisenhower's — the unintimidating Everyman as hero. But it had more specifically traceable causes as well. One cause was Reagan's shrewd concentration on *domestic* policy. That is the meat and potatoes of our politics, the thing on which most elections hinge. Yet modern Presidents forget or suppress this basic information. There is not only more immediate glamour, but a greater sense of control, when a President deals with foreign powers than when he tries to placate blocs of the American electorate. Ceremony itself seems more substantial at state dinners for foreign rulers than at a reception for high school teachers.

Recent Presidents have immersed themselves in foreign policy, so thoroughly that at last they could not resurface. President Nixon had the patience and determination to thread a devious course toward China, plotting its every turn in long sessions with Henry Kissinger. Welfare reform, by comparison, bored him, and he let it take a shape at odds with his own campaign promises, untroubled by the discrepancies. When it came to tricky planning on the domestic front, he called on the expertise of Tony Ulasewicz. Mao demanded a Kissinger. For Daniel Ellsberg, a Colson would do. Nixon dismissed his own country's internal affairs as "building outhouses in Peoria."

John Kennedy aspired to office with a misconception that it made him "Commander in Chief" of all the American people. He was so fascinated by international relations that he devoted all of his famous inaugural address to the subject, omitting domestic matters entirely. President Carter went to the Oval Office with dreams similar in scale if more pacific in content. He hoped to create an entirely new policy toward Third World countries and the USSR. At first he staked his reelection hopes on a treaty in the Middle East. Then he relied on the first surge of support for him when American hostages were taken by Iran — only to become a hostage to that crisis himself.

The President is blessed with a power that can turn overnight into a curse: the power to change Air Force One from pumpkin to hero's chariot just by taking off from Andrew's Air Force Base on the way to some foreign capital. When Nixon could not land his great plane at civilian airports in America without heckling from demonstrators, he was still given a hero's welcome in Tel Aviv. It has been the desperate ruler's resort, since before the time of Shakespeare's Bolingbroke, "to busy giddy minds/With foreign quarrels." American Presidents have even entertained the softer hope that *composing* foreign quarrels, instead of stirring them up, can distract voters from a humdrum reality like the price of bread. But election results offer little support for that hope. Entirely aside from the Iranian crisis, Carter's chances for reelection were sealed when he entered the election year with an inflation rate running to two digits. That is tantamount to resignation.

It would have been easy and natural for Reagan to compensate for his inexperience in dealing with (or even seeing) other nations by foreign-policy activism. His anti-Communist rhetoric over the years led in that direction, and so did the cries of immediate peril over SALT [Strategic Arms Limitation Talks] provisions, Russian advances, allied disorder. Yet all the feverish rhetoric did not produce a hyperkinetic first few months in office, like Kennedy's attempt to forge a "first hundred days" of foreign victories comparable to FDR's domestic onslaught. Reagan was in no hurry to deal with unfamiliar parts of the world. More to the point, he retained a performer's feel for his audience. He knows you cannot leave an audience, to go off and study the arcana of diplomacy, and expect to have it waiting for you when you finish.

His first rule is not to lose the crowd—you may never get it back. The electorate does not follow missile counts day by day, but it knows how much it pays for groceries. Reagan's first concern, therefore, remained "the free market system" at home. The grain embargo was hurting the Soviets—which was, for Reagan, a strong argument in its favor. It was also hurting American farmers—which was a fatal consideration. Lifting the embargo was the first decisive thing Reagan did in foreign policy, because he was looking to its domestic effect.

Reagan not only steered clear of the temptation to huddle with fellow princes, he defied another maxim dear to modern presidents—that one must do the hard but necessary things during one's first year in office, a year of honeymoon and bated opposition, before opponents rally with accumulating grudges. The immediate problem to be addressed can be foreign or domestic. In 1916, 1940, and 1964 Presidents who had just taken office or returned to it by promising to keep America out of war felt they had to begin preparing the nation for war. Carter bit the bullet on Panama. Nixon began the difficult process of achieving détente with China and Russia. On the domestic front, Roosevelt tried to pack the Supreme Court right after his 1936 reelection. Johnson used the penitent mood of the nation after his predecessor's assassination to push through a civil rights bill that had been stiffly resisted while Kennedy lived.

Reagan disregarded all this accumulated wisdom about investing political capital at once in order to draw dividends of popularity when they are needed down the road. His was a politics of immediate, not deferred, gratification. The compelling task he set himself in his first year was a large tax cut, something for which there is always a certain popular support, whatever the misgivings expressed by keepers of the nation's books. Jimmy Carter had a core to his political beliefs—the need to seek human rights in a peaceful way with the Soviet Union and in the Third World. He tried to accomplish the difficult preliminaries of this task in his first year. If Reagan had felt a similar commitment to the difficult parts of his moral program—e.g., to the social agenda of the New Right calling for prayer in schools, an end to abortion, and suppression of pornography—he might have spent his early days of popularity working for them. But he made his first assignment the inflation that had plagued Carter. To counter that in a *popular* way meant not only consciously putting off any pledges of return to an older morality—more dangerously, in the eyes of some White House advisers, it meant letting foreign matters wait on domestic.

The first indication of Reagan's priorities was the grain embargo. President Carter had imposed it in response to the Soviets' invasion of Afghanistan. It had severe effects on the Russian economy, primarily by cutting back feed for livestock. Yet Reagan lifted it at a time when Soviet armed forces seemed poised to invade Poland during the height of the Solidarity campaign. The new President's Secretary of State argued that the embargo must be retained, for a while at least, as a bargaining point in that crisis. Instead, new grain contracts were written with promises not to reimpose the embargo—a matter that led to some recrimination when Poland, under Soviet pressure, imposed martial law. Not only were the grain contracts now untouchable; their status gave Europeans an excuse to resist other sanctions suggested by America—steps like shutting down work on the Russians' oil pipeline to Europe.

There were other early signs that Reagan's heart was in domestic affairs rather than foreign. Much of his campaign had been based on the "window of vulnerability," supposed to be opening even as he came into office. The remedy he had campaigned on was a movable MX-missile plan developed and promoted during the Carter administration. But this ran into domestic opposition in a region where Reagan was especially strong, the Southwest. Reagan had already placated this group by the appointment of James Watt, a symbol and spokesman for the "sagebrush rebellion," as his Secretary of the Interior. A movable MX would not only require federal control of huge tracts of the Southwest; it would affect the "water politics" in states most dependent on that precious commodity. Reagan instructed his Secretary of Defense to find another "basing mode" for the MX—which began the slide of that missile into a token program, drastically cut back, one housed in the very silos Reagan had called vulnerable.

Moves like these convinced Reagan's hard-line followers that he had come to preside over an edgier détente, not to end the era of negotiation; that he would use brisker rhetoric while completing some of the things Kissinger had begun. For true believers, Reagan was repeating the defection of Eisenhower, who gave the New Deal its first Republican sanction rather than dismantling it. Their fears seemed confirmed when the limits of the unratified SALT II were observed throughout Reagan's first term, despite his attacks on that "fatally flawed" treaty in the campaign. Relations with the People's Republic of China were continued, though he had attacked Carter for establishing them. Arms control talks were continued, though Reagan had never approved a single arms treaty in the past and his own favored experts shared his view that the Russians cannot be trusted to observe any international agreements. All this was less a surrender of Reagan's campaign positions than a refusal to deal with foreign matters energetically while domestic politics absorbed his time and energies.

The President did not keep his thoughts at home for lack of strong pressures toward activism abroad. The most clamorous demands came from Alexander Haig, appointed in part to placate the Kissinger faction in the party, and resented by cold warriors for that reason. Yet by 1986 Kissinger himself had been cultivating the Reagan camp for some time, backing away from the negotiatory flexibility Reagan criticized in the 1976 campaign. Kissinger distinguished his own form of détente from what he ridiculed as Jimmy Carter's weakness, and called for a show of strength. In April of election year 1980 he was telling the American Society of Newspaper Editors that "somewhere, somehow, the United States must show that it is capable of rewarding a friend or penalizing an opponent."

Haig, fresh from the attempt to mount his own presidential campaign, shared Kissinger's sense that détente could only be revived in conjunction with a bellicose stance; Nixon, after all, had achieved détente on some issues while (and partly because) he was continuing the Vietnam war. And Haig thought he was in a position to use his old mentor's bureaucratic maneuvers to continue his policies. But the balancing act that urges forward tough and conciliatory lines in conjunction can only be performed by one who maintains control of all the "signals" being sent in apparently opposite directions. Kissinger could concentrate decision-making powers in his office at the National Security Council (cutting the Secretaries of State and Defense out of the action) because his President was using him for that purpose. Haig made the mistake of thinking Ronald Reagan would allow a similar concentration, not because Reagan had a Nixonlike devotion to foreign policy, but out of his very inexperience. The whole Haig period in the Reagan administration looks like a dogged attempt to keep performing Hamlet's lines though everyone else was playing *Measure for Measure.*

Kissinger had staged, by inauguration day, a reorganization of the NSC that his critics called a bureaucratic coup d'etat. Haig tried to enact the same revolution-by-memorandum on January 20, 1980. The 1968 "NSDM 2" document drew all lines of policy together under one man at the NSC; Haig's "NSDD 1" ran them to the Secretary's office at the State Department. Reagan was not Nixon, and men close to the President still feared Haig's presidential dreams. Some of these men wanted to run foreign affairs themselves (Richard Allen, for instance, in Kissinger's old office at the NSC). Others did not want them run at all, at least for a while — until the economic program could be passed. The result was that for most of Reagan's first term no one really ran foreign policy. And President Reagan barely noticed the omission. He was not even talking to Haig. Secretary of Defense Caspar Weinberger was buying arms from all directions and discouraging their use in any sector. Eugene Rostow was talking about START [Strategic Arms Reduction Talks] negotiations in order to stop all prior negotiations. Senator Helms was monitoring U.S. embassies. Reagan, so different from Nixon, was not himself the Secretary of State — and neither was anyone else.

At first Haig thought he could personify the recovery from Carter's paralysis. He quotes wistfully Senator Paul Tsongas's words at his confirmation: "You are going to dominate this administration." Despite his own disclaimers, Haig agreed. He made it to the cover of newsweeklies as rapidly as Kissinger had. Haig even thought he had his own Vietnam to run, but with a big advantage: it was a miniature replay of that struggle, winnable, to be executed on our terms and on our turf. Kissinger said it was time to win one somewhere, and Haig thought he knew where — El Salvador. In his rare private meetings with Reagan he repeated, "Mr. President, this is one you can win." Haig thought of El Salvador as a "good" Vietnam, one where all the advantages lay with America. Now it was the Communists who had a long and difficult supply line. Their arms came, according to Haig, through Cuba, no longer down a misnamed Ho Chi Minh "trail" which was actually a huge sponge of forest trickling men and arms through numerous pores and capillaries. Haig thought that aid to government troops in El Salvador would make them prevail as soon as we cut off the rebels' support by threatening to "go to its source" in our own backyard, Cuba.

He found surprisingly few allies in the Reagan administration, despite all the anti-Communist appeal of his little war, and despite a shared resolve to reverse Carter's "human rights" approach to Latin America:

> Some advisers, especially his [Reagan's] highest aides, counseled against diluting the impact of his domestic program with a foreign undertaking that would generate tremendous background noise in the press and in Congress. The Secretary of Defense [Weinberger] genuinely feared the creation of another unmanageable tropical war. . . . The Joint Chiefs of Staff, chastened by the experience of Vietnam, in which our troops performed with admirable success but were declared to have been defeated, and by the steady decline of respect for the military and of military budgets in the post-Vietnam period, resisted a major commitment.

When the Reagan administration finally found a war small enough to win, it would be in Grenada. America's invasion would be partly justified there on the grounds that so small an island should not have so large an airport.

Even Jeane Kirkpatrick, who was identified with tough Central American policies in many minds, became at first a rival and then a bitter foe of Haig. The two were equally touchy about White House slights, but instead of making an ally of her, Haig (following Kissinger's loner policy) emphasized the irrelevancy of a mere UN Ambassador's role to the formation of policy in the State Department. She, in turn, thought Haig had borrowed her views and then made a mess of them by his bungling procedures.

Kirkpatrick was widely credited with the distinction between "authoritarian" and "totalitarian" governments as a touchstone for American policy. The former are said to be personal in their despotism, corrupt but of limited effect throughout the society, while the latter are programmatic, reaching into the lives and thoughts of every subject. Actually, in her overpraised *Commentary* article on this matter, she had discussed "traditional versus revolutionary autocracies." That was her twist of language on the contrast between authoritarian and totalitarian governments, which is a rather obvious one. It had become popular in neoconservative circles well before her article appeared in November of 1979; Ernest Lefever, who led the administration's first assault on Carter's human rights policy, had put it in the customary language for the Heritage Foundation over a year before Kirkpatrick's article appeared: "In terms of political rights, moral freedom and cultural vitality, there is a profound difference between authoritarian and totalitarian regimes." So Haig was not specifically stealing from Kirkpatrick when he told the Trilateral Commission, shortly after the inauguration, that

> the totalitarian model unfortunately draws upon the resources of modern technology to impose its will on all aspects of a citizen's behavior. . . . [But] the authoritarian regime . . . customarily reserves for itself absolute authority in only a few politically sensitive areas.

Mrs. Kirkpatrick was called the discoverer of this doctrine since her article was one of the few citable works on foreign policy that Reagan had actually read (at the suggestion of Richard Allen).

According to Kirkpatrick, traditional dictatorships are not as onerous as Communist regimes because "maintaining a culture requires less repression than does the effort to radically alter it by administrative decision." On this basis, the Reagan administration supported "constructive engagement" with the government of South Africa—though it was hard to imagine a regime more intrusive into the daily life, marriage, employment, and residence of subjects than the Botha regime with its passbook system. And in time Reagan had to adopt a program of mild sanctions toward South Africa in order to prevent Congress from acting even more harshly. President Carter was attacked by Kirkpatrick for "destabilizing" the regimes of autocratic friends like Somoza of Nicaragua and the Shah of Iran. Yet spontaneous anger of the rulers' own population forced Reagan to withdraw his early support for Jean-Claude Duvalier in Haiti and Ferdinand Marcos in the Philippines— though Kirkpatrick was speaking for both governments to the very end, as she had comforted the generals in Argentina during the Falklands war.

Kirkpatrick's is the classical theme of European conservatism—that maintaining "traditional culture and roles" is less disruptive of ordinary life than ambitious efforts to reform society as well as the state. Yet there is often popular support for such reform efforts, even if they involve hardship and a self-imposed discipline. Example after example of this has presented itself to Americans in the anticolonial movement that swept the globe after World War II. American observers like Kirkpatrick saw all this activity in the "so-called Third World" as an epiphenomenon to Soviet aggression. South Africa was supported on the grounds that black rulers who came to power during anticolonial wars led regimes more intrusive into the lives of ordinary people than had the colonial administrators. The charge is quite true, since colonial rulers did not want to disturb the goose unduly, just take the golden egg from it. Determination to prevent that has led people after people to submit to rigors enforced by their own kind rather than be harvested seasonally by foreigners.

There is nothing surprising or new in the voluntary submission to dictators of a people's choice—even Hitler, Mrs. Kirkpatrick's model of a totalitarian ruler in her first treatment of the theme, was democratically elected. Many less despicable governments have been popularly sustained despite repression of large segments of the population—Andrew Jackson's America, for instance, despite its treatment of black slaves and the "savage" native Americans. Fidel Castro has been more popular with Cubans over the span of his reign than was Fulgencio Batista. One may say this "should" not have been; indeed, Henry Kissinger *did* say that of Chile, where he thought citizens had no right to choose against their own interests, as Kissinger read those interests for them, by voting Communist. But it is hard to distinguish the denial of a people's right to rule themselves, even badly, from any other denials of freedom, especially when the denial is imposed by a foreigner.

In any case, Reagan had to back off from his support for "authoritarian" regimes in Argentina, South Africa, Haiti, and the Philippines. But he did this gracefully, with his gift for declaring setbacks victories. In fact, he tried to use these "democratic" victories as endorsements of his administration, and even drew a parallel he had at first denied. He came into office supporting Marcos because he was authoritarian, and therefore different from Daniel Ortega in Nicaragua, whose regime Reagan was trying to overthrow by aiding the contras. After the fall of Marcos, former supporters of Kirkpatrick like Reagan's communications director Patrick Buchanan said that aid to contras in Nicaragua would be an equivalent to, or continuation of, the democratic "revolution" (actually an election) that had brought down Marcos. Overnight an authoritarian regime had become just like a totalitarian one.

Carter had been mocked as irresolute and wavering in his attitude toward other nations. Yet his positions were not nearly as mutable as Reagan's, who reversed himself on relations with the People's Republic of China, on the European pipeline, on keeping Marines in Lebanon, on holding a summit without an agenda, on swift reprisals against all terrorists, on visiting a death camp in Germany, as well as on sanctions for South Africa and support for Duvalier and Marcos. Yet, far from hurting himself by these reversals, Reagan usually benefited by them, since the original position was often ill-considered. But the astonishing thing was that he was perceived as following a consistent (strong) course through all the zigs and zags. This came in largest part from Reagan's easy way of avoiding accountability for mere facts, for accuracy or consistency. But it also came in some measure from his refusal to become obsessed — or even involved — with the niceties of foreign politics. Secretary Haig was expressing personal grievance when he wrote, "The necessity of speaking with one voice on foreign policy . . . simply never took hold among Reagan's advisers." But many observers with no sympathy for Haig came to the same conclusion during Reagan's first term.

When George Shultz finally established his authority as Haig's successor, he avoided his predecessor's worst personal clashes, the disputes over turf that had doomed the imperious Haig, even as he continued the policies Haig had tried to establish — a retaliatory attitude toward Communist terrorists in Central America and elsewhere, combined with a search for arms control and stable relations with the Soviets. But where Haig's form of détente ran into personal problems with the Arms Control and Disarmament Commission, Shultz found the President's Strategic Defense Initiative blocking all approaches to a treaty; and on retaliation he found Caspar Weinberger as little disposed to send troops for the Shultz State Department as for the Haig one. There were no longer five or six foreign policies, as in the first years of the Reagan administration — more like two or three. But the public tended not to notice this because their President, so close to them in his continuing addresses and ceremonial appearances, did not notice either. He knew that the public mind is not disposed toward foreign quarrels unless it has been kindled to it by a President trying to show off his prowess among other leaders.

Reagan's very provincialism formed a bond with his fellow citizens and a bastion for his office. He had traveled little in other countries before taking office, and he was not going to acquire that taste. Reagan went late and reluctantly to his first summit with a Soviet leader (in the final year of his first term), all the while playing down the meeting's significance, denying it would address substantive issues. (Early in his term, he had made such issues the requirement for a summit, in order to avoid holding one.) When Reagan had to be abroad, he addressed domestic issues even in a foreign land. A trip to Canada became a "Shamrock Summit," played—like his visit to "the ancestral home" in Ireland itself—for American voters. His address at the Normandy beaches provided some of the choicest footage in his 1984 campaign film, as did his worship at a religious service with GIs in South Korea. Even the troubles of his Bitburg visit [to a German cemetery where Nazis were among those buried] arose from an initial attempt to find an analogue for Arlington Cemetery abroad and to avoid touchy political issues. Other Presidents experienced an influx of power as they moved farther off from American shores, but President Reagan just felt the distance widening between him and his audience. His instinct proved as useful as it is unusual. Others felt fully "the President" only when away from home. He never really left home.

Document

Report of the President's Special Review Board

JOHN TOWER, EDMUND MUSKIE, AND BRENT SCOWCROFT

B. FAILURE OF RESPONSIBILITY

The NSC system will not work unless the President makes it work. After all, this system was created to serve the President of the United States in ways of his choosing. By his actions, by his leadership, the President therefore determines the quality of its performance.

By his own account, as evidenced in his diary notes, and as conveyed to the Board by his principal advisors, President Reagan was deeply committed to securing the release of the hostages. It was this intense compassion for the hostages that appeared to motivate his steadfast support of the Iran initiative, even in the face of opposition from his Secretaries of State and Defense.

In his obvious commitment, the President appears to have proceeded with a concept of the initiative that was not accurately reflected in the reality of the operation. The President did not seem to be aware of the way in which

From the *Report of the President's Special Review Board,* February 26, 1987.

the operation was implemented and the full consequences of U.S. participation.

The President's expressed concern for the safety of both the hostages and the Iranians who could have been at risk may have been conveyed in a manner so as to inhibit the full functioning of the system.

The President's management style is to put the principal responsibility for policy review and implementation on the shoulders of his advisors. Nevertheless, with such a complex, high-risk operation and so much at stake, the President should have ensured that the NSC system did not fail him. He did not force his policy to undergo the most critical review of which the NSC participants and the process were capable. At no time did he insist upon accountability and performance review. Had the President chosen to drive the NSC system, the outcome could well have been different. As it was, the most powerful features of the NSC system—providing comprehensive analysis, alternatives and follow-up—were not utilized.

The Board found a strong consensus among NSC participants that the President's priority in the Iran initiative was the release of U.S. hostages. But setting priorities is not enough when it comes to sensitive and risky initiatives that directly affect U.S. national security. He must ensure that the content and tactics of an initiative match his priorities and objectives. He must insist upon accountability. For it is the President who must take responsibility for the NSC system and deal with the consequences.

Beyond the President, the other NSC principals and the National Security Advisor must share in the responsibility for the NSC system.

President Reagan's personal management style places an especially heavy responsibility on his key advisors. Knowing his style, they should have been particularly mindful of the need for special attention to the manner in which this arms sale initiative developed and proceeded. On this score, neither the National Security Advisor nor the other NSC principals deserve high marks.

It is their obligation as members and advisors to the Council to ensure that the President is adequately served. The principal subordinates to the President must not be deterred from urging the President not to proceed on a highly questionable course of action even in the face of his strong conviction to the contrary.

In the case of the Iran initiative, the NSC process did not fail, it simply was largely ignored. The National Security Advisor and the NSC principals all had a duty to raise this issue and insist that orderly process be imposed. None of them did so.

All had the opportunity. While the National Security Advisor had the responsibility to see that an orderly process was observed, his failure to do so does not excuse the other NSC principals. It does not appear that any of the NSC principals called for more frequent consideration of the Iran initiative by the NSC principals in the presence of the President. None of the principals called for a serious vetting of the initiative by even a restricted group of disinterested individuals. The intelligence questions do not appear to have been raised, and legal considerations, while raised, were not pressed. No one seemed to have complained about the informality of the process. No one called for a thorough reexamination once the initiative did not meet expectations or the manner of execution changed. While one or another of the NSC principals suspected that something was amiss, none vigorously pursued the issue. . . .

fifteen

THE ECONOMY TODAY

In the late 1970s and early 1980s, the American economy faltered. Inflation, a problem ever since the Vietnam War, gave way to a recession that was just lifting when Jimmy Carter took office in 1977. His effort to pursue an expansionary policy led to mounting deficits, increases in the money supply, and double-digit inflation that moved out of control. Compounding the difficulties was the mounting energy crisis. A source of concern ever since the Arab world began increasing oil prices in 1973, it created problems that could not wait and fostered a sense of urgency in the nation's quest for stability in economic affairs.

Commentators differed in their reactions to American problems. The selections in this section show contrasting assessments of the sources of difficulties and conflicting prescriptions for what should be done.

On the left, economist Lester C. Thurow is one of the most able proponents of the need for a major government effort to promote equity among citizens as hard decisions about the economic future are made. In this selection, taken from *The Zero-Sum Society,* Thurow argues that any decisions about resource allocation create winners and losers, and it is necessary to recognize who will be hurt, for they can stop progress toward common goals.

George Gilder, a spokesman on the right, disagrees with Thurow's contention that careful regulation is necessary to assure economic growth. An influential economic and social analyst, Gilder suggests that regulation squelches creativity and undermines initiative, thereby causing stagnation for the entire society. *Wealth and Poverty,* from which this selection is taken, helped shape the thinking of the Reagan administration, as it argued for the need to ease restraints, encourage investment, and in that way support rich and poor alike.

The document in this section provides a counterpoint to the selections that precede it. It comes from the opening of Michael Harrington's *The New American Poverty.* An articulate author, speaker, and political activist, Harrington made a major contribution with an earlier book, *The Other America,* published in 1962, which helped spark the war on poverty in the next few years. Now Harrington contends that we have a new class of poor to care for, and he makes a plea for those Gilder would leave to the devices of a free and unfettered economy.

The books by Thurow, Gilder, and Harrington provide the best introduction to the current debate over the course of the American economy. To pursue the issues raised further, the next step is to go to the books themselves, consider the full treatment by each author, and then turn to the specific sources used in each account. All of the authors write in the popular press as well, and their arguments can be followed in contemporary magazines and journals. For a good overview, by the former Director of Management and Budget, of how the Reagan administration attempted to deal with economic issues, see David A. Stockman, *The Triumph of Politics: Why the Reagan Revolution Failed* (1986).

The Zero-Sum Society

LESTER C. THUROW

After decades of believing in their economic invulnerability, Americans were jolted by the 1973–74 Arab oil embargo. The actions of a few desert sheiks could make *them* line up at the gas pump and substantially reduce *their* standard of living. Sudden economic vulnerability is disconcerting, just as that first small heart attack is disconcerting. It reminds us that our economy can be eclipsed.

When the shutdown of a major oil exporter for just a few months in 1979 once again resulted in the convulsions of gas lines, it was possible to ask whether that first mild heart attack was not the harbinger of something worse. Seemingly unsolvable problems were emerging everywhere—inflation, unemployment, slow growth, environmental decay, irreconcilable group demands, and complex, cumbersome regulations. Were the problems unsolvable or were our leaders incompetent? Had Americans lost the work ethic? Had we stopped inventing new processes and products? Should we invest more and consume less? Do we need to junk our social welfare, health, safety, and environmental protection systems in order to compete? Why were others doing better?

Where the U.S. economy had once generated the world's highest standard of living, it was now well down the list and slipping farther each year. Leaving the rich Middle East sheikdoms aside, we stood fifth among the nations of the world in per capita GNP in 1978, having been surpassed by Switzerland, Denmark, West Germany, and Sweden. Switzerland, which stood first, actually had a per capita GNP 45 percent larger than ours. And on the outside, the world's fastest economic runner, Japan, was advancing rapidly with a per capita GNP only 7 percent below ours. In our entire history we have never grown even half as rapidly as the Japanese.

While the slippage in our economic position was first noticed in the 1970s, our economic status was actually surpassed (after just half a century of delivering the world's highest standard of living) by Kuwait in the early 1950s. Kuwait was ignored, however, as a simple case of a country inheriting wealth (oil in the ground) rather than earning it. We failed to remember that our supremacy had also been based on a rich inheritance of vast mineral, energy, and climatic resources. No one inherited more wealth than we. We are not the little poor boy who worked his way to the top, but the little rich boy who inherited a vast fortune Perhaps we had now squandered that inheritance. Perhaps we could not survive without it. . . .

Up to now, we have comforted ourselves with the belief that the economic growth of others would slow down as soon as they had caught up with us. It was simply easier to adopt existing technologies than to develop new technologies—or so we told ourselves. But as other countries have approached our productivity levels, and as individual industries in these countries have begun to be more productive, the "catching-up" hypothesis becomes less and less persuasive.

In the period from 1972 to 1978, industrial productivity rose 1 percent per year in the United States, almost 4 percent in West Germany, and over 5 percent in Japan. These countries were introducing new products and improving the process of making old products faster than we were. Major American firms were reduced to marketing new consumer goods such as video recorders, which were made exclusively by the Japanese. In many industries, such as steel, we are now the ones with the "easy" task of adopting the technologies developed by others. But we don't. Instead of junking our old, obsolete open-hearth furnaces and shifting to the large oxygen furnaces and continuous casting of the Japanese, we retreat into protection against the "unfair" competition of Japanese steel companies. The result is a reduction in real incomes as we all pay more for steel than we should. As a result, our economy ends up with a weak steel industry that cannot compete and has no incentive to compete, given its protection in the U.S. market.

This relative economic decline has both economic and political impacts. Economically, Americans face a relative decline in their standard of living. How will the average American react when it becomes obvious to the casual tourist (foreigners here, Americans there) that our economy is falling behind? Since we have never had that experience, no one knows; but if we are like human beings in the rest of the world, we won't like it. No one likes seeing others able to afford things that they cannot.

As gaps in living standards grow, so does dissatisfaction with the performance of government and economy. The larger the income gap, the more revolutionary the demands for change. Today's poor countries are in turmoil, but it should be remembered that these countries are not poor compared with the poor centuries ago. They are only poor relative to what has been achieved in today's rich countries. If we become relatively poor, we are apt to be just as unhappy. . . .

UNSOLVABLE PROBLEMS

. . . [O]ur problems are not limited to slow growth. Throughout our society there are painful, persistent problems that are not being solved by our system of political economy. Energy, inflation, unemployment, environmental decay, ever-spreading waves of regulations, sharp income gaps between minorities and majorities—the list is almost endless. Because of our inability to solve these problems, the lament is often heard that the U.S. economy and political system have lost their ability to get things done. Meaningful compromises cannot be made, and the politics of confrontation are upon us like the plague. Programs that would improve the general welfare cannot be started because strong minorities veto them. No one has the ability to impose solutions, and no solutions command universal assent.

The problem is real, but it has not been properly diagnosed. One cannot lose an ability that one never had. What is perceived as a lost ability to act is in fact (1) a shift from international cold war problems to domestic problems, and (2) an inability to impose large economic losses explicitly.

As domestic problems rise in importance relative to international problems, action becomes increasingly difficult. International confrontations can be, and to some extent are, portrayed as situations where everyone is fairly sharing sacrifices to hold the foreign enemy in check. Since every member of society is facing a common threat, an overwhelming consensus and bipartisan approach can be achieved.

Domestic problems are much more contentious in the sense that when policies are adopted to solve domestic problems, there are *American* winners and *American* losers. Some incomes go up as a result of the solution; but others go down. Individuals do not sacrifice equally. Some gain; some lose. A program to raise the occupational position of women and minorities automatically lowers the occupational position of white men. Every black or female appointed to President Carter's cabinet is one less white male who can be appointed. . . .

A ZERO-SUM GAME

This is the heart of our fundamental problem. Our economic problems are solvable. For most of our problems there are several solutions. But all these solutions have the characteristic that someone must suffer large economic losses. No one wants to volunteer for this role, and we have a political process that is incapable of forcing anyone to shoulder this burden. Everyone wants someone else to suffer the necessary economic losses, and as a consequence none of the possible solutions can be adopted.

Basically we have created the world described in Robert Ardrey's *The Territorial Imperative.* To beat an animal of the same species on his home turf, the invader must be twice as strong as the defender. But no majority is twice as strong as the minority opposing it. Therefore we each veto the other's initiatives, but none of us has the ability to create successful initiatives ourselves.

Our political and economic structure simply isn't able to cope with an economy that has a substantial zero-sum element. A zero-sum game is any game where the losses exactly equal the winnings. All sporting events are zero-sum games. For every winner there is a loser, and winners can only exist if losers exist. What the winning gambler wins, the losing gambler must lose.

When there are large losses to be allocated, any economic decision has a large zero-sum element. The economic gains may exceed the economic losses, but the losses are so large as to negate a very substantial fraction of the gains. What is more important, the gains and losses are not allocated to the same individuals or groups. On average, society may be better off, but this average hides a large number of people who are much better off and large numbers of people who are much worse off. If you are among those who are worse off, the fact that someone else's income has risen by more than your income has fallen is of little comfort.

To protect our own income, we will fight to stop economic change from occurring or fight to prevent society from imposing the public policies that hurt us. From our perspective they are not good public policies even if they do result in a larger GNP. We want a solution to the problem, say the problem of energy, that does not reduce our income, but all solutions reduce someone's income. If the government chooses some policy option that does not lower our income, it will have made a supporter out of us, but it will have made an opponent out of someone else, since someone else will now have to shoulder the burden of large income reductions.

The problem with zero-sum games is that the essence of problem solving is loss allocation. But this is precisely what our political process is least capable of doing. When there are economic gains to be allocated, our political process can allocate them. When there are large economic losses to be allocated, our political process is paralyzed. And with political paralysis comes economic paralysis.

The importance of economic losers has also been magnified by a change in the political structure. In the past, political and economic power was distributed in such a way that substantial economic losses could be imposed on parts of the population if the establishment decided that it was in the general interest. Economic losses were allocated to particular powerless groups rather than spread across the population. These groups are no longer willing to accept losses and are able to raise substantially the costs for those who wish to impose losses upon them.

There are a number of reasons for this change. Vietnam and the subsequent political scandals clearly lessened the population's willingness to accept their nominal leader's judgments that some project was in their general interest. With the civil rights, poverty, black power, and women's liberation movements, many of the groups that have in the past absorbed economic losses have become militant. They are no longer willing to accept losses without a political fight. The success of their militancy and civil disobedience sets an example that spreads to other groups representing the environment, neighborhoods, and regions. . . .

PARALYSIS

At the end of the 1970s our political economy seems paralyzed. The economy is stagnant, with a high level of inflation and unemployment. Fundamental problems, such as the energy crisis, exist but cannot be solved. We have lost the ability to get things done. A successful man-on-the-moon project could be launched in the 1960s, but in the 1970s energy independence in beyond our reach.

Lacking a consensus on whose income ought to go down, or even the recognition that this is at the heart of the problem, we are paralyzed. We dislike the current situation, we wish to do something about our problems, but we endure them because we have not learned to play an economic game with a substantial zero-sum element.

But as in all boilers, when the steam rises it reaches a limit. Will the operator develop a good control valve that solves the necessary problems, or will the pressure, in time, become so intense that the lid blows off? Or have we simply reached the point where some future economic historian will say that our day in the economic sun has come to an end? . . .

SOLVING THE ECONOMIC PROBLEMS OF THE 1980s

When viewed together, the problems of the 1980s share both a common set of causes and a common set of cures. Energy, growth, and inflation are interrelated on many fronts. Without growing energy supplies, economic growth is difficult, and rapidly rising energy prices provide a powerful inflationary force. Inflation leads to public policies that produce idle capacity and severely retard growth.

To adjust to a rapidly changing pattern of energy supplies, the energy industry needs to be deregulated. But eliminating regulations, protection, and subsidies is also one of the essential ingredients in any successful program for stimulating economic growth. Because of its value elsewhere in the economy and because it involves the fewest net costs, the elimination of regulations, protection, and subsidies becomes the preferred route to controlling inflation. Upward price shocks are deliberately counterbalanced with planned downward price shocks.

Solving our energy and growth problems demand that government gets more heavily involved in the economy's major investment decisions. Massive investments in alternative energy sources will not occur without government involvement, and investment funds need to be more rapidly channeled from our sunset to sunrise industries. To compete we need the national equivalent of a corporate investment committee. Major investment decisions have become too important to be left to the private market alone, but a way must be found to incorporate private corporate planning into this process in a nonadversary way. Japan Inc. needs to be met with U.S.A. Inc.

A united front cannot be created, however, by simply trying to bulldoze energy, growth, and antiinflation policies down the throats of all those who would be hurt. The losers in this process may not be a majority of the population, but they are certainly large enough to prevent any such policy from being adopted.

A high-quality environment is important, and even if it were not, the time has come to admit that many people think that it is important. Unless we are to be permanently bogged down in fighting about the environment, goods and services simply have to be produced in ways that do not result in environmental deterioration. This means more expensive goods and services. Utility executives may not like stack scrubbers, but it is more important to get coal-fired power plants built than to argue about stack scrubbers. Resistance to those who demand reasonable environmental controls is silly since with a rising standard of living (and it is rising) more and more people are going to move into the economic classes that want a clean environment. Environmentalism is the wave of the future. As such, it makes much more sense for those who are interested in economic growth to reach an accommodation with it than to try to resist it.

If protection, regulations, and subsidies were eliminated, large numbers of individuals would suffer economic losses. If such a policy is ever to be adopted, we have to develop techniques for paying compensation to the individuals who are going to be hurt. Support for failing firms should be minimized, but support for individuals to help them move from sunset to sunrise industries should be generous. It should be generous for the simple reason that if it is not, we will not be able to adopt the policies that the country needs.

Economic growth also means that we must fully utilize the skills and talents of the economic minorities that are now kept out of the mainstream of economic activity. While our economy has survived for a very long time with large income gaps between blacks, Hispanics, American Indians, and women on one side, and white males on the other side, the world has changed and it is difficult to imagine that it can survive as well in the future. But even if it could, old levels of performance are no longer good enough. To reach the levels of productivity reached by others, we have to eliminate this divisive issue. It is not an issue that is going to fade away.

Similarly, we have to stand ready to prevent income gaps between the rich and the poor from increasing. The last twenty years have been marked by success on this dimension, but it will be more difficult to be successful in the next twenty years since we are entering a period of rapidly rising inequalities. Active government involvement in promoting economic growth will also make some Americans richer. We have to ensure that the bottom 60 percent of the population does not fall behind, for if we don't, we won't be able to adopt the growth policies that we need. This means that transfer payments will have to continue to grow for the poor and the elderly, and that our income tax system is going to have to be reformulated to keep the after-tax incomes of the second and third quintiles of our households rising in pace with the rest of the economy.

When one reviews what must be done — massive public investments, budget surpluses to generate more savings, large compensation systems, increases in income transfer payments, and tax cuts for the lower middle class — it is clear that one of the basic ingredients of future progress is a tax system that can raise substantial amounts of revenue fairly. If energy is to be deregulated and the massive income redistributions that are implicit in this policy attenuated, substantial amounts of revenue will be necessary. Some of this may come from taxes on energy — a large excise tax on gasoline consumption — but some of it will have to come from general revenue. If good compensatory systems are to be devised for those who make economic sacrifices in the interests of society, large amounts of general revenue will be necessary. If we are to increase income transfer payments and cut taxes on low-income families that are being squeezed by energy prices and growing inequalities in market earnings, fair taxes will have to be collected from the rest of the population.

At the moment, our tax system is so unfair that it simply isn't capable of doing what is demanded of it. We have to have a tax system that will be perceived as fair. Such a tax system would make it possible to raise the revenue that needs to be raised, but it would also make it possible to adopt the expenditure programs that need to be adopted. More public money for process R&D will make some individuals rich. There is nothing wrong with this if those rich individuals at the same time pay their fair share of taxes.

The need to construct a fair tax system simply emphasizes our primary need. Our society has reached a point where it must start to make explicit equity decisions if it is to advance. The implicit, undefended, unanalyzed equity decisions that have been built into our tax, expenditures, and regulatory policies of the past simply won't carry us into the future. To implement public policies in the future we are going to have to be able to decide when losers should suffer income losses and when losers should be compensated. We have to be able to decide when society should take actions to raise the income of some group and when it should not take such actions. If we cannot learn to make, impose, and defend equity decisions, we are not going to solve any of our economic problems. . . .

DECISIONS TO BE MADE

Whatever the process for getting there, and whatever the specifications of economic equity, there are four major decisions that everyone must make.

First, what is the minimum economic floor to which you will let any individual or family sink regardless of the cause of their failure? Unless you are willing to tolerate starving families in the streets, this is a question that must be answered by everyone. I suggest a minimum floor that would provide a standard of living just half as large as that of the average American.

Second, what is to be the distribution of economic rewards for those that participate in the economy? I suggest that structure of rewards that now exists for fully employed white males.

Third, given that tax revenue must be collected to finance government expenditures, how should this burden be distributed? Given a fair distribution of economic rewards in the marketplace, a proportional tax system is desirable, but without large variances among individuals with the same real income. To the extent that the distribution of market earnings has not reached the desired level, a progressive tax system should exist to move the distribution of take-home incomes toward the desired goal.

Fourth, what compensatory payments should be made when public policies cause large income losses? One can be a purist and answer "never," but I argue that we need a generous system of transitional aid to individuals, but not firms.

THE POLITICAL PROCESS

While this has been [an essay] on economic problems, these problems and their solutions focus attention back on our political process. Does our inability to act reflect fundamental irreconcilable divisions that no political process could overcome, or is there something wrong with our political system? Some of our paralysis is due to irreconcilable differences, but some of it is also because of a political process that cannot make decisions when all decisions result in substantial income losses for someone.

This is not a fault shared by other forms of government to the same extent. Everywhere else in the industrial world, parliamentary forms of government have demonstrated that they can penalize automobile driving, even when everyone drives and loves it. Very high taxes can be levied on gasoline elsewhere, but not here.

Our problems arise because, in a very real sense, we do not have political parties. A political party is a group that can force its elected members to vote for that party's solutions to society's problems. With a majority and minority party, the majority is expected to solve the nation's economic problems. If it can't, it is replaced in the next election, and the minority becomes the majority. Responsibility for success is clear, and failures can be punished.

Instead of having two parties, we have a system where each elected official is his own party and is free to establish his own party platform. Parties are merely vague electoral alliances. But this means a splintering of power that makes it impossible to hold anyone responsible for failure. No elected official can be expected to solve the problems by himself. Failure can always be blamed on someone else. There is no majority that must solve problems or be held accountable. In comparison, the diffusion of responsibility that we so often castigate in proportional representation seems mild. We have the ultimate in proportional representation, where every elected official is a one-man political party.

When no one can be held responsible for failure, it becomes possible for everyone who contributed to the failure to be reelected time after time. Each individual member of Congress reports to his constituents that his solutions to the problems were killed by someone else, but he is fighting hard. He or she can also report that they also successfully fought to prevent their particular electorate from having to suffer any of the costs that would have occurred if someone else's solutions to the problems had been adopted. Being successful in stopping programs that would hurt their electorate, and giving the appearance of working toward solutions, each congressman can be reelected with the problems unsolved. Since no one has the power to solve the problems, no one can be fired for not solving the problems.

But not having accountable, integrated political parties fails us in an even more fundamental way. Since all economic solutions require decisions about the distribution of income, we should be voting political parties up or down based on how they are going to allocate the economic losses necessary to solve our problems. Not having political parties with a common position on this issue, there is no way that voters can come to a majority or minority position on who should bear the inevitable losses. Each individual congressman is free to argue that all of the losses should be allocated to someone else's congressional district, and this is exactly what his voters want to hear.

Presidential candidates cannot shift the losses to someone else's electoral district quite so easily; therefore they retreat to the position that they can solve the problems without hurting anyone. We are told about the large economic gains that each of us will make if they are elected, but losses either don't exist or are quietly ignored.

To pretend that there are no losses, however, is to guarantee that once elected, a president will not be able to impose the necessary losses. He has been elected on the basis of no losses for anyone, and he has no electoral mandate to impose the losses. In contrast, a British conservative government was elected on the platform of tax cuts for the rich and tax increases for the lower middle class. Having been elected on this redistribution platform, the laws implementing it could be quickly passed. In our system, proposals that yield economic losses come as a surprise, are treated as a betrayal, and result in fierce political resistance that makes it impossible to impose the programs.

There is no easy path for getting from here to there, but somehow we have to establish a political system where someone can be held responsible for failure. This can only be done in a system where there are disciplined majority and minority parties. Every politician with his or her own platform is the American way, but it is not a way that is going to be able to solve America's economic problems.

As we head into the 1980s, it is well to remember that there is really only one important question in political economy. If elected, whose income do you and your party plan to cut in the process of solving the economic problems facing us? Our economy and the solutions to its problems have a substantial zero-sum element. Our economic life would be easier if this were not true, but we are going to have to learn to play a zero-sum economic game. if we cannot learn, or prefer to pretend that the zero-sum problem does not exist, we are simply going to fail.

Wealth and Poverty

GEORGE GILDER

Wealth and poverty are the prime concerns of economics, but they are subjects too vast and vital to be left to economists alone. Although economists have provided me with some of my most valued counsel . . . this . . . is in part an essay on the limitations of contemporary economics in analyzing the sources of creativity and progress in all economies. . . .

The belief that the good fortune of others is also finally one's own does not come easily or invariably to the human breast. It is, however, a golden rule of

From *Wealth and Poverty,* by George Gilder. Copyright © 1981 by George Gilder. Reprinted by permission of Basic Books, Inc., Publishers.

economics, a key to peace and prosperity, a source of the gifts of progress. It is the belief that finally confounded the predatory economics of mercantilism, in which nations used regulation and beggar-thy-neighbor trade campaigns to gather surpluses and bullion. It was this golden rule that inspired the first great book of economics, *The Wealth of Nations.* It was this belief that David Hume proclaimed in 1742, at the end of his essay, "Of the Jealousy of Trade:" "I shall therefore venture to acknowledge, that, not only as a man, but as a British subject, I pray for the flourishing commerce of Germany, Spain, Italy, and even France itself. I am at least certain that all nations would flourish more [with] such enlarged and benevolent sympathies toward each other."

The golden rule finds its scientific basis in the mutuality of gains from trade, in the demand generated by the engines of supply, in the expanded opportunity created by growth, in the usual and still growing economic futility of war. On this foundation have arisen most of the world's economic gains since the times of Smith and Hume. Its abandonment during the tariff wars of the thirties precipitated, deepened, and prolonged the Great Depression. Its continuing survival is our greatest patrimony as a free people. But it is a belief that is always in danger of erosion and attack.

A prominent source of trouble is the profession of economics. Smith entitled Book One of *The Wealth of Nations,* "Of the Causes of Improvement in the productive Powers of Labour and the Order according to which its Produce is naturally distributed among the different Ranks of the people." He himself stressed the productive powers, but his followers, beginning with David Ricardo, quickly became bogged down in a static and mechanical concern with distribution. They all were forever counting the ranks of rich and poor and assaying the defects of capitalism that keep the poor always with us in such great numbers. The focus on distribution continues in economics today, as economists pore balefully over the perennial inequalities and speculate on brisk "redistributions" to rectify them.

This mode of thinking, prominent in foundation-funded reports, best-selling economics texts, newspaper columns, and political platforms, is harmless enough on the surface. But its deeper effect is to challenge the golden rule of capitalism, to pervert the relation between rich and poor, and to depict the system as "a zero-sum game" in which every gain for someone implies a loss for someone else, and wealth is seen once again to create poverty. . . . [A] free society in which the distributions are widely seen as unfair cannot long survive. The distributionist mentality thus strikes at the living heart of democratic capitalism.

Whether of wealth, income, poverty, or government benefits, distributions always, unfortunately, turn out bad: highly skewed, hugely unequal, presumptively unfair, and changing little, or getting worse. . . .

In every economy . . . there is one crucial and definitive conflict. This is not the split between capitalists and workers, technocrats and humanists, government and business, liberals and conservatives, or rich and poor. All these divisions are partial and distorted reflections of the deeper conflict: the struggle between past and future, between the existing configuration of industries and the industries that will someday replace them. It is a conflict between established factories, technologies, formations of capital, and the ventures that may soon make them worthless—ventures that today may not even exist; that today may flicker only as ideas, or tiny companies, or obscure research projects, or fierce but penniless ambitions; that today are unidentifiable and incalculable from above, but which, in time, in a progressing economy, must rise up if growth is to occur.

Except in the very short run, growth does not consist of the kind of booming demand and rising productivity—the sale of more soap and Chevrolets—that the president discusses with the Business Roundtable when they gather to consider how to stimulate the American economy. Growth may not even spring from what most of the business establishment calls investment: the repair, duplication, and expansion of existing capital plant and equipment. Existing systems become more expensive and less appropriate as time passes and conditions change. Their reproduction is often a burden on growth, a diversion from always necessary investment in new technology. Long-term growth can be virtually defined as the replacement of existing plants, equipment, and products with new and better ones.

Sir Henry Bessemer, the creator of the Bessemer method of large-scale steel production, vividly described such a nineteenth-century moment of discovery and displacement. In 1854, after his first breakthrough in tests for making steel, he wrote:

> I could now see in my mind's eye, at a glance, the great iron industry of the world crumbling away under the irresistible force of the facts so recently elicited. In that one result the sentence had gone forth, and not all the talent accumulated in the last 150 years . . . no, nor all the millions that had been invested in carrying out the existing system of manufacture, with all its accompanying great resistance, could reverse that one great fact.

Bessemer was right. Although the adaptation and diffusion of his method took far longer than he expected, Bessemer's invention indeed ended by wreaking ghost towns and bleak motionless factories from the British Midlands to eastern Pennsylvania. By the last decades of the nineteenth century the Bessemer system was producing some 85 percent of America's steel output, replacing wrought iron everywhere in the vast extension of railroads. But the Bessemer technique also was to succumb to change. By 1910 the open hearth process, with its radically different capital plant, had usurped Bessemer and had taken over some two-thirds of the steel market in the United States.

As [Joseph] Schumpeter so memorably wrote, "Creative destruction is the essential fact about capitalism . . . it is by nature a form or method of economic change, and not only never is, but never can be stationary. . . . The fundamental impulse that sets and keeps the capitalist engine in motion comes from the new consumer goods, the new methods of production or transportation, the new markets, the new forms of industrial organization that capitalist enterprise creates."

In the struggles of creative destruction neither large nor small companies have a decisive advantage. In general large companies are most valuable in making incremental (though cumulatively very large) productivity improvements and in extending their markets into the world economy, where political and financial clout are often more important than innovation. Small companies are collectively far less efficient. But they are also more likely to create totally new items. Large firms can sometimes succeed in buying or forming subsidiaries, such as Exxon's Zilog and Vydec, that display much resourcefulness in imitating and improving the innovations of others. What large firms lack is the fertility of numbers and the flexibility of uncommitment. Although any particular small firm may be less creative than a large corporation, the millions of small businesses together are the prime source of creative destruction—the chief initiators of valuable change.

The very virtues of size—the economies of scale they offer—are the corollary of their vices: their huge and settled investments in particular capital and management practices. Without expressing any hostility toward the large corporations, one can maintain that the struggle between past and future is in part a struggle between David and Goliath, and this struggle will never end. Although Schumpeter himself came to underestimate the changeless implications of the imperative of change—and many contemporary economists astonishingly imagine that we are now entering a stationary or stagnant technological age—creative destruction is always the essence of growth.

From this fact arises the central question about any system of political economy, any platform of a political party, any inspiring scheme of leadership: will it allow the future to prevail? Will it favor the promise of the unknown against the comforts and passions of the threatened past? Little else matters. As at every other point in the harrowing course of human history, current technologies and productivities are inadequate to a rapidly growing and, above all, increasingly demanding world population. As at every other historical epoch, faithless and shortsighted men attempt to halt the increase of knowledge and the advance of technology; they dream of "stationary states," "economic equilibria," "alternative lifestyles," "diminishing technological returns," "ecological stasis," and "a return to nature," all the while mumbling of "the threat of scientific progress." Such fantasies, endlessly refuted and endlessly recurrent, are the prime obstacle to the survival of civilization.

The problem emerges with ever more insistent urgency in every modern state. Governments everywhere are torn between the clamor of troubled obsolescence and the claims of unmet opportunity; between the sufferers of aging pains and the sufferers of growing pains; between enterprises shrinking from competition or asking subsidies for their errors and companies seeking human and capital resources to create new products and new markets for them.

Socialist and totalitarian governments are doomed to support the past.

Because creativity is unpredictable, it is also uncontrollable. If the politicians want to have central planning and command, they cannot have dynamism and life. A managed economy is almost by definition a barren one, which can progress only by borrowing or stealing from abroad.

After a trip to the Soviet Union Luigi Barzini described the results of "progressive" leadership in that vastly endowed land. Many operating Russian factories, Barzini said, resemble nothing so much as beautifully maintained and managed industrial museums for nineteenth-century machinery, all oiled, buffed, and polished like an old Packard ready for presentation at a rally of antique cars. Except in the vital realm of national defense, where Soviet businesses must compete with the United States, communism in general is a purely reactionary system, a kind of dream come true at a conference of industrial archaeologists. This creative sterility can in theory be overcome by socialist countries that "plan" for freedom and change (that is, become partly capitalist). But as a practical matter it is on capitalism we must rely to unleash the forces of creative destruction that can save the world in its perpetual crisis of population and scarcity.

Nonetheless, as capitalist governments weave themselves ever more deeply into the economic fabric, capitalist and democratic political systems enlist themselves more and more on the side of the established order—on the side of stagnation and against creative growth. A democratic legislator normally supports the most powerful businesses and cultural influences in his constituency. Labor unions, deeply important in the politics of all non-Communist countries, normally back the interests of the large companies they have already organized. Bureaucracies often are closely allied with the industries they regulate, particularly when the regulations—together with excessive taxation—so damage the industry that, like the American railroad and utility corporations, they finally fall helplessly into the arms of the state.

Detailed systems of regulation understandably tend to favor the products and patterns of behavior that have been adjusted to the rules—the "good" companies that can be easily understood and supervised by the existing expertise of the incumbent regulators. Innovation always has unpredictable and possibly dangerous results. In early stages, it is always uncertain, inefficient, and if it is based on new scientific findings, even inscrutable. Any fail-safe system of regulation to prevent environmental damage, work-place hazards, and every possible peril to consumers would never have permitted the launching of an airplane, let alone an industrial revolution. Regulators must always rely on existing knowledge, commanded by existing scientific disciplines and their leading proponents.

Yet scientific expertise is nearly always as narrow as it is deep, and established scientists resist change as doggedly as any other establishment. William Shockley was one of the inventors of the transistor, one of the heroic innovators of the modern age. But in the early 1960s he was as blind to the potentialities of the semiconductor as he is now to the genetics of intelligence. Most scientific breakthroughs are made by men in their twenties or early thirties. The National Laboratories, the Food and Drug Administration

(FDA), the Environmental Protection Agency (EPA)—all used by government to appraise the products of civilian science—are full of men who are past their prime, emotionally and intellectually committed to earlier technologies, and deeply resistant to progress. Asking them to judge the implications of new breakthroughs in fusion energy or microbiology is like using railroad technicians in the nineteenth century to appraise the plans of the Wright brothers.

These realities do not preclude regulation. But they suggest its inevitable pitfalls and grave unaccountable costs. The more comprehensive the regulatory systems, the more surely they will be dominated by mediocrities, and the more surely mediocre will be the growth of the U.S. economy. Excessive regulation to save us from risks will create the greatest danger of all: a stagnant society in a changing world. The choice is not between comfortable equilibrium and reckless progress. It is between random deterioration by time and change and creative destruction by human genius. Our current regulatory apparatus is in danger of becoming an enemy of creative destruction. . . .

Understandable or not . . . the hostility of politicians toward the chief sources of wealth in America makes most of them—regardless of their professed beliefs in progress and equality—reactionary defenders of the old plutocracy against the forces of innovation and progress. Politicians who have prevailed in ruthless rivalries of wit and risk become natural allies of bureaucracy and privilege and diehard opponents of economic growth and vitality. Yet politicians, through their lives of ambition and adventure, are spiritual kin of entrepreneurs. Politicians, if they consider their own careers, and their final attainment of a fortune in prestige, should be able to comprehend the dynamics of capitalism and the necessity of great rewards for triumph against great odds.

The future of American capitalism depends on this shift of the political order from a reactionary defense of the past to a progressive embrace of the future. In the anomalous world of American politics, this change almost necessarily entails overcoming the "progressive" trends in the society.

Our central problem arises from a deep conflict between the processes of material progress and the ideals of "progressive" government and culture. Equality, bureaucratic rationality, predictability, sexual liberation, political "populism," and the pursuit of pleasure—all the values of advanced culture—are quite simply inconsistent with the disciplines and investments of economic and technical advance. The result is that all modern governments pretend to promote economic growth but in practice doggedly obstruct it.

Material progress is ineluctably elitist: it makes the rich richer and increases their number, exalting the few extraordinary men who can produce wealth over the democratic masses who consume it. Material progress depends on the expansion of opportunity: geniuses identify themselves chiefly through their works rather than by their inheritance or test scores. Material progress is difficult: it requires from its protagonists long years of diligence and sacrifice, devotion and risk that can be elicited only with high rewards, not the "average return on capital." Material progress, although democratically demanded, is procedurally undemocratic: it means the expensive support of activities thoroughly beyond the ken of the people, and often even of their leaders. Material progress is radically unpredictable (to foresee an innovation is in essence to make it): the most important developments happen on a frontier where things are forever slipping slightly out of control. Material progress is inimical to scientific economics: it cannot be explained or foreseen in mechanistic or mathematical terms.

All those who seek a rational and predictable world—a system of scientific management and control—can prevail only by thwarting material and scientific progress. A world without innovation succumbs to the sure laws of deterioration and decay. As resources predictably dwindle, governments will extend their controls. Distribution becomes paramount. Planning works. Even such a somber certitude seems better to many than the notion of a continuing and incalculable struggle to extend the mastery of man over nature and to increase the fund of material wealth.

It is the idea of economic futility—not capitalist growth—that gives license to the culture of hedonism and sensuality. In an imperfect and suffering world, the possibility of progress implies a responsibility to attempt it. Only in a world of socialistically managed "limits to growth," where human effort, enterprise, and creativity can never long prevail over needless poverty and suffering, can the progressive dream of sexual liberation, leisure, redistribution, and sensual pleasure lose its onus of decadence and injustice.

The dream of stagnation exalts the politician as well as the hedonist. Only in a stationary economy can government no longer defer to scientists, technologists, and businessmen as the heroes of the age. In the stationary state all that matters are the works of power and bureaucracy: mass behavior and its regulation. Conservation, distribution, and control become crucial values. Economists, too, come into their own. Without the surprises of creativity, their models can actually predict the future.

In a world without material growth, poverty will increase nearly everywhere. But experts will come forth with new rationales for ignoring, in all but rhetoric, the plight of the global poor. Just as the alleged laws of classical economics doomed the workers to subsistence wages, the new laws of contemporary ecology doom them to a stagnant world economy. . . .

. . . [W]hat is the source of the ideas by which intellectual progress occurs? The answer, we may agree, is chance. Theories arise spontaneously and mysteriously, by intuition or happenstance. This mystery constitutes the crucial problem of intellectual history. . . .

The crucial rules of creative thought can be summed up as faith, love, openness, conflict, and falsifiability. The crucial rules of economic innovation and progress are faith, altruism, investment, competition, and bankruptcy, which are also the rules of capitalism. The reason capitalism succeeds is that its laws accord with the laws of mind. It is capable of fulfilling human needs because it is founded on giving, which depends on sensitivity to the needs of others. It is open to faith and experiment because it is also open to competition and bankruptcy. Capitalism accumulates the capital gains not only of its successes but also of its failures, capitalized in new knowledge. It is the only appropriate system for a world in which all certitude is a sham.

The dynamics of economic growth thus consist of the fundamental process of all growth and development in nature and thought: a largely spontaneous and mostly unpredictable flow of increasing diversity and differentiation and new products and modes of production. Business begins with a new idea, a better mousetrap, and expands into a differentiated industry of mousetrap marketing, maintenance, and hygiene, leading to a proliferation of mousetrap-related activities, from weasel traps to bear traps, from rat poison to door-to-door household goods, perhaps climaxing with a breakaway mouse meat short-order empire, selling Big Mickeys to teenagers. The pattern of development is usually the same (ideas have an inherent tendency to split up and specialize as they are applied). But the process is nonetheless unpredictable, full of the mystery of all living and growing things (like ideas and businesses).

In order for this process to fructify through the system, there must be activity beyond the system's control. The new production must usually be done by individuals whose work and ideas are not subsumed by a larger institution (the builders and sellers of mousetraps will not look with favor on the diversion of their earnings into a fast-food chain). There must be room for individuals to find their own unexpected way of dividing and specializing labor, originating and adapting new goods and services. These individuals and their new ideas are the way an economic system grows and changes; they lead to the small businesses and new activities that are finally joined with others in new systems, which often become rigid and unresponsive, unless they can continue to assimilate or shoot off new products and processes. It is this very conventional but absolutely crucial interplay of chance, change, and growth that economists so often ignore.

The key thing to notice about this process is that most of its motive activities take place beyond the view of the statistician. It is a personal and psychological drama that decides whether a man dares to borrow and take risks to carry out an innovative idea that all the statistics show will probably—like two-thirds of all new businesses in America—fail within five years. This decision will be affected by government; it will be much deterred by high taxes and interest rates; but it will most essentially express an impulse of faith, a belief in the future, and a sensitivity to the needs of others, even if unstated. Economists who themselves do not believe in the future of capitalism will tend to ignore the dynamics of chance and faith that largely will determine that future. Economists who distrust religion will always fail to comprehend the modes of worship by which progress is achieved. Chance is the foundation of change and the vessel of the divine. . . .

In the United States today we are facing the usual calculus of impossibility, recited by the familiar aspirants to a master plan. It is said we must abandon economic freedom because our frontier is closed; because our biosphere is strained; because our resources are running out; because our technology is perverse; because our population rises; because our horizons are closing in. We walk, it is said, in a shadow of death, with depleted air, poisoned earth and water, and a fallout of explosive growth showering from the clouds of our future in a quiet carcinogenic rain. In this extremity, we cannot afford the luxuries of competition and waste and freedom. We have reached the end of the open road; we are beating against the gates of an occluded frontier. We must tax and regulate and plan, redistribute our wealth and ration our consumption, because we have reached the end of openness.

But quite to the contrary, these problems and crises are in themselves the new frontier; are themselves the mandate for individual and corporate competition and creativity; are themselves the reason why we cannot afford the consolations of planning and stasis. The old frontier of the American West also appeared closed at first. It became an open reservoir of wealth only in retrospect, because the pioneers dared to risk their lives and families in the quest for riches, looking for gold (of which there was relatively little in the United States) and finding oil (then of little use). Only in retrospect were the barrens of Texas and Oklahoma an energy cornucopia, the flat prairies a breadbasket for the world, or Thomas Edison a catalytic genius and Henry Ford the salvation of capitalism in the grips of an earlier closing circle. The future is forever incalculable; only in freedom can its challenges be mastered.

The economists, who make the case for stasis and planning in these terms, formulate point by point the case against themselves. The closing circle, the resource crisis, the thermal threat, the nuclear peril, the "graying" of technology, the population advance, the famine factor, and whatever else is new in the perennial jeremiad of the rational budgeteer and actuary of our fate—all these conditions are themselves the mandate for capitalism. To overcome it is necessary to have faith, to recover the belief in chance and providence, in the ingenuity of free and God-fearing men.

This belief will allow us to see the best way of helping the poor, the way to understand the truths of equality before God that can only come from freedom and diversity on earth. It will lead us to abandon, above all, the idea that the human race can become self-sufficient, can separate itself from chance and fortune in a hubristic siege of rational resource management, income distribution, and futuristic planning. Our greatest and only resource is the miracle of human creativity in a relation of openness to the divine. It is a resource that above all we should deny neither to the poor, who can be the most open of all to the future, nor to the rich or excellent of individuals, who can lend leadership, imagination, and wealth to the cause of beneficent change.

The tale of human life is less the pageant of unfolding rationality and purpose envisaged by the Enlightenment than a saga of desert wanderings and brief bounty, the endless dialogue between man and God, between alienation and providence, as we search for the ever-rising and receding promised land, which we can see most clearly, with the most luminous logic, when we have the faith and courage to leave ourselves open to chance and fate.

Reinhold Niebuhr summed up our predicament:

Nothing worth doing is completed in one lifetime.
Therefore we must be saved by hope.
Nothing true or beautiful makes complete sense in any context of history.
Therefore we must be saved by faith.
Nothing we do, no matter how virtuous, can be accomplished alone.
Therefore we are saved by love.

These are the fundamental laws of economics, business, technology, and life. In them are the secret sources of wealth, and poverty.

Document

The New American Poverty

MICHAEL HARRINGTON

The poor are still there.

Two decades after the President of the United States declared an "unconditional" war on poverty, poverty does not simply continue to exist; worse, we must deal with structures of misery, with a new poverty much more tenacious than the old.

Structures of misery. The idea was a commonplace when one thought of Appalachia a generation ago. An economy controlled by absentee corporations neglected basic investments, which eroded the physical and social infrastructure as well as the tax base. People fled this impossible situation, so there were even fewer human resources, which made further investment unlikely. That in turn further eroded the physical and social infrastructure as well as the tax base. Under such conditions, poverty is not merely an episode or the fault of some heartless Scrooge, but the ongoing product of the organization of disorganization.

Now there are new structures of misery. In the winter of our national discontent in 1982–83, when there were more jobless Americans than at any other time in almost half a century, a young worker walked through the milling, sometimes menacing men on East Third Street in Manhattan and asked the City of New York for a bed at the Municipal Shelter. One of the reasons he was there was that there are steel mills in South Korea. That is, the poor—and the entire American economy—are caught up in a crisis which is literally global. Yet one cannot simply blame changes in the way the world is run for what is happening on East Third Street, or in the *barrios* of Los

Angeles, the steel towns of the Monongahela Valley, and the backwoods of Maine.

The great, impersonal forces have indeed created a context in which poverty is much more difficult to abolish than it was twenty years ago. But it is not the South Koreans—or the Japanese, the West Germans, or anyone else—who have decided that the human costs of this wrenching transition should be borne by the most vulnerable Americans. We have done that to ourselves.

One reason is that this economic upheaval did not simply strike at the poor. It had an enormous impact on everyone else and, among many other things, changed the very eyes of the society. In the sixties there was economic growth, political and social movement, hope. What was shocking was that poverty existed at all, and the very fact that it did was an incitement to abolish it. I simplify, of course. Even then, as I pointed out in *The Other America,* suburbanization was removing the middle class from daily contact with the poor. In our geography, as in our social structure, we were becoming two nations.

Moreover, the optimistic sixties often overlooked the systemic nature of its own poverty. I remember a quintessential political cocktail party of those times. It was during the 1964 Presidential campaign at the Dakota, perhaps the most chic apartment building in New York City. A leading trade unionist was talking to some of the intellectual elite. We are going to the moon, he said. Why can't we put an end to the slums? He, and almost everyone else there, knew that our capacities were boundless, that we could deal with ghettos as well as outer space. But there are no people on the moon, no landlords, no silk-stocking districts reluctant to welcome the ex-poor into affluent neighborhoods. Lunar exploration posed technical problems; abolishing poverty raised issues of power and wealth.

Few people realized this in 1964, so there was a social war without a human enemy. The opposing forces were abstractions: hunger, illiteracy, bad housing, inadequate motivation, and the like. It was innocently assumed that ending the outrage of poverty was in everyone's interest. It was not until the seventies, during the debate over Richard Nixon's Family Assistance Plan, that a Southern congressman bluntly stated the more complex truth. If the government provided a minimum income to everyone, "Who," he asked, "will iron my shirts and rake the yard?"

But even if there were more than a few illusions in the sixties, they facilitated some very real gains. There were many of the working poor who, in a decade of falling unemployment, fought their way out of poverty. The aging made dramatic gains through Medicare and increased, indexed social security benefits. Blacks successfully eradicated legal Jim Crow; Chicanos and Filipinos created a union in the fields; even Appalachia registered some gains. If the antipoverty program turned out to be a skirmish rather than an unconditional war, it nonetheless made some significant advances.

In the eighties it is not simply that structural economic change has created new poverties and given old poverties a new lease on life. That very same process has impaired the national vision; misery has simultaneously become more intractable and more difficult to see.

In the seventies and the early eighties, we had both inflation and recession, which subverted the established liberal wisdom; the highest unemployment rates since the Great Depression; and a consequent loss of political and social nerve. Crises, particularly at first, do not make people radical or compassionate. They are frightening, and most people concentrate on saving themselves. Thoughts of "brothers" or "sisters," who are moral kin but not one's blood relatives, are a luxury many cannot afford. It was not an accident that the Economic Opportunity Act of 1964 proclaimed that its goal was "to eliminate the paradox of poverty in the midst of plenty." It is somewhat more problematic to summon the average American to such a struggle in the midst of declining real wages and chronic unemployment.

At the same time, the process of suburbanization, which puts the poor out of sight and mind, has proceeded apace over the past two decades. The central cities have become reservations for the marginalized, as distant from the everyday consciousness as are the Navajos in the empty reaches of the Southwest. In 1982 *The Economist* of London wrote that the security forces in the shopping malls of America were there "to insulate their clientele from the undesirable elements of the real world—and those elements are as likely to be the poor and unwashed as the snow and the sun." "With less physical community," the article went on, "street life in cities will diminish and become less varied, criminals will gain ascendancy, buildings will become like fortresses." That is not, of course, an exercise in futurism; it is a sober description of what is going on in the United States.

So the national vision has been impaired in a number of ways. As men and women turned inward to face their own relative deprivation, it became harder to see anyone else's absolute suffering; and the Balkanization of American social structure only made things worse. More broadly, where the sixties spoke of possibilities, the eighties were forced to become aware of limits, which some assumed, wrongly, were ugly necessities to be imposed on those at the bottom of the society. In the process, America has lost its own generous vision of what it might be. . . .

The poverty of the eighties is different from all those poverties that preceded it.

Around 1970, the United States joined the global economy for the first time and the American poor began to suffer from the international division of labor in unprecedented ways. Of course, this country had been involved in foreign trade from the earliest days of the Republic. But if America had long been important for the world, the world was not too important for America. We were the technological pioneers, the inventors of the second industrial revolution of steel and mass production, as well as of the third, electronic industrial revolution. After all, we had an internal market so much larger than any other that it was not especially crucial for us to be concerned about foreigners. Even today, after more than a decade of relative decline, the gross national product (GNP) of the United States is six times that of France, four times that of West Germany, three times that of Japan, and twice as big as that of the Soviet Union.

But this country rebuilt the European and Japanese economies after World War II, made a handsome profit in the process, and did the job too well. Our former clients in West Germany and Japan became fierce competitors. At the same time, trade became more important for the United States than ever before. In the seventies, exports almost doubled (from 9 percent to 17 percent) and the imported portion of the internal market more than doubled (from 9 percent to 21 percent). The West Germans and the Japanese, however, proceeded to sell "turnkey" plants—complete factories ready to start up—to South Korea and other Third World countries. With the spread of multinationals—corporations without a country to be loyal to—there was an unprecedented internationalization of the economy.

Suddenly the industrial geography of a good part of the United States— its mass-production heartland—no longer made as much sense as it once had. That did not simply menace the traditional working class with a new poverty, but by beginning to reshape the occupational structure of the United States, it also threatened a new, mainly immigrant working class and undercut the struggle of blacks, Hispanics, and other minorities who suffered from the effects of an institutional economic racism. . . .

. . . [A]t the same time . . . a technological revolution also restructured America from within. In the auto industry, for instance, it is well known by everyone that a significant portion of the men and women laid off during the 1982–83 recession will never get their jobs back. The companies, like many other corporations, had found a certain utility in the recession. It allowed them to shut down obsolete plants, which also meant destroying living communities, and to plan for more efficient, robotized, automated production. This process is still very much in progress. It has transformed agriculture and the factory, and it is now invading the office.

These massive international and national trends have created the basis for the new structures of misery in the America of the eighties, for a poverty more difficult to defeat than the indignities of twenty years ago. . . .

. . . [T]he most basic single point [here] is that if the new poverty is so much more intransigent than the old, it is not a fate. The structures of this misery were created by men and women; they can be changed by men and women. That, we shall see, is easier said than done—but it can be done.

I have long thought that perhaps we are all on an arduous pilgrimage which might—only might—lead us to our own humanity. There are times when the pilgrimage halts, when the people are exhausted from wandering in the desert, when the reports of the Promised Land over the Jordan seem preposterous. So it has been for a while in the United States. It is not that men and women have lacked courage and decency. It is that bewildering, distant forces have perplexed them and subverted their capacity for hope. But one day there will be a stirring, and—perhaps hesitantly at first—the long column will begin to move once again. . . .

It is my modest hope that when the pilgrimage begins again, when the time for the antipoverty idea has returned, this . . . might point out a path or two. It is my deeper hope that when that day comes, when we join, in solidarity and not in noblesse oblige, with the poor, we will rediscover our own best selves — that we will regain the vision of America.

sixteen

THE NUCLEAR QUESTION

The nuclear question is the most pressing issue in the United States today. Ever since American atomic bombs obliterated the Japanese cities of Hiroshima and Nagasaki, the world has had to deal with more potent forces of destruction than ever before. As atomic weapons gave way to hydrogen bombs and intercontinental ballistic missiles joined arsenals in the 1950s, both the United States and the Soviet Union developed the capability of destroying all life of earth.

Occasional efforts at arms control enjoyed moderate success. The Limited Test Ban Treaty of 1963 prohibited atmospheric testing. Strategic Arms Limitation Talks culminated in a SALT I agreement of 1972 and a SALT II treaty of 1979, though the latter measure was never ratified in the United States. But arsenals grew as agreements were signed, and destructive capabilities increased.

In the 1980s, after a period of dormancy, a protest movement revived. Physicians for Social Responsibility, in hibernation after the 1963 Test Ban Treaty, became active once again. The Union of Concerned Scientists resumed its opposition to nuclear weapons. And Randall Forsberg, first a staffer at the Stockholm International Peace Research Institute, then head of her own Institute for Defense and Disarmament Studies in the United States, offered a new idea for arms control: a mutual and verifiable nuclear freeze.

The freeze idea took hold. Town meetings, first in Vermont, then elsewhere around the country, considered and endorsed the proposal. In 1982, Senator Edward M. Kennedy, a Democrat from Massachusetts, and Senator Mark O. Hatfield, a Republican from Oregon, introduced a joint congressional resolution calling for a weapons freeze. While aimed at implementing one particular action, their proposal was really part of a larger effort to bring an escalating arms race under control.

In the first selection reprinted here, "The Case for a Freeze," Kennedy and Hatfield defend their resolution. They counter the Reagan administration's talk of a "window of vulnerability" with the assertion that there is now a "window of opportunity" for arms control. They propose, in short, a "firebreak" to circumscribe the arms race.

Not everyone agreed that a freeze was the answer. Christopher M. Lehman, director of the Office of Strategic Nuclear Policy in the Department of State, argues in "Arms Control vs. the Freeze" that while fear is the guiding force behind the freeze movement, fear alone cannot prevent nuclear war. He claims that while the freeze is superficially attractive, it would undermine the policy of deterrence, which has prevented nuclear war in the post–World War II years. The Reagan administration's initiatives—Strategic Arms Reduction Talks (START) and Intermediate-Range Nuclear Forces (INF) discussions— would, Lehman suggests, offer more hope for success.

The document in this section is the Kennedy-Hatfield resolution itself. After introduction in Congress, two dozen senators and more than 150 representatives signed their names as sponsors. In August 1982, the House of Representatives defeated the resolution by a 204–202 vote, but later came back and passed it. In the November elections, numerous communities and several states endorsed the proposal. Although the measure never became national policy, it may well have created the pressure that rejuvenated the administration's arms control efforts and thereby contributed to the INF agreement to destroy a whole category of nuclear weapons.

For further background on the nuclear question, Robert C. Williams and Philip L. Cantelon provide a good introduction in their anthology *The American Atom: A Documentary History of Nuclear Policies from the Discovery of Fission to the Present* (1984). John B. Harris and Eric Markusen, *Nuclear Weapons and the Threat of Nuclear War* (1986), is another useful anthology. The Harvard Nuclear Study Group (Albert Carnesale, Paul Doty, Stanley Hoffmann, Samuel P. Huntington, Joseph S. Nye, Jr., and Scott D. Sagan), *Living with Nuclear Weapons* (1983), is a jointly written assessment of the nuclear predicament that provides both historical perspective and policy alternatives. Gerard H. Clarfield and William M. Wiecek, *Nuclear America: Military and Civilian Nuclear Power in the United States, 1940–1980* (1984), is a readable overview of diverse nuclear issues. Jonathon Schell, *The Fate of the Earth* (1982), is the most eloquent—and influential—plea to bring the arms race under control.

The Case for a Freeze

EDWARD M. KENNEDY AND MARK O. HATFIELD

In 1963 when President [John F.] Kennedy, in a commencement address at American University, proposed high-level negotiations with the Soviet Union on the issue of nuclear testing, he was trying in a single but sensible stroke to break a deadlock that had lasted for years. He had dismissed the counsel of some advisers that his offer would be perceived as American weakness. He had listened with disbelief to the argument that the rest of the details had to be worked out before we could ask the Soviet Union to agree to the general principle of an atmospheric test ban. After his address, in the remarkably short span of two months, the remaining details were disposed of and the Test-Ban Treaty of 1963 was signed.

Today there are some officials who, like their counterparts two decades ago, believe that a freeze followed by major reductions in nuclear arsenals is improbable and who argue, in effect, that peace is also impossible. Too many defense experts who have grown up with the arms race have become accustomed to guiding it. The agreements negotiated in SALT I and SALT II have not prevented steadily higher levels of weaponry. As Senators, we supported SALT II because we thought the country and the world would be better off with it than without it. It offered a number of limits of nuclear weaponry; without it, there would have been no limits at all on Soviet and American buildups. But in fact, the SALT II Treaty, which was never put before the Senate for a ratification vote, was mostly a means of setting down rules for limiting the arms buildup, instead of stopping the arms race and then reversing it.

The SALT process has failed to deal with critical technological advances in weapons and continuing increases in the number of warheads. In 1960 the United States and the Soviet Union together had 6,500 strategic nuclear warheads; today they have 17,000. By 1985, when the SALT II Treaty would have been due to expire, there would have been somewhere between 22,500 and 24,400 such warheads. Though the treaty was the product of long, hard work against the background of stiffening political resistance to arms control, it may have been the best that could be achieved at the time, at least in domestic terms. But the effort to conciliate the political opposition largely failed. Some critics who originally wanted no treaty at all charged that the treaty did not do enough. Many advocates of arms control agreed, but nonetheless argued the comparative advantage of the SALT II limits.

The weakness of the SALT process in addressing technological breakthroughs has plagued efforts at arms control for the past decade. The first SALT agreement ignored the advance called MIRV, multiple independently targetable reentry vehicles, which meant that a single ballistic missile could carry several warheads, each aimed at a separate enemy city or military

From *Freeze! How You Can Help Prevent Nuclear War,* by Edward M. Kennedy and Mark O. Hatfield. Copyright © 1982 by Edward M. Kennedy and Mark O. Hatfield. Reprinted by permission of Bantam Books.

installation and each sufficient to obliterate it. Many experts felt that SALT did too little to stop the qualitative arms race and restrain ongoing scientific revolution in weaponry.

In the 1980s, technology has marched on. Guidance systems have become increasingly and exquisitely accurate; a missile may now be able to fly 5,000 miles and land within a few hundred feet of the intended target. But exquisitely accurate land-based missiles may also be vulnerable to the other side's exquisitely accurate missiles. Even in a decade governed by SALT II, both could pass beyond the "first-strike" threshold, where either side might assume that it had first-strike capability and first-strike vulnerability simultaneously. The inexorable development of nuclear technology is heading inevitably to a world bristling with hair-trigger nuclear missiles and governed by a "use them or lose them" nuclear psychology. Like sulfur coating a matchstick, the layering of nuclear technology on top of other disputes could erupt in nuclear war any time Americans and Soviets rub each other the wrong way.

Once this strategic Rubicon has been crossed, the possibility of accidental war will rise to an even more dangerous level. On 147 occasions within the past 20 months, U.S. computer malfunctions have signaled a Soviet strategic attack. Four of the incidents were severe enough so that orders were issued to move our strategic forces to a higher state of alert. Once, a mistake caused by a programming error flashed a warning of a Soviet submarine attack. According to the Pentagon, it took six minutes for U.S. command authorities to make a positive identification of the mistake; in a few minutes more, if there had been no mistake, a fusillade of Soviet submarine missiles would have struck our coastal cities. On another occasion, a false signal was flashed from satellites that mistook the rising of the moon for the launching of Soviet missiles.

Some defense analysts behave as if the purpose of arms control is, at most, permanent management of the arms race. But it is unlikely that it can be managed forever and more likely that it will finally manage to destroy much of civilization forever. A nuclear freeze, followed by reductions, is not the only avenue to arms control, but it is the only idea which can stop the spiral of nuclear arms development without the self-defeating delays of endless negotiation over what constitutes equality. In a matter of months, the two superpowers, assuming their goodwill, could reasonably work out verification procedures for a freeze. The former Chief of Naval Development, Admiral Thomas Davies, says:

> Now the virtue of the freeze is to prevent the continued increase of weaponry and the worsening of the situation during a prolonged negotiation. In fact, the history of our negotiations [for arms reductions shows] that they are lengthy and difficult, and during that time there is always a great increase in the number of warheads deployed. So I would say that the freeze is the only practical way to go at that problem.

To freeze first and then negotiate reductions makes sense on many levels. It recognizes the urgency of taking a step that is as simple as it is practical, and that is more feasible now than it has ever been before, because both sides are so nearly equivalent in their arsenals of annihilation.

The freeze agreement would be a firebreak, encircling and containing a weapons race threatening to break out of control. Once armaments and technological advances are stopped at present levels, the two superpowers can negotiate phased and balanced reductions. The Kennedy-Hatfield resolution calls for such reductions "through annual percentages or equally effective means." George Kennan, our former Ambassador to the Soviet Union and our foremost expert on that country, and Admiral Hyman G. Rickover, Director of Naval Nuclear Propulsion under seven Presidents, have argued eloquently and compellingly for deep cuts of at least 50 percent in the nuclear armories of both sides. These cuts could be achieved by the end of this decade, if we mutually agree to reasonable reductions of 7 percent a year. This is the approach proposed in the Kennedy-Hatfield resolution, and suggested by the Senate Committee on Foreign Relations in 1979, which sought sustained major reductions from SALT II ceilings on weaponry.

As the process of reductions moves along, it will be in the interests of both the United States and the Soviet Union to direct their reductions to vulnerable land-based missiles that also provide particularly rapid and precise offensive capability: weapons that could seriously unbalance the basic retaliatory equation which yields mutual deterrence. In short, a freeze on nuclear weapons followed by reductions from their current levels can strengthen deterrence as the purpose of our defense, diminish the risk of accidental nuclear war, and curtail the incentives for the hair-trigger use of nuclear weapons during an escalating crisis.

A freeze will enhance, not reduce, our overall security, because it will prevent the development of more powerful Soviet rockets and block their further deployment of existing weapons. A freeze will prevent one side from perfecting its capacity for a first strike against the other by prohibiting the testing and production of such weapons; the result will be a substantial reduction in the fear of a U.S. or Soviet preemptive attack.

A freeze will also help to strengthen our economy and other areas of our national defense, both of which have heavily suffered from neglect and from the cost of this nuclear buildup. The $90 billion that a freeze alone could save in the next five years could be spent on conventional defenses and domestic priorities. In fact, the strategic arms race is crippling our capacity to meet human needs. We are cutting immunization for children in order to finance the weapons that may someday kill them. Every new shelter for a missile means more spending, a bigger deficit, and higher interest rates, but fewer homes for families. Every new warhead guidance system that can read enemy defenses means there will be more schools where more students will never learn to read. Every new escalation that could mean death at an early age across the earth also darkens the golden years of senior citizens who rely on Social Security, Medicare, and Medicaid, all of which are in danger from cutbacks due to the budget crisis.

The nuclear buildup is an extremely important aspect of the current economic distress. The B-1 bomber alone will cost more than all the job training programs enacted by Congress in the past 20 years. In short, the two greatest issues of our time—the prosperity of the economy and the probability of survival in the nuclear age—are inextricably intertwined. Not only could a freeze save at least $18 billion annually; negotiated reductions could save billions more. A process of mutual nuclear restraint is a needed defense against the prospect of endless budget deficits.

As we have noted, some of the savings from a freeze can be reallocated to improve the readiness and the reliability of our conventional forces. But just as important, when the total burden of military expenditures on the budget is lessened, we will have the resources for the revitalization of our industries and the restoration of America's competitive position in the markets of the world. We will have the funds to develop, and share, alternative energy sources. These tasks are at the heart of the great national security challenges of the 1980s; they are the central arena of testing for the United States, which cannot endure as an insecure or failing economy amid international economic disarray and deprivation.

An eloquent warning of the costs of the arms race came three decades ago from the leader of Republican conservatism. This is what Senator Robert Taft of Ohio said in 1951:

> No nation can be constantly prepared to undertake a full-scale war at any moment and still hope to maintain any of the other purposes in which people are interested and for which nations are founded. In short, there is a definite limit to what a government can spend in time of peace and still maintain a free economy, without inflation and with at least some elements of progress in standards of living and in education, welfare, housing, health and other activities in which people are vitally interested. In my opinion, we are completely able to defend the United States itself. The one great danger we face is that we may overcommit ourselves in this battle against Russia. Let me say that no one is more determined to resist the Communist aggression in the world than I am, but we cannot afford to destroy at home the very liberty which we must sell to the rest of the world as the basis for progress and happiness. In short, a war against Communism in the world must finally be won in the minds of men.

The costs and dangers of the arms race are not new to this administration or to this budgetary crisis. Since World War II, with occasional exceptions, we have paid an accelerating price to prepare for World War III. In 1982 the economic burden of the effort weighs heavier and heavier upon Americans and Soviets alike. President Reagan has observed of the Soviet Union: "Their great military build-up . . . at the expense of the denial of consumer goods . . . has now left them on a very narrow edge." But it is not the adversary alone that now suffers from major economic difficulty. There is no question that if we continue to run an expensive, escalating arms race, we run the risk of Sovietizing our own economy. Investment capital has been drained by the crunching combination of massive increases in military spending, massive deficits, and the resulting scarcity of credit. When resources and strategic materials shortages are factored into the equation, unprecedented military spending may make it impossible for our society ever to return to its previous peaks of prosperity.

We must start retooling now for the future economic character of states from Oregon to Massachusetts, and Michigan to Louisiana. We cannot afford to imitate our adversary by limiting economic progress so that strategic military spending can multiply, vacuuming up every kind of resource. Generally our government has sought to budget federal dollars in ways that leverage private capital formation, jobs and thriving communities; but excessive defense spending actually means more, not less, unemployment. The military has the least multiplier effect of any dollar we spend, while the highest multiplier comes from a dollar spent on preventive medicine and health. Strategic spending is capital intensive, not labor intensive. Every billion dollars that we spend on the MX missile program will hire 17,000 people, while the same $1 billion could hire 48,000 hospital workers or 65,000 people in the building trades, or 77,000 teachers, police officers, and firefighters.

Few will deny the costs of the arms race in economic and human terms. Instead, opposition to a nuclear freeze, followed by reductions, has focused on military and technical issues. There are certain experts who claim, in effect, that the freeze is a nice but impractical idea. They resist the notion that an issue which was formerly the exclusive province of a professional elite has now become a matter of public debate and intensifying citizen concern. Of course, the management of the nuclear arms race since 1945 has not been a model of success. One argument which freeze opponents are raising now — that the issue is too complex and too important to be left to the people — echoes the argument of an earlier generation that the popular effort to end the Vietnam war was a mistake, or the parallel argument of 1982 that American policy in El Salvador and Central America should be decided in secret.

A number of other analysts and former officials who decry the present arms control stalemate regard the freeze as nothing more than a popular movement which may be beneficial in pressuring the administration, but which does not make sense as national policy because, they say, our strategic forces are not equal to those of the Soviet Union. In fact, there are many experts who favor the Kennedy-Hatfield resolution, ranging from former Secretaries of State and Defense to former CIA executives to America's most capable scientists. There is not a single sensible military or diplomatic official who would trade our strategic forces for the Soviet arsenal. At the present time, the United States is fully capable of defending itself by retaliating fully against any Soviet nuclear attack. America is secure today, and a freeze will preserve that security for the future. Despite all the talk of a "window of vulnerability," this nation and the Soviet Union are at approximate equivalence in strategic nuclear power. In the event of an immediate freeze, we would have 9,400 available strategic nuclear warheads and the Soviets would have 7,500. Even if a Soviet first strike destroyed all American land-based missiles, we would still have a retaliatory capacity of at least 4,000 warheads at sea and in the air. Even congressional testimony from military experts makes reference to the "rough parity" between the two countries. The Defense Department's military posture statement last year stated explicitly that a condition of parity continues to prevail. The current nuclear balance is relatively stable; deterrence still works. By freezing now, we would avoid an age of perceived first-strike threats in which the Soviets would face their own window of vulnerability and which could tempt either side to launch a preemptive strike. And it is that new arms race, not the present situation, which could irrevocably shatter the present balance.

We stand now at a unique moment in the history of the nuclear age where a freeze can work and must be tried. Rather than a window of vulnerability, we now have a window of opportunity for arms control. That window could be slammed shut in the coming years. It is no longer merely enough to call for reductions in nuclear weaponry without calling for a freeze as a first step, and as the only way to keep the window of opportunity open. Critics charge that the Soviets would have no incentive to reduce their arsenals after a freeze. They call for building new systems in order to pile up bargaining chips for negotiations with the Kremlin. But in the past, the arms race has been needlessly perpetuated by this bargaining-chip theory, because both sides feel forced to match new and threatening developments with their own. MIRVs, multiple independent warheads, were defended as a bargaining chip during the SALT I talks. So the United States continued to deploy them and then we were told that they were too important to bargain away.

In contrast, after a freeze both sides will have a vested interest in reductions, since they will still be saddled with weapons which do not add to their security or the effectiveness of their deterrent, which detract from the overall stability of the nuclear balance, and which they can no longer work to perfect. For those whose real aim is a new buildup, the rationale that we need reductions, but not a freeze, is merely a rationalization for amassing the B-1, the MX, and other new strategic weapons while engaging in protracted negotiations with the Soviets. Frankly, often during negotiations, the United States and the Soviet Union have behaved like fevered patients whose temperature rises from 103 to 104 degrees and who think they're getting better because they're getting sicker at a slower rate.

Past agreements have also been defective because they have not prevented impending leaps in the sophistication of weaponry. Thus the Vladivostok accord and the SALT II Treaty permitted the development of cruise missiles. The military planners saw the loophole and proceeded to rush through it with a weapons system in which they had previously shown only minimum interest. Where there is a loophole, it will almost certainly be exploited. Where a system is permitted, it will be pursued; otherwise, the thinking goes, the adversary will gain an advantage. A comprehensive freeze already in place during reduction talks would plug past loopholes and prevent future ones for the simple reason that it would impose a general moratorium on any and all additions to nuclear arsenals.

Critics of the freeze next suggest that it would leave the United States behind the Soviets in nuclear weaponry in Europe. Officials in the Reagan Administration have presented varying statistics to prove this proposition, citing an inferiority ranging between three-to-one and six-to-one. But such critics exaggerate the facts and distort the true situation in Europe, where the United States, according to the authoritative International Institute for Strategic Studies, has 1,168 available warheads and the Soviets have 2,004. With such numbers each nation has enough to blow up the continent many times over. In any event, the Kennedy-Hatfield resolution rejects a freeze in Europe alone. We are calling for a global freeze. In case of a Soviet nuclear attack on NATO, the United States could call on its entire nuclear arsenal to respond. For the administration to suggest that it no longer relies on this option would signal a major and destabilizing change under which Europe would no longer enjoy the protection of America's nuclear umbrella.

The real and present danger to the NATO alliance, by the estimate of former Under Secretary of State George Ball, is the uncertain and unclear attitude of the United States with respect to the nuclear issue. The sense of apprehension in Europe has been amplified by American discussion of limited nuclear war and nuclear warning shots and by American insistence on the neutron bomb, a malignant scientific breakthrough designed to destroy people through "enhanced radiation" while minimizing damage to buildings and equipment. Campaigns for unilateral European disarmament gain strength when Washington sounds casual about nuclear conflict and seems uninterested in arms control or unable to achieve progress. Given this record, it is "grotesque," in Secretary Ball's phrase, for the administration to suggest that the Kennedy-Hatfield freeze will undermine the American position in Europe. To the contrary, it can reassure the Europeans that this nation is finally being serious about reducing the risk of accelerating nuclear competition.

Other critics of the resolution have focused on the question of verification. The Kennedy-Hatfield resolution specifically calls for a verifiable freeze. What cannot be verified will not be frozen. But there are many experts who agree that a freeze is largely and sufficiently verifiable. We can have high confidence that one critical aspect of the freeze, deployment, can be verified through "national technical means" — that is, satellites and listening posts equipped with sensors — and through data exchange and restrictions on concealment. A second critical aspect of the freeze, testing, can also be verified by such means together with unmanned seismic stations and opportunities for on-site inspection — both of which the Soviets have already accepted in principle in the recent negotiations for a Comprehensive Test Ban Treaty. In the past, the United States has regarded such measures as fully adequate for verifying SALT restrictions on deployment and limits on nuclear weapons testing, and they would be fully adequate for verifying these aspects of a nuclear weapons freeze.

A freeze on production of nuclear weapons may be harder to verify, but our intelligence is so well developed, according to former Under Secretary of Defense William Perry, that we have been able to "monitor Soviet activity at the design bureaus and production plants well enough so that we have been able to predict every ICBM before it began its tests." It may be that some form of on-site inspection will be necessary to closely verify production and to check certain limited aspects of testing. To presume that the Soviets will not permit any such inspection overlooks the record of the Comprehensive Test-Ban Treaty negotiations, now postponed by the Reagan administration, where the Soviets have agreed to the principle of on-site verification.

Even areas where there may be verification problems, such as some areas of production, do not present serious difficulties, since verification in other areas would assure overall enforcement of the freeze. Indeed, Herbert Scoville, onetime Deputy Director of the CIA, contends that a freeze is *easier* to verify than a treaty like SALT I or SALT II. Such treaties contain complicated limits on numbers and modifications of missiles and planes; to detect a violation requires continuing and exact measurements of a vast array of possible and prohibited activity. With a freeze, however, a violation would be known if the adversary did anything new at all. And even the one-for-one replacement that would be permitted by a freeze could be verified with high confidence.

We are also told by critics that a freeze will interfere with arms control negotiations now planned or underway. But as we have seen, it could be years before any overall agreement is concluded. Meanwhile a comprehensive freeze can break the fever of the arms race and bring the thermonuclear temperature down. It can also contribute to progress on the formidable problem of nuclear proliferation, the spread of the bomb to other nations, including unstable regimes in the Third World. American and Soviet appeals against such proliferation tend to fall on cynical ears so long as our own nuclear production moves ahead. A freeze can draw a line not only across the arms race, but across the attitudes of the world. It would give the superpowers the moral authority to deal with the gathering disaster of proliferation. It would deprive aspiring nuclear powers of the too ready excuse that they have every right to acquire the bomb so long as we are striving to augment our own massive arsenals.

The Indian nuclear explosion in 1974 forcefully reminded the world of the deadly threat of proliferation. Pakistan has reacted predictably by trying to catch up with India. We now have an arms race in the subcontinent. Where one nation becomes a nuclear power, however modest, neighboring states feel driven to get bombs of their own; this process is globalizing the deadly logic of nuclear threat and counterthreat. And this, in turn, could set off a nuclear confrontation between the United States and the Soviet Union.

Expanding numbers of nuclear weapons around the world could encourage terrorism in the form of nuclear blackmail. The possible scenarios are chilling. Suppose that Libya, long frustrated in the quest for a nuclear bomb of its own, receives a gift from Pakistan as an act of Islamic solidarity. Colonel Qadhafi then brandishes the bomb against the state of Israel, which he is sworn to destroy. The crisis escalates and engages Qadhafi's Soviet allies and Israel's American allies; there is a regional and then a global nuclear catastrophe.

A credible and effective strategy to prevent such nightmares depends on a number of mutually reinforcing steps. We must strengthen international nuclear safeguards against the diversion of nuclear materials from peaceful to military uses. We must restrain reckless commerce in nuclear energy, by prohibiting the transfer of plutonium reprocessing and uranium enrichment equipment and technology, and by insisting on control of spent nuclear fuel. We must seek more nuclear weapons-free zones such as the ones in Latin America.

The key to all of these developments is greater adherence to the current Nuclear Nonproliferation Treaty. A freeze, followed by reductions, can promote that. It is exactly what the treaty itself calls for. By embarking on such a course, the United States and the Soviets can prove that at last, they are observing their pledge under Article VI of the treaty:

> Each of the parties . . . undertakes to pursue negotiations in good faith on effective measures relating to cessation of the nuclear arms race at an early date and to nuclear disarmament, and on a treaty on general and complete disarmament under strict and effective international control.

In effect, a freeze would also be a comprehensive test ban between the superpowers. They could then move to expand it into more formal sanctions against all nuclear tests or explosions.

Finally, some critics suggest that a freeze proposal will be dismissed outright by the Soviet Union. They point to the Soviet rejection of the so-called "deep cuts" suddenly proposed by the Carter administration in 1977. In fact, that experience argues for the more modulated, less complicated strategy of an initial freeze followed by negotiated reductions. The 1977 proposal was highly specific; it asked for agreement to detailed cuts before agreement to the principle of deep cuts. After analyzing the details, Soviet leaders almost certainly interpreted the proposal as locking them into a position of nuclear inferiority. A freeze today would mean a more nearly equivalent balance. In any event, the possibility of rejection by the Soviets is hardly an argument against the desirability of trying for a freeze. If there is any case in history where the imperative of bold initiative applies, it is the nuclear arms race. In the search for arms control, nothing ventured is truly nothing gained, and perhaps in the end, everything truly lost.

In reality, much of the attack on the freeze resolution is a disguise for a different and more unsettling position. The 1983 budget proposal asks for funds to "successfully fight either conventional or nuclear war." This is the first time that any budget proposal has ever said any such thing. We must continue to insist that the American purpose is to deter a nuclear exchange, not to fight one. We must reject the concept of a limited nuclear battle. Admiral Noel Gayler, former Director of the National Security Agency, has acidly dismissed the musings of the limited war theorists: "I have no confidence in the imaginary situations and chess games that a certain school of analysts dreams up. Real war is not like these complicated tit-for-tat imaginings. There is little knowledge of what's going on, and less communication. There is blood and terror and agony, and these theorists propose to deal with a war a thousand times more terrible than any we have ever seen, in some bloodless, analytic fashion. I say that's nonsense. We deceive ourselves, and we deceive our opponent into believing we have aggressive intentions that we do not have." Indeed that is the danger: someday the nuclear war-game theorists may actually find themselves playing the game for real.

The fascination of some experts and politicians with such games, or their attachment to traditional approaches to arms control, has spurred a constant effort to find some simple argument, any simple argument, to dismiss or deflect the freeze proposal. When the critics come to admit, as former Secretary of Defense Harold Brown recently did, that a complete freeze "if immediately and fully implemented and completely verified" might be in the American national interest, they often shift ground and begin charging that even the attempt to negotiate a freeze would be dangerous, because the U.S. might stop building but the Soviets would continue to build. But if the two sides can agree in principle to a freeze, they can also agree to an interim moratorium while the details of the plan are discussed. It would be plain common sense to begin freeze talks with a "negotiator's pause" to hold weaponry constant. A similar pause was put in place and it was effective prior to the 1963 test-ban negotiations.

And sometimes critics even suggest that a nuclear weapons freeze will not, by itself, eliminate the danger of nuclear war. The freeze which they first assailed as too ambitious is then attacked as insufficient to be meaningful. In reality, it is a first but essential step back from the nuclear precipice; it can stop the arms race from rushing over the edge of that precipice, and subsequent reductions can truly move us back to a safer place, farther from the brink.

When these arguments do not avail, the opponents of a freeze offer a counterfeit version, such as the Jackson–Warner resolution introduced in the Senate this spring and supported by the Reagan administration, which calls for a freeze at "equal" levels after "sharp" reductions in nuclear arsenals. This is a false freeze which begins with the assertion that there is, at present, "a nuclear force imbalance." The implication is that the United States must build more to catch up and only then negotiate reductions, or that the Soviets must agree to "unequal reductions," in the phrase of administration arms negotiator Eugene Rostow. According to that scheme, the Soviet Union would give up more of its strategic power than the United States. The prospect for such a negotiating posture hardly seems bright. In any case, lengthy negotiations for reductions before a freeze could lead to frantic production and development of new weapons in the meantime, as each side seeks bargaining chips and marginal advantages. A false freeze calls for running faster before we stop. It is a recipe for putting off the freeze and getting on with the arms race.

Freeze opponents who offer these counterfeit resolutions concede a critical point. By favoring a freeze later, they have, in effect, admitted that a freeze as such is feasible and verifiable. They have agreed to the principle; now they are only haggling about the timing. But ordinary citizens increasingly understand how vital an issue timing is. They are not interested in a "freeze" that is only a cover for another round of the arms buildup; they want a real freeze, and they want it *as soon as possible, as comprehensive as possible.* The Kennedy-Hatfield resolution may not prevail immediately in the Congress or inside the administration, but the people can, and will, keep the pressure on. They will organize, raise their voices, and cast their votes.

The Kennedy-Hatfield resolution, by combining a mutual freeze and major reductions, provides the most promising way to move back the hands of the Doomsday Clock. It is time, perhaps the last period of time we shall have, to cease debating the preferred options of certain experts and public figures who think that there is a better way to dot the *i*'s or cross the *t*'s of arms control. The freeze concept has the inestimable political virtues of simplicity and practicality. Its benefits to humanity are readily apparent to ordinary human beings, rather than to only a select handful of scientists and strategic analysts. There would be no mistaking the moral implications of an agreement to stop the arms race now, and an intense national and international campaign for ratification could be effectively mounted. To a world increasingly apprehensive over the awesome dangers and technological complexities of the arms race, a freeze offers the symbol and the substance of hope.

Arms Control vs. the Freeze

CHRISTOPHER M. LEHMAN

Over the past year [1982], the nuclear freeze movement has brought to the forefront of public discussion a deceptively attractive, simple solution to the arms race — freeze it! Calling for an absolute prohibition on the production, testing, and deployment of nuclear weapons and their delivery systems, advocates argue that a freeze can truly bring about a halt in the arms race and reduce the dangers of nuclear war.

The nuclear freeze has been as popular as it is simple. But is it really a plausible path to meaningful arms control, or is it a distraction that makes genuine arms control far more difficult to achieve?

There has been much debate on this question, and surely there is more to come. However, a serious review of the issue forces the conclusion that the

From Christopher M. Lehman, "Arms Control vs. the Freeze," in *The Nuclear Weapons Freeze and Arms Control,* edited by Steven E. Miller. Copyright © 1984 by Ballinger Publishing Company. Reprinted by permission of the publisher.

nuclear freeze proposal has serious drawbacks as to make it unsuitable as the basis for meaningful arms control.

THE FREEZE AS SENTIMENT

The rapid growth of the nuclear freeze movement is a phenomenon which cannot be fully explained. However, it is clear that a number of factors were instrumental in boosting the visibility and the political clout of the freeze movement, and they all have a common element—fear. The fear of nuclear war has once again spawned a movement of concerned men, women, and children who demand that we avoid Armageddon.

The roots of the freeze movement go as far back as we care to look, but its more recent impetus has come from the increased attention to defense issues and the undeniable growth in the Soviet threat. The 1980 election in large part turned on the question of defense, and the Reagan Administration has made the rebuilding of U.S. defenses a central element of its program.

The continuing public focus on threats to U.S. security and the huge defense expenditures necessary to meet those threats have helped to create a backlash or an aversion to matters related to defense. This aversion has been particularly strong with respect to our nuclear arsenal where a major modernization of our nuclear forces has served to rekindle strong anti-nuclear sentiment. Anxieties were boosted even further by several statements by Reagan Administration officials concerning nuclear weapons and nuclear war, and since then some politicians have sought to exploit anti-nuclear sentiment for ballot-box gains, and authors and publishers have cashed in as well.

The fear and anxiety that is so much a part of the nuclear freeze movement is, of course, understandable. There have been dangerous developments in the nuclear balance in recent years, and a nuclear war would most certainly be unimaginably horrible. But it takes more than fear to prevent nuclear war. It takes a dual strategy of deterrence and arms control.

The very foundation of peace in the nuclear age has been America's strategy of deterrence. Since the earliest days of our possession of nuclear weapons, the United States has sought to prevent war by discouraging aggression against the United States and its allies. By threatening any aggressor with the certainty of unacceptable levels of destruction, an uneasy peace has been maintained. The history of the twentieth century makes it sadly clear that peaceful intentions and good motives alone never stop aggressors. Military strength does, and the strategy of deterrence has been highly successful in protecting America's security since the end of World War II.

But America has pursued a dual policy since the end of World War II. In addition to maintaining strong military forces for deterrence, we have also vigorously pursued arms control as a complement to our policy of deterrence.

Thus while anxiety over the threat of nuclear war is well warranted, we cannot let fear dictate our response. The proven course of deterrence and arms control is the best means of preventing nuclear war and preserving the peace. A nuclear freeze would be harmful to deterrence and to meaningful arms control and thus a freeze should be rejected.

THE FLAWS OF THE FREEZE

The arguments against the nuclear freeze proposal are many and would apply to most, if not all, of the various freeze formulae that have been proposed. The most popular freeze proposal, and the one which has earned *the* nuclear freeze label, is the Congressional Resolution introduced by Senators Kennedy and Hatfield and its companion measure introduced in the House of Representatives. This resolution calls for an immediate mutual and verifiable freeze on production, testing, and deployment of nuclear weapons and their delivery systems. This proposal is surely well intentioned, but it will not help accomplish effective arms control. In fact, if a freeze were to be implemented, it would endanger American security and the security of our allies.

The first, and probably the strongest, argument against the nuclear freeze proposal is that a freeze would preserve the current high level of nuclear forces, and would thus preserve an unequal and unstable strategic balance.

The experts have hotly debated the exact status of the strategic balance for years, but there is no debate that the balance has shifted dramatically in recent years in favor of the Soviet Union. There is debate over whether parity still exists, but there is little opposition to the view that present trends cannot continue without directly harming the security interests of the United States.

As a result of a massive 15-year military buildup, the Soviet Union has now surged ahead of the United States in every static measure of strategic power except one—total strategic warheads. In missile throwweight, missile warheads, ICBMs, SLBMs, and even strategic bombers, the Soviet Union has gained the advantage; and qualitatively the Soviet Union has caught up as well. . . .

In addition to numerical advantages, the average age of Soviet strategic weapons and their delivery systems has come down considerably while the average age of U.S. systems has gone up. According to U.S. Department of Defense figures, 77 percent of Soviet systems are less than five years old, while 77 percent of U.S. systems are in excess of 15 years of age.

Thus, if a freeze were implemented, the United States would be frozen with aging systems with no opportunity to modernize those forces to ensure a strong and credible deterrent.

Our current strategic weapon systems will also become increasingly vulnerable over time, and a vulnerable deterrent is an invitation to catastrophe. The vulnerability of our land-based missile force is already a matter of major concern. While the freeze would lock us into these and other current systems, the freeze would not prevent advances in conventional air defenses or anti-submarine warfare that could threaten the remaining two elements of our strategic triad. But a freeze would prevent the production of the Stealth bomber and other advances that could counter steadily improving Soviet air defenses. Similarly, the freeze would prevent the production of new Trident submarines and other efforts to stay ahead of advances in anti-submarine warfare.

In short, a nuclear freeze would weaken deterrence over time and thus make nuclear war more rather than less likely.

The present nuclear balance in Europe is also one which should not be frozen in its present state. A freeze now would give the Soviet Union an overwhelming nuclear advantage in intermediate-range nuclear weapons in Europe to the detriment of our own and our allies' security.

A second important argument that flows from the first is that by freezing at today's high and unequal levels a nuclear freeze would undercut our START and INF negotiations and make the prospects for actual arms reductions less likely.

The United States is currently engaged in two separate negotiations with the Soviet Union seeking nuclear arms reductions. In those negotiations, the United States has put forward dramatic reductions proposals: in START, the U.S. is calling for one-third reductions in ballistic missile warheads, and a cut in the number of deployed missiles to about one-half the current U.S. levels. In the INF negotiations, the U.S. has proposed the elimination of a whole category of intermediate-range ballistic missiles. The Soviet Union has responded with counterproposals that also envisage arms reduction. While the Soviet proposals have not been acceptable to the United States, it is important to note that the principle of reductions has been accepted. This is quite significant, especially in view of the fact that the recent SALT II negotiations produced a draft treaty which would have allowed both sides to almost double their nuclear warhead inventory within the terms of the agreement.

Thus, in a very real sense we have already moved far beyond a freeze, and we should not waste the months and years it would take to negotiate the terms of a verifiable nuclear freeze if, in fact, that were possible. Supporters of a freeze may believe that a freeze agreement could be easily arrived at, but experience has shown that any meaningful agreement would require agreed definitions, counting rules, and other details which would unavoidably complicate the implementation of the conceptually simple nuclear freeze proposal.

Aside from the complexities of implementing a freeze, U.S. agreement to a freeze would destroy Soviet incentives for accepting an arms reduction agreement. A freeze at today's force levels would preserve the Soviet Union in a position of relative advantage. The Soviets thus would have every incentive to prolong a freeze and avoid coming to an agreement on arms reductions to lower but equal levels.

Unless the United States and its allies demonstrate their will to take the actions necessary to restore the nuclear balance, the Soviets will have little incentive to agree to reductions in their own forces. Indeed, the Soviet Union initially refused our offers to negotiate on INF systems while they deployed several hundred SS-20 missile systems. They agreed to come to the negotiating table only when it became clear that we and our NATO allies were determined to take steps to counter those SS-20 deployments unless an arms control agreement were reached. A unilateral U.S. withdrawal from the allied "dual track" decision of 1979, which has consistently been endorsed by all NATO governments, would also cause serious doubt on American leadership of NATO and our readiness to fulfill our commitments to the defense of Europe.

Similarly, the freeze would leave the U.S. with a vulnerable land-based missile system, an aging and less credible bomber force, and a submarine fleet which faces block obsolescence in the 1990s. The Soviet Union, on the other hand, would have an arsenal of newer, heavier ICBMs, newer ballistic missile-firing submarines, and over 250 modern Backfire bombers built during the 1970s. Under these circumstances, there would be little reason for the Soviet Union to agree to reductions.

A third important argument against the nuclear freeze is that it is just not verifiable in many important respects. Simply prefacing a freeze proposal with an incantation that it must be mutual and verifiable just doesn't make it so.

As proposed, a freeze would cover production, testing, and deployment of strategic nuclear weapons. However, of those three categories, only deployment is verifiable with high confidence, and there are exceptions to that. Verifying a ban on nuclear testing would be extremely difficult, and the possibility of surreptitious testing at lower-yield levels would be significant. With respect to production of nuclear weapons, however, the task of verifying a freeze becomes unmanageable. Even with on-site inspection, the possibility of detecting the production of nuclear weapons would be low.

Thus inadequate verification alone is sufficient argument against the nuclear freeze as proposed.

THE FREEZE IGNORES DETERRENCE

There are other arguments against the nuclear freeze, but they are mostly subsidiary to those mentioned here. However, there is one additional criticism of the freeze that needs to be made. The freeze proposal ignores deterrence. It assumes that deterrence is stable and easily maintained no matter what the strategic nuclear balance sheet looks like. It assumes that the vulnerability and looming obsolescence of U.S. strategic systems will not affect the viability of deterrence. In short, it assumes that the concept of minimum deterrence is valid—that so long as the United States retains the capacity to destroy a few Soviet cities then deterrence will prevail.

This simple view of deterrence has been rejected by every administration since Eisenhower as being inadequate and incredible and therefore dangerous. Deterrence requires capable and survivable nuclear forces on both sides so that neither side can expect advantage under any circumstances by initiating the use of nuclear weapons. Allowing gross imbalances in the level or capabilities of nuclear forces would be destabilizing. Allowing our nuclear forces to be vulnerable to a pre-emptive disarming first strike would only invite attack and greatly increase the probability of war.

These are things we must not allow to happen, yet these are the very things which a nuclear freeze would mandate.

THE FREEZE IS BAD ARMS CONTROL

The arguments against the nuclear freeze are powerful and persuasive. It is a superficially attractive concept, but one which has hidden within it serious flaws that make it unsuitable as the basis for serious arms control. A substantial number of respected arms control experts have supported this view, and even some who support the freeze concept do so as a means of building political pressure in support of arms control while recognizing the internal flaws of the actual nuclear freeze proposal. Respected journals such as the *New York Times,* the *Washington Post,* and the *Wall Street Journal* have all editorialized against the freeze.

Those who support the concept of a nuclear freeze need to stop thinking with their heart and start thinking with their head. We all share the common goal of avoiding the catastrophe of nuclear war. We all share the desire for peace. But we all have a responsibility to work toward practical solutions to man's most serious problem.

The practical solution, in my view, is the proven course of deterrence and arms control. That has been the course adopted by every administration in the postwar era, and it is the course which the Reagan Administration is vigorously pursuing.

We are now engaged in two nuclear arms control negotiations with the Soviet Union—START and INF. The United States has put forward serious arms reduction proposals at the negotiations, and the Soviets have made serious counter-proposals.

It is time for all those who truly desire arms control to support the arms control efforts which the United States is now pursuing. These negotiations seek deep reductions in the levels of nuclear weapons. A freeze at today's high levels of nuclear weapons would be a step backward.

Document
Joint Resolution

ON NUCLEAR WEAPONS FREEZE AND REDUCTIONS (S. J.RES. 163)

Whereas the greatest challenge facing the Earth is to prevent the occurrence of nuclear war by accident or design;

Whereas the nuclear arms race is dangerously increasing the risk of a holocaust that would be humanity's final war; and

Whereas a freeze followed by reductions in nuclear warheads, missiles, and

From *Hearings before the Committee on Foreign Relations, United States Senate,* 97th Congress, 2nd Session (1982), pp. 4–5.

other delivery systems is needed to halt the nuclear arms race and to reduce the risk of nuclear war: Now, therefore, be it

Resolved by the Senate and House of Representatives of the United States of America in Congress assembled,

That (1) as an immediate strategic arms control objective, the United States and the Soviet Union should—

(a) pursue a complete halt to the nuclear arms race;

(b) decide when and how to achieve a mutual and verifiable freeze on the testing, production, and further deployment of nuclear warheads, missiles, and other delivery systems; and

(c) give special attention to destabilizing weapons whose deployment would make such a freeze more difficult to achieve.

(2) Proceeding from this freeze, the United States and the Soviet Union should pursue major, mutual, and verifiable reductions in nuclear warheads, missiles, and other delivery systems, through annual percentages or equally effective means, in a manner that enhances stability.